STOUT HEARTS

The British and Canadians in Normandy 1944

Ben Kite

With a Foreword by
Field Marshal the Lord Bramall KG GCB OBE MC

Helion & Company

Helion & Company Limited
26 Willow Road
Solihull
West Midlands
B91 1UE
Tel. 0121 705 3393
Fax 0121 711 4075
Email: info@helion.co.uk
Website: www.helion.co.uk
Twitter: @helionbooks
Visit our blog http://blog.helion.co.uk/

Published by Helion & Company 2014
Designed and typeset by Bookcraft Limited, Stroud, Gloucestershire
Cover designed by Euan Carter, Leicester (www.euancarter.com)
Printed by Gutenberg Press Limited, Tarxien, Malta

Front cover – Clifford Brown of the Somerset Light Infantry quenches his thirst after the
capture of Mont Pinçon, 7 August. (Imperial War Museum B8787).
Rear cover – Infantrymen of the 8th Canadian Infantry Brigade take a brief rest during
their advance into Caen as a Sherman tank kicks up more dust, 18 July. (Lieut. H. Gordon
Aikman / Dept. of National Defence / Library and Archives Canada / PA-129128).

ISBN 978 1 909982 55 0

British Library Cataloguing-in-Publication Data.
A catalogue record for this book is available from the British Library.

For details of other military history titles published by Helion & Company Limited contact
the above address, or visit our website: http://www.helion.co.uk.

We always welcome receiving book proposals from prospective authors.

To the men of the Allied armies who served in North West Europe 1944-45

'With stout hearts, and with enthusiasm for the contest, let us go forward to victory'
Extract from General B L Montgomery's personal message to all Allied soldiers on
the eve of D-Day. 'To be read out to all troops once embarked, June 1944'.

Contents

List of Photographs

List of Diagrams

List of Maps

In colour section

Key to maps. We have followed the Second World War convention of showing British and Allied Symbols in red and German and Axis symbols in blue.

Foreword

There have been so many books written on Normandy that the publication of another one might initially seem rather superfluous. But *Stout Hearts* is different. Most books have so far focused on narrating the sequence of the various battles, describing the factors which have influenced their outcome and debating the various merits of Allied and German armies. There is also a further genre of books satisfying the needs of a rather smaller readership which cover individual equipment or units. What has been missing is a book that attempts to describe, for the uninitiated, how an army actually operates in war; how it integrates with the other two Services and what it was like for those involved. *Stout Hearts* fills this gap, explaining how the many different arms and units within 21st Army Group operated during the Normandy campaign. How, for instance, does the artillery know precisely where to drop its shell? How does an individual tank operate? How are the wounded cared for? How were the Air Force and Navy able to support them?

As someone who landed at Juno Beach on D+1 and fought in the front line through most of the Normandy Campaign until I was wounded, Ben Kite's explanations bring back many emotive memories of the realities, the noise and appalling destruction of those stirring and dangerous days; and I can vouch for their authenticity and accuracy. I also believe that his fascinating descriptions of operational procedures and tactics interspersed, with numerous personal accounts of how individual soldiers faced up to those dangers and realities, will be of interest to all students of military history who would wish to have a clear idea how a battle is orchestrated, managed and professionally carried out.

With so many personal memories myself I am glad Ben Kite has chosen the Normandy Campaign as the background to his study of an Army at War and I warmly commend it.

Field Marshal the Lord Bramall, KG, GCB, OBE, MC

Acknowledgements

This book has taken a number of years to produce and would not have been completed without the support of a wide range of people and institutions. I am particularly grateful to Dr Rob Johnson, as Director of Oxford University's Changing Character of Warfare programme he encouraged me in translating an embryonic idea into a finished first book. Dr Simon Trew of the Royal Military Academy at Sandhurst, an acknowledged Normandy expert, was also kind enough to lend helpful criticism of the book. Understanding the complex techniques and science behind some of 21st Army Group's organisations was aided by a combination of veterans, historians and military officers.

Brigadier Jeremy Bennett helped me better understand the mysteries of artillery, Colonel Simon Stockley explained combat engineering and Mr Bart Cookson, formerly of the Royal Tank Regiment, expanded my knowledge on the use of armour in battle. I am also thankful for Captain Peter Stocking and Dr Justin Pepperell for ensuring I was factually correct in medical and surgical aspects. Finally, Mr Norman Franks was kind enough to lend his deep expertise on air power and help me comprehend the air contribution to the campaign.

I have hugely appreciated the large number of veterans who have ensured that my historical understanding of the Army of 1944 has stayed on track. A full list of those who have helped is enclosed at the back of this book, but I would particularly like to single out Sydney Jary, Joe Lawler, Jon Majendie, Ian Hammerton, Ken Tout and Jack Swaab. Most of all I am indebted to Field Marshal the Lord Bramall for both his frank advice on an early manuscript and his most generous foreword.

This book's greatest strengths are the veteran's own stories. The majority are extracted from autobiographies and I am therefore very grateful for either the author's permission, or those of his family, to reproduce them within this work. I have done my utmost to try and find the original author or descendants, on the very few occasions where I have been unsuccessful I ask the copyright holders forgiveness and hope they will feel I have done the original author's work justice. I am also very grateful for the relatives of those records held in the Imperial War Museum archives, particularly those who also provided photographs. Again where I have been unable to locate copyright holders and ask permission, I hope they forgive me and enjoy seeing their relatives' work in print. Needless to say I am hugely grateful to the staff at the National Archives, Imperial War Museum and many other regimental museums who freely gave their time and advice. I would particularly like to single out Major Boris Mollo, curator of the Kent and Sharpshooters Yeomanry Museum who, with his fellow trustees, have allowed me to use a number of their photographs in this book. I wish them the best of luck as they establish their regimental museum at Hever Castle. I would also like to thank the staff at the Air and Army historical branches who have also been particularly helpful in allowing me to access and use their crown copyrighted images. I would particularly like to single out Jo Bandy and Bob Evans in the Army Historical Branch and Mary Hudson in the Air Historical Branch.

I feel I have been blessed in finding an excellent publisher in Helion. Duncan Rogers and his team have been helpful and enthusiastic about the book and made generous allowances for photos, diagrams and maps. I should add that George Anderson was particularly skilled in translating a rough intent into very clear graphics for which I am very grateful.

This book has taken a long time to complete – it would never have been finished were it not for the tolerance of my wife, Elsa, as well as my two young daughters, Jemima and Lucy. My final thanks, however, go to my father. No other person has had to plough through quite so many drafts of this book and yet his patience never tired and he has continued to offer welcome criticism, advice and encouragement throughout. Thank you Dad.

1

Introduction and Campaign Overview

My experience on numerous battlefield tours is that people, whether soldiers or civilians, are always interested in how an Army actually 'works' on operations, how its various arms and services interact on the battlefield to produce an overall operational success. There are many detailed explanations on the various instruments within this orchestra of war which will help the reader understand how a battle is waged. The reader will also note that these explanations are interspersed with many personal accounts from the actual combatants. These veterans' anecdotes are vital. They bring the book to life and illustrate the important point that whatever the particular procedures, tactics and equipment, warfare remains a collective human endeavour. You cannot comprehend how an Army works without understanding the men within it who have to serve in conditions of extreme danger, confusion and fatigue. This is important because although aspects of warfare change, human behaviour essentially does not. General Patton captured it superbly in a letter he wrote to his son on D-Day itself:

> To be a successful soldier you must know history…What you must know is how man reacts. Weapons change but man who uses them changes not at all. To win battles you do not beat weapons—you beat the soul of man of the enemy man. To do that you have to destroy his weapons, but that is only incidental. You must read biography and especially autobiography. If you will do it you will find that war is simple.[1]

Including veterans' accounts also fulfils the secondary aim of this book, to capture the serviceman's experience in one of the most complex and daring military operations in the history of warfare.[2]

In explaining how an Army works I have concentrated on the British and Canadian[3] 21st Army Group, resisting the temptation to broaden the scope and include the US Army in Normandy; to have done so would have made the book too rambling. Moreover by focussing on the 'particular' the 'general' point is often easier to understand. For example, studying a British Casualty Clearing Station in Normandy will facilitate better comprehension of the general principles of surgical and medical support in any modern battle. Similarly, in some chapters I have selected a particular equipment to focus on and paid less attention to other similar types. In the chapter on artillery, for instance, I describe the gun drill of the 25-pounder and how a Field Regiment operates, but do not give the same attention to the 5.5-in gun or Medium Regiments. If you have a good understanding

---

1. Patton papers, George A Patton Papers, Manuscript Division, Library of Congress.
2. D'Este, Carlos, *Decision in Normandy* (New York, Konecky and Konecky, 1994), pp.13-14.
3. I will frequently refer to this Army Group as 'the British' Army Group. This does not mean to denigrate the Canadian contribution but reflects the shorthand terminology used at the time.

on how a 25-pounder unit operates, you will have a general understanding of how any other artillery unit functions.

Why select Normandy in particular? Principally because 21st Army Group was the largest and most complex organisation the British have placed into the field in living memory. It was also the most decisive, intense battle the British fought in the Second World War, where the best elements of the German Army were engaged and defeated and where casualty rates began to approach the level of the First World War. In addition the success of 21st Army Group was dependent upon both naval and air support and these are also covered. Finally, as the Normandy campaign occurred towards the later stages of the War the British organisation and equipment had begun to reach a mature level. It therefore has the most relevance for modern readers.

This book will enable you not only to understand the battle of Normandy rather better, but also the Second World War more generally. Understanding equipment, tactics and procedures and how tired, frightened serviceman used them, will allow the reader to better appreciate the complexity of land operations and reveal the difficulties and challenges all armies and all soldiers must overcome in order to emerge victorious. The challenges of military operations are all too frequently glossed over in many military histories that fail to understand that 'easy' things are often incredibly hard to achieve in war, that however sound a plan may be, it will rarely survive contact with the enemy and finally that all armies usually have to innovate and adapt tactics and equipment as they fight.

As we mark the 70th anniversary of the Normandy campaign it is worth reminding ourselves that the victory in Normandy was by no means a foregone conclusion and the success of the Allies stems from both many individual sacrifices, the organisational efficiency of 21st Army Group and the overall defence effort. My final point is to ask you to keep in mind one vital factor, the importance of morale, how it dominates almost every chapter and how the army is utterly reliant on the quality of its soldiers and their commitment and courage. This book does not focus on the debates over the quality of generalship, or which side was 'best'. It focuses on an institution that inflicted the greatest defeat Hitler's armies ever suffered in the West, together with the servicemen who collectively made it work. I hope I have done their efforts justice.

CAMPAIGN OVERVIEW

> If anybody had told me then that in four years I should return with Winston and Smuts to lunch with Monty commanding a new invasion force, I should have found it hard to believe.[4]
> The Diary of Field Marshal Lord Alanbrooke, 12 June 1944

21st Army Group in Normandy was led by General Sir Bernard Montgomery and comprised two armies; Second British Army under Lieutenant-General Sir Miles Dempsey and First Canadian Army under Lieutenant-General Sir Harry Crerar. Each Army was composed of several corps, three being the norm but these would be altered as required throughout the campaign. In Normandy there were initially four corps; I Corps, VIII Corps, XII Corps and XXX Corps. Initially all were placed under Second British Army, however once II Canadian Corps had landed First Canadian Army was properly constituted and the order of battle was altered once more. General Montgomery left the activation of HQ First Canadian Army until quite late in the campaign, some have suggested that this was possibly because he did not have much faith in its Canadian commander, Lieutenant-General Crerar.

The corps were usually composed of three divisions. Some of these formations had so far never seen any action in the Second World War (e.g. 15th Scottish Division) and others had not been deployed

---

4   Bryant, Arthur, *Triumph in the West*, (London, Reprint Society, 1959), p.172.

since Dunkirk (3rd British Division). A few had served in the North African and Italian campaigns and were brought back at Montgomery's insistence to give his new Army Group some experienced formations (51st Highland, 7th Armoured and 50th Northumbrian Divisions for example). In addition to the various divisions there were a number of 'independent' brigades. These included the commando brigades as well as armoured brigades equipped with Sherman cruiser tanks (e.g. 4 Armoured Brigade) and tank brigades equipped with Churchill infantry support tanks (e.g. 31 Tank Brigade). These brigades would be loaned to corps or divisions when required. At Army and Army Group level there were also concentrations of engineers, artillery, medical and logistic units who could be used to support whichever corps was the main effort for a particular operation.

As well as bringing veteran formations back to England, Montgomery was also careful to transfer a number of former Eighth Army staff into HQ 21st Army Group, this importantly included his Chief of Staff, Major General Francis De Guingand, as well as his head of intelligence, Brigadier 'Bill' Williams. These key staff all arrived about the same time as General Montgomery took up his appointment in January 1944. Prior to Montgomery's arrival, the planning for the invasion had been conducted by a team led by the Chief of Staff to the Supreme Allied Commander (COSSAC), Lieutenant-General Sir Frederick Morgan. This staff had selected Normandy as the invasion area based upon a number of key factors. Firstly Normandy possessed several wide, open beaches that were sheltered from the prevailing westerly winds by the Cherbourg peninsula. Secondly it was within range of fighters based in southern England, which would make securing air superiority over the bridgehead easier. Finally it was further away and therefore a less obvious assault area than the Pas de Calais, this fact would be exploited by a highly effective Allied deception plan.

The initial COSSAC-originated OVERLORD plan called for an assault by three divisions, on three beaches, with two brigades dropped by air and follow on divisions disembarking over the same beaches. The Allied military and political leaders approved this plan at the Quebec Conference in 1943.

Figure 1.1 The Allied command team, front row left to right: General Montgomery, General Eisenhower and General Bradley. Back row: General Crerar, General Simpson (Ninth US Army) and General Dempsey. (Barney J. Gloster, Library and Archives Canada, PA-136327)

General Montgomery reviewed the plans, once he had been appointed as Commander-in-Chief, 21st Army Group. He dismissed them as too small in scale and with the support of the newly appointed Supreme Allied Commander, General Eisenhower, pressed for an expansion of the initial D-Day assault. General Montgomery proposed a landing of five divisions each on separate beaches, with three airborne divisions dropped to guard the flanks. By expanding the scale of the initial landings Montgomery believed he could deliver a less congested bridgehead, better able to withstand German counter-attacks. These proposed changes to the original plan necessitated a delay till a point when extra landing craft would be available and a new D-Day of early June 1944 was agreed upon.

Following the assault itself the Allies would land a total of thirty-nine follow on divisions in Normandy. These would include twelve British, three Canadian and one Polish division under 21st Army Group as well as twenty-two American and one Free French division under the American General Omar Bradley. Despite the increase in scale of the assault there was still considerable concern over the inevitable strong German counter-attacks against the bridgehead (see Map 2), the Allied plan would mitigate this German response in two ways. Firstly through Operation FORTITUDE; a deception plan aimed at convincing the Germans that the main Allied invasion would come through the Pas De Calais and not Normandy. This deception was based on a fictitious US Army Group, supposedly in East Anglia and southern England, under General Patton. Secondly by massive air attacks on German lines of communication in France and the low countries; known as the 'Transport Plan'. The air assets available included the Strategic Air Forces heavy bombers which were used to destroy rail yards and key bridges over the Seine and Loire. This would disrupt German efforts to deploy their reserves towards Normandy and effectively isolate the battlefield.

This latter activity was controlled by General Eisenhower's Supreme Headquarters Allied Expeditionary Force (SHAEF). Eisenhower had Air Marshal Tedder as his deputy and three subordinate Commanders in Chief (CinC) to manage the Air, Sea and Land Battles. Air Marshal Sir Trafford Leigh-Mallory was appointed the Air CinC with command of both the British 2nd Tactical Air Force and the American 9th US Air Force. The British Admiral Sir Bertram Ramsay was the Naval CinC and he had two subordinate fleets under his command; the Western Naval Task Force which would support the American forces and the Eastern Naval Task Force which would support 21st Army Group (see Maps 3 and 4). Finally the CinC of the land battle for Normandy was General Montgomery who as well as commanding 21st Army Group's British and Canadian Armies would also exercise authority over General Bradley's First US Army. This would be until General Patton's Third US Army was properly constituted in France, at this point Montgomery would hand over his responsibilities for overall control of the land battle to General Eisenhower who would assume the dual role of both the Supreme Allied Commander and the Land Commander. Though Patton's Army was firmly established by 1 August, Eisenhower did not take control of the land battle until 1 September.

The British part of the D-Day plan was to assault on three separate beaches (see Map 5). 50th Northumbrian Division would land on the western GOLD beach, 3rd Canadian Infantry Division on the central JUNO beach and the 3rd British Division on the eastern SWORD beach. The British 6th Airborne Division would also land by parachute and glider on D-Day to the east of the beaches. Their task was to protect the British flank by occupying a bridgehead over the River Orne and capturing key bridges for future use (including the famous Pegasus Bridge – see Map 6).

To the west of the British the American First Army would come ashore on OMAHA and UTAH beaches with two airborne divisions, the 82nd and 101st Airborne divisions, dropped to protect their flanks and safeguard the routes from the beaches. General Montgomery had stressed in his pre-invasion planning the importance of securing the town of Caen (12 miles inland) on D-Day. This town was the centre of a number of road junctions and its early capture together with the open ground to the south-east would offer the Allies a strong advantage. The assault on D-Day was undoubtedly a success though opposition was fierce on some beaches. Disappointingly for the Allies 3rd British Division were not able to take Caen on D-Day itself, indeed the town would not finally fall to the British until mid-July. Although 3rd British Division was initially criticised after the war for this failure, most now accept that the poor D-Day weather hampered their efforts and that the objective was unrealistic. Only one Allied division (50th Northumbrian) actually managed to obtain its inland D-Day objective (see Map 5).

From D-Day onwards the British advance encountered German panzer divisions which were being rushed into the area on a daily basis. Within the first week of the landings the British were facing a tough defence bolstered by 21st Panzer Division in the east, 12th SS *Hitlerjugend* Panzer Division in the centre and, to its west, the Panzer Lehr Division. But the Allies were also landing their follow on forces including some of the veteran divisions from the Desert war (see Map 7). An opportunity seemed to present itself to the British on 12 June when a gap in the German defences to the East of Caumont became apparent.

7th Armoured Division were tasked to exploit this gap during Operation PERCH and succeeded in reaching the town of Villers Bocage. However this penetration was curtailed dramatically when a complacent 7th Armoured Division was ambushed by Tiger tanks led by German 'panzer ace' – Michael Wittmann. The experience so shocked the veteran armoured division that it humbly retreated, and it was quickly becoming apparent that the British tanks were no match for the better armed and protected German Tiger and Panther tanks. Additionally this disappointing performance by 7th Armoured Division was coupled with a reportedly poor showing by 51st Highland Division east of the River Orne, leading some observers to raise doubts about the ability and performance of some of the Desert divisions. Some accused the veteran soldiers of being a little too wary and 'canny'.

The failure of Operation PERCH led Montgomery to seek another method of capturing Caen and pressuring the German eastern flank to tie down the Panzer divisions. This led to Operation EPSOM, an attempt by the newly arrived divisions of VIII Corps to cross the River Odon, capture the important feature of Hill 112 and outflank Caen to the west (see Map 8). This operation would involve the use of 43rd Wessex Division, 15th Scottish Division and the 11th Armoured Division. Operation EPSOM would also be preceded by a divisional attack from 49th Division onto the Rauray spur (Operation MARTLET) which dominated the EPSOM battlefield. Operation EPSOM was scheduled to take place in mid-June but a Channel storm between 19-21 June slowed the arrival of VIII Corps' divisions in Normandy and caused a few days delay. Operation EPSOM lasted from 26 June to 3 July, it did not achieve its overall objectives but did create a thin bridge-head over the River Odon (known as the 'Scottish Corridor'). It also succeeded in not only tying down the panzer divisions in place but also committing the newly arrived 1st SS Panzer Corps (9th and 10th SS Panzer divisions) into a counter-attack against the EPSOM salient. Forewarned by ULTRA intelligence the German counter-attack against the salient was beaten off by the British formations supported by strong artillery and air support.

During the June period the American First Army had succeeded in cutting the Cotentin peninsula and advancing towards the important harbour of Cherbourg at its tip. Cherbourg fell on 29 June but the deliberate damage done to the port by the Germans meant it could not be put to use until early August. Nevertheless by the end of June Montgomery's plan for the British and Canadian forces to tie down the main enemy forces in the east, including the bulk of the German Panzer divisions, was becoming effective. It would allow the Americans, still under General Montgomery's control, to 'develop an offensive southwards in order to open a gap pivoting on Caumont.' Montgomery went on to explain that 'Through this gap was to pass the remainder of the US forces which would on the right enter and clear the Brittany peninsula, and on the left sweep south of the bocage country to the area LAVAL – MAYENNE – ALENCON – LE

MANS.' The American offensive known as Operation COBRA could not be launched by the Americans until late July. Therefore the British had to continue tying down the German eastern flank throughout the month of July until the US 1st Army was ready to attack. Given the increasingly bloody battle the British were fighting and their growing infantry manpower shortages this was a demanding task. General Bradley said as much in his memoirs after the war:

> For three weeks he had rammed his troops against those panzer divisions he had deliberately drawn towards that city as part of our Allied strategy of diversion in the Normandy campaign. Although Caen contained an important road junction that Montgomery would eventually need, for the moment the capture of that city was only incidental to his mission. For Monty's primary task was to attract German troops to the British front that we might easily secure Cherbourg and get into position for the breakout.
>
> In this diversionary mission Monty was more than successful, for the harder he hammered toward Caen, the more German troops he drew into that sector. Too many correspondents, however, had over-rated the importance of Caen itself, and when Monty failed to take it, they blamed him for the delay… We desperately wanted the German to believe this attack on Caen was the main Allied effort.[5]

To that end Operation CHARNWOOD was launched with the aim of capturing Caen on 8/9 July by I Corps (3rd Canadian Division, 59th Division and 3rd British Division) (see Map 9). Preceded by a large, arguably ineffective, air attack by heavy bombers, the attack was partially successful and cleared a portion of the town. On 10 July XII Corps (15th Scottish Division, 43rd Wessex Division and 53rd Welsh Division) launched an attack from the bridgehead over the River Odon (now known by British soldiers as 'Death Valley') onto Hill 112. This attack (Operation JUPITER) failed to capture the peak of Hill 112 despite intense fighting that caused heavy casualties on both sides. On the British western flank, XXX Corps (50th Northumbrian Division, 59th Division and 49th Division) continued to try and push south towards Villers Bocage once more, but again with limited success. The final major British offensive before the Americans launched Operation COBRA was launched by VIII Corps to the east of the River Orne between 18 and 21 July and known as Operation GOODWOOD.

GOODWOOD involved the three British armoured divisions (see Map 10); 11th Armoured, the Guards Armoured and 7th Armoured. The offensive, which was again supported by heavy bombers, failed to reach its final objective the Bourguébus ridge, though the area south of Caen was cleared by II Canadian Corps during Operation ATLANTIC which was conducted simultaneously. This newly captured ground would assist future offensives south towards Falaise. On the eve of COBRA, II Canadian Corps launched Operation SPRING (22-25 July) an attack south towards the Verrières Ridge and this prevented the 9th SS Panzer Division from being transferred to the American front. On 23 July, 1st Canadian Army was established in Normandy and took command off I Corps and II Canadian Corps as well as responsibility for the eastern end of the bridgehead. The Americans launched Operation COBRA on 25 July; by this time the British and Canadians had tied down the vast majority of the Panzer divisions in their sector preventing them from hindering the American offensive.

Once COBRA was launched Montgomery switched his offensives from the eastern end of the bridgehead to the centre using Second British Army to launch Operation BLUECOAT which involved three separate corps. The aim of Operation BLUECOAT was to capture Mont Pinçon, a large massif that dominated the centre of the German defensive position, and protected the

---

5   Bradley, Omar, *A Soldier's Story*, (New York, Henry Holt and Company, 1951), p.325.

American Army's left flank as it advanced south. The operation started on 30 July, however XXX Corps, in the centre, made little progress whereas VIII Corps advancing from Caumont to the west of XXX Corps made rapid advances and secured an area to the east of the town of Vire (see Map 11). In this area they were heavily attacked by German forces but were able to safeguard the American flank. Mont Pinçon itself finally fell to XXX Corps on 7 August.

As well as safeguarding the American flank, Operation BLUECOAT had also drawn away some of the German panzer divisions that had been facing the Canadian Army at Caen. As a result of this the Canadian Army was able to launch two operations; TOTALIZE (8 August) and TRACTABLE (14 August) along the Caen – Falaise road (see Map 12). By 16 August the Canadians had succeeded in capturing the town of Falaise, but they were unable to close the northern end of the Falaise Gap and link up with Third US Army advancing from the south until 21 August.

With the bulk of the German Army destroyed in France, 21st Army Group swung round to advance in a north-easterly direction towards the Belgian and German frontier. First Canadian Army would advance on the left, clearing the Channel ports as they went. Second British Army would advance on the right, conducting an assault crossing of the River Seine at Vernon on 25 August. This assault was undertaken by 43rd Wessex Division and was known as Operation NEPTUNE (see Map 13).

Progress after the crossing was extremely rapid, with XXX Corps pursuing the Germans with three armoured divisions under its command. Brussels was liberated on 3 September, and Antwerp on 4 September (see Map 14). However, by this stage the Allies had begun to run out of supplies and there was an unavoidable pause on the Belgian/Dutch border for logistical reasons. This pause allowed the German Army to recover and stabilize their frontline. It would take another major operation (Operation MARKET GARDEN launched on 17 September) to renew the offensive, the failure of which would dash Allied hopes of ending the war by Christmas. 21st Army Group also had the task of clearing out the German garrisons in the various channel ports. The assault on the port of Le Havre on 10 September by I Corps (OP ASTONIA) was the largest of these operations and required significant air support and engineer assistance to breach the fortress defences – it is widely regarded as a model of combined arms operations.

2

'Closing With The Enemy' – The Infantry

First, all battles and all wars are won in the end by the infantryman. Secondly, the infantryman always bears the brunt. His casualties are heavier, he suffers greater extremes of discomfort and fatigue than the other arms. Thirdly, the art of the infantryman is less stereotyped and far harder to acquire in modern war than that of any other arm.

Field Marshal Earl Wavell[1]

Normandy highlighted once more that it is the infantry who, through close combat, ultimately determine battlefield success. In the attack; it would be the infantry's role to close with and complete the destruction of the enemy. In defence; it would be the infantry who had to hold their positions in the face of tremendous counterattacks and by repelling these assaults, inflict a level of destruction the Germans would not recover from.

Victory in Normandy would largely be down to the infantry's performance in a violent interaction with the enemy, where terrain advantages would be exploited by either side in order to maximize the effects of their own firepower and movement. This encounter would test commanders to the full as well as requiring stoicism, initiative and courage by the individual infantryman. For in the infantry, perhaps more so than any other arm, the level of 'fighting spirit' was critical.

This chapter will examine the men, their weapons and how they were organized as well as touching upon the major 'operations of war'; the attack and defence. This will provide a tactical frame to view the infantryman's role as well as a wider understanding of how an Army coordinates and executes offensive and defensive operations.

In subsequent chapters various units and types of equipment will be analysed, their performance judged on various technical parameters. The quality of the British infantry is however determined by the quality of the man. Training was critical in this regard and the army believed an infantryman should be highly skilled in moving, observing and employing his weapon effectively on the battlefield. This movement and observation was termed 'fieldcraft' and was a particular feature of the training of infantrymen. Fieldcraft emphasized four aspects. Firstly that soldiers needed to rely on their own weapons and expertise in tactical movement, concealment and surprise. Secondly fieldcraft was offensive and did not mean using ground to cower in a hole out of the enemy's fire but as a hunter uses it – getting closer to the prey in order to kill. Thirdly that observation was paramount in offence and concealment paramount in defence – 'This is a war of concealed posts, of camouflage. You cannot kill the enemy unless you can find him. You cannot even start to attack him, if you do not know where he is.'[2] Finally it was stressed that cover from view was not the same

---

1   Wavell, Archibald Feld Marshal, *In Praise of Infantry,* First published in *The Times*, 19 April 1945.
2   *Infantry Training Part VIII – Fieldcraft, Battle Drill, Section and Platoon Tactics* (War Office, March 1944), p.3.

as cover from fire; an infantryman should do all he could to move away from enemy fire unseen – but only so that he could subsequently bring his own weapons to bear against the Germans.

British soldiers were taught a number of individual tactical methods of movement; 'the roll', 'the monkey run' and the 'leopard crawl', methods of moving stealthily at night were also covered and included the 'ghost walk', 'cat walk' and 'kitten crawl'.

A soldier's individual field craft included camouflage techniques; these were taught not merely to protect the soldier, but to help him work his way forward undetected and attack the enemy or surprise him from an unlocated defensive position. The soldier was taught a number of camouflage and concealment techniques. Firstly he must alter the 'tone' of his appearance so that it would match his surroundings. In lush green Norman countryside he would adopt dull clothing, apply dark blanco on his web equipment and darken his white skin with camouflage cream, soot, blanco or even cocoa. Secondly he must prevent the 'shine' of an uncovered helmet giving him away by tying strips of hessian and local foliage to the helmet net. The foliage would also serve to disguise the distinctive 'shape' of the helmet and could also be applied to the square shape of the small pack and his webbing pouches for similar reasons.

In addition to these techniques the soldier was warned about moving too close to water and casting reflections in it, or silhouetting himself against a uniform background, such as the sky. He was taught not to look over the top of cover, particularly smooth linear surfaces like walls or fallen trees, but rather to observe round the side or through the cover, knocking a brick out of a wall for instance. Finally the value of mis-direction was emphasized, the technique of distracting the enemy and causing him to focus on what he thinks he ought to see, a dummy tank, gun or slit trench for instance, rather than the actual position the infantryman was occupying.

Figure 2.1 Rifleman R R Schwabe of the Regina Rifle Regiment mans a loophole in Vaucelles, 23 July. (Lieut. Ken Bell, Library and Archives Canada, PA-131387)

These techniques could also be used to successfully detect the enemy. For instance when observing at night the infantryman learnt to keep low to the ground and extend his skyline thus increasing the chances of an enemy silhouetting himself against it. In addition to visual methods, the art of locating a firing enemy through the 'thump' of the weapons discharge rather than the 'crack' of a round as it passed overhead was practiced. This knowledge could be taken even further and the training manuals emphasized that a more experienced man could:

> … 'read the battle' from the sound of firing from both sides. Every burst of small arms fire, every shell or mortar burst from the enemy or from ourselves, has been fired with an object. A good man can interpret them all.[3]

Having been taught how to conceal himself and take advantage of cover the infantryman would then need to understand how to select a fire position. This application of weapons and soldiers to the terrain itself was the first step in minor tactics and infantry work in general. It demanded from the private soldier the highest standards of both weapon training and fieldcraft, one without the other was usually of little value. The optimum fire position would have provided the infantryman a good view of the ground or target to be covered by his weapon, cover from both enemy observation and fire, a covered approach to the position and finally the ability to operate his weapon freely taking advantage of its unique characteristics. These could include enfilade fire for the Bren gun over open ground or a close flanking shot on a tank from a Projector Infantry Anti-Tank (PIAT) on a likely tank approach.[4]

Though the infantry were equipped with a variety of weapons, the No.4 Lee Enfield .303 rifle was the primary one. It was a bolt-action rifle that was fitted with a double-column ten-round magazine which could be charged either one round at a time or by using a five round charger. The weapon could accurately engage targets up to 550 yards, though typical engagements were usually less than 150 yards. The rifle was also fitted with a spike bayonet, known to soldiers as the 'pig sticker', a handy weapon for close quarter battle.

The Lee-Enfield had many strengths; its bolt action was designed to allow an infantryman to fire, eject and load rounds easily from a prone position. Its accuracy and reliability, particularly when fired as part of a section, was also devastating. Lieutenant Sydney Jary, a platoon commander with the 4th Somerset Light Infantry, recalls engaging a squad of attacking Germans:

> I was briefing my runner, Private Thomas, behind the house when I heard the cry: 'Sir, they are charging us.' Sure enough, from about one hundred and fifty yards ahead, a well spread out line of about twenty Germans were putting in a bayonet charge. Brave lads they didn't stand a chance. I gave no orders except 'cease fire'. Not one got within seventy yards of us.[5]

The alternative individual weapon for the British infantryman was the Sten 9mm sub-machine gun, it was common throughout the Army but in the infantry was normally only issued to radio operators and commanders. The Sten was a crude weapon that operated on the blowback principle with a fixed firing pin on the face of the bolt. When cocked the bolt was at the rear, operating the trigger would cause the bolt to fly forward pick up a round from the magazine, feed it into chamber and fire. When the round was fired the breech on the Sten would not be locked, instead

---

3   *Infantry Training Part VIII – Fieldcraft, Battle Drill, Section and Platoon Tactics* (War Office, March 1944), p.42.
4   Ibid., p.44.
5   Jary, Sydney, *18 Platoon* (Winchester: The Rifles, 2009), p.116.

the recoil action was used to push the bolt back to the rear from where the firing cycle would continue as long as the trigger remained depressed. This clumsy movement within the body of the weapon, as well as the 'pistol type' 9mm rounds meant that the Sten was an inaccurate weapon and had an effective range of 100 yards. The 9mm rounds were loaded into a 32 round magazine, the rounds converging into a single column feed that was notorious for jamming and causing stoppages. Equally serious were the safety implications of the open bolt design. Dropping the Sten could easily cause the bolt to slide forward and inadvertently fire a round; accidents were tragically frequent. Despite all of these handicaps it remained a popular weapon for close quarter battle and was frequently taken on patrol, its 500 rounds per minute making up for its other disadvantages. Private Stanley Whitehouse of 1st Black Watch witnessed the Sten's lethality on a patrol:

> Taffy suddenly cocked his head and looked back the way we had come. Grainger and Aitch, heads together, were muttering over the map when Taffy put one hand over the sheet to attract their attention and pointed to the rear. We peered anxiously through the greenery and my heart must have skipped a beat. Ambling towards us, following our trail, were a dozen or so Germans, about thirty yards away. By their nonchalant, carefree attitude, with weapons slung over their shoulders, it was obvious they had not seen us and were not expecting trouble. Our corporal, calm and complete master of the situation, gripped his Sten and leaned over to Aitch.
>
> You come with me," he whispered, 'and the rest of you stay here. And for God's sake don't fire unless you hear me start shooting. Then get anything that comes your way.
>
> The two NCOs melted away to the left and were soon lost among the trees, leaving the four of us waiting and wondering. My throat was so dry I could hardly swallow. We looked at each other with misgivings as the enemy approached…fifteen yards, now ten. I was waiting for Grainger and Aitch to come behind them and yell 'Hande Hoch', the signal for the rest of us to step out and show the enemy that they were surrounded and that surrender was their only option. But it was not to be. Violent bursts of Sten fire came from our left, destroying the deathly hush that was always an integral feature of no-man's land. The Germans half turned in panic, trying to unsling their rifles, but the unrelenting fire chopped them down. Above the firing we could hear cries of pain that were abruptly cut short, ending in gasps and groans. Now the rest of us fired into the group, sending the field grey figures milling around and stumbling. Within seconds it was all over.[6]

For firepower though the Bren light machine gun was the most important weapon available to the infantry platoon. One was issued for each rifle section and the two-man team that operated the Bren was usually referred to as the 'gun group'. The team consisted of a No.1 who carried and fired the Bren and a No.2 who loaded and spotted targets as well as carrying the spare magazines, barrels and toolkit. Helpfully, the Bren fired the same .303 rounds as the Lee Enfield which were loaded into a 30 round magazine, though to ease pressure on the springs normally only 28 rounds were loaded at any one time. Spare Bren magazines were normally shared out amongst the infantry section, each soldier carrying two magazines. The Bren's bipod provided a stable firing position that gave the gun an effective range of up to 600 yards, though typical engagements were at much shorter ranges. The Bren's accuracy also stemmed from the gas-operated closed bolt system, this allowed propellant gases to be vented from a port towards the muzzle end of the barrel. The gases operated a piston which in turn moved the breech block, this system disturbed the firer's

---

6   Whitehouse, Stanley and Bennett, George, *Fear is the Foe: A Footslogger from Normandy to the Rhine*, (London: Robert Hale, 1988), p.91.

Figure 2.2
British infantrymen armed
with a Sten and Bren gun
man a building in Faub de
Vaucelles near Caen, 19 July.
(Imperial War Museum
B7749)

Figure 2.2
British infantrymen armed
with a Sten and Bren gun
man a building in Faub de
Vaucelles near Caen, 19 July.
(Imperial War Museum
B7749)

position less and increased the weapon's accuracy. During prolonged firing the Bren's barrel would inevitably become progressively hot and before this reached a critical temperature the No.2 would quickly change the barrel using the carrying handle above the barrel to grip it without burning his hands. Although a popular weapon, the Bren's closed breech and magazine fed method of operation meant it had a much slower rate of fire than its German counterparts; the MG34 and MG42 'Spandau' machine guns. The Bren only had a cyclic firing rate of 500 rounds per minute, much slower than the Spandau's 1,200 rounds per minute. Whilst nowhere near as accurate as the Bren the Spandau's suppressive firepower was often a critical superiority in the close country of Normandy where ranges were generally short and accuracy less of an issue. Lieutenant Sydney Jary compared the two:

> Like most infantry subalterns trained in the UK for the invasion of Europe, I was convinced of the excellence of our Bren light machine gun. After 40 years, I still view the Bren with affection. It was excellent, particularly as a highly portable and accurate infantry section weapon invaluable in the attack. However, when it came to a firefight between a German and a British platoon, their MG34 and MG42 won hands down. I remember my first reaction to actual infantry warfare in July 1944 was one of amazement at the crushing firepower of these very rapid-firing guns. It seemed to me that the German infantryman seldom used his rifle. He was a carrier of boxes of light machine gun ammunition of which they seemed to have an endless supply. Our Bren gunners usually fired in short bursts of about five rounds, which not only conserved ammunition but also avoided the gun barrels overheating. Our theory was that, unless one hit the target with the first burst, the opposition would go to ground and subsequent bursts would be unlikely to be so effective. The Germans thought otherwise,

Figure 2.3 A German paratrooper equipped with an MG 42 machine gun. (Bundesarchiv, Bild 101I-587-2253-15, photo: Toni Schneiders)

firing in long sustained bursts, the object of which seemed to me to be to keep us pinned to the ground regardless of the ammunition expenditure.[7]

The infantryman was also equipped with grenades, of which there were two main types; the No.36 grenade and the White Phosphorus grenade. The No.36 grenade or 'Mills bomb' consisted of a metal grooved 'pineapple body' weighing 1lb 11 oz. The body contained a central striker, held in place by a hand-lever that in turn was secured by a pin. The thrower would simply have to pull the pin, release the hand-lever and throw the grenade. Average soldiers could throw the grenade 50 feet or so, yet the grenade splinters were lethal up to 100 yards, consequently the thrower would have to ensure he and his comrades were protected behind some form of cover when it detonated. The grenade was an ideal weapon for posting in bunkers or trenches as well as house-clearing. At the beginning of the war the grenade had a time delay of seven seconds before detonation, it was soon realised that this was too long and allowed the enemy to either take cover, or worse still throw the grenade back, the timing was therefore reduced to four seconds. Lieutenant Balsom, of 1st Norfolks, recalls using grenades during an attack:

Just in front was a mound of earth and on its far side an entrance covered by a camouflaged ground sheet. As I approached, a grey-clad figure drew the ground sheet aside, saw me and ducked back in again.

---

7   Jary, Sydney, *18 Platoon* (Winchester: The Rifles, 2009), pp.53-54.

I registered a young, pale, frightened face but my only thought was that I could not leave an enemy soldier behind our backs as we moved forward. I took a 36 grenade from my belt and attempted to pull the safety pin but my hands were too cold to close the ends of the split pin before withdrawing it. I sheltered against the bank of earth while it seemed to take an age to press the ends of the pin closed against my belt buckle so that I could pull the pin and throw the grenade into the dugout. I waited for the explosion but had no time to see the result and ran on until we gained the ditch alongside the track.[8]

The British soldier was also provided with White Phosphorus grenades, which were used for producing a smoke screen. The grenade's exploding action caused the phosphorus in the grenade to ignite producing dense clouds of white smoke, the burning phosphorous also made it a useful incendiary device too.

The large quantities of weapons, ammunition, rations and other paraphernalia the infantryman had to carry meant that a load bearing system was essential. To that end the 37-pattern webbing system was provided, which came with an assortment of pouches as well as a small pack. Each infantryman would have his own personal preferences about what to put where, Private Rex Wingfield, 1st/6th Queen's, describes the advice he was given by an old soldier in Normandy about how to use his webbing:

He brought my webbing equipment over and emptied my pouches. A Bren magazine, grenades and cartridge clips poured out.
'That's the drill book way. Now look at mine.'
The pouches were further from the buckle than mine. I asked why.
'When you crawl, you may as well crawl comfortably without them sticking in your guts. Not too far round, mind, or they'll interfere with your arm movements. Now empty the pouches!'
I did so. In the left pouch were two bars of chocolate, boiled sweets and a tin of cigarettes. In the right was a 77 smoke grenade and clips of ammunition were packed tightly on top. I looked at him questioningly.
'I'm right handed, so if I want anything the right hand is the one I use. That's why ammo is in the right pouch. Fags are essential, but not a matter of life and death, so they go in the left-hand pouch. First things first, mate. No Bren mag? We always carry them in a box with the gun, so that we don't get them scattered in a hot spot. 36 grenades? Watch!'
He took two grenades and clipped them by the safety lever to his belt near his right buttock. The safety-pins were firmly splayed out.
'If I'm lying down or standing up I can get at them easily. Now, where do you keep your money?'
'Right-hand trouser pocket!' I said.
'O.K. Feel mine! Much more important than money!'
I felt his pocket on his thigh. It wasn't there.
'Round the back mate!'
The corner of his pocket was stitched to the back of the leg, drawing the whole leg round to the rear. The pocket contained more clips. The map pocket on his left thigh was full of letters. The field dressing pocket was empty. The dressing was tucked in his blouse.[9]

8   Lincoln, John, *Thank God For The Infantry* (Stroud: Sutton Publishing, 1994), p.118.
9   Wingfield, Rex, *The Only Way Out* (London: Hutchinson, 1955), pp.58-59.

However tactical training and equipment was only a small part of what made an efficient infantryman. The Army had witnessed both the moral collapse of their French and Belgian Allies in 1940 as well as its own Singapore debacle where 80,000 British troops surrendered to a smaller Japanese force. Much of the reason for this defeat would be put down to 'defeatism' or a lack of 'guts' by the Army's senior leadership and British training manuals of the day unsurprisingly stressed the requirement for aggression amongst infantrymen:

> In this war men may be surrounded or may have deliberately penetrated deeply behind the enemy's main positions, fighting in isolation, unsupervised by a senior commander. They may have accomplished their immediate task and be in a position where there is no chance of praise or punishment or supervision. The ability to decide to carry on fighting and use their initiative will depend not so much on obedience, uniformity and subordination as morale, and the enthusiasm, initiative, and aggressiveness which spring from it. False discipline, the kind which is not founded on high fighting morale, may lead to a dangerous sense of complacency. True discipline is the harnessing of enthusiasm.
>
> For this war, more than ever, we need this enthusiasm, this determination to destroy the enemy, this high fighting morale which makes discipline a source of pride, and initiative a matter of course, so that each man will act intelligently and bravely without waiting to be told what to do when a new and surprising situation arises. We need fighting morale. To generate high morale each man must be aware of his own genuine skill and power as a fighting unit, and feel his own importance to his comrades and nation; he must know of the efficiency and high morale of his comrades and be infected by the energy, vitality and enthusiasm of his officers.[10]

Heady stuff indeed, however Lieutenant Sydney Jary's rare experience in commanding the same platoon (18 Platoon, 4th Somerset Light Infantry) from August 1944 to VE day makes him eminently qualified to judge what makes a good infantryman. He offers an alternative perspective, highlighting some surprising qualities a soldier would require to endure frontline service:

> Had I been asked at any time before August 1944 to list the personal characteristics which go to make a good infantry soldier, my reply would have been wide of the mark.
>
> Like most I would no doubt have suggested only masculine ones like aggression, physical stamina, a hunting instinct and a competitive nature. How wrong I would have been. I would now suggest the following. Firstly sufferance, without which one could not survive. Secondly, a quiet mind which enables a soldier to live in harmony with his fellows through all sorts of difficulties and sometimes under dreadful conditions. As in a closed monastic existence, there is simply no room for the assertive or acrimonious. Thirdly, but no less important, a sense of the ridiculous which helps a soldier surmount the unacceptable. Add to these a reasonable standard of physical fitness and a dedicated professional competence, and you have a soldier for all seasons. None of the NCOs or soldiers who made 18 Platoon what it was resembled the characters portrayed in most books and films about war. All were quiet, sensible and unassuming men and some, by any standards, were heroes.[11]

---

10 *Infantry Training Part VIII – Fieldcraft, Battle Drill, Section and Platoon Tactics* (War Office, March 1944), p.38.
11 Jary, Sydney, *18 Platoon* (Winchester: The Rifles, 2009), p.117.

An infantryman would rarely operate as an individual but usually as an integral part of his ten-man section. This section would be commanded by a corporal who would normally divide his team up into a group of six riflemen, which he would accompany, and a Bren gun group of two, which his section second in command (a lance corporal) would lead. There were many tasks that the section commander was responsible for; administration, sentry duties, trench digging etc. but perhaps his most important task was to tactically control the section. This included directing what formation his section would adopt as they manoeuvred across country, which usually depended on the terrain and the perceived enemy threat. He could choose the 'Blob' of 2-4 men which gave good control and concealment, or 'single file' which was useful for advancing alongside certain linear types of cover like hedgerows, but was poor for delivering fire to the front. The section commander could also select 'irregular arrowhead' which allowed the section to deploy rapidly to either flank; but was hard to control or finally the 'extended line' could be chosen, which as it was both hard to control and vulnerable to fire from the flank was really only utilised for the final assault.

At other times the section commander would be responsible for detailing the specific targets, arcs of fire and observation for his section's soldiers as well as controlling the rate of fire of his men. This latter task was important for either conserving ammunition or controlling the effect their fire was having on the enemy. For instance a section commander when suppressing an enemy position may, just at the moment an assault goes in, increase the rate of fire from 'deliberate' to 'rapid' to ensure that the enemy's heads are kept down at the critical moment.

There were three sections to a platoon, which would be commanded by a second lieutenant or lieutenant. The platoon HQ would consist of a platoon sergeant, a runner (to pass messages, either down to the sections or back to company HQ), as well the platoon commander's servant known as a batman. A servant may seem an extravagance on a battlefield but the platoon commander was usually too busy leading the platoon and rarely had enough time to prepare his own meals or dig a slit trench, these tasks would therefore fall to the batman. The platoon HQ was equipped with a No.38 radio set for communications back to company HQ, the radio set being carried and operated by the platoon signaller. An infantry platoon signaller had a thankless task, the radio was unreliable, heavy and also marked him out as a key target for snipers. As Private Stanley Whitehouse observed it also reduced the effectiveness of one of the five senses with dangerous consequences:

Figure 2.5
Private R L Randolf of
the 1st Bn the Canadian
Scottish Regiment
armed with a 2-inch
mortar, 12 June.
(Lieut. Donald I. Grant,
Library and Archives
Canada, PA-131431)

As we stalked down Norman lanes Batey always stayed just behind the platoon commander with his earphones on, ready to pick up radio messages. But when we were shelled or mortared he was unable to hear the tell-tale whines and often continued advancing while the rest of us crouched in a roadside ditch. He complained loudly to all who would listen and when something thudded off his helmet while the rest of us lay flat on our bellies, his invective was unfit for chaste ears. Eventually we agreed that I should walk behind him and on hearing a whine or screech of anything unfriendly approaching I would slap his pack hard. It worked quite well, except when occasionally, in my haste to 'hit the dirt', I forgot to warn my mate. Then he would say nothing, but his scornful look as I sheepishly got to my feet was far more effective than mere curses.[12]

Platoon headquarters also had a 2-inch mortar, this exceptionally simple weapon could fire either High Explosive (HE), Smoke or illuminating bombs out to 500 yards, the platoon normally carried 30 bombs, some of which would be scattered amongst other infantrymen to share the load. The mortar had no bipod; but simply a short stubby baseplate at the end of its 21-inch barrel. The mortar was lined up against the target using a white vertical line, the bomb dropped down the barrel and fired by pulling a trigger at the base of the mortar, the fall of shot was then adjusted till the bombs fell in the target area. Crude and simple the 2-inch mortar may have been, but it worked, allowing the platoon to put down an effective smoke screen or a modest weight of HE (The HE bombs weighed approximately 2.25lb). The 2-inch mortar was usually operated by a two

---

12 Whitehouse, Stanley and Bennett, George, *Fear is the Foe: A Footslogger from Normandy to the Rhine* (London: Robert Hale, 1988) p.58.

man team, although one man could fire it if needed, the mortar gave off a small smoke cloud when fired so the weapon was usually operated from behind cover to disguise its signature.

For its anti-tank defence the platoon would usually be given one of the three PIAT weapons that were normally held at company level. There were few weapons produced by the British in the Second World War that were quite as bizarre as the PIAT. The PIAT was designed to launch a 2.5lb shaped charge bomb, placed in the open cradle at the front of the weapon, using a powerful spring that would detonate a cartridge on the base of the bomb. The PIAT had an effective range of about 115 yards, though the bomb was not powerful enough to penetrate the frontal armour of Tiger or Panther tanks and a shot at the rear or sides of the tank was the only realistic method of attack against these targets. Firing the weapon was an awkward affair, first the weapon had to be cocked which involved placing two feet on the weapon's padded butt and pulling and twisting at the same time. This required considerable dexterity and strength and was hard to do standing up, let alone when in a prone position or a slit trench. The soldier would then get into a firing position and pull the trigger, holding onto the PIAT like grim death if he wanted the recoil to re-cock the weapon rather than face doing it manually once more. On firing, the bomb would reportedly 'wobble' through the air and on impacting the target its shaped warhead would detonate and penetrate the armour. Because the shaped charge warhead was reverse detonated there was the reasonable risk that the base of the bomb would fly directly back at the firer. Unpopular and bizarre a contraption though the PIAT was, it reportedly accounted for 6% of German tanks destroyed in Normandy (the RAF as a comparison accounted for 7%).[13] Company Sergeant Major Harrison, 4th King's Shropshire Light Infantry, successfully used one during Operation BLUECOAT. His company commander recounts the story:

> Arming himself with the platoon's PIAT, he took a shot at the tank as it withdrew slowly down the road. The bomb hit the sloping front and bounced harmlessly off. The Panther withdrew another seventy yards and stopped. Harrison stalked it for several minutes and eventually located it ten feet beyond a hedge, its crew dismounted and standing, talking together in hoarse whispers. In a cold sweat he pushed his loaded PIAT cautiously through the hedge, whereat a bramble stalk caught the muzzle and the bomb fell off.
>
> That made me hopping mad,' said Harrison to me later, 'So I stamped five yards down the road, yanked the brushwood out of the way, shoved the PIAT through the hedge and pulled the blasted trigger.' The bomb went off like a clap of thunder and nearly concussed Harrison – but it put paid to the Panther, and must have given its nearby crew a rare shock.[14]

Three infantry platoons would make up a rifle company and there were normally four rifle companies in an infantry battalion (A, B, C and D companies). A rifle company was commanded by a major with a captain as his second in command and a warrant officer as a company sergeant major (CSM). The company would also be supported by a company quartermaster sergeant (CQMS) and a storeman who would ensure that sufficient ammunition, rations and other essential stores were available.

The battalion also had within its structure a support company (Sp Coy) consisting of Mortar, Anti-Tank, Carrier and Pioneer platoons. These support platoons were essential to the infantry battalion's operations. Though other heavier weapons might exist within the brigade or division

---

13 French, David *Raising Churchill's Army: The British Army and the War against Germany 1919-1945,* (Oxford: Oxford University Press, 2000), pp.88-89.

14 Thornburn, Ned, *The 4th KSLI in Normandy* (Shrewsbury: 4th Bn KSLI Trust, 1990), p.109.

Figure 2.6 An infantryman prepares to fire a PIAT anti-tank weapon, 9 August.
(Imperial War Museum B8913)

the beauty of the battalion's own support weapons was that its commanding officer did not have to ask anyone's permission to use them and could employ them wherever and however he saw fit.

The mortar platoon was commanded by a captain, with a lieutenant as a second in command, it was equipped with six 3-inch mortars which were divided into three sections of two mortars each, each mortar section being commanded by a sergeant. With a maximum range of 2,800 yards the 3-inch mortar was very much a close support weapon, the range being altered by a combination of changing the elevation of the barrel as well adding a series of augmenting charges to the tail of the bomb (Charge I – 500 to 1,500 yards and Charge II – 950 to 2,800 yards). The high trajectory of the 3-inch mortar meant that it was very effective when firing against targets which were behind steep cover or generally out of reach of flat trajectory weapons, for this reason it was particularly useful in built up areas.

As the level of 'effective fire' could only be obtained by firing two or more mortars on a target they were rarely used individually and normally the minimum of a mortar section would be employed on any given task. The advantage of splitting the mortar platoon into sections was that more of the battalion's frontage could then be covered, though it did make command and control more difficult. The mortar fire itself was controlled by observers either located in an Observation Post (OP), or mobile and moving with the rifle company. On most occasions the OP was connected to the mortars themselves by land line as wireless communications often proved too unreliable. In the attack mortars would assist in the supporting artillery fire plan and were often sighted so that they could fire 1000 yards beyond the objective, greatly assisting in the post attack re-organisation. In defensive engagements the mortars would be used to engage areas that could not be adequately engaged by small arms fire, as well as to support friendly counter-attacks.

Figure 2.7
A 3-inch mortar crew of the
Regina Rifles Regiment near
Bretteville-l'Orgeuilleuse,
9 June. (Lieut. Donald I. Grant,
Library and Archives Canada,
PA-128794)

Mortars were also allotted Defensive Fire (DF) tasks in exactly the same manner as the artillery, these techniques will be covered in detail in the later chapter on artillery.

One of the most important elements of the infantry battalion was the anti-tank platoon. Whilst the PIAT could, in favourable circumstances and at very short range, defeat German armour it was the anti-tank platoon, equipped with the 6-pounder anti-tank gun, that provided the infantry battalion's main integral defence against tanks. The platoon was split into three sections and each section was equipped with two 6-pounders commanded by a sergeant. Lieutenant B T W Stewart was the second-in-command of the 1st Tyneside Scots Anti-Tank Platoon and gives a good description of the 6-pounder gun:

> The 6-pounder looked like, and was, a serious gun. It fired solid rounds and exploding shells which were obviously useful for demolishing walls but not for killing tanks. The gun had a split trailer which was opened as soon as the gun was unlimbered from its towing Loyd carrier, so that the two legs of the trailer roughly formed a 45 degree stabilizer, the base plates digging into the ground as the gun was fired. The wheels were not removed, so the gun was ready for movement at all times, either by carrier or manhandling. The gun 'layer' and 'loader' were protected by a shield which stopped shrapnel splinters.
>
> The 6-pounder was a high velocity gun and a very sharp crack accompanied its firing – I fear we all paid dearly in later years for the enthusiastic and frequent practice which formed the basis for the Platoon's success at Rauray. My hearing has never been the same since. Just before action in Normandy, the familiar 6-pounder ammunition was replaced or augmented by Sabot – a tungsten 'dart' encased in a plastic sleeve which disintegrated as the round was fired, leaving the dart to travel twice as fast as the old 6-pounder solid-round and with infinitely greater penetration. The dart, if a hit was achieved, made quite a small hole in the tank's armour but then whizzed round around the inside causing great damage to crew and

Figure 2.8 Infantrymen of the Highland Light Infantry attach drag ropes to a 6-pounder anti-tank gun, Thaon, 6 August. (Lieut. Ken Bell, Library and Archives Canada, PA-131365)

equipment. Not having been trained in the use of Sabot, we only knew of these rounds in theory and we were probably less effective than we had been with the familiar 6-pounder round. The extra velocity changed the trajectory as well as making it less necessary to 'lay off' (allow for speed of the target). On the other hand there can be little doubt that when we achieved a hit it was more likely to penetrate.[15]

The 6-pounder had many virtuous points, its high muzzle velocity (up to 2800 feet per second) meant that it had an accurate flat trajectory with a short time of flight and the shot was also filled with a tracer composition that allowed the observer to track the round in flight. The gun was very mobile; not only could it be towed by jeeps or carriers, it was also light enough (22 1/2 cwt) to be manhandled over rough ground and with practice could be brought into action from any number of unlikely firing positions. It had a free traverse of 90 degrees which was shoulder controlled by the layer, this design allowed the layer to feel as if the gun was an extension of his body thus making it easier to aim. The simple gun drill meant that a good crew could fire 12 rounds per minute,[16] though accuracy was usually more important than rate of fire. Lieutenant Stewart describes the firing drill:

15 Baverstock, Kevin, *Breaking the Panzers*, (Stroud: Sutton Publishing, 2002), p.xxx.
16 *Small Arms Training Volume 1 Pamphlet No.27 6Pdr, 7-cwt. Anti-Tank Gun*, (War Office, 1944), pp.1-2.

The perfect sequence of action was: (1) Unlimber the gun from the Loyd carrier and unload box of ammunition (once the gun was in position the carrier could then widen its role carrying food, ammunition and wounded for the local rifle company). (2) Face gun barrel to enemy and open trailer legs. (3) Load. The breech block was opened by hand, a round pushed in and block closed by loader who then raised his hand to show that the gun was ready to fire. (4) Aim. The layer (aimer) would be looking through his telescope and adjusting his aim as the loader was doing his part. (5) Fire. On the command of the Gun Detachment Commander, the gun would fire at the designated target. The layer had to use his judgment, possibly helped by the Commander, about the speed of the enemy tank and the Commander's orders about range. The Commander would be giving his target information to the layer as soon as the gun was in position. The loading would be automatic. Thus: 'Enemy tank, 2 o'clock, speed 20, range 500. If the first round travelled over or under the tank, the Commander would order: 'up 200!' or 'down 200!', and the aimer would adjust his telescope accordingly. Getting a hit fast was important before fire was returned by the enemy. As I previously mentioned, we practiced this sort of drill endlessly, on parade grounds and in the countryside so that it became instinctive. Of course, in battle, the confusion of moving targets, some using smoke to conceal their whereabouts, made accurate estimates of range and speed, which required laying off ahead of the tank (unless the speed was very slow), difficult. In short however good the drill, and I think we were as good as any, judgment and luck played a major part.[17]

The 6-pounder did have one or two limitations; it had a very pronounced muzzle flash which could quite easily give away its position, therefore careful siting and concealment were vital. The considerable blast from the gun also made observation of the shot difficult; the observer frequently controlling and adjusting the guns from an upwind flank. Finally the shock of discharge also caused the gun to 'bounce', particularly before the spades had dug-in, sometimes unsettling an inexperienced crew. Perhaps the principal disadvantage though was that the Armour Piercing (AP) solid shot could not penetrate the frontal armour of some German tanks, this meant that the 6-pounder would need to be sited to achieve flanking shots.

To take advantage of flanking shots the guns would be deployed to engage tanks as they approached the defensive position along predicted approach routes, known as 'tank runs'. Although the anti-tank platoon commander would determine gun areas and arcs, the gun would normally be sited by the section commander. He would position it so it could engage the tank with enfilade fire from a defilade position, or to put it another way hit the side of the tank by firing from a flank. This enabled the gun to engage the tank's thinner side or rear armour and helped prevent the enemy from locating the gun through its pronounced muzzle flash. Guns were never sited to engage tanks frontally except in emergencies. Ideally the gun's arc of fire should also include obstacles or broken ground, which would slow the enemy tanks and make them easier to engage.

Concealment and mis-direction were important factors in siting the gun, helping to hide it from the tank or being engaged by enemy observed mortar or artillery fire. The 6-pounders would be sited so that they could provide mutual support to each other, should one gun be attacked by tanks the others could assist it by engaging the attacking tank.

The gun and its crew were vulnerable to attacking infantry accompanying the tank, consequently a Bren gunner was an integral part of the crew. He was usually sited to a flank where his fire would be used not only to engage supporting infantry but to ensure the tank crew remained 'closed down' (i.e. the hatches shut) and therefore had a much more restricted view. As a single Bren gunner can only deliver a modest weight of fire, protection against sizable enemy infantry forces

---

17 Baverstock, Kevin, *Breaking the Panzers* (Stroud: Sutton Publishing, 2002), p.xxxi.

would be provided by siting the 6-pounder within a larger infantry company's defensive layout. Alternate positions for the gun to move to once it had fired a number of shots were routinely identified and considered another important tactic that would increase the gun's chances of survival.[18]

The battalion also had a carrier platoon within support company. This was equipped with thirteen Universal or 'Bren' Carriers which were open topped light-armoured tracked vehicles. They were often used for command and control, reconnaissance purposes or as a mobile reserve or fire unit. Bren carriers were not only present in the carrier platoon but also deployed throughout the battalion for a variety of other purposes too. The mortar platoon used them to carry their mortars and ammunition and the anti-tank platoon used the very similar Lloyd carrier to tow its guns. Even the commanding officer of a battalion possessed one, its high mobility and modest protection helping him to move around the battlefield and maintain control of his unit. The impressive utility of Bren carriers will mean that they are frequently mentioned in this book, not just because they were useful but because of the great affection that existed for these remarkable little vehicles. Lieutenant Sydney Jary captures this feeling as well as explaining why Bren carriers were so admired:

> Her name was Lizzie she was our maid of all work and for eleven months, from the Normandy bocage to Bremerhaven, D Coy 4th Somerset Light Infantry quite shamelessly took her for granted.
>
> I suppose she really belonged to the CSM and her primary role was ammunition resupply, if necessary under SA [Small Arms], shell or mortar fire. However she was coy about tanks and antitank guns, particularly 88s. She was loaded with lots of .303 and 9mm SAA, 2-inch mortar bombs (HE, smoke and illuminating) and bombs for the horrid PIAT …
>
> … Her paint was scarred by bullet, shell and mortar splinter strikes some of which had penetrated her front mudguards. I suspect that many contemporary soldiers do not appreciate the devastating effect SA, shell and mortar fire has on battalion soft-skinned transport – why do radiators always get holed first? It always seemed to me that even one stray shell near any of our transport produced a fatally holed radiator. Lizzie was impervious to all this and was able to go where Bedfords, Fords and Chevrolets feared to tread.
>
> She was a dirty wench and often went unwashed. In the Normandy summer she was invariably coated with fine dust. During the winter battles she was covered with mud or, sometimes, with snow. Unlike some of her sisters, she was reliable and totally faithful, and survived to live with the family until, like all old soldiers, she just faded away.
>
> The British soldier can make unreasonable demands and Lizzie rose to everyone. I think it would be fair to state that some defensive positions were only tenable because Lizzie made them so.[19]

Whist its speed, low silhouette and light armour gave it a degree of protection, travelling in a carrier near the frontline was still a hazardous business. Captain George R Blackburn was a Canadian Artillery Forward Observation Officer and recalls one risky trip during the Verrières ridge battles. His account illustrates not only how other arms as well as the infantry used carriers, but also how concealment, movement and observation are just as important for frontline vehicles as they are for individual infantrymen:

> When you tell Ryckman that once over the crest he'll be in full view of the enemy all the way down into the village, and that he'll have to 'tramp on it' if he is to make it, he merely shrugs

---

18 *Small Arms Training Volume 1 Pamphlet No.27 6Pdr, 7-cwt. Anti-Tank Gun* (War Office, 1944), p.88.
19 Jary, Sydney, "I love my Bren Carrier", *British Army Review*, No.112, pp.71-72.

as if to say 'what the hell,' and starts grinding the carrier slowly up the slope at an angle meant to gain the greatest concealment before turning onto the road itself. The cool, deliberate, and remarkably quiet way he manoeuvres the sluggish machine up the slope is very reassuring. But when the carrier at last tips over the brow of the ridge and noses down, the breadth and depth of the sunlit panoroma lying before you is even more startling than you imagined it would be. In the clear morning air, you can see for miles, far beyond St Martin, now laid out below you two kilometres away.

And it's clear that if you have an unobstructed view so must all the Germans' dug-in tanks and camouflaged 88s out there – each of them capable of destroying you with one shot from distances far beyond that first crest and the high ground they still hold over on the right, across the Orne. It's as though you're riding a shooting-gallery. You duck as the carrier dodders over the crest, almost stopping as Ryckman changes gears from the bull-low used to climb quietly up the steep route – for though he's highly skilled and moves smoothly and swiftly to change up to high gear, it still takes time to get a sluggish carrier rolling.

Even when he has it roaring down the slope with accelerator pressed to the floor, you know you're offering an easy target for guns that fire missiles faster than the speed of sound. The way is as straight as a Roman road all the way down to the village, without a house, a tree, or anything to obstruct their gun's view. And on all sides there is chilling evidence of their accuracy: the slope on the left is dotted with burned-out tanks; and down on the bottom-land on the right, close to the Orne, is an appalling clutter of burned-out half-tracks, carriers and even a smashed Jeep.

You find yourself holding your breath. Ryckman has the carrier roaring wide-open now, passing very close to the edge of a yawning cavity along the left side of the road, a quarry or gravel pit clearly marked on the map.

You're halfway there…Then suddenly there's a heart stopping metallic wham! Ryckman involuntarily lets up a bit on the accelerator before realizing It's only one of the tracks taking a slap at the underside of the carrier body. Before he gets full power back on, to take up the slack in the tracks, both of them are slamming away at the undersides of the carrier, making a terrible racket. If the Jerries have been dozing they surely are awake now, and hastening to man their guns.

But the village with its sheltering buildings is getting close. The stubby church tower over in the southeast corner, near the map reference you're headed for, is plainly visible.

Now you're passing a large orchard on the right. Only three or four hundred yards more and you'll be among the first buildings . They must be withholding their fire until you get so close that they'll be absolutely certain not to miss. You find yourself breathing, Oh please, not now…now that we've almost made it!

Suddenly, from the orchard on the right, a soldier leaps out onto the road, directly in the path of the carrier, and waves his arms over his head, frantically signalling you to stop.

Even at a distance, the tall, raw-boned man with a great shock of jet-black hair that no helmet could completely hide, is instantly recognisable as Gunner Lewis Milton Bryan, a member of Waddell's crew. As the braking carrier rolls up to him, barely halting in time, he's jabbing his left hand urgently towards a track leading off to your right. And when Ryckman skid-turns in that direction, Bryan hops up on front of you yelling urgently, 'Get going! Back in there among the trees. Fast! You're under observation here – he still holds half the village.[20]

20 Blackburn, George, *The Guns of Normandy* (London: Constable, 1998), pp.283-285.

Figure 2.9 A Bren carrier of the Toronto Scottish (M.G.) Regiment, near Tilly-la-Campagne, 8 August. (Lieut. Michael M. Dean, Library and Archives Canada, PA-131368)

The battalion also contained a small team of snipers, usually under the control of the intelligence officer. These soldiers required a very high level of fieldcraft and marksmanship to fulfil their role of harassing the enemy, killing key commanders and countering the German's own snipers. The snipers usually operated as a pair, one observing and one shooting, they were equipped with the standard Lee Enfield .303 rifle fitted with the No.32 telescopic sight. The rifle's bolt action proved useful in that the firer could wait to eject the empty cartridge when he deemed it safe, avoiding detection by the enemy. It takes a special type of soldier to make a sniper, Lieutenant Robert Woolcombe, 6th King's Own Scottish Borderers, recalls one of his battalion's own snipers:

Then there was Johnstone 43. He was called Johnstone 43 to distinguish him from Johnstone 63, and Johnstone 75, and from Johnstone 04, and all the other Johnstones. He came from somewhere around Gala, with a lilting, good-natured voice and a head that was very bald and pink. With an easy smile and the soft answer, he worked in the Company Office as a second clerk and assisted Black Douglas in the stores. But he, too, was a countryman, and the murmur of streams, the sighs of far woods and of breezes over the braes were in the soul of Johnstone 43, and in his voice. Especially streams. Streams with fish. The tributaries and waters of the Tweed.

He also happened to be a crack rifle shot, and was taken from us into the small team of battalion snipers run by the Intelligence Officer. Lord Wavell, it will be remembered, said that the ideal infantryman should be a combination of cat burglar, gunman, poacher, with a seasoning of devilry in him, and Johnstone 43 was all these things in his gentle way.

Time and again he crept out ahead of the Battalion frontage in Normandy to ply his craft. There was another man with him: a leathery, burly, jolly man with remarkable pale blue eyes, who came also in the first place from 'A' Company, called Bell. And very, very tough. The two worked as a pair – the snipers always worked in pairs. They were inseparable and soon established a grim reputation for themselves...Then Bell was killed. I saw him lying in a cart track near an orchard, covered by a gas cape with only his boots sticking out. And there was a shadow over the face of Johnstone 43 as he went his way, a look one had not seen there before; and he smiled less. And on across North-West Europe he went out and laid up with his telescopic sights and did his deadly work. Bell must have been avenged a hundredfold. Long before the campaign was finished he had been awarded the Distinguished Conduct Medal, and his escapades were many. But all this he survived, to return to his braes and streams of the Tweed, no longer of necessity Johnstone 43.[21]

One of the major tasks for snipers was to combat their direct counterparts; the German snipers. Sergeant Major Charles Martin of the Canadian Queen's Own Rifles noted an enemy sniper outside Carpiquet had wounded several riflemen and decided to neutralise him. This required some care as he knew only the general target area the enemy sniper area was operating from:

Harold would come with me with his telescope. It takes two – one to spot the larger target with the telescope and a riflemen to sight, adjust, aim and keep the precise target more or less in view through telescopic sights mounted on one of our regular .303 rifles.

About two o'clock in the morning we moved out 250 yards or so, which put us nicely 100 to 150 yards from our target area. We made a blind and a small trench with some cover. We were in some kind of cabbage field. You must be very careful in digging your slit trench to distribute the dirt along the cabbage rows so that when daytime arrives, it will not look new or freshly dug. And the trench must not disturb the crop. Under the hot sun, uprooted cabbages would dry out and change colour. It would not take an enemy long to spot the change and to realize someone had dug-in. Since we were so close to them you can imagine we took a lot of care with our digging that night.

From dawn to the following dusk, we had to stay completely hidden – no movement, no talking, no coughing, because sound carries so easily. The sniper had a partner and we located them both about noon. Two enemy soldiers meant two shots from us which doubles the chance of being spotted. I would have to fire once at the sniper, then cock and aim again at the partner while Harold, with the telescope, would try to guide me to him. Well, to give ourselves a break as far as getting away, we decided to wait till just before dusk.

Harold was on the telescope and I had the rifle. Two rounds got them both. We were lucky; had the enemy observer been on the job with his own telescope, he would have spotted us immediately. Harold had done his job perfectly. You need an observer who can tell you exactly where you've hit first time, then guide you successfully and very quickly for the second shot. It is difficult, but we did it.[22]

The battalion might also be reinforced by assets from the divisional support battalion, this was an infantry battalion whose soldiers were employed to serve either the Vickers Medium Machine Gun (MMG) or the 4.2-inch mortar. There were three MMG companies and one Heavy Mortar Company within the Divisional Support Battalion. The Heavy Mortar Company was divided into three platoons with 4 mortars in each, the 4.2-inch mortar fired a bomb weighing 9.1kg and

21 Woolcombe, Robert, *Lion Rampant* (Edinburgh: B&W Publishing, 1994), p.27.
22 Martin, Charles, *Battle Diary* (Oxford & Toronto: Durndurn Press, 1994), p.35.

Figure 2.10 Vickers machine guns of 2nd Battalion Cheshire Regiment supporting an attack by 50th (Northumbrian) Division against the village of Hottot-les-Bagues, south-west of Tilly-sur-Seulles, 11 July. (Imperial War Museum B6940)

could reach ranges out to 4,200 yards. The mortars were either grouped as a battery or split up to reinforce a particular brigade.

The MMG companies each contained three platoons of 4 guns, a total of 12 Vickers per company, or 36 per battalion. The infantry brigade within an armoured division also had an independent machine gun company, organized in the same manner as the MMG companies in the support battalions of the infantry divisions. There were many ways that the MMG companies could be employed, but they most commonly fired in the in-direct fire role, sometimes concentrated as a battalion, with machine-guns shooting on a large number of pre-selected targets under a divisional fire plan. On other occasions they were placed under command of a brigade in their division. It was also frequent for each MMG platoon to be detached from their company and placed in support of, or under command of, an infantry battalion.

The Vickers MK IV was a beautifully engineered machine gun and by making a belt-fed weapon available to the infantry the limited firepower of the Bren gun was partially compensated. The MMG was mounted on a 50lb Tripod with three tubular legs which had cross bars on the bottom to dig into the ground. The rear leg was the longest and extended to the rear, the front legs extended forward and at an angle to each sides, all of the legs could be adjusted for height as required and locked by means of a jamming handle onto the central pedestal. At the top of the pedestal was a crosshead where the gun itself was attached to the tripod and could pivot 360 degrees, though the gun was usually locked onto a particular point of aim. The gun was elevated back and forth using a small elevating handwheel.

The Vickers machine gun weighed 40lbs and its belt-fed mechanism delivered 500 rounds per minute through a combination of the recoil of the gun and some gas-assistance. The 250 round belt came flaked in an ammunition 'liner' which was opened by tearing off a soldered flap, the belt itself was made of canvas webbing with the ammunition held in pockets by cross stitching.

At the rear of the gun were two wooden traversing handles, to fire the gun the No.1 would hold the handles with both hands placing his index fingers over the top of the handle brackets. He would then raise the safety lever centred in front of the thumb piece. Once the thumb piece was pressed the gun fired, the No.1 holding the traversing handles loosely and applying no vertical or horizontal pressure to them, simply allowing the gun to jump freely whilst he held up the safety lever and kept the thumb piece depressed. The firer could raise the guns elevation during periods of firing by using the elevating handwheel. To make small lateral changes the gunner can apply a 'tap' to the traversing handles, literally a glancing blow using the back of hand, this was sufficient against the controlled resistance to move the gun small measured degrees left or right. The effect was important in increasing the gun's 'beaten zone' – the predicted ellipse where the rounds would impact; 'tapping' was a delicate art which took frequent practice.

To keep the barrel cool through sustained firing a two-gallon condenser can was used to fill the barrel casing with water through a screw plug at the top. The can was then attached to the barrel casing by a rubber condenser hose allowing steam vapour to cool and be recycled.

A bracket on the left rear side of the breech casing allowed a dial sight to be fitted to the gun. Essential if the gun was to be fired in an indirect role using the same, directors and aiming posts as artillery and mortars use. In the direct fire role a normal 'iron' sight with a sliding mechanism to alter the range was used, the firer simply aiming the gun through the aperture and front sight onto whatever target he chose. Lieutenant Reginald Fendick was a MMG platoon commander with the 2nd Middlesex, the Divisional Support Battalion for 3rd British Division:

> Our guns could engage targets up to a maximum of 4,500 yards. When firing 'rapid' each of the platoon's four guns could put down about 250 rounds per minute (x 4 guns), so the platoon fire power was not insignificant: 1,000 rounds per minute. While the cyclic rate of fire of the Vickers was in the neighbourhood of 500 rounds per minute, we fired approximately 25-round or 5 second, bursts, with pauses between. The 'normal' rate of fire was one belt in 2 minutes, and 'rapid' one belt in 1 minute, a belt holding 250 rounds.
>
> One great characteristic of the water-cooled Vickers gun was that it could be fired continuously for very long periods, as long as you kept water in the barrel casing. The water boiled after a minute or so of rapid fire, or a little longer at normal rate, but a hose from the barrel casing carried the steam off into a two-gallon can of water, called the condenser can, where it was condensed. When the water in the gun boiled low, the condensed water in the can could be poured back into the casing in a few seconds. However the water in the condenser can would also start to boil quite quickly from the steam passing into it, and then the condensation action ceased, and a cloud of steam would start to rise from the condenser can... not desirable if there was any danger that the gun position could be seen from Jerry-land. If we were to do a long shoot, we always arranged to have plenty of extra water available.[23]

The infantry battalion was therefore a combination of rifle companies who would conduct the actual close combat and a supporting infantry cast of mortars, anti-tank guns and medium machine guns. However just as it is important to note that the infantryman is measured by his 'fighting spirit' as well as good training and equipment. It is equally important to understand the 'battalion' was not simply a sterile organizational bureaucracy. A good battalion had a heart and a spirit that was usually unique and though the war had significantly mixed up regimental cap badges and geographical recruiting areas, it is noticeable just how much the 'regimental spirit' still mattered to conscripts, territorial soldiers as well as regular serviceman. Reginald Fendick, the

---

23 Fendick, Reginald F, *A CANLOAN Officer* (Buxton: MLRS Books, 2008), pp.56-57.

machine gun platoon commander mentioned previously was part of the 'CANLOAN' scheme, where Canadian Army officers were used to make up for a lack of officers in British infantry regiments. He served throughout the campaign in North-West Europe with the 2nd Battalion, The Middlesex Regiment, 'the Die Hards', and clearly felt part of their family:

> No matter what paths a soldier may follow throughout his career, his feelings for the unit with which he fought in battle must always remain the strongest. I wore uniforms and badges of one sort or another for 38 years, and have much pride and many good memories from all that service, but my pride in having been a Die Hard takes second place to none of the others.[24]

Essentially a battalion with a 'good spirit' was far more likely to perform than a poor one; regardless of the circumstances it found itself in or the level of support it received. Good battalions such as the 5th Duke of Cornwall's Light Infantry or the 1st Norfolks were to carve famous names for themselves over the campaign, others would conversely be considered 'unlucky'. As we shall examine further in the chapter on command and control the most dominant factor in nurturing a good 'spirit' within a unit was leadership. Good leadership could put right a 'bad' battalion, conversely toxic leadership could destroy a 'good' one. Generating the right 'atmosphere' and fighting morale within his unit was considered to be one of the principal duties of a good commander.

A good, well-led battalion, composed of highly motivated, trained and equipped infantrymen still needed to be tactically directed well if it was to achieve its mission. Ensuring that the forces within an infantry battalion were both deployed and employed correctly was not a simple matter and required considerable planning and flexibility from the commanding officer and his small staff. To aid them in their planning and judgment battalion officers were educated in tactics and taught a series of principles that could be used as a handrail and potentially applied to certain operations. As an example when coordinating an attack officers were taught to consider which of two categories the enemy defence's fell into. Were the enemy positions prepared hastily? Had they insufficient time to construct extensive obstacles and fully coordinate their anti-tank and defensive lay out? If this was the case the battalion's officers might consider rapidly attacking these positions, taking advantage of the enemy's lack of preparation. This was known as a 'quick attack' and had a degree of risk involved in sacrificing the attacker's own preparation and reconnaissance time for speed. If it was to be successful it required a simple decentralized plan as well as a slick, familiar and well-practised 'battle procedure' that allowed attached arms, such as engineers or artillery, to deliver their support very quickly.

On the other hand the battalion's officers might consider the enemy's defences fell into a second category, one where there had been sufficient time to organize defences properly with obstacles, a fully co-ordinated fire plan and well sited dug-in positions. To attack this type of defence required a 'deliberate' attack, one where the planners needed time to conduct reconnaissance and study the intelligence in detail. This would allow them to produce a plan that exploited weaknesses in the enemy positions and fully coordinated all available resources in support of the attack.

Whichever type of attack was planned; there were a number basic points the officers recognised as important if the operation was to be successful. Firstly the attack should be organized in depth and on a narrow front; this maintained the momentum of the attack and created a deep penetration; the idea was to hit the enemy hard in one place and keep on hitting hard. Follow on forces also played an important role in mopping up bypassed enemy positions after the assault

---

24 Ibid., p.226.

Figure 2.11 Infantryman of 15th Scottish Division supported by Churchill tanks advance during Operation Epsom. (Crown Copyright)

wave had passed over the enemy's defences. Secondly the attack should always start from a firm base and continue to secure firm bases as the attack progressed. This reduced the effectiveness of the highly predictable German counter-attacks and prevented the assaulting forces from losing the initiative. Thirdly the attack should be supported by fire up to and beyond the objective, the artillery 'Fire Plan' would work to the timings of the assaulting infantry and armour. It was important to include targets beyond the objective to protect the troops once they had accomplished their mission. Fourthly once an initial breach had been made the assaulting troops should turn outwards and get behind the enemy positions on the flanks, this widened the frontage of the attack and prevented the enemy from sealing off the initial breach. It was important that at this stage the supporting weapons (anti-tank guns, mortars, MMGs, artillery etc) were brought forward as quickly as possible to support the progress made and defeat any counter-attacks. Finally it was critical that the impetus of the advance was not allowed to die down, maintaining the momentum of the attack required correct positioning of fresh troops as well as rapidly reorganizing those that had already been assaulting.

In any attack there was always a preparatory phase. In a quick attack the time available for this would be cut to the bone, lest the enemy use it to better prepare his defences, conversely in a deliberate attack much more time was available. Time could be used for improving routes to the start line, dumping ammunition or engineer stores forward and generally organising the concentration and assembly areas. Time was also used to gather the best available intelligence and conduct further reconnaissance, by patrols or aircraft for example, ensuring the layout of the enemy defences was better understood. The preparatory phase sometimes allowed assaulting troops the opportunity to study the ground they would be attacking over from an OP or vantage point. Lieutenant Robert Woolcombe's company visited a forward Canadian outpost in Norrey prior to their attack on Operation EPSOM:

> There was a thick, uneasy quiet. Now and then a figure slunk between the buildings on an errand for water cans or on its way to a command post. One of them was inaptly ensconced over a latrine pit. There was no talk. It was mid-afternoon and the sun beat down, and stubble was on faces and that watchful look when a man knows if he shows his head he gets a piece of lead through it. We met Hugh, the IO who was already up there, and who introduced us to the Canadian company commander in his command post.

'As long as you fellers don't bunch, and go quiet,' they told us. 'We get mortared if we show any movement, but it's all right if you keep to the houses…'

We clambered through a farmyard into the shambles of a house, and keeping well back from the yawning windows on the upper floor, with our camouflage veils pulled over our faces looking beyond. There before us were the rolling cornlands, with their great hedgerows, trees and clumps of wood, and the concealed villages of that awful country that was to become known as the Scottish Corridor. We knitted ourselves to our maps, then gazed beyond the window again, keeping right back against the opposite wall…The hidden stream called the Mue…St Manvieu…La Gaule… Cheux. Names on the map. Names in all their foreboding, screened from us, brooding there among the pregnant cornfields. And rising out of the distant trees, like fate, we could just see the top of St Manvieu church tower…

'Look just in front of that wood.' Said Hugh – 'you can see the head of a sentry.' Far in front was a tiny dot on the ground.

'You can make him out through the binoculars,' said Hugh.

I raised my binoculars. Very small, but quite clear, was a distant Wehrmacht helmet level with the top of a slit-trench. It moved slightly. The first German of the war that I had set eyes on. There, whoever he was, my enemy.

Then we went out into an adjoining orchard. Extending further again from this was the start line for our attack. There was a hedge around the orchard, and a Canadian platoon had positions here. Never had we seen slit-trenches dug so deep. Fire steps had been built in order to see out of them, while burrowed into the soil off the trench floors were recesses in which the men not on stand-to were sleeping…

… They were helpful and only worried about our drawing fire on to them, and we left them to it again. We had done our best for their sakes, but something must have been seen, for they got another dose shortly afterwards.[25]

To ensure that the assaulting troops were launched into the attack in good order, the British carved up the real estate behind the front line; allocating each unit a series of Areas, Forming Up Points (FUP) and a Start Line (SL). This common geography cut down on confusion and ensured that soldiers had a shared understanding of what preparation they should be undertaking, where they should be conducting it and when they should do so. A significant amount of early preparation for the attack would take place in the 'Concentration Area', it was normally sighted well to the rear and was a good place for the assaulting troops to deliver and receive the relevant orders for the attack. The more peaceful setting allowed troops to properly study air photographs or maps and particularly difficult stages of the attack might be rehearsed or talked through in greater detail. The 'Orders' for the attack were formally given by the platoon and company commanders to ensure they were as tailored and relevant as they could be, on occasions the unit's commanding officer might also brief the battalion collectively and explain the nature of the future operation.

From the Concentration Area the troops moved to the Assembly Area. This was where the assaulting troops would normally 'marry up' with their supporting arms. The Assembly Area was normally 1-5 miles from the front line and was both secured and concealed from enemy view. In the Assembly Area the final preparation of weapons and equipment were undertaken, rations and ammunition were replenished and the wireless sets 'netted in'. Lieutenant Robert Woolcombe describes the actions in the assembly area before Operation EPSOM on 26 June:

25 Woolcombe, Robert, *Lion Rampant*, (Edinburgh: B&W Publishing, 1994), pp.47-49.

Arriving from Secqueville into the forward assembly area. 3am in the drizzling rain. Pitch dark, with the minute-hand slipping leadenly to the dawn. Digging shallow pits as a precaution against enemy counter-shelling, and huddled with my batman, head to toe, with our anti-gas capes spread over us for some warmth. Then more fitful sleep, until at 5.30 the sentries stole around the silent positions with muttered words, shaking inert figures in the ground back to consciousness.

We woke dully, shivering. Still dark, and the drizzle still falling. With two hours to the barrage.

The blowing of the petrol cooker sounded from the barn, where the cooks were preparing breakfast. Then a subdued jangle of mess tins, the occasional glow of a cigarette end, and a straggling queue of men with slung rifles: shadowy blurs forming for porridge, 'compo' sausages, biscuits and tinned margarine, and a mug of steaming tea, in the first glimmer of dawn.

Inside the barn on some sacks sat the Company officers. We ate and said little. Gavin, weather beaten, with the steady grey eyes. Duncan, whose big moustache was suddenly obvious again, although one had seen it a thousand times. They exchanged trivialities without a word about the battle. Danny, Alastair and myself swopping desultory comments of a more relevant kind-

'Hour and a half to the barrage. …'

'Weather's bad for flying …'

'Any more 'Chah? …'

… Green camouflage cream was shared out in grubby palms and smeared over our faces – we never bothered to use it again. Weapons were carefully cleaned and oiled. Magazines loaded. Bayonets fixed. Midday rations – slabs of bully beef and cheese with more biscuits – packed into haversacks. The boiled sweets and chocolate stowed into a handy pocket. Cigarette tins into another…The men quietly chatting and smoking in little groups, in their platoons. Everyone admirably controlled, but an air of tension about them. None quite knew what battle would be like. And we waited for H Hour.[26]

The troops would move from the Assembly Area to the Forming Up Point (FUP), at this stage control of the assaulting troops was critical and to prevent soldiers taking a wrong turning guides were routinely used and the routes usually marked with signs and mine tape. The FUP and Start Line would usually be secured by a force already in place. Siting the location of the FUP was critical, it was particularly important that it was concealed from the enemy's view and his direct fire weapons. The Start Line was normally located at the forward edge of the FUP, and the FUP therefore needed sufficient space to allow units to deploy into their assaulting formations, this was no easy matter where tanks as well as infantry were involved and guides were again often used to prevent chaos. Good direct entrances and exits into the FUP were critical, if tanks had to approach from a flank then there would have to be a change of direction in the FUP, with a consequent increase in engine noise. If it was dark[27] there was also the risk that the tank crews might lose their sense of direction. Whilst in the FUP a pre-H-Hour bombardment would normally commence, focusing the soldier's minds on the coming attack. Lieutenant Jocelyn Pereira of the 5th Coldstream Guards took part in a battalion attack near the village of Le Busq in early August:

We consulted our watches – it was time to go.

26 Woolcombe, Robert, *Lion Rampant* (Edinburgh: B&W Publishing, 1994), pp.52-53.

27 Whilst it was unusual for tanks to operate at night it was common for them to move into the FUP in the pre-dawn darkness for an early morning attack.

Figure 2.12
British infantry and Cromwell tanks
pass each other east of Le Beny Bocage.
(Soldiers of Gloucestershire Museum)

To get to the start line we merely had to follow the same route that we took earlier in the day, so there were no worries about finding the way and we knew exactly how long it would take – ten minutes down the road and there were the outposts of the 11th Armoured Division; left turn down a path through a small wood and we came to the cluster of farm buildings where the R.A.P. was to be established; still going left through the barns and out-houses, we found the entrance to the sunken lane; and then after another ten minutes we reached the big gap in the hedge and the track that was to mark the inter-company boundary here we halted. A tangle of hazel and brambles topped the banks on either side, filling the lane with dark shadows and cool patches where the grass was still quite moist with dew despite the heat of the day. The whole length of the lane was full of men, taking up positions by the gaps so that they could scramble out into the fields beyond when the time came, and having a last cigarette in the few moments of quiet that remained. Michael Willoughby, whose company was to attack on the right, and Francis Brown, who had taken over No.1 Company on the left, came down to our command post in the centre to have a last word before the 'off'. Quietness lay over the whole scene like a blanket, as oppressive as the stifling heat – not a gun fired, nothing marked the steady progress of the minutes, then suddenly the mortars in the field behind us began to fire. It was the opening signal and everyone began to scramble out of the lane into the fields beyond.

'Bang, bang, bang, bang, bang,'

'Well, here we go – what a long time they take to come down!'

'Crump, crump, crump, crump.'

'Any news on the wireless yet? No? Of course not; there couldn't be yet.'

'Bang, bang, bang, bang, bang.' went the mortar bombs; they seem to get caught up in the clouds.

'Crump, crump, crump.'

We stepped out of the lane, through an orchard and then down the side of a large cornfield. In the shadows of the lane one had become unaccustomed to the glare – it felt like stepping out on stage.[28]

Once H-Hour arrived the signal was given for the troops to move across the Start Line. By this stage it was possible that the enemy had figured out what was going on and the FUP and Start Line could both be under either enemy direct or indirect fire. Private Ted Jones of 4th King's Shropshire Light Infantry remembers a difficult period whilst waiting at the Start line during Operation GOODWOOD:

When we arrived at the start line we were already being shelled and mortared, and our Section Leader ordered us to dig shell-scrapes to give us some protection. This was quickly started when suddenly I had a knock on the head and my steel helmet fell off. I recovered my helmet to discover a bullet lodged in the camouflage net. I thought that this was getting too close for comfort and speeded up my digging when there was a flash in front of my face and blood dripping on the ground. I quickly got into my shell scrape and, getting a small mirror from my pack, I could see that the end of my nose had been grazed by another bullet. After a little while I picked up enough courage to have a look round to see if I could pin point where the bullets were being fired from. I came to the conclusion that they must have been fired from extreme range as there was no cover except in the far distance. Soon we got the order to start the advance and I was glad to be on the move away from that hot spot.[29]

The likelihood of German shelling of FUPs and Start Lines meant the British would only keep assaulting troops in the FUP for as short a time as possible. The Start Line itself was usually square to the objective and often sited along a linear feature such as a track or a line of trees, this helped the soldiers recognise it on the ground and identify their 'Centre Line', or axis of advance. Correctly identifying the Start Line was important as H-Hour was always the planned time that the first assaulting troops would cross the Start Line. As virtually all timings in the plan would be based off H-Hour it was critical that the assaulting troops crossed the Start Line at the right time. H-Hour was particularly relevant to the supporting artillery, mortar and MMG fire plans and it was vital that the assaulting troops kept up with this fire. The ideal attack would have the assaulting troops arriving at the edge of the enemy position as the last shells of the fire plan were crashing down. It was important however to take the safety distances for weapons like the 25-pounder artillery gun (150 yards) into account to prevent friendly fire causing casualties amongst assaulting troops. Lieutenant Geoffrey Picot, 1st Hampshires, describes leading a platoon attack supported by artillery fire:

To help us on our way we are to have a rolling barrage of artillery fire, moving forward at a predetermined speed, about 100 yards every minute. The barrage will make the enemy cower at the bottom of their slit trenches or in the cellars of their buildings. If we arrive at these positions the instant the barrage lifts we can kill or capture them all. But if the enemy spring to their firing positions before we get there they will be able to mow us down mercilessly.

All depends on our keeping up with the shellfire. 'Lean on the barrage', we have been taught in training.

It is better to risk casualties from the occasional shell from your own side falling short than

---

28 Pereira, Jocelyn, *A Distant Drum* (Aldershot: Gale & Polden, 1948), pp.52-53.
29 Thornburn, Ned, *The 4th KSLI in Normandy* (Shrewsbury: 4th Bn KSLI Trust, 1990), p.66.

to allow the enemy a few seconds to recover.

I place a section of ten men in front, in line abreast. I follow immediately behind, with the other twenty-five members of my platoon strung out behind me. The barrage starts and we move with it. For ten minutes I do not stop shouting.

'Keep up the pace. Don't slacken. Keep up the pace. Keep up. Don't stop. Keep up.'

A soldier complains 'But there's a Spandau firing at us from over there on the right. I had better take it on.'

'No,' I yell. 'Don't stop for anything. Fire the Bren back at him from the hip if you like, but keep up, keep moving, keep up, don't stop.'

Another soldier reports: 'Two wounded enemy here, sir, we can't leave them.'

I reply: 'Yes, we can. Leave them. Leave everything. Just keep up with the barrage, that's all we've got to do. Keep up. Keep up. Don't lose the barrage.'

'It might be dangerous to leave them,' the soldier persists.

'Shut up,' I bellow. 'Don't stop. Keep up. Keep up!' There are plenty of shells landing every-where. I'm not surprised there's some wounded.

One of my men reports: 'There's movement on our left sir.'

'Fire as you go with anything you've got,' I reply. 'But don't stop. Keep up, keep up. Faster, faster, keep up.'

I see a salvo of shells fall around our objective. A few seconds later Corporal Daley, a regular soldier who is commanding my leading section, enters through the front door of the house and I go in through the side door. We have got there without being seriously impeded at any stage of our 1,000 yard advance.[30]

The British Army knew that the artillery fire would not destroy a determined enemy in dug-in positions, but they were clear about taking advantage of the covering fire's temporary suppressing effect and gave some salutary advice to attackers in their Infantry Training Manuals:

(i)   Apart from direct hits from shells or bombs few if any of the enemy will be killed by your covering fire. Do not therefore expect to find only dead men when you assault. A well trained enemy with good morale will begin firing again as soon as your own supporting fire ceases for safety reasons.

(ii) Therefore, you should do five things:-

First, begin the assault immediately your supporting fire stops or lifts. The enemy may be a bit 'rattled' and his shooting may be wild. Therefore, do not give him time to recover his composure.

Second, before you assault, get two Brens in position at very short range, to give you intimate close support over the last 200 yards. These Brens, if well placed, will be able to shoot you right on to and over your objective.

Third if necessary be prepared to use smoke.

Fourth, be prepared to fire from the hip during the assault all other weapons you have with you.

Fifth, search all enemy positions thoroughly with the bayonet.[31]

Ultimately the effectiveness of the covering fire and the resistance troops met when assaulting the enemy position would depend upon the German's 'fighting spirit'. There were occasions when

---

30 Picot, Geoffrey, *Accidental Warrior* (Sussex, Book Guild, 1993), p.252.
31 *Infantry Training Part VIII – Fieldcraft, Battle Drill, Section and Platoon Tactics* (War Office, March 1944), p.21.

the bombardment and threat of assault was enough to cause the enemy to cut and run. Lieutenant Robert Woolcombe found this to be so when assaulting German positions on Hill 112, it is worth noting the short period spent at the FUP and also how the Start Line was sited on a geographical feature the attacking troops would recognize as they crossed it in the dark:

> To the roar of the guns we were off. Down through the valley and upwards to the shattering reverberations of the big 'Five-fives' plastering the objectives, and the 'crumps' of the counter bombardment smashing down through the woods around us. Long columns of steel-helmeted shapes, hands gripping the bayonet frog on the belt of the shape in front, moving up the Hill. Fixed bayonets momentarily gleaming in the quick flicker of yet another explosion. Here and there men dropping, and a huddled form being carried downhill on a stretcher. Over our shoulders the night sky back to the sea was revealed an amazing sight. There snapped into life, the unwavering beams of 'Monty's Moonlight.' The inky fields riotously winking and sparkling with myriad gun flashes, and over all, that spiteful thunder crashing on the Hill close above us.
>
> It was estimated we should have to endure a five to ten minutes halt on the start line. We emerged from the trees, and wheeled right, along the reverse slope, across a bleak flat ploughed field. A road bank became visible ahead: the start line. We shook into formation and lay down. Far in front, in direct line with us, sounded the cold-blooded chirps of a 'Nebelwerfer' and the sparks of a stick of rockets streaking upwards into the night. We picked out their wailing across the sky above the din. There were one or two warning shouts of 'Keep flat!' Closer came the wailing, crying over the sky for what seemed an eternity. 'A' Company froze to the earth. Down it moaned…down… one's fingers gripped and twisted the very soil. One's lips wrenched into a tight, silent 'Please God, Please God.'
>
> The lot fell on 9 Platoon. There was a succession of sickening eruptions. A stunned silence. A few agonized, lonely cries…'Stretcher-bearer!' …And when, the next minute, the signal came for 'A' Company, Danny and a handful of men arose and marched forward.
>
> We went in with Bren guns firing tracer from the hip. The Brens had been issued tracer for morale effect against the enemy. We reached our first objectives to find them pulverized. The enemy foxholes were strewn with greatcoats, Wehrmacht caps, respirator containers, mess tins, even post-cards and letters to the Fatherland; but grabbing their weapons and ammunition, the defenders had got out of it.[32]

If the Germans had sufficient time to prepare their defensive positions then the attack became a much tougher proposition for the assaulting British infantry. Obstacles including mines and barbed wire would frequently be built around the defences and these were almost always covered by enemy direct and/or observed indirect fire. Assaulting troops could forego supporting fire, opting for an infiltration into the enemy's position using stealth and surprise, but if they were discovered too soon there was always a risk of terrible losses and outright failure. Corporal Proctor, 4th Somerset Light Infantry recalls a horrendous experience on the night of 12 July at Hill 112:

> At 0100 hours we rose silently from our slits and began to move forward up the hill. The intention was to infiltrate quickly forward, then rush the German positions with the fervent hope that this stratagem would succeed where the Cornwalls had failed.
>
> 16 and 17 Platoons, commanded by Sergeant Oxland and Partridge respectively, led our advance. All went according to plan until our leading elements reached the brow of the hill.

---

32 Woolcombe, Robert, *Lion Rampant* (Edinburgh: B&W Publishing, 1994), p.86.

The Germans were alert – in fact it seemed as if they had foreknowledge of our attack and had been luring us forward – waiting silently until all of D Company was fully exposed before inflicting upon us their murderous attack. Quickly we went to ground, but our leading sections were caught on the brow of the hill where the enemy had constructed their first barbed-wire defence. They appeared to have an inexhaustible supply of small arms ammunition and mortar bombs, keeping us pinned to the ground which was hugged with grim determination…

… the leading sections were having trouble at the barbed-wire defences which they had to overcome at any cost. It proved an impossibility as the enemy's defensive firepower was too strong and intense.

Nothing prepared me – nor any of us really – for what happened in the following minutes. The leading section commander was attempting to scramble through the barbed wire… a single enemy bullet pierced his belly and as a result exploded a phosphorous grenade he carried in his webbing pouch. Struggling in desperation he became entangled in the barbed wire and hung there, a living, screaming human beacon. His only release from the fiery hell, as he must have known, was to plead for someone to shoot him as quickly and mercifully as possible.

A single well aimed shot from a compassionate but no doubt appalled officer, put the lad out of his blazing hell. Even in death the horror continued as the phosphorous burned into the now lifeless body. Many a silent prayer was murmured as we witnessed our comrade's instant funeral pyre. His manner of death was a salutary lesson to us all – never again did we carry phosphorous grenades in our webbing pouches.

It was obvious our attack was doomed to failure, and it was no surprise when the signal was given to withdraw. We moved quickly back to our defensive positions – a very chastened company indeed.[33]

On other occasions the assault could be thrown into chaos by the fire from a well-hidden and previously un-located German position, perhaps one firing from a flank. On 19 July, during Operation GOODWOOD, 4th King's Shropshire Light Infantry were tasked to assault the village of Hubert Folie and encountered such problems. Captain Clayton of B Company described the encounter:

After a time we were ordered to continue the advance across the Caen/Vimont railway line, which ran at right angles to our front. We did so in open order with two platoons up, then myself with Coy HQ in the centre, followed by one platoon with the remainder of Coy Headquarters in the rear. We covered nearly a mile and a half with not much more than 500 yards to go to Hubert-Folie, things were beginning to look rosy when, without warning, we were enfiladed from our left by machine-gun fire from the high railway embankment. In a matter of seconds the swishing noise of the bullets through the corn had accounted for almost a third of my weakened Coy. My Wireless Operator, Lance Corporal Whelan, was shot through the head but miraculously survived, and altogether it was quite a party.

I shouted for 2' Mortarmen and Prosser (our 'B' Coy Centre-Forward) answered. Both of us were rather glad to know that somebody was still alive. He put down smoke on our left flank. Sergeant Kelshaw, using his loaf as always, came up with the Company Carrier, under cover of which I ran forward to a transverse hedge to see what was doing. We roughly pinpointed the enemy positions, which were dug into the railway embankment and concealed in haystacks. We gathered a 'battery' of three Bren guns to fire alternately so as to give continuous

33 Proctor, Douglas, *Section Commander* (Bristol: Sydney Jary Publishing, 1990), pp.5-6.

fire while we organised the men as we had left into two platoons, one of which was to be the fire platoon while the other 'pepper-potted', one section advancing at a time. This was only successful for about 100 yards, when we were once again pinned down.

Colonel Reeves now came up to see what was the matter. In spite of my instructions to the contrary, he stuck his head out round the hedge to see for himself what was happening. We hooked him back in time to save his head from being blown off by a machine-gun burst! In the meantime George Edwards, who was behind us with 'C' Coy had read the battle. In addition to thickening up our smoke screen he also put in a left hook to help, but this was also pinned down.[34]

Whilst the two leading companies were pinned down, the Carrier Platoon was brought up and succeeded in outflanking the Germans to the left and inflicting heavy casualties on them. The KSLI were then able to continue their advance. On many occasions armour would be available to support the infantry assault by providing direct fire support onto the machine guns and defensive positions that were to be assaulted. The doctrine and training before the war had been confusing to say the least, with thoughts of tanks leading the infantry in and then standing to a flank. The reality that was exposed in Normandy was that it was usually better for the infantry to lead the tanks in. Sergeant Greenwood was the troop sergeant of the Churchill-equipped 9th Royal Tank Regiment, and remembers his squadron assaulting Eterville in support of 4th Dorsets during Operation JUPITER.

We reached the crest …and there were the enemy running for cover…towards Eterville and the trees ahead. Our Besa opened up…every bush and shrub: every tree: every haystack: anything and everything that could hide a body…was raked with machine-gun fire.

Our infantry were now among and ahead of us…and soon, prisoners started to come in: odd couples of Jerries popping up from the corn, hands raised…scared to death.

At least three haystacks were now on fire from our incendiary machine gun fire. The smoke from them was a bit of a nuisance, blowing across our front. Ahead, lay the trees immediately in front of Eterville: they were my worry. Jerry had a habit of concealing Tigers and Panthers in the woods. They usually open fire when we are too close to take evasive action… and one hit from an '88 at 400 yards …!

Very soon we opened up with HE on the village…there were as yet no signs of any 88s. The infantry kept steadily on…walking warily through the deep corn, but always going forward… forward. Our Besa fire passed over them, but it must have been uncomfortably close. Grand fellows those infantry lads: so brave and calm.

I felt terribly grateful towards them when I saw them amongst the trees: they would report any hidden AT guns and tanks. My vehicle was behaving well…and putting down smoke fire: crew worked splendidly: damned hard work too. And how we smoked cigarettes! Pedder solved the match problem by getting his lighter to work with gun buffer oil! And in the midst of an action! Mortars were still troublesome: as good as any airforce to Jerry!

Time has no meaning during action: some time during the fight, Very lights were seen from the village, and we knew the infantry were 'in': they had done a grand job and occupied the place with remarkable speed. We just remained on the high ground…keeping on the alert from any armour…and a possible counter-attack.[35]

34 Thornburn, Ned, *The 4th KSLI in Normandy* (Shrewsbury: 4th Bn KSLI Trust, 1990), p.74.
35 Beale, Peter, *Tank Tracks – 9th Bn RTR at War 1940-45* (Stroud: Sutton Publishing, 1995), pp.73-74.

Figure 2.13 Infantrymen of A Company, 5th Battalion the Wiltshire Regiment,
led by their Section Commander, advance to the River Seine.
(The Wardobe: The Museum of the Berkshire and Wiltshire Regiment)

Although supporting fire was helpful, there would always come a point in the final stages of an attack when the platoon or section would have to cover its own approach to the enemy position, this was achieved by what was known as 'Fire and Movement' or 'Pepperpotting'. Fire and Movement simply meant that one group would always be either firing or firm in a position from which fire could be opened, whilst the second group would be moving. This practice would continue and alternate between the two groups, keeping the enemy suppressed but slowly closing on the enemy, until the infantry were close enough to deal with the position, normally by posting a No.36 Grenade into the trench or dugout. Lieutenant Sydney Jary's experience was that once the assaulting force arrived on the position all resistance ceased and there was 'no need to run around the enemy position shooting people in slit trenches. A boot up the backside is the maximum force necessary to show who has won and to assemble prisoners.'[36] The German infantryman was however sometimes not such a pushover. Lieutenant D H McWilliams recalls the last stages of the attack by 9th Camerons on the German positions at Cheux during Operation EPSOM. These positions were manned by members of the 12th SS Panzer Division which had already established a fearsome reputation. When 9th Camerons finally reached Cheux it had advanced over one and a half miles trying to keep contact with the rolling barrage moving forward at 50 yards per minute.

Ahead lay a sinisterly quiet orchard, in which my binoculars detected certain humps which were almost certainly German slit trenches with substantial head cover. If that cover had been really effective, it would mean that, under it, crouched survivors from the barrage which had passed that way a short time ago, leaving many shell holes as its calling cards. I spent a few minutes, crouching behind a low mound tracking from one side to the other with my binoculars, accompanied by a rifleman who, although he had a record of many visits to the 'glass

36 Jary, Sydney, "I love my Bren Carrier", *British Army Review*, No.112, pp.71-72.

house' for various military offences, had proved himself a soldier of sterling worth when the 'muck and bullets' had begun to fly. Suddenly I heard a dull thump and his flow of sotto voce conversation was abruptly cut off. Although I could not, without exposing myself foolishly, establish the nature of his wound, his complete silence was a pretty clear indication of fatality. There was now no doubt that we had a fight on our hands, and after hosing the likely spots with Bren gun fire, we went in, at full alert and moving in bounds from one piece of cover (mostly apple trees and the thicker the better) to another. It was not long before I spotted a Schmeisser barrel projecting from a slit trench, and my dive for cover (the roots of an elderly and substantial tree) was of exemplary speed. Beside me, I found another of our reinforcements, this time a 'beardless boy' who had just completed his training after less than twelve months service. He proved a real fire-eater, and I had almost forcibly to restrain him from executing a solo charge with his rifle and bayonet, while I fished for one of my '36' hand grenades. Aware of branches just above me, I had fears about what might happen if my arm was snagged during the recommended over-arm bowling action, so I tried it under-arm, and was delighted to see the grenade end up right on top of the head cover. As soon as it exploded, I was alongside the trench pumping bullets at the helmeted head I could see rocking backwards and forwards inside. My victim was probably already hit by grenade fragments, but this was no time to take chances.

The capture of the orchard was very much a bomb and bullet matter, with little employment for the bayonet, which was, however, useful for the uplifting effect it had on our morale and the correspondingly adverse effect it, hopefully, had on the enemy's.

At one point, a young German leapt out of his trench just in front of me shouting 'Kamerad!' Unfortunately, and in his panic, he forgot to leave his rifle behind him in the trench and, before I could summon up my scanty German to my assistance (on cool reflection, 'hande hoch' would have done), one of my men, acting, I am convinced, on nothing more than a conditioned reflex, fired from the hip and solved the problem for ever. When all is said and done, it remains foolish to delay one's surrender until the enemy is among you, his mind full of memories of lost comrades and personal narrow escapes from death.

As I was passing another trench, a hand suddenly reached out and, with the utmost deliberation, placed a 'stick grenade' at my feet. It so happens that the stick grenade, like our 36, had a delay fuse of three or four seconds and, in that time, I managed, in a credible imitation of a scalded cat, to cover quite a few yards, before hurling myself flat. After the detonation, with murder in my heart – the explosion had killed a Jock who had had less time than me to react – and accompanied this time by a Bren gunner, I returned at high speed, and the two of us emptied our magazines (twenty-eight rounds in his case, a mere ten in mine) through the roof. At that range, we were confident that bullets leaving at about 2,200 feet per second would easily penetrate that sort of head cover.

As the scene of mayhem unfolded, our CO joined us. He was in great fettle, and seemed to be positively enjoying himself and perfectly happy about the way in which we were conducting our business. By the time he left, we had the situation fully under control and Cheux was ours. I recall making a maniacal suggestion that I should take my platoon forward as a fighting patrol to establish how far the enemy had retreated but, by the grace of God, he did not take me up on the offer.[37]

Many of the larger assaults by the British in Normandy featured multiple battalions advancing in extended line across open cornfields. The ground, the scale of these attacks as well as the prescribed artillery and armour support came with command and control dilemmas that sometimes restricted

---

37   Lt D H Williams papers, Ref 15132, Imperial War Museum.

Figure 2.14 Infantrymen of the Gloucestershire Regiment advance towards the village of Cahagnes. (Soldiers of Gloucestershire Museum)

the manoeuvre of platoons and sections and a junior commander's freedom of action. This was certainly a frustration felt by Lieutenant Sydney Jary:

> Infantry had to fit into the big picture, rarely operating without artillery and armoured support. The most successful actions fought by 18 Platoon were fought without the support of either. We had learned in a hard school how to skirmish, infiltrate and edge our way forward. The right or left flanking platoon attack, so beloved of the Battle School staff, would rarely succeed in the Normandy bocage. I remember with horror being 'locked' into the timetables of meticulously planned large battles. These invariably left the junior infantry commander no scope for exploitation. If you found a gap in the enemy defences, adherence to the artillery programme, which rarely could be altered, effectively stopped any personal initiative.[38]

There were however many smaller attacks that did take place. Indeed though the Normandy bocage limited observation for artillery observers and reduced intimate armoured support to the infantry, it did afford a certain amount of cover to assaulting troops to attack or outflank an enemy position. Private Stanley Whitehouse recalls such an assault, and illustrates the difficulty in identifying well concealed positions within the hedgerows:

> Because of the dense thickets and narrow, winding byways, which were veritable tank traps in themselves our armour deserted us to find an easier route and we were left on our own. We pushed forward painstakingly, through the thick, almost impenetrable growth and began clearing a more open sector of scrubland when it happened. A Spandau opened up with its

38 Jary, Sydney, *18 Platoon* (Winchester: The Rifles, 2009), p.19.

unmistakeable purr – like cloth being torn – and our lead section was chopped down. I hugged the ground closely as the cries of the wounded rang in my ears.

'Stretcher-bearers,' someone shouted.

'Come on you chaps,' said Lieutenant Yates, crawling up to our section. 'Let's get up there and help them. Follow me.' He led us off at an angle away from our wounded mates, into denser scrub, and then swung towards the stricken section, actually coming out ahead of them. Two were dead, three wounded, and the other two seemed all right, just too terrified to speak or move. I had seen this happen before. The sudden shock and the sight of dead and wounded mates could render lads completely immobile and speechless.

Whilst Private Stanley Whitehouse and his comrades were dealing with the casualties, the company and platoon commanders were attempting to accurately locate the enemy and formulate a quick plan of attack:

The enemy machine gun fired again.

'There sir, over there sir,' someone shouted, pointing to a tangle of logs and fallen trees about 250 yards away.

'Right, my man, you've had your chips,' said the company commander quietly as he verified the position through his glasses. 'I'll contact the 3-inch mortars and when they've finished take your chaps in quickly, Yates. We're running well behind time, y'know.'

'Right sir,' the lieutenant nodded…

…The mortars crashed down on the strongpoint and we advanced, only to be checked by another Spandau burst. Ironically our sole casualty was the old wag, shot in the knee. He was in severe pain, but could console himself with having received a Blighty wound, and not a few of us would have swopped the 'pain for the gain'.

Another mortar salvo straddled the logs and then, led by our platoon commander, we rushed forward blazing away. We were surprised to find not just a few logs, but a solid well constructed fortification of interwoven logs, with diggings and a tunnel for a quick exit. Two SS men were spread-eagled on the ground, one dead, but the other merely dazed. Sgt Edmonds slapped his face roughly and tipped the German's water-bottle over his head.[39]

On many occasions assaults would be conducted either within towns or with the objective of taking them; such fighting in built up areas comes with many special challenges. Soldiers found it generally much harder to locate the enemy and as the fighting was often conducted at very close quarters, with comparatively heavy casualties, the nervous strain on soldiers was particularly telling. Troops were often confined to houses with movement restricted and the streets becoming the 'killing area'. The numerous floors in a house also meant that it took many troops to clear and hold a house; this systematic clearing needed to be conducted very thoroughly as it was all too easy for the Germans to re-emerge and re-occupy supposedly 'secured houses'. Lieutenant Robert Woolcombe summarises his experiences of urban fighting:

The art of street fighting was to see without being seen. The disadvantage usually lay with the attackers. Vicious bursts of Spandau fire ripped across the back gardens and splayed into door-ways and windows of the houses. A man racing round the corner of a building heard warning shouts of 'Look Out!' from his friends already inside, and as he dived through the door a

---

39 Whitehouse, Stanley and Bennett, George, *Fear is the Foe: A Footslogger from Normandy to the Rhine* (London: Robert Hale, 1988), pp.55-56.

stream of bullets streaked over his head, splattering into the wall the other side of the room at chest height, with the plaster and brick-dust flying. From nowhere out in the fields came the angry, snarling 'brrrr!-brrrp!-brrrr!' of the same bullets leaving the barrel of the weapon that fired them; but beating the speed of sound to be embedded in the brickwork beside you. Split seconds were the division between survival and oblivion to cross from point to point you picked up your life and ran with it. Sometimes it was the carefully aimed rifle shot, cracking through the room like the lash of a heavy whip, and for a moment a stab of shock left you almost too weak to move. Or you climbed into an attic for a good OP then hurled yourself backwards, as with a hideous clatter of broken tiles streams of bullets pierced the roof, sprayed to and fro by enemy machine-gunners. The living rooms in the houses a shambles. Broken crockery, nick-nacks, pictures and furniture strewn about, covered with dust and rubble.[40]

Attacks into built up areas often resolved themselves into a series of almost independent platoon operations. For each attack a platoon would normally split itself down into three groups. The first group would clear the house, the second form a firm base of support to protect the house clearing group and the third to provide a reserve to meet the unexpected. A platoon could clear a whole street, but this would normally require knocking holes in walls and 'mouse-holing' from house to house, or using sewers and back gardens. Where the enemy was strong each sector might have to be systematically cleared by a series of bites, on other occasions, where the enemy was weak, the attacking forces would try to drive wedges on a narrow front converging towards a key objective. Troops would move along these axes with strong points between axes cleared up afterwards. Lieutenant Sydney Jary recalls such an occasion in the assault on Vernonnet on 28 August.

The Spandau, as we later discovered, was only thirty yards up the lane on the right and obscured by the high wall. There seemed to be no way of attacking it without the whole company retracing its steps along the river bank.

Douglas [Major Douglas Garner, Lieutenant Jary's company commander] called a hurried 'O' Group to give out orders for this move, but as I was about to leave my Platoon for this, Corporal Proctor pointed to a door in the wall on the far side of the lane. This was immediately opposite the intersection of our lane along the riverbank and the lane, complete with Spandau, which went to the right. The door, sagging on its rusty hinges, had once been painted light blue most of which had peeled off. If we could dash across the lane and through the door before the opposition had time to fire, the wall would give us cover from view and cover from fire – providing of course that there were no Germans in the orchard beyond.

A glance at the door from behind the corner where Sergeant Partridge had been hit suggested that it had not been opened for years. Douglas, with sixth sense, appeared at my side and decided to give the plan a try. We both thought that if I could get through the gate and then run up behind the wall to a position opposite the Spandau, one 36 Grenade lobbed over the wall would eliminate the opposition. As we were unsure at that time how far up the lane the gun was sited, we would have to draw its fire in order that I could accurately place it from the other side of the wall.

Douglas his most impressive chief instructor's voice, snapped at me: 'If that door does not open after one good push you will leap back here at once, understand?' What he didn't know was that I had no intention of trying a second push.

Not giving myself time to think, I sprinted across the lane and with both arms outstretched rushed at the door. There was little resistance and it fell off its hinges into the orchard. I

---

40 Woolcombe, Robert, *Lion Rampant* (Edinburgh, B&W Publishing, 1994), p.163.

tripped over it and, looking up, found Sergeant Kingston from 18 Platoon and Corporal Douglas from 17 Platoon standing beside me. I think they both felt that I could not be trusted on my own.

Not one burst of fire came down the lane. So, still not knowing quite where the gun was, I called back through the doorway asking Douglas to get someone to draw the enemy's fire after I had moved thirty yards along the wall. A few moments later, a long burst of Spandau fire reverberated through the wall immediately opposite where I now crouched. I pulled the pin from my grenade, let the lever fly off and, after counting three tossed it over the orchard wall. There was the usual 'Crump!' I remembered so well from grenade ranges, and a clatter of feet as one or two people ran back up the lane towards Vernonnet. Later, at the rear of the town we found their shattered bodies. They had bled to death from the awful wounds inflicted by the jagged pieces of the 36 Grenade.

In no time Corporal Proctor was calling to me from the other side of the wall. He said that the Spandau, an MG 42, was still there and spattered with blood, While I was shouting over the wall urging Corporal Proctor and 18 Platoon to get up the lane as fast as possible, a rifle bullet slammed into the wall not an inch from Corporal Douglas's head. Turning to me, he pleaded: 'Have we got to stay here?[41]

Whether the attack was a quick or deliberate one, in an urban or rural environment, once the objective was taken it was vital that it should be organized for defence against possible counter-attacks and turned into a firm base for further advances. However immediately after an assault the only force on the position would be the exhausted and possibly depleted assaulting infantry with perhaps some surviving armour. It was therefore vital that supporting weapons including anti-tank guns, mortars and machine guns were brought up as quickly as possible. In addition because the attacker usually assaults with a 3 to 1 ratio in his favour there would never be sufficient existing trenches on the captured enemy objective. New positions would therefore need to be dug. Ammunition would be checked and replenished, a supporting artillery/mortar Fire Plan established and the arcs of the anti-tank guns and machine guns coordinated. Forward companies would push out patrols and OPs to give warning of enemy attacks. The reorganization phase was a vulnerable time usually marked by a bout of shelling and an inevitable German counter-attack. On 10/11 July the 5th Black Watch captured Collombelles but found their objective was overlooked and that the flanking battalions had failed to capture their objectives. The commanding officer, Lieutenant Colonel Thomson, describes what happened once the objective was taken:

At about 0300 hours Bn HQ having been established as planned and all supporting arms having been ordered forward, I went to the X Roads already having visited A Coy and found the digging in of infantry, M.M.G.s and A/Tk guns well in progress there and everything satisfactory, except that one 17-pdr had not been sited and had been sent back by the Troop Comdr to ST HONORINE. He told me it was impossible to find a position for it, and I accepted his statement. On arrival at the X roads I met and talked to the A/Tk Troop Comdr and he informed me that his weapons were in position and that digging was in progress. He said that the positions were not perfect but would do. He pointed out the position of the guns and I was satisfied that the area of fire covered the X roads from attack by tanks from the CUVERVILLE direction and from the south. I then saw the Sqn Comdr of A Sqn, 141 Regt R.A.C. and learned that his tanks were in position to carry out the tasks allotted. I did not feel that it was my duty to interfere with the siting of the tanks, but I was satisfied that the

---

41   Jary, Sydney *18 Platoon* (Winchester: The Rifles, 2009), pp.26-27.

Figure 2.15 Private W Wheatley of A Company, 6th Battalion Durham Light Infantry fires his Bren gun from a ruined house in Douet near Bayeux. (Imperial War Museum B5382)

positions occupied by them were fully protected against enemy infantry by my own infantry. I then satisfied myself regarding D Coy and the Company Comdr informed me and I was able to see for myself that the Coy position was sound.'

From there Lieutenant Colonel Thomson moved to the C Company position and saw that they were deployed correctly, but was then informed by a Brigade liaison officer that the unit on his right flank, 1st Gordons, had failed to capture its objective.

It was clear by this time that every movement was clearly observed from the factory area, and heavy and continuous shelling and mortaring developed on the actual areas occupied by the troops. To make matters worse, digging had been very difficult and slit trenches were not much more than one to two feet deep. I spoke on the wireless to my Brigadier and warned him that unless something was done quickly on my right that my position was bound to become very difficult, and he assured me that he fully appreciated that, and that something would happen soon. Shelling and mortaring continued, and was for a period of four hours, quite continuous, and easily the most severe of my experience. At one time 63 shells landed in the restricted area of my HQ in three minutes, and that was common throughout all the positions occupied. I repeat that no cover existed except at the X roads itself and every movement was clearly visible to the enemy who overlooked the positions from a distance of a few hundred yards on three sides. At about 0500 hrs rather ineffectual infantry attacks began to develop which were easily beaten off, but some infantry and automatic weapons managed to get behind the leading Coys, having advanced from the area of COLLOMBELLES. At about 0600 hrs or earlier, Tiger tanks (only five of which were seen) were reported approaching from the S.E. and by about 0700 these had closed to within 300 yds. By this time several of the eleven Shermans had been brewed up and the situation was becoming increasingly difficult. The 17-Pdrs had not opened fire but it is possible that they were blinded by the D.F. which I was asking for fairly continuously. By 0745 hrs my D Coy Comdr reported to me, and indeed it was obvious from my own observation, that all the tanks had been knocked out except one, which was withdrawing. He also reported to me that the 17-Pdr gun crews had passed his Coy HQ making for ST. HONORINE, one of their guns being destroyed. I will make no further remarks regarding these gun crews as I believe their actions have been the subject of another and obviously more impartial report. D Coy Comdr told me that the enemy tanks were very close and were shooting up the buildings with their 88s and what was he to do. I said he must hang on, but that I would consult with the Brigadier and told him that to hold the positions of my leading Coys would result in their destruction piecemeal as the A/Tk defence had collapsed, and my own 6-pdrs could not be brought to bear. He then ordered me at about 0900 hrs to withdraw to ST. HONORINE, and this move was completed under cover of continuous smoke by 0930 hrs.[42]

The 5th Black Watch suffered 25% casualties in the action at Colombelles. It highlights not only the typical speed and ferocity of German counter-attacks but that the arrival of supporting arms and tying them in to a defensive framework is not sufficient in itself if the objective is on ground that cannot be defended effectively.

Although the British were generally on the offensive in Normandy, German counter-attacks were a particular feature of their tactics, a predictable tactic the British heavily exploited by using considerable quantities of artillery and air delivered firepower to break up German attacks. However this response would have been ineffective had it not rested upon a solid infantry-held framework of defensive positions, which tracked and slowed the momentum of the German counterattacks, allowing them to be struck by the massive British firepower.

In a similar manner to the planning of offensive operations British officers were taught a series of tactical principles and techniques to assist them in the coordination of defensive operations. The British categorized defensive operations in two ways. Firstly there was the 'deliberate' defence, this was undertaken when out of contact with the enemy, it allowed time for detailed reconnaissance and planning to select and site ideal positions on ground of the defender's choosing. The 'deliberate defence' also allowed time for the construction and concealment of positions without any enemy ground interference. Whilst this was the ideal option the circumstances of a battle, an anticipated and imminent German attack for instance, might dictate that a 'hasty defence' had to be assumed. This allowed less time for the construction, concealment and detailed siting of positions, the defender often only being able to make some local re-adjustments to his troop's existing dispositions. A 'hasty' defence was not necessarily a temporary or short-term defence and the British commander would progressively adjust, coordinate and generally improve his defensive layout as defensive operations became prolonged.[43]

When planning his defensive operation the commander would break up the ground to be defended in a logical manner. The first task was to identify the 'Vital Ground' this was ground, the possession of which was critical for the defence of a particular area. Vital ground was laid down by the next higher commander and his subordinate would then have to arrange a defensive layout that secured it. The practice of identifying vital ground was usually held at a reasonably

42 TNA: WO 171/1268, 5th Black Watch War Diary, Report by Lt Col C N Thomson D.S.O. on the action at Collembelles on 10/11 July 1944 (23 July 1944).
43 *Infantry Training Volume IV Tactics – The Infantry Battalion in Battle* (War Office, 1952), p.112.

high level; the brigade commander normally being the lowest commander with this authority and it served as an effective way of coordinating a subordinate's defences. Having identified the vital ground the commander would then divide the defensive area into a framework of brigade and divisional 'sectors', within these would be a 'defended area' usually of battalion strength within which 'defended localities' of company or platoon sized strength would be sited. Finally within the defended localities infantry sections would construct defended posts, which, in most cases, would be one or two simple slit trenches.

When laying out his defensive dispositions the commander would be conscious not only that the vital ground, identified by his immediate superior, must be denied to the enemy by either one or more 'defended localities', but that if the vital ground fell in to the enemy's hands he would have to launch a counter-attack to re-occupy it. For this and some other tasks he would usually constitute a reserve or counter-attack force. The commander would also ensure that his positions were sited in 'depth' this meant that his front line was not one thin line but a series of posts or localities that stretched backwards. Depth was an important concept for a number of reasons, firstly it would prevent the enemy from being able to recce and observe the whole defensive layout and secondly it would help break up the enemy attack and impetus through a process of gradual attrition. Finally a position with depth allowed the defending commander time to appreciate the enemy's intentions and adjust his Fire Plan or deploy his reserves appropriately.

The commander would attempt to make his defensive positions as well concealed as possible. The attacking enemy might initially have the initiative but surprise could be achieved and the initiative re-gained if the positions were well concealed and the reserve unlocated by the enemy. The commander would also understand that any position that could be observed or identified by the Germans could also be neutralised at a point in time that suited the enemy. He would therefore ensure that considerable attention was made to ensuring that camouflage was effective, movement on the position by day restricted, noise and light emissions limited and track discipline adhered to. Siting his defences on the 'reverse' as opposed to 'forward' slope of a hill was a common tactic used by both sides to keep positions out of their enemy's direct line of sight and fire. The commander would also realize that the Germans would try and probe his defences to identify DFs and machine gun fixed lines and he would ensure that there were strict guidelines about who could call down such important fire support and under what conditions. Lieutenant-Colonel Derek Mills-Roberts commanded 8th Commando on Breville ridge. He highlights how concealed positions greatly strengthened his infantry battalion's defensive position:

> It was now time to dig in and fortify our position in the farm area. The farm and its immedi-ate surroundings formed a natural fortress, and although we would be isolated from other British troops we would have a secure footing on the ridge whatever happened. The Germans were in Breville and only about four hundred yards separated the outskirts of that place from the farm orchard. The obvious place for us to dig our defensive line was along the extreme border of the orchard facing Breville, but I decided against this and dug along the line of the hedge some seventy yards back within the orchard. The reason for this was that if you dig in an obvious or suspected place you will inevitably be shelled and mortared. These were our main positions and in front of them I ordered standing patrols to be placed which could give us full and accurate information of any enemy advance upon the orchard.
>
> Our defensive perimeter had to be complete by darkness. Under the screen of vigilant patrol activity the Commando dug-in. We were well used to this and had carried out experiments far in excess of the ordinary standard entrenching tool which was of limited use. Half the men carried miners' picks and the other half carried general-service shovels, which had been specially foreshortened to facilitate digging – they were all experts in this digging business. Whatever happened, the camouflage of the area had to be preserved

Figure 2.16 An infantryman of D Company Regina Rifles Regiment on guard duty in
a forward post in Normandy, 10 June. (Lieut. Donald I. Grant, Library and
Archives Canada, PA-131423)

– movements across the grass which would leave tracks for spying aircraft next morning
were to be avoided. Two strips of barbed wire were hastily tacked on either side of the
hedge in which our weapon pits were situated, to prevent clumsy oafs treading on the
grass and making tracks. Two hours later I was pleased to see that the place was taking
shape…

The night passed with patrol activity taking place between both sides and speculative fire from
German snipers which hoped to draw a response from 8th Commando, however Lieutenant
Colonel Mills-Roberts' men held their fire and did not disclose their positions. Shortly after dawn
German field guns opened up, the heaviest concentrations falling on the forward edge of the
orchard, where they suspected the British positions to be and which had been avoided by 8th
Commando for precisely that reason.

After the shelling, on came the German infantry. When they reached the edge of the orchard
they hesitated and came through looking rather puzzled –surely this place should have been
manned by us. Where were we? They entered our defensive rectangle, two sides of which
bristled with rifles and light machine-guns. Not a shot was fired. They were well through the
hedge and some sixty yards through the orchard towards us before the Bren guns opened up.
There was chaos in the orchard. The killed and wounded lay still, those who were unwounded
came on, but gradually the advance of the first wave of Germans lost its impetus.
    Simultaneously our artillery was pasting the German forming-up position in Breville, and
the battleships were hammering the road beyond, where further enemy reserves were probably
being moved up.

One most important feature of our defensive position was that the Germans could not see what was happening in the orchard till they came up a slight rise to the first hedge. [This illustrates the advantage of a 'reverse slope' position.][44]

The commander would also ensure that his defensive positions were mutually supporting, through either interlocking or overlapping arcs of fire. Positions that were not mutually supporting could be easily isolated by the enemy and defeated in detail. A strong defence consisted of positions that could not only protect themselves but bring fire to bear on any Germans attacking friendly flanking positions.

The Germans could be expected to attack or infiltrate from any direction and not simply frontally. For that reason although most of a platoon's defended posts would be sited to bring the maximum weight of fire to bear upon the most likely enemy approach, some would be positioned to achieve all-round defence. At a larger scale; in a defended locality or a defended area, platoons or companies would also be sited to achieve this effect. Major Ned Thornburn, 4th King's Shropshire Light Infantry, describes how he sited a hasty defence position at Les Grand Bonfaits Farm during Operation BLUECOAT on 3 August. This position would undergo attack by 9th SS Panzer Division for several days and was cut off from its battalion for a considerable period, but the strong defensive layout allowed it to repel German attacks and hold on:

My first consideration in laying out a defensive position was always to secure the best possible view of the enemy's approach. This took precedence over the actual field of fire, though to some extent the two go together. With the unstinted support of the artillery which we enjoyed in an Armoured division, fields of fire for our Brens were less vital. My second consideration was to ensure that the platoons could all support each other. This implies a triangular layout. Finally, I would always aim to be in the open, where one is less easy to pin-point rather than along hedgerows or under trees. At Bonfait the position was centred on an orchard, which had a frontage of 75 yards facing Le Busq (the next village to the east) and a depth of perhaps 40 yards. 16 and 17 platoons were forward of the two 'ends' of the orchard's 75 yards frontage, and 18 Platoon was to the right rear with observation of the road running from Point 218 to Le Busq at a range of 200 yards. This left us a field of fire of 400 yards to the north-east, east and south-east across cornfields. Company HQ was in the orchard itself along its rear edge, which was 50 yards forward of the farm. It certainly was a lovely position, as Colonel Max testified when he saw it for the first time thirty years later.

We dug-in during the night and were reinforced at dawn with two platoons from 'A' Company and two or three of the Battalion's Anti-Tank guns. 'A' Company's platoons were used to complete the all-round defence of the position. The squadron of 3rd Royal Tanks reached us just as darkness fell.[45]

The forward edge of all the various defended localities was usually known as the Forward Defence Line (FDL). The commander would attempt to destroy the enemy in front of this line by deploying the maximum weight of fire on the approaches to his defended localities. Good riflemen could generally shoot with confidence at ranges up to 500 yards, though their most effective killing range was 300 yards or less, accordingly platoon positions were normally sited to have a field of fire of up to 400 yards. Artillery and mortar fire would also be planned to break up an attack well before it reached the FDL covering avenues of approach as well as possible enemy

44 Mills-Roberts, Derek, *Clash By Night* (London: Kimber, 1956), pp.102-108.
45 Thornburn, Ned, *The 4th KSLI in Normandy* (Shrewsbury: 4th Bn KSLI Trust, 1990), p.110.

assembly areas or FUPs. Bringing down this indirect fire was usually done with FOOs but an infantry commander could also request it. Lieutenant Robert Woolcombe's platoon was part of a company defensive position south of the River Odon, when it came under attack. His company commander (who went by the nickname of 'Heid the ba') was instrumental in breaking up the German attack by calling down artillery:

> By this time there was a lot of movement in the flax, and we were clearly about to be attacked. 'Heid the ba' stood up in his trench and screamed for platoon commanders. Again one left the trench, but crawling now. Converging from the other side was Danny, and wriggling over the road a bear-like lance-sergeant called 'Gibb,' who had been in the Company since the outbreak of war, and was now in charge of 8 Platoon. Then a bullet smacked into 'Heid the ba's' parapet, kicking up a little spurt of earth at his back. As if pulled on one string, the three platoon commanders flinched then resumed crawling. But 'Heid the ba' never even noticed. And the next moment an extraordinary sound was unloosed at us. Right along the line of the flax the enemy raised a war-cry. From end to end the shout resounded, and 'A' Company fixed its bayonets, stood to its parapets, and prepared to resist.
>
> Another shout went up. At the back of one's mind, confusedly, were the boys' books of childhood and their stories of dramatic bayonet charges of the other war. And naturally we had all been trained in the parry, thrust and butt stroke. And here we were, then: my platoon was the largest; we had fourteen men. There were six men left in 9 Platoon and eight men in 8 Platoon and a few in Company Headquarters.
>
> But it must be said that 'Heid the ba' now saved 'A' Company. He was a fanatic, of course. He stood up in his trench in full view, and yelled into his wireless for gunfire. His voice must have told every German for miles that here was a British company commander calling for artillery support, but he seemed to have a charmed life.
>
> Everything happened rapidly. Back came the answer from the functionary known as 'Shelldrake': 'Then keep your heads down!' In the nick of time came a violent outbreak of battering far to the rear. We ducked and the air was loaded with the sibilant screeching of shells that plunged and raked along the ghastly line of the flax, one or two shorts exploding practically on top of us.
>
> There was silence after that, and their stretcher-bearers were busy. It took them four hours to evacuate wounded and bury their dead.[46]

Assaults from dismounted German infantry were problematic enough, but the commander would also be concerned about the threat German armour posed and would try and predict where the German tanks might attack him, where they could best be destroyed and what arcs of fire were necessary to achieve this aim. He would give arcs to the anti-tank platoon commander who would conduct the siting of the anti-tank guns themselves. If they were lucky the battalion might be reinforced by the 17-pounders of the Royal Artillery anti-tank regiment which, with a much better armour penetration capability than the battalion's own 6-pounders, would improve his defensive strength immeasurably. Sergeant Swaddle, 1st Tyneside Scottish, had a section of 6-pounders and gives an excellent description of their action during the Rauray Battle on 1 July. You will note the mutual support between the guns and the arcs of fire against 'tank runs':

> We settled in to check the guns and ammunition. As I said before, 'A' Section guns (No's 1 and 2), on the left flank had taken over the DLI [Durham Light Infantry] guns already

---

46 Woolcombe, Robert, *Lion Rampant* (Edinburgh: B&W Publishing, 1994), p.100.

there to save making any noise. No.2 gun, with Cpl J. Drysdale as detachment commander, covered the road on the left, with my own gun, No.1 to the right of it interlocking with its arc of fire. To my right came 'B' Sections guns (No's 3 and 4) commanded by Sgt Watson…

…As the battle started we stood by our guns, most of the trouble coming in on Sgt Watson's position (No.3). I was listening to the gun shots but could not help to see the tanks off Sgt Watson. Everyone was on alert first as riflemen until tanks appeared on our front. Five tanks came along the road, three carried straight on and the other two came through the fence of the field in front, towards my gun. No.1 gun team then took up position. I gave instructions for the two tanks to be allowed to get within 100 yards of us. They appeared to be moving across towards Sgt Watson's gun on our right. We attacked the second tank first. On firing our first shot, we found although we could see the tank through the sights, the shot went into the embankment 5 feet in front of us, so as a team we pushed the gun forward placing the barrel over the embankment. Our second and third shots killed the second tank. We then turned to the first tank and hit the target with two shots. It stopped dead. We had fired five rounds of Sabot. I then began to wonder about the other three tanks and if they had troubled the other gun, so I left my team with instructions to stay in their trenches and use the gun if needed, I was going to see what we could do from our No.2 gun.

On approaching the gun, I found that it had taken a direct hit on the barrel, ripping the slide right off. One man was wounded in the legs (Pte Allen). I told him to make his way back down the hedge as there was bound to be some first aid behind, but he could not walk or crawl and he asked me to take him out. With the help of L/Cpl Barclay, we took him to safety, running all the time under small arms fire with Hughie on our shoulders.[47]

Another important increment to the battalion's defensive firepower were the Vickers MMGs. They were accurate up to a range of 2,000 yards and had a long narrow beaten zone (i.e. at 1,000 yards the beaten zone is 300 yards long by 5 yards wide the beaten zone becoming shorter but wider as the range increases). The MMG was usually sited in depth to give overhead fire however its flat trajectory and long beaten zone meant that on level ground its fire should fall at least 400 yards in front of friendly forces. The MMGs were most effective when firing from a flank and were often employed in this capacity as well as being used to fire on fixed lines at night. For protection the machine guns were usually sited within the company defended localities with some kept back in depth to assist in any counter-attack. The MMGs like the other supporting weapons would usually be dug-in, but on occasions a hasty defence was required and this brought some risks. Lieutenant Reginald Fendick of 2nd Middlesex describes when his machine guns were supporting the Royal Ulster Rifles who had gone into temporary defence near Sannerville during Operation GOODWOOD. From his position he could observe a château 500 yards away and a barn slightly nearer:

We could see considerable enemy movement all around the area of the château, and along the line of the trees and hedges in front of it, bordering the far side of the wheat field. I had no doubt that we were also visible to them as the strip of wood we were in was treed, but had little undergrowth and there was a platoon of RUR in it with us.

The first thing I did after getting into action was to have all four guns lay on the barn, and ordered rapid fire with swinging traverse all along its ground line and the eve line, the two levels where Jerry would be if he was inside. We chewed it up thoroughly and a few minutes later saw 8 or 10 Jerrys running back from it, towards the trees and château beyond the field.

47 Baverstock, Kevin, *Breaking the Panzers* (Stroud: Sutton Publishing, 2002), p.88.

I ordered rapid fire on them and saw two or three fall, one of whom was helped on by a mate who went back for him. Then I put down continuous fire on the area of the Château.

At one point I saw clearly, through my binoculars, a German officer standing in front of the Château, looking at us through his. He disappeared promptly when we fired at the Château.

Almost immediately a German Spandau opened fire and a duel commenced between the two sides, the British were unable to locate the German gun, but the Spandau bursts were also initially high.

However his last burst, a long one, was right on. He started a slow traverse just beyond the left end of our gun line, and raked across to our right, kicking up the ground right along our whole gun line. We had shallow scrapes by this time, and the chaps on the guns ducked as the fire approached them and no one, and no gun, was hit. But I was standing up right just behind my No.1 right-hand gun. As the burst swung toward me, I went flat, parallel to the line, with my head to the right and my heels down. The fourth-to-the-last shot of his burst struck the side of my left boot, and came out through the centre of the sole, ripping the sole off. The last three rounds of his burst stitched the ground by my side, a foot or two away, but were stopped by a slight fold in the ground, which was about half as high as my body.

It is amazing how, in a situation like that, one experiences everything as though it was in slow motion. Although that gun was firing at a very high rate of fire, I could hear and count each bullet as it arrived and buried itself in the earth beside me. The one which hit my boot felt like I'd been slammed on the sole of the foot with a baseball bat, and numbed the foot, so I didn't know if I'd been wounded or not. I lay where I dived, and Sgt Crossman crawled over, lay beside me and cut my boot off, telling me I'd been hit and it would start to hurt in a minute.

But when he got the boot off, my sock wasn't cut; the bullet had angled through along the edge of my foot inside the boot, without nicking me. So I put the boot back on and took a few deep breaths, while a bunch of Paddy's, who'd watched the whole thing with great interest, grinned at me and one said 'Lucky that time'.[48]

Although there was clear direction from senior commanders on the defensive layout of a position, it would be the platoon and section commanders who undertook the detailed siting of positions and other necessary defensive arrangements. The platoon commander's own judgement and reconnaissance were key to this task, he would try to imagine how the enemy might take his post, what their approaches, likely FUPs and so forth might be. He would sometimes lay down on the ground and look in all directions considering what fire is already coming in front of and behind his own post and how much more fire is required to fill the gaps. In common with his senior officers he would also take into account the all-round defence, mutual support and concealment of his platoon's positions and site his small platoon headquarters so that he could maintain communications effectively with his sections. The platoon commander would give a priority of work to construct the position, this might entail clearing a field of fire or digging trenches before erecting barbed wire.

The section commander would be given an arc to cover with his fire by the platoon commander, he might also be given a special fire task; to shoot down a particular approach, or to fire across the front or flank of a neighbouring platoon for instance. The platoon commander would also point out to the section commander where the enemy might attempt to obtain observation of their

---

48 Fendick, Reginald, *A CANLOAN Officer* (Buxton: MLRS Books, 2008), p.80.

Figure 2.17 A 6-pounder gun of 3rd Anti-Tank Regiment is towed by its carrier near Gouy, 30 August. (Lieut. Donald I. Grant, Library and Archives Canada, PA-132421)

position from and what support was available from artillery, mortars and machine guns as well as their targets. He would then supervise his men as they dug their positions and constructed the defences.

Slit trenches were the normal battle position used, other cover could be used but often had disadvantages. Sunken roads and railway cuttings might look tempting but were marked on maps and were a frequent 'shell trap'. A building's walls could splinter and some were not thick enough to stop even a small arms round. In addition these sorts of linear features often caught the eye, were easy to range on and did not protect those sheltering from any shells bursting behind the cover. Shell holes might seem to be a ready-made weapon pit; but control was difficult when a section was occupying more than one and overcrowding one shell hole could have disastrous consequences. Infantry were normally discouraged from using buildings as fighting positions as substantial work was usually required to make sure they could withstand heavy fire. However both the British and Germans swiftly realized that the typical stone-built Norman farmhouse was unusually solid and they were often integrated into defensive frameworks.

The standard fire trench was normally designed to hold two or three men and was adapted to suit each particular site and weapon, it was usually 2 feet wide at the bottom with steep vertical sides and would usually have neither parapet or parados[49] but simple elbow rests dug out of the ground. To avoid silhouetting the occupant's heads, careful attention was paid to the background behind the trench. Some form of overhead cover was almost always constructed, but the occupants would need to be careful that it did not restrict their view or fields of fire. The section's slit trenches were usually dug close enough so that the section commander's orders could be shouted

---

49 The parapet is the raised area in front of the trench caused by the earth or 'spoil' dug out of the trench, the parados is the raised area behind.

across. Sergeant Major Charles Martin describes the seriousness with which digging was done by his fellow Canadians in the Queen's Own Rifles:

> Our number-one priority was making a hole. In our training days, we all had the small trenching tool most people have seen in photographs or films. It was useless. Within hours after D-Day, every second man had a regular round-bladed shovel; one in every section had a pickaxe. Two men could make a decent place for themselves in about an hour.
>
> In training we'd been content with a nice enough six-foot trench, three feet wide and three feet deep. After D-Day, we learned to be more exotic. In fact, there was some competition to see who could create the most elegant trench. So you'd find in some of them such valuable comforts as mattresses, blankets and other household items that served to make in-ground living a little better. All these things would have come from farmhouses. But the men claimed the objects were lost. They had simply found them. Another development was the roof. We found that if we were under fire, it was better to build a trench in an L shape and to roof over the longer part.
>
> Making the roof took us another step beyond the simple fox-hole. You could make a good roof using doors from barns or houses. Sheet metal could do the job. There were also knocked-down trees that were put to good use. Then the whole roof was covered with dirt, and the mattress and blankets suddenly had 'a room of their own.' In the small and exposed part of the L we might have a Bren or a Piat. One man was always on watch; the other could take a rest.
>
> All this digging and construction required camouflage. The roof could not look like a roof and the excavated dirt could not look like dirt. This required some ingenuity. If you left anything around to advertise your spot, it wouldn't be long before the enemy sent his calling card.[50]

Support weapons would require slightly more complicated trenches which would take a little longer to dig in, Lieutenant Reginald Fendick describes a Medium Machine Gun trench as well as the soil of Normandy:

> Slit trenches were our standard accommodation, and we became expert judges of European soil. Positions were often rated in our minds, not by tactical considerations, but by the degree of difficulty in digging in. Across N W Europe we encountered every extreme, from very soft and easy to flinty hard.
>
> Some of Normandy wasn't bad, the cultivated fields were good soil when dry, but terrible when wet. A lot of the soil there was very gritty and abrasive, and when muddy it impregnated our serge battledress material and turned it into something resembling sandpaper, which quickly rubbed one's flesh raw. Some spots were very stony, and one could only get down with vigorous application of a pick as well as a shovel…
>
> …Our MG slit trenches were always dug with a sunken platform to the front, large enough to take the spread legs of the tripod and low enough for the casing of the gun to clear the front parapet and permit a full traverse. The main slit was immediately behind the gun platform and deep enough for the gun numbers to stand comfortably behind the gun. A space to allow the No. 2 to stand beside the gun was often dug around the right hand side of the gun platform. The standing height was often provided by a fire step, with the floor of the main slit

50 Martin, Charles, *Battle Diary* (Oxford & Toronto, Durndurn Press, 1994), pp.41-42.

considerably deeper. In wet weather, a sump pit might be dug at one end of the main slit, to hold some of the surplus water.[51]

The advantage of the slit trench in providing protection for the defenders was stressed repeatedly in training. It was also made clear that it was not a place to cower thinking only of one's survival but as a temporary refuge from which the defenders would need to 'come alive' at the earliest possible moment, putting down the maximum weight of direct and in-direct fire:

i)   In a weapons slit men are comparatively safe against all forms of fire, except a direct hit from a shell or bomb. Such a direct hit is a matter of chance and is exceptional.
ii)   While the fire is falling round the weapons slit, the enemy infantry are working nearer, taking advantage of the fire which is keeping the heads of the defenders down.
iii) For safety reasons, these advancing infantry cannot normally get nearer than 100-200 yards; so long as the high trajectory fire on your post (their objective) continues.
iv)   Therefore the moment the enemy fire ceases look up at once, and you should get a very good view of the attackers, probably thoroughly out of breath by now, assaulting over the 100-200 yards they still have to cover. They will probably be in the open (if your defended post is well sited) and will be assaulting with little or no covering fire. So hold your fire until they are right close up and they should all be dead men. They are in the open you are under cover.[52]

The Germans would use their mortar and artillery not only to support their attacks and to neutralize defenders, but also to harass and degrade front line troops over a protracted period. German fire became a habitual aspect of frontline life that would slowly erode the strength of the infantrymen who could do little more than shelter in their slit trenches, it illustrates the reason that Sydney Jary rated 'sufferance' as such an important characteristic for an infantrymen. Such shelling was particularly stressful for those occupying slit trenches by themselves. Robert Woolcombe describes such a period in Belgium in the Autumn of 1944.

And here in A Company, was the compact little entity of Company Headquarters in this sandy soil, with the battered houses along the village street about a hundred yards at our backs. Where everyone was sharing a slit trench with someone else, as usual, except me, by some chance. Which was not so good. For the world was consisting of heads. Heads of sentries. Heads of relief sentries. Lurking heads. Heads chewing bars of chocolate, and expression-less. Heads slightly oscillating as rifles were cleaned. Heads that sometimes blew their noses on dirty handkerchiefs. Heads that looked at one another across the tops of their trenches throughout the day-light hours. Hour after Hour. Those heads of 'A' Company. Heads under steel helmets with unshaven faces, with all the imponderable fortitude of the British soldier upon them. Heads that all disappeared below the ground as if pulled by the same string whenever another load of shells came down: but nobody else in my trench. Nobody to share a laboured joke; no solid body drawing a cigarette in the corner opposite. Even my signallers a universe away, the other side of three or four feet of this earth.

I used to wonder what all the other heads were doing at that moment. Inanely one tried to visualize them, but each trench was a world of its own, with infinite distance separating it from its neighbour: each separate world, sheltering its human life, on its own particular

---

51   Fendick, Reginald F, *A CANLOAN Officer*, (Buxton: MLRS Books, 2008), p.61.
52   *Infantry Training Part VIII – Fieldcraft, Battle Drill, Section and Platoon Tactics* (War Office, March 1944), p.21.

brink of eternity. One never remembered these imaginings in Normandy, and alone in the trench you grasped the floor of it and twisted the sand in your hands: and down came more sand, tumbling down the sides as the trench shuddered from near misses. And because there was nobody there, there was nobody to overhear; so one spoke aloud. The Lord's Prayer, the Creed, the General Confession – they were my repertoire, and I went through the lot. Sometimes on the spur of the moment, I composed my own. When I reached the end, if the shelling still continued, I started over again at the beginning. When at last there came a stunning silence all the heads bobbed up again, and looked round to see if all the other heads were the same, and I was once more the company commander. If someone was hit, the stretcher-bearers would be already doubling out to his cries, and when the next dose came over the string was pulled and we all ducked again.[53]

As a unit's time spent in defence grew longer, efforts would be made to inflict damage on the enemy opposite without either giving away carefully concealed positions or prompting a withering retaliatory action. One method of achieving this aim was to employ 'shoot and scoot' tactics. A battalion's mortars would often be used in this manner, their ability to deploy from their carriers quickly set up and fire their rounds before conducting a rapid get away suited this purpose admirably. The Vickers MMGs could also be brought into action in a similar manner as Lieutenant Robert Fendick highlights:

No1 Pl moved back to the Coy HQ 'rest' area. From there we went out daily to various uninhabited spots (where the enemy retaliation to our fire wouldn't be a hazard to dug-in Infantry positions) and carried out harassing shoots. These were 'shoot and scoot' operations. Sometimes our shoot would be timed to coincide with a shoot on the same target by our 4.2-inch mortars or artillery.

We'd be given a target and the number of belts to be fired, usually no more than two or three minutes of Indirect Fire. I would park the platoon under cover, on carriers, while I went forward and found a suitable gun line. While I was working out the fire control problem, my DR (Murley)[Despatch Rider] would go back and bring up the gun carriers. They would roar up as fast as possible, the sections would pile out with guns, tripods, ammo etc., and the carriers would tear off back into concealment.

I would indicate the gun line, the guns would be mounted and laid very quickly (we were often in enemy view), get the prescribed belts away and then the only order I'd give was 'Go'. The carriers dashed forward, the guns were thrown in, often not even dismounted, and we got the hell out of it as fast as possible.

If we were lucky we finished the shoot and were away before Jerry had time to locate us and get his mortars on to us. His location and counter-fire drills were usually very fast and accurate, so if we were too long in action or he was quick, we finished and went out of action through whatever he chose to throw at us.[54]

Another way of hitting back at the enemy was by conducting fighting patrols or raids, the British conducted patrols far more extensively than the Germans, they not only believed that this prevented their soldiers becoming stale or stagnant when occupying static defensive positions, but also felt it was a way of dominating the enemy and maintaining the initiative. The fighting patrol was keyed by specific intelligence; usually gained through a preceding reconnaissance patrol.

---

53 Woolcombe, Robert, *Lion Rampant* (Edinburgh, B&W Publishing, 1994), p.155.
54 Fendick, Reginald, *A CANLOAN Officer*, (Buxton: MLRS Books, 2008), p.54.

Figure 2.18 Bren gunners of the Highland Light Infantry of Canada man a slit trench,
20 June. (Lieut. Ken Bell, Library and Archives Canada, PA-131432)

The British would frequently be supported by armour during their defensive engagements, however armour was primarily designed for offensive mobile action and when tanks were supporting a unit in defence their role would normally be as a counter-attack force or to block a penetration of the defensive position. For this purpose the armour was usually kept centralized and slightly to the rear. When the FDL had become static tanks were also called forward to engage particular targets, one might think that this would be a tonic for the infantry they supported, but the German's efficient retaliatory fire meant that this was not always a popular course of action as Lieutenant Reginald Fendick recounts:

On the second or third day I was with the platoon, a troop of four Sherman tanks of our supporting 27th Independent Armd Bde pulled up against the outside of our hedgerow and swung their guns almost over our heads. I went to their Troop Comd and asked him to go elsewhere, as if he fired he was sure to bring counter-fire down on us. He said he'd been sent up to engage a suspected Jerry Tank on the far slope and wouldn't be staying, 'and anyway, mortars don't bother us.' I pointed out that we did have to stay, and mortars did bother us, but his mind was made up.

His tanks duly fired a few rounds each and then the crews got out for a smoke before leaving. Within moments we heard the familiar distant thump as the Jerry mortars fired, and we dived into our holes while their bombs were in the air. The tank crews scrambled into their tanks and buttoned down their hatches, but the Troop Comd had been standing talking to me and was too far from his tank. I'm afraid I rather rubbed in his remark about mortars not bothering him, as he huddled beside me in my slit trench while we endured 5 or 10 minutes of accurate stonking....[55]

55 Ibid., p.54.

There were occasions where armour was split up and used to provide intimate defensive support to the infantry. The mere presence of tanks in these circumstances inevitably had a powerful moral effect, additionally the extra firepower the tanks main armament was able to bear could be decisive and their inherent mobility allowed them to concentrate fire power at critical places and points in the battle. These small parties of tanks were particularly useful in helping the infantry beat off either armoured or infantry attacks. Captain J S Highmore, 1st Tyneside Scottish, recalls directing a Sherman of 24th Lancers:

> About mid-morning, my right-hand platoon (18 Platoon) reported German Infantry working their way down a typical bocage hedge towards the anti-tank gun position (No.5) and Company HQ. They were engaged with small arms fire which would have been pretty ineffective because of the valley between the high banks topped with trees and thick hedging. I remember climbing on top of the Sherman tank parked in the Company HQ area (another one here had been knocked out by this time I think) and asked the Commander if he could fire a few rounds of HE to explode in the branches of the trees above the ditch and stop the enemy infiltration. He obliged effectively because nothing further developed from that hedge.[56]

Whilst the frontline infantrymen in the forward positions would bear the brunt of the German onslaught; those at battalion or other headquarters would also be under pressure. A defensive battle was a complex and nerve wracking business for commanders, coordinating the many aspects of the fire plan, understanding which assault is the enemy's main effort, when and where to deploy the reserve all required considerable attention. The picture would be a confused one, with communications often difficult or non-existent as a result of signal line cut by artillery fire, or runners frequently being unable to get through with vital messages.

In theory the defensive plan would have included disrupting the enemy long before he got to the FDL. Intelligence sources would hopefully have identified the German's approach triggering the air force to begin breaking up and disrupting the enemy formations, this fire would be supplemented by artillery and other indirect fire support as the enemy came closer. The German's final detailed approaches would potentially be detected by OPs, patrols or a screen to the British front, the defender's would try to channel them further, through an obstacle plan of wire, mines and ditches, into an area where withering coordinated fire from anti-tank and anti-personnel weapons could be brought to bear on him. However battles never go quite according to plan and small parties of Germans might be able to approach the defensive position, using darkness or fog to cover their movement, in these circumstances it would be the alertness of the sentry and the troops in the forward slit trenches which would determine whether the enemy achieved surprise. On such occasions hand to hand fighting was a very realistic possibility. Private Stanley Whitehouse recalls such an instance when serving with 1st Black Watch. Armed with a Schmeisser and a PIAT he shared a trench with a fellow private who went by the nickname 'Popeye', together they prepared for a long vigil separated by a hedge from their neighbouring slit trench. After some time he observed the distinctive German helmets silhouetted against the night skyline:

> 'Enemy front!' I bawled. 'Enemy front!' Pointing the Piat towards the silhouettes I fired. A mighty explosion erupted down the lane, followed by weird shouts and screams. Training now took over. After firing at night move your position or hide. Being unable to move I ducked. It was not a second too soon. A long burst of the dreaded Spandau raked the front of our 'slitter', hurling my small pack, pouches and pistol over my head and away into the night. Luckily

---

56 Baverstock, Kevin, *Breaking the Panzers* (Stroud: Sutton Publishing, 2002), p.99.

the Schmeisser, its spare magazines and the grenade fell into the trench. The enemy were now roaring, as though making a charge, but were still invisible. I stuffed the spare magazines into my blouse, grabbed the Schmeisser and emptied it in their direction, spraying it from side to side. Even before the firing stopped there were more screams and guttural shouts. I looked down at Popeye, who all this time had been crouched low in our 'slitter'.

'Why aren't the other buggers shooting?' I gasped. He just stared grimly into the gloom. I heard more German voices, as though orders were being shouted. Changing the magazine, I fired again and was surprised at the amount of flash and sparks coming from the automatic. Realizing that these would pinpoint my position I emptied the magazine and ducked.

Swoosh! I felt the wind on the back of my neck as a Panzerfaust (a bazooka) bomb skimmed the top of our trench and exploded in the hedge…

…I stood up quickly, finished off the magazine and crouched again. There was barely time to draw breath before another bazooka bomb zoomed in, showering us with dirt. I was now too terrified to be frightened – if that makes sense. I felt I was about to be killed and there was nothing I could do about it. To combat my 'bomb-happiness' I stood up and hosed another magazine down the road, this time finding relief by shouting, 'Come on you bastards, come on.' I was becoming hysterical, but the shouting seemed to release a pressure valve and I clipped on another magazine – the last – and emptied it in the general direction of the enemy.

Private Whitehouse had expected other sections to come into action as well, but a lack of mutual support amongst his platoon's positions, as well as a broken firing pin on the neighbouring sections Bren gun, meant his trench would have to fight an isolated battle:

I heard a roar and turning saw a huge German rising from the opposite ditch and pointing a Panzerfaust at us. I froze as he climbed out and crossed the road towards us, snarling and uttering horrible guttural sounds. I was convinced that this was my last moment on earth. In sheer, futile desperation I picked up the grenade and threw it at him without bothering to pull the pin; in any case, he was too close. The grenade hit his body and bounced away.

Screaming deliriously now he was on the edge of our 'slitter', still pointing the bazooka at our heads. Like two puppets on the same string Popeye and I simultaneously jerked our hands in the air and croaked 'Kamerad!' But the German made a fatal mistake by ignoring our offer to surrender. Had he ordered us out of the trench we would have complied readily. Instead he emitted a ferocious bellow and lifting the bazooka high slammed it down on our heads. As the weapon connected with my steel helmet I felt a tremendous jarring through my whole body, my knees buckled and every atom of breath was forced out of my lungs. I recall groaning, 'Oh Mum' – and then blacked out.

Private Whitehouse was unconscious for only a few seconds, when he recovered it was to hear the cries of a comrade being strangled in a nearby ditch:

I could hear desperate, panicky cries coming from nearby, and as objects gradually registered I saw two figures thrashing frantically in the water-filled ditch alongside our 'slitter'. The big German was now trying to hold one of our lads under the water, though I could not see who it was. Some unknown force compelled me to climb out of the trench, in slow motion, it seemed, grab my Schmeisser and close in on the German. Bent low, with his powerful hands holding one of my mates down, he was unaware of my presence. The sub-machine gun was empty and I therefore had no killing weapon, the thought of which drained my confidence. Nevertheless I raised the Schmeisser and smashed it down with all my strength on the German's helmet and struck my mate. The German never flinched. I tried again, with the same result. Christ, I thought, I'm killing one of my mates. A head appeared above the water, gurgling and spluttering.

'You're hitting me,' a thin voice cried out.

The next blow had to count. This time I reversed the gun and, holding it by the barrel, aimed for the German's curved spine, the only part of his body that seemed to be exposed. The Schmeisser's pistol grip had a steel band edging and it was this that I brought down with all the force I could muster on to the big brute's backbone. He screamed with pain and straightened up, clutching his back. I was vaguely aware of his victim, still coughing, crawling away into the gloom.

Standing upright, this Goliath of a man turned on me. His face was blacked up accentuating the whiteness of his teeth, which he gnashed in pain and anger. His eyes too were white, startlingly white and evil looking as he glared at me. He stretched out his massive arms toward me and I tried to step back. But my feet stuck in the mud, and now bereft of all strength, I fell back with a splash into the ditch. He leaned over me as I cowered under the hedge and then I heard a distinct 'pop', which seemed no louder than a cork exiting a bottle. With a grunt the German staggered, and grabbing at his side keeled over alongside me. I looked up and saw Popeye holding his smoking rifle. It was the first shot he had fired all night. But what a telling shot! Without it I would not have survived.[57]

Whilst the Allies often overmatched the Germans with both material and numerical superiority, there would be frequent occasions when the Germans, attacking with their habitual determination, were able to achieve a potentially crushing local superiority. These were the moments when British battalions literally held on by their fingernails to prevent either being overrun or a German breakthrough. The capable German armour often posed the greatest threat and although the PIAT could account for tanks at close range and in favourable circumstances, it was the 6-pounders of the anti-tank platoon that formed the linchpin of many battalion's defended areas. The anti-tank platoon's success would often be determined by skill in firing, canny fieldcraft and strong nerves. As this official account from the Rauray battle illustrates, being an anti-tank gunner required a particularly calm form of courage as well as native cunning:

On 1 July at Rauray, a 6 Pdr anti-tank gun belonging to a battalion of a Highland Regiment [1st Tyneside Scottish] was ordered to occupy a very forward position near three knocked-out Shermans. It was not possible to move up until dark when the detachment manhandled their gun forward and started to dig it in. The enemy kept on putting up flares and firing at these men, so that it was extremely difficult to work. These difficulties increased as the night went on, and the detachment was eventually compelled to lie flat and dig with their hands. At first light they noticed a blown up 6-Pdr nearby. They put this gun in position again and camouflaged it so as to look as though it was in action.

At 0650 hrs, enemy tanks were seen approaching from the village of Brettevillette. Someone excitedly shouted 'Tanks – look out.', to which the gun detachment replied, 'That's all right – we can see them – keep quiet'. Gradually about 20 tanks came into view and the detachment commander gave 'Engage!'. At that moment, the layer was wounded so the detachment commander took over his duties.

The leading tank was now getting uncomfortably close, but as it kept head-on to the gun, it was allowed to continue. Two other tanks, farther off offered their flanks and they were

---

57 Whitehouse, Stanley and Bennett, George, *Fear is the Foe: A Footslogger from Normandy to the Rhine* (London: Robert Hale, 1988), pp.96-100.

promptly shot up. Then, when the leading tank was 150 yards away and still closing, the detachment fired at its front and set it on fire.

Altogether the detachment killed nine tanks from this position – one head on at 150 yards and the remaining eight sideways on at an average range of about 400 yards. The gun had only 24 rounds of Sabot shot and ran out of ammunition after getting its ninth tank. More ammunition had been sent for but had not arrived. It was therefore decided to withdraw and join a gun detachment of a nearby anti-tank battery. Some hours later, the detachment took over another gun and succeeded in killing a tenth tank, thereby reaching double figures in one day. On the other hand, owing presumably, to the careful siting of the first gun, not a single shot was fired at it. All the enemy fire was directed at the three derelict Shermans and the decoy 6-pdr.[58]

Though a German attack might be defeated on the framework of defended localities and posts, there would still be occasions when defenders would have to restore the position, coping with infiltrators who had worked their way past the FDL or even having to launch counter-attacks to recapture positions that had been lost to the enemy. On the evening of 1 July, Corporal Cowie, section commander with the 1st Tyneside Scottish's reserve Company (D Company) was called forward during the Rauray Spur battle to recapture the positions of B Company. Sometimes the attackers may have rehearsed the counterattack plan and many of the arrangements would have already been laid on. On many occasions however the counter-attacks were a little more ad hoc:

At 'H' Hour we formed up with myself leading and emerged into the field, and at a semi-crouch, advanced up the left side of it towards 'B' Company's position. About thirty or forty men were following me, in single file tactical formation. A few yards behind me was my own Bren gunner, Taffy Jones, with the gun strapped across his chest so that he could fire it from the hip, behind him the No.2, then the new Company Commander, Capt J. R. Alexander, with the remainder of 'D' Company. On looking round later, I found that our attacking force seemed to stretch back some considerable distance. Providing I kept my head down there was cover on the left, i.e. a small bank and hedge. There were several yards to go before reaching the end of the field which seemed to slope up –our objective being 'B' Company's slit trenches just beyond it. There was no cover on the right just an open field with an amazing number of 'brewed up' tanks. I felt somewhat exposed. Everyone, including the company commander, looked white and tense. I felt OK, although I do not know how I looked. Being an NCO in any case, one had to set an example. I think I did this day.

Local support was much in evidence. I could hear behind me, as promised, 'Pipey' McKay's Bren guns, and the tanks of the 24th Lancers firing their Besa machine gun. The 'big stuff' from the enemy was still flying about and it was anything but quiet, one could not hear what one said even if it was bawled out. About a third of the way up the field, bullets started slashing through the grass at my feet.

I could have been hit either standing up or lying down, So I just carried on at the same pace, except I was now crossing my fingers and muttering a silent prayer that I would not be hit. The only time we would have had to pause and hit the deck would have been if we had been 'stonked' by mortars on the way up. We weren't. The small arms fire continued, bullets pinging and whining all around me. I had no idea where it was coming from. It may have been from the front, or it could have been from the hedge on the other side of the field. The

---

58 Operational Research Section account drawn from Baverstock, Kevin, *Breaking the Panzers* (Stroud: Sutton Publishing, 2002), p.81.

following day, we found a dead SS soldier with a Spandau in this hedge, almost at the point opposite where I was when the small-arms commenced. However, I believe it was Colour Sergeant McKay who had kept his word and was chopping down every blade of grass in front of me in case Jerry was occupying a position en route to our objective.

With a few yards to go to the end of the field, I ran up the small slope until my head was level with the ground of the field beyond. About a couple of yards ahead of me were several slit trenches, and a group of Jerry Infantry were scrambling out of these towards a screen of trees about four hundred yards to the rear. They had probably seen us when we had been advancing and had realised that we were intent on taking over the position again. Taffy Jones joined me at the top of the slope and I grabbed his Bren and fired several bursts after the fleeing Germans, they were zigzagging towards the trees and running fast.[59]

Whether attacking or defending, infantry combat in Normandy was a bloody and brutal affair that reinforced Field Marshal Lord Wavell's comments at the beginning of this chapter. Though the supporting arms and services played a vital role in Normandy, ultimately all engagements were decided by the infantry. The infantry's frontline role came at a crippling price though, infantry casualties in Normandy were proportionally larger than any other arm. Despite the infantry only accounting for 15% of 21st Army Group manpower, 63.7% of the casualties amongst soldiers were infantrymen. To put a little context to these figures Lieutenant Sydney Jary noted that 4th Somerset Light Infantry's casualties from Normandy to VE Day were 47 officers and 1,266 Other Ranks killed or wounded (a battalions strength was normally 36 Officers 860 Other Ranks). In his own platoon of the original thirty-six NCOs and soldiers who had landed in Normandy, only one NCO remained with the platoon at the end of the war.[60] The intensity of the fighting in Normandy dwarfed other parts of the campaign, 15th Scottish Division were in action for 325 days in North-West Europe, yet during their first action in Normandy, the five day EPSOM battle, they suffered 25% of the total casualties they would incur for the whole campaign. These casualty rates inevitably meant that battalions, companies and platoons were frequently understrength. Lieutenant Jary recalls the under-manning in his platoon and the handicaps of fighting with depleted numbers:

> Despite reinforcement, the Platoon was still not brought up to full strength. It never was, throughout the remainder of the campaign in Europe. When, just over a month before, I had taken command of the Platoon, its reduced strength of seventeen NCOs and soldiers gave me some concern. For Mont Pinçon we were even weaker: just two sections of six men each. Experience in Normandy had removed any anxieties regarding commanding an understrength platoon. In the attack, particularly at night, a platoon at full strength is just too big to manoeuvre quickly. Three rifle sections of about seven men each, plus Platoon Headquarters, was the ideal. In defence it was a different matter: the more riflemen on the ground the better.[61]

The British gravely underestimated the numbers of infantry casualties they would sustain in the War. Even before the campaign in Normandy began General Montgomery was acutely aware that the manpower supplies of infantry would run out quickly leaving him little alternative other than to split up and disband battalions (e.g. 1st Tyneside Scottish) or divisions (e.g. 59th Division).

---

59 Ibid., pp.142-143.
60 Jary, Sydney, *18 Platoon* (Winchester: The Rifles, 2009), p.122.
61 Ibid., p.34.

Figure 2.19 Riflemen of 5th Battalion Wiltshire Regiment waiting under a bridge for the order to move to the River Seine. (TThe Wardobe: The Museum of the Berkshire and Wiltshire Regiment)

Figure 2.20 Men of 2nd Battalion Royal Warwickshire Regiment advancing through a wheatfield during the final assault on Caen. During the preliminary bombardment, 450 Royal Air Force heavy bombers had dropped 2,500 tons on the town. (Imperial War Museum B6618)

The impact of both casualties and constant danger would inevitably have reduced the combat effectiveness of the infantry battalions, it would be difficult to absorb replacements and those that had survived would inevitably become jaded. A similar process was undoubtedly occurring within the German Army. Indeed veteran infantrymen have frequently been surprised at the modern perception of the German capabilities being superior to the British, as well as the direct criticism of British infantry prowess. Lieutenant Sydney Jary comments:

> Over the past twenty years it has become the custom for some of our younger military writers to extol the professional ability of the Wehrmacht whilst decrying that of our own fighting arms, particularly our armour and infantry.
>
> This has perplexed me because it runs contrary to my experience, My 18 Platoon were better soldiers than any we fought. So was 'D' Company and the whole 4th Battalion, The Somerset Light Infantry. Admittedly it was a good battalion but I find it hard to believe it was unique. This tendency among writers is understandable. They are too young to have taken part in the operations about which they write and therefore have had to rely on official records and personal interviews with those who were present…
>
> …Although they lost, the German soldiers and their families are proud of their exploits, many of which were considerable. It is of course, very much in their own interest to encourage the theory and myth that, although superior as fighting men, they were beaten only by numerically superior forces and firepower. In my experience this was not so. In many attacks the prisoners we took outnumbered our attacking force and German units who would continue to resist at close quarters were few indeed. Unlike us they rarely fought at night, when they were excessively nervous and unsure of themselves. Where we patrolled extensively, they avoided it. I can remember only one successful German patrol and not one successful night action. If our positions had been reversed I doubt they would have performed better than we did.[62]

The passage of time may provide us with a more objective perspective, one that argues that the British infantry were more than a match for their German counterparts and played the most significant part in the Battle of Normandy by tying down, fixing and attriting the cream of the German Army. This required support from the other arms and services of the Army, the Royal Air Force and, as we shall see in the next chapter, the Royal Navy. Nonetheless it was the infantry in Normandy who took on the lion's share of the work suffering the heaviest of casualties and reinforcing Lord Wavell's words that 'all battles and all wars are won in the end by the infantryman.'

---

62 Ibid., pp.16-17.

3

'Neptune's Trident' – Naval support

O Lord, we thank thee for the protection afforded us by the Royal Navy. Who brought us safely over the Channel. Who covered our landings. And who with the Merchant Navy, have brought to us safely all our wants. And for all those who have laboured so willingly in our Docks and Ports.

Second British Army Thanksgiving Service on Conclusion of the
Campaign in North-West Europe 1945

The Normandy campaign was initiated by the largest amphibious operation ever attempted by man, an operation on such a vast scale that it is unlikely it will ever be repeated again. This amphibious element of Operation OVERLORD was known as Operation NEPTUNE and the tasks faced by the Allied navies must have daunted the most courageous of planners. The Naval forces firstly had to ensure the safe arrival of the troop convoys for an assault on a hostile shore, this included minesweeping operations to clear lanes through the large German minefields in the Channel. Secondly, they had to suppress the German beach defences with a naval bombardment. Thirdly, land the assault forces, their vehicles and equipment onto the beach itself and finally disembark the follow-on forces and reinforcements at as high a rate as possible and without interruption. It was anticipated that 'building-up' the Allied forces would have to be done over the beaches for only the first five to six weeks after the landing, until the port of Cherbourg was captured and operational.

The Naval planners recognized that Operation NEPTUNE required a large and varied fleet of Naval ships. Minesweepers were needed to clear the passages through the German minefields. Battleships, monitors, cruisers and destroyers would engage and neutralise the enemy coastal defences as well as support the army in subsequent operations inland. Destroyers, frigates and corvettes, would be required to protect the convoys as they crossed the channel from both German surface threats and the *Landwirte* group of thirty-six U-boats that the Germans had earmarked to attack the invasion convoys. This mixed Allied fleet would include both the larger vessels of the Navy but also smaller units such as the Allied coastal patrol craft, that would help counter the German fast attack craft including the dreaded E-boats and torpedo boats. Finally, perhaps most importantly, there would need to be a plethora of landing craft and assault shipping to land the Army on the beaches themselves. The Navy was not entirely alone in these tasks; in their efforts to counter the submarine and surface menace they would be supported by the Allied air forces, including the RAF's Coastal Command. Additionally their bombardment tasks would also be conducted in close coordination with the Allied Expeditionary and Strategic Air Forces. Operation NEPTUNE was a truly joint operation.

To command and control this mammoth amphibious operation Admiral Sir Bertram Ramsay, the commander of the Allied Navy supporting OVERLORD, divided his forces into a British

Figure 3.1 A convoy of Landing Craft Tanks containing 3rd County of London Yeomanry
passes the Isle of Wight. (County of London Yeomanry)

Eastern Task Force (under Rear-Admiral Sir Phillip Vian) and an American Western Task Force
(under Rear-Admiral Alan G Kirk). Each Task Force was then further sub divided to provide the
assaulting and bombardment forces for the actual beach areas themselves. For the three British
beaches these were Force S (Sword), Force G (Gold) and Force J (Juno), the assault forces for the
American beaches were Force O (Omaha) and Force U (Utah). In addition there were two 'Follow
Up Forces', one for the British and one for the American beaches, which carried the supporting
divisions that would land after the initial assault formations.

One of the early challenges facing the Naval planners was the loading and assembly of the
various shipping in the UK. Once the Army had completed its 'Q' or logistic appreciation it gave
detailed requirements of what the invading forces would require in France and by when. This
included not only the troops themselves, but all their vehicles, equipment, ammunition, stores,
rations and so forth. These were then 'tactically loaded' into the available shipping, a process that
ensured that the Army's highest priority items were also the first elements of the cargo ready for
unloading at the other side. To aid this process the assault Forces were allocated specific loading
and assembly areas in southern England, as an example Force 'G,' which would land on Gold
Beach, was allocated the port of Southampton to load and given Southampton Water, the Solent
and Spithead areas to assemble their convoys. Force S, which was landing further to the east,
was given the ports of Portsmouth, Newhaven and Shoreham to load and the waters around
Portsmouth, Spithead, Newhaven and Shoreham to assemble their assault shipping into convoys.
The minesweepers and escorts attached to these assault force convoys also used these same ports,
but the larger bombarding ships would sail from Belfast and the Clyde and the coastal forces, who
would play a significant role in countering the German E-boat threat, would operate out of their
usual bases of Dartmouth, Portland, Newhaven and Dover.

Having assembled this fleet the Allies had to pass it through the very large German minefield
that ran the length of the channel. It was understood at the time that the Germans had a coastal
channel south of this belt which they used for their inshore traffic, the Allies assessed that this

would still be clear of mines at the time of the assault. Consequently the area of this channel was selected to be the 'lowering position'; the point from which the smaller landing craft would be cast off from their mother ships before their run in to the beaches. The NEPTUNE planners believed that the Germans would have mined inshore of this coastal channel and therefore these additional areas would also need to be swept to allow the Landing Craft to access the beaches and the bombarding ships to move freely into their firing positions. The minesweeping plan therefore consisted of three parts. Firstly for each assault force/beach area two channels were swept through the main mine barrier by a flotilla of fleet minesweepers; these channels would be subsequently widened as soon as was practically possible. Secondly the areas inshore of the coastal channel would be widened as required to provide areas for bombardment and other tasks and clear the landing craft channels leading to the beach. Thirdly the minesweepers would try to keep all of these areas clear of mines following the assault. This latter task was based on an assessment that German aircraft would drop an assortment of sea mines into the crowded Allied anchorage after the invasion.

The Germans possessed a variety of sea mines, each of which worked in a different way and required a different technique to render them safe. The large German minefield that crossed the channel and formed the first part of the NEPTUNE minesweeping task consisted of 'Contact' mines. These are the mines beloved by moviemakers and consisted of a large metal ball with horns protruding from it, the ball being partially filled with air to keep the mine buoyant. If a passing ship were unlucky enough to strike one of the horns it would cause a glass tube to break releasing an acid into an internal battery, which would complete a detonating circuit and cause the mine to explode. Contact mines were normally laid by dropping them from rails over the stern of a ship, but they could also be laid by submarine or air. The Contact mine contained a mooring weight, which would anchor it to the seabed, and sufficient cable to allow the mine to rise to a point a few feet below the surface of the sea. As the tidal variation in the channel would raise and lower the depth of the sea; it was considered best to cross a minefield in a shallow draught vessel at high tide, when there was a good chance of passing over the mines without striking them. Minesweepers were designed with a shallow draught for precisely this reason.

The minesweepers would deal with these contact mines by the use of a 'sweep'. This was a long wire hawser that the minesweeper towed behind it. At the outer end of the cable would be an Oropesa float, essentially a buoyant metal tube with a flag attached to it. Two attachments a 'Kite' and an 'Otter' were attached to the cable, these were simply rectangular metal boxes with a series of angled vanes inside. As the water moved through the vanes the Kite box would pull the wire down below the surface of the sea to a depth which was controlled by a separate wire connecting the Kite directly to the ship. The 'Otter' box used the water flow over its vanes to push the wire and Oropesa float away from the ship. The wire hawser of the sweep essentially worked as a cutting device, one of the wire strands of the hawser was twisted in the opposite direction to the others and this created a saw-tooth cutting effect as the sweep contacted and rubbed along the mine's mooring cable. If the cable's cutting action did not work a series of v shaped clamps were also attached to the wire, these attachments would detonate on contact with the mine's mooring cable and also help cut it. Once the mine's mooring cable was cut; the buoyant mine would float to the surface and the minesweeper's crew would fire at it with rifles or machine guns, If they hit one of the horns the mine would detonate noisily but harmlessly, alternatively if they missed the horns but struck the ball they would create enough holes for the sea to seep in, the mine to lose its buoyancy and sink to the bottom of the sea.

There were two risks to the minesweepers when carrying out these duties, firstly that the mine might get caught up in the sweep but not get cut, a constant lookout was therefore kept upon the sweep, the strain it was under and the noise it was making. If a 'trapped' mine was discovered the sweep would simply be cut. If a mine was not discovered through this close monitoring then it would become alarmingly obvious as the sweep was being reeled in, at this point the mine would probably be only a few feet from the ship. This required quick action with an axe to cut the wire, usually done as close to the winch as possible to reduce the lethal effect of the wires whiplash. The other threat that the minesweeper faced was in hitting a mine head on, to mitigate this threat the minesweepers would operate in formation with each ship in echelon to one side, much as combine harvesters do when cutting a large wheat field. The ships would then steer a compass course that would hopefully keep her inside an area just swept by the minesweeper ahead with her own sweep covering the vessel behind. Clearly the leading minesweeper was most at risk as unlike the others she was not moving through swept water on the first leg of the sweep. On D-Day this was mitigated by having shallow draught motor launches sweep in front of the larger fleet minesweepers who could sweep to a greater width and depth. Identifying successfully swept areas was critical and during sweeping operations it was normal for trawlers to follow the minesweepers and drop red and white dan buoys to mark the cleared lane. The dan buoys were used on D-Day but were subsequently replaced by the more permanent 'ocean light' buoys controlled by the Trinity House organization.

On D-Day itself a total of 265 minesweepers were used in the largest minesweeping operation of the war. From an area known as 'Z' (just south of St Catherine's point on the Isle of Wight), five channels had been selected which headed towards the Normandy coast and the five invasion beaches, each channel was then split into two, one for the fast ships (12 knots) and a second for slower vessels (5 knots). All through the night of 5 June the ships steadily cleared lanes, navigation was reportedly particularly challenging and a combination of radar and taut wire measuring gear (which involved trailing a thin wire behind the boat to measure distance over ground) had to be used to ensure accuracy. At the conclusion of their sweeps all the flotillas had cleared channels within one cable (200 yards) of the planned position and within a few minutes of the time allocated in the NEPTUNE plan.

Having completed this task the minesweepers then cleared an area parallel to the beaches in which the bombardment ships could take station and the landing ships unload their troops, stores and equipment. Brendan A Maher was a RN officer on Motor Launch ML137 and gives a good account of the sweeping operations that were undertaken in the night before D-Day:

> Our role in the invasion had placed us as the first ship in Channel 9, one of the ten channels that were to be swept. Channel 10 was the most easterly channel; Channel 1 was at the extreme western edge of the American landing zone. Our task was to sweep mines to leave a safe depth for the larger fleet sweepers of the 1st Flotilla, led by *Harrier*. They, in turn, swept at an even greater depth and width to clear the water necessary for the larger invasion vessels coming in behind them. Channel 9 was one of the approach channels for Canadian troops, who were in the landing ships behind the minesweepers. It led straight to Sword Beach, its direction being due south (magnetic) on a line directly terminating at Ouistreham.
>
> During the night sweep across the English Channel toward France, the tide turned shortly after midnight. This necessitated hauling in the minesweeping gear from one side and streaming the gear from the other. In order to do this, it was necessary to proceed slowly or stop altogether while performing the manoeuvre. The plan called for us to turn around and head back north slowly to permit the change of sweeps and then, once the sweeps had been changed, to turn around southward and resume the approach. It was necessary for all ships in the sweeping group to do this at the same time; as no signals were permitted on the radio, the signal to make the turns was given by the brief exposure of a small light on the masthead of the *Harrier*. It was crucial that this signal be seen by every ship so that they would turn together. A clear recollection is of the intense strain of watching from our stern to where the *Harrier* was following somewhere in the total darkness and very stormy sea. The *Harrier*'s light flashed

briefly at 0026, and the entire manoeuvre was completed by 0155, at which point we were once more headed toward France.

Once off the Normandy coast the plan called for the minesweepers to remove themselves into the unswept water outside channel 9 and allow the assault craft a clear run to the beach

> We did so by turning westward into the mined waters between Channels 9 and 8. Here we began to haul in the sweeping gear, but a German artillery bunker seemed to have selected us as a target; shells began to drop around us. To get out of the range of the German guns, we were compelled to cut the sweep wire that we were hauling in. We then replaced the missing sweep from our spares. Later, in clear daylight, I could see the bunkers on the beach through binoculars, but they had already been overrun by the Canadians and were no longer firing.
>
> As we moved out of the way into the mine field, we watched the endless panorama of landing craft and ships of all kinds heading toward the beach, bombarding the German positions further inland, moving this way and that, and turning sharply to avoid mines and other obstacles.[1]

Once the main minefield had been breached, the Naval bombardment of hostile coastal defences could commence. This bombardment, planned in conjunction with the air forces, had a number of aims, firstly to neutralise all batteries capable of firing on the sea approaches or the beaches themselves; secondly to neutralise or destroy the beach defences and finally to support the Army once ashore by engaging mobile batteries, counter-attacking formations and defended areas. The bombardment forces consisted of battleships, monitors, cruisers and destroyers, all of which were split up amongst the Assault Forces and came under their command and control. All bombarding ships had been given specific targets prior to the assault, whilst the battleships and cruisers generally engaged the heavy batteries; the destroyers were allocated sectors of the beach defences in front of the assault forces to which they were attached. These destroyers were not only given specific targets but were also allowed to use their own discretion; giving priority to targets such as guns firing at our own forces, pillboxes, machine gun posts and observation posts. Midshipman Colin Lawton served on the destroyer HMS *Serapis,* he kept a diary and describes his ship's actions on D-Day vividly:

> Just before dawn we moved forward again, the dim outlines of two battleships and a monitor could be seen moving silently towards the coast. At 05:00 they opened fire at the flanking batteries near Le Havre.
>
> A quarter past five and the time had come – with a dozen other destroyers and innumerable small craft, preceded by the BYMMS, we closed the shore. The first signs of dawn were already in the sky and the faint outline of the French coast was soon visible; a thin grey strip, so inoffensive in appearance, but held by an unscrupulous enemy...
>
> Soon after 06:00 the 'lowering positions' were reached where the large transports stopped to drop off their small landing craft. We were now five miles (8 km) off the shore, but there was no sign of the enemy; only an occasional tracer spurting upwards at an odd bomber and the sound of gunfire to the east.
>
> We passed the transports and, in single line, some eight destroyers continued slowly towards the beach which was now easily visible; a long strip of yellow sand behind which rose rows of houses all along the front of the little town of Ouistreham. We were now only three

---

1   Maher, Brendan, *A passage to Sword Beach* (Annapolis, Maryland: Naval Institute Press, 1996), pp.118-119.

miles (5 km) off those sinister dunes, but no flashes of gunfire came from them. Either they were holding their fire or our bombers had knocked out their batteries; we did not know, but waited in a state of tension. One or two cruisers had turned their attention to our particular beach and we could see the shells bursting, some just short of the beach, some on it and others amongst the houses behind.

By 07:00, the LCTs (Landing Craft Tank) were passing us and slowly moving forward to the northern shore of France – the moment the world had been waiting for had come at last. It was now our duty to fire as many shells as possible at the pillboxes and beach defence positions during the thirty-five minutes before 'H' Hour. The roar of gunfire was shattering non-stop, every ship around us was firing, broadside after broadside thundered along the line – it was devastating. More LCTs were coming up and we cheered them on as they passed us.

At 07:15, the heavy American bombers came over, too high for us to see, but we could hear their solid drone as they passed over the beach in their formations. Suddenly, a corner of the beach became a flickering mass, little spurts of flame springing up all along the ground and, before we realised what had happened, the air was split with the roar and thunder of falling bombs. This was precision bombing. Again and again it happened, the earth quivering as the ripple of flashes appeared concentrated in such a small area. How anything could have lived through this ordeal was beyond conception. Five minutes to zero hour – still the bombers came and still the bombardment continued. There was now so much smoke on the beach it was difficult to see and the air was full of the pungent smell of cordite. A new, awesome sight attracted our attention – rocket ships which were lying about a mile offshore had opened fire. Like streaks of red flame, the rockets shot upwards in groups of twenty, only to disappear into the cloud of smoke which enveloped the beach. Our own gunfire seemed pathetic in the face of those terrible weapons; it was a sight that can never have been equalled. The whole area seemed alive with flame and drifting smoke.[2]

As Colin Lawton highlights it was not just the larger Naval ships that would provide the fire support to the assaulting forces. The Royal Navy had also equipped a series of landing craft with a variety of heavy weapons and whilst the destroyers engaged targets from their positions on the flank of the assaulting forces, these specialized craft would accompany the normal Landing Craft right up to the beach. The LCT (Rocket) was one such craft and produced a fearsome amount by firing one thousand rockets in one large carpet. The rockets themselves were laid out in banks and were fired in a carefully calibrated sequence to prevent the craft from rocking too violently from side to side. As one can imagine the heat and flame of the rockets launching prevented any member of the LCT (R) remaining on deck during firing. The rockets were aimed through radar and the mutual efflux caused them to move apart so the fall of shot was much bigger than the LCT itself. After firing the crew would remain below deck for thirty minutes to allow the craft's sprinkler system to cool down the red-hot deck. Any misfires were simply thrown overboard.

A much smaller version of the LCT (R) the Landing Craft Assault (Hedgerow) (LCA (HR)) was also developed, this differed slightly from the LCT (R) in that its aim was to explosively clear a lane through the mines and wire on the beach with 46 'Hedgehog' mortars that were normally used for anti-submarine work. Forty-five LCA (HRs) were towed by other vessels to Normandy, some foundered and only twelve actually fired their mortars. As well as developing rocket and mortar landing craft the Navy had also equipped some LCTs with guns, known as Landing Craft Guns (LCGs), which were sited on the flanks of the assaulting forces. An LCG was equipped with

---

2   Lawton and Thomas, "In a Royal Navy Destroyer on D-Day", *Military History Journal* Vol 9 No.5 – June 1994, c/o South African Military History Society.

Figure 3.2 HMS *Warspite* and HMS *Ramillies* bombard the Normandy coast, 6 June.
(Crown Copyright)

Figure 3.3 Naval and army officers on the bridge of HMCS *Algonquin* watch the Normandy
coast being bombarded, 7 June. (Lt Richard G. Arless, Library and Archives Canada, PA-140084)

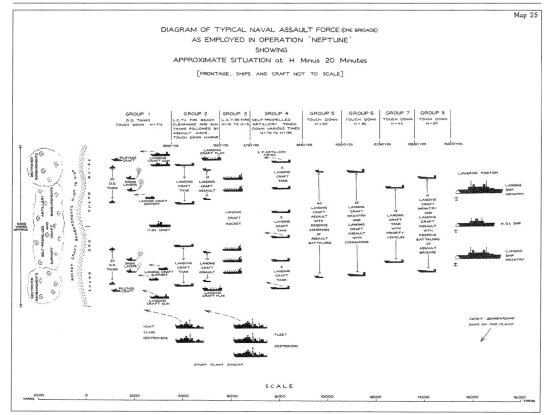

Diagram 3.1 Typical fire support.

eight 20mm Oerlikon machine guns and either two 25-pounders or 4.7-inch guns (the same gun as equipped many destroyers). Though she would not actually beach the LCGs extremely shallow draft would allow it to approach the shore with the other landing craft and provide the most intimate fire support. LCTs were also adapted to produce Landing Craft Flak (LCF) which provided the assault force with the necessary anti-aircraft fire. To convert an LCT into an LCF the bow ramp was welded shut and a roof built over the tank deck upon which several light anti-aircraft guns would be positioned; a typical configuration would be eight Oerlikons and two quick firing 'Pom-Poms'.

The final element of fire support came from the self-propelled guns of the Royal Artillery who would fire on the beach defences from their own LCTs during the run-in. This was being attempted for the first time in Normandy, Lieutenant Gregson RA was on one of the LCTs approaching GOLD beach with his self-propelled guns. He was supposed to have been given the range to the shore by a Fairmile Patrol boat equipped with a mast mounted radar, sadly this vessel had not turned up and he had to calculate the range to shore manually, adding 2,000 yards as a safety measure:

> There was France! A low grey misty line far ahead. I wondered for the hundredth time how I was to measure the range when H-Hour minus 20 minutes came to commence our barrage. Where the hell had that Fairmile got to? The No.1s were busy preparing their guns, the ammunition on deck was being unboxed, muzzle covers and gun covers stowed, and camouflage nets rolled back.

The coastline grew clearer and larger so that we could now see the outline of woods and as the minutes to H-Hour dwindled, so the details of the coast emerged. All was peaceful, just the throb of our engines and the hiss of the water and the smell of diesel fumes from our funnel. Our infantry in the LCIs must have been about 1,000 yards ahead of us but we could barely see them and they might have been much more. I thought the coast might now be 3,000 yards off. Our barrage time of H-20 minutes was approaching so I shouted fire orders: 'Troop target…H.E. charge 2…Zero lines …Angle of sight zero…five thousand (yards range)…Fire by order…Five rounds gunfire.' Without an accurate range to the beach I could not fire our barrage close ahead of our infantry, so added 2,000 yards to estimated range for safety. While the No1.s raised their hands to signify 'Ready', I set the range clock then as the synchronized second-hand crossed the line of H-20 mins, I ordered 'Fire!' The noise and concussion of four guns so close together and fitted with muzzle brakes, was terrific. Wreathes of smoke appeared on the beaches and inland. Our shooting would at least awaken the French countryside and perhaps unsettle a few German supporting troops. We repeated the five-rounds gunfire again and again until the paint began to blister on the gun barrels. Our last rounds of deck ammunition were fired just as H-Hour struck.[3]

Having succeeded in suppressing the beach defences with both naval and air firepower there were still a number of obstacles in the beach that could prevent the craft from landing. Some of these would be dealt with by the Royal Engineers once the tide was out and will be covered in the next chapter, others would be dealt with by the twelve Landing Craft Obstacle Clearance Units (LCOCUs). These twelve man frogmen teams were tasked to deploy from LCAs to destroy the various obstacles in place using explosives. However a time delay, the unexpectedly high tide and powerful surf hampered the LCOCU efforts and there were nowhere near enough lanes cleared for the assault. These beach obstacles would present a problem throughout the day with landing craft having to pick their own way through the hazards.

For the actual assault on the beaches the Allies had developed a variety of landing craft to suit the different purposes required in the assault. For the first waves of assaulting infantry there were the small Landing Craft Assault (LCA); these were launched out at sea from davits on their mother ship, the Landing Ship Infantry (LSI), which had also accommodated the assaulting troops during the cross-channel passage. For the second wave of infantry there were the Landing Craft Infantry (LCI), these larger seagoing vessels could cross the channel under their own steam landing troops directly on to the beach. For landing the Allied vehicles there were Landing Craft Tanks (LCT) which would be used in the assault itself and the larger Landing Ship Tank (LST) which would be used later in the invasion for disembarking the subsequent follow on forces. These last two vessels could also cross the channel unassisted.

So how did the army actually assault the beaches? Ironically on most beaches the first 'craft' that was planned to arrive at the beach was not a boat at all but that remarkable amphibious invention; the Duplex Drive (DD) Sherman tank. The DD Sherman was a normal tank fitted with an inflatable canvas skirt around its hull, when the screen was filled with air and raised by its crew the freeboard of the tank was increased and the amount of water displaced greater than the actual weight of the tank itself; allowing the vehicle to float. The DD tank was powered by two propellers at the back which gave the tank an overall speed through the water of about 4 mph. To see over the screen the commander stood on the turret itself and steered by using the large tiller he had available or gave instructions to the driver who could swivel the propellers. On landing on the

---

3   Lund, Paul and Ludlam, Harry *I Was In The War Of The Landing Craft* (London: W Foulsham, 1976), pp.165-166.

beach the screen would be deflated and lowered allowing the tanks armament to be immediately brought to bear and the tank to go into action. Five DD tanks could be carried in an LCT and it was intended that they should be launched about four miles off-shore. However the tanks were only capable of operating in slight seas with waves of one foot in height, on D-Day itself the waves were approaching six feet in height and the decision was usually made to launch the tanks either closer to shore or land them directly on the beaches. This was a sensible decision as the rough seas not only carried a risk that the tank would be swamped but would also slow the speed of the tank through the water causing it to arrive too late to support the infantry.[4] Lieutenant Stuart Hills was a DD Tank Troop Leader with the Sherwood Rangers Yeomanry, his LCT had closed to within 600-700 yards of Gold Beach and the ramp lowered:

> We were the front tank on the LCT, poised at the top of the ramp and clearly silhouetted a perfect target for the German gunners. To make matters worse, the steel hawsers holding the ramp were not quite tight enough, and we would be in danger of tipping over when we launched, so we had to wait precious moments while this was rectified. In those few moments a shell slammed into the water just in front of us, then one on the side of the ramp and another on the starboard beam. Sergeant Sidaway was wounded and Bill Enderby too, in the arm, and it was surely only a matter of time before a shell hit us.
>
> I gave the order, 'Go, go, go.' Geoff Storey moved into gear and we lumbered slowly down the ramp and flopped into the sea. Geoff engaged the propellers and we were on our way. I was still standing in my bridge position on the back of the tank, feeling terribly exposed and trying to peer over the canvas screen, while at the same time issuing orders to the driver and crew. The sea was rough and the struts holding the screen were hard pressed to do their job properly; possibly the screen itself had been damaged by one of the shells. At any rate, without it we would not be able to keep afloat for long. We had gone about fifty to seventy yards in the water towards the beach when it became clear that something was seriously wrong and it certainly was not just the canvas screen. The tank was shipping water from the bottom. In the driver's compartment, Geoff Storey was already knee-deep and he shouted, 'We're taking water fast.' Arthur Reddish slipped into the co-drivers compartment and engaged the bilge pump; it worked but the damage below must have been huge and soon water was pouring from the driver's compartment on to the deck. It is my guess that one of the shells that had landed so close to us had damaged the plates beneath the tank. Here there was no real armour, and this part of the vehicle had been exposed while on the ramp. But whatever the cause, we were without doubt sinking and sinking fast...
>
> ...I gave the order to bail out or abandon ship. Corporal Footitt had the presence of mind to pull the ripcord to inflate our yellow dinghy, and Sam Kirman, our only non-swimmer, put it over the side. The tank was now virtually awash and we did not have long. I frantically scrabbled about inside the turret to retrieve my map case, but without success. Trying to work quickly and calmly in a sinking tank is hard at any time and, with shells dropping close by, it was harder still. Everything became tangled up, so I gave it up as a bad job, ripped off my earphones, jumped out of the turret and just fell into the dinghy, all our personal possessions went to the bottom of the sea.[5]

---

4   Most commanders made such pragmatic decisions; the exception was on Omaha beach where, despite the heavy seas, DD tanks of 741st Tank Battalion were put into the sea far from shore. Of the 29 DD tanks only two made it to the shore.

5   Hills, Stuart, *By Tank into Normandy* (London: Cassell, 2002), pp.75-79.

Figure 3.4 No. 4 Commando heads for Ouistreham with the support of Sherman DD tanks from 13/18 Royal Hussars, 6 June. (Crown Copyright)

Jim Ruffell, RNVR commanded an LCT carrying the DD tanks of 4th/7th Royal Dragoon Guards in the landings on Gold beach. Like many others he was concerned about the sea state and elected to land the tanks directly onto the beach:

We were supposed to launch the tanks three miles out, 60 minutes or so before H-Hour, to enable them to swim to shore and be in position to advance with the first wave of assault troops. But a little bit of drama was taking place. We knew the limitations of DD tanks in rough weather and it was rough. There was no doubt in my mind that to launch these crack troops would have had even worse results than the Charge of the Light Brigade at Balaclava. A furious bout of signals started between my craft and that of the flotilla officer. Thank God my utter conviction that to launch was suicidal was finally upheld and it was decided to beach the whole flotilla and put the tanks ashore dry.

With an hour to waste before we beached, we milled around three miles off shore. The Germans opened fire, but they had arranged their gun emplacements so that the embrasures faced the beach to give cross fire and present solid concrete to the open sea. They just couldn't get their guns round. They kept firing away, dropping shells into the small bit of ocean. We kept outside their extreme angle of fire and enjoyed the extravagance.

Finally we approached the shore. Our formation changed from two divisions in line ahead to line-abreast. We were the first LCT to hit the beach, the doors went down and the 4th/7th Royal Dragoon Guards rolled forward. The first tank ran into trouble a few yards up the beach, but the others were off in a flash.

All our training in LCTs demanded dropping a stern kedge anchor as we beached. On this, our critical landing, I decided that if I dropped an anchor it might well foul on a German obstacle, so no anchor was dropped. I relied on the speed of the tanks getting off, and the lightened load getting us clear if I came astern straight away. This I did. We were afloat and away in a minute, but not before I had seen the guns of the tanks already in action against their first objective.[6]

Whilst some of the DD tanks launched out at sea did founder; the majority on the British beaches did make the shore even if they were sometimes a little late and had to be dropped directly onto the beach by their LCTs. The combination of amphibious DD tanks and the various 'funnies' of 79th Armoured Division appeared to achieve a high level of tactical surprise on the Germans. Sergeant Leo Gariepy was a Canadian DD tank commander who was able to successfully swim his tank ashore onto Juno beach:

> More by accident than by design, I found myself the leading tank. On my way in I was surprised to see a friend – a midget submarine who had been waiting for us for forty-eight hours. He waved me right on to my target and then made a half turn to go back. I remember him very distinctly standing up through his conning hatch joining his hands together in a sign of good luck. I answered the old, familiar sign – to you too bud!
>
> I was the first tank coming ashore and the Germans started opening up with machine gun bullets. But when we came to a halt on the beach, it was only then that they realized we were a tank when we pulled down our canvas skirt, the flotation gear. Then they saw we were Shermans.
>
> It was quite amazing. I still remember very vividly some of the machine-gunners standing up in their posts looking at us with their mouths wide open. To see tanks coming out of the water shook them rigid.[7]

With the DD Tanks having been slowed by heavy seas, it was often the LCTs carrying the 79th Armoured Division's 'funnies' which ended up as the first to arrive on the beaches. These LCTs were about 112 feet long and could travel at speeds up to five and a half knots, carrying fifty-five men and eleven vehicles. Their small length and shallow draft (it drew only 3 feet at the bow) meant that they were frequently the scorn of those in other ships. 'I wouldn't go outside the harbour in a thing like that!'[8] one officer recalls being told by a fellow Naval officer. An LCT had a small crew, of two officers and ten ratings all of whom were accommodated in the vessel, the crew in quarters behind the engine room and the two officers in a box behind the bridge. Like most landing craft personnel the crew were almost always members of the Royal Naval Volunteer Reserve (RNVR), rather than regular Royal Navy personnel (the latter were normally retained for service on the larger capital ships). The crews of the LCTs might have been forgiven for developing an inferiority complex, one young Midshipman recalls being invited onto the Battleship HMS *Duke of York*:

> The journey up the side of the massive capital ship was something to remember, but so was the intense interest which her captain expressed in how we lived. He punctuated his rapid pacing up and down his quarter deck with frequent darts to stare over the side at the upper works of the LCT, and then asked where I slept.
>
> 'What in that box? Good God! What, the captain as well? Good God!'
>
> Another walk up and down the vast expanse of holystoned deck and then another dart to the side to see where the crew lived. 'Good God! Really – in there?'[9]

---

6   Lund, Paul and Ludlam, Harry, *I Was In The War Of The Landing Craft* (London: W Foulsham, 1976), pp.162-163.
7   Lewis, Jon, *Eyewitness D-Day* (London: Magpie Books, 2004), p.117.
8   Lund, Paul and Ludlam, Harry, *I Was In The War Of The Landing Craft* (London: W Foulsham, 1976), p.136.
9   Ibid., p.135.

Figure 3.5 Tanks from 3rd County of London Yeomanry offloading from an LCT onto Gold Beach, 7 June. (County of London Yeomanry)

Figure 3.6 The tank of Major Woods MC, wades ashore from an LCT onto Gold Beach, 7 June. (County of London Yeomanry)

The LCT was equipped with two Oerlikon 20mm guns, mounted on either side of the bridge. They were for both anti-aircraft defence and perhaps more usefully in Normandy for suppressing the enemy on the beach. Midshipman John D Lund recalls his LCT landing on Gold Beach in the first wave and the steady nerves required of those operating the Oerlikons:

> A number of 88mm shells missed us as we made the run-in; they came from a beach pillbox on our port bow. Above and beyond this were several seaside boarding-houses from which a large amount of small-arms fire was coming. Unfortunately the gunner on the port Oerlikon was an inexperienced youngster and was more than a little disconcerted about the small arms fire going in his direction. The starboard gunner, A/B Franks, walked over to the port Oerlikon, strapped himself to it and proceeded to pour four pans of ammo into the pillbox. This put the 88mm out of action fortunately, as it could have clobbered our first tank as soon as the ramp door was dropped, making it impossible for the remainder of the tanks to disembark. It was afterwards found that the Oerlikon gunshield had been hit three times and the guns ready use locker had been pierced twice, one bullet having gone into a drum of Oerlikon ammo. This drum was very gingerly carried to the side and dropped overboard. A/B Franks received the DSM for his brave action.[10]

The LCTs were some of the smallest craft to cross the channel independently, their diminutive size and shallow draft often resulted in a very uncomfortable crossing, few were expected to survive D-Day unscathed. In a pre-invasion briefing Lieutenant R B Davies, RNVR, who commanded LCT 647, had asked what they should do after landing their tanks on GOLD Beach 'There was hesitation and consultation on the platform, and then a candid staff officer said, with great charm, 'As a matter of fact, we hadn't included you in the Turnround Organization at all. However if you do get off the beach you'd better go to the waiting position and join a convoy back here.' Extracting the landing craft was one of the most risky moments for the crew. Once the passengers and vehicles had been disembarked, a combination of a lightened load as well as a rising tide should theoretically have made the process relatively easy. In addition most landing craft were equipped with a kedge anchor and winch which allowed the craft to pull itself back into the water. As Lieutenant R B Davies' LCT approached Gold beach and identified their landing mark the flotilla's six craft manoeuvred into line abreast covering a mile of beach where they would land their 79th Armoured Division 'funnies' in the first wave of Allied troops onto the beach:

> Tanks were manned and revving up, the ramp door eased, two hands aft by the kedge wire, all of us dressed and armed and provisioned against a probably enforced stay ashore, feeling and looking like pirates. The squadron commander circled round in his headquarters craft and hailed us all in turn. 'Can you see your beach marks? – O.K., beach at full speed. Good luck!'
>
> A terrific 'Whoosh' sounded on our starboard quarter and we saw the streaks of 500 rockets rising shorewards from one of our rocket craft. We made for our beach, allowing for the strong easterly tide and going in at full speed. This last minute order made me wonder how our reel of kedge-wire would take it, for even at normal speeds it needed careful control.
>
> The last mile coming up-no opposition yet noticeable –then suddenly hundreds of flashes right along the sand dunes. 'Here it comes,' I thought, 'Coast batteries opening up at the last

---

moment.' But nothing came and I realized that the flashes were the rocket explosions from those we had seen launched seconds before. However, something was flying around – my tin hat registered a 'ping'. One or two plumes of water were shooting up here and there but we could see nothing likely to fire stuff that big. There was a pillbox on our port bow – point-five or similar we thought. It was spitting away at us and our port gunner on the Oerlikon got well on to it with his first burst. His second put tracer right inside and the box just blew up. We were due to beach at 7.23am – the last few hundred yards –strong cross-tide as expected – next craft to starboard had hoisted a child's wooden horse as mascot – more shell splashes – ramp door partly lowered – 'Stand by kedge…Let go.' And roughly what I feared happened. The kedge dropped and our speed jerked the wire drum off its frame, the wire jammed and the anchor bounced along behind us at the end of fifty feet of useless wire – but we were there. I felt us take the ground and continued pushing at full speed to make sure of it. She was slowing up now. On our port side three survivors from a DD tank asked for assistance. 'Get them aboard if you can, ' I told two of the lads. Then 'Down Ramp' and the Royal Engineers went ashore…

…The shell splashes were coming from the right, we saw, from a gun emplacement a mile along the beach near where the flotilla officer's craft had landed. The craft was still there. The others were then kedging off –their kedge wires had survived. The signalman told me the three tank survivors were aboard.

Figure 3.7 Aerial photo of the landings on Mike beach, Juno to the west of Courseulles, 6 June. (Air Historical Branch)

The Army were ashore. Now, apart from the F.O.'s craft we were the only craft still on the beach. The splashes were coming closer – we were almost a broadside target. For a long minute the rising cross-tide took charge as we moved slowly ahead dragging a useless kedge, before No.1 had dashed aft from the ramp door and, with an engine-room Chief, cut the kedge wire so that I could go astern. We slewed round immediately, providentially facing the troublesome gun and presenting the smallest target. We were still well afloat and still slewing broadside to the beach. I decide that rather than going astern I could get quicker results by continuing the turn with a hard-a-starboard rudder and engines full ahead, which I did. Two splashes went up, one either side of us as we turned; we gathered way, completed the turn, and unbeaching right against the rule book, we got clear.[11]

Following close behind the DD Tanks and 'funnies' of the first wave would come the infantry in the Landing Craft Assault (LCA). The LCA was a wooden landing craft clad with armour, it could carry a platoon of 31 soldiers who were seated in three parallel benches that ran along the length of the craft. At the bow of the craft were two hinged armoured doors and beyond that a ramp which would be lowered manually by a simple wire and pully system. Bren guns could be fired from two ports at the front of the craft. The LCA benefited from a low silhouette, very shallow draft and silenced engines, its armour plate was also sufficient to protect the troops from both small arms fire and shell splinters. The craft was crewed by four personnel, a coxswain, two seamen and a stoker, a naval officer would be responsible for a group of four LCAs. In common with the LCTs most of the crew were RNVR though a large number of LCAs were also crewed by Royal Marines. The LCAs were not capable of crossing the open sea in all weathers and were therefore carried on the davits of a Landing Ship Infantry (LSI), such as the SS *Glenroy*. The LCA passengers and crew would also be accommodated on these ships, thirty seven of which were employed off the British beaches on D-Day. When the LSI reached the lowering position 5-11 miles off shore, the LCAs would be lowered to the loading deck level where the Platoon would cross on gangways into the craft's stern, a rifle section occupying each one of the three benches. The tricky part would then be lowering the heavily laden craft into the sea and casting off from the ship itself; this was never simple in a sea with a swell. The bowman and sternsheetsman would stand by the snatch blocks and try to cast off at the same time and when there was still slack in the 'falls' or ropes. Once the craft had cast off from the ship it would join the other LCAs which made up its twelve craft flotilla and move in line astern towards the beach, the formation changing to extended line as it prepared to assault the beach. Sub Lieutenant James Leslie, RNVR, was the boat officer on loan to 538th LCA flotilla carried by the LSI *Empire Broadsword* at Sword Beach:

We were called in the small hours and going on deck I saw that it promised a dark and lowering day with a lumpy sea running and a cold wind. I could find no comfort in the weather so I went below to have a good breakfast and after that got into my gear. After I had stowed my papers and spare ammunition about me I took my wristwatch off its strap and knotted it into a condom through which I could wind it and read the time. I also put three pound notes in another condom so that should I be left to my own devices in France I would have some currency. I packed a small ammunition box with a spare jersey, some chocolate which I had saved and a bottle of liquor, and got into my craft, LCA 796, and watched the troops climb aboard it. They were East Suffolks, a quiet and nonchalant bunch. They all seemed to be Eighth Army men, veterans of too many battles to be overmuch impressed by another, even though it was the greatest raid in history.

---

11 Ibid., pp.160-162.

Figure 3.8 Infantrymen of the Royal Winnipeg Rifles in a Landing Craft Assault (LCA) en route to land at Courseulles, 6 June. (Library and Archives Canada, PA-132651)

We lowered in the semi-darkness into a jabble of broken water around *Broadsword*, took station on our navigation leader and, sliding left and right over a semi-beam sea, started our run for Normandy.

On the run in to the beaches the troops on Lieutenant Leslie's LCA chatted, played cards or smoked. Thermos containers of food or tea were opened, though many troops were too sea sick or nervous to think of eating.

We increased to maximum speed for the last 2,000 yards run in and on nearing the beach saw that the obstacles were intact, still very much awash with the high tide blown up by the recent wind. We decreased to as slow a speed as possible, and my coxswain, Corporal Smith, took the side-slipping craft carefully into the first line of obstacles (Element C). I swore at a Teller mine which came dangerously close and involuntarily held out my hands to fend the bloody thing off, but in the last line of obstacles we were severely holed for'ard. On touching down we found that the ramp was damaged and the small steel doors between it and the well of the craft could not be opened, so the troops had to leave us over the catwalks down the sides.

Getting back to *Broadsword* was the problem. The size and shape of the hole in the bow was too much for one of the plugs we carried. Meanwhile shells threw up fountains of sand around us and there was uproar to our left heralding the arrival of an LCT which smashed her way through the obstacles to get her tanks ashore. The tanks deployed themselves along the beach in front of us and I thought we might shelter under them until we could make a sortie on the remaining houses on the beach road, but the tanks attracted sundry flying scrap iron and I reluctantly decided that staying ashore was 'no go'. Going backwards out of the beach obstacles was worse than coming in, but Corporal Smith got us safely to their seaward edge, where the craft began to sink despite our efforts to plug the hole. Corporal Lynch came along in LCA 1341 just as we went under and we rapidly transferred to that craft, which had also been damaged and turned out to sea.[12]

The poor weather conditions and incoming tide meant that the sea level had risen much higher than had been anticipated. As a result many of the obstacles were now partially covered by the sea, making landing the assault craft a much trickier proposition.

The final Landing craft that was used in the assault phase at Normandy was the Landing Craft Infantry (LCI). These were built in America to a British requirement which had identified that a larger craft than the LCA was needed, one that could embark troops in the UK, cross the channel under its own steam and land the soldiers directly onto beaches. There were a number of different LCI variants produced but most were about 158 feet in length and steel hulled, they could carry anywhere between 80-210 troops who would disembark the craft down two bow gangways. The vulnerability of these narrow gangways and the larger size and silhouette of the craft meant that LCIs were generally thought inappropriate for use in the first assault wave. However in Normandy they were employed in this role on a number of beaches. The LCI had a crew of 3 officers and 21 men who would sail the vessel across the Channel and man the four 20mm Oerlikons. Lieutenant Sidney Henry RNVR, commanded LCI 300 which carried troops of the Norfolk Regiment from Newhaven to Sword Beach:

> The colonel whom I carried wanted his three LCI to land opposite a gap in the sand dunes defined from the excellent low-level aerial photos which had been taken. We landed at H-Hour at precisely the spot he wanted but unfortunately the gap led to a building which looked as though it had been a hotel but was now full of Germans firing down on us from the windows with what appeared to be mortar rifles. On the run-in to the beach I ran on to a submerged beach obstacle which holed the engine-room and detonated a mine under No.2 troop space – then holes started appearing in the decks where the mortars were hitting. The explosions stunned every one momentarily and then we all shook ourselves and swung into action. The Oerlikon gunners started blasting the hotel, the fo'c'sle men lowered the ramps and I dashed off the bridge to pull my first lieutenant out of the water where he had been blown by one of the blasts. Then followed the grim task of sorting out the dead and wounded – removing all effects from the dead and giving the wounded temporary first-aid.
>
> By this time our gunners had silenced the enemy fire and the troops had got up the beach unscathed and disappeared over the sand dunes. I looked round and found we were the only one of the flotilla left on the beach and I pulled off and headed for a cruiser which took my wounded. The motor-mechanic kept telling me that the level of the water was rising in the engine room but there was nothing I could do, and after casting off from the cruiser I heard an ominous hissing which indicated that the water had reached the air intakes. We were then drifting about 10 miles out – and rather alarmingly towards the Seine and German-held Le Havre. We buried the dead at sea. The only weights available were sections of the galley stove which we dismantled and the young matelots, who had been considerably shaken by the day's events, thought it all very callous, not knowing that landing craft commanders had been expressly forbidden to bring any bodies back to the UK, so as to avoid choking the embarkation ports.

12 Ibid., pp.151-152.

Figure 3.9 Infantrymen in an LCA going ashore from HMCS *Prince Henry* off the Normandy beachhead on 6 June. (PO Dennis Sullivan, Library and Archives Canada, PA-132790)

Figure 3.10 Troops disembark from a Landing Craft Infantry (LCI) at Bernières, Juno Beach. (The Wardobe: The Museum of the Berkshire and Wiltshire Regiment)

By now the stern was under water and if we remained afloat we looked like finishing up in the Seine and 'in the bag'. Fortunately I managed to flash up an LCI in the distance and she steamed up and took my crew off; then with four of us still aboard, all on the bridge in case she took a sudden dive, the LCI towed us back to Newhaven. Imagine my feelings when, rather pleased with myself at having got my craft back despite everything, I was confronted by an irate harbour master shouting 'Don't bring that bloody wreck into my harbour!' Muttering imprecations against all 'base wallahs' we beached the craft on the shingle outside the harbour.[13]

Once the initial assault phase was over the naval commanders could begin the rapid build up of troops ashore. In this instance the carrying capacity of the Landing Ship Tanks (LST) would be critical. The LST was over 300 feet in length and could carry 2100 tonnes. It had a spacious hold that allowed vehicles to be carried either in its internal tank deck or, using an elevator or ramp, on the main upper deck. Vehicles would usually exit the craft through the clam shaped bow doors directly on to 'Rhino' ferries or the beach itself. Landing such a large craft up a sloping beach was not as easy as it sounds. As the craft approached the shore the large forward ballast tanks would be empty, and the aft tanks would be filled with seawater; this would tip the bow of the ship up so that she struck the sloping beach lightly, sliding up it and getting as close to the water's edge as possible. Once beached, the forward ballast tanks would be filled up to keep the bows heavy and prevent the ship from floating off the beach as the tanks or other vehicles disembarked and made her progressively lighter and more buoyant. When all the cargo had been discharged she emptied all ballast tanks and attempted to float off, going full astern with the engines. This was rarely sufficient to get her off and additional help from a kedge anchor, which was dropped at 500 or 1,000 ft from the shore on the run in, might be necessary. Tides were clearly an important consideration in beaching the LST, ideally the ship landed with a rising tide, got rid of its freight quickly before it was swamped by the rising water, and backed off at a higher tide. Whilst the LSTs had been designed to beach and dry out on an ebbing tide there were concerns that repeatedly doing this would weaken the hull over time and on many occasions the 'Rhino' was used to take vehicles from the LST to shore.

The Rhino was a 180-foot long raft constructed from a series of steel tanks joined by a frame of steel girders. The raft was powered by two outboard motors and equipped with wooden ramps that would allow them to offload the vehicles onto the beach, bulldozers would then be used to push them back out to sea again. Sometimes LSTs would moor three to four miles out at sea, in which case the Rhino ferry would often have a 'Sea Mule' in assistance, essentially a miniature version of itself that could act as a tug. The Rhinos were strong rafts and larger ones were capable of carrying up to thirty lorries at a time. Although these rafts were very effective they did not often inspire confidence in some of their passengers. Gunner W. T. Jones of 3rd Regiment Royal Canadian Artillery records his scepticism:

Our Gun HI was to be the first towed gun of the regiment to land. We were to land on 'Mike' sector of 'JUNO'. This was the plan, but what action goes to plan? On our run-in to the beaches, about three miles from the shore we were ordered out of the landing order and fell back about five miles. Here we circled for hours, which seemed like days as the seas were rough and we weren't sailors. We had been told our beach exit was plugged and closed to vehicles.

---

13 Ibid., pp.153-154.

Figure 3.11 Vehicles disembark on Juno beach from Landing Ship Tanks (LST) at low tide.
(The Wardobe: The Museum of the Berkshire and Wiltshire Regiment)

Finally, our turn came and in we went. The tide, however was now not suitable for a direct landing, i.e. ramp down, drive off, as we had rehearsed for many months. Major Scott informed the gun sergeants we would be loading on a small 'Rhino' raft. This was the first time we had heard about 'Rhino' rafts and we sure weren't crazy about the word 'raft'. There were the usual derogatory remarks about the Canadian Brass. We were assured that four Bren gun carriers and guns could fit on these rafts 'if properly handled'. Out from the beach purred our raft, a low-slung affair with steel decking and no railings, powered by two outboard motors and crewed by two REs who looked about forty years old. How they did it without loss of life and limb I'll never know, but they did.[14]

In addition to the Rhino rafts the highly successful, American built DUKWs[15] (pronounced 'ducks') were also used to offload the amphibious shipping during the build up. This six-wheeled amphibious truck was able to carry 2.5 tonnes from the ship to the shore in a small open cargo bay in the middle of the vehicle. Charles Wales was a driver with 633rd Company Royal Army Service Corps (RASC), which was converted to DUKWs in January 1944, he describes his arrival in Normandy in an LST:

On board an LST we arrived off the beaches on the evening of D-Day, but remained on board the LST overnight. And then on the morning of D+1 we went ashore. I, being the last on the LST, was first off. On approaching the shore there was a Beachmaster equipped with

14 Robin Neillands and Roderick De Norman, *D-Day 1944: Voices from Normandy* (London, Weidenfeld & Nicolson, 1993), p.187.
15 The DUKW derived its name not from a military acronym but from the civilian maker's internal categorization of its vehicles (D = a vehicle designed in 1942, U = utility, K= front driven wheels and the W = two powered rear axles).

a bat in each hand, signalling us to a position ashore between the underwater obstacles and some wrecked landing craft. All our DUKWs had been preloaded with cargoes before leaving England – I had flamethrower liquid, stored in cylinders. We'd be carrying supplies ashore and then six stretcher casualties each from the Casualty Clearing Stations back to an LST offshore. An LST could accommodate three DUKWs inside, bow to stern. After unloading the stretcher cases we would back out and go to a designated ship to load up again, and back to the shore with more supplies.

Operating a DUKW was not simple, when exiting the LST at sea the DUKW would run down the ramp until the DUKWs buoyancy lifted its front wheels off the ramp, if the driver was not quick enough in engaging the propellers there was a danger that a cross sea could quickly catch the DUKW's bow and sweep it sideways causing it to become entangled in the chains supporting the ramp. If the driver took the run into the water too quickly there was a danger that the bow of the heavily laden DUKW would dip too low into the water and the weight of the DUKW (and its flooded cargo hold) would take it straight to the bottom. Entering the sea from the beach was a much simpler process as Charles Wales describes:

> The procedure was to halt at the water's edge, engage the propeller, select second gear, and then apply full throttle. She'd shudder at the first few breakers, then lift and perform just like a motor boat. At the top speed of 6 mph you'd use a gallon of petrol a mile.

As the build up on the beaches developed the unloading process became more organised and much easier. Each ship would carry a large black board on its bridge that helped the DUKW drivers identify the ship Beach Control wished them to unload. In addition mobile cranes began to be brought ashore to help unload the DUKWs. After a while the DUKWs work became almost routine:

> We operated from Jig Sector of GOLD for 80 per cent of the time. There was a wide concrete slope from the road down to the beach, and Beach Control was at the foot of this slope. A nearby field was used like a taxi rank. You had to park around the perimeter, and as vehicles were called for by Beach Control we all moved around the field like taxis. Here was a chance to top up with petrol from jerry cans on the stern deck, or have a cigarette.
>
> Ships to be unloaded provided a spring line from bow to stern, with a steel hook adjacent to the hatches. Coming alongside we would connect the hook to the DUKW, turn the steering wheel away from the ship's side and open the hand throttle to a fast tick-over, so holding the vehicle hard against the ship. A Jacob's ladder was provided to allow the Pioneer Corps men to descend into the DUKW to unload. Supplies were loaded by rope nets, but large shells like 5.5in were loaded loose in wooden trays.[16]

The Naval planners had initially anticipated that the use of Rhinos, DUKWs and amphibious shipping would reduce as both Mulberry harbours were to come on line, albeit at a limited initial capacity, within a week of D-Day. In addition it was hoped that American forces would be able to capture the port of Cherbourg intact and the Allies could begin to use this great harbour. In fact the German demolition of Cherbourg's harbour facilities was so extensive that it was not fully operational until mid-August.

---

16 Bruce, Colin, *Invaders: British and American experience of seaborne landings 1939-45* (London: Chatham, 1999), pp.147-150.

The Mulberry harbours are one of the most famous aspects of the Normandy campaign, even today the project's ambition and engineering skill take one's breath away. The idea developed slowly, indeed it took a number of field trials to establish Major Allan Beckett's design of roadways, flexible bridging units and floating pontoons as the basis of the Mulberry harbours. This floating roadway was known as 'Whale' and some 10 miles were ordered for the two Mulberry harbours at Arromanches and at Omaha. The roadway was suspended on pontoons known as 'Beetles' which were anchored to the seabed using a 'kite' anchor especially designed by Major Beckett. So impressive was the kite anchor's holding power that few could be recovered at the end of the war. The roadway would end with a 'Spud' pierhead where the ships would unload or discharge their cargoes. The spud was able to operate in all tides by the use of four legs which rested on the seabed upon which the spud slid up and down.

The harbour's framework consisted of a large number of concrete caissons known as 'Phoenixes' which would be used as breakwaters, piers and connecting structures. The harbour itself was protected by a floating breakwater known as 'Bombardon' and a series of blockships that were sunk in place known as 'Gooseberries'. Additional gooseberry blockships were also sunk off the beaches to give a little shelter to the landing craft that were still landing directly on to them. Although the Mulberry at Omaha beach was permanently put out of action in the storm of 19-22 June, the harbour at Arromanches, which became known as Port Winston, was kept in service for 8 months until the port of Antwerp was successfully opened. All the elements of Mulberry had to be towed across the channel, the larger phoenixes by powerful tugs.

Assembling the Mulberry harbour was the responsibility of a team of Royal Engineers. They surveyed the harbour and demolished areas of the town of Arromanches to allow easier access and exits for the large volumes of vehicles that would disembark or unload at the harbour. The invasion marked the first time the Royal Engineers had ever assembled the various units of the harbour – unlike almost every other aspect of the invasion there had been no opportunity for a rehearsal. The overall contribution of the Mulberry harbours is frequently debated, particularly after the Americans elected not to repair their own storm-damaged harbour off Omaha beach. However 35% of the total British stores were landed through the Mulberry harbour at Arromanches compared to 50% over the beaches and 15% through the small French harbours of Port en Bessin and Courseulles. The total number of British forces discharged between 6 June and the end of August consisted of 829,640 men, 202,789 vehicles and 1,245,625 tons of stores. Whether they came across the open beaches or at the Mulberry harbour the scale of build up was impressive.

Whilst the build up took place the naval planners knew that they would have to protect the Normandy anchorage and cross-channel shipping from the various German threats which would be marshalled against it. Though the large units of the German surface fleet were in a very weak state an attempt was made by the German Navy to dispatch destroyers from Bordeaux to attack the bridgehead. On their way north they were attacked by RAF Beaufighters and forced to put in at Brest. They then departed that port and were met in the early hours of 9 June by the destroyers of the 10th Flotilla (HMS *Ashanti, Haida, Huron, Eskimo, Javelin* and the Polish ships ORP *Blyscawica* and *Piorun*). After an intermittent action one of the German destroyers was sunk, one driven ashore on the Ile de Bas and the remainder damaged and withdrawn to Brest. There were no further significant attempts by the Germans to use large vessels to attack the invasion shipping.

The U-boat threat was also treated seriously by the Allied navies, Coastal Command had instituted what was described as a 'solid wall of air patrols' over the south-western approaches. These patrols were so effective that within the first 48 hours of the invasion, 22 attacks were made on U-boats of which two were sunk (U955 and U970) and seven others sufficiently damaged as to cause them to return to harbour. In the period 8-12 June a further four U-boats were sunk and the German commanders recognized that only those U-boats fitted with Schnorkel could realistically hope to survive in the Channel. Consequently the German Navy ordered all U-boats without

Schnorkels to return to Brest. Although those U-boats that were fitted with Schnorkel would continue to operate in the Channel they could only do so at much slower speeds, greater discomfort and considerable risk; the shallow Channel waters were generally unfavourable for submarine operations. The U-boats did achieve some success torpedoing HMS *Mourne*, 45 miles north of Ushant, and HMS *Blackwood,* 20 miles north-west of Cap de la Hague. It is however noteworthy that the first sinking of an Allied merchant vessel by a U-boat only occurred some three weeks after D-Day. The U-boats were able to pick up the pace a little later on in June and successfully torpedoed 5 ships[17] (none of which sank) on 29 June, but the Allies were also able to inflict a heavy rate of attrition on the U-boats, on this same day the Germans lost their twelfth boat to a combined effort by Liberator aircraft and ships of 3rd Escort Group. Despite the best efforts of the German U-boats their effect in delaying the Allied build up was minimal.[18]

Though the main German surface fleet and U-boats could be dismissed as merely nuisance value to the Allies, the threat posed by German mines and their smaller coastal and torpedo craft was more potent and caused the Allies considerable problems. That German mines were still causing difficulties after the main German mid-channel 'contact minefield' had been breached prior to D-Day may seem surprising. But once the site of the invasion was confirmed the Germans were able to deploy a number of 'influence' mines directly against the anchorage. These influence mines were usually laid by aircraft and designed to sink to the bottom of the sea where they would rest on the seabed. There they would detonate not on direct physical contact but, depending on which type of influence mine was used, in reaction to either the sound, the magnetic field or the pressure of a passing ship. The magnetic mine was probably the most widely used influence mine by the Germans in World War Two. It operated on the principle that a ship's metal hull has a magnetic field around it, a magnetic needle was therefore placed inside the mine and allowed to swing freely on its axis. When a vessel passed over the mine the needle would be deflected by the ship's magnetism and used to initiate a detonator in the mine. Magnetic mines had the advantage of being easy to lay by aircraft but as they had to rest on the seabed were really only effective in relatively shallow water. Magnetic mines had been used since the beginning of the war, but once the Allies discovered how this new German weapon worked they fitted their ships with a degaussing band, a neutralizing electrical circuit tailored to each ship's unique magnetic character. Whilst 'degaussing' would provide ships with a passive defence against mines it did not neutralize the mine permanently and therefore the proactive sweeping of magnetic mines was undertaken by wooden minesweepers (principally the 105 foot Motor Mine Sweeper (MMS) and the slightly larger British Auxiliary Mine Sweeper (BAMS).

These wooden hulled mine sweepers had a reduced magnetic field which allowed them to pass over the mines (though they were still fitted with a degaussing band to neutralize even their modest signature). A generator on board the minesweeper passed a strong current down one of two large, thickly insulated cables it trailed from its stern. These two cables were of two different lengths, one was normally 525 yards long and the other 200 yards long. At the ends of both cables was a large copper electrode, when the current was passing along one of the cables during the sweep the salt water conducted the electricity to the other cable and created a magnetic field similar to that of a ship, this would cause the magnetic mine to detonate a safe distance astern of

---

17   Four liberty ships in convoy E.C.M.17 were torpedoed at 1545, three of them (*James A Farrel, James A Treutkan* and *H. G. Blasdel*) were towed by tugs to the Solent; the fourth (*Edward M House*) continued with the convoy. Three hours later S.S. *Empire Portia* in convoy F.M.T. 22 was torpedoed, she was successfully towed to the Solent by LST 416.

18   RN Historical Branch, *Battle Summary No.39: Operation Neptune Landings in Normandy* (London: Naval Staff, 1947), p.147.

Figure 3.12 The invasion fleet off Courseulles, the v-shaped structure is one of the 'gooseberries' and comprised of sunken blockships. (Crown Copyright Army Historical Branch)

the minesweeper. During sweeps the generator would reverse the flow of the electrical current and change the polarity of the field, to comprehensively clear all types of magnetic mines.

Magnetic sweeps were normally conducted between pairs of minesweepers, this was because the combination of cables not only created a larger magnetic field but also moved it further away from the two ships. This was a useful benefit as one of the particular risks to magnetic sweeping was the damage that was done to the cables after each detonation. Great care needed to be taken by crews in inspecting the cables and repairing any cracks in the insulation with an insulating compound and tape, failure to do so would mean the artificially generated magnetic field would be present all the way to the crack and the minesweeper might well have its stern blown off. Brendan Maher on ML 137 observed the American minesweeper, YMS 350, conducting magnetic sweeps off Cherbourg on 2 July and believed that cracks in the cable were the cause of her sinking:

> 2.25pm saw us back alongside ML 143 and continuing our disturbed sleep. Supper over I was standing at the top of the Wardroom companion-way watching mines detonating astern of a US Minesweeper when suddenly she began to heel over. 'SOS' flickered from her signal lantern. A hurried shout, a roar of engines, and we and ML 257 were racing to the doomed vessel. Slowly and gracefully she listed over to port and began to settle stern first. We hove to about twenty yards away and lowered scrambling nets, flinging life-belts over the side. The officers jumped leisurely over the side, having first disposed of their confidential papers in weighted bags, and as the bow rose more steeply two ratings appeared from the focs'le hatch and shouting in dismay, leaped into the water.[19]

Acoustic mines were also laid by the Germans, the technology in this instance was a little too rudimentary to be effective and it was hard for the mine to accurately distinguish ships noises and determine their proximity. The usual Allied countermeasure was a large sound generating boom that was deployed in front of the ship, designed to detonate the mine well ahead of the minesweepers bow. A much more significant threat came from the new German 'oyster' mines laid in considerable numbers after D-Day, this secret weapon had been kept in reserve by the Germans to specifically disrupt shipping in the invasion area; and for the Allies there were no immediate counter measures available. The oyster mine worked on the basis that a ship will displace an amount of water equivalent to the weight of the ship, and that as the vessel moves this displacement of water will create a variation in the vertical pressure on the seabed. The oyster mines took

---

19 Maher, Brendan, *A passage to Sword Beach* (Annapolis, Maryland: Naval Institute Press, 1996), pp.143-144.

advantage of this effect by having two water filled chambers separated by a diaphragm that was sensitive to changes in the vertical pressure. A small hole in the diaphragm allowed water to pass slowly through to take account of slow pressure changes due to of tidal fluctuations, but a rapid change in pressure caused by a ship passing overhead caused the diaphragm to remain inflexible and the differing pressures in the two chambers activated a switch in the mine's detonator.

The new mine was fortunately discovered by the Allies when a German aircraft inaccurately dropped its payload of oyster mines amongst houses behind Sword Beach. Counter measures to the mine were developed over time and these included towing large ship like, unsinkable objects over the mine or using explosives to generate a vertical pressure wave. Neither were particularly successful and it seems the most effective measure adopted was simply to require vessels to slow down in the anchorage, speeds slower than 4 knots did not seem to set the mines off. The problem the German influence mines posed was never truly mastered by the Allies, in the first ten days of the operation eleven vessels were mined, though this began to increase and in the third week of the operation the British losses rose to 12 warships and 7 merchant ships sunk, including the SS *Derrycunihy*. The SS *Derrycunihy* was transporting the 43rd Recce Regiment (formerly the 5th Bn Gloucestershire Regiment) to Normandy and had been anchored offshore on 24 June. The Regiment's padre, Eric Gethyn-Jones, describes what it was like to be in a ship mined by the Germans.

An hour before Reveille (put back to 8.30am to conform with ship's routine) a landing-craft came alongside and orders were given to steam to Gold Beach and unload in greater safety. A few moments later, with the first throbs of the donkey engine, there was a violent explosion and the whole ship heaved and shook.

Scrambling back onto the bunk from which I had fallen, I thrust my head through the porthole. The mental impact was strange, producing an almost dreamlike reaction, when I saw the aft rail disappearing in a foamy turmoil reminiscent, on a large scale, of a pot of boiling water. To verify the facts, I opened the cabin door leading to the aft deck. Confirmation came as the door flew open.

The shock was bewildering because of the suddenness of the unexpected and catastrophic turn of events. An hour before, I had walked out of that door, across the deck, and climbed down the ladder into No.4 hold to return my communion set to the Doctor's 'White' Half-Track. Now there was no deck; only a foaming and turbulent patch of water in which objects, some human, were bobbing about.

The top of the mast stuck out of the water at a jaunty angle, and I saw the jagged sides of the ship which had, clearly, split in two. The stern rails, visible when I had looked out of the porthole moments before, had now disappeared. The stark reality produced a peculiar feeling, for suddenly everything seemed to be going in slow motion as the realisation came that No. 5 hold was under several feet of water, and that No.4 hold was represented by a gaping hole into which, from the doorway, one could not see.

What were my reactions and thoughts?

I remember, first, saying to Doc Ellis 'The ship has split in half!' to which he replied 'Come out quickly, padre' and second, being terribly frightened and wanting to panic. I was, I suppose as near to cracking point as one can be without crossing the fateful line.

I picked up my boots, put them on and laced them up. This foolish action (I ought instead to have followed Doc Ellis out of the cabin at once, in case the forward section keeled over and sank) gave me time, like Nehemiah of old, to pray 'to the God of Heaven' and to steady my nerves, and enabled me to act rationally when I came out on deck.

There was bustle, but no noise or panic, while in the sea I saw masses of floating debris, some bobbing heads, and patches of oil spreading rapidly. The Doc and I ran aft and discovered that part of No.4 hold was still above water and that inside there were three figures floating. A small raft was thrown down and a rope fixed to the rail of the superstructure on which we stood. Then an R.E.M.E staff sergeant and I went down. At the same time, a large M.G.B. drew alongside the wreck.

In the hold, the three wounded men were collected on to the raft. Two had broken arms, while the third man was much more seriously injured. We called up the M.G.B. for a rope. This was tied around one of the men, under his arms, and we shouted, 'Pull!'

Rough on the poor chap?

Well, yes; but it would have been rougher still had the fuel oil, which now covered the water in the hold, been ignited by the ammunition lorry blazing on deck a few yards above our heads, or if the final plunge had taken place. The second arm patient received the same crude treatment.

Padre Gethyn-Jones realized that the third wounded man would not have survived being pulled up by a rope and instead a 'Robertson stretcher' similar to those used to evacuate immobile casualties from mountainsides was found amongst the MGB's equipment:

The stretcher descended, and a few minutes later, trussed up like a fruit tree in transit, the injured man was pulled up gently and taken aboard. The staff sergeant followed and then, from the still floating half of the ship, they lowered a rope ladder down to me. Less than a minute later the fuel oil in the hold was alight, ignited no doubt, by a tracer-round from the ammunition truck, or a burning fragment…

…It was clear now that the water-tight doors between the engine room and holds 1 to 3 were intact, and that part of the ship was in no immediate danger of sinking. All non-essential personnel had been ordered down the ropes into the waiting boats. Only the C.O., the Quartermaster, and one or two others remained, busy removing important papers. I ran back to my cabin to collect some kit; the bulk of it had been in the M.O.s half track in No.4 hold, and was now on the seabed. The cabin was ablaze and all I could rescue was my mackintosh. I then slid down the rope, followed by the Quartermaster and the C.O.[20]

Of the 500 members of 43rd Recce Regiment on board the *Derrycunihy*, 150 were wounded and 180 were missing. It would take many weeks before the regiment could be brought back up to strength and take its position in the line as intended.

Whilst the larger surface vessels in the German Navy had little effect on the build up, smaller coastal and torpedo craft were more of a threat particularly early in the invasion period. As well as a limited number of torpedo boats (which looked like small destroyers) the German navy had several flotillas of E-boats and R-boats in the Normandy area. The E-boat (called Schnellboot or S-boot by the Germans, meaning 'fast craft') was essentially a fast attack craft. It used its very high speed of 43 knots and stealthy low silhouette to sneak up on shipping and then extract quickly. It was designed for coastal waters and good sea conditions and was armed with two torpedoes as well as a mixture of 20mm and 37mm cannon. One characteristic of the E-boat was that its torpedo tube track channels were very distinctive, a cut away effect in the hull made them easily recognizable from the air, a trait which will prove important later in this book. E-boats usually operated in flotillas and given Allied air activity in the channel would depart harbour in darkness and return before first light. Even then Allied use of 10cm and 3cm, Air

---

20 Gethyn-Jones, Eric, *A Territorial Army Chaplain in Peace and War* (East Wittering, West Sussex: Gooday Publishers, 1988), pp.91-94.

to Surface Vessel (ASV) radar made the E-boats detectable and the crews had to rely heavily upon their passive FuMB radar detection devices and their vessel's high speed to avoid attack. The E-boat concentrations in Cherbourg and Le Havre were of most concern to the Allies and the E-boat attack on the 'Tiger' convoy which sank three LSTs was a painful reminder to naval commanders of the German craft's capabilities. Also in the area were a number of German R-boats, the equivalent of a British Motor launch. R-boat is an abbreviation of the German *Raumboot,* meaning sweeping boat and these craft were primarily used for patrolling and minesweeping.

On the first day of the invasion four German torpedo boats from Le Havre (*Mowe, Jaguar, Falke* and *T-28*) attacked the Allied fleet off Sword beach, taking advantage of an Allied smokescreen covering the assault force from the Le Havre coastal batteries. The little flotilla fired eighteen torpedoes which missed the larger capital ships, including the battleships HMS *Warspite* and *Ramillies,* but succeeded in hitting the Norwegian destroyer *Svenner* amidships and sinking her. In the next 72 hours the E-boats successfully attacked several cross-channel convoys, though usually not without loss to themselves. During the night of 7/8 June E-boats attacked a convoy of LCTs and LCIs returning from the beachhead and although the escorting Motor Launch 903 put up a spirited defence, two LCTs were sunk. Lieutenant Robert Loveless, RNR, was the No.1 of LCT Y 921 returning from Omaha beach.

> As the tide rose the shelling was resumed and we were not sorry to join a flotilla of craft heading for home. We were making what appeared to be a normal passage into the night, except that both the skipper and myself were on the bridge, when suddenly there was a hissing sound and then an almighty bang, followed by lashings of water. I was knocked out and on coming to was surprised to find myself lying quite whole and flat on the bridge duck-boards. All was silent, the engines stopped. The skipper too was just recovering consciousness and had opened a confused eye. My immediate thought was to jettison the confidential books. This entailed jumping down the bridge ladder into the wardroom, stumbling over the recumbent third officer, lifting an enormous safe off the bulkhead and tossing it into the sea. I was at a loss afterwards as to why I had done this, especially as there was some money in the safe, but the ritualistic action obviously cleared my mind and I was able to take note of the state of the ship. Most of the crew were dazed but the Chief was doing a good job assessing the structural damage – we had been torpedoed. The engine-room bulkhead was fractured badly and the bows and welldeck appeared to be hanging on by a thread, and just as I appreciated this interesting piece of news someone told me that the helmsman had been hit in the jaw by a dislodged compass ball and was subsiding into a state of concussion. I tried to help him and was distinctly annoyed by a call to abandon ship. As I was working out what to do about a broken jaw and the loose teeth of the now unconscious helmsman, our frail plywood dinghy pulled away from the craft into the silent night, but the small group of men by the starboard Oerlikon were by no means prepared to leave. Within minutes it seemed there came another call –'Belay the last pipe – she still seems to be floating!' – and the dinghy shamefacedly returned.
>
> There was no sign of any other craft – the flotilla had orders not to stop. And so we made for home like dozens of other damaged craft which staggered back with pumps working over-time, except that we were shelled – inaccurately – by a US destroyer. She sent up a star shell too and then wished us luck after learning we required no help.

Figure 3.13 A German E-boat enters a reinforced concrete shelter.
(Bundesarchiv, Bild 101II-MW-2681-34, photo: Vorländer)

The inquiry held on our return established that it was an E-boat which had torpedoed us – we were lucky that it hadn't come in and finished things off with its guns while most of us were knocked out. Our Sister vessel had been sunk without trace over to our starboard.[21]

The responsibility for protecting the Cross Channel convoys and dealing with the enemy forces outside the assault area fell to the Naval Commanders in Chief at Portsmouth and Plymouth and the Vice Admiral at Dover. Thus the waters north east of Cherbourg near Pointe de Barfleur became the scene of fierce fighting between the E-boats working from Cherbourg and the MTBs supported by Frigates and Destroyers from Plymouth working west of the 'Spout' (The Spout was the name given to the system of channels that connected the 'Z buoy, south of the Isle of Wight, to the northern limit of the assault area). In the east, activity was centred around Le Havre, as the invasion developed so too would a MTB close blockade of Le Havre and a defence line of destroyers and MTBs to the east of the Spout. In the British anchorage off Normandy itself the Eastern Task Force Commander in HMS *Scylla* developed a line to the east of the British beaches and ships known as the 'Trout' line, this was held by LCG and LCF anchored one cable apart. Two or three divisions of MTBs under his control were then stationed to the north east of the anchorage and in addition destroyers patrolled north of these.[22] As one can imagine command and control of these various units was no easy matter and sometimes confusion could result. Any vessel that strayed out of the anchorage and beyond the 'Trout' line at night was certainly taking its life in its hands. Lt W S Strang RNVR of 55th MTB Flotilla recalls being tasked to investigate a stationary E-Boat. Just as he was on the point of giving the order to open fire the suspect vessel:

---

21 Lund, Paul and Ludlam, Harry, *I Was In The War Of The Landing Craft* (London: W Foulsham, 1976), pp.170-171.

22 RN Historical Branch, *Battle Summary No.39 Operation Neptune Landings in Normand* (London: Naval Staff, London: 1947), p.108.

Switched on his navigation lights, and I saw he was a 'B' class M.L. The *Scylla* still could not believe it, and Pat Edge kept saying over the R/T 'Sink him sink him,' until I told him that the target was M.L. 243, that we were speaking to him and that I recognized the C.O. (Even afterwards when I met the C.O. ashore he could not believe how near destruction he had been by cheerfully anchoring outside the anchorage). No sooner were we finished with him than off we were sent to investigate some L.C.Ts., which turned out to be our own again anchored out of position. They gave us rather a warmer reception by firing (over us, fortunately) till we closed them and identified ourselves.[23]

As well as checking on unidentified vessels near the anchorage the MTBs would have the major task of intercepting the German E-boats, torpedo boats and other craft based out of Le Havre. There were a variety of MTBs operated by the Royal Navy off Normandy, the Vosper Type II was typical and one such craft was operated by Lieutenant Commander D G Bradford DSC RNR, of the 55th Flotilla on the eastern flank of the invasion. His Vosper was 73 foot in length and had a speed of up to 40 knots, it was equipped with two torpedo tubes, a 6-pounder quick firing gun, a 20mm Oerlikon machine gun and two .303 twin machine guns. On the night of 6 June his flotilla had its first encounter with enemy boats trying to attack the flank of the anchorage. On this occasion he had a unit of four boats:

We had been assigned a patrol on the east flank of the landing about 10 miles due west of Le Havre and just on the edge of a mined area. Tony Law, with the Canadian unit, was lying about 3 miles to the north of us.

About midnight six craft approached us from the east at fairly slow speed – obviously enemy. We got under way and steamed to the north for half a mile to wait on their line of advance, and I warned Tony that things were beginning to happen. They were five R boats and a T.L.C. [An armed trawler] obviously out on a mine laying sortie. The visibility was moderate – a damn dark night, but no mist. I led towards them and formed into quarter line for a gun battle. They must have seen us practically as soon as I fired rockets to illuminate them. We opened fire at about 500 yards' range, closing rapidly, and the return fire was pretty close and hot, though a bit straggly, as if their hearts weren't in it and their Senior Officer couldn't make up his mind what to do. I don't blame him. There they were – caught with six or eight mines in each boat – some five tons of highly temperamental explosive set on deck, where it wouldn't do the least good if it was hit. They scattered as we charged in, altering round to the east and going up to full speed. The T.L.C. altered to the south to make for their occupied coastline and I let him go, wishing to concentrate on the R boats, which were the more important.

'Our guns were hitting them, and we could see the flashes as the Oerlikon shells tore in. One R boat got a direct hit with a 6-pounder shell and started to fall back crippled. They commenced making smoke to try to cover themselves, but we were on their windward quarter and it only served to silhouette them. They were jettisoning their mines as fast as possible – we could see the splashes as they went over the stern.

In the excitement I had forgotten the minefield – but not so my navigator. He suddenly howled up the voice pipe, 'Sir, we are a mile inside.' However, the R boats were there too, so there couldn't be more danger for us than for them. They stopped making smoke when it was obvious that it only helped our shooting – but two of them were smoking involuntarily

23 Scott, Peter, *The Battle of the Narrow Seas – A History Of Light Coastal Forces in the Channel and North Sea 1939-45* (London: Country Life, 1945), p.196.

– showing flame and noticeably slowing down. I thought we had them cold and was quite chirpy – the first scrap with our German counterparts in the assault area, and we were caning them in no mean manner. Suddenly there were a couple of tremendous explosions in the water quite close to my boats – mines. Life was starting to be difficult. I could slow down and lose the R boats, or go on and risk it taking a chance with all my boats. More mines started to go up, some round the R boats, and then suddenly the last R boat in their line exploded in a vast sheet of flame – either we had detonated a mine on board by gunfire or it had hit a submerged mine. That decided it. I altered course hard over to starboard and reduced speed, content with our victory and thinking in terms of 'We'll play again another day.' We picked our way out, slowly and daintily, everyone talking in whispers and walking around on tiptoe. Even so we detonated mine after mine, some quite close, others farther away being apparently countermined by the near ones. We got out shaken up a little, but still whole, having set off twenty-three mines. Our Gods were certainly with us that night![24]

Ultimately the German attack craft menace was neutralized not just by the Allied patrol craft but by a combination of naval, air and land operations. It would be the movement of the American VII Corps up the Cotentin peninsula to the port of Cherbourg itself that would cause the Germans to evacuate their naval forces from there during the period 12-13 June. Allied intelligence picked up that many of the E-boats had moved to Le Havre and this prompted the RAF to launch one of the most technically impressive air raids of the war against this concentration of targets on 14 June. We will examine this raid in more detail later on. Though the E-boat threat was eventually neutralized, there were still many more challenges and hardships for the naval forces to endure. Not all of these perils would be as a result of enemy action.

Sea conditions in the Channel, even in summer, can often be poor and 1944 was no exception. Historians are right to emphasise the effect of the 'Great Storm' which arose on 19 June where winds gusted to Force 7 and waves averaged 8 feet in height. The storm lasted for 72 hours and only began to ease on 22 June. In the British area damage to shipping was severe, six LCTs were driven ashore and broke their backs and one LCT was capsized. LST 386, three coasters and HMS *Colsay* were also damaged by grounding. HMS *Tasajera* was dragged onto a blockship off the Mulberry harbour, HMS *Diadem* collided with a Rhino and HMS *Fury* was driven ashore. One Army estimate was that the gale had delayed the unloading of 20,000 vehicles and 140,000 tons of stores.[25] Some LCTs were however able to take advantage of the shelter the Mulberry harbour's blockships, or those off the beaches, provided but great feats of endurance and seamanship were still required:

The gale caught us while alongside a merchant ship and made loading impossible. At midnight we broke adrift, lay off and anchored. An hour later the sea was still rising and we were dragging with 60 fathoms of cable out so we gave up and anchored in the lee of the 'Gooseberry'. About half an hour after this another LCT parted her kedge wire and arrived alongside with more than a polite bump. We secured her from the for'ard bollards and allowed her to stream downwind of us, veering our own cable to 60 fathoms. A third LCT arrived during the night and was also made welcome. We now had three craft hanging on to one slender cable, which was asking for trouble. To avoid the prospect of all three of us breaking adrift and piling up together on the beach, which was uncomfortably close, it was decided to muster all the old

24 Scott, Peter, *The Battle of the Narrow Seas – A History Of Light Coastal Forces in the Channel and North Sea 1939-45* (London: Country Life, 1945), p.194.

25 RN Historical Branch, *Battle Summary No.39 Operation Neptune Landings in Normandy* (London: Naval Staff, London: 1947), p.141.

iron and odd shackles that could be found and shackle it on to our cable, letting it slide down to the bottom to provide more grip on the seabed . When the gale eventually moderated our grateful friends went their several ways leaving us with the problem of getting all that old iron up from the bottom together with our anchor. It proved to be a slow and painful process and a very much over heated winch motor heaved a sigh of relief when we had done.[26]

Some landing craft commanders took refuge by driving their craft ashore. This was in many ways the most serious aspect of the storm, 800 craft were stranded on the beaches, causing an immediate shortage of ferry craft once the storm abated. As an example of the 14 Rhino ferries in the British area that were operationally fit before the storm only 2 were working afterwards. Energetic salvage work was undertaken by port repair parties brought over from the UK after the storm and 600 craft were refloated at the next spring tide on 8 July. Landing craft commanders were well aware of the risks in beaching in a storm and the damage it might do to their craft, but many felt they had little choice:

I tried to go alongside the 'Gooseberry' but it was too rough to do even this. During the morning as I steamed around as best I could, a landing barge out of control smashed against our side and hooked on. The barge's coxswain had busted his leg and after much struggling he was heaved aboard with the rest of his crew. Conditions became so bad with the barge smashing against us that even the bollards began to pull out against such a terrible strain, and I had to order the barge to be cut adrift. After messing about all day with sea conditions getting even worse, I decided that the only thing to do was to get on to that beach. From about a mile out I could see that the beach was completely littered with all types of LC as far as the eye could see. Luckily I spotted a small gap between two of these craft and promptly headed for it, despite the objections from the principal beachmaster and his party – objections which became all too obvious as I drew closer and, with about a foot to spare on either side, crashed on to the beach. The beachmaster told me to get the hell out of it, and being a little nervy and fed up, I replied that if he wanted my LCT off the beach then he was the best bloke to take it off! A few large gins made us the best of friends…[27]

Some of the larger craft were able to last out the storm out at sea. Sub Lieutenant Dudley Roessler was an officer on an LCT (R) which had been sent to Sword Beach:

When the weather started to turn bad we sought permission either to return to the U.K. or to enter the Mulberry harbour at Arromanches. Both requests were refused and we attempted to anchor, but with 200 fathoms of our anchor wire out astern there was no holding. Recovering the cable was a great hazard. Huge waves crashed over the quarterdeck and several times I was swept off my feet holding on nearly upside down for all I was worth. Two of the crew were dashed against the bulkhead and had somehow to be got inside without further injury to them and without the sea flooding down into our must vulnerable region –aft. Finally we reeled in all the cable and got under way. Then for the next few days and nights as the storm blew we steamed up and down off the Calvados Reef. Cooking was impossible. Messdecks and magazine were awash. The C.O. went down with some bug and we tried to get him to

---

26 Lund, Paul and Ludlam, Harry, *I Was In The War Of The Landing Craft* (London: W Foulsham, 1976), p.184.
27 Lund, Paul and Ludlam, Harry, *I Was In The War Of The Landing Craft* (London: W Foulsham, 1976), pp.183-184.

Figure 3.14 The Mulberry harbour at Arromanches takes a battering during the storm of 19-22 June. (Crown Copyright)

take M&B 693[28] which was all we had. The midshipman and I went watch-and-watch and clung grimly on to our little open box of a bridge. Up and down, up and down, hour after hour, day after night and night after day. Each turn into the gale took nearly a mile to achieve. We worked up to full speed, waited for a procession of lesser waves and flung the wheel over hoping to get round before the wind bashed us back again. To turn into the beach was impossible because we would have run downwind onto the reef.

Finally after the storm had begun to abate and we had at last got our anchor down again I was sitting on the after capstan enjoying the smell of the first hot food for a week and taking a message from a little LCQ (landing craft administration) which had popped out to ask us to report our state. I was just preparing a reply when there was an almighty explosion under my seat and I was flung high in the air, even more impressive walls of water than we had seen all week rising all around me. Then I seemed to hit the deck again just as it was coming up for the second time. When all that was over I got up found that I could still walk although with a dreadful pain in my lower spine and a horrid feeling in my guts. Then I saw that we had got a nasty list and were settling fast. We had activated an acoustic mine.[29]

There was also great risk for those further out at sea. The regimental history of the 91st Anti Tank Regiment (5th Argylls) recalls their journey during the great storm, and the problems they had with their armoured M10 tank destroyers in the holds of their ungainly LSTs:

28 Produced by the firm May and Baker, it was used to treat sore throats, pneumonia and gonorrhoea.
29 Lund, Paul and Ludlam, Harry, *I Was In The War Of The Landing Craft* (London: W Foulsham, 1976), pp.184-185.

When we reached the open sea we quickly discovered that the behaviour of a heavily laden L.S.T. in bad weather is unique; it has a capacity for rolling all ways at once which fortunately is unrivalled by any other kind of sea-going vessel. In the middle of the first afternoon out a message was received which said conditions were so bad that the whole convoy was to turn back except 91st A.-Tk Regt which was operationally required. So with one destroyer as escort L.S.T.s V86, V87 and V88 continued banging their hearts out in the heavy seas. The tremendous and terrifying rolls, which shook the equanimity even of the crew, eventually had their effect. On V86 the lift, which was used to raise on to the upper deck the vehicles driven in through the open bows, collapsed and took with it a 3-ton lorry loaded with 17-pdr ammunition. The whole tangle of lift, lorry, ammunition and steel cables landed on top of the carriers parked below, smashing down the thin metal superstructure built round them as part of their water-proofing. Fortunately no-one was hurt, and later when we reached calm water the lift was miraculously repaired; even the lorry was a runner, though a rather uncertain one.

On V87 the results of the storm were more serious. The tremendous rolling of the ship placed on the chains which secured the M.10s to the deck a strain far in excess of expectations, and in consequence some hooks straightened out like soft wire and two tanks broke loose. The decks of an L.S.T. are of metal, and the sides consist of thin metal sheeting in a double skin, the space in between the skins being fitted as accommodation for the crews of the vehicles loaded on board. The roar of the steel tracks of the tanks across the deck was horrible, and the crash with which they piled up against and eventually smashed the inner skin made the whole ship shudder. The captain – yachtsman brother of Doris Duke – altered course to avoid the beam sea, and a working party went down into the hold. To secure the two wandering tanks was an extremely difficult task, but it was done, and the working party stayed below the whole afternoon checking and strengthening the chains. In this work Lieut. Crosby distinguished himself. When it seemed at last that everything possible had been done and the party was about to leave the hold, three more tanks suddenly and unexpectedly came adrift. Sergt Adams of G Troop was pinned between two of them end on, but it was possible to release him very quickly by driving one forward. He suffered bruises and a cracked pelvis and went back to England. Much worse, Driver Tommy Orr of 146 Battery was caught between two tanks side by side which made releasing him more difficult. When he was got out he was dead… when we anchored off the coast of Normandy that night few of us by then retained even a semblance of interest in the events on land.[30]

During the entire period of Operation NEPTUNE nine hundred and seventeen Allied craft ranging from warships to Rhino ferries were either damaged or destroyed. On many of those occasions significant loss of life would result. Even in the crowded waters of D-Day itself rescue was by no means assured for those who found themselves in the sea. We last met Sub Lieutenant James Leslie, RNVR on LCA 1341 as it was returning from Sword Beach to the LSI *Empire Broadsword*:

The enemy opened up on us as we beat it out to sea followed by other LCAs all making for their mother ships. We had to keep a fair way on our craft to get out of enemy range and were just about a safe distance off when the ramp caved in and LCA 1341 dived head first into the swell. We were washed aft and quickly made our way on to the stern sheets and then into the water before she slipped under.

For some reason I wasn't wearing my usual Mae West but some uninflatable lifebelt which,

30 Flower, Desmond, *History of the Argyll and Sutherland Highlanders: 5th Battalion, 1939-45* (Edinburgh: Thomas Nelson & Sons), pp.96-98.

Figure 3.15 A photo taken at midday on the 6 June showing men of 5th Battalion the Royal Berkshire Regiment assisting 9th Canadian Brigade in getting ashore on Juno beach. (The Wardobe: The Museum of the Berkshire and Wiltshire Regiment)

when I hit the water, started to take me at speed towards the bottom. I looked upwards and saw the sunlight above glimmering through the surface disturbance – and it was going upwards and away from me fast. I swam towards it with all my might and swam and swam until at last I broke surface, where I first of all jettisoned my tin hat; I saw my infant son's photo in the crown of it as I heaved it off. I then discarded the ammunition I had in my battledress pockets, together with my belt and holster, and tried to get my boots off. Who in heaven's name decreed that our bootlaces had to be made fast with reef knots? I could not get those boots off and I tore my oilskin trousers to shreds without effectively getting rid of them either. My lifebelt was worse than useless and I swam around looking for something to give buoyancy. A fellow swimmer kindly let me share a boathook he was clinging to but we both went under, so I thanked him as civilly as the circumstances allowed and wallowed on more under the surface than on top. I was getting a little desperate when I came across a thermos box. The lid was missing and it had a fair amount of water inside; foolishly I tried to scoop this out, only to cause it to take in much more, so I gave that idea up and decided to make the best of what providence had provided. My little box and I went up and down the swells, both of us making heavy weather of it.

How long this went on for I have no idea, but then I saw a small LCT not far away with a burning tank still in its hold. I could see that her crew had no eyes for what might be passing overside, busy as they were with hoses, so when some of the Marines in the water made towards her I called them back and told them to bunch up as previously so as to make the biggest target for a lookout to spot; but two of them, my coxswain and stoker, did not appear to hear me and swam on. Soon afterwards our luck turned and we were seen by the DSOAG's ship (Deputy Senior Officer Assault Group). They put down a scrambling net for us and I wearily propelled my little box to the ship's side, where I let it go and tried to get aboard. I wasn't too successful and was hoisted up by a ginger haired rating who I was later surprised to see was only about half my weight and size. Of the thirteen of us who had taken to the water eleven were saved; sadly the two lost were my coxswain and stoker.[31]

Operation NEPTUNE was an admirable success. The naval forces achieved tactical surprise and delivered the Allied armies ashore. Though the mid-June gale and German actions inflicted delay and damage to Allied shipping the build up was still able to be developed. Perhaps most critically the rate of troops, equipment and logistics pouring into Normandy exceeded the German's own efforts using their land lines of communication. This was a point conceded by the German Admiral Krancke who after noting through German radio intercepts the amounts being unloaded by the Allies in Normandy commented 'The amounts quoted represent many times the reserves of material and men moved up to the front by us, and offer a clear picture of the enemy's superiority and of the advantage of seaborne supplies, given sea and air superiority.'

With the Royal Navy having established them ashore, it would now be up the Army to complete the task of assaulting the beach defences and subsequently defeating the German Army in Normandy. The Army could be grateful that the Royal Navy had landed them at the right place and at the right time, but the obstacles and fortifications that the Germans had constructed had been carefully designed to turn the beaches into a killing ground for the disembarking infantry and armour. It would be the Royal Engineers who would breach these obstacles and help the Army cross the beaches, the first of many supporting tasks that this Corps would perform across the continent of Europe.

---

31 Lund, Paul and Ludlam, Harry, *I Was In The War Of The Landing Craft* (London: W Foulsham, 1976), pp.150-153.

4

'First in Last Out' – Engineers

The Sappers really need no tribute from me; their reward lies in the glory of their achievement. The more science intervenes in warfare, the more will be the need for engineers in field armies; in the late war there were never enough Sappers at any time.

Field Marshal Montgomery, 1945

Engineers are the essential enablers in warfare. Armies by their very nature need to move in order to engage the enemy or to occupy ground and in Normandy the Royal Engineer's primary role was to support this mobility. However the Sappers were not just in the business of creating freedom of manoeuvre, they were equally vital in hindering the enemy's mobility and setting the conditions to live and fight. This chapter will begin with the meticulously planned engineer operation to assist the D-Day assaulting forces in breaching Hitler's Atlantic wall. It will also focus on the engineer operations required to hinder the enemy's movement or ability to concentrate forces, including bridges being blown or prepared for demolition. After covering some of the general tasks engineers are routinely required to deliver, the chapter concludes with the Engineer river crossing operations over the River Seine in late August.

The planners at SHAEF believed the engineers would have to undertake a number of different tasks for the invasion. These included tackling underwater and beach obstacles to allow landing craft to beach, clearing minefields and helping to destroy enemy fortifications. Once these initial tasks were completed the engineers would be required to aid Allied mobility by establishing tracks up the beaches, as well as lateral ones across them, creating or improving new exits from the beach and constructing additional inland routes. As a precaution against German counterattacks the engineers would also need to be prepared to assist in the construction of a number of defences. This exhaustive list of demands was finished off with a number of more specialised tasks including the provision of water supply and airfield construction.[1]

The D-Day assault landing presented one of the most demanding problems ever encountered by engineers. The experience at Dieppe in 1942 had reinforced the importance of having assault engineers readily available to overcome German defensive fortifications and obstacle belts. Without intimate support from engineers during the actual assault it was judged extremely unlikely that the Allies would succeed in getting off the beach. These Allied concerns were understandable when one considers the vast array of defences and obstacles the Germans had placed on, or near, the Normandy beaches. As General Rommel stated, these obstacles had been designed to stop the attackers 'in the water, not only delaying him but destroying all enemy equipment while still afloat'.[2] The Germans also understood that obstacles of any type are only truly effective if covered

---

1   Pakenham-Walsh, Maj Gen R P, *The Second World War 1939-45, Military Engineering (Field)* (War Office, 1952), p.116.

2   Pakenham-Walsh, Maj Gen R P, *The History of the Corps of Royal Engineers* Volume IX (Chatham: W & J Mackay, 1958), p.327.

Figure 4.1 Low-level photograph showing German soldiers building defences on one of the
beaches used by the Allies on 6 June. (Crown Copyright Air Historical Branch)

by direct fire or observed artillery and mortar fire. Consequently the siting of these obstacles was
coordinated with a series of strong points along the beaches as well as defended artillery battery
positions further inland.

Information on the obstacles, known as 'beach intelligence' was obtained from numerous air
photographic reconnaissance flights, special forces' beach reconnaissance and experience from
other theatres. It was found that the German obstacles were designed to have a specific effect. The
first elements were the anti-landing craft obstacles, these prevented the approach of assault landing
craft and most were placed between the high and low water marks. There were many different
types of anti-landing craft obstacles, these included floating rafts of heavy timber about 18 feet by
4 feet, timber ramps and steel or timber stakes usually driven into the beach at an angle pointing
out to sea. 'Hedgehogs'; composed of three steel rails welded together centrally were also present
together with Steel tetrahedra, or tripods of rails. Finally there existed 'Element C', a vertical steel
framework about 7 feet high by 9 ½ feet wide, these were of Belgian origin and had been originally
designed to be connected together to form a continuous anti-tank obstacle.[3]

The majority of the anti-landing craft obstacles would have either anti-tank mines or shells with
press igniters attached to them, both of which would detonate when struck by a landing craft. The
Sapper teams that were tasked to deal with these anti-landing craft obstacles were known as the
'Obstacle Clearance Teams'.

The second category of obstacles laid by the Germans were above the high water mark and
were designed to interfere with the passage of tanks, vehicles and personnel over and off the
beaches. These included wire (both coils of 'Dannert' wire as well as complex 'spider webs' of low

---

3   Ibid., p.328.

wire entanglements two to three feet above the ground), anti-tank ditches, concrete walls, mines and flooded areas, furthermore the roads leading off the beach were blocked by craters, debris or concrete obstacles. If life was not difficult enough for the Allies the pre-existing sand dunes and sea walls might also hamper their exit off the beach. The Sappers that would deal with these obstacles were known as the 'Gap Crossing Teams'.

Mines were a common feature in both sets of obstacles. But there was some good news: the Allies, based on the British experience of coastal defence in 1940, correctly believed that the Germans were unable to surface lay mines below the high water mark. However, mines would still present a significant challenge throughout the Normandy campaign, Alfred Lane was an assault engineer on Sword beach and describes the various types of mines employed by the Germans:

> A 'Teller' Mine, for example, was about the diameter of a large dinner plate, an inch or two thick, containing enough high explosive to blow man and vehicle to pieces. Besides having a detonating fuze for downward pressure, it also had two screw holes into which – all too often – were inserted small pegged booby switches, one which could be felt with sensitive fingers along the outer edge, which would then indicate that the other could be found underneath at the 'four o'clock' position. It had for some time been the usual disarming and safety practice to simply unscrew and separate the fuse from the mine charge, but it had lately been discovered, after many people had been killed in the unscrewing process, that safety depended on turning the fuse a precise number of times, which were certainly not to be exceeded. Removing the fuse here would be the death trap. It may be evident, therefore, that to find this type of mine was one thing, making it safe was another!
>
> The 'S' mine was in every way an anti-personnel mine. It was one that must, I believe, have caused many British casualties in World War Two. It can best be described as a device having two small metal pots – like jam jars – with a smaller one being inside a slightly larger one. The inner jar contained approximately 360 ball bearings. A peculiar antenna on the mine was a detonating system having three switches, i.e. press, trip and release, which meant that it could be activated by walking on it, tripping off a loose wire leading from it and by cutting or releasing a taught wire attached to it. When triggered by any one of these switches the smaller jar containing the steel ball bearings would be propelled or hurled like a jack-in-the box into the air to a height of six to eight feet before exploding and scattering the ball-bearings like bullets.[4]

The 'S' mine was normally disarmed by placing a pin in a hole in the side of the three pronged pressure sensor. This would stop the sensor from being depressed and de-activate the mine. The sensor could then be safely unscrewed from the body of the mine and by removing three plugs from the top of the mine the detonators also removed. Both the 'S' mine and Teller mine were easily detected by the standard MK IV Mine detector of the time, as described by Alfred Lane:

> It was big, heavy and very clumsy to use. It was a rather complicated gadget which involved carrying a box of tricks in the form of a large pack strapped to my back – altogether a bundle of equipment far removed from the metal-detector types that followed in later times. With the earphones, the buzz pitch – the variation of which was the 'reading' by which the detection of metal objects could be made – was also more of a noise than a tune, having too much interference for reliability. Our minesweeping drill was fairly simple and straightforward. I would move forward with the detector, making semi-circular sweeps, the edges of which would be

---

4   Lane, A, *What More Could a Soldier Ask of a War?* (Lewes: The Book Guild, 1990), p.94.

Figure 4.2
Members of the Royal
Canadian Engineers
sweep the verges for
mines near Vaucelles,
20 July. (Lieut. Ken Bell,
Library and Archives
Canada, PA-131385)

well-defined and marked by good stiff white marking tape. In this way cleared and uncleared areas in the minefield would not be confused because of the method of working in 'lanes'.[5]

The Germans were well aware that Allied mine detectors would pick up the metal components of their mines and had therefore developed alternatives:

> The 'Box' mine and 'Schu' mine were wooden cased mines which were deliberate non-metal mines to defy discovery by metal detectors, which formerly had been extensively and successfully used against the more conventional metal mines. Prodding the ground patiently and laboriously was the only way of tackling the problem. There was, however, always the danger of becoming a little careless, particularly after some barren patch by prodding a little too hard. The 'Schu' mine was the smallest of the German mines, having only about four ounces of explosive – sufficient to take some blighter's leg off and cause him blindness as well.[6]

The normal drill in mine clearing would be for the 'detector operator' or 'prodder' to mark the mine's location, he would be followed by one or two sappers who would lift and disarm the mines. The following sappers would also lay the tape to mark the safe lane. Whilst this sounds ordered and controlled in practical terms such a drill would be very hard to achieve under fire.

Though dismounted sappers from Royal Engineer Field Squadrons would overcome many of the obstacles, mines and defensive fortifications, help was also at hand in the form of a number of vehicles specifically developed to support both the obstacle clearance and gap crossing teams. These vehicles were grouped into 79th Armoured Division and became known as the 'funnies'. Each vehicle was designed to overcome one particular type of obstacle and therefore each engineer

---

5   Ibid., p.46.
6   Ibid., p.94.

Figure 4.3 A Sherman flail tank. (Crown Copyright)

team had a mixed and tailored variety to overcome all of the obstacles in its specific sector of beach. Additionally once the vehicle's primary task was accomplished it could continue to assist the assaulting troops either as a normal tank or armoured vehicle. There were three main vehicles that conducted assault engineer tasks on D-Day; Sherman 'Crab' flail tanks, Armoured Vehicle Royal Engineers (AVREs), and armoured bulldozers.

One of the first vehicles to land on D-Day would be the 'Crab' or flail tank. This was a normal Sherman tank with two large arms that jutted forwards; between these arms a rotating drum would rapidly spin chains flailing the ground in front of the tank. This flailing action provided a mechanical method of detonating mines without causing damage to the tank. The use of flails to beat a path through a minefield was quicker than using dismounted sappers and could be done under small arms and shellfire. It had the useful secondary effect of tearing through barbed wire. Whilst in the process of flailing the Sherman's turret and gun would be reversed over its back deck, however once the task was completed the turret could be traversed forward again and the Crab operate as a conventional 'gun' tank. The Crabs were not operated by Royal Engineers but by members of the Royal Armoured Corps (e.g. 22nd Dragoons), however when clearing mines they were performing a classic combat engineer role and on D-Day itself they formed an integral part of the 'gapping team'. Flail tanks did have some drawbacks. Firstly as each mine detonated, damage to the chains would result, this would inevitably mean that after a while the flail was no longer clearing the ground thoroughly. Secondly over undulating ground the fixed arms might raise the drum to too high a level and cause the chains to spin without actually beating the ground. Finally, although quicker than hand clearance methods the Crabs would still have to slow down to between one and one and a half miles per hour when flailing. This slow speed would make them vulnerable to enemy anti-tank fire and it was therefore important to support flail operations with separate tanks to provide over watch and covering fire. In clearing a safe passage through the minefield the flail tanks would usually work in pairs with the rear tank slightly offset from the forward tanks to ensure a lane of sufficient width was cleared. Ian Hammerton, a flail tank troop leader of 22nd Dragoons, describes his experiences as he approached JUNO beach in a landing craft:

'In a moment the LCT grounded on the shore, a sailor in the bows sounded the depth and the ramp went down. The time was 0715: H Hour.

When the first Flail went out, the lightened craft surged forward a few feet. The second Flail followed and again it surged forward but there was a 'crump' and the craft lurched as the ramp struck a mine on a submerged beach obstacle. Now it's my turn.

'Driver, Advance!' I order and as we pass over the ramp, a damaged hinge breaks and we lurch, my tank's rotor jib striking another tetrahedral and exploding a shell attached to it. But we are moving onto the wide sandy beach where Jock Stirling and the second flail are already beating up to the wall. I can see the bridge AVRE moving through the beach obstacles behind them when there is an explosion on the turret and the bridge falls uselessly. The AVRE tries petarding the sea wall for some time but without success.

That means Plan 2, so I move up to the foot of a concrete ramp leading to the top of the wall and blow my Cordtex.[7] Paddy Addis, my gunner clears the barrel and I sight through it just as we did at Orford and we fire high explosive at one corner of a railway-steel gate called 'Element C' which is blocking the top of the ramp. I carry on aiming and firing until Element C is a wreck. We then back off to let another AVRE climb the ramp and push the wreckage away, but it tips over on its side, one track off the ramp. Another AVRE goes up the narrow ramp and pushes the wreckage to one side – and sets off a mine which halts it on top of the wall.

I move up to the foot of the ramp, dismount to attach the tow-rope to the wreckage which we drag backwards to the sea out of the way. The tide is coming in fast now with the onshore wind. I signal to Jock and the second Flail to go up the ramp to start flailing inland. It takes a few minutes as they have to line up carefully on the ramp the foot of which is already under water, but they are up. Just as we are about to follow, Collinge my driver says: 'Sir, the water's coming in up to my knees.' Then the engine dies, we are flooded because of having to clear the turret ring.

'Bail out!' I yell. Almost before the words are out of my mouth Dogger Butler, the co-driver, a tall gangling man has come out through the turret past me…We help each other up and I leave my crew to set up the machine gun on top of the wall while I run to Jock's tanks which have halted about fifty yards down the path. They have struck so many mines that they have stopped to replace some damaged chains.[8]

As Ian Hammerton alludes to in the account above the flail tanks would usually be followed by the Assault Vehicle Royal Engineers (AVRE),[9] this vehicle was based upon a Churchill tank usually a MK III or IV. The most significant modification to the Churchill was the removal of its 6-Pounder gun replacing it with a 'Petard', a spigot mortar which could throw a large 40 pound mortar bomb about 150 yards. This demolition bomb, or 'flying dustbin' as it was sometimes called, was designed to destroy concrete fortifications or walls. To breach a substantial concrete wall a section of three AVRE would engage the target. The leader would fire a single round aimed at the base of the obstacle three feet above ground level. The other two AVRE would then aim

---

7   This was to remove the waterproofing around the turret ring.
8   Hammerton, Ian, *Achtung Minen!* (Lewes: The Book Guild,1991), p.76.
9   Sometimes abbreviated as AVsRE when there were more than one.

Figure 4.4 AVREs on the move. The Petard mortar can be seen
clearly. (Crown Copyright Army Historical Branch)

three feet either side of their leader's initial shot. After that all three AVRE would then fire a foot
above their last shots until a breach was made.

Against bunkers similar tactics were also used, though an actual breach was often not necessary as the concussive effect of the bomb would normally 'neutralise' the defenders. The Petard's
bomb was not fed through a breech inside the turret, as would be the case in a normal tank, but
had to be loaded externally. This was achieved by traversing the turret until the barrel was above
the co-drivers hatch where the 'Demolition NCO' would, having assembled and fuzed the bomb,
open the hatch and push the bomb upwards into the barrel until spring catches gripped it. The
barrel would then be returned to the firing position and the AVRE would engage its target. This
drill meant that the soldier need only expose his hand outside the armoured vehicle for the briefest
of moments. It also created much needed space inside the turret for the Engineer stores, including
fourteen petard bombs as well as shaped explosive charges and Bangalore torpedoes. The Churchill
AVRE was an excellent vehicle to carry the sappers, its heavy armour protected the crew, whilst
convenient side doors allowed them to dismount easily in order to place charges, clear obstacles or
carry out other sapper tasks.

The AVRE was provided with a number of fittings that allowed it to take a range of attachments.
This meant that there were many different AVREs for specific obstacles, though four variants
were most commonly used. This included firstly the 'Fascine AVRE', which had bundles of brushwood or chestnut palings (Chespale) resting in a cradle at the front of the AVRE. Fascine AVREs
were used to cross small anti-tank or other ditches, the commander would drive up to the ditch,
pull a quick release device and the bundle would simply roll into the ditch. Secondly an 'Assault
Bridge' AVRE variant was used to carry a Small Box Girder bridge. The AVRE would approach
the obstacle and a hand winch used from inside the tank would lower the bridge, when the bridge
was two feet off the ground explosive charges would be detonated to sever the cables and allow
the bridge to fall across the obstacle. This bridge could normally span gaps of about 30 feet or so.
Thirdly the 'Bobbin or Track Laying AVRE' was used to lay a carpet of Hessian strengthened by
steel scaffolding tubes across soft patches of sand on the beach. It deployed this track as it travelled

from a large circular drum, which provided a firm, albeit temporary, surface on the beach for heavy vehicles. Finally the AVRE Boase Bangalore would push two long pipes of explosive into obstacles such as sand dunes or barbed wire. The pipes would be detonated to blow a gap in the dune or wire through which vehicles could pass. The AVRE Boase usually carried a carpet of connected logs to then line the gap for following vehicles.

The other type of vehicle often employed by the Royal Engineers was the armoured bulldozer. These would be used to remove debris or obstacles by either pushing or towing whilst under fire. The most common bulldozer employed on D-Day was the D7, this was a standard bull dozer with an armoured shield fitted around the driver and cab. Sherman tanks fitted with dozer blades had been ordered and were used extensively later on in the campaign, but none were ready in time for D-Day.

The Allies intended assaulting at low tide with the DD Sherman tanks landing first, followed by the Infantry and Engineers. Each of the three attacking infantry divisions would require eight exits to be open by H+45 minutes and this tight timeline required the obstacle clearance teams and gapping teams to be landed almost simultaneously. Each team was configured differently to tackle the precise obstacles and defences that would be encountered on their particular sector of the beach. For example some teams included Assault Bridge AVREs if a sea wall was expected and others Boase Bangalore AVREs or log carpets if a sand dune blocked the exit off the beach. Though the AVREs and Flail tanks were all drawn from 79th Armoured Division they would be split up and work in conjunction with dismounted sappers drawn from a variety of engineer field regiments, including those integral to the assaulting infantry divisions. Captain Low, who commanded 2 Troop of 77 Assault Squadron, gives a good account of how these AVREs and flails all worked together on Sword Beach. In his landing craft were two Sherman flails commanded by Sjt Smyth and Cpl Nash, both of 22nd Dragoons, a plough commanded by Major K du B Ferguson, a Boase Bangalore and carpet commanded by himself, a bridge commanded by Sergeant Myhill and a bobbin commanded by Corporal Gregory. His LCT was just about to land near a building known as 'Sad Sack villa':

Figure 4.5 Two AVREs, the one on the left is mounting a 32ft small box girder (SBG) bridge. (Crown Copyright Army Historical Branch)

Two Oerlikon guns on the craft were being used both against the aircraft and the houses on the beach, which contained snipers and machine guns, whose sole purpose in life was to make the bridge of the craft uninhabitable. I scrambled down to my tank, ordering LCpl Parsons and Spr Manuel to cut holding ropes on fascine bundles on the ports side of the craft. We then climbed into the tank as the door was dropped.

Ahead of us was a gun which was apparently concentrating on the troop upon our left. Sjt Smyth ran his flail up to high water mark and began flailing straight for the gun. Cpl Nash followed widening the gap. Maj Ferguson ran his AVRE off the craft and began to attempt to clear obstacles on the beach. I followed out with the Boase carpet, running up to the gun and turning right along the flail path.

Sjt Smyth had flailed a second path up to the sand dunes and this I used to push the Boase Bangalore into a sand dune about six feet high. During this time Sjt Myhill was running up the beach with his bridge. He dropped it on the edge of the gun position but apparently experienced trouble in releasing the bottom end. He leaped out of the turret and dealt with it.

I was experiencing trouble in cutting the rope tackle on the Boase Bangalore, which had been pushed very easily into the dune, as snipers kept up a steady hail of lead whenever I appeared. I ordered Sjt Myhill to carry on through to the second lateral in my place. He could not display his windsock as it had been shot off, and I ordered Cpl Gregory, who had been sitting hull down in the water, forward to use his. By this time grenades were being flung at my tank, so I poked my head out and dealt with the offender, then cutting the Boase Bangalore loose. Drawing back from the dune I saw the Bangalore explode having been hit. It made a good gap in the dunes, but I did not drop the carpet on it as both flails had gone forward. The beach was being shelled, and snipers were very active. Running back along to the bridge we started to mount it, but the right support of the carpet was blown away and the logs dropped on to the bridge. We drew back and stopped. Sapper Young, Corporal Parsons, Sapper Manuel and I got out attached a tow-rope to the last log, and the AVRE pulled the carpet back off the bridge. Some Pioneers were lying behind and at the side of the tank under cover. These I ordered to help straighten out the carpet to form a straight run on to the bridge. We eventually did the job, but for four logs, on our own. We nipped back into the tank and crossed the bridge, and the anti-tank gun. The Infantry who had landed behind us were now pushing forward. As we reached the top of the bridge, I saw Cpl Nash standing behind his flail which had struck a mine, breaking a track.[10]

Each assaulting division was provided with eight gapping teams and each team was required to create one exit and mark it by flying a windsock when successful.

Whilst the gapping operations were in progress the obstacle clearance teams were disembarking. Obstacles from a depth of 10 feet to 4 feet 6 inches were the responsibility of the Landing Craft Obstacle Clearance Units of the Royal Navy, and those from 4 feet 6 inches to 0 feet were a sapper responsibility. The Engineers had expected to encounter the obstacles out of the water when they touched down, but a strong on shore wind and small delays in landing by the Royal Navy meant that many obstacles would be submerged. Each D-Day beach area (e.g. SWORD) was divided into beaches (e.g. PETER, QUEEN, ROGER, OBOE) and sub divided further into sectors (e.g. QUEEN–WHITE or QUEEN-RED). These sectors were each allotted a squadron of Royal Engineers with five supporting AVREs for obstacle clearance. The detailed 'beach intelligence' the Allies had on the layout of the obstacles came into its own at this point. As an example

10 *Royal Engineers Battlefield Tour: Normandy to the Seine*, Prepared under the direction of Chief Engineer British Army of The Rhine, HQ BAOR, 1946, p.78.

on QUEEN WHITE it was correctly assessed that the obstacles were in four rows. These were laid out from the dunes to the sea as two rows of hedgehogs, a row of stakes and a row of ramped stakes.

The plan was for the Engineers to land shortly after H-hour, at this time the tide was expected to be lapping the bottoms of the ramped stakes. The engineers would tackle the obstacles starting with the ramped stakes and working their way up the beach to the two rows of hedgehogs. AVREs would assist the dismounted sappers by towing porpoises (waterproofed steel sledges carrying ammunition and explosives) onto the beach, and then either running the obstacles down or towing them away with pre-prepared slings. The dismounted sappers had also prepared numerous water-proofed charges to blow obstacles in situ.

Lieutenant I C Dickinson was Second in Command, 3 Troop, 77 Assault Squadron and responsible for clearing the obstacles on QUEEN-WHITE Beach:

> Suddenly we saw the first row of obstacles loom out of the smoke. They were ten feet high and consisted of a vertical log capped by a Teller mine, and reinforced on the seaward side by a ramp. The LCT moved in, and we found the obstacles were in 4 feet of water instead of being on dry ground as had been intended. We beached against the side of one of the ramps, the door was dropped, the gapping team went ashore and carried on with their job. Whilst gapping was in progress the obstacle team disembarked.
>
> The conditions we met were very different to what we had expected. Firstly and most important, the sea was rough and up to 4 feet up the ramped stakes, secondly there were Teller mines on every stake and shells on all the hedgehogs. This we took in as we came ashore. Soon we had more trouble. 629 Field Squadron's LCIs landed in a bunch on the left of the LCTs, and suffered heavy casualties from machine guns on disembarking. One of the obstacle clearance AVsRE could not disembark from 4 Tp's LCT, and LCT 110A was an hour late in arriving. As a result, the right hand sector of WHITE beach had two AVsRE and their crews, and the left hand sector one and crew. One of the AVsRE received a direct hit killing two of the crew, and that left two AVsRE with twelve men to do something about clearing the obstacles on WHITE beach.
>
> We began by removing shells from the hedgehogs and stacking them in German weapon slits. We then towed the obstacles away. The main problem, however, was the Teller mines on the stakes. We had been given orders to save these mines for future use, so, as soon as a flail had completed its flogging it was taken into the sea to act as a platform, and we went from stake to stake removing the mines. The waves were breaking over the top of the turret, and so the commander had to keep closed down, while the man on the outside removed the mines. Then we received the unwelcome attention of a machine gunner in one of the beach villas who after some very poor shooting at 75 yards range, succeeded in scoring an outer. By this time the waves were too high, so we had to come ashore just before the flail engine gave out. The mines were removed from the back of the tank, and put in disused German defences. On our sector of the beach we did not put up any navigational beacons for the Navy, as had we done so they would have assumed that the sector of the beach bounded by these was clear which was not the case. We then kept the roads off the beach open, and kept the traffic moving in whatever way we could.
>
> When the tide began to go down, all the obstacle clearance teams began to clear the beach, and by nightfall had accomplished their task. Meanwhile, the gapping AVsRE made their way to their pre-arranged RVs and proceeded to sort themselves out for their next tasks.[11]

---

11 Ibid., p.82.

Major Giddings commanded 629 Field Squadron. His sappers all wore assault jackets instead of web equipment for their obstacle clearance duties. In these vests they carried personal kit and rations; a demolition pack containing six 8lb charges with initiators and fixing wires. An axe or a shovel, wirecutters, pliers and a cordage sling were also taken. However on landing Major Giddings realised his team's major difficulty would be the tide and onshore wind.

> Here beside us were the obstacles we were to clear away, but not in the circumstances we expected; for to our surprise and momentary dismay, they were standing in about seven feet of water, instead of being, at the worst, in shallow water, so that it seemed that our carefully worked out clearance drills would be useless. We passed through the first row, turned and moved along between the rows, studying the eight-inch diameter stakes each with a Teller mine or impact fused shell fixed to its head. I well remember the effort of concentration required to get the craft near enough to make an examination, but not to make a bump.
>
> I decided the removal of the mines and shells was an urgent matter. The stakes themselves could wait. So I ordered assault jackets and demolition packs to be taken off, Mae Wests to be kept on, and men to get to the stakes and remove the mines. The attempt was partially successful, but the sea was cold and running too strongly for us, and men quickly became exhausted in the water or were swept away.
>
> We nosed our way through the obstacles and felt our craft ground on the beach, on the Continent at last. It must have been about eight o'clock. Ramp down – door open – and we plunged into water up to our waists, wading ashore with waves breaking over our shoulders and feeling cold from our plunge. We took our demolition packs with us, but left the assault jackets in the LCA. We mistakenly hoped to retrieve them later, but that LCA never returned, and we bitterly regretted the loss of the essentials we had so carefully packed.

Major Giddings set his two parties to work in dismantling the timber ramps in two to three feet of water.

> I felt a peculiar blow on my upper arm and thought I must have been hit, but I could see or feel little, so there seemed no need to do anything about it.
>
> We were only able at this time to clear some small areas towards the top of the beach, but it heartened us to see the craft nevertheless still coming in. When at high tide we could do no more, we turned to laying the beach lateral roadway above high water mark. Dumps of Sommerfeld[12] and Chespale had sprung up as if by magic. Tools were short, but anything was made to serve.[13]

As the day progressed and the tide receded Major Giddings' men were able to resume their obstacle clearance duties, though enemy opposition still hampered their efforts:

> Mortaring on the beach was still heavy. I met our second in command; it was a tonic to see him ashore, clean, dry and cheerful. I myself feeling wet, dirty, hungry and a little weary. Half an hour later I heard he had been killed by a mortar bomb.
>
> It was now well in the day and the tide was falling. We got hold of a bulldozer and an AVRE and really set to on obstacle clearance. First the mines and shells were removed and stacked to a flank. The pile grew to a monstrous size, and, because of one delay or another, had

---

12 Sommefeld is a type of metal trackway.

13 *Royal Engineers Battlefield Tour: Normandy to the Seine*, prepared under the direction of Chief Engineer British Army of the Rhine, HQ BAOR, 1946, p.84.

not been demolished before the tide rose again. I remember my dread lest some unsuspecting craft should be shattered by an outsize explosion if the pile went up, but no such thing happened to my knowledge. The bulldozer and AVRE then neatly ran over the timber obstacles, breaking and rooting them up, while my party cleared up behind. Concrete tetrahedral obstacles were dealt with in the same way, and to our joy we were able to put our demolition drill into effect on a row of hedgehogs. Everything went satisfactorily and spirits rose higher and higher as eventually the whole beach was cleared.

In the evening I reported to an Aid Post to get my arm treated, and was detained for evacuation.[14]

Who actually reached the beach first; DD tanks or gapping teams and who actually made the gaps is still uncertain, events on D-Day were confused to say the least, nonetheless exits and gaps were made successfully on most British and Canadian beaches. As an example on QUEEN-WHITE Beach, there were four exits open within one hour and on QUEEN-RED Beach three exits were open after one hour forty-five minutes and the main lateral road inland was cleared shortly after. All elements suffered heavy casualties in the process, the 22nd Dragoons reportedly lost half their flail tanks during the assault. Though the obstacles had been cleared and gaps created the strongpoints that covered these obstacles still needed to be dealt with. The nucleus of these strong points was often based on one or more guns, ranging in calibre from 155mm to 37mm and protected in concrete emplacements or pillboxes. These were supplemented by mortars and machine guns and inevitably surrounded by wire and minefields. Diagram 4.2 shows how the machine guns were typically sited for all-round defence, whereas the larger guns (47mm in this case) were placed to give a mutually supporting cross fire over the beach. There were living quarters, magazines and first aid quarters too, all under reinforced cover. The emplacements typically had walls 3 feet 6 inches thick and a roof 5 foot thick reinforced with steel 'I' beams. Concrete shelters and casemates usually had steel doors; the entrances were normally tucked around internal corners and typically covered by a loophole. The machine gun posts were often in 'Tobruk' emplacements; which consisted of a metal ring round the top on which a crosspiece carrying a central pivot for the machine gun revolved, usually twin Spandaus.

Some of these forward fortifications had been put out of action by the initial armoured assault of DD tanks, AVREs and flails, others would however require an infantry assault backed up by intimate support from their integral assault engineers.

These engineers were allotted to each assaulting infantry company and divided into mine clearance and assault demolition teams. The infantry/sapper method of dealing with a strongpoint and its protective wire and mines would be as diagram 4.1 illustrates.

Infantry would blow a gap in the wire at A and B with Bangalore torpedoes. The mine clearance teams under covering fire from the infantry would then send detector teams to clear and mark a one yard wide lane to point C. Infantry would then blow gaps in the wire at C. The infantry and assault demolition teams would then assault through the wire, the five man assault demolition team assisting in the destruction of the pillbox either by the use of its flamethrower or by placing a 'Beehive' shaped charge on either the roof of the bunker or its side. Beehives could come in a number of sizes from 15 to 75lb; they could penetrate up to 2 metres of concrete, the effect of which would be lethal to the bunkers occupants. The most common type of 'Beehive' shaped charge was a 40lb version, known as the 'General Wade', this was carried in most AVREs.

---

14 Ibid., p.84.

Diagram 4.1
Assault engineer
tactics.

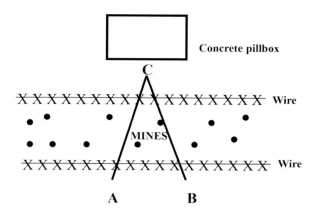

MINES

A   B

Concrete pillbox

Wire

Wire

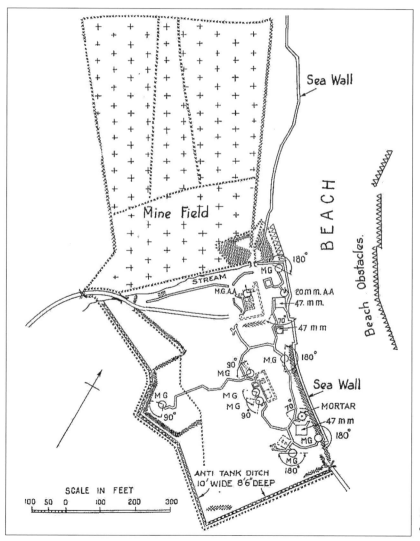

Diagram 4.2
Typical German
infantry strongpoint
on Normandy coast.

Major R M S Maude describes the use of mine clearance teams during the assault on the HILLMAN fortified position sited behind SWORD Beach:

> The second position (HILLMAN) was some 500 yards further south and proved much more formidable. It was manned by a regimental headquarters and about one platoon of infantry with two infantry guns and machine guns. The whole position was approximately circular and about 500 yards in diameter on high ground commanding the whole area up to the beach. It was surrounded by a minefield 15 yards deep and contained a number of concrete machine gun positions and deep shelters all connected by deep trenches.
>
> The position was approached from the north, where the grass was sufficiently long to allow covered approach to the outer minefield area. It was decided to attack from this point, and a mine clearance team was detailed to breach the minefield there. Lt A Heal RE led a party of four sappers. Working in two parties each of two men with a mine detector, tracing tape and wire cutters, these parties working on their stomachs in the long grass, and covered by fire from the infantry, cleared and marked two paths through the minefield. The inner wire was breached by Bangalore torpedoes placed by the infantry and infantry assaulted through these gaps with A Company [1st Suffolks]. A Company (Major G Riley) captured the first concrete post but then found themselves under such intense fire that they were unable to maintain the position, and after the company commander had been killed they were forced to withdraw. It was then decided that the position could not be captured without the assistance of armour. Lt Heal was then ordered to widen the gap through the minefield to allow tanks to enter the position. This was done in about one hour, although the gap was now under small arms fire, and a gap eight yards wide was cleared by hand. Two sappers were wounded in this operation. The position was now assaulted again by 1 Suffolk supported by two troops of Shermans and was captured after heavy fighting.[15]

On occasions the Petard on an AVRE could be employed in support of assaulting troops. Captain A Low recounts using three AVREs in support of 41 Commando RM's attack on a German strongpoint at Lion-sur-Mer:

> Capt Mclennen took the first section of 41 RM Cdo up the road, and I in my AVRE took the second section 20 yards in the rear. Lt Tennent followed up in the rear with the third section. Heavy fire from riflemen on either side of the street was quietened down by Besa fire.[16] Capt McLennen had a Petard bomb loaded and it was ignited by bullets. He stopped, and a gun which was not known to be there opened up, the first shell striking the drivers visor and severely wounding the driver. A second shell penetrated the turret, killing Cpl Shea the demolition NCO.
>
> At this juncture, men began to come out of the tank which was filled with smoke, the smoke mortar bin having been hit. Spr Norris was seen covered in blood staggering back down the road. I covered him while he came down as far as the tank where another man attended him. Commandos then dashed for cover taking wounded with them. A smoke screen from Capt McLennen's AVRE now covered the gun position. Capt McLennen was seen to jump out of his tank and was hit possibly by hand grenades which were being thrown at the time.
>
> I moved up using the AVRE in front as cover from the gun. Covered by me, Lt Tennent came up on the right. Heavy fire was coming from a house on the left, which was believed to

---

contain a mortar position. I fired one round of Petard at it. Fire ceased. Lt Tennent came up level, but his loaded Petard became ignited and the gun opened up again hitting him in the turret and killing the wireless operator Spr Treadrea. Lt Tennent reversed down the road, but was hit again and had to abandon the AVRE with the Petard bomb still burning.

I tried to advance to use the Petard as a mortar, but the co-drivers plate was hit wounding the demolition NCO Cpl Parsons. The tank was reversed, but another shell hit the driver's visor block, wounding the driver and upsetting the controls. More Besa was fired at the gun but it was too well dug-in and I decided to abandon tank. As the crew was beginning to bail out, the turret gun mantlet was hit and the gunner killed. The crew bailed out and took cover with some commandos behind a wall.

It would take a further two days before the strongpoint at Lion-sur-Mer was captured. Some enemy strongpoints had been deliberately bypassed by the British as they tried to advance quickly inland. The radar station at Douvres la Deliverande, a D-Day objective, was a particularly tough strongpoint and would only fall on 17 June when assaulted by 41 Commando RM with significant engineer support. The position consisted of two strong points deeply dug-in with reinforced concrete protection; surrounded by a belt of mines and wire 40 yards deep. The defences included five 50mm anti-tank guns, numerous 20mm, light automatic cannon and 'Tobruk' shelters. LCpl H B Sorensen was an AVRE driver with 26 Assault Squadron and recalls attacking through one of the three lanes to penetrate the defences:

At about 1700hrs [17 June] we moved into the attack. We were to make a direct attack across the minefield, and to clear lanes through this belt which was about forty yards deep, flail tanks or Crabs of B Sqn 22 DGNs were employed. Each Crab was followed by three AVsRE, my own being second in line.

We had penetrated about one third of the minefield before anything happened. But then came under heavy anti-tank fire. The fact that I was wearing headphones, together with the noise of the engines, prevented me hearing the noise of the gunfire. But every now and then I could see a column of dust and smoke go up as a shell landed, and the flashes from the 75mm guns of the Crabs as they replied. As we moved through the minefield, I removed my gloves to light a cigarette. Smoking inside tanks is strictly against orders and I was to suffer for this later.

When we got through the belt of mines, the Crabs pulled to one side and we opened up at short range with both Besas and the petard at any target we could find. I remember seeing two direct hits on concrete shelters by my gunner, which completely demolished them.

The AVRE in front of me succeeded in getting its offside track in a deep trench and was stuck there immovable. My commander gave me the order to overtake on the left. As I did so there was a terrific concussion and my vehicle gave a lurch. My instrument panel lights went out as well as all the interior lights. My first impression was that we had hit a mine, and I tried the steering to see if the tracks were intact. As I did so I saw my co-driver lying with a terrible wound in his head. He was unmistakeably dead, and I then realised we had been hit by a shell. The next moment the whole of the driving compartment caught fire. I was almost suffocated by flame, but managed to open the hatch over my head enough to scramble through. As I was climbing out the ammunition in the hull Besa was exploding and a piece of shrapnel hit me in the right leg. I jumped clear and ran for a bomb crater about fifteen yards away. As I jumped into it I was joined by my wireless operator and my gunner. Hardly had we dropped into it than my tank blew up. The force of the explosion may be gathered from the fact that the turret, which weighs about ten tons was later found fifty yards away.

When we had recovered from the first effects of shock, we found we were all severely burned about the hands and face, the burns on my hands being due to the fact that I had removed my gloves to light that cigarette! I decided to try and get to the ditched tank to get the first aid kit which is carried outside an AVRE in the rear. Imagine my feelings when, after having crawled about twenty yards, I found the container for the first aid kit full of nuts and bolts. On my way back I saw the other tank crews place their 70lb charges on top of the underground emplacement and lie 'doggo' until they were blown. I joined the crew of the ditched AVRE and we set out to see if we could 'winkle' out any enemy that might be above ground. We were joined by men of the Royal Marine Commando, who had come in to mop up. The white flag appeared and the job was done.[17]

As the campaign developed another fearsome vehicle from 79th Armoured Division was brought into action to defeat dug-in enemy and pillboxes. Known as the Crocodile it was a standard Churchill tank converted into a flame-throwing tank. The tank towed a lightly armoured trailer in which the fuel was stored. When in operation the fuel ran through a pipe entering the tank through the bottom of the hull and then to a projector located in front of the hull machine gunner. To operate the flamethrower the gunner would turn on a fine spray of petrol and then ignite it. Once ignited the flame fuel itself could be turned on and the target properly engaged. The flame could be used in either a long squirt or fired higher in short blobs to fall in trenches or behind low cover. Unignited fuel could also be sprayed on a target and then set on fire when required. Having expended its flame the trailer could be ditched and the Crocodile operate as a normal gun tank. The crew were members of the Royal Tank Regiment but were part of the 79th Armoured Division and often used in conjunction with assault engineers. Crocodile commander Andrew Wilson recalled supporting infantry during operation EPSOM:

Suddenly the hum of the headphones cut out. It was the Sqn Comd, Maj Barber calling us forward. We were going in to flame. At the start of the first rise Maj Barber was waiting with the Infantry CO. He made an up and down movement with his clenched fist, which was the sign for opening the nitrogen bottles on the trailers.

'Got where we are?' said Barber pointing to the place on his map. His finger moved to an orchard four hundred yards away stayed there for a moment, then moved to a field beyond it.

'There are some Spandaus there. Flame them out. The Infantry will follow you. A troop of tanks is waiting to cut off the enemy at the back.' I wanted to ask 'How do you spot Spandaus?' but it sounded too silly. With the other troop leaders, I ran back to the tanks. The crew were closing the trailer doors.

'Mount' I shouted and they climbed in and slammed down the hatches.

'Driver advance, Gunner, load HE.' The troops moved forward in line abreast; my tank was on the left. As we came through a hedge mortaring started everywhere and infantry were crouching in half dug foxholes, trying to protect their bodies from the burst of the bombs. We went through a couple of fields. Any moment now we should see the orchard. I reached down and put on the switch that let up fuel into the flame gun. Suddenly it came into view: a bank of earth, another hedge and beyond it the orchard. 'There you are. Dead ahead driver' the driver slammed into second gear. The tank reared up for a moment, so you couldn't see anything but sky; then it nosed over the bank and through the periscope I was looking down a long empty avenue of trees. Somewhere in this avenue, someone was waiting to kill me. 'If only I knew what to look for?'

---

17 Ibid., p.120.

Figure 4.6 A Churchill Crocodile flame-throwing tank.
(Crown Copyright Army Historical Branch)

My sergeant and corporal moved their tanks alongside mine. I ordered 'Co-ax, fire' but there was no target to indicate. The gun roared filling the turret with bitter fumes which made my eyes smart. Through the periscope, I saw the other troops start to flame, the yellow fire seeping through the trees. 'Better get my own flame going. Flame gun fire!'

'I heard the hiss, the slapping of the fuel striking the target. The fuel shot out, spraying the trees paving the ground with a burning carpet. The tank ran through it.

'Slap it on, flame gunner, all you've got!' The flame leapt out with an unbroken roar. The driver was slowing it up uncertain where to go.'

Suddenly the leader of the other troop called across the wireless:

'Hello Item Two, don't go into this lot. Let them have it from where you are.' I saw nothing but blazing undergrowth. Surely no-one would have dared to stay there. But I kept the troop on the edge of the field, pouring in the flame, till the fire rose in one fierce red wall.

Then the gun gave a splutter like an empty soda-water siphon. The other troop had finished, so I turned my tanks and followed. Beneath the trees with smouldering leaves, the British infantry were coming in with fixed bayonets.[18]

The majority of Sapper tasks were focused on supporting British mobility, but it is also important to mention the Royal Engineers efforts in countering the German ability to manoeuvre across the Normandy Battlefield. These counter-mobility tasks were generally adopted in the initial stages of the Allied assault when the bridgehead was far from secure. The measures taken were inevitably modest in their approach, as the Allies wished to resume the offensive as soon as possible and did not want their own obstacles to subsequently handicap them.

---

18 Wilson, Andrew, *Flamethrower* (London: Corgi Books, 1973), pp.56-58.

On D-Day itself the greatest counter-mobility tasks were connected to the flank protection mission of 6th Airborne Division. Part of the plan would involve the blowing of several bridges over the River Dives, these demolitions were known as 'preliminary demolitions' i.e. those that are detonated immediately in order to form an obstacle. There were a number of service explosives available for these demolitions. These included Ammonal (or the similar Ammotal or Baratol explosives) whose slower rate of detonation created a 'pushing' effect and was used for producing craters and destroying the abutments of bridges. Gun-cotton was also used and had a much higher rate of detonation producing a 'shattering' effect, it typically came in slabs and was used to cut steel girders. Commercial explosives such as gelignite were available but not widely used as, unlike Ammonal and Gun-cotton, rifle bullets, shell splinters and other battlefield hazards could inadvertently detonate them.

The other explosive charges that could be used were the previously mentioned 40lb General Wade or other 'Beehive' shaped charges. These used a hollowed out cone at the end of a cylinder to canalize the force of the explosion and so produce a punching or penetrating effect. They would be supplemented by Camouflet charges to create craters in the abutments of a bridge increasing the size of the gap and making any subsequent crossing effort more difficult. The task of demolishing bridges over the River Dives was given to 3rd Parachute Squadron who would drop at 0050 hrs with 8th Parachute Battalion. The first troop was to destroy the bridge east of Troarn with Wade charges; the second troop was to destroy two bridges at Bures by cutting the spans and destroying one or two abutments. The Third Troop would drop with 1 Canadian Parachute Battalion and destroy a bridge at Robehomme, a culvert near Le Hoin and a bridge at Varaville.

Major J C A Roseveare who was OC 3rd Parachute Squadron describes his part in the night's operations:

> On landing I suspected we were in the wrong position as I could see no high ground to the east, and Stirling aircraft were running from all directions dropping Paratroops. Several gliders landed close by – they were not RE ones. My stick commander, Lieut Lack, and the SSM set about collecting the stick at the containers, which were well concentrated and illuminated by the 'Thomas'[19] devices which worked well.
>
> Paratroops dropping around appeared to belong to every Para Bn in the Div. I contacted Capt Tait of the Independent Parachute Company,[20] who said we had been dropped in the wrong place and this was DZ K. I found this hard to believe. We gathered as many 8 Para Bn and 3 Para Sqn men as possible and kept them moving down to a track junction… There I contacted Capt Juckes, and we reorganized. Considerable signs of battle were coming from the SW, and it was obvious that the later numbers in the sticks must have struck trouble in the area Ranville-Le Marquet. Our position was confirmed by a signpost at the crossroads…
>
> On taking stock, we appeared to have a recce boat, a MK II Camouflet set, 4/500lb of plastic explosive and 45 General Wade charges besides an adequate number of accessories, beehives etc. and the HQ link 68 set and one 18 set. We had only six trolleys, however, sufficient anyway to carry out some form of demolition on our three bridges. The following officers were present – OC, Capt Juckes, Lieuts Shave, Forster, Breese, Wade and Lack. No 8

---

19 A small light on the container which activated on hitting the ground and helped the paratroops find the container. Conversely, other paratroops commented that recovery of containers was, at the height of June, very difficult.

20 Pathfinders parachuted ahead of the main force to mark the drop zone.

Para Bn officers were apparent but there were some 20/30 other ranks chiefly from the Mortar and MMG Pls. About 40 sappers and NCOs were present.

I then endeavoured to organize the party for the approach march. In the absence of any 8 Para Bn officers it proved rather difficult to persuade the 8 Bn other ranks to take the lead even under sapper officers, so eventually the point section consisted of Capt Juckes, myself and a few stout hearted sappers who were not hauling the trolleys. As we moved off to the accompaniment of Mortar and MMG fire, a jeep and trailer with medical stores joined the party. The time was about 0230 hours. The route followed was Herouvillete-Escoville-road junction 140703. The march which was fortunately unopposed was a feat of endurance by the sappers hauling the heavily laden trolleys. Many were limping with DZ injuries, but they all pulled their weight on the trying gradient up to the road junction.

On reaching the road junction at about 0400 hours, two 8 Para Bn officers materialised. One was the Mortar Officer. I ordered them to take up a defensive position with all the 8 Para Bn personnel and hold the area of the road junction. We then redistributed the stores amongst the transport available. All the medical stores were unloaded in the timber yard, and all General Wade charges were loaded on the jeep and trailer. All plastic explosives and the Camouflet set were loaded on the trolleys.

Major Roseveare then ordered Captain Juckes to proceed with the main body of the sappers to attack the bridges around Bures whilst he led an eight-man team with a jeep and trailer to attack the Troarn bridge:

We set off down the road at a moderate pace with everyone ready with a Bren or one of our several stens for any trouble. Just before the level crossing, we ran slap into a barbed wire knife rest road-block. One Boche fired a shot and then went off. It took twenty minutes hard work with wire cutters before the jeep was freed. We then proceeded on, leaving behind, it transpired later, Spr Moon; two scouts were sent ahead to the cross road 160676. As they arrived a Boche soldier cycled across complete with rifle. On being dragged from his bicycle he protested volubly, and we made the mistake of silencing him with a Sten instead of a knife.

The town was now getting roused, so we lost no time and everyone jumped aboard while I tried to make the best speed possible. As the total load was about 3,000lbs we only made about 35mph. At the corner 163678 the fun started, as there seemed to be a Boche in every doorway shooting like mad. However, the boys got to work with their stens and Spr Peachey did good work as rear gunner with the Bren. What saved the day was the steep hill down the main street. As the speed rose rapidly we careered from side to side of the road, as the heavy trailer was swinging violently, and were chased out of town by an MG 34 which fired tracer just over our heads.

On arrival at the bridge, which was not held, we found Spr Peachey and his Bren were missing. 39 General Wade charges were immediately placed across the centre span, a cordtex lead was connected up, and the charges fired. The demolition was completely successful – the whole centre span being completely demolished giving a gap of 15 to 20 feet. The time taken was about five minutes.

I decided Troarn would not be a healthy spot to return to, so we drove the jeep up a track due north towards Bures, as far as possible, and then ditched it. Lt Breese made a recce of Bures which led him to believe it was occupied. It was now about 0500hrs. The party therefore swam several streams south of Bures and took to the woods. A good deal of MG42 fire from the direction of the road junction 140703 made me alter my plan, and I decided to make for Le Mesnil which was reached at 1300 hours.[21]

Captain Juckes' party also successfully destroyed the two bridges at Bures. The other type of preliminary demolition that could be made was that of cratering a road, a very easy process using a 'Camouflet set'. Cratering would require the sapper party to bang a tube into the ground and insert some gun cotton primers and electrical detonators on the end of a line which would be pulled to initiate the charge. This modest explosion would leave a small chamber and tube. Powdered Amatol would then be poured in until the chamber was half full; another set of primers and detonators would be inserted and the rest of the chamber filled with more Amatol and the tube removed. The wires would then be trailed back to a dynamo which would be used to initiate the charge.[22] Detonating the Camouflet would leave a large crater in the road which would usually be supplemented by laying anti-tank and anti-personnel mines. Like all obstacles the crater would only be effective if it was covered by direct fire or observed indirect fire and could not be easily bypassed.

The alternative to a preliminary demolition was a 'reserved demolition', this was used to prepare a bridge for demolition (or crater a road) but not actually initiate it until the appropriate moment. It was less common than a preliminary demolition because the Engineers could not move on to another task and infantry would also be required to guard the potential obstacle and firing party. Nonetheless reserved demolitions had obvious utility if friendly forces were withdrawing across the obstacle. Immediately after D-Day a number of reserved demolitions were placed upon the bridges over the River Orne and the Caen canal in case a German offensive pushed the Allies back and these waterways needed to be turned into an obstacle. Alfred Lane describes the process needed to prepare these bridges and ensure that they were constantly ready to be demolished if required:

> Here then our ditch, being the point of initiation for the possible demolition of the bridge(s), contained the nerve endings and beginnings for the 'big twitch' in any awkward development. Fuse, cable, exploder/test box, etc., were all connected and within easy reach of both my companion and I as we waited tense and alert for the worst to happen…It was late night as we peered into the misty dark direction of the forward bridge and towards the enemy somewhere not far beyond. Jerry, we knew, was no more than a mile or two away, which allowed little time or warning in the event of a sudden push or infiltration through the bridgehead shell, which was certainly not impenetrable by a particularly desperate foe. We kept our eyes skinned and our limbs ready for the dreaded emergency of setting the fuse alight and activating the detonating handle of the exploder.
>
> It should be explained that the demolition layout and task before us followed our usual sapper practise of having two alternate ways of detonating the charges in case of the failure of any one of the methods through battlefield incident (shelling etc.), fault or accident. The two methods involved two different circuits (or ring mains), one of them being standard electric wire cable connected to the series of electric detonators (dets electric No. 33) which – after careful testing and calculation of the connected circuit's Ohms resistance – would normally be activated by the electric current generated manually via the handle of the exploder box. With this method a small battery –powered test box would be used to pass and receive a low

21   *Royal Engineers Battlefield Tour: Normandy to the Seine*, prepared under the direction of Chief Engineer British Army of the Rhine, HQ BAOR, 1946, p.73.

22   Barber, Neil (ed), *Fighting With The Commandos* (Barnsley, Pen & Sword, 2008), p.58.

Figure 4.7 A Sherman crosses the Canadian-built 'Winston Bridge', a Class 40 Bailey Bridge over the River Orne at Caen. (Crown Copyright)

inactivating current so that a positive meter reading of a flickering needle ensured that the many connections were properly made and that the circuit was complete and ready for the generated activating current.

The second method was the use of a circuit (or ring main) of 'American Cortex' which might best be described as explosive cord (or cable) which had the explosive (or detonating speed) of 2,000 feet per second. This was connected to the main demolition charges by a series of knots and bindings etc... being itself initiated by safety fuse (burning rate at two feet per minute) inserted into an ordinary detonator (detonator No.27) which together with a primer would explode the cortex.[23]

As the Allied build up continued and the critical moment passed, the requirement to blow the bridges over the River Orne and Caen Canal no longer existed and the demolitions were removed.

With the bridgehead secure there were many other general tasks that needed to be conducted by the sappers. Constructing the Mulberry harbour and the RAF Advanced Landing Grounds are covered elsewhere in the book but it is worth considering some of the less dramatic but equally vital aspects of sapper work that allowed the bridgehead and Army to function. Without clean water for instance the ability of any soldier to operate would be doubtful and it was a sapper responsibility to provide potable water for the Army. The 43rd Wessex Division newsletter of 30 July recorded the Royal Engineers work in this regard:

'We were sent forward to establish a water point within three quarters of a mile of Jerry' continued Corporal Donoghue 'We got here at five o clock in the evening and said we'd have the plant working by seven. It might have been a little sticky at times but we made it in spite of Oscar [nickname for German Mortars]. He punctured three of our water tanks. We patched them up again. But at one time there was water everywhere except in the tanks.

23 Lane, A, *What More Could a Soldier Ask of a War?* (Lewes: The Book Guild, 1990), p.83.

'We're open from four in the morning until eleven thirty at night; and get a lot of casual night callers too, our retail trade is tremendous! The troops come along with their trucks loaded up with Jerrycans to be filled. But the Infantry who come straight out of battle to fill their water bottles are the ones. They're really grateful it's a delight to see their faces,' said the corporal.

'We test the water for poisons while the Royal Engineers erect the plant.' Explained Corporal Bailey of the RAMC. 'Jerry hasn't attempted to poison the water yet as far as I know. We chlorinate all the water and the troops are only allowed to draw drinking water at the official points. The position is not too bad over here. I think the supply job we've just done must be a record. We kept the whole of our Division supplied and others too. We believe in being open to all, you see the notice 'Water Point – Quite Free – All Invited'.

'There's old faithful said Cpl Donoghue pointing to the purifying plant alongside. 'Oscar knocked her about a bit – she's like a sponge. We plugged the shrapnel holes with bits of rag and wood, she's taken more bashings than I'd like to take and she's still grinning.'

Another sapper task that literally saved lives was the disposal of booby traps. Normandy was littered with booby traps, it was a skill that the Germans had perfected and cost the lives of many Allied soldiers. Alfred Lane describes being approached by an infantry RSM for assistance:

He explained that he had been looking around for some REs to remove a nearby danger to members of his own unit. We were led to a deserted or abandoned German armoured truck which was tucked away in a corner of a small field. The RSM thought that it was booby-trapped, and was indeed found to be so when I examined it. The vehicle appeared to be designed or adapted as a transporter for Teller mine. Inside the vehicle were racks upon which were a number of mines neatly stacked and secure. It was no doubt a sort of German 'quickie' system of distributing and laying mines rapidly to close the gaps caused by the increasing shortage of manpower in German lines of defence. It was, or should be, all too obvious that such an abandoned vehicle loaded with mines – which were themselves designed to hold booby-trap switches – would be a trap.

After careful examination I discovered two booby-traps, one a 'pull switch' which would be activated by opening the back door of the vehicle. The other was a 'press switch' booby-trap and had been placed under a stiff cover on the driver's seat. A live mine was attached to both igniter switches. Other mines in the rack could also be presumed to be made sensitive so that one big hell of a hole in the ground would be made if any the booby traps were triggered. This was one disarming job I would trust only myself to do, and, as I didn't like the idea of possibly being another 'missing person', I told Tommo to watch proceedings (or at least the vehicle) from a relatively safe distance. The RSM had already vanished! I was not – or indeed could not – be absolutely sure that the two booby traps I found, and tackled successfully, were the only ones around. It was always a possibility that something more cunningly devised could be concealed underneath or within the mechanism of the vehicle. I therefore fastened a scribbled warning note to the window. 'Some booby-traps removed. Handle with extreme care![24]

It is also worth recalling the large road building and route maintenance the Engineers were also required to conduct. Between D-Day and the end of August the British landed 202,789 vehicles of different types into the crowded beachhead. The simple country roads of Normandy

---

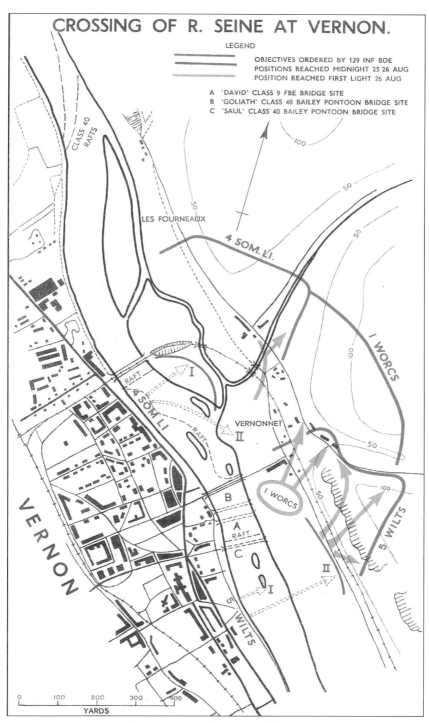

Diagram 4.3 Crossing of Seine.

were never designed to cope with such traffic volumes, one main road in the bridgehead recorded a peak total of 13,000 vehicles a day moving in one direction and 5,200 moving the opposite way. Not only were the Engineers required to repair and improve routes broken up by the heavy traffic but they were also tasked to construct entirely new roads. Major tank cross-country routes were constructed to prevent tracks from tearing up existing roads, by passes were also constructed around the major towns. Bayeux was one such example where 7 Army Royal Engineers constructed a 4 mile-long bypass right around the town. The road was 21 feet wide and had side drains on either side as well as a surface of Sommerfield track and Chespaling covered with sand and gravel, the road opened for traffic on 2 July. The Engineers had hoped to use the quarries in the vicinity of Caen to provide the stone for its roads, but the failure to capture the city early on meant the sappers had to use a poorer quality of limestone which failed to stand up to the heavy traffic nearly so well. Of course there were other sources of stone available as Major Vernon illustrates:

> On 16 August the Company moved to Ecouches about 3 miles from Argentan, which was still burning and almost completely destroyed, we had been given the task of constructing a by-pass around Argentan for the all important 'Diamond Route'. With the aid of a Company of Pioneer Corps much additional transport and mechanical equipment and portable lighting sets for working at night. The Company worked for four days and nights non-stop. In parts a chalk sub-strata was graded to make a fine surface, houses demolished and any further material required was available in large quantities from the battered town close by. The resulting road stood up to continuous and heavy Army traffic for some time.[25]

Once the Allies were able to break out of the bridgehead, the sapper requirement to support the Army's mobility was renewed, and included bridging major rivers. The assault crossing of the River Seine at Vernon by 43rd Wessex Division on 25 August, illustrates the challenges for sappers in crossing waterways. The operation was made more complicated in that it occurred during the break out and pursuit phase of the Germans by the British. At this stage of the campaign the Allies therefore wished to maintain their momentum and 'bounce' the Germans over the River Seine rather than produce a deliberate meticulously prepared plan that would allow the Germans a chance to recover. This hasty crossing therefore meant that the minimal amount of time would be available to organise Sapper support, which would include the provision of assault boats, rafts to ferry across individual vehicles and the construction of the three necessary bridges. Essentially the Allies were sacrificing preparation time for speed.

The British planners had studied the available intelligence carefully and deduced that the river was 600 to 650 feet wide, 10 feet deep and had a current of 2 knots. The river bed was made of silt with slight gravel and had steep banks which varied in height from 10 to 15 feet. The gap for bridging estimates was taken as 900 feet. The pre-existing road bridge known as the Pont de Vernon and the railway bridge had both been destroyed in May by the Allied air forces as part of the pre-invasion 'Transport Plan' to isolate the Normandy battlefield. They were so badly damaged that they could not be repaired quickly enough to assist the assault crossing. It was noted an island existed to the west or downstream of the road bridge, although the channel on the far side of this island was closely studied through air photographs a false conclusion was reached that it was a small obstacle. This would come to affect the left assaulting battalion in due course.

A major river crossing requires considerable engineer effort, consequently 43 Wessex Division were appropriately resourced with extra engineer regiments for the operation. The Royal Engineer

---

25 Major D R Vernon papers, Reference No.339, Imperial War Museum.

Commander at XXX Corps allotted the three major engineer tasks for Op NEPTUNE as follows.[26] Firstly 43rd Wessex Division's own integral engineer regiment would build a Class 9 Folding Boat Equipment (FBE) Bridge. The FBE was a lightweight bridge which could only take vehicles such as jeeps, 6-pounder anti-tank guns and Bren carriers up to 9 tonnes (hence the term Class 9). This bridge would be called 'SAUL'. Secondly, 7 Army Engineer Regiment would build a Class 40 Bailey pontoon bridge. The Bailey bridge was a wonderful innovation, made up of rectangular panels of angle iron 5 feet high and 10 feet long. Knee brace members and end panels could all be bolt-connected to join these panels together into a strong box girder construction. The panels could also be pinned together in a variety of different combinations according to the span and load carrying requirements of the bridge. The Bailey bridge would take longer to assemble than the 'SAUL' Class 9 FBE Bridge, but importantly it could carry the heavy tanks needed to defend the bridgehead and subsequently attack from it. This first Bailey bridge at Vernon would be called 'GOLIATH'. Finally 15 (Kent) Engineer Regiment would build a second Class 40 Bailey pontoon bridge (DAVID). This regiment would also construct and operate rafts whilst the first Bailey bridge, GOLIATH, was being built. These Class 40 rafts, which could be quickly assembled, would be able to take over limited numbers of heavy vehicles; including the tanks, which would be desperately needed to support the infantry in the bridgehead. The Bulldozers, which would be required to prepare the exit routes on the other side of the river, would also be taken across the River Seine by this raft. However before they began building rafts and bridges, 15 (Kent) Engineer Regiment's first task would be to operate the 'Stormboat' assault craft and take across the two assaulting battalions 5th Wiltshires and 4th Somerset Light Infantry.

The Stormboats were wooden assault boats powered by an Evinrude outboard and capable of carrying fifteen fully loaded men. They were heavy craft and required working parties of thirty men to carry them to the river. 4th Wiltshires would provide these work parties as well as act as the 'in-place force'; a role that required them to defend the town of Vernon and the home bank from where the assault across the River Seine would take place. A 'hasty' crossing inevitably is more confusing and chaotic than a deliberate crossing where more time is allowed for greater planning, reconnaissance and preparation. The hasty assault crossing of the Seine was no exception. 4th Wiltshires underestimated the time taken to drag the Stormboats through the town to the waters edge and of the eight boats to cross at 5th Wiltshire's location only two had reached the bank at H Hour (1845 Hrs 25 August). Lieutenant Colonel Fayle, CO of 15 (Kent) GHQ Troops RE, recalls the assault:

> The preliminary bombardment commenced starting with HE and changing after 10 minutes to HE and smoke mixed.
>
> When the assault was due to commence we got out into the garden and lying behind some trees we had a good view of the river. However, owing to the smoke it was very difficult to see anything, but we heard the sound of the Stormboats starting soon afterwards and the Boche replied with a good deal of Spandau fire. After some time there I decided I would go off and see my own troops and I got down to the river after a certain amount of running and crawling, where I eventually met the officer (Lt Bellamy) in charge of the Stormboats on the right battalion front. He was slightly wounded and told me that the first wave on his side consisted of two boats, but that they had run into a sandbank midstream and had been heavily fired on and the boats damaged and most of the occupants killed or wounded; he had escaped serious wounds himself and had got back and re-organized the remaining boats which had got about

---

26 *Royal Engineers Battlefield Tour: Normandy to the Seine*, prepared under the direction of Chief Engineer British Army of the Rhine, HQ BAOR, 1946, p.122.

a platoon over the river but the battalion commander had shut down the crossings until after dark, so the men were at that time under cover.[27]

Though locals had assured the engineers that the shallows were passable by craft, the two craft that set off containing members of 8 Platoon, 5th Wiltshires also grounded on a sand bank two thirds of the way across. The smoke screen then began to dissipate and German machine gunners slaughtered the occupants. Other boats joining in the crossing experienced similar difficulties but slowly the few survivors in the initial waves began to subdue the resistance on the other side. Sergeant R C Hunt went across the Seine in one of the Stormboats' later waves, landing in the left assault battalion's area (4th Somerset Light Infantry), his task was to recce landing sites for a Class 9 raft. He describes the journey:

> We made our way to the river bank with a Stormboat driver. As we were about to embark a German MG concealed further upstream on the other side of the river opened fire on us, and a few unhappy moments ensued. The bullets were hitting the bank all around us so we dashed for cover. We tried again a few moments later when the smoke had thickened and this time we were more successful. We swung our bows offshore and feeling rather like clay pigeons headed for the clump of fir trees just upstream of the railway bridge. In the trees we found the Gunner FOO [Forward Observation Officer] already operating (to him must go the distinction of getting the first British vehicle across the Seine) and an odd assortment of boards and logs laid on the muddy bank where the jeep had been manhandled ashore from the storm boat.
>
> Contacting an officer of the Somerset Light Infantry, we went forward and with him towards the obstacle ahead. Halfway across the open ground a sniper got busy and caused us to dodge but we gained the cover of the trees lining the bank of the other 'river'. This proved to be an obstacle of some magnitude, some sixty feet wide with steep muddy banks and deep mud at the bottom.

Sergeant Hunt tried to get over this other river and off the island to find an unloading point for his class 9 raft, he moved under cover along a bank until he arrived at the railway bridge that was the only means of egress from the 'island':

> They were negotiating this bridge by walking along a ledge over the water and holding on to the parapet wall. Owing to the fire from the German MGs higher up the hill, crossing over the open bridge was a somewhat hazardous project at this time.
>
> An infantryman was lying behind a Bren on the top of the railway embankment and as we passed below him he announced, apparently to us, 'I can see 'em' …and then 'shall I fire?'. As no one else seemed to be inclined to proffer advice I said 'Go on, have a go' and we left him shooting merrily.
>
> Returning to the river bank we crossed again to the Vernon side without anything untoward happening…

Sergeant Hunt was then dispatched back across the River the next morning to continue his task of recceing a suitable off loading point for class 9 rafts.

> Things appeared to be much quieter than on the previous evening. We loaded into a storm boat and had reached a point about half way across the river when an MG opened fire, again

---

27 Ibid., p.128.

Figure 4.8 Three riflemen and a Bren gunner of A Company 5th Battalion the Wiltshire Regiment embark in assault craft during their crossing of the River Seine at Vernon. (The Wardobe: The Museum of the Berkshire and Wiltshire Regiment)

from further upstream; this time we were less fortunate and the boat was riddled with bullets along one side. The driver was hit in the face and shoulder and lost control of the boat, which fortunately continued on a course for the bank, which we hit a few minutes later. This was a lucky escape for although there were bullet holes all along the boat, with the exception of the driver, no-one received more than splinters. Deciding that hostilities could not have entirely ceased, we commenced to crawl along the muddy bank, upstream towards the small island, and continuing along the bank of the backwater. Gaining the cover afforded here by the trees, we left the bank and climbed up on to the flat ground amongst the trees. As we did so we saw immediately in front of us a German with an MG in a slit trench. He had had enough of it and at once put up his hands.

A little more warily now … a few moments later a shout came from another member of the party, and I turned to witness another German hastily ridding himself of his rifle. We sent both of these back to the tender care of the infantry and pushed on again. We were now confronted by another water obstacle, but this time sufficiently narrow to permit a comparatively easy crossing. We eventually found a suitable point for off loading, at a point some fifty yards downstream of the road bridge. The same afternoon a class 9 raft ferried across the first bulldozer, and this immediately went to work improving the ramp and exit to the main road.[28]

28 Ibid., p.128.

The next priority for the sappers would be to build the floating bridge so that light vehicles, especially the anti-tank guns vital for bridgehead defence, could quickly cross the river. Lieutenant D R Silvester describes the construction of this bridge by 43rd Wessex Division's integral engineer regiment.

The class 9 FBE bridge was built to take across the anti-tank guns, carriers and maintenance vehicles of the assaulting infantry division; speed therefore was essential. 553 and 204 Fd Coys, which were to bridge the Seine arrived on the high ground overlooking the town of Vernon at about 1630 hours 25 Aug by which time the recce parties were already at work down in the town. The bridging was due to commence two and a half hours later at the same time the assault went in.

At 1850 hours there was a short sharp bombardment on the far bank of the river by the Divisional Artillery, and at 1900 hours the assault commenced. A foothold was however not immediately established on the far bank, a number of boats being sunk, and several DUKWs getting stuck on submerged islands. The actual bridging operation therefore was unable to commence until 2100 hours.

Since 1900 hours the two field companies had been harboured in the town just behind the water front, awaiting the word 'go'. With them was the RASC transport carrying all the bridging equipment. Within a few moments after the companies had been told they could commence building, lorries were down by the river bank and boats were being offloaded. There were three platoons engaged in building rafts, and between them they had to build thirty-four. Some of the building sites were slightly protected from enemy fire by an island in midstream. In spite of this however an amount of enemy tracer came towards the building sites, and there was intermittent shelling. As a result there were a number of casualties, including an NCO in charge of one of the building parties who was killed on his raft.

Although these incidents and others, such as boatloads of wounded infantry landing on the building sites, slowed down the building somewhat the last raft was completed by 0345hrs.

In the meantime the construction of the approaches and landing bay was being disrupted. The platoon responsible needed to use a bulldozer to level out the existing steep banks but it came under fire constantly and the work did not commence until the far bank had been cleared further.

Work was recommenced at first light 26 Aug and at the same time it was decided to moor the rafts in the lee of the island. Owing to the strong current this was found to be a very difficult job, and as the bulldozing and landing bays came along quickly in daylight with very little interference from Jerry, it was decided to bring rafts straight into bridge.

Half a dozen rafts were brought into bridge without much difficulty then the opposition decided to take an interest in things. The next few rafts were subjected to accurate sniping and machine gun fire, and after a raft had been peppered killing one of the crew, wounding several others and killing the officer who was trying to bring it into bridge, it was decided to stop work on the bridge until the snipers and machine gunners, who were the cause of all the trouble, had been routed out from the cliff face over the river. Previous fire from the companies own Brens on to suspected enemy positions had been ineffective.

The Germans in question were eventually located by the infantry and taken prisoner. Work on the bridge was able to carry on; it was finally completed at about 1800 hours 26 Aug and the badly needed anti-tank guns rolled across. There was intermittent shellfire in the area, but traffic continued to cross all night. The next morning at 1130 hours a DR was crossing the bridge when an unlucky shell hit him, directly knocked out the centre bay of the bridge and damaged two adjoining bays. Spare rafts were brought down to fill the gap, and the bridge was in operation again within two hours.[29]

While SAUL Bridge was being completed, 7 Army Troops Regiment RE were building the first Class 40 Bridge (GOLIATH) and concurrently 15 (Kent) Engineer Regiment were constructing the Class 40 raft to take across the first tanks. Captain Tanner describes the construction of the raft and exits which would be vital in getting the first tanks across the river before the bridge was built:

> I took a small party across the river on a pontoon to select an exit on the far bank. I did not know how far downstream the bridgehead extended at this time, or who or what was on the far bank; but we got across safely. As we expected we found an island opposite our building site, so we moved downstream as it was better to have the current with the raft when going across loaded. There seemed to be very few possible exits, because the river was exceptionally low and there was soft mud on the banks; but we eventually chose a site which could be made suitable with a bit of work on it. It was clear, however that the round trip on the raft would be a fairly long one.
>
> As we were returning across the river after midnight, we heard the sound of oars downstream, and in the darkness saw the dim outline of a boat, crossing from west to east; but it was not a suitable moment to pursue it, as we had to get back to report the result of our reconnaissance. Building the raft was going ahead when we got back, so L/Sjt Guy, who had been across the river with me, was despatched with a party and some suitable timber from a nearby woodyard to go and prepare the far bank exit.
>
> Work on both banks progressed slowly owing to the mud and darkness, so caution was thrown to the winds and lorry headlamps were switched on, on the near bank. An occasional shell arrived but fortunately did no harm, and work now went on apace.
>
> Shortly after 0600 27 Aug, the first tank was rafted across. [In fact this tank immediately got stuck in the mud at the exits and had to be towed out by the subsequent tank which was landed at a better spot downstream]
>
> The far bank exit gave constant trouble, so a new exit was selected and hurriedly prepared still further downstream, making the round trip almost half a mile. It was therefore decided to move the whole site downstream, and a new site giving a run almost straight across the river was selected and prepared by bulldozing a ramp down to the water on both banks. Rafting on the new site went on more quickly and was continued until the class 40 Bailey pontoon bridge was opened in the evening.[30]

As the Class 40 raft came into operation the GOLIATH Bailey bridge was being constructed by 7 Army Troops RE. Their commanding officer Lieutenant Colonel Lloyd describes the operation:

> OC 71 Fd Coy and I went across the Pont to look at the far bank. There were a lot of huge logs and lumps of masonry where he would have to build the landing bay, otherwise his job looked straight forward enough. During the morning and early afternoon the Field Companies did their mine clearance (NIL result) and detailed recces, interrupted frequently by enemy fire. By 1530 hours 26 Aug things were quiet, and the Chief Engineer sent us word to start the job.
>
> 73 Fd Coy built from the near bank, 71 Fd Coy from the far bank, 72 Fd Coy launched the pontoons initially, and built the floating bays latterly. 343 Coy Pnr Corps was divided among

---

29 Ibid., p.127.
30 Ibid., p.132.

Figure 4.9 Infantry of the Hampshire Regiment cross the River Seine at Vernon. They are marching on 'SAUL', the Class 9 Folding Boat bridge. 'GOLIATH', the Class 40 bridge, is to the right. (Imperial War Museum B9743)

the three Field Companies. 73 Fd Coy had a stiff job with their landing bay. They had to deal with a very large bomb crater, and to cut away a lot of the masonry facing wall before they could start. Then they had a downhill launch involving extra preventers. The other snag was the approaches, which cost both 73 and 71 Fd Coys a lot of effort. Others have told how the site was stonked twice at an interval of a quarter of an hour on 27 Aug. Shortly beforehand I was with OC 72 Fd Coy at his pontoon launching place when shells were arriving down by the railway bridge. He guessed the Germans were ranging for us. We sent off a 'Shelrep' but I didn't put out any warning. Nearly all our casualties were in the second stonk and on the far bank. They included both of the small dozers which had been ferried over, also the ramp lorry (hit and burnt out in Vernnonet). The first thing to cross the bridge was a dozer at 1745 hours, but work was still going on particularly on the approaches, so we didn't open it to operational traffic until after 1930 hours – i.e. approximately 28 hours after the Chief Engineer ordered us to start on it. The length of the bridge excluding ramps was 694 feet...Our casualties were 20 (RE –10., RASC –1, Pnr Corps –9).[31]

The three bridges allowed the bridgehead to expand rapidly and the exploiting armoured divisions of XXX Corps (Guards Armoured and 11th Armoured Division) to continue the pursuit of the German Army into Belgium. The Royal Engineers would continue to be prolific bridge builders across Europe as each river was encountered.

Figure 4.10 A Class 40 raft operated by 584 Field Company Royal Engineers carries a Sherman tank across the Seine at Vernon on 27 August. (Crown Copyright Army Historical Branch)

Figure 4.11 The GOLIATH class 40 Bailey pontoon bridge at Vernon nears completion, The DAVID class 9 FBE can be seen alongside. (Crown Copyright Army Historical Branch)

The crossing of the Seine highlights how Engineer success is utterly dependent upon making sure that the correct stores and specialised equipment are available at the right time and at the right place. For this to occur a detailed and accurate knowledge of the obstacle or gap to be crossed is essential, the impact of turning up with a 30 foot assault bridge to find the ditch is 40 feet across is all too obvious. For D-Day itself such information could only be obtained by air photographic intelligence, Special Forces reconnaissance and other high-level intelligence sources or agencies. However once the British were ashore then engineer reconnaissance could be used to ensure the information about the obstacle was as accurate as possible, this would be particularly important in a 'deliberate attack' where there was more time available for preparation. Engineer reconnaissance usually required sappers to be placed with normal infantry or armoured patrols to find out specific answers to engineer questions, the resulting information about the ground and natural or man-made obstacles is known as 'Engineer Intelligence'. The account of an Engineer reconnaissance patrol by Corporal R W V Ganter of 275 Field Company, part of 51st Highland Division, on 8/9 September is useful in highlighting the techniques and hazards in such work. The patrol occurred two days before the assault on Le Havre (Operation ASTONIA) and sought to confirm details on an anti-tank ditch, two craters and the surrounding minefields. His account illustrates that obstacle or gap crossing was not an affair unique to D-Day but a problem that was encountered on many other occasions in Normandy as well as later on in the campaign.

Corporal Ganter's team would have been conscious that previous patrols had been engaged in the same area on the previous six nights. It was one and a half miles from the Forward Defence Lines to their objective and as they neared the main road upon which it was located the patrol slowed to a snail's pace, halting every ten steps or so:

> When I saw it I thought 'Some crater! And I was told it was twelve feet across'. That crater was forty to forty five feet across and nearly twenty feet deep. We examined it for mines but could find none. The earth on the top was very soft and we sank in over six inches when we trod on it. The bottom of the crater was soft oozy mud, and we didn't attempt to go down in case we couldn't get back. We examined the road between the crater and the road fork very carefully for anti tank mines, but saw none, though there were many little mounds of spoil that looked like mines.
>
> On reaching the fork we turned sharp right and went ten yards up the left fork to the second crater. The distance between the two craters was about forty feet and they had been blown in line with the anti tank ditch. We found no mines on the road up to the second crater, nor round the edge of it, nor in it. I had been told that this crater was going to be bridged by the 32 foot assault bridge carried by the Assault RE, but in measuring it I found it to be thirty two feet across and between fifteen and twenty feet deep. Getting to the far side of the crater to measure it up was quite a job, due to the steep walls and mud, and the SEAFORTH officer who took the string across got into a real muddy state.
>
> Clayton and I now started to sweep along the edge of the anti tank ditch, of which this leg ran nearly due north and south. We commenced where the ditch met the 32 foot crater, and had only gone ten paces when a mine was detected. It was a Teller, buried about nine inches in the spoil from the ditch. We found another Teller twenty paces further on. We swept for another hundred and fifty yards, but found no more mines, so we turned and swept back again, keeping ten yards from the ditch and parallel to it. We found nothing until we had nearly reached the road again, when we found a Teller practically in line with the first one we had found.
>
> At this point the rain ceased for a few minutes and the moon shone out with all its light. It was like daylight. Putting my mouth close to Clayton's ear I suggested getting into the crater,

only fifteen yards away. The next thing I knew was that Clayton asked 'WHAT?' in a voice that was nearly a shout. Grabbing his arm I put my finger to my lips, but again he shouted 'WHAT?' He had been wearing the earphones of the detector and picking up so much metal and shrapnel that his hearing must have become dulled. However getting him by the arm, I got us both down into the crater, where his ears became normal again. Standing in the crater were the two SEAFORTHS with mud well over their ankles.

It began to rain heavily and Corporal Ganter realizing this was an opportunity set to work again measuring the width and depth of the anti-tank ditch and finding it to be twenty-one feet across and between fifteen and twenty feet deep.

The next thing to find out was if there were any mines in the bottom of the ditch, the bottom was all soft mud and about three feet wide. Clayton, still having the detector, started to sweep along the bottom. After sweeping for about two hundred yards along the ditch, Clayton and I had a little conference and decided there would be no mines in the ditch, and packed the detector away in its haversack.

Having established the nature and type of obstacles the recce patrol could at last turn its thoughts to heading home. However this would not be without its difficulties:

The SEAFORTH officer and man then passed by us in the ditch, Clayton following them, leaving me to come up behind carrying the detector. They must have gone about twenty yards, and I had only gone three, when there was a 'Bang!' and I felt a nasty thump on my left foot. Our first thoughts were 'S Mine', and we all threw ourselves down in the bottom of the ditch. After waiting for what seemed an eternity, and nothing having happened, we realized it must have been a form of warning device and not an S mine, so we expected every second to hear some mortars being thrown across at us. I took out the detector again and searched the area of the explosion but found no trace of any metal. Nothing came over, however, and the only noise above the rain was the squelch of our gym shoes as we continued along the bottom of the ditch, sweeping the whole time. After a further hundred and fifty yards we came to the end of the ditch.

Here after a short conference, the detector was packed away again and it was decided to make a quick recce of the enemy side of the ditch. The SEAFORTH officer started to climb up the slope at the end of the ditch which was not so steep as the sides, and had got over half way up when 'Bang!' and everybody's thoughts were the same – 'S Mine'. The officer jumped over the top of the ditch and lay down and we three got down pretty quickly in the bottom. But it was no S mine, just another warning charge. Surely we thought, the enemy must fire something at us now. But no, nothing at all. After keeping down for ten minutes we made our way out of the ditch around to the enemy side. Here we found a minefield started about twenty yards from the ditch and ran its entire length. We did not reconnoitre this field, as it was not so necessary to have information about mines on the enemy side of the ditch as about mines on our side of it.

Getting back to the road junction again, we walked two hundred yards back from the ditch and swept on either side of the road for a hundred and fifty yards. We found no trace of mines, but there were plenty of poles [anti-glider obstacles] and anti-airborne wires in the area. We repeated this operation two hundred yards further on, and again found no trace of mines.

After sweeping four hundred yards from the ditch we knew our recce was over. All we had to do now was to get back. The return was safely made, although we had one or two false

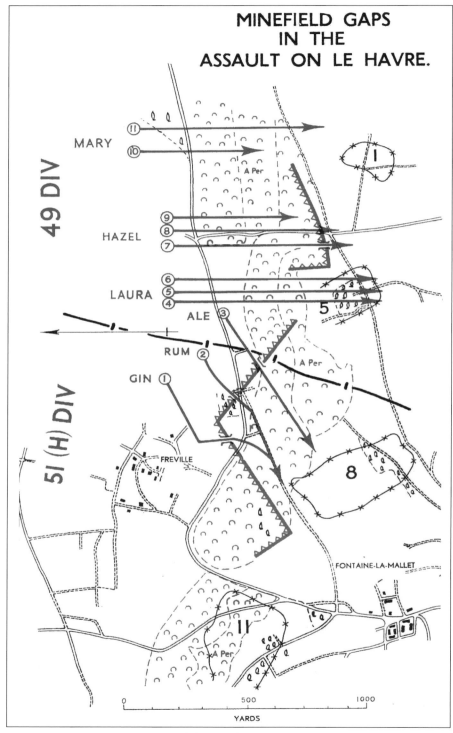

Diagram 4.4 Attack on Le Havre.

Figure 4.12
Sapper C W Stevens
of 18th Field
Company Royal
Canadian Engineers
uses a mirror to check
the underneath of a
Teller mine, 22 June.
(Lieut. Ken Bell,
Library and Archives
Canada, PA-136278)

alarms on the way, and it was with a feeling of relief that we had done something worth doing, and the information we brought back was considered of great interest.[32]

The information brought back by Corporal Ganter and other sappers who reconnoitred different parts of the Le Havre defences allowed the relevant commanders to organise the 'lane' teams. These composite teams assaulted the fortress of Le Havre over eleven separate lanes as illustrated in diagram 4.4.

What shines brightly in these anecdotes is the quality of the sappers. Few JNCOs in the Army would routinely have the responsibility thrust upon Corporal Ganter for instance. Major Martin Lindsay the Second-in-Command of 1st Gordons wrote in his diary of his admiration for the sappers who had supported him throughout the campaign in North-West Europe.

I certainly take my hat off to these men. It is all the same for the assault RE – either building bridges or clearing roads of mines in places where the enemy cannot fail to know that we need bridges or roads, and therefore always under fire. It is different for us who have a job to do and then are able to dig in. I would put the unpleasantness, by which I mean the danger, of soldiering in the campaign as: firstly, field companies RE, secondly, infantry; and thirdly, either airborne formations (who have long rests at home between operations) or tank crews (who are not called upon to fight so often as infantry).[33]

Combat engineers are the critical enabler for infantry and armoured movement on the battlefield. However combat with the enemy itself is often typified by the combination fire and movement together. The next two chapters will cover how fire support was delivered by both artillery and the supporting air forces.

---

32 Ibid., p.122.
33 Lindsay, Martin, *So Few Got Through* (London: Collins, 1946), p.248.

5

'Queen of the Battlefield' – Artillery

> Although I am an Infantryman, in my opinion the arm of the Service which did most to win the last war was the Royal Regiment of Artillery.
>
> General Horrocks[1]

The extensive use of artillery and indirect fire by 21st Army Group was arguably the strongest feature of British operations during the Normandy campaign. The Royal Artillery was widely recognised as the most mature and professional branch of the British Army and had perfected both its techniques and organisation throughout the war. To say it was well resourced would be an understatement, eighteen per cent of the men in 21st Army Group were gunners (as opposed to 15 per cent infantry for instance) and if one takes into account those non-gunners providing logistical or other support to the artillery then this figure rises to about a third of the Army Group's total strength. By mid-1943 over 700,000 men were in the Royal Artillery, which made this single regiment almost as large in manpower as the Royal Navy.

The artillery was also one of the few areas where the British equipment compared favourably with their German counterparts. However the gunners' success stemmed not just from numbers or quality of equipment but from a series of innovations in tactics, techniques, procedures and organisation. These included shrewd investment in target acquisition (sound ranging, flash spotting and Air Observation Posts) as well as surveying and meteorological capabilities. Arguably the most significant of tactical innovations was the Royal Artillery's ability to centralise control of the guns under various Commanders Royal Artillery and yet de-centralise the availability of its 'fire'. This enabled artillery to deliver fire support across boundaries to units in entirely different formations and ensured that the guns were efficiently used and never 'idle' or kept in reserve. The Royal Artillery's system of enduring affiliation's between its batteries and combat units also ensured that Royal Artillery commanders usually had an intuitive understanding of the units they supported, their operations and what their requirements for fire support would be. Trust between different units is an important element in any Army and this system of affiliation encouraged close individual relationships between the gunners and the units they supported. The effect was to generate considerable confidence within the Army in the capabilities and dependability of the Royal Artillery.

The organisation of the gun regiments themselves had developed during the war. The majority of gun regiments were 'field' regiments equipped with either the towed 25-pounder gun or, if they were supporting an armoured brigade, the Self-propelled 25-pounder gun or 'Sexton' which was

---

1   Horrocks, Lt Gen Sir Brian with Belfield, Eversley and Essame, Maj Gen H, *Corps Commander* (London: Sidgwick & Jackson, 1977), p.36.

Figure 5.1 A 25-pounder gun of 'D' Battery, 3rd Regiment, Royal Horse Artillery at Boissey, 21 August. (Imperial War Museum B9543)

mounted upon a Canadian Ram tank chassis. A field regiment had three eight gun batteries each of two troops of four guns, this meant that the field regiments could permanently affiliate a battery to each of the three combat units in an infantry or armoured brigade. Whilst fire support was delivered in a combined battery mission for greater effect, each troop of four guns was regarded as a 'fire-unit' and could independently generate a viable amount of fire through its own gun position and command post. There were three 25-pounder field regiments in an infantry division (one for each of its brigades) giving a total of 72 available guns. The fire of these field regiments was usually available to the affiliated battalions and brigades unless required on higher priority tasks elsewhere. The Commander Royal Artillery (CRA), with his staff at divisional headquarters, directed these tasks in accordance with the divisional commander's priorities. This arrangement meant that artillery fire could be quickly concentrated on a single target by the 24 guns of the regiment (known as a 'Mike' target) or the 72 guns of a division (an 'Uncle' target).[2]

In addition to field regiments there were medium and heavy artillery gun regiments. These would be grouped into an Army Group Royal Artillery (AGRA) and although normally attached to a particular Corps they were usually employed as an Army resource and would be used in support of specific operations regardless of any affiliation. There was no standard organisation for an AGRA, but they usually consisted of one field regiment of 25-pounders, four medium regiments and one heavy regiment. As well as being made available to a Corps for specific operations

---

2   Mike and Uncle were the old phonetic words for the letters 'M' and 'U'.

they could also concentrate their fire against a single target (known as a 'Victor' target).[3] The flexibility this system provided was highlighted by the XXX Corps commander, Lieutenant General Sir Brian Horrocks:

> Neither the Germans, the Russians or even the French, who were always supposed to be the masters of artillery fire systems, could approach the accuracy or the weight of concentrated fire power which, on my Corps front, I had at my disposal in a matter of minutes. To simplify and speed up the call for a concentration of artillery fire, only code names were necessary. Thus, if I wanted the fire of all seventy-two 25-pounder field guns of any division to be concentrated on one target, my Gunner Brigadier [The Corps Commander Royal Artillery or CCRA] would merely have to get in touch with Brigadier RA at the Division concerned and ask for an 'Uncle' target to be fired. If a target was sufficiently important to warrant all, or most, of the Corps artillery being employed this was called a 'Victor' target… In a matter of minutes, therefore, about 400 guns could be brought into action where I wanted them. This system of predicted fire not controlled by an observer, was made possible by a combination of excellent surveying, good communications and a high degree of flexibility at the guns. Finally these concentrations could be fired in any weather by day or night and were thus far more reliable than any air strikes which were always very dependent on the weather.[4]

But it wasn't just the senior officers who were impressed, the Royal Artillery were held in high regard by the combat units themselves because of their ability to support them with 'observed' concentrations of fire. This role was undertaken by the Forward Observation Officers (FOO) and their three-man teams; it was critical in repeatedly breaking up German attacks and assisting British offensive operations. FOO parties were usually the most forward deployed of Royal Artillery personnel and their hazardous role was reflected in a high casualty rate.

The FOOs were drawn from the troop commanders of the field regiment's batteries. They would be affiliated to a particular company or squadron with their battery commander acting as the combat unit's artillery adviser and the gunner regimental CO the brigade commander's adviser. This system of 'affiliation' was disturbed as little as possible so mutual confidence and shared techniques could prosper. It was unique to the British Army and stemmed from an innovation between 3rd Royal Horse Artillery and 9th Australian Division during the 1941 siege of Tobruk, the idea subsequently spreading. The FOO's duties were to observe and report the tactical situation, maintain close contact with the supported arm, deliver the required fire support at the earliest moment and to direct and control the fire of the allotted guns. These latter guns could be allocated not just from the observing officer's own battery but those of the regiment, the division or even Corps artillery drawn from the AGRA. FOOs were usually equipped with a Bren Carrier and 3 wireless sets, though those supporting armoured units operated from specially adapted tanks. The FOO was supported by an OP assistant (usually a bombardier) and a driver/signaller. Captain Jack Swaab who was a FOO with the 5th Black Watch describes in his diary the preparation of a FOO's equipment prior to an operation:

> Today we are getting what in the Army is known as 'teed up' or 'laid on' or simply organised. Wireless sets checked, batteries filled, maps marked, chinagraphs sharpened, bootlaces tested,

3   Townend, Lt Col Will, "Gunners in Normandy: Notes on Artillery organisation and equipment", *Journal of the Royal Artillery*, Spring 2010.

4   Horrocks, Lt Gen Sir Brian, with Belfield, Eversley Belfield and Essame, Maj Gen H, *Corps Commander*, (London: Sidgwick & Jackson, 1977), p.177.

stens and revolvers cleaned, rations, petrol and water loaded, binoculars cleaned, compasses tested, vehicles checked, cable checked – these are only a few of the larger and more important things one has to do before going forward with an attack. I alone have 3 wireless sets – a No.22 to communicate with the battery commander and guns, a No. 18 to talk to the infantry, and a No. 39 if my remote control cable from me to my wireless in the carrier is destroyed. That is if my OP is away from the carrier which it nearly always is; you then have what is called a remote control unit by which you work the No. 22 as much as ½ a mile away.[5]

The FOO's ability to observe, direct and control the guns was vital to a combat unit's operational success and this meant that he sometimes had to occupy some particularly exposed and dangerous positions. Captain Stu Laurie of 4th Field Regiment, Canadian Royal Artillery recorded a particularly hazardous OP location whilst serving as a FOO during Operation SPRING with the Royal Hamilton Light Infantry:

Leaving the carrier back in the sunken road, I go forward about fifty yards, accompanied by MacAleer [his OP assistant], who as he goes unreels the remote control cable that will link us to the big [No.22] radio set in the carrier behind us. We take shelter behind a stone wall where one of our anti-tank guns has just been knocked out, and the crew is lying dead around it. Peering over the top of the wall, I see a great big Tiger tank just down the slope in front, with several officers standing around it directing its fire. Just then one of our tanks comes up and shows itself on the fringe of a little wood only about one hundred feet from where we are. The shot from the Tiger peels a silver groove right across its turret. And though it doesn't catch fire or anything the metallic rip is god-awful –even at one hundred feet! What it must have sounded like to those guys inside the tank! Anyway they get the hell out of there in a hurry.

That Tiger has control over the whole ridge where we are, and when I stick my head up and try to pin down a map reference, he starts shooting at me with 88mm solid shot – not at the centre of the wall, but chopping away both ends. First he hits this end and then the other, knocking off a bit more wall with each shot. And he keeps this up until the wall, which was about fifteen feet long to start with is down to about six feet. In the meantime Major Wren and the Colonel [The battery commander and Gunner CO respectively] are still keeping the guns engaged and all I can get to use is a section [two 25-pounder guns] or sometimes a troop [four 25-pounder guns].

Oh I get some shells down, but nothing of consequence, nothing you could call real fire, before we have to leave. MacAleer and I are now alone – the few Rileys,[6] who'd been out in the field with us, having disappeared when the tank started shooting. With our wall disappearing, our only hope is to make it back to the carrier in the sunken road. As we get set to make the dash, I see MacAleer preparing to reel up the remote control cable, and I have to yell at him, 'Forget your damned remote control and get the hell out fast!' And running like the devil we make it back the fifty yards or so to the sunken road where there is some protection. There we pile into the carrier and pull out with the remote control bouncing behind us.[7]

Having observed and identified an appropriate target the FOO's next step was to judge what effect the supported infantry or armoured unit would wish to have upon it. This judgement was based upon the number of guns available, the importance of the target and the capabilities of both

5   Swaab, Jack, *Field of Fire: Diary of a Gunner Officer* (Stroud: Sutton Publishing, 2005), p.184.
6   Nickname for RHLI infantryman.
7   Blackburn, George, *The Guns of Normandy* (London: Constable, 1998), p.251.

Figure 5.2 A Universal or Bren carrier of 4th Field Regiment Royal Canadian Artillery
at Vaucelles 18-20 July. (Lieut. Ken Bell, Library and Archives Canada, PA-153423)

the artillery pieces and the shells they fire. It is these shells which are of course the real 'weapon' of the artillery.

There were two shells routinely used by 25-pounder equipped field regiments in Normandy; High Explosive shell (HE) or Base Ejection (BE) Smoke shells. A solid shot Armour Piercing (AP) round was also available for use against enemy armour and had been used extensively in the Desert. However by 1944 the use of the 25-pounder guns in the anti-tank role had become rare, the Army having been finally equipped with capable anti-tank guns, such as the 6-pounder and 17-pounder. All British artillery shells were painted, both to protect the shells from rust and aid identification; HE was yellow, smoke was a vivid 'Brunswick' light green and AP rounds were black. The effect of the HE shell could be adjusted by changing the fuze screwed into its nose. For example HE with a Direct Action fuze would burst upon immediate contact with the ground making it suitable for use against troops and guns in the open or under light cover. It was therefore often used for offensive or protective covering fire, for harassing fire and wire cutting, the shell could also have a concussion effect on buildings and would damage an enemy tank's tracks or cause other superficial harm. The HE shell when fitted with a Graze Fuze allowed a tiny time delay between the shell hitting the ground and detonating. This meant that it could penetrate certain targets before exploding and consequently it had a greater destructive effect on buildings, strong cover and trenches. There also existed an HE shell with a time fuze; these produced an airburst that was primarily used for ranging purposes. It would not be until proximity fuzes were introduced later in the war that a more dependable anti-personnel air burst became available to the British.

The Base Ejection smoke shell used a carrier shell with a time fuze to eject burning smoke canisters some 300 feet above the ground. These would then fall to the ground and burn for 75-90 seconds producing a smokescreen that was used to prevent enemy observation. It could also be used as a method of ranging field guns especially with air observation. Smoke shells would normally generate white smoke, but red smoke shells were also used to mark enemy positions for attack by Allied aircraft. Thick and enduring smoke screens could be generated for significant periods of time, though care was needed. Attention had to be paid to the wind which would clearly effect the build up of the screen and the tendency for the smoke to hug the ground meant that the FOO had to ensure the enemy were not in a position to see over its inevitably limited height (effectively about 50 feet). Lieutenant Colonel Fanshawe, CO of the 86th Field Regiment (Hertfordshire Yeomanry) RA describes the process:

> Some Div commanders would demand a smoke screen lasting for hours to guard a flank or screen a hill. This wasn't difficult to work out, one had to get the wind speed and direction off the meteor telegram, decide how many points of origin[8] were required and allot the guns to them, and fix the rate of fire which as far as I remember was pretty slowly – 1 round per gun per minute. Even then to fire one all day took a great deal of ammunition and a great deal of dumping.[9]

As well as reacting to unexpected enemy activity on an impromptu basis the FOO also had to produce 'programmed' shoots. Programmed shoots generally meant a fire plan coordinated with the supported troops, the fire being either scheduled to occur at a specific time or held on call in case the need arose. The British attempted to categorise the effect or purpose of a 'fire plan' into Covering Fire (CF), Defensive Fire (DF), Harassing Fire (HF) and Counter Battery Fire (CB). In offensive operations the Royal Artillery would produce Covering Fire (CF) to neutralize the enemy as friendly forces conducted an attack, it would use barrages or concentrations of HE to achieve this as well liberal quantities of smoke. Offensive operations would usually be supported by counter battery operations and if air support was being employed, counter–flak operations or 'apple pie' shoots would be laid on.

The 'barrage' tended to be the dominant feature of British offensive fire plans, with concentrations against specific targets supplementing the barrage. A barrage could be stationary or move forward in front of the assaulting troops, 'quick barrages' could be ordered over the radio and were usually rectangular in shape 'ordinary barrages' were irregularly shaped, usually quite large and generally issued as traces to be overlaid on maps. Given the typical size and depth of German defensive positions barrages would inevitably have to move over the German position to give effective covering fire. This could be done by either a 'creeping' barrage, one that moved slowly from one line to the next, a 'rolling' barrage', where several lines were engaged at once the line slowly moving forward lifting from the nearest line one by one or, a 'block' barrage where a number of lines were engaged at the same time and all lifted and moved on to another set of lines simultaneously. Barrages were quite flexible and could wheel and turn or even move back depending on the effect required. Ultimately the speed with which the barrage moved was determined by the speed of the assaulting troops. Armour was believed to be able to advance about 200 yards per minute and infantry 100 yards per minute though these planning figures were clearly dependent upon the terrain. Barrages were expensive in the allocation of guns required to service them, a regiment

---

8   These are the points of origin of the burning canisters on the ground and not the location of the artillery piece that fired them.

9   Memoirs of Maj Gen G D Fanshawe 1943-45 (Part IV), Royal Artillery Institution archives MD 1661.

of 25-pounders could be expected to generate a barrage of 400 yards frontage, with two batteries firing on the forward line and the third engaging a line in depth. Given the maximum range of the 25-pounder was 11,800 yards[10] a 25-pounder barrage planning range was normally to a maximum depth of 8,000 yards. The medium regiment's artillery would normally be used to extend the depth of the barrage by using their longer ranges or employed where the greater destructive power of the 5.5-inch gun's 80lb shells, or the 7.2-inch gun's 202lb shell was most required.

The smaller destructive power of the 25-pounder was not necessarily a handicap; it reduced safety distances considerably; 150 yards distance if it was being fired overhead and 200 yards if fired from a flank. This allowed the assaulting infantry to 'lean into the barrage' a practise that as we have seen was well understood by the infantry.

During a defensive operation Defensive Fires (DF) would be used to cause damage to enemy forces, disorganising and breaking up his attacks in the process. These DF's could be a standing barrage but were normally a concentration and a unit would always have one DF (SOS) target, placed on the most likely enemy approach, as part of its fire plan. The unit's supporting guns would always be layed upon this target when not in action to ensure the quickest response. The scale and rate of fire on a DF task was typically three minutes 'intense' for field regiments (five rounds per gun per minute or 360 rounds per regiment). George Blackburn, a 4th Canadian Field Regiment FOO recalled calling in a DF (SOS) as a response to a German attack at Eterville:

> It comes in just as the sun is going down, beginning with a flurry of mortars, 88mm airbursts, and a hail of machine-gun tracers lacing the orchard. The tracers are coming from the right front, but from some distance away, judging from the faintness of their staccato bur-rup, bur-rups, barely distinguishable among the hammering Brens and mortar explosions over on the right. And it's clear the tracers, streaking mostly through the upper remnants of the trees, are originating from a point much lower than the orchard, probably from that skinny copse some 400 yds south of here, just east of the road you earlier studied whilst waiting for your rounds to land – a good forming up point, providing a concealed route almost right up to the village.
>
> On your map you find a DF (Defensive Fire) target marked precisely where you want to bring down fire. But when you pick up the remote microphone to call the guns, its dead – the line again cut by a piece of mortar or shell. Scrambling out of your hole, you run crouched over as fast as you can back to the carrier and huddle down tight against its steel flank, just outside where Kirby is sheltering. Kirby's ears are covered with big, puffy earphones and you have to tap him on the shoulder. When he uncovers his left ear, you give him the DF target number and the order 'Fire!' for transmittal to the guns. In an incredibly short time of less than a minute, shells are rustling overhead, and a great furore of overlapping roaring explosions starts rolling up from the area of the copse…your guns have just squelched an enemy attack of some consequence (no more tracers skitter through the trees and the popping and chattering of small-arms fire down in the village seem to have stopped).[11]

The British also categorised fires for Counter Battery (CB); designed to neutralize or destroy enemy targets, as well as Harrasing Fire (HF) which was used to hamper enemy movement to the front, hinder the conduct of their operations and generally lower their morale. The most important point about programmed shoots, of whatever type, was that all of the targets were pre-selected and

---

10 A 25-pounder could fire up to 13,400 yards with charge super but they would overheat after 40 rounds so this was not really a practical proposition.

11 Blackburn, George, *The Guns of Normandy* (London: Constable, 1998), p.121.

Figure 5.3 Gunners of the Medium Regiment of the Royal Canadian Artillery clean their 5.5-inch gun south of Vaucelles, 23 July. (Lieut. Ken Bell, Library and Archives Canada, PA-131382)

the technical work at the guns was therefore done in advance. This meant that predicted fire (not needing correction by observation) would be forthcoming with maximum speed and accuracy.

The formulation of the fire plan would require the coordination of the battery commander at unit level and the artillery regimental commanding officer at brigade level. At both divisional and corps level the Fire Plans were directed by the Royal Artillery commanders and an example of such a Fire Plan can be seen in Appendix H along with the Commander Royal Artillery's comments.

The battery commander had other important responsibilities as well as the fire plan, these included advising the armour or infantry battalion CO as well as siting the FOO's observation posts till he was satisfied he had achieved adequate observation across his unit's front. The battery commander would move with the infantry or armoured CO most of the time, ensuring that the effort of his battery's guns conformed to the CO's plan. The battery commander was often given broad latitude by his gunner CO and he was expected to use his initiative on the engagement of targets, or deviate from the Fire Plan if required without reference to the gunner regiment. He remained in command of his battery of eight 25-pounder guns using his battery command post to assist him in this task, this was important because, unlike him, the battery command post was located at the gun lines with the two gun troops. Major Robert Kiln a battery commander with the 86th Field Regiment (Hertfordshire Yeomanry) describes how he controlled his subordinate FOOs and developed a fire plan:

> We were holding a section of our front line and knew from aerial reports that a German attack was expected. I had one forward OP, Garton Ash, to give me warning of any German build up, and a second officer, in this case our subaltern Tony Dorling, forward with the advance company. With my Tactical HQ, I was dug into a ditch alongside the infantry battalion head-quarters. My fire plan against a German attack was carefully worked out. Using maps only, I

had put myself into the position of a German commander attacking our position and marked out as our targets the routes he was likely to use to attack us; this sunken lane, that belt of trees; where his mortars would be sited; where his forming-up position would be behind that hill or this wood; where his headquarters must be put in that farm. Each of these positions was pre-recorded as a target. Of course, we could not see these positions, and could not record them directly with observed fire, but we registered a known feature on the map close to our lines that we could see by firing our guns on it and recording its range and bearing. Using that recorded target as a base, we recorded all the other targets indirectly. Once the German attack was under way, I tried to visualize where the Germans would be and brought down the regiment's guns on forming-up places, then the approach routes, with a switch to their presumed headquarters.

With his two OPs forward Major Robert Kiln was confident he could observe the later stages of the German approach:

> The defence plan was simple; if the Germans reached the wood, our troops would fall back several hundred yards to prepared positions in the wood itself, alongside six Churchill flame-throwing tanks. Once our infantry had withdrawn, we would shell the edge of the wood then the infantry and Churchill tanks would counter-attack. It was similar to many such actions and memorable to me for its complete success. We fired as we planned and the action ended with few casualties on our side and the Germans flung back and being chased in a horrible fashion through the trees by the flame-throwing tanks. Over 100 prisoners were taken and while one of the captured German officers was being interrogated the battalion Intelligence Officer called me over and said 'Bob you ought to hear this'. The German officer told how his infantry division had moved up to Normandy from near Bordeaux, partly by rail, but mostly by night on foot, and how they had been put in to attack our positions. I quote (in translation):
>
>> It was terrible, we formed up to move forward and your guns shelled us so we moved to a little wood and the shells followed us. Even our headquarters in the farm was shelled. Then we moved forward down a lane and the shells followed us, and then when we got to your positions, you had gone and more shells came down on us. Then the few of us that were left were chased by horrible flame tanks. It is enough! We lay in a ditch then surrendered. I have had enough of war.[12]

The gunner regimental CO would be located at brigade HQ with a small team. Here he would act as the brigade commander's adviser on gunner matters. He would also be responsible for the deployment of his regiment, allotting the zones and tasks to his batteries as well as directing their general movement. Much of this detailed staff work and coordination would be managed by Regimental HQ which was geographically situated amongst the regiment's batteries. He would also ensure that the fire plan at brigade level accorded with the brigade commander's intent and would control and manage the overall ammunition expenditure by his batteries accordingly. As the only officer, other than the brigade commander, above the rank of major in the brigade HQ the Royal Artillery CO had great power and influence. Lieutenant Colonel G D Fanshawe describes his role with 8th Armoured Brigade:

---

12 Kiln, Major Robert, *D-Day to Arnhem with Hertfordshires Gunners* (Welwyn Garden City: Castlemead Publications, 1993), p.114.

I formed a sort of Tac HQ consisting of myself with my tank with two No.19 sets, a jeep with a 19 set and an IO with a 19 Set. All the sets were on the Regimental net except the second tank net which was on the net of the unit or formation to whom I was in direct support, obviously I couldn't speak on it but I could hear what was going on.

The Tac HQ stayed at or about the Bde HQ. The gun line was in charge of the 2IC. The BC's and troop commanders were with the units they were in Direct Support of, or acting as LOs to other units or formations with whom we were In Support of. My life followed a general pattern – in the evening go to the Bde 'O' Group and make up a fire plan if in Direct Support or find out what the plan was if only In Support, go to bed and then up at dawn or whenever. Subsequently life varied, if in Direct support –stay at Bde HQ – but more often when In Support, leave a LO with a set on the Regimental Net to transmit any calls for fire to the RHQ and go round any OPs that one could reasonably safely get at. In the afternoon visit the RHQ and some of the guns.[13]

During an operation itself the CO of the gunner regiment and his Tac HQ would be busy adjusting the Fire Plan and manoeuvring the regiment to support the battle as required. R A H McCree who served in the Tac HQ of 116 Field Regiment gives a description of their support to 176 Brigade, 59th (Staffordshire) Division as it crossed the River Orne on 7-8 August. The reader may wish to note the actions and decisions the CO of 116 Field Regiment takes on behalf of the brigade commander, as well as the artillery fire that is concentrated from elsewhere in support of 176 Brigade:

The [Bde] Commander decided to include BRIEUX in his bridgehead. 6 N Staffs were to attack at 1900hrs. A fire plan was arranged to soften BRIEUX with Field and Medium artillery from 1830-1900 hrs and then to give protective fire beyond the village until 1930 hrs. The conference broke up at about 1500hrs and on the way back an OP[14] was selected from which to observe the attack on BRIEUX…At about 1800 hrs the CO arrived at the OP to register softening fire on BRIEUX as this was close to our Start Line. The Regiment had moved up during the day and at this time theatre grid data had arrived, so a change to that grid was ordered and no time remained for registration. At 1830 the fire plan opened and 6 N Staffs had two Companies ready to attack at 1900hrs. The fire fell well.

After about 5 minutes the enemy opened up on the OP and Bn areas with shell and mortar. His DF fire we thought, but this illusion was soon dispelled by a message from Major Pettit (Battery Commander with 7 Norfolks) saying that a counter-attack had started in his area. The Brigade commander had not yet reached the OP area. Major Kell (Battery commander with 6 N Staffs) was therefore advised of the counter-attack and told to tell the Battalion CO of 6 N Staffs to ask to put off his BRIEUX attack. This was ordered to proceed.

From that time onward the CO was kept busy converting information messages into calls for fire from the Div Artillery and attached regiments. At first 'Uncle' targets were ordered; but as reports of more and more areas from which enemy were attacking came in it was difficult to keep pace with requirements. The CRA [At Division] suggested putting regiments on the areas for longer periods at slow rates. He arranged for support from a regiment of 53 Div in addition to 6 Field and 59 Medium of 3 AGRA. Much firing was done despite great difficulty with wireless, which it seemed the enemy was jamming. As darkness fell the battle died down and all OPs reported their areas held, a somewhat optimistic picture.

---

13 Memoirs of Maj Gen G D Fanshawe 1943-45, Royal Artillery Institution archives MD 1661.
14 This seems to be an OP for the Bde Tac HQ to view the battle rather than a specific gunner OP.

Figure 5.4 A 5.5-inch gun of a British Medium regiment firing near Vallee, August.
(Crown Copyright)

The view from the OP was not so good. Men of 6 N Staffs had straggled back past us in some numbers. Many Churchill tanks could be seen burning and the flames from houses lit the sky. No more could be done from the OP and we returned to [Bde] Main HQ just behind the hill. Here the commander sent for LOs and the picture resolved itself about midnight. The Tank Bn had been virtually 'brewed up', they said that 6 remained. 6 N Staffs had been caught on the move and lost the best part of two Coys. They were ordered to protect the bridge. The crossroads was lost. Communications with the other Bns was lost but they were believed to be intact.

Taken by and large it was a great battle for the gunners and those across the river excelled themselves throughout. They kept continual watch and their communications were perfect. Our regiment fired 1,000 rounds per gun at their request during the attacks on 7/8 Aug.[15]

The movement and deployment of the guns themselves would also exercise this command team of regimental and battery commanders. The CO of the field regiment would normally select the gun area for the batteries in consultation with the brigade staff and the divisional Royal Artillery staff. Battery commanders would be given a zone for their battery, which reflected the needs of the battalion they were supporting. Each battery commander would then select a central point in his zone, the batteries of a field regiment normally being within 1,000-2,000 yards of each other if the ground was suitable. This proximity facilitated surveying, communications and ammunition supply as well as mirroring the typical brigade frontage in Normandy. A 'reconnaissance' (or 'G' Party) as well as a preparation party would occupy the new position in advance of the arrival of

---

15 Cree, R M H, 'The Crossing of the River Orne', Royal Artillery Institution archives MD 1843, pp.3-4.

the 'main body' which would contain the guns and ammunition groups. Within the battery positions the troops of four 25-pounders would deploy a few hundred yards apart, with the right hand gun being known as the 'pivot gun'. This meant that a field regiment presented six dispersed and separate gun positions complicating the enemy's counter-battery efforts.

The four guns in the troop would normally deploy 20-30 yards apart, in a curved line so that they could all respond if attacked by tanks on the flank. The troop Gun Position Officer (GPO) would select individual gun 'platforms' having taken direction from the Battery Command Post Officer (CPO). The ideal gun position would have a low crest about 500 yards in front of it, this gave them a clear field of fire in case they came under tank attack and provided some cover from enemy flash spotting. Once the guns and ammunition limbers had been towed into place the gun tractors and any other superfluous vehicles would be moved to wagon lines about half a mile away. Not all positions were perfect and those on forward slopes, exposed to enemy view, risked inevitable problems. Captain Stephen Perry records one poor position for his Sexton self-propelled guns. It is a rare instance of artillery firing AP shells in Normandy:

> August 3rd. We move off and at 0800 hours arrive in our new gun area half a mile west of Jurques. But what a gun position! We are on a forward slope overlooked by a long ridge 2000 yards in front, but the Commander Royal Artillery (CRA) of 43rd Division has ordered us in here despite our CO's attempts to dissuade him, so here we have got to stay.
>
> At 1130 the inevitable happens and we are heavily shelled by 105mm guns, but luckily there are no casualties because we have a sunken lane behind the guns which provides good cover. At 1200 the 105s come over again and we remain safe and sound in our sunken lane; but here is something quicker than a 105, probably an 88, perhaps it is a Tiger. I take a dekko through my glasses and there is the flash, and the tank, sitting just below the skyline. What a target for him 24 SPs all lined up on a forward slope within easy range. Well, we will have a go at him. I grab the first three chaps I can see and jump onto E subsection's SP. As we get up, Sgt Fielding gets hit by a high explosive shell, but the rest of us are alright. Tulloch jumps into the driving seat and I direct him onto the tank and lay the gun for the first round. Just after it is fired there is a hell of a bang and G Sub's SP is covered in dust and smoke – it has had a direct hit. It will be us next if we do not get a move on. We bracket him with 4 rounds, but he has spotted us, because an armour piercing shot digs into the ground four yards in front. Then starts a ding-dong battle, round for round. We are getting them off as fast as we can and back comes the reply at the same rate. Why hasn't he hit us heaven knows! I am becoming deaf and my ears hurt like hell every time a round goes off. With the eleventh round a cloud of smoke comes up from the Tiger. Gosh this is exciting, we have hit it. Keep going! AP expended, oh blast! Well, fire HE but the first round is short and we raise the elevation and get half a dozen rounds off before he waddles off pouring smoke from his turret. Well that is that, he is damaged but not dead. However, it's as well we tickled him up or he might have got all our guns.[16]

It was normal within a battery position for the troop command posts to be positioned to the flank of the guns with the battery command post somewhere between the two troops. The guns in each position would then be numbered from the right, the pivot gun being number one. The enemy mortar threat meant that guns, ammunition and the CP were all routinely dug in, a very physically demanding task:

16 Kiln, Major Robert, *D-Day to Arnhem with Hertfordshires Gunners* (Welwyn Garden City: Castlemead Publications, 1993), pp.135-136.

Figure 5.5 A 'Sexton' self-propelled 25-pounder gun in Normandy 1944. (Crown Copyright)

There'd been some chance for sleep in the quads while they waited to move off, and during the long slow move, but once here all hands were needed to put the guns in action and keep them serviced while the pits were dug. And it was well after dawn on July 19 before the gunners could turn to digging personal slit trenches into which half of them might tumble for some sleep…To form a gun pit (18 feet in diameter and 3 feet deep) requires the excavation of some 28 tons and to dig an ammo pit (12 feet wide, 18 feet long and 3 feet deep) to receive the cases of shells and 125 cases of propellant charges, representing 1,000 rounds per gun, calls for the excavation of another 24 tons earth.[17]

Whilst the guns and their ammunition were being dug-in the battery's guns would be aligned against the battery's 'zero line'; a theoretical bearing which would cross the frontline at right angles. This would mean that their barrels were all parallel and the process of 'laying' or aiming them onto a target collectively was simplified. This procedure was usually done using the 'director' a surveying equipment on a tripod, or a distant known aiming point (e.g. a church steeple). The process involved recording the angle between the gun and the director and setting that angle on the gun dial sight's main scale; the gun was then traversed until its dial sight was aimed at the director at which point it was now 'laid' on the zero line. Two gun aiming posts, (effectively white sticks) were then planted about 50-100 yards from the gun, the angle was recorded to both of them using the sight's main scale. One was selected for current shooting and the dial sight laid upon it and the slipping scale (sometimes called the shooting scale) was adjusted until it read Zero and then clamped to lock it to the main scale. This procedure sounds complicated but was in practise quite simple, the technique meant that all the crew had to do to aim a gun was receive changes in direction or bearings from the zero line; these were known as switches and were easily applied using the slipping scale. During fire missions all the gun crew's 'layer' needed to do to check he was still firing in the right direction between rounds was keep the relevant gun aiming posts in his dial sights and because the gun aiming posts were near (unlike a distant church steeple) this could

17 Blackburn, George, *The Guns of Normandy* (London: Constable, 1998), pp.201-202.

be achieved in conditions of low visibility such as darkness and mist. Checking the lay would be quickly done after each round was fired because the gun's position will have been disturbed by its recoil action.

Concurrently the regimental survey team would be integrating the 'pivot' gun into the regimental, divisional and theatre Grid. This meant that each gun would be accurately placed on the surface of the earth generating greater and more accurate concentration of fire by massed guns on individual targets. George Blackburn describes the occupation of a gun position:

> Immediately battery and troop advance parties each consisting of a subaltern and an ack (a highly trained technical assistant) are sent forward to lay out their allotted positions and plant their gun-marker flags to allow the regimental survey party to carry their survey work right up to the marker of each 'pivot gun' (the right hand gun of each troop of four). The survey party will, first, establish the pivot gun's position on the face of the planet in terms of the numbered grid overprinting on the 1/25,000 map and second will pass to each 'director' (survey instrument) set on a tripod in front of each troop position and orientated to an identifiable aiming point, a precise 'grid bearing'. So that when the guns arrive the troop will be ready to pass on to each gun for its 'dial sight' the 'zero-line' (a grid bearing arbitrarily drawn by Divisional HQ through the middle of the enemy front). Thus all guns will be in accurate relationship to each other on 'Regimental Grid' and their barrels will be parallel to each other, as a starting point for setting ranges and switches to targets.[18]

After the survey party had finished there would be considerable activity and shouting by the gun position officers of each troop putting their guns on line.

> Standing with their acks, some fifty yards in front of the guns, working their directors with the aid of wavering lamps – electric, they call out to each of their four guns in turn a reverse bearing in degrees and minutes so the gun-layer can set it on his dial sight and traverse his weapon left or right, until his sight is looking directly into the lighted lens of the director and he knows he is laid on the zero line.[19]

Despite the complexity of siting the guns the occupation of a gun position was a quick and a well-practised drill, usually taking little more than 10 minutes from the time the main body entered the new gun position for the guns to be ready to fire.

The guns could now fire at either programmed targets, as part of a fire plan, or at impromptu targets being 'ranged' in by an observer normally a FOO. In the latter case a clear and simple communications procedure between the observer, the battery and troop command posts and the guns themselves was required to ensure rapid and accurate fire. The first stage would be for the observer to decide the nature of the target (is it a troop, battery, or regimental target?); the ammunition required (including shell type, fuze and charge), the location of the target, which could be either a grid map reference (given as 'Map Reference 123456 height 250 feet' for example) or a switch from the Zero line and a range from the guns (e.g. 'Zero, 5 degrees, 4500'). The observer would then order the method of fire stating they should 'concentrate' so that all the shells converged precisely on his target or that they 'distribute' their fire, which increased the frontage or width of the falling shells. If the target is a minor one then this information would be sent directly back to the battery or troop command post. If it is a major

---

18 Ibid., p.55.
19 Ibid., p.59.

Figure 5.6
Lieutenant L W Spurr directing the fire of the 25-pounder guns of 4th Field Regiment Royal Canadian Artillery near Antwerp. (Lieut. Ken Bell, Library and Archives Canada, PA-145559)

target, perhaps a regimental 'Mike' target, then it would pass through the Royal Artillery regiment's HQ and the batteries would be tasked by the adjutant. If the target justified the use of more guns than the twenty-four 25-pounders the regiment possessed i.e. it is a divisional target (Uncle) or a Corps target (Victor) then it would be passed to the Royal Artillery staff at divisional HQ who would decide if the targets justified additional effort. The FOO would often send his information back in two packets, firstly the target and nature of the ammunition would be provided which would allow the ammunition to be prepared and the relevant guns 'warned off' for the task. The detailed target location itself could then be worked out by the observer and sent subsequently.

Whatever type of target this information would ultimately find its way to one or more battery or troop command posts tasked to deliver the fire. At the command post the target would be converted, on an artillery board, onto a bearing 'line' and distance 'range'. The battery command post would then produce the firing data required for the guns taking into account the muzzle velocity of the guns (based upon the propellant charge size and barrel wear), a standard weight for the type of shell, the air temperature, the barometric pressure and the strength of the wind. They would also take into account the temperature of the propellant which was measured regularly on the gun position itself. These calculations were aided by a plethora of graphs and range tables to factor in any deviations from standard conditions. In addition a 'Meteor' telegram would be received every two hours from the Royal Artillery survey regiment, which provided the necessary weather data in Normandy itself. Having made his calculations the Gun Position Officer would order specific fire control orders to the guns themselves through a local tannoy or intercom system or by shouting. A typical order from the Gun Position Officer to the crews of the guns could be:

HE,[20] 117,[21] Charge 3,[22] zero 346 degrees,[23] angle of sight 2 degrees,[24] right ranging[25] 7700,[26] fire.

On receiving the order the six man gun crew of a 25-pounder would spring into life. The No.1, a SNCO in charge of the gun crew, would call out the orders and supervise the process particularly the laying and loading of the gun. The No.3, or layer, seated on a wooden seat at the left of the gun would adjust the dial sights and ensure he was elevated and traversed correctly. The No. 2, who stood to the right of the gun, would open the breech using the breech lever. The No. 4 was the loader and would place the shell into the breech. The projectile would be rammed home by the No.2 to ensure that the driving band (a ductile strip of copper built into the shell) had engaged with the barrels rifling. Making sure the shell was rammed properly home was important for three reasons; firstly it would ensure that the rifling would spin the shell successfully in flight giving it added stability, secondly it would stop the shell falling back down the barrel, and finally it would prevent the propellant gases escaping forward of the shell whilst in the barrel, which would effect the shells muzzle velocity.

After the projectile has been rammed home the No.4 would place a brass cartridge case containing the propellant in the breech. The No.2 would then close the breech and on the command 'Fire!' by the No.1 the layer (the No.3) would fire the gun using the firing lever on the gun's left side. The second in command of the gun detachment (No.6) and the No.5 would be preparing the ammunition; this would include screwing on and setting the appropriate fuzes on the shells, as well as placing the small charge bags into the brass cartridge case. There were three charges that gave different muzzle velocities and therefore different potential ranges and these were all configured at the gun. These propellant charges came in three small cloth bags; for charge 1 the red bag was required, charge 2 meant that the white bag should be placed with the red bag into the cartridge and charge 3 meant the further addition of a blue bag. A small cap was placed over the top of the cartridge to stop the propellant catching fire from any embers still burning in the breech. The brass cartridge case used in the 25-pounder gun not only acted as a container for the propellant charge and the cartridge that initiated it, but also contained and prevented the expanding propellant gases from escaping backwards. Larger guns like the 5.5-inch did not have cartridge cases but used the breech itself to contain the expanding gases, this meant that the breech block was more complicated to open and close and that the bottom of the barrel would have to be swabbed with water between firing to extinguish any burning embers.

Having received the command from the No.1 the layer pulls the firing lever and a firing pin in the breech block strikes the base primer in the cartridge case. This initiates the cartridge tube firing pellets of gunpowder into the propellant. The propellant, which is a low explosive, burns and produces rapidly expanding gas at incredibly high pressures and speeds, this enormous energy causes the projectile to move forward and as the copper driving band engages the rifling in the

---

20 Type of shell; in this case a High Explosive Shell.

21 Fuze type; in this case No 117 a direct action fuze which functioned on hitting the ground. This was the standard fuze.

22 The size of propellant charge to be placed in the gun cartridge behind the shell. This determines the muzzle velocity of the shell and its range. In this case Charge 3 is being used which will give a range of 10,790 metres.

23 The angle of deviation from the zero line, which of course the gun is normally laid upon.

24 The elevation, which, in conjunction with the muzzle velocity, will determine how far the shell will go.

25 This means only two guns from the right section of the troop will open fire to allow the observer to correct or 'range' the target.

26 The range itself.

barrel the round begins to spin. Clearly this is all happening incredibly quickly and the massive acceleration forces are used to activate a switch in the fuze thus arming the shell for the first time. It also causes the barrel to recoil and then subsequently move back on its hydraulic recuperating gear, into its original position. At that point the layer can check his aim, the breech can be opened once more by the No.2 and the firing cycle repeated.

With the shell now spinning through the air the Command Post would inform the observer that a shot was on its way by saying 'shot over!'. The observer would then observe the fall of shot relative to his target. He would correct the gun's aim by giving directions in yards such as 'Right 50, add 200', these would then in turn be converted at the Command Post to a new angle of sight and adjustment to the zero line. The observer will keep bracketing the target until the shells are on the target and then order the necessary round of gunfire from each gun e.g. 'All 5 Rounds gunfire'. The reader will now see the benefits of 'programmed' fire as opposed to impromptu firing. Programmed fire allowed time for planning and meant that all the necessary calculations had been previously made and the fire could be effected so much quicker with the observer simply having to call in the recorded targets number – 'Target Mike 7' or 'DF 26'. It was frequent practise for any impromptu fire mission to be subsequently recorded as a target, effectively 'programming' it for future use. There were many variations to this technique and of course sometimes the observer would not be able to see the target and would be relaying information from an infantry or armoured officer. One popular technique used frequently in Normandy to maximise the surprise and shock of massed artillery fire on a target was to allocate a time for the shells to land together. Lieutenant Colonel Fanshawe explains:

> The expression TOT (Time On Target) became very popular, this meant the order would go out over the various wireless Nets through the LOs – 'Uncle Tgt, Uncle Tgt, Uncle Tgt, MR 1234, 1230hrs, Scale 4') The CPO and GPO worked out the line, Range, Angle of Sight, added the appropriate Meteor, looked up the time of flight, which was taken off 1230 hours and fired 4 rounds a minute for 5 minutes. Very simple and about 5-10 tons of old iron would drop within 100 yards of the target in the space of about 15-30 seconds, in some circumstances less.[27]

This was an important technique because the greatest damage by shellfire is usually achieved in the first minute or so of it landing on an enemy position. Speed was always a fixation for the gunners and the whole process of calling down fire could be very rapid indeed, as George Blackburn records when he brought down shellfire against a suspected enemy OP in a derelict tank:

> You establish as quickly as possible the map reference of that damned tank, which is relatively easy, it being on the side of the hill in direct line with the road that bends right just before reaching it. You call over the wall to Elder [His OP assistant], now jammed in a very small trench with the remote control he's managed to drag over here, 'Able Troop target – map reference 985638 – right ranging – fire!' All you want is to see one round. If it lands anywhere close to that damned tank you'll go into 'fire for effect' maybe five rounds gunfire…Estimating the range from gun to target at about 4,200yds, you figure the shell will take about eight seconds to come up from the gun when it does fire.[28] And when at last you hear Elder calling out the

---

27 Memoirs of Maj Gen G D Fanshawe 1943-45, Royal Artillery Institution archives MD 1661.
28 At Charge 3 a 25-pounder shell, leaving the muzzle at 1,460 feet (or 488 yards) per second takes 2.05 seconds to travel 1,000 yards.

Figure 5.7 25-pounder guns and their 'Quad' tractors advancing towards Vire, 2 August. (Imperial War Museum B8478)

message he's received from the guns its sounds like 'Shot – four thousand.' Meaning of course the range at which the shot was fired.

You start counting to yourself 'Hippopotamus one, hippopotamus two, hippopotamus three…' before you reach seven there's a sizzling overhead, and before you can get your glasses up, WHAM, there it is an orange flash in the middle of a violent puff of rolling smoke very close to the tank. As you do a running vault over the wall, you call to Elder –'Five rounds gunfire – fire!' Kneeling down just inside the wall, waiting, it feels so safe and secure you decide there's no way you're going to go out there again. Somehow they let you get away with it once but luck like that can't last…But when you hear the guns thumping, you've got to see those shells land and the only way is to jump back onto the road, You get down on one knee and get the tank in your glasses just in time to see the shells bursting all around it. No correction is needed – in fact you almost imagine a couple of rounds hit it… satisfied you take the wall in a running leap and join Elder in his cramped trench.[29]

Whether the gun crew were delivering programmed or impromptu fire missions the work at the guns was often physically very demanding:

Serviced by its entire crew it blasts away at unseen targets on the ridge across the river. Stripped to the waist, the gunners haul and carry shells removing safety caps, adjusting charges, loading and firing them like robots – not even looking up when a big hostile shell lands directly in front of the troop with a horrendous roar, sending up a great black spout of steamy mud and smoke.

29 Blackburn, George, *The Guns of Normandy* (London: Constable, 1998), pp.114-15.

Figure 5.8
Two Canadian Gunners
hump ammunition
around a gun position,
20 June. (Lieut. Donald
I. Grant, Library and
Archives Canada,
PA-169262)

The gun layer, hunched over on his seat, his wet back glistening with the falling rain, a soggy cigarette hanging from the corner of his mouth, never takes his eye far from the rubber eyepiece on the dial sight, as he maintains a constant rhythm, his deft hands constantly touching gear wheels ensuring the lay remains on the aiming point, and pulling the firing lever each time he hears the breech block close.[30]

In some cases the six man gun crew of a 25-pounder would be reduced to a three-man crew to allow a degree of rest. This caused some issues in that there was a greater risk of errors creeping in as the supervising and checking role of the No.1 was reduced. Movement of ammunition was an equally tiring activity around the gun position. The ammunition for 25-pounders was delivered with the standard No.117 fuze already fitted and packed in steel boxes of either 2 or 4. The brass cartridges were placed in steel boxes of eight each individually packed in its own waterproof wrapping with spare primers being provided. There were 224 rounds of this ammunition available in the ammunition trailers which accompanied each towed gun, the pair being pulled by the gun tractors or 'Quads'. Any further ammunition would have to come from the Royal Army Service Corps Ammunition Troop who would dump the ammunition at the gun positions where it would be dug in. George Blackburn describes the physical demands of managing this ammunition:

Each six-man gun crew slogging back and forth through the mud and dark with 138 boxes of shells and 69 boxes of propellant charges carries more than ten tons 300 yards. By now when weary gunners try and pick up a box of shells it feels as though it is anchored to the earth, and the very awkward twisting lifts required to lower them into the pits (and haul them out again when later they are needed) puts a wicked strain on back muscles aching for sleep.[31]

---

30 Ibid., p.208.
31 Ibid., p.202.

This method of operation was standard across gun regiments and though the numbers, calibres and sizes of guns and gun crews[32] varied between field, medium and heavy regiments, the procedures, planning and pattern of life was broadly similar whichever gun was being served.

It is important to briefly mention the Royal Artillery's role in the provision of naval gunfire support. This large calibre indirect fire played a key role in the Normandy campaign and though it was unable to provide fire as the advance moved significantly inland it was in a position to support most of the key offensives. It also continued to have an important role during the clearing of the Channel ports providing fire support during the seizure of Le Havre by 49th West Riding Division and 51st Highland Division (10-12 September) for instance. The special characteristics of naval guns, not least their flat trajectory which meant a greater probable error of range, required a specialist unit to direct and adjust their fire. These were Combined Operations Bombardment Units. In principle one unit supported a Corps with the unit CO being the Chief Bombardment Liaison Officer with the Naval Task Force. There were junior Bombardment Liaison Officers on the bombarding ships too, advising them on military matters and interpreting Army requests for fire. Each Combined Operation Bombardment Unit troop was able to generate seven Forward Observers Bombardment (FOB) teams, who were in direct contact with their allocated ship and the Bombardment Liasion Officer on it. Alex Cameron explains:

> My boys and I moved to join the Canadians. The colonel gave me a great welcome and immediately took me out of his barn to point out a Church Tower 400 yards away which he wanted me to demolish as it was a German observation post. I had to tell him that when firing 14-inch shells, which I knew were the armament of the ship to which I was 'attached', our orders were to keep at least 1,000 yards away. You can imagine what he said – I took on the target, never having before heard a 14-inch shell in the air, after the CO agreed to tell all his men to keep their heads down. In those days when the shell was five seconds away from its landing point the ship sent by morse the signal 'SSS' (Splash, Splash, Splash) this gave the observer time to get his field glasses up to his eyes to observe the shell burst and make any corrections to ensure if possible that the next round hit the target. In this particular case no correction was required, the navy had proved their undoubted ability, the church tower came tumbling down.[33]

The Naval bombardment system allowed the Royal Navy's considerable firepower to be used in a timely and effective manner. This was a huge advantage given that a destroyer's firepower was equivalent to a field regiment and a cruiser's the equivalent of a medium regiment. The Royal Navy was able to deliver such a large amount of firepower because firstly the weight of the shell was much larger, a battleship's 14-inch gun could fire a shell weighing 2,000lbs seventeen miles inland, but also because the mechanical loading methods in the ship meant that a higher rate of fire could be achieved.

Effective though the Royal Artillery's system of ground based forward observers was, they were clearly limited by the field of view determined by the terrain itself. This meant that enemy targets in significant depth would not be visible to them. Whilst intelligence sources such as air photo reconnaissance and signals intercept would play their part in uncovering these targets, the Royal Artillery had their own system of target acquisition which was to prove useful not just for attacking enemy positions in depth but also for countering the effect of artillery and mortar fire on British positions. Given that 70% of the British casualties in Normandy were caused by mortar

---

32 As an example the 5.5 Inch guns and the 7.2 Inch guns both had a crew of 10.

33 Cameron, I, 'Memoirs of a Fishermans Son', Chapter 13 – http://igcdadsmemoirs.blogspot.com/.

Figure 5.9 An Auster Air Observation Post. (Crown Copyright Air Historical Branch)

fire the requirement for effective counter mortar fire was a particularly pressing issue. Of the target acquisition capabilities available to the British in Normandy perhaps the most successful was the Air Observation Post (Air OP).

The primary role of the Air OP was to control artillery with the pilot/observer usually acquiring his own targets. The Air OP in Normandy was equipped with the Taylorcraft Auster MK IV light aeroplane, this hardy aircraft required only a short, basic airfield, minimal maintenance and its two man gunner crew of pilot and observer were capable of observing and directing all types of fire. The Auster squadrons, of 16 aircraft each, were theoretically part of 2nd Tactical Air Force, but were allocated on the basis of one squadron to each Army Corps and the RAF exercised little say in their operational use. The Auster's ability to land almost anywhere meant siting an Advanced Landing Ground was simply a process of finding a suitably large field. Captain Ian Neilson, 652 Squadron landed on D-Day and describes the process:

> I set out on my James 125cc two stroke motorcycle in the usual cloud of blue smoke to reconnoitre the three possible Advanced Landing Grounds (ALGs) which we had selected in advance from the vertical air photographic cover. I went up the road to the south through St Aubin D'Arquenay and found the first area – off to the east of the road leading down to the River Orne and the 'Pegasus' Bridge. It was littered with wrecked gliders, parachutes and anti-landing poles. It soon became obvious that even if we cleared suitable lanes for our aircraft, the whole place was in full view of the opposition to the east across the Orne valley. There was also very little tree cover and that was on the west side near St Aubin…I went off in a north-westerly direction towards field No. 2… The second field was alongside and to the north of the lateral road running eastwards from Douvre. In addition to a number of large trees on its eastern side, it also turned out to be a minefield. Having rapidly decided that this was not acceptable, I went south – westwards toward Perier and the village and farm of Plumetot. Our third choice was a large area – in fact, three fields to the east of the farm and its orchards, with large trees on the south. Apart from various obstacles such as anti-landing poles, electric pylons, a large concrete water tank and quite a lot of wire fences, it seemed

acceptable. The surface was smooth and there were no dead animals. There was good cover for many vehicles. Having returned to collect the ground party, it now being breakfast time on D plus 1, we demolished all that was required at Plumetot and that evening were 'operational'. A radio message to Captain Linton at 3 Div enabled him to get a message through to the Sqn who were by now at Selsey Bill. At 0815 hrs on D plus 2 the first five of 652 Sqn's 16 Auster IV aircraft arrived to be followed during the next few days by the remainder.[34]

The Austers normally flew at a very low height and over friendly forces; they were in fact forbidden to fly within 2000 yards of a known enemy position or above 600 feet. But this modest height coupled with the agility of their aircraft allowed them to focus deep into the enemy's depth. One Auster observer described the technique used:

> The aeroplane skimmed the trees and the guns fired. As they did so the pilot pulled up into a steep climb, arriving at the top of it as the shells fell on their distant target. A few seconds of steady flight to observe and transmit the next fire order, and a swift swoop down to tree-top level whilst the guns were re-layed and fired. Here was a sector where leisurely flying at 1,000 feet was 'not on'.[35]

One might have expected the casualty rates amongst these Auster aircraft to have been high, but their low profile meant they were hard to detect and their slow speed and manoeuvrability meant they were hard to shoot down too:

> During the afternoon there was an amusing incident for us as spectators when an Auster artillery spotter plane was attacked by a Focke-Wulf 190. At least, the Focke Wulf tried to shoot down the little plane. The German pilot hurtled towards the Auster, which simply flew round a large elm tree and back along the other side of the hedge. Flying round in as tight a circle as he could manage, the German again came for the Auster, but the latter came down almost to grass level and hopped over the hedge and round another tree. The slow speed of the Auster was greatly to its advantage, and after a few more fruitless passes the German decided he had been around for too long and beat it for home.[36]

To improve the aircraft's survivability a protection plan was frequently created, giving each Air OP flight a 'refuge' strip close to its allotted zone with a troop of 40mm Bofors Light anti-aircraft and Local Warning radar and ground observers.[37] In many cases the Air OP aircraft were most vulnerable when at their Advanced Landing Ground which in Normandy were inevitably very close to the enemy front line and well within artillery range. As a result many squadrons took the precaution of borrowing a bulldozer to excavate pits down which the aircraft was run. The pits would be deep enough for the wings to be almost at ground level, which helped to minimise damage from shell splinters during enemy artillery fire. Captain Ian Neilson describes the pattern of life for the Air OPs.

34 Neilson, Captain Ian, 'Normandy 1944: The Role Of the Air Observation Post', Royal Artillery Institution archives MD 2878.

35 Parham, Maj Gen H & Belfield, E, *Unarmed into Battle: The Story of the Air Observation Post* (Winchester: Warren & Son, 1956), p.77.

36 Hammerton, Ian, *Achtung! Minen!* (Lewes: The Book Guild, 1991), p.95.

37 Routledge, Brigadier N W, *History of the Royal Regiment of Artillery: Anti Aircraft Artillery* (London: Brassey's, 1995), p.317.

Figure 5.10 An Auster Mk IV AOP aircraft of 652 Squadron flies over a 3rd British Division 25-pounder field gun at Cresserons, 6 July. (Imperial War Museum B6626)

In Normandy our sorties were usually of about 20-30 minutes duration depending upon the fire task and the amount of enemy fighter interference. We were enormously impressed by the weight of fire and accuracy of the bombarding ships of the Navy. Our radio links with the Bombardment Liaison Officers on board the bombarding ships and with all the Field and Medium Regiments worked well – in spite of having to twiddle knobs: there were in those days no automatic crystal controls and push buttons. In addition to the three 25-pounder Field Regiments of 3 Div, we had the Medium Regiments of 5 AGRA and the Naval Guns of HMS *Rodney*, *Warspite*, *Belfast*, *Diadem*, *Mauritius* and the 15-inch guns of the Monitor HMS *Roberts*.

The height of our sorties depended on the nature of the target, the time of day and likelihood of FW 190 interference. We carried out much counter-battery registration and harassing fire – as well as full Regimental; (Mike) and Divisional (Uncle) targets – even the very occasional Corps (Victor) target. One had always to be careful to avoid our own shells and on one occasion I observed a large shell – clearly a 5.5-inch – passing onwards and upwards beneath my left wing.[38]

During the period D+2 to 30 June, 652 Air OP Squadron would fly 856 sorties and conduct 458 shoots. Their effectiveness was highlighted by 10th SS Panzer Division in their 'Lessons from the Normandy Front':

But the greatest nuisance of all are the slow-flying artillery spotters which work with utter calmness over our positions, just out of reach, and direct artillery on our forward positions.

---

38 Neilson, Captain Ian, *Normandy 1944: The Role Of the Air Observation Post*, Royal Artillery Institution archives MD 2878.

In addition to its attached Air OP squadrons each corps had a dedicated survey regiment. The batteries within the regiment were affiliated to each of the corps' divisions giving them a troop for sound-ranging, a troop for flash spotting and a survey troop which we have seen assisted the regiments in accurately mapping their own guns locations.

The Flash Spotting Troop consisted of four flash-spotting posts and a plotting centre. The task of the post was to observe German gun and mortar muzzle flashes or indirect sky flashes using a tripod mounted binocular known as the 'Instrument, Flash Spotting No.4'. These bearings would be sent back to the plotting centre and triangulated with the bearings from the three other posts who had hopefully witnessed the same 'flash'. The task was complicated by the German use of flashless propellant and the difficulty for the plotting centre to ascertain that all the posts were reporting on the same flash at exactly the same time.

The Sound Ranging Troop located German artillery and mortars by measuring the sound waves as they hit a series of deployed microphones. Each troop deployed two 'Advanced Posts', with its associated microphones, as well as a Sound Ranging Command Post; the latter performing as a recording and computing centre. When activated the microphones used electrical pens to plot a trace line of the sound waves on a roll of sensitive paper. The microphones could pick up three types of sound waves; the 'gun-wave'; the actual noise of the gun firing; the 'shell-wave'; the noise of the shell in flight and the 'burst-wave' the noise of the shell bursting. The microphones were also sufficiently sophisticated not only to detect the point of origin of the shell but also its calibre. There were limitations though, firstly the microphones could quite easily get swamped by the perpetually high levels of surrounding noise; a particular problem given the very intense fighting in Normandy. Secondly it was impractical to keep the microphones permanently activated and therefore the Advanced Post was deployed at least 800 metres in front of the line of microphones to switch the recorder in the Sound Ranging CP on and off. Perhaps most significantly the sound ranging equipment initially deployed to Normandy could not detect the German 81mm mortar; arguably the most troublesome weapon the British were encountering. It would take the deployment of the more sensitive '4-pen' sound recorder in July before this gap in capability was closed.

The British did note during the campaign that the GL Mark III radar (An Anti-Aircraft Radar) was picking up mortar trajectories at 7,000 yards and Nebelwerfer trajectories at 11,000 yards. Though field trials during the Norman summer met with mixed success a decision was made to establish two radar batteries (1st Canadian Radar and 100 British Radar Battery) with specific counter mortar roles, these were eventually deployed in January 1945.

All target acquisition data was sent to the Counter Battery Officers at corps and divisional HQs. They would collate this intelligence with other sources to produce constantly evolving Hostile Battery Lists which would be integrated into Fire Plans where appropriate. The British counter battery efforts became more effective as the battle of Normandy evolved; this was sometimes borne out by PW interrogation reports that indicated that as soon as the German crews fired 5 or 6 rounds from their mortars they would immediately dive into the nearest slit trench.

As well as the threat from German artillery and mortars the D-Day planners also recognised the danger German air attack posed to the landings and subsequent build-up. Senior commanders insisted that full Anti-Aircraft (AA) cover was integrated into their plans. This AA support would be coordinated with the RAF who had already caused significant losses amongst the Luftwaffe in France and were confident in their ability to maintain air superiority during the day, though less assured of their ability to cope with night attacks or low-level intruders. The responsibility for ground based Air Defence fire rested with the Royal Artillery who, with the 21st Army Group planners, prioritised the areas to be protected by AA. These included the beaches, the Mulberry harbour and Port-en-Bessin, airfields, the bridges over the River Orne and Caen canal and finally the beach maintenance area's dumps. As 21st Army Group's strength grew in Normandy the close protection of the forward troops would also become a high priority together with key centres of communication particularly Caen and Bayeux.[39]

The control of the AA organisation within 21st Army Group rested with GHQ AA troops who advised on AA matters and commanded the various AA brigades not assigned to the Army commanders. AA brigades and units assigned to an Army were often allocated to a Corps and commanded by the Corps Commander Royal Artillery, the same individual responsible for 'normal' artillery. A division's AA capability rested with its integral light anti-aircraft regiment of 40mm Bofors. As well as supporting the various corps and divisions there were a number of separate 'defended areas' which came under the responsibility of an Anti-Aircraft Commander. As one example the 'Mulberry' harbour had 30 x 40mm AA guns on barges, 4 x 40mm guns on the block ships, 36 x 20mm guns on the piers and 34 x 40mm guns on the various concrete caissons. These were all controlled by a HQ Command ship which was itself armed with 16 x 40mm guns and acted as the seaborne control for early-warning raid information and any restrictions on firing. These restrictions on firing were imposed by the RAF Sector and Group HQs in Normandy and were designed to allow the fighter aircraft as much of a free hand as possible and prevent AA guns firing on friendly aircraft.

Information on these restrictions would be passed to the AA gun sites through the Tactical Air Command's sector operations rooms and ground control centres, they in turn would have received information on inbound enemy aircraft from the many mobile radars that were deployed in Normandy. This information would pass through an AA operations room before reaching the gun site.

The Royal Artillery had two types of AA regiment in Normandy. Heavy Anti-Aircraft (HAA) regiments were equipped with 24 x 3.7-inch guns and were supported by two radars. Firstly a tracking or 'fire direction' radar (No II mark 3 tracking radar) and secondly a tactical radar, (either a GLII or one of the newer No.4 Mark III) which gave longer range information and was used to steer the fire direction radar. The second type of AA regiment was the light anti-aircraft (LAA) regiment, which were normally equipped with three batteries of 40mm guns with 18 guns in each battery.[40] The Bofors gun was a reliable and effective gun operated by a crew of seven. The No. 2, seated on the left side of the breech, propelled the gun through a 360-degree traverse whilst the No. 3, seated on the right side of the breech, elevated the gun. Between them the No. 4 loaded the four-round clips of 40mm ammunition into the auto-loader which fed the breech, he also fired the gun by depressing a foot pedal. The gun fired 2lb shells with a velocity of 2700 feet per second that were effective up to a height of 5,000 feet. They were fitted with direct action fuzes to detonate on impact, but if the shell failed to hit a target the tracer burnt through and detonated the shell in the air which prevented it from falling to earth and injuring men on the ground.

The No.1, a sergeant, was in command of the gun and its crew and he stood directly behind the gun and gave the order to fire. He followed the enemy aircraft through sights of rings and radial bars to assist the layers in applying the necessary range and approach angle to the target. Sometimes he would direct the gun to engage an individual aircraft, on other occasions he would fire into a group to break up a formation; a rope was sometimes tied to the ankle of the No.4 which was held by the sergeant who would pull his foot off the firing pedal when he wanted him to stop. No.5 and No.6 would prepare and pass loaded ammunition clips to No. 4 under the watchful eye of a Lance Bombardier (No. 7).

---

39 Routledge, Brigadier N W, *History of the Royal Regiment of Artillery: Anti Aircraft Artillery*, (London: Brassey's, 1994), p.302.

40 Ibid., p.306.

The gun crew had to be constantly vigilant. A FW190 could fly at 400mph and it was quite possible that a low level aircraft would be undetected by the radar warning system and no warning received at the gun position. Consequently active guns would be permanently manned in daylight by a team of three with the remainder of the gun crew rushing to assistance when an action started. Gunner Jim Holder-Vale, 121st LAA Regiment, describes what it was like to be in action against German aircraft around the Caen canal bridges:

Early on D+1 the bridges were attacked by a number of fighter-bombers, all guns opened fire immediately; they would have been spotted by the gun crews. When you are sitting on the gun there is little doubt that you know where your shells are going, as they are all tracer, and you would be well aware if your shells hit your target. Our gunners used to their advantage an optical illusion called a 'line of sight'; when the shells were on a collision course with the target you get an illusion that the red line of tracer is entering one end of the plane and emerging from the other, so the gun would be switched to automatic firing and the foot held down on the pedal. This would increase the rate of firing and the numbers of shells hitting the target say 2-3 or more, this decreases the chance of plane or pilot surviving. These attacks continued for five days during which time the gunners shot down 17 confirmed 'category one hits'. We had obtained some small swastika transfers which the gun crews affixed to their gun for each plane destroyed, they looked impressive.[41]

The Royal Artillery also had a number of searchlight regiments equipped with three batteries of 24 searchlights, these were normally the 150cm projector fitted with a No.2 Mark VI SLC radar to focus it. These regiments were used to support nightfighter operations but composite units were also formed of LAA and Searchlight batteries and used to provide 'canopy' defence for key areas such as airfields. By D+6 a pattern had emerged in the Luftwaffe's tactics, during daylight fighters and fighter-bombers would attack flying low, using cloud cover and approaches screened by ground. At night, raiding was being conducted by Ju 88 bombers appearing in numbers up to 30 and using jamming techniques including the dropping of small strips of metal to disrupt radar. HAA methods were conventional, searchlights were useful and barrages prepared over key points, by 4 July GHQ AA troops had claimed that their units had shot down 84 aircraft. The congested beachhead meant that Luftwaffe night time missions were bound to cause some damage, though never significant enough to hinder the build-up meaningfully.

Luftwaffe ineffectiveness meant that the AA units could be used for other tasks. As we have seen already the AA GL Mark III radar began to be used to track mortars and at the Royal Navy's request the same equipment was used to observe German aircraft dropping sea mines in the approaches to the Mulberry harbour and Port-en-Bessin. These cliff top radar sites were able to give naval forces the bearing and range of where the mine was released assisting the Navy's mine-sweepers dramatically. Searchlights were also used as 'movement light' or 'artificial moonlight', a technique where they 'bounced' their illuminating beams off a cloud base and onto a particular piece of ground. It was seen as particularly useful during offensive operations where the assaulting force could use the cover of darkness for its approach and then have increased light levels (what one might recognise as twilight) for the action on the position itself. As one example movement light played an important role in ensuring safe passage through gaps in minefields during the assault on Le Havre.

The HAA 3.7-inch guns were also sometimes used in the indirect role against ground targets. During Operation TOTALIZE 109th HAA regiment fired a total of 3,600 rounds mainly in a

---

41 Searching for Gunner Whitaker, Royal Artillery Institution archives RAI A/C 2005.08.04.

Figure 5.11 A 40mm Bofors anti-aircraft gun near an advanced landing ground in Normandy.
(Crown Copyright Air Historical Branch)

counter battery role. The LAA 40mm Bofors gun was also often in demand, its automatic 40mm cannon could give useful close range fire to assist infantry working from cover to cover and its sensitive percussion fuze gave an air burst effect amongst the trees, it was also used for bunker busting.[42] However the exposed Bofors guns were vulnerable to any German reaction and could not afford to loiter for too long near the frontline.

Despite these useful secondary roles the Luftwaffe's diminishing strength meant that by the end of the Normandy campaign, the size and manpower demands of the AA system were seen as excessive. The acute crisis in infantry manpower meant that many soldiers in AA regiments were compulsorily transferred into the infantry during the campaign.

21st Army Group capitalised upon the Royal Artillery's considerable strengths particularly their ability to mass and concentrate fire with speed and flexibility. Respect for the gunner's expertise was universally high, but perhaps appreciated most by the infantry. Lieutenant Sydney Jary commented: 'I doubt if any experienced infantry officer would deny that the Royal Artillery, during the Second World War, were the most professionally competent people in the British Army.[43]

This gratitude and admiration undeniably stemmed partly from a healthy respect for the efficiency and professionalism of the gunners, but there was another selfless quality that was admired by the frontline arms too. This letter from the wounded battery commander of 477 Battery to the widow of Captain Paul Cash, one of the FOOs, touches upon these other strengths:

---

42   Routledge, Brigadier N W, *History of the Royal Regiment of Artillery: Anti Aircraft Artillery* (London: Brassey's, 1995), p.317.

43   Jary, Sydney, *18 Platoon* (Winchester: The Rifles, 2009), p.60.

Someley Officers Convalescent Hospital
Ringwood
Hampshire
9 August 1944

Moira my dear,

I have been meaning to write to you for a long time but could not get hold of your address. Now I have heard the tragic news of Paul's death is confirmed. Nothing I can say can alleviate the awful loss you have suffered. I also have lost a very dear and loyal friend. I know no details of Paul's death but can tell you something of the action on July 10 in which Paul was slightly wounded. During an attack by the 7th Hampshires on the village of Maltot on the Orne we got into a very sticky place. Paul was in a tank but had to abandon this when things became too hot. My scout car was knocked out by a 88mm. Paul Atkins was wounded and had to be left behind when the infantry withdrew.[44] Thus Paul, Blinks [Lt Joseph Blincow] and I had ourselves with only two wireless sets. We were stuck in a ditch on the outskirts of the village with Colonel Ray and the remains of his Battalion HQ and one Company. The Boche were counterattacking from both sides, we therefore put shellfire on three sides of us and brought it in as close as we dared. Paul and I did this between us – he observing and I on the wireless – until I was wounded in the hand. I then left him to carry on the job as we seemed to have beaten off the enemy. I then spent the rest of the day commanding and encouraging part of the defences, I was again slightly wounded in the leg and later in the arm. By this time things were very serious and none of us expected to get out alive. The Boche were sweeping our position with machine gun fire and shot up both our carriers and wireless sets with 88mm. Paul got the blast from one of these in his mouth which was badly swollen but was otherwise all right.

Another Battalion arrived to relieve us in the nick of time and we collected our party together to withdraw as we could do nothing further without communications. At this time Blinks went up to show the tank commander where an 88mm was shooting from. However the gun fired at that moment and blew up the tank and poor old Blincow. Paul and I found our way back to Brigade HQ where we told our story to the CRA and colonel, we then went to a dressing station from which Paul returned to take command of the Battery while I was evacuated. That was the last I saw of Paul. I have since had no word from anyone on the other side although I have written begging for news. During that Battle Paul was magnificent although I know he realised as I did that it would be a miracle if we survived. I had a word with the CRA about him when I was at Brigade HQ.

It breaks my heart to think of your happy life being broken like this and of young Bill[45] growing up without Paul to help him. Is there any way in which I can help you now or in the future. I shall be at the depot waiting to go back from the 21st onwards. I wonder If I could see you – if you would like to hear more from me. Anyway please do not hesitate if there is anyway in which Pam and I can help. Please keep in touch with us until this beastliness is over, as I think it soon will be and we may then be able to be of some assistance. God bless you my dear.
Hubert

---

44 He was later recorded as being killed during this action.

45 'Young Bill' grew up to become the Rt Hon Bill Cash MP; he has kindly allowed this letter, which rests in the Imperial War Museum archives, to be published.

The history of the 7th Hampshires recalls that 'Captain Paul Cash, a young artillery FOO, was instrumental in saving the reverse at Maltot from being catastrophic.' Capt Paul Cash was killed on 12 July by an airburst shell, his soldiers buried him at a farm near Château de Fontaine and he was subsequently re-interred at St Manvieu cemetery near Cheux alongside Gunner Clifford Carpendale a fellow member of the 477 Battery OP Party killed during the same action. The gunner's professionalism and efficiency were undoubtedly important in establishing a high reputation for the Royal Artillery but the courage and self-sacrifice of gunners like the 477 Battery OP party created a reputation for reliability and dependability. This formed the basis of a deep reservoir of trust between the gunners and their affiliated infantry and armoured units. Few other arms have come close to matching it.

Figure 5.12 A 5.5-inch gun firing at night during an offensive in the Odon valley near Évrecy, 16 July. (Imperial War Museum B7413)

6

'By Air to Battle' – Air Power and Support

It is abundantly clear that all modern land operations are combined Army/Air operations. Technical developments in the air weapon continue apace and their possibilities are bounded only by the imagination. It follows that land operations are likely to be influenced more and more by air action.

Field Marshal Montgomery October 1945[1]

General Montgomery understood that the RAF's contribution would be critical to the success of the Normandy land battle and air support would have to form an intimate part of 21st Army Group's operations. But as well as the close air support, air interdiction, air superiority and reconnaissance tasks, air power's contribution also included the projection of a powerful land force behind enemy lines. The important role played by airmen in establishing the 6th Airborne Division in Normandy, as well as the actions of the airborne soldiers themselves would be an important element of D-Day's success and delivered a number of advantages for the British as they subsequently prosecuted the Normandy campaign.

The 6th Airborne Division performed a critical flank protection mission by occupying the high ground which separated the River Orne from its neighbour, the River Dives, six miles to the east. Within this overall flank protection role there were a number of specific tasks that the division had to accomplish. These included capturing the bridges over the River Orne and Caen Canal at Bénouville, neutralising a coastal defence battery at Merville, destroying a number of bridges over the River Dives (which we saw Major Roseveare's team accomplish in Chapter 4) and finally occupying an area of ground that would protect the invasion area from German attacks emanating from Le Havre and Rouen to the east. Major General Richard Gale, commander 6th Airborne Division, describes the overall plan:

> The bridges at Bénouville were to be seized by a glider coup de main, consisting of three gliders at each bridge carrying in all a company of infantry found from the 52nd (Oxford and Buckinghamshire Light Infantry) under the command of Major R.J. Howard. Brigadier Noel Poett's 5th Parachute Brigade was to take over from Howard as soon as they had landed and then to defend the whole area until the 3rd Division arrived at the bridges. Thereafter they were to secure a firm base at Ranville and Hérouvillette.
>
> The bridges over the River Dives were to be tackled by Brigadier James Hill's 3rd Parachute Brigade and one battalion was to capture and silence the coast defence battery which was

---

1   Montgomery, Field Marshal B L, 'Some Notes on the use of Air Power In support of Land Operations', HQ BAOR, October 1945, p.29. Held in Joint Doctrine and Concepts Centre, Shrivenham.

Figure 6.1 Hawker Typhoon Ibs of 198 Squadron taxi out for a sortie from their dispersal
at B10 Plumetot, July. (Crown Copyright Air Historical Branch)

located at Merville. Thereafter this brigade was to hold the high ground forming the water-
shed between the rivers Orne and Dives.

So much for the initial assault. No more than these two brigades could be carried in one lift
and so I had to wait for my glider-borne or airlanding brigade until the afternoon of D-Day.
Even then I could only get two battalions, for the third, the 12th Devons, had to be brought
in by sea. On its arrival I planned to use the 6th Air-Landing Brigade, commanded by the
Honourable Hugh Kindersley, to thicken up the defence of Ranville and Herouvilette and to
seize and hold the village of Longueval on the River Orne.[2]

The task of flying in the Division's 6,000 parachutists, towing the Army's 280 gliders and dropping 20,000 equipment containers would fall to the RAF's 38 and 46 Groups and would come under
the overall operation name of TONGA. Operation TONGA was divided into three separate phases.
Phase One took advantage of the tactical surprise airborne operations can achieve, by landing a small
team of six gliders, each carrying a Coup de Main party, at Landing Zones X and Y to seize the
bridges at Bénouville. These bridges needed to be captured intact in order to maintain a secure route
between the rest of 6th Airborne Division and the invasion forces landing west of the River Orne and
Caen canal. The Horsa gliders were the main glider used by the British on D-Day, it was just over 20
metres long and made of a plywood skin over a wooden frame. The glider could carry 31.5 tonnes, a
load which could include vehicles, trailers and light guns or simply 29 soldiers who would sit in a set
of two rows of wooden seats that ran along the sides of aircraft. The inside of the glider looked like
a smaller version of a London underground train, the floor of the Horsa was corrugated to prevent
slipping and there were two small sliding door exits for the soldiers to disembark through. One was
at the port side near the glider's nose and the other to the rear of the aircraft on the starboard side.

The Horsa had two pilots who sat side by side; the controls were similar to a normal aircraft's
with the obvious exception that there were no throttles or engine controls. Perhaps the most
important fixture was the tow-rope release handle which allowed the pilot to disengage from the

---

2   Gale, Gen Sir Richard, *Call to Arms* (London: Hutchinson, 1968), p.137.

Figure 6.2 A 6-pounder anti-tank gun is manhandled onto a Horsa glider at an airfield in England, 6 June. (Crown Copyright Air Historical Branch)

tug when he wished to land. There was a duplicate handle in the tug itself should they need to cut the tow for various reasons. In addition a 'Cable Angle Indicator' highlighted what was termed the 'angle of dangle'. The instrument effectively allowed the glider pilot to fly at night or in periods of low visibility either slightly above the tug (known as 'high tow') or slightly below it (known as 'low tow'), flying directly behind the tug was not an option as the slipstream would cause the glider to shake violently and the tow-rope to snap. The tow-rope was attached to the Horsa's wings at two points and carried a telephone cable which allowed the glider pilots to communicate with the tug aircraft – normally a Halifax, Stirling or Albermale bomber, but a Dakota was sometimes also used. The Horsa glider had enormous flaps which allowed it to dive steeply after casting off and brought it in to land quickly, with a landing speed as low as 70 mph. A set of undercarriage was provided, but these would often break off on rough Landing Zones. British gliders were not piloted by the RAF, but by personnel from the Army's Glider Pilot Regiment. These pilots were all SNCOs who would fly the gliders during the airborne operation and then subsequently operate as soldiers on the ground.

In Phase One of Operation TONGA the Bénouville bridge gliders would be towed by Halifax aircraft across the channel disengaging over the coast at 7,000 feet. This deliberate decision to cast off further away than normally the case would ensure a silent approach that would prevent the enemy from detonating the bridges. Flying in darkness over unfamiliar enemy territory to land first time at a tiny unmarked, unilluminated point next to a bridge, called for superb flying qualities. That the pilots did so using nothing more sophisticated than stopwatch and compass methods is astonishing. Private Denis Edwards of 2nd Oxfordshire and Buckinghamshire Light Infantry was one of the soldiers aboard the very first glider (piloted by Staff Sergeants Jim Wallwork[3] and

---

3   Staff Sergeant James Harley Wallwork was awarded a DFM. A hugely experienced glider pilot, as well as Op TONGA he flew operations at Sicily, Arnhem and during the crossing of the Rhine.

John Ainsworth) to land in Normandy at the bridge over the Caen canal at Bénouville. He recalls their dramatic arrival:

> From a height of some six thousand feet we headed downwards at an ever increasing speed until we were within a thousand feet of the ground, then levelled out and glided more slowly downwards to make two sweeping right-hand turns before the final approach and run-in to the selected landing zone.
>
> With our bodies taut, weapons gripped tightly, the senior pilot yelled 'Link arms' and we knew that at any moment we would touch down. The time was now 0015 hours. We all held tight and braced ourselves for the landing. For about forty or fifty yards we bumped forwards, bouncing in our wooden seats as the craft lost contact with the ground and came down again with another bump, a tug, a jerk and, for a few moments at least, it seemed as if we were in for a smooth landing.
>
> As the thought flashed through my mind, the darkness suddenly filled with a stream of sparks as the underskids probably hit some stony ground. There was a sound like a giant sheet of cloth being ripped apart, then a God-almighty crash like a clap of thunder and my body seemed to be moving in different directions at the same time. The glider came to a juddering halt and I found myself at an uneven angle and peering into a blue-greyish haze. From somewhere outside tracer-like streams of multi-coloured light zoomed towards me.
>
> The noise ceased and was replaced with an ominous silence. Nothing and no-one moved. God help me we must be all dead, I thought. People began to stir in the gliders shattered interior. The door of the glider had been right beside my seat, but now all there was left was a mass of twisted wood and fabric and we had to smash our way out.
>
> As I hit the ground I glanced quickly around from beneath the glider's tilted wing and immediately saw the canal swing bridge structure towering above me. The pilots had done a fantastic job, bringing the glider to a halt with its nose buried into a canal bank within about seventy-five yards of the bridge. I glanced back at the glider and saw that the whole front had been smashed inwards, almost back to the wings. I had been sitting just below the forward edge of the wing. There had been some twenty feet of glider forward of my seat – now there was just a twisted mass of wreckage.[4]

The two pilots survived the crash though both were injured badly having been catapulted through the Perspex canopy of their cockpit. They had fulfilled their promise of ensuring that the Horsa landed not only as close to the bridge as possible, but also rammed its way through a wire entanglement surrounding the bridge. Not for nothing was this described by Air-Chief Marshal Trafford Leigh Mallory as one of 'the most outstanding flying achievements of the war'.[5] The soldiers of 2nd Oxfordshire and Buckinghamshire Light Infantry were able to capture both bridges intact and hold on to them until 5 Parachute Brigade and then 3rd British Division relieved them. The operation at Bénouville highlights the strength of all airborne forces, the ability to use air power to cross obstacles and enemy defences, taking advantage of surprise, shock and confusion to seize operationally important objectives. The bridge over the Caen canal is now called 'Pegasus Bridge' after the shoulder flash of the British Airborne troops, the bridge over the River Orne 'Horsa bridge'.

Phase one of Operation TONGA also included the dropping of the Pathfinders of 22nd Independent Parachute Company. Pathfinders are responsible for securing and marking the

---

4   Shannon, Kevin and Wright, Stephen, *One Night In June* (Shrewsbury: Airlife Publishing, 1994), pp.44-45.
5   'Heroes of Pegasus Bridge', *The Independent*, April 2009.

Figure 6.3 A Halifax bomber tows a Horsa glider, 5 June.
(Crown Copyright Air Historical Branch)

parachute Dropping Zones (DZs) and the glider Landing Zones (LZs), their role is critical to the accurate landing of the main airborne assault force. In phase one of TONGA the Pathfinders were to mark the DZ/LZ 'N' where 5 Parachute Brigade would parachute and land gliders, as well as DZs 'K' and 'V' into which 3 Parachute Brigade would drop. Sadly little went according to plan, Private Frank Ockenden was a pathfinder and describes the challenges encountered in marking DZs/LZs on D-Day:

We were trained in the use of the Eureka-Rebecca and Glim Light. The Eureka was radar equipment that sent out a signal so that the pilots of the tug aircraft, which was fitted with Rebecca, homed on it to release the gliders or drop parachutists on the LZ or DZ. Like every-thing else it was very fragile and very easily damaged when dropped and should have been treated with more care. A lot of the trouble that arose on the LZ and DZ was the fault of the ground staff back in England through lack of maintenance. A lot of the batteries were no good and we were not to know until the last minute, which in a lot of cases was too late…

…As we flew over the Channel the sky seemed to become lighter and the waves were breaking over the shore as we passed over the coast. Gunfire was making little red blobs in front of us but we could not hear a thing because of the engines. When the red light came on we were already hooked up in case of a hit by flak, but so far it was no worse than flying in a thunderstorm. Someone said five minutes to DZ. We all stood up and took up positions ready to jump. This was it! No turning back and no calling it off this time. Someone shouted 'Green light on! Good luck boys.' I thought we would need it. Out the plane we went. Done it lots of times – just like dropping on Salisbury Plain.

Hit the ground with a bump. I never saw it as we came in lower and lower, the ground got darker. No damage done so I got out of my chute and looked around. It didn't look like any of the models or maps we had studied for hours. Found Tommy Green, but nothing of Taffy Burt. Heard heavy gunfire to my right and guessed it came from Caen. Tommy was doing a recce and when he came back I told him that I thought we were in the wrong place. We then

Figure 6.4 Paratroopers from 5th Parachute Brigade on board their aircraft, waiting to take off from Keevil Airfield, England, on 5 June. (Crown Copyright Air Historical Branch)

heard planes and down floated some paras. A sergeant came running over. '7th Battalion, mate?' he said. 'No. 8th,' I replied. 'Bloody hell, they've dropped us in the wrong place. We worked our way over in the direction of Troarn towards the LZ. When we got there it was pandemonium. There were aircraft going in all directions over the DZ.

What a balls-up! When I got there I bent over the Eureka to activate it when something hit me on the back of the head. Tommy told me later that a lad from the 13th Battalion had knocked me out with his boots as he was coming in to land by parachute. We saw one glider land and REs running all over the place with a Polish trolley. Guess it must have been Major Roseveare's men who were to blow the bridge at Troarn. Just as we made our way to the woods we saw a glider come straight down nose first and hit the ground about 80mph. It just scattered all over the place – never saw anyone left alive.[6]

The pathfinders were widely scattered in the parachute drop and unable to carry out their role of marking the DZ/LZs clearly. Many of the beacons, holophanes or glim lights for DZ/LZ 'V' were lost and the lights that were deployed could not be easily seen by the aircraft because of the tall standing crops. One Pathfinder team was also dropped on the wrong DZ, not realising that a mistake had been made they set up their beacon anyway. All of these events served to add to the confusion that inevitably accompanies any airborne operation; particularly night ones.

The second phase of Operation TONGA, consisted of the main parachute drops of 3 and 5 Parachute Brigades together with a small number of glider landings. The paratrooper's Stirling or Dakota aircraft would formate over their Fairford and Keevil bases flying to a Group RV over Bognor Regis (for those going to DZ/LZ N), Littlehampton (for DZ K) and Worthing (for DZ

---

6   Shannon, Kevin and Wright, Stephen, *One Night In June* (Shrewsbury: Airlife Publishing, 1994), pp.50-52.

Figure 6.5 Aircraft and gliders based at Tarrant Rushton in Dorset prepare to take off and reinforce the 6th Airborne Division as part of Operation MALLARD on 6 June.
(Crown Copyright Air Historical Branch)

V). They would then use the Southern Gee radio navigation chain to navigate over the Channel to their target RVs, crossing the French coast at low altitudes (about 1,000 feet). At this point the crews would begin to try and identify their landmarks, though visibility was initially good (7-10/10ths cloud cover at 2,000 to 4,000 feet) the RAF bombing of the Merville battery created a lot of dust and smoke as the night progressed and some pilots mistook the River Dives for the River Orne. The aircraft were engaged with anti-aircraft fire as they crossed the coast causing some to take evasive action, often knocking the now standing paratroopers to the floor. In the final 'run in' to the DZ the aircraft, flying in groups of three, would reduce height further to about 600 – 1,000 feet and slow their speed to 135 mph. A red light would appear over the parachute door warning the paratroopers that they were approaching the DZ, this would turn to green when the navigator believed he was over the drop zone.

The paratroopers were jumping with static lines that would automatically deploy their parachute as they left the aircraft, British Airborne forces were not equipped with a reserve chute so any failure of the parachute deploying was catastrophic. On seeing the red warning light turn green, the dispatcher directed the paratroopers' exit from the aircraft using either the side door of the Dakota or the hole cut in the floor of the Halifax, Albermale or Stirling aircraft. An aircraft travelling at 135 mph will swiftly cover a large amount of ground and getting the paratroop 'stick' quickly out the aircraft increased the likelihood they would land accurately on the DZ in as tight a group as possible.

Once outside the aircraft the slipstream will push the paratrooper sideways and he will fall for about a second and a half before the strop, which is still attached to the aircraft, pulls out the static line and then the parachute itself. The canopy then swiftly opens with a reassuring crack and the feeling of rapidly falling is pleasantly arrested, though the paratrooper is still falling faster than it sometimes appears. In the short period of time he has in the air there is a lot for the paratrooper to do, he will firstly try and make sure he is away from other falling paratroopers, he will then try and kick out any twists he has in the shroud lines connecting him to his parachute and let down any equipment bundles he may have attached to himself so that they dangle on a piece of rope beneath him. If he has any time remaining in his short drop he will try and steer away from any obstructions. Steering the parachute was done simply by grapping a clutch of shroud lines and causing the canopy to collapse slightly on one side moving it awkwardly in that chosen direction.

It is hard for a paratrooper to judge the precise moment that he will hit the ground, especially at night, he will therefore position his body to absorb the shock of impact early on. This will entail keeping the legs together, soles parallel to the ground and when he eventually strikes the ground flexing through the ankles, knees, hips and back, finishing with a roll. Having landed the paratrooper will then operate his quick release gear, discard his parachute, pick up his weapon and other items from the equipment bundle and move off to his designated rendezvous (this assumes he is on the right DZ and recognises his surroundings which was not a universal D-Day experience). Parachuting at night, from low altitude, with many other aircraft in the sky can be hazardous. Lieutenant D A Breese dropped into DZ 'N' during Phase 2 of Operation TONGA:

> Arrive airfield, assemble stick, check aircraft with crew, tea car and RAF Padre come round, all in excellent spirits, one sapper has his ukulele. Emplane about 2000 hours, engines started, aircraft move from echelon to line astern for takeoff. Beautiful summer evening, fine sunset. Take off flying V's of three, my aircraft left hand of leading V. Uke put in lavatory, everyone looking very cheerful, ragging and singing. Sit with navigator as we fly NW to join other formations, then south over LARKHILL district. Open tea containers after crossing coast about 0030 hours D-Day. Well over channel – line of green marker lights still continues from land. 20 mins to go, hook up, check equipment, strap kitbag to my leg and switch off lights in aircraft. 15 mins, 'action stations', can just make out French coast and what appears to be AA fire. Sparks fly past door, think they must be from port engine until realise it is tracer which fortunately misses. Loud noise like stick on railings, SAA through the wing.
>
> 5 mins, stand to door, find great difficulty in balancing on doorway because of my weight, awkwardness of kitbag, jinking of aircraft and the fact that I have to twist round to put both hands on release switches. [As the lead man in the stick Lt Breese had to pull the switches to release the equipment containers] Running in, more jinking, red on, 'tap', green on press five switches simultaneously and jump, awkward exit, see plane just flashing away. 'Chute fully developed, look around, can't recognise the DZ at all. Heavy landing all very quiet, stand up to get out of harness, burst of MG somewhere, so lie down as per the book. Flash my torch as agreed signal for closing in. No one about, still fail to recognize a single feature of DZ. Realise on seeing a deep pit that we have been dropped on 5 Para Bde DZ at RANVILLE instead of 3 Para Bde DZ at Touffreville.[7]

The Germans had flooded areas around the River Dives and those that were not dropped accurately onto the DZs, possibly because the pilots had mistook the River Dives for the Orne, sometimes landed in this inundated area. John Speechley from 9th Parachute Battalion was one:

> As I was going down I could definitely hear voices of alarm and trouble. I heard a mass of glass go, that was to my left. I was looking at the ground and I said to myself 'Bloody hell, I'm looking at the reflection of the moon on the water. Bugger this! So I turned my cords 180

---

7   *Royal Engineers Battlefield Tour: Normandy to the Seine*, prepared under the direction of Chief Engineer British Army of the Rhine, HQ BAOR, 1946, pp.71-72.

degrees to have a look around the other way, and it's still all reflection. 'Shit! I'm in trouble.' I thought I was on the edge of the sea.

John Speechley prepared for a water drop by inflating his life jacket and sliding out of his parachute harness, preparing to drop fifteen feet above the water so the parachute would not smother him:

My heart's beating, I can't swim, not with this bloody lot [Pack etc.] let go. I went in and I sat on my arse, looked up. I could see this green flickering, it was the moon shining up top. So I felt down; this was grass not mud, and I realized it was a flooded area. I stood up and I'd got the water just by my Adam's apple. Bloody hell! I heard people in trouble. You could hear 'Help, bubble, bubble', y'know, one here one there. It's just a case of survival now. I walked this way, I walked the other way. I walked another way and made a bit more headway, and I got it down to my ammunition pouches. I'm looking around and I went right round 360 degrees. I can't see a bloody thing; a top of a tree, a row of trees…I looked in one particular direction and it looked too straight. That's a railway line got to be. So I made my way there, slightly to the right, bit to the left, bit too deep. I was following the contours of the meadow. In the end I got almost to it and it turned out to be a road…

…A bloke said, 'Halt, who goes there?' Well, now I've got to think. There's that much been going on, what with the aeroplane noise and firing. I heard the click of a rifle bolt. Got it 'PUNCH'! 'JUDY'! Well it was Corporal Dowling. He said, 'Don't bugger around in there, get out!'

'That's all right for you. I can hardly bloody walk.'

So he said , 'Get hold of this,' and he gave me the butt of his rifle. I took one stride to get hold of it and went straight under. I didn't realize there's a drainage ditch been built in it, all of eight feet deep plus the flooding. I'm crawling among the reeds and I came up. He hit my helmet, I felt where his butt was and he got me out. My head was really pounding. I was loaded, had to let the water out of my trousers. This mud, oh it stunk![8]

Paratroop Engineers were also dropped in Phase two of Operation TONGA. Their tasks included the dismantling of glider poles and other German obstacles on the various LZs to prepare for the main glider landings that would occur later that night (Phase three of TONGA). Lieutenant John Shinner was one of the Sappers involved in this task, his journey in a 620 Squadron Stirling, highlights the threat posed by German anti-aircraft fire. He was due to drop at 0100 hrs but only the last two minutes of the flight would be overland; however as they crossed the coast the plane came under anti-aircraft fire and shrapnel peppered the aircraft.

One bit nicked my right arm – it didn't hurt, but felt a bit numb. The sky seemed to be full of vivid flashes and orange streaks. Suddenly there was a flash and burst of flame inside the aircraft –astern of where I stood. In a matter of seconds the whole of the inside of the aircraft was blazing. Each of the sappers had been carrying plastic explosives in the form of 'sausages' (for the demolition of obstruction poles on the LZs) and one poor chap had his hit, and it burned fiercely. Five or six of us at the forward end of the fire were forced towards the main spar by the flames. I felt the flames singeing my face and yelled to someone to get the escape hatch off to let out the suffocating smoke. I told one of the sappers (Reardon-Parker) to go forward to the radio cabin to find out what the situation was. He contacted one of the crew,

8   Barber, Neil, *The Day the Devils Dropped In* (Barnsley: Leo Cooper, 2002), pp.55-56.

Figure 6.6
Discarded parachutes and
Horsas litter Landing Zone
'N' between Ranville and
Amfreville, 6 June.
(Crown Copyright Air
Historical Branch)

but obviously things were badly wrong up there, because they passed the order to jump and then immediately cancelled it. In any case we could not have got out past the blaze between us and the hole.

Almost immediately after this the nose dipped, there was an horrendous rending and crashing, and I had the sensation that we were being rolled over and over. It seemed to go on for an awfully long time. When all movement stopped I became aware of something (fuel?) swilling over my face and that there was a fierce fire burning in the forward part of the aircraft, a few feet away. I also realised that I couldn't move of my own accord because I was hanging upside down, by one leg, on my static line, which had become entangled with the roof of the aircraft.

If I didn't do something I was going to cook in the very near future. Again my luck was in, and the urgent action required was taken by another survivor who came staggering my way. I yelled to him to cut me loose and in two seconds his fighting knife had done the job and we were both on our feet. We only had a few feet to walk, because just behind where I had been hung up, the fuselage was broken off and there was a pile of wreckage and dead and injured men. We couldn't see any sign of the tail!

We two set about getting some of the injured out. As far as I could tell – I was pretty dazed and shaken – there were few of us on our feet, three or four men alive but badly injured, and the others dead. The front part of the plane was a raging furnace and there was obviously nothing to be done for the aircrew. We pulled out two of the injured sappers but couldn't shift the third man who was very firmly trapped in the wreckage.[9]

---

9   Williams, Dennis, *Stirlings in Action With The Airborne Forces*, (Barnsley: Pen & Sword, 2008), pp.82-84.

Thinking they were south of the DZ the small party of injured sappers set off to reach Allied forces but unfortunately encountered a German patrol they were forced to surrender to. Despite the non-arrival of Lieutenant Shinner's aircraft the obstacles were removed and two landing strips 1,000 yards by 90 yards were cleared for the arrival of the first main group of glider landings at 0330 hours. Staff Sergeant Johnny Bowen was piloting a Horsa glider in this the third phase of TONGA, his second pilot was Captain John Smellie:

> We were first away at 0119 hours and I remember that a red flare was fired as we took off. Much later, I learned that this was a signal that half our undercarriage had fallen off. We flew north to begin with, to Southam, and at first there was no-one with us, but then other gliders and tugs arrived and we got into formation line astern. Crossing the Channel, I saw one German Me109 fighter and below us, American gliders heading west. These latter were all showing full lights!
>
> Near Le Havre we met anti-aircraft fire and suddenly emerging from cloud we found that we were near the landing zone. Squadron Leader Reggie Trim, our tug pilot, yelled 'Pull off Johnny we're there.' I released the tow-rope and descended at about 115mph. Another glider passed me and, as I flew over the triangle of lights and positioned myself in the lane between the obstructing poles, I saw that the other glider had hit a pole and was blocking my path. I eased back the wheel, but still hit his fuselage as I flew over. This changed my path and one of the poles smashed into the port side of my cockpit, leaving John Smellie with nothing in front of him. As I eased back to land, having lost the other half of my undercarriage, the nose wheel hit a ditch and came up inside the glider. Then we were safely down with no injuries and load intact – the time was 0324 hours.[10]

Other Horsa's would carry vehicles and heavy equipment, essential items of hardware if the paratroopers were to successfully defend themselves against German armour. Loading Horsa gliders required the jeep, trailer or gun to be manoeuvred up a ramp and manhandled through ninety degrees into the fuselage of the Horsa. Once the glider had landed, 'quick release' bolts in the tail would be unfastened and the whole tail section was supposed to simply fall away and a ramp deployed. This rarely worked well and sometimes Cortex was used to explosively remove the tail. Although his landing was a particularly bumpy affair Bill Musitano's glider was unloaded perfectly easily:

> As we approached the coast of France, in Horsa PF803, we saw the flak come up. Much of it was tracer and as we flew on at 160mph, it passed us by in fast moving streaks. It was now that we discovered a major problem. The wind had been forecast as blowing from south to north, but was in fact blowing from almost the opposite direction. The green 'T' was only visible from the air when approaching into wind. These had been laid out 'as briefed', but we were approaching into wind. As the 'T' was not visible we had to rely on the navigator of the Halifax to tell us when to release. He was good, but maybe thirty or sixty seconds out. I remember he said 'Now' and I pulled the 'tit' and we were free. A gentle turn to starboard showed us the 'T' and I believe I said to Paddy 'It's too far away!'
>
> With our full load, the vital seconds delay in pulling off, meant that we were going to land half a mile short of the LZ. I put on half flap to get maximum gliding distance and we waited. We were gliding at around seventy, perhaps ten above stalling point, when up came a row of trees. I pulled up and cleared them, then a small field and another row of trees. She

---

10 Shannon, Kevin and Wright, Stephen, *One night in June* (Airlife Publishing, 1994), p.101.

Figure 6.7 A jeep being unloaded from a Horsa glider during an exercise in England, 19 April.
(Crown Copyright Air Historical Branch)

still hadn't stalled, so I aimed her between two of the trees, which cut the wings off, and we collapsed onto a stone wall with a bump. The wall cut the nose of the Horsa clean off, just behind where we were sitting, but didn't damage the load or the passengers, although I think we were all a bit shaken. The cortex band near the tail was blown and we got the jeep and the gun out intact.[11]

Other gliders were less fortunate in unloading their vehicles. Staff Sergeant Ashby's was carrying one of the bulldozers required to further clear and improve the major LZs:

We landed without damage. Having, as our first contribution to the invasion, regaled ourselves with mugs of tea from the enormous vacuum flasks thoughtfully provided, we set to work to get the bulldozer out. The Horsa was of the side-loading type, so we let down the strengthened section of fuselage designed for such purposes, fixed the stanchions underneath to hold it up, and positioned, from it to the ground, the steel U-section troughs, down which the bulldozer was supposed to descend.

Unfortunately it didn't! The Sapper got the bulldozer out of the glider all right and into the ramps, but there it stuck. The caterpillar tracks were a very tight fit and the ramps cannot have been absolutely parallel. If the bulldozer would not go down, neither would it go back up, however hard and often the driver tried.

I remember thinking that, having brought it all that way at no little trouble and expense, we could hardly leave the machine suspended in mid-air. Something drastic would be justified. Hailing a jeep which happened to be nearby, I attached ropes from it to the props under the loading platform and had them jerked out from under. That did the trick. The bulldozer

---

11 Ibid., p.126.

crashed to the ground, happily undamaged and the right way up. The Sapper, whose name I never did know, drove it off and within the hour it was working clearing the LZ.[12]

The bulldozer Staff Sergeant Ashby's glider was carrying was to prepare for the final major wave of glider landings (known as Operation MALLARD). These were scheduled for 2100 on 6 June and would land the final major element of 6th Airborne Division, including the 6th Airlanding Brigade, onto two landing zones; LZ 'W' (108 gliders) and LZ 'N' (146 gliders). LZ 'W' was marked with two parallel landing strips and LZ 'N' had four, one of which was reserved for the large Hamilcar gliders. The Hamilcar glider was available in much smaller numbers than the Horsa gliders and carried the heaviest of equipment including the 17-pounder anti-tank guns and the Tetrarch light tank. The Hamilcar was also made of a wooden frame with a plywood skin but there were some steel beams used in its construction to reinforce key areas. At 21 metres in length it was not much longer than a Horsa glider but was much wider and higher, the pilots entering the cockpit on top of the aircraft through a 15 foot ladder. The Hamilcar's load was accommodated in a large cargo hold resembling the inside of a small wooden barn, the vehicle crews would often remain inside the tanks or Bren carriers during the flight and would start the engines during the run in so they could deploy quickly through a hinged door at the front of the aircraft.

Sergeant 'Jock' Simpson was a second pilot on a Hamilcar which landed on Phase three of operation TONGA with a 17-pounder anti-tank gun, he also helped prepare for the OP MALLARD landings the following day:

> A short time after midnight we rolled down the runway and took off, heading towards the Channel and wondering what lay in store for us. The atmosphere in the glider was electric as our passengers, the gun crew, were rather excited as they were unable to see anything and consequently, kept calling on the radio telephone until Tommy Taylorson got mad, told them to 'shut up' and said that he would keep them informed when anything transpired.
>
> As we crossed the Channel, tense but calm, we could see the white wakes of the ships of the sea-borne forces as they made their way across the water. The flight was uneventful until we approached the French coast, where we encountered medium and light anti-aircraft fire coming from Le Havre. Fortunately we escaped being hit, but our Canadian tug pilot, Flying Officer Baird, was hit by a bullet between the toes. Some strong adjectives were heard over the radio telephone, but he carried on and did not falter in his duty…
>
> …As we approached for the landing we could see that the area was obstructed by masses of poles standing in the ground and obviously placed there by the Germans as landing obstacles. However we were very relieved when we realised that our wings were too high, seventeen feet above the ground to be affected, but unfortunately that was not the case for the Horsas landing in the same area, as their wings were below the height of the poles –consequently they sustained severe damage.
>
> After we rolled to a stop we got out, opened the nose door and released the valves on the landing legs, allowing the Hamilcar to settle on the skids. When the load was released the tractor pulled the gun and ammunition down the ramps.[13]

The MALLARD landings of 6 June marked the conclusion of the deployment of 6th Airborne Division. The Division would continue to be employed as an infantry formation until 5 September, when it was recovered back to the UK. The use of both the British and American

---

12 Ibid., p.104.
13 Ibid., pp.120-122.

Figure 6.8 The controllers signal all-clear to a waiting Halifax tug towing a Hamilcar glider, 5 June. (Crown Copyright Air Historical Branch)

airborne forces in Normandy has attracted much debate with critics arguing that they were a costly distraction of Allied resources and highlighting the confusion of misdrops on the night of 5/6 June. That the 6th Airborne operation was often chaotic and costly cannot be denied but despite these losses the Division's objective to secure the left flank of the bridgehead was achieved. The specified tasks were also a success; the bridges at Bénouville were captured intact, the battery at Merville neutralised and the bridges over the Dives were destroyed. Once thickened up by the arrival of 6 Air-Landing Brigade and 1 Commando Brigade the bridgehead east of the Orne was secure and presented the invaders with a considerable advantage. The commander of 3 Parachute Brigade, Brigadier James Hill, had prepared his men for the confusion of D-Day by stating 'Gentlemen do not be surprised if chaos reigns; it undoubtedly will'. That the objectives were achieved despite the misdrops, crashes and overall confusion speaks much for the 'Airborne attitude' of carrying on in the face of adversity and the unexpected.

The surprise and dislocation that the British Airborne drop had on the German command was much more profound and they took some time to fathom what exactly was going on. One can imagine their shock when it eventually dawned on the Germans that without warning and in little over five hours, key bridges had either been captured or destroyed, a critical coastal battery silenced and there was now a powerful defensive position equipped with anti-tank guns astride one of their key counter-attack routes. It highlights the advantage those with Airborne forces possess in being able to use air power to achieve operational objectives with great surprise and rapidity, as well as sowing chaos amongst the opponent's command structure.

That 6th Airborne Division and the Glider Pilot Regiment had to have the closest relationships with the RAF to undertake its role is obvious. But such a relationship with the air force was also important for the more conventional ground units and formations of the Army. In particular close-cooperation with the affiliated 2nd Tactical Air Force would be essential if 21st Army Group were to fully exploit the Allies' massive air superiority.

2nd Tactical Air Force (2nd TAF) was an independent air command composed primarily of squadrons of the RAF and Royal Canadian Air Force (RCAF) as well as some individual French, Czech, Dutch, Norwegian and Belgian squadrons. 2nd TAF was led by Air Marshal Sir Arthur Coningham from his headquarters at RAF Uxbridge where he directly controlled an independent Strategic Reconnaissance Wing specialising in day and night air photography, as well as four subordinate Groups. Two of these 'Tactical' Groups, 83 and 84 Group, were allocated to each Army.

83 Group was the first to operate from Normandy and supported Second British Army, it was comprised of 11 Wings which gave a total of thirteen squadrons of Spitfire IXs, ten Typhoon squadrons and six squadrons of Mustangs. In theory all were capable of both air combat and ground attack tasks, but the Typhoon was more suited for ground attack and was used almost exclusively for that role. The Spitfires and Mustangs were mainly used as air superiority fighters though they also attacked ground targets too. Each 'Tactical Group' also had a reconnaissance wing of three squadrons of tactical reconnaissance (TAC/R) aircraft (Mustangs) and one Spitfire photo reconnaissance (PR) squadron. Finally the Tactical Group also had control of five squadrons of the Royal Artillery's Auster Air OP aircraft, though they were usually placed directly under the command of each of the Army's corps.

84 Group consisted of 16 squadrons of Spitfire IXs, eight squadrons of Typhoons and five squadrons of Mustang IIIs, it also had a reconnaissance wing consisting of two squadrons of TAC/R aircraft and one for PR. 84 Group was affiliated to the First Canadian Army and began to arrive in Normandy from late July once HQ First Canadian Army had been properly constituted.

Second Tactical Air Force's order of battle also contained a 'base defence Group' (85 Group). This had the latest air superiority fighters including four squadrons of Spitfires and two of Tempest Vs. The Group also had six squadrons of Mosquito nightfighters predominantly the Mark XIII version. Its role was to remain operating over the UK and protect the vast concentration areas of southern England as well as the lines of communication across the channel. Other Mosquito nightfighters would also fly across the channel each evening to interdict German night raiders. Finally 2 Group, a Light/Medium Bomber Group, had been detached from Bomber Command and placed under the command of 2nd TAF. It brought with it four squadrons of Mitchells, two of Boston IIIs and six Mosquito VI fighter-bombers.[14]

It had been envisaged that as early as possible a significant number of squadrons would use forward bases in Normandy. These aircraft would belong to Wings which would each be given a 'Sector of Responsibility' over Normandy. The Wing's role was to command the three squadrons and support them with intelligence, maintenance, flight control, catering, accommodation, transport and medical facilities. Each squadron was commanded by a squadron leader and would consist of three flights of four aircraft or alternatively two flights of six. A squadron normally had a total of 18 aircraft giving them a few spares to cope with unscheduled repairs and routine maintenance. Each aircraft was assigned a crew chief and maintenance team including an armourer, an instrument and electrical specialist, an engine mechanic and an airframe mechanic. There were also other unassigned ground crew who were used as a 'reserve' to help out with the more demanding servicing requirements; such as engine changes. The squadron also possessed an adjutant, a medical officer, an engineering/technical officer and an intelligence/operations officer.[15]

The requirement for good forward airfields led the RAF to press strongly for the early capture of the area south-east of Caen where the ground seemed ideal. The Army's failure to capture

---

14 Ellis, L F, *Victory in the West* Volume 1 (London: HMSO, 1962), p.556.
15 Clark, David, *Angels Eight* (Bloomington Indiana: 1st Books, 2003), p.194.

Figure 6.9 Typhoon pilots of 121 and 124 Wings discuss operations at B2/Bazenville on the 14 June. (Crown Copyright Air Historical Branch)

this ground early in the campaign led to significant criticism from some Air Force commanders, though the Army did recognise their responsibilities to the Air Force in this regard. Indeed Army responsibilities were not limited to capturing sufficient real estate but also in providing sufficient engineer and logistic resources to help construct and maintain the airfields.

The Army built airfields in Normandy on a progressive basis. At the earliest stage of invasion Emergency Landing Strips (ELS) were constructed where aircraft in trouble could put down. The ELS would then be subsequently developed into Refuelling and Re-Arming Strips (R&Rs) and finally Advanced Landing Grounds (ALGs) would be built and allocated on the basis of one per wing, with an RAF wing commander in charge. This large engineering task was given to five RE Airfield Construction Groups,[16] who built a total of 20 new airfields between 7 June and 8 August (see Map 15). There were some slight variations in the design of each of these airfields; if a fighter ALG was to be built the runway would have to be 1,200 yards long. Whereas 1,650 yards was required for fighter-bombers, who required a longer takeoff because of the extra weight they carried. There were also a number of alternative surfaces used by the RE in creating the runways. Sommerfeld tracking was available, though its tendency to rip the tail wheels off aircraft meant Square Mesh Track (SMT) was the preferred option. This metal mesh, similar to that used in the construction industry to reinforce concrete, was simply pegged down with large metal stakes. The best technical solution to create a runway was recognised as Pierced Steel Planking (PSP). However this heavy material required such a significant amount of shipping space that it was generally used to provide hard standing for aircraft and was only ever used as the main runway material at B17-Carpiquet ALG (All British Airfields began with a 'B', American Airfields began with an 'A').[17] Whatever airfield surface the engineers elected to

---

16 12, 16, 23, 24 and 25 Airfield Construction Groups RE.

17 Shores, Christopher and Thomas, Chris, *2nd Tactical Air Force* (Hersham: Ian Allan Publishing, 2005), pp.141-142.

use, it could not be laid without significant preparatory work, including levelling and grading the surface, cutting through hedgerows and removing trees. The Airfield Construction Group would also have to set up the ALG's essential services including power, lighting, water, latrines and defensive structures.

Each Aircraft Construction Group consisted of an HQ company, two companies of REs, two companies of pioneers and one company of mechanical and electrical engineers; a total of 800 men in all; equipped with bulldozers, scrapers and rollers. One of the first units to arrive was 23 Airfield Construction Group who were tasked with constructing a 1,650 yard tracked airfield for three squadrons of Typhoon fighter-bombers at Le Fresne Camilly (B5). The ALG would initially be constructed without taxi tracks and dispersals until further stores became available. Lieutenant Colonel R H Havers gave a description of the task:

> Before entering the concentration area the CRE [Commander Royal Engineers] had visited 121 Airfield Commander and discussed with him in general terms the layout of his airfield. The field was for Typhoon fighter-bombers which were heavier and more stable on the runway than Spitfires, but, when taking off with tail up, there is only six inches of ground clearance between the tip of the prop and the ground before take off. They do not 'scramble' off the field, but usually take off in pairs so that large marshalling areas at the ends of the runway are not essential. The relative positions of Airfield HQ, Ops and Int, Aircraft and MT maintenance areas, bomb storage areas etc are variable according to the desires of each Airfield Commander and if not agreed in principle beforehand, will certainly have to be adjusted to the satisfaction of the RAF.

After establishing contact with HQ I Corps he moved to La Deliverande where Commandos were mopping up the last elements of German resistance and with his company commanders began the process of planning the building of the airfield on the site itself:

> The ALG site was almost that indicated on the multiplex map. An alternative site crossing the road south of Le Fresne Camilly was turned down as it cut a main advance artery. Although it was more in the wind, the site proposed was approved by the CRE and his RAF adviser. Permission was obtained to divert the lateral road which ran north of the site if necessary. This was found unnecessary in spite of the dip in the ground in front of 'flying control' which was graded to the prescribed limits after the removal of the hedge. Initially there was only enough SMT available for the runway itself, and the rate of delivery from the beaches prevented the full use of the pioneers and slowed up the progress somewhat, although it had all arrived by the last date of the plan. From D plus 4 onwards the lower end of the field was subjected to spasmodic 88mm shelling which lost, in all, one and a quarter working days. There were no casualties, except one MACK whose petrol tank was split by a splinter, and little damage to the track. Most of the shells fell in the untracked areas. There were considerable misgivings in the Group about SMT, which was fairly new to airfields at that time, and much trouble with billowing in front of wheels of landing aircraft had occurred in England . Only a fortnight before the construction, a War Office experiment carried out by 23 Airfield Construction Group and 121 RAF Wing, to try and reduce the number of clips and the overlapping of rolls to one square mesh, had proved a failure through excessive billowing. As a result of this the overlay was fixed at two squares and ninety six clips per roll. In addition special screw pickets were provided to pin down the track to the ground, and crimping tools to take out set waves were provided. Although the screw pickets tended to work loose in dry weather, there was no trouble at all when aircraft landed and the maintenance party had very little to do. The screw pickets were later discarded and a system of stretching the rolls by lorry winch and yoke

Figure 6.10 Square Mesh Track (SMT) is laid during the construction of B19 Lingevres. (Imperial War Museum CL 710)

Figure 6.11 Royal Engineers of an Airfield Construction Group prepare a new Landing Ground in Normandy using Square Mesh Track (SMT). (Crown Copyright Air Historical Branch)

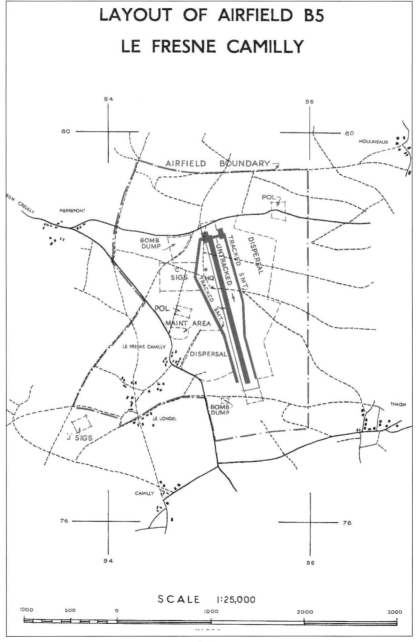

Diagram 6.1 Airfield at Le Fresne (B5).

Figure 6.12 An RAF servicing commando fusing 3-inch rocket projectiles stacked at an Advanced Landing Ground in Normandy before they are fitted to Typhoon aircraft. (Crown Copyright Air Historical Branch)

produced by the late Lt Col L F Hancock OBE CRE 16 Airfield Construction Group was used with complete success.[18]

Although the Airfield Commander's arrival was interrupted by a bout of German shelling, he reportedly expressed complete satisfaction with the field. The Typhoons operating from B5 made 1,365 operational sorties in July entailing three thousand aircraft movements over the track.

As the Normandy bridgehead size remained smaller than expected the plans on constructing the airfields had to be adjusted. The failure to capture the ground south-east of Caen in particular meant that the Airfield Construction Groups would have to try and secure alternative sites for their airfields. No easy matter in what was becoming a very congested bridgehead as Lieutenant Colonel G C Clark relates:

Orders had now been issued by I Corps for the reconnaissance and, if possible construction of a second ALG (1200 yard fighter strip) near Plumetot. Once more the site lay on magnificent cornland and presented few difficulties from a constructional point of view. The main difficulty was to obtain an area clear of troops, not only for the men working on the strip but for the field itself. In the congestion which existed at that time in that part of the beachhead it appeared difficult to convince other people that an airfield really did require the space it does.

---

18 Havers, Lt Col R H, 'The Construction of ALG B5 at Le Fresne Camilly', taken from *Royal Engineers Battlefield Tour – Normandy to the Seine,* prepared under the direction Commander Royal Engineers, British Army of the Rhine, 1946, p.116.

AGRAs, supply points and medical units littered the ground and it was only after much argument, some of it regrettably acrimonious, that we were able to get on with the job.[19]

Given the paucity of landing strips in Normandy, the care and maintenance of the fragile Sommerfeld or SMT strips was uppermost in pilots' minds, even when trying to land a severely damaged aircraft. Flying Officer J G Simpson a Typhoon pilot in 193 Squadron:

There was an occasion when I had to land wheels-up, not much problem, it's a bloody great engine so unless you make an absolute 'Charlie' of it you don't come to much harm. There were things to remember however, for on some airfields in France we had up to five squadrons so there wasn't a lot of room. You couldn't put a damaged aircraft down on the runway or the Wing CO would have your 'guts for garters' as that would mean ripping up the carefully laid tracking and then nobody could operate. So you had to put it down by the side; you didn't want to go into the nearby fields as the crash wagons couldn't reach you. So we had a spot which was earmarked for forced landing which usually ended in a terrific cloud of dust. We had problems with dust in Normandy but at least you could throw it over the aeroplane so it wouldn't catch fire.[20]

In the early part of the operation the Spitfires and Typhoons would use the newly constructed landing grounds as R&R strips returning to bases in southern England each night. Pilot Officer G Clubley from 181 Squadron describes the process:

We went over to Normandy a few days after D-Day. The army had bulldozed a strip for us –B6 it was called – and the initial idea was for us to go over first thing in the morning. The Army had positioned Jerry cans of petrol for us, and little groups of men who had been trained to turn round aircraft refuel and rearm us from stock piles of rockets etc. At night we'd fly back to southern England. It was a nice theory but the timing was a little critical! I remember the first one I did, only four of us; we landed and as we did so the mortars started. The Germans were just over the other side of us and had been waiting to see the dust from our strip start to rise. Fortunately there were slit trenches.[21]

To ensure that ground crew were immediately available after the landings, six RAF Servicing Commando Units (SCU) were established and brought ashore early on 7 June. Each SCU comprised two officers and 148 men. They would provide a refuelling and re-arming service for any aircraft operating in the Normandy beachhead, managing the fuel and ammunition dumps and carrying out repairs and servicing. When the ALG was finished by the sappers, the Wing's own support staff would be flown or shipped across and the SCU would move on. In the initial stages the refuelling was rudimentary and slow with only jerry cans and funnels available, furthermore SCU crews were often supporting different types of unfamiliar aircraft. Flying Officer S J Eaton, 257 Squadron records one incident:

We had one nasty experience when our Servicing Commandos were refuelling us on one occasion and to our horror we found all our cockpit hoods had been pulled. We had a jettison handle and they had pulled these instead of turning the Coffman starter which looked very

19 Ibid., p.118.
20 Franks, Norman, *Typhoon Attack* (London: William Kimber, 1984), p.185.
21 Ibid., p.120.

Figure 6.13 A Typhoon IB of 184 Squadron piloted by Pilot Officer Ian Handyside kicks up dust as it accelerates along B2/Bazenville on 14 June. (Crown Copyright Air Historical Branch)

similar. Nobody could put them right so we had to wait for some of our own ground people to be sent out from Hurn to put them on again.[22]

The first emergency runways had been ready for use by 7 June and by 18 June three of the ALGs had been occupied by Spitfire-equipped Wings. The first Typhoon Wing, No. 124, would occupy B6 Coulombs on 20 June. The presence of fighters and fighter-bombers in France gave a marked advantage to the Allies; a Spitfire flying from southern England in an air superiority role could spend only one hour operating over France, the same aircraft based a few miles from the front in Normandy, could spend up to two hours on task. The availability of airfields in France also meant that damaged aircraft did not have to run the risk of crossing the Channel. In the pre D-Day attacks by Typhoons on coastal radars in France, fourteen Typhoon pilots were forced to either ditch or bail out over the channel, only nine of which were rescued.[23]

By the end of June, 83 Group was complete in Normandy and operating entirely from its own landing grounds, but as the various wings settled in to the airfields a serious problem became apparent. At most airfields the engineers had simply bulldozed the surface of the airfield and laid SMT on its surface, whilst this provided a firm surface it did not stop billowing clouds of dust, which were found to have an abrasive effect on the engines. The Typhoons with their large air intakes under the propeller were particularly badly affected. The OC of 181 Squadron, Squadron Leader C D North Lewis, commented:

The big problem in Normandy was that the Typhoon had no air filter and when we went over we were just operating off bull-dozed strips with nothing on them at all. As soon as you started up the Typhoons there was something like a major dust storm blowing in fact it was so bad at

22 Ibid., p.122.
23 Thomas, Chris, *Typhoon Wings of 2nd TAF* (Oxford: Osprey Publishing, 2010), p.60.

times that you couldn't see whether the pair in front of you had taken off, you just had to go when you thought they'd cleared and so if anything had gone wrong in front there was always the danger of bumping into them. After we'd been over for some days, someone, probably at command HQ, got worried as to whether the dust was causing any wear on the engines, so they did a check and found that an enormous number of engines had excessive wear, so we all flew back to England and all the aircraft were checked and those that had excessive wear, had new engines put in. They also rigged up a make-shift air filter, put in a kind of cotton wool effort. It did give you a performance penalty but as we rarely got embroiled with German aircraft it didn't really matter. In a curious way that affected us right till the end of the war, because there was always a shortage of engines.[24]

The dust did not solely affect the engines but other parts of the aircraft too:

The dust in Normandy was also affecting the ammunition belts, which were heavily oiled, and the automatic ejection of the shell cases and clips became clogged with dust as it got up underneath through the ejection shoot. So out came a team of boffins from Farnborough to sort this problem and everyone was interested in the time scale. They said they would have the problem conquered in no time at all – two or three months! We all said that was no good to us but Chiefy Schaefer, our flight sergeant armourer on 181 Squadron, solved the problem quite simply. He glued pieces of toilet paper to the chutes so that when a pilot taxied out, dust didn't get in; when you fired your guns in the air, of course, the first shells just tore through the paper.[25]

General Montgomery was clear what the immediate priority for any air force was: 'the winning of the air battle, and with it the achievement of a favourable air situation, is at one and the same time the primary task of the air forces, and the greatest contribution they can make to the land battle. It is in fact a pre-requisite to military success.'[26] For the Normandy campaign this air superiority task was given to the Spitfires and Mustangs of 83 and 84 Group. These aircraft were initially controlled from fighter controllers on the Navy's ships but, once established ashore, the task was passed to 83 Group's Control Centre on 10 June. This Centre, in conjunction with the US 9th Fighter Control Squadron, would control all Allied fighter aircraft over the bridgehead and direct them to intercept German intruders. The Spitfires and Mustangs were excellent air superiority aircraft and compared favourably with even the best German fighter, the FW190. Hugh Godefroy who was a Wing Commander in 127 Wing, flew a captured FW190 before the campaign and was therefore able to contrast it with his own Spitfire:

The things I discovered about the comparative performance of the Spitfire IXb proved invaluable to me in the next two years. In level flight and high speed the 190 flies slightly nose down. With a higher wing loading than the Spitfire, the 190's maximum rate of climb was attained at an airspeed of about 240 miles per hour. The Spitfire IXb's maximum rate of climb was attained at 160 miles per hour. Thus if you were foolish enough to try to follow the 190 in full throttle at the same angle, you would soon find that he was above you. On the other hand,

24 Franks, Norman, *Typhoon Attack* (London: William Kimber, 1984), p.135.
25 Flying Lieutenant H Ambrose quoted in Franks, Norman, *Typhoon Attack*, p.135.
26 Montgomery, Field Marshal B L, 'Some Notes on the use of Air Power In support of Land Operations', HQ BAOR, October 1945. Held at Joint Doctrine and Concepts Centre, Shrivenham.

if you pulled away and held the Spitfire at an air speed of 160, you would climb at a much steeper angle and end up with a height advantage.

Below 20 thousand feet in level speed runs there wasn't much in it either way. But once above 20 thousand feet, the Spitfire IXb's second blower kicked in giving it the advantage. If Jamie Rankin, who was flying the 190, followed the favourite German technique of flicking over on his back and going straight down, he would pull away from me in the first two or three thousand feet. After that the Spitfire IXb could gradually catch him. Jamie never tried to turn inside me in the Spitfire, we all knew that wasn't possible. That was an advantage that all British fighters enjoyed. At the end of the trials I came to the conclusion that I would still prefer the Spitfire IXb.[27]

The already iconic Spitfire was both a beautiful, effective and popular aircraft to fly; Canadian Pilot Bill Olmstead describes his first encounter with the Spitfire:

My attachment to this aircraft was instantaneous and total. With my parachute strapped to my back, I stepped onto the left wing root, moved up one short pace and entered the cockpit through the open hatch door. With some shifting I positioned myself in the metal bucket seat moulded to accept the parachute pack, which then acted as a comfortable cushion. The Sutton harness straps were positioned over my shoulders and hips to hold me securely in position. My body seemed to fill the cockpit space completely, putting the controls within easy reach. I looked at the throttle and pitch control quadrant mounted ahead of the hatch with trim tabs and radiator regulators immediately below. The doughnut-shaped control column moved easily in every direction. I noted the gun button was in the OFF position. Directly in front of my eyes were the major flying control instruments, the air speed indicator, the altimeter, the directional gyro and the turn and bank dial, all neatly centred, allowing the pilot to look forward at all times. Every instrument detailing the condition of the engine or the fuselage was easy to read and reach. About fifty different knobs, switches, dials, buttons, tabs and controls were to be my constant guides in the future, and I was determined to understand them completely.[28]

Whether taking off from Normandy, or from the UK, the start up procedure for a Spitfire was almost identical:

I primed the engine and gave the thumbs up sign to the 'Erk' (mechanic) to give the engine power from his electric cart. The Merlin caught immediately with a cough and a stutter, which quickly smoothed into a quiet, throbbing burble as I throttled back. The machine vibrated slightly seeming to come alive suddenly in response to the engine's song of power, a very distinctive and easily identifiable sound. I hooked up the oxygen tube and plugged in the radio cord after closing the hatch door. At my signal the wheel chocks were removed, freeing the aircraft to move forward. Slowly moving ahead, I found there was no forward vision on the ground, the view being completely blanked out by the long nose and the broad engine cowling. By bursts of the throttle and shoves on the rudder pedals and brakes, however, the nose could be swung from side to side, which allowed me to see enough to keep the aircraft on the taxi strip without 'pranging' some obstruction.

27 Clark, David, *Angels Eight* (Bloomington, Indiana: 1st Books, 2003), p.191.
28 Olmstead, W, *Blue skies – the autobiography of a Canadian Spitfire Pilot* (N.p., Stoddart Publishing, 1988), p.23.

At the down-wind end of the runway. I ran the engine up to test the magnetos. No serious drop. I was ready for and received permission from flying control to take off. I made a last quick check of the brakes, trim, flaps contacts, pressures, undercart and radiator, ensuring everything was in order. I opened up the throttle smoothly. The engine responded with a deep-throated roar typical of the Rolls-Royce Merlin and the Spit accelerated rapidly. Christ how she accelerated I could scarcely believe how quickly she gathered speed with the pressure forcing my whole body tight against the contoured seat. As more power was added there was a strong tendency for the aircraft to swing to the right, and I countered this by increasing pressure on the left rudder pedal. Faster and faster, the tail up now as the control surfaces gained effect with the increasing speed. After what seemed a short take-off run, the Spit freed itself from the ground at 100mph. My speed built up rapidly as I moved the wheels-up lever. Within a minute the aircraft was clean, responding instantly to even the lightest touch on the controls.[29]

Large English airfields like Tangmere and Hurn had wide concrete runways and parallel stretches of grass that allowed up to four or six aircraft to take off simultaneously. In Normandy the ALG's runway was inevitably narrower and only two aircraft could take off at the same time. Once airborne the squadron would concentrate as quickly as possible and if necessary formate with other squadrons, a quarter of a mile apart and separated by 1,000 feet in height.

Within the squadron each section would normally be given a colour ('red' section, 'blue' section and 'yellow' section were the most common) and each aircraft within the section had a number. This facilitated command and control in the air and allowed different types of formation to be used. The most popular formation used when cruising was to fly in three sections of four aircraft each, this was known as 'finger four'. The 'finger four' formation had the aircraft flying in a similar pattern to the fingernails in an outstretched hand. The Section Leader (Red 1) would be the furthest forward with his wingman (Red 2) to one side and slightly behind. The final two aircraft in the section (Red 3 (the second in command) and 4) would be on the opposite side and also slightly behind. Each aircraft would fly at different altitudes (50 feet or so difference) and, if able, keep 300 feet of separation between them, this allowed sufficient space for the pilots to search for the enemy, whilst ensuring the aircraft were not so close that pilots spent all their time concentrating on keeping station.[30] Each squadron had slight variations to this technique depending on the CO and how experienced his pilots were.

The Finger Four formation was flexible enough to allow the section to alter course easily – the pilots simply crossing over. When the squadron flew together the squadron leader's section would normally be in the middle with blue section normally 200yds to the right of him and yellow section 200yds to the left. A variation of 'finger four' was 'fluid six' this was normally used when a squadron was carrying out a ground attack mission with the twelve aircraft split into six carrying bombs and six providing cover. Squadrons would use either the 'finger four' or 'fluid six' formation to cruise to a target or to intercept enemy aircraft. If a squadron intercepted the enemy the sections would immediately break into pairs, with each lead man attacking an enemy aircraft. The wing man would try to stay with his leader and make sure his rear was clear, this allowed the leader to concentrate on shooting down the enemy aircraft. Flight Lieutenant Neil Russell of 416 Squadron RCAF describes a dog fight on 28 July where this practise was used:

I was Green Two on front line patrol and we were vectored to west of Lisieux. We climbed above cloud 7,000 feet and saw approximately 50 Liberators at 11 o clock, at 15,000 feet. 20

---

29 Ibid., p.23.
30 Clark, David, *Angels Eight* (Bloomington, Indiana: 1st Books), p.189.

Figure 6.14 RAF Spitfires flown by Norwegian pilots over France during a routine fighter sweep, 13 June. (Crown Copyright Air Historical Branch)

– plus Focke-Wulf 190s (FW190s) were seen to half-roll and attack the Liberators, then break down into our formation. I followed Green One into a steep climbing turn to port but was a bit behind. At that moment a FW 190 started to come down at nine o' clock to me. As he came down I got in a 2-second burst from 45 degrees (machine gun and cannon) at 300-400yards. He then turned right and down I got onto his tail very easily. I fired three or four 2-second bursts hitting him on the fuselage and right wing. Large pieces came off his fuselage, there appeared to be an explosion and a great deal of flame and smoke. He went down and I got another burst (2-second machine guns and cannon) and part of his right wing came off. He then went spinning straight down and burning. He appeared to be about 2,000 feet at that time. The squadron was then ordered to reform so I did not see him hit the ground.[31]

To be a successful fighter pilot there were a number of 'dog fighting' techniques that were essential to learn. Keeping yourself between the enemy and the sun was an important advantage as was the ability to get on and stay on the enemy's tail. The 'head on attack' was a nerve-wracking technique with an all too obvious hazard as Flying Officer K A J Trott of 197 Squadron found out on 11 July:

As I came out of cloud I noticed a solitary ME 109 coming towards me. I lined up for a head-on attack, firing my cannon. The next minute I realised I would have to break to avoid collision. As I did so my starboard wing collided with the wing of the 109 and I felt my head hit the cockpit cover and my left shoulder the side of the cockpit. My helmet, oxygen mask, goggles and revolver holster were torn from my body and I hurtled into space with only my parachute intact. I realised I would have to pull the ripcord as my altitude was only about

---

31 Ibid., p.300.

3,000 ft. The next moment my canopy opened and I lost consciousness. I came round to find myself hanging from a tree in an orchard surrounded by several armed Germans.[32]

If an enemy pilot succeeded in getting onto his tail then the pilot's very survival would depend upon his ability to 'break'. This could be done by a number of methods. A sudden turn, dive, or deceleration might work or alternatively a well timed 'skid' or yaw to one side. In addition to these tactics there were a number of manoeuvres developed by expert pilots in both world wars. There is of course the famous 'loop' a quick 'breaking turn' or a 'barrel roll' where the pilot flicks the aircraft over on its back while climbing and then does a roll again climbing slightly to adopt the same direction. Many pilots would use the *Immelmann* manoeuvre, named after the German World War One pilot who introduced it. In this technique the pilot pulls into a steep climb, turns it into a loop but flicks out at the top of the loop to resume a normal flight attitude.

These manoeuvres would be used by expert pilots instinctively, allowing them to move into advantageous positions or break contact. It became a real test of flying skill and nerves as the dogfight progressed and the altitudes became lower and lower. In addition to performing these manoeuvres the pilot needed to be an accurate shot, this often required him to 'aim off' the speeding German aircraft, a practise that was known as deflection shooting. Many who have fired weapons at moving targets can appreciate the skill required when both firer and target are moving at speeds up to 400 mph in three different dimensions. Flying Officer Willie Warfield, 421 Squadron RCAF, recalls a low-level dog fight on 15 June:

> I was flying Blue Two behind Blue One as he attacked an Me 109. Two Me 109s bounced us from six o' clock and I broke 180° port. Blue One broke into sun. Both 109s turned with me but one flicked out, the other spiralled down but I managed to keep with him after completing four rolls. This 109 dove to the south of Caen and it took me approximately eight to 10 miles to close with him. I opened fire approximately 600 yards at 0 to 5° deflection, corrected and immediately the 109 streamed coolant from the port side. I fired my second burst from 300 to 400 yards with 0 to 5° deflection, a long one and strikes appeared all over the 109 which finally disintegrated. When I broke off attack another 109 was on my tail so I steep-turned through trees about 10 feet off the deck and was cutting him off and getting into position to fire when he either flicked in or hit a tree, and catapulted into an open field and exploded. No one was about to confirm either, but my camera was on throughout the first attack and before I was able to attack the second Me 109, I was able to take a cine film of it crash into the ground. Also a picture of the first 109 that crashed into a wood, setting trees and undergrowth on fire. The attack commenced about 1200 feet and ended up at zero feet and I probably attained 450 mph closing on the first Me 109.[33]

The success of Mustang and Spitfire pilots in achieving daylight air supremacy over Normandy allowed the ground forces to operate largely unmolested and the fighter-bombers and bombers to attack ground targets largely unhindered by the Luftwaffe. Nonetheless this all came at the cost of a number of Allied pilots; indeed of the Canadian Spitfire squadrons the average number of pilots killed per squadron between 6 June and the end of August was 6.4, over half a squadron's strength.

32 Shores, Christopher and Thomas, Chris Thomas, *Second Tactical Air Force – Volume 2* (Hersham: Ian Allan Publishing, 2005), p.216.

33 Clark, David, *Angels Eight* (Bloomington, Indiana: 1st Books), p.216.

Figure 6.15 A Visual Control Post operating from a Humber scout car in 83 Group's sector of operations, 24 July. Major Colin Gray, the Army liaison officer, points out the coordinates of a target to Squadron Leader Sutherland, who will relay the request to the Army/Group composite HQ. VCPs operated close to the frontline, normally near to a Brigade HQ. (Crown Copyright Air Historical Branch)

It may have been small consolation that German Luftwaffe fighter squadrons suffered twice the loss rate of Spitfire squadrons.[34]

The Tactical Groups would also provide British and American forces with 'Close Air Support'; essentially immediate attacks at the Army's request on targets they were engaging. In addition 'General Air Support' was also provided by the RAF and focused on attacking targets not in close proximity to friendly ground forces, but immediately behind the battlefront. These targets could include bridges, road and rail lines of communication as well the supply transport itself.

There were a number of ways the aircraft could identify targets to attack. They could find their own targets by flying an 'armed recce' or alternatively respond to an Army call for fire support. The Army requests were passed through Air Support Signals Units (ASSU) officers at brigade, divisional and corps HQs known as 'tentacles'. These could communicate not only with each other but also with the joint Army Air Support Control (AASC) HQ Centre and the ASSUs located with the RAF Wings themselves. This meant that all Army headquarters were made aware of the RAF Tac/R reports as well as details of close-support strikes that might affect their troops. The approval of targets at the AASC HQ Centre was based on a judgement of the target's priority and its proximity to the 'bombline' – a line projected forward of friendly troops beyond which aircraft were permitted to attack targets freely. If the target was accepted the Army Liaison Officer attached

---

34 Ibid.

to the RAF squadron would then brief the aircrew using air photographs and maps marked with friendly and enemy locations.[35]

This provided a quick response for pre-planned tasks, but it was not suitable for immediate requests. The system was therefore supplemented through the provision of Forward Control Posts (FCP) that could communicate directly to the aircraft as well as the army formation and ASSU HQ. If the target was urgent the FCP would short circuit the system and 'cut in' to handle the request directly and manage the aircraft's mission. Good though the FCP system was it still depended upon information sent back from the battlefield and therefore further decentralization was afforded through the use of Visual Control Posts (VCPs) or 'Contact Cars'. These were usually armoured cars which contained a Forward Air Controller (FAC), normally an experienced RAF ground attack pilot. This individual would communicate direct to the aircraft overhead and identify targets to him using the terms one pilot would use to another. The results of the mission would be communicated back to the contact car who would then inform the ASSU network.

Even quicker turnaround times were achieved if a 'Cab Rank' of aircraft were available; these would be in a holding pattern behind the frontline and called forward by the FCP/Contact Car as required.[36] Flight Lieutenant G J Gray, 181 Squadron, describes the process:

> We would just take off, wind up to 7,000 feet behind the lines and then went down on your target. You could be back and landed in twenty minutes having fired your rockets. We'd then rearm, refuel and away we went again.
>
> Quite often from these forward airfields the only way to contact HQ was on the air, because there might not be any good communications on the ground. We mostly spoke in clear language, never in code, except when co-operating with the army when you'd have special map squares. Colours of the day changed each day and you wrote these on the back of one's shammy leather gloves – so you'd get through several pairs a week! Even so we tried not to talk at all on the R/T except in an emergency. We used hand signals or would waggle our wings. The only times we spoke was when the enemy was sighted or you as a leader would say, 'Going down now,' or 'Going down in five seconds – R/Ps [Rocket Projectiles] on'.
>
> The army would fire red smoke shells, say into a corner of a wood and that was your signal for attack. If they didn't fire the smoke then we weren't allowed to attack even if we could see the enemy. This was because they were so close to our own lines that we might possibly mistake them, but more often than not all we did was go down and fire our rockets where the red smoke was and have no idea what the results were, for the Germans were very well camouflaged. I was amazed when we did eventually catch up the front lines and saw some of the damage we had done. The fragmentation rockets we had cut soft stuff absolutely to ribbons –little bits, around two or three inches.
>
> There was always a chap in a forward tank who could speak to you in the air and he'd say, 'Red smoke going down now, go to square four, section 6,' or something, wherever they wanted support. We'd be hovering around at about 7-8,000 feet till we got more or less into the area where this chap wanted you and then we'd see the red smoke go down and we'd dive in and bash where the smoke landed. He had a visual siting of the enemy always and could fire his smoke pretty accurately. Sometimes he would say it was a bit short so fire 200 yards in front of the smoke, which was what we did.[37]

35 Gooderson, Ian, *Air Power at the Battlefront* (London: Frank Cass, 1998), p.24.
36 Ibid., pp.26-29.
37 Franks, Norman, *Typhoon Attack* (London: William Kimber, 1984), p.140.

The air-ground coordination was far from perfect however. The commander of 51st Highland Division, Major-General Bullen-Smith, made the following points in a letter to his higher headquarters on 14 June:

> Even under existing conditions, where a bombline is given which is thought to be simple, grave errors are made by the RAF. Further, when targets are given to the RAF which are on, it is thought, easily recognisable features, similar very grave errors have been experienced.
>
> An example of this happened yesterday evening. I asked for an air attack to be made on the village of DÉMOUVILLE 1067. The nearest tps of mine to this village were at TOUFFREVILLE 1368. The target lay on the main rd CAEN–TROARN, yet, for over an hr, beginning at the time selected by me and accepted by the Air for the attack on DÉMOUVILLE, my troops in the wood at 1370, and Airborne Tps further north, were bombed, shot at by rockets, and machine-gunned by Typhoons. As soon as the attack began yellow smoke was put up. Yellow triangles were laid and vehs and ambs were pulled into the open, yet the aircraft persisted in their attack.[38]

The primary aircraft in attacking Close Air Support ground targets was the large, aggressive looking Typhoon fighter-bomber. Introduced in 1942 and originally designed as a high-speed interceptor the aircraft had an unpromising first year in service. Pilots complained of an engine that cut out unexpectedly and a tail with an alarming tendency to fall off. By 1944 these issues had been resolved and the pilots began to appreciate the Typhoon's qualities as a very stable low-level firing platform, one that could carry significantly more ordnance than other fighters. It therefore began to be converted for use as a fighter-bomber in the ground attack role. The aircraft was fitted with four 20mm cannons which were very effective against soft skin vehicles and light armour. In addition the Typhoon could also be equipped with bombs, normally two 500lb and one 1,000lb bomb, or alternatively eight 3-inch rocket projectiles fired from four rails underneath each wing. The rocket itself was little more than a cast iron tube with a 3-inch diameter motor and a 60lb warhead screwed to the end.

These were effective against a range of targets, including German armour, although a tank could only be destroyed by a direct hit from the rocket itself. The setting up and maintenance of the aircraft's armament was the responsibility of RAF ground crew armourers such as Des Sheppard of 137 Squadron:

> The four cannons were all set to converge at a point directly in front of the aircraft at a set distance. This varied according to the pilot or even target. The idea was to set the gun sight against boards we made and erected about 25 yards in front of the aircraft, with coloured discs worked out mathematically to where the cannon shells would meet at, say 250 yards. Then we took the breech-block back and dropped in a sort of telescope which you'd look through. It had an angle mirror and you could see out along the gun barrel and then one armourer (one would work in pairs normally) would adjust the cannon after releasing the lock nut, then move the cannon, while the other man guided him to which way it should move, so as to pick up the view of the coloured disc on the board…
>
> Working on the main planes of the Typhoons was not easy. It was so high and so steep when the plane was sitting on the ground for working on the gun bays, which were covered by two big folding panels which were unscrewed and folded up. This gave you a big opening where the cannons belt feed ammunition boxes were, But because it was so steep if you didn't

38 TNA: War Diary of 51st Highland Division, WO 171/1527 Air Support – 14 June 1944.

Figure 6.16 A Typhoon IB of 183 Squadron displays its four 20mm cannon.
(Crown Copyright Air Historical Branch)

have some support, you'd just be hanging on trying to stop yourself sliding off. So we had big wooden platforms made which were cut at the same angle as the wing, so that when you clipped that over the edge of the gun-bay (but in reverse) you were level.

When we were sliding the rockets onto the rails it was important that the two saddles at each end were square and rode well down the rail when we put them on, we didn't only push the rocket down once, we slid it backwards and forwards a few times so that there would be no kind of stoppage when it was fired. We would clean the rails with a slightly oily rag but that was all that was necessary.[39]

Close support missions were normally carried out with 6-8 aircraft. For an attack to be effective visibility could be no less than 2,000 yards and the cloud base no lower than 5,000 feet (or 3,000 feet if only strafing with 20mm cannons). The major threat to the Typhoons came from German AA guns and therefore the nature of this fire largely determined the tactics employed. The Germans possessed large quantities of small caliber AA fire (e.g. 12.7mm) which was effective up to 3,000 feet and could not be seen by Allied pilots. Anti-aircraft fire of 20-40mm calibre was also widely used and usually automatic, it was easily seen by pilots and effective up to 6,000 feet, to avoid this fire the normal cruising altitude of 7,000 to 8,000 feet was adopted. The heavier 88mm guns could easily reach this height; but were not automatic and generally inaccurate against fast moving Typhoons. Flying Officer J G Simpson of 193 Squadron gave his views on Flak:

39 Franks, Norman, *Typhoon Attack* (London: William Kimber, 1984), p.85.

Figure 6.17 German 20mm anti-aircraft artillery mounted on a half-track scan the sky for Allied aircraft in Normandy, June 1944. (Bundesarchiv, Bild 164-12-6-09A, photo: Wilfried Woscidlo)

The thing that worried most of us quite a bit was the fact that the Germans would put up a carpet of 20 and 40mm stuff. Little white puffs you could get out and walk on. Round about 3-4000 feet this was and one had to dive through it. You didn't think of the shells that were coming up and had not yet exploded, unless they hit you! It seemed much safer to go through the white puffs rather than fly around and try to screw your courage to dive down through it.

I think on the low level shows you never saw the flak that hit you, and I personally felt very much afraid of flak on a low level op. After an attack and you begin to pull up you are a better target for the light flak and there's no doubt that the German gunners were a pretty brave lot.[40]

If the target was heavily defended the pilots would normally make a steep 60° dive at 7-8000 feet and fire all eight rockets in one salvo at 4,000 feet. If the target was lightly defended then the pilots would, from a height of 3,000 to 4,000 feet, make a shallow dive of 20 or 30° and then, at 1,500 feet height and 1,000 yards distance from the enemy, ripple the rockets in pairs. Many pilots however also came down much lower, firing rockets and cannons together at 250 yards and heights of 500-600 feet. Belgian Pilot Charles Demoulin of 609 Squadron describes a typical attack on 9 August:

We arrive west of Falaise at 3,000 feet, in radio contact with the attack control, called 'Cab Rank'. I'm surprised to recognize the voice of the controller – it's my old friend Monty Van Lierde (he returned to us in 123 Wing a few weeks later and took over command of 164

---

40 Ibid., p.204.

Figure 6.18 A still from the gun camera footage of a 181 Squadron Hawker Typhoon showing a rocket projectile travelling towards a group of German vehicles.
(Crown Copyright Air Historical Branch)

Squadron). There could be no better guide than Monty, whose calm voice gives me the form precisely and in a tone of friendship as he mixes French and English.

'Allo Charles. Tanks and staff cars in F4, behind the Farm. Flak in the wood – Bonne Chance!'

'Thanks, Monty. OK boys, orbit left.'

As we turn left, I plot the coordinates on my map, scan the ground, then pick out the poorly camouflaged targets round the Normandy Farm.

No flak yet. As usual they don't want to show themselves before we go down, so as to take us unawares. Just wait, friends! In a moment it will be your chance!

Three-quarters of the way round my turn, I am perfectly positioned up-sun to spoil the aim of the flak as we go down in our shallow dive on the Panzers. Now I can see the tanks clearly and I start diving with the first section. I send the other four Typhoons to look after the flak boys in the wood.

'Red Section – we go for the armour. Blue Section enjoy yourselves with the guns in the wood go!'

As soon as they realize that we have seen them, the Germans let go at us with everything they've got and tracers zip past on all sides. But nothing except a lucky shot can stop a Typhoon diving at 500mph. Blue section neutralizes the wood with rockets and cannon and we soon have a free hand. The first tank grows in my gun sight and I let go two pairs of rockets that get him on his left side. I pull up an inch, and fire at a staff car which goes up in smoke as the shells strike home.

A steep turn to port, and from the corner of my eye, I see my No.2 climbing behind me while Nos 3 and 4 are busy shooting up a line of lorries that go up in flames. Down again and this time I choose a juicy half-track under a camouflage net and get a direct hit with my last pair of rockets. A little further away, a small black Citroen jumps and explodes, as my guns go silent with the long hiss of compressed air that marks the end of my ammunition.

Figure 6.19 Armourers fit rocket-projectiles to the under-wing racks of a Typhoon IB at B6/Coulombs on 16 June. (Crown Copyright Air Historical Branch)

> I climb back to 2000 feet to watch the slaughter. In a dozen places there are still sporadic explosions under the thick black smoke that billows towards the sky, and flames are coming out of the farm roof.[41]

Accurately hitting the target with rockets was notoriously difficult. Not only were small targets like tanks and AFVs hard to identify but the rockets themselves were inherently inaccurate. The rockets when fired left the aircraft launch rails at 150 feet per second, the cordite would burn for one and a half seconds accelerating the rocket to 1,000 feet per second. This relatively slow launch speed meant that the slightest yaw or skid when the pilot fired his rocket could affect the point of aim dramatically. In addition a strong cross wind could cause the rocket to drift on its journey to the target. Consequently the pilots approach would often have to be determined by wind direction rather than tactical considerations like the position of the sun or enemy flak. To complicate the pilot's problems further the large engine cowling of the Typhoon also presented problems. Flying Officer S J Eaton of 257 Squadron explains:

> When dive bombing you formed your echelon port or starboard, depending which way you were going, and literally it was a question of peeling over – there was no other accurate way of doing it. It was no use just pushing the nose forward because the Typhoon had a very broad nose and you couldn't see down over it. In-experienced pilots used to get lost on these sorts of things because they hadn't learned to keep in line with their leader. Usually rather like a tail chase, one follows straight down and when ground flak starts and the Germans start aiming for the leader and under deflecting because of the angle of the dive etc. it was usually the pilot down the line who got into trouble. On a lot of trips those who were Nos 3 and 4 of

41 Demoulin, Charles, *Firebirds! Flying the Typhoon in Action* (Shrewsbury: Airlife Publishing, 1986), p.130.

sections were hit more often. I soon found out from this experience of seeing what happened and I always weaved behind until the last moment possible and then straightened up, but never in a dead line with my leader – it was absolutely fatal. This was why it was inevitably the newcomers to the squadron who were hit for they were not around long enough to learn how to avoid this type of fire.[42]

If damaged by flak the aircraft might be sufficiently high enough and over Allied lines for the pilot to consider baling out as Charles Demoulin experienced:

As I'm regrouping the squadron again, I feel my plane judder and the engine vibrates. My radio is silent and there is a big hole with the wind whistling through the fuselage, just behind my seat: things are going to go from bad to worse…

Instinctively, I climb towards our lines not very far from the target, and I watch my temperature gauge climbing towards the red danger zone. I won't make base. Surprisingly calmly, I nurse my wounded plane towards the safety of our lines before I have to abandon her. Near Caen, the flames start melting the engine cowling and the acrid smell of black smoke fills the cockpit. It's time to go: canopy jettisoned, straps undone and stick in the belly – barrel roll and exit…

A sharp blow on my shoulders, a white mushroom above my head and I land quite peacefully in an orchard, narrowly missing an apple tree. All in one piece, and already surrounded by Scottish tank crews who seem to want to throw out a party.[43]

The pilot's alternative to baling out would be to stay with his damaged aircraft, given the low levels the Typhoons would operate at, this was sometimes an unavoidable choice. It was certainly a dilemma presented to Flying Officer H G Pattison of 182 Squadron:

On the break I felt about five strikes underneath me; not surprising as there was intense heavy and light flak in the target area. Breaking left had put me on the safety course from the target and my immediate reaction was to check the instruments. To my surprise, the oil pressure was falling rapidly, and within five seconds, stopped at zero coincidentally with the propeller coming literally to a shuddering halt as the engine seized. The whole airframe shook but did not fall apart. Then came decision time to pull up from the deck and bail out or to continue as far as possible with excess speed and hope to force land behind our lines. I quickly opted for the latter course and kept going. On the way I switched off fuel and all electrics, then tightened my straps.

Speed was obviously decaying fairly rapidly and at, I suppose, 250 mph I decided to pull up and look for somewhere to put down as all I could see were trees. My lucky star must have been shining brightly as, at about 200mph, I saw a large clear space ahead. This turned out to be a ploughed field, or at least, it was very rough. Speed dropping to 150mph I jettisoned the hood, selected flaps down and started pumping like hell. Fortunately they went down and I was committed.

The available space did not look too generous so I had to force the aircraft onto the ground at, I guess, somewhere between 120-140 mph – rather fast! After two or three ricochets it stayed down and we ground to a halt with clods of earth flying everywhere including into the cockpit. Sudden silence while I disembarked and crawled under a wing tip – fortunately

42 Franks, Norman, *Typhoon Attack* (London: William Kimber, 1984), p.79.
43 Demoulin, Charles, *Firebirds! Flying the Typhoon in Action* (Shrewsbury: Airlife Publishing, 1986), p.116.

there was no fire – then the silence became very noisy. German tanks to the east, British tanks and artillery to the west and me in the middle being fired on by both sides. Needless to say I was somewhat concerned as to what might happen in such an exposed position. After 30-45 minutes of enormous twitch, the firing stopped and a Canadian army captain drove out in a jeep and picked me up. I was debriefed at his HQ and a kindly gentleman instructed a soldier to furnish me with a tumbler of Scotch. It was quite full and only a little was lost due to a trembling hand on its way to my lips.[44]

Regular low-level flying into a wall of flak caused the Typhoons to receive the heaviest casualties of 2nd TAF. Fifty-six per cent of the total Typhoon force engaged between 6 June and 1 September were killed as opposed to 41% of the Spitfire force or 32.8% of the Mosquito force. Additionally whereas Bomber Command crews could expect a fixed 'thirty mission' tour and Spitfire tours were fixed at 'two hundred operational hours', the shortage of Typhoon pilots meant that for many there was no alternative but to keep on flying. Squadron Leader H Ambrose commanded 181 Squadron and had also flown with 259 Squadron:

We were all tired. I shouldn't have gone on myself; I had done my 100 trips by November 1944, but I went on and on and was then promoted so I kept on. No one seemed to take much notice or check up, but I know at the end of the war I was really tired. I finally did 389 ops and I still can't believe I did it.[45]

An inevitable consequence of heavy casualties was a growing shortage of Typhoon pilots. However the Typhoon squadrons had already established a reputation as a 'Chop' squadron, an RAF term for a unit where the odds of surviving were poor. Wing Commander Desmond Scott raised his concerns of the growing shortage:

After I explained my fears to our Group AOC, 2nd TAF circularized all Spitfire squadrons asking for volunteers. Those pilots who did accept would return to England and complete a conversion course at our Group support unit at Lasham before being posted back to a Typhoon squadron.

The response was most disappointing. Not a single Spitfire pilot applied. So it was necessary to withdraw them, even if unwillingly, from their respective squadrons, which was not the happiest of situations. Few took kindly to their new role, and some even un-ashamedly illustrated their anxiety when interviewed either by myself or Wing Commander Dring. Others philosophically accepted their transfer to rocket-firing Typhoons and acquitted themselves well in the weeks that followed.[46]

Though at a sobering cost, the effect the Typhoons had on the Germans was dramatic, but perhaps in ways that might be surprising. In August a field study was made by the Second Army's Operational Research Section on the effects of air attacks on armoured formations by examining destroyed and damaged German vehicles in the Falaise Gap. The study highlighted that in some cases Allied pilot's claims of destroyed vehicles were greatly exaggerated, but also that many German vehicles, including tanks, were simply abandoned rather than being destroyed. This is surprising given that a tank could only be destroyed by a direct hit from a rocket and that

44 Franks, Norman, *Typhoon Attack* (London: William Kimber, 1984), p.144.
45 Ibid., p.230.
46 Scott, Desmond, *Typhoon Pilot* (London: Arrow Books, 1982), p.120.

Figure 6.20 Typhoon pilots of 121 Wing back from operational sorties on 16 June are debriefed at B2/Bazenville. On the right, leaning over the table, is Squadron Leader Ingle-Finch, commander of 175 Squadron. Behind him, wearing sunglasses, is Squadron-Leader Pitt-Brown of 174 Squadron. (Crown Copyright Air Historical Branch)

Figure 6.21 Workmen tend to a de Havilland Mosquito plane on an aircraft runway. (Ronny Jaques, Library and Archives Canada, e000762768)

a rocket's inherent inaccuracy meant the safest place to be was probably in the tank itself. This was a point understood by some German prisoners of war who noted that experienced crews remained in their tanks during air attacks, which often only inflicted superficial damage (cannon strikes or near misses from bombs). Whereas inexperienced men would frequently bail out when aircraft attacked.[47] The Typhoon attacks may not have destroyed German tanks in the numbers either claimed or generally supposed, but the destruction of supporting soft skin vehicles and the effect on the enemies 'will' was decisive. There are innumerable examples of German attacks stalling or breaking up after the intervention of Typhoon Close Air Support strikes.

The Light and Medium Bombers of 2 Group also supported 21st Army Group. Equipped with Mosquitoes, Bostons and Mitchells they operated from airfields in England and were used on General Support tasks rather than Close Air Support roles and were specifically tasked to 'cause maximum delay to the movement by road and rail by enemy forces at night'.[48]

The twin-engined, wooden framed Mosquito was the lightest bomber in 2 Group and had a maximum speed of 370mph at 13,000 feet with a service ceiling of 32,000 feet. It could carry a bomb load of 2,000lbs for a distance of 1,270 miles or alternatively 1,000lbs for 1,650 miles. It had a crew of two and was armed with four .303-inch guns and four 20mm guns.[49] A good example of the sort of mission flown by 2 Group's Mosquitoes is that of 11 June when Mosquitoes of 464, 487 and 107 squadrons attacked petrol tankers at the rail yard in Chatellerault. This mission was as a result of a request by the Army received at 1945hrs. The Mosquito crews were at their aircraft at 2000hrs and their engines were started at 2015. As there was no flight plan for this short notice mission, the commanders, Wing Commanders Irving Smith and Bob Iredale, simply drew a straight line from the easterly entrance route of the battle area to the target, measuring distance and direction. A different route, avoiding flak, was handed to them just as they were about to leave but in order not to delay the mission any further they elected to measure this in the air. A target map was also passed in these last few moments but in the confusion it was left behind, its absence only being discovered once the aircraft were airborne. Wing Commander Irving Smith described the mission:

> We set course in cloud in formation at 1,000 feet and made the whole trip between six and eight thousand feet using Gee as the only navigation aid. We broke cloud forty miles from Le Mans and then flew along the base of the cloud until we went off our map. We then went down on the deck and flew two courses, which my navigator had been able to scribble on a piece of paper. On the run-up to target I flew 7 degrees further north across the main double track railway leading south from Tours. I intended to find the line and fly along it to the first big town then find the marshalling yards. This would have been Chatellerault. Twenty miles from the target No.3 got a definite pinpoint and took over the lead. He then flew a course only 2 degrees different to the one we were steering and attacked from 100-150 feet. I bombed the northern end. No. 2, Flt Lt J B Ellacombe, bombed the south end and Flt Lt WJ Runciman the centre. We then flew out on a reciprocal, climbed to 7,000 to 8,000 feet and returned in cloud. North of Bernay my No.2 warned me of the presence of a 'snapper' who made a tentative attack from port beam about 1,000 yards away. He then disappeared. Iredale's formation went into cloud for two minutes to evade him then continued course to the target at ground level.

47   ORS 2nd TAF/No. 2 ORS Joint Report No.3 'Rocket Typhoons in Close Support Missions quoted from *Air Power at the Battlefront* Ian Gooderson (London: Frank Cass, 1998), p.116.

48   Bowyer, Michael J F, *2 Group* (London: Faber and Faber, 1992), p.368

49   Ellis, L F, *Victory In the West* Volume 1 (London: HMSO, 1962), p.563.

Wing Commander Bob Iredale continues the story:

> We reached the target and attacked from the south. I saw 487's successful attack and I cannoned a goods train at the south end of the rail junction and bombed trains in the station, but I could not identify whether they were petrol tankers. After bombing I decided to reconnoiter this very long railway line at low level until it was too dark to do so. Between the target and Châteaudun many trains were attacked, mostly troop trains stationary in small sidings.[50]

The Mosquitoes had arrived over the target a mere two hours after the target message had been received in England, it demonstrates the quick response the AASC was able to generate for even 'General Support' requests from the Army. Operations by the RAF's 2 Group, as well as other bomber squadrons, quickly began to have a profound effect on the German ability to move troops, even at night. An order within a German Panzer division highlighted the issue:

> The ever-growing danger of air attack necessitates the strictest observation of orders concerning black-out…under no circumstances will lights – even tail lights – be allowed, No dashboard lights will be allowed and care is to be taken in lighting cigarettes. All machine-guns will remain in position and fire will be opened only against direct attack.[51]

The Medium bombers of 2 Group consisted of two twin-engined American built aircraft: Bostons and Mitchells. The Mitchell had a top speed of 292 miles an hour at 15,000 feet with a service ceiling of 20,000 feet, it could carry 4,000lbs of bombs for a distance of 1,660 miles or 6,000lbs of bombs for 965 miles; it had a crew of five and an armament of five .5inch guns. The Boston had a top speed of 320 miles an hour at 11,000 feet with a service ceiling of 24,500 feet and could carry 2,000 lbs of bombs for a range of 1, 570 miles or 4,000lbs of bombs for 710 miles. It had a crew of four and an armament of four .5-inch guns.[52] Squadron Leader Malcolm Scott DFC, who served on Mitchells, describes the 10 June daylight attack on the headquarters of Panzer Group West at Château de la Caine, 12 miles south west of Caen. The large force of Mitchells would bomb from medium height with their full bomb load of 4,000lbs, made up of eight 500-pounders. Rocket firing Typhoons would also attack at low level and Spitfires acted as fighter escorts. Initially the morning briefing scheduled for 1030 had to be deferred because of heavily overcast sky and thick cloud. However as the day progressed Squadron Leader Scott recalled the weather slightly improved and a briefing was arranged and the aircraft took off:

> The bombers climbed steadily, circling over base as they formed up, before setting course at 2022. Over Selsey Bill they were joined by another 18 aircraft of 226 Squadron led by their commanding officer, Wg Cdr Mitchell. Soon after, 33 Spitfires took up their escort positions, close escort being provided by Mark Vs from an Air Defence Great Britain Squadron while three Mark IX squadrons of 84 Group flew high and low cover to the Mitchells. One 226 Squadron aircraft had to abort with mechanical trouble. Two others from 180 Squadron turned back before bombing; one with an oil pressure problem and the other with an instrument fault. Yet another suffered bomb release failure and brought its bombs back.

50 Bowyer, Michael J F, *2 Group* (London: Faber and Faber, 1992), p.374.
51 Ibid., p.380.
52 Ellis, L F, *Victory in the West* Volume 1 (London: HMSO 1962), p.563.

Two of the four Typhoon squadrons flew their 'spare' aircraft also and of the 42 Typhoons taking part in the operation, two from each squadron were 'fighters' with no rockets but fully–loaded cannon, the remaining 34 were all rocket-firing 'Tiffies'. The plan was for the Typhoons to attack in two waves with 30 minutes between them, the first wave's attack on the parked vehicles and tanks to coincide with the assault by the bombers, the second wave's task was to 'clear up'.

The Chief of Staff of Panzer Group West, General von Dawans, was reportedly dining with his staff officers in the Château's large dining room. On hearing the air raid sirens the head-quarters staff exited the building to view the aircraft never imagining that they were the target. At the moment the raid began General Geyr von Schweppenburg, the commander of Panzer Group West, arrived at the Château in his staff car. The timing of his arrival would nearly cost him his life:

Seventeen 'Tiffies' from 181 and 247 Squadrons loosed off 136 rockets from 2,000 feet with devastating effect.

Above at 12,000 feet, the three squadrons of 139 Wing spread in a 'vic', with the Mitchells of 226 Squadron flying tight up behind 180 Squadron in the No. 4 position, converged on the target in boxes of six aircraft. At 2115 the Mitchells released 536 x 500 lb bombs with great accuracy and saturated the château and the whole target area. Great clouds of dust and debris, flame and smoke rose into the air. Geyr von Schweppenburg and another officer were wounded, but von Dawans and the remainder of his staff perished in the attack.

Four 'fighter' Typhoons meanwhile swept into the nearby village of Montigny, shooting up the place with their cannon. As the Mitchells swung onto a north-westerly course after drop-ping their bombs some Flak was experienced from Caen, but no real damage was suffered. By the time the second wave of RP Typhoons arrived on the scene, the château was a charred and smoking ruin and the radio trucks and other vehicles were scattered and scorched wrecks. The 'Tiffies' fired their rockets and cannon into any outbuildings that remained standing. All the bombers were down by 2225 (2025 GMT) and there was an immediate call for a 'turn round' for night operations. At de-briefing the elated aircrews of each squadron reported on the complete success of the operation. Almost everyone claimed to have seen their bombs fall on the target or close to it; Flak had been light, there was no enemy fighter opposition and the raid appeared to have taken the enemy defences completely by surprise.[53]

In addition to 2 Group's bombers, 21st Army Group could call for support from Bomber Command and the US 8th Air Force. In March 1944 these forces, against the wishes of their commanders; Air Chief Marshal Sir Arthur Harris and Lieutenant-General Carl Spaatz, had been switched from strategic air campaign targets over Germany to support Operation OVERLORD. The destruction that these heavy bomber assets did against the lines of communication in France and the low-countries was immense, it succeeded in greatly delaying the German's ability to rapidly counter the Allied bridgehead. After D-Day General Eisenhower still retained the ability to give 'strategic direction' to these air forces and the Allied ground and air commanders began to consider how and when heavy bomber aircraft could provide close support. The principle advan-tage that the British Lancaster and US B-17 Flying Fortress would provide compared to other 2nd TAF aircraft was the weight of their fire power. The Lancaster could carry 14,000lbs of bombs on

53 Shores, Christopher and Thomas, Chris, *Second Tactical Air Force* (Hersham: Ian Allan Publishing, 2005), p.148.

Figure 6.22 A Lancaster bomber in flight. (Crown Copyright Air Historical Branch)

14 available bomb hooks. A typical load would therefore be ten 1,000lb bombs and four 500lb bombs. Although the B-17 could carry comparatively less (6,000lb) it had 40 bomb hooks and could therefore carry a greater variety of loads including 250lb, 100lb or even 'clusters' of 20lb fragmentation bombs. The B-17's ability to carry two hundred 20lbs fragmentation bombs was an attractive quality as the large craters created by 1,000lb and 500lbs often affected the Army's subsequent mobility.

At the army commander's requests heavy bombers were used on a number of occasions in Normandy either against German 'Fortress' positions, such as Le Havre, or to saturate German front line positions in order to achieve a breakthrough, such as Operation GOODWOOD. There were differences between the methods employed by the RAF's Bomber Command and the USAAF's bomber force. The RAF bombed in succession, each bomber aiming individually, guided by a Target Indicator previously laid by a specialist 'pathfinder' aircraft and radio instructions from an accompanying airborne 'Master Bomber'. The USAAF bombed in very fixed formations, with only the formation leader aiming his bombs, the other aircraft in the formation simply releasing theirs at the same time as the leader.[54] The use of heavy bombers in a close support role was unpopular with many of the air chiefs who felt it to be a distraction for Bomber Command and argued that the work should be done by either Tactical Air Forces or the Army's own artillery. Nonetheless when they were used their effect was often astounding. Lieutenant Richard von Rosen, a Tiger tank company commander in 503rd Heavy Tank Battalion recalls the effect of the bombing prior to the launch of Operation GOODWOOD:

> I was awakened early in the morning by engine noise, and saw the first bomber waves approaching. From then on we were subjected to heavy air bombardment, which lasted for two and a half hours without interruption. It was like hell, and I am astonished that I survived it. I was unconscious for a while after a bomb exploded just in front of my tank, almost burying me alive. Another tank, about thirty yards away, received a direct hit, which set it on

---

54 Gooderson, Ian, *Air Power at the Battlefront* (London: Frank Cass, 1998), pp.128-129.

fire instantly. A third was turned upside down by the blast – a Tiger weighed fifty-eight tons and yet it was tossed aside like a playing card. It shows what sort of hell we found ourselves in. It was so nerve shattering you couldn't even think. Then suddenly the bombing ended and the following silence was uncanny. Two Tigers were completely destroyed, and two so severely damaged that they could not be used. All the rest were completely covered by earth and had to be dug out. The engines were full of dust and the air-cooling systems were not functioning. All weapons were put out of adjustment by the shock effect. Fifteen men in my Company were dead. Two, who could not stand the terrific nervous strain of the bombardment, had committed suicide. Another had become insane and had to be sent to an asylum.[55]

Conversely the effect on Allied troops of witnessing heavy and medium bombers being used in close support could be very positive. Major Blacker of 23rd Hussars recalls watching the same attack:

Dawn broke mistily on 18 July; it was obviously going to be another gloriously sunny day. Gradually, as the light grew stronger, we could see the whole armoured brigade drawn up in its full battle array. Tanks, guns, half-tracks, carriers – it really was a most impressive, indeed thrilling sight. As the mist rolled away we heard in the distance the drone of a vast number of bombers. And then appearing over the horizon behind us and coming in an apparently never ending stream, were the big black Lancaster's of the RAF, while high above them spitfires twisted and rolled. The bombers passed over our heads and began to unload their bombs on the villages that flanked our advance. Immediately the whole area erupted in grey and brown clouds of dust, which completely obscured our view. Next came the Marauders, the medium bombers, white and glistening in the sun, flying straight down the middle of the corridor, dropping fragmentation bombs along the path of our advance. Again the whole area disappeared in a tremendous swirl of dust. By this time all the chaps were tremendously excited, waving, cheering and shouting at the tops of their voices. And then tragedy – one of the Marauders dropped a bomb short and killed a complete crew. This sobered everyone up. We settled down into our tanks and got ready to advance.[56]

Sadly such short bombing by Allied bombers over their own troops was not unheard of. In some cases it was a case of mistaking the target or poor navigation but in others there was also a tendency for the bombing to creep back. Flight Lieutenant Campbell Muirhead a bomb aimer on Lancasters explains:

It's this 'drop-back' that they keep on and on about at briefing: bomb aimers lying there, thumb poised over the tit all ready to press and the target sliding slowly – oh, so slowly – up the graticule: and they can't wait – their thumb drops just that fraction of a second before the target is fully on the cross graticule and, gradually, if one or two bomb-aimers act similarly, the entire bombing effort more or less creeps backwards until it's the area before the target which is getting it, not the target itself.[57]

The consequences of heavy bomber loads falling on friendly forces prior to an assault could be disastrous. One occasion when RAF bombers caused heavy casualties by short bombing was

55 Major General von Rosen papers, Staff College archives.
56 Operation Goodwood Staff College Battlefied Tour, Staff College archives, 1954, p.23.
57 Campbell Muirhead, *The Diary of a Bomb Aimer* (Tunbridge Wells: Spellmount Publishing, 1987), p.35.

during a mission to support II Canadian Corps during Operation TRACTABLE on 14 August. Bombardier J G Perry who served with a 51st Highland Division artillery regiment recalls the experience:

> We were in open country about 5 miles south of CAEN on a beautiful sunny afternoon. The time was 2 pm. We knew that a big attack was going in, in the area of, or towards the direction of Falaise, to be preceded by a very large force of Lancasters (some said 1,000) & which we were to support by artillery fire simultaneously.
>
> The first few squadrons passed over flying very straight on a south-easterly direction, evidently loaded with bombs. Their main objective was a wood about 4 miles south of us which Jerry was reported to be occupying in force & bombing was thought to be the only thing to move him.
>
> I was off duty at the time & had just finished a letter to my wife. There was then a gap in between the squadrons overhead when apparently from nowhere a stick of bombs fell approximately two fields to the north of our position. The weather had been dry for some days and they obviously hit something very vulnerable as the area for perhaps a mile square was obliterated with smoke and dust.

The next wave of Lancasters compounded the error and dropped several 1,000lb bombs in the field adjoining the original one where Polish tank squadrons, AA, Canadian reserves and British and Canadian artillery were situated. Bombardier Perry and his comrades sensibly took cover:

> I was in a fairly shallow slit trench face downwards (about 2 1/2 feet deep). It wasn't my own slit trench which was about 150 yards away. The bombing continued after that as wave after wave came over and released their loads. All Hell was let loose and the earth jumped up and down as each stick of bombs crept near to where I was. All sorts of thoughts kept flashing in my mind as I lay there, my loved ones, home everything that was dear to me and finally as I was gradually getting buried alive a prayer.
>
> A split second afterwards I had a feeling of peaceful satisfaction that I had said the prayer. A stick of bombs came whistling down much nearer than any before and I felt instinctively that I was to get it, this was it. I remembered counting the bombs as they fell in quick succession each one nearer than the last. One 2-3-4-5-6 after that I couldn't even think because 2 noises like thunder which deafened me literally lifted me out of the trench, dropped me back in and plastered earth and debris on top of me. My brain had almost ceased to function but subconsciously I had the governing feeling that I had on one or two previous occasions when I had thought it was all over and that was I must not Panic.
>
> I began to pull my knees up towards my stomach. At first I realised that if I didn't make a tremendous effort in a second or so I would suffocate. My knees moved and I got a bit of leverage & heaved for all I was worth (mentally thanking God that I had a strong leg, back and stomach muscles). Finally when I was beginning to feel that all was over I saw a small shaft of daylight under my eyes. I took a deep breath then I rested for a second – another deep breath and then a heave for all I was worth.
>
> The patch of daylight widened but I couldn't get any further with the heaving. I supported what I had already moved as best I could and I was able to think more clearly again. I began to dig upwards with my fingers towards the light and eventually got my head out – another short rest and then one shoulder and then the other. After that it was comparatively easy. I lay panting on God's good earth. Then I realised that another squadron was coming over. I nearly panicked then, but almost immediately came the thought – I mustn't

panic. I dragged myself to my feet and forced myself to walk to my own slit trench. I got there before the next lot came. My own trench was comparatively heaven and inhabited by a Canadian. I dived in and we huddled together sideways until the bombing stopped.[58]

Bombardier Perry was lucky to have only suffered minor injuries as there were many Allied casualties. A subsequent court of inquiry attributed the mistake to poor navigation by the pathfinders in the second wave, but usually the vast majority of aircrews did their utmost to bomb accurately despite the personal risk involved. Flight Lieutenant Campbell Muirhead, the Lancaster bomb aimer, describes a mission in support of OP CHARNWOOD on 7 July:

Another daylight op. We were told that very accurate bombing was essential – 'bring the things back if you can't be sure of your aiming point.' This because we were bombing only 1 1/2 miles ahead of our troops (Canadians, evidently). My sighting was not right so I didn't press the tit. I told Vernon [Flying Officer Vernon the pilot] to go round a second time. God, the language which came over that intercom! Interspersed with references not only to my complete inadequacy as a bomb aimer, but also to my parentage. Can't exactly blame them – there we were, the only Lancaster left over Caen and what flak there was beginning to concentrate on us. But there was no way I was going to drop 13,000lbs of high explosive when there was the slightest possibility of the dreadful stuff killing or wounding our own troops: would have taken the load back to Wickenby first. However, I got a perfect sighting on that second run (despite what was still being said over the intercom) and placed my bombs exactly where I wanted them.

Despite that second time round, on the way back we caught up with the stragglers ('B' for Baker being brand new and with that extra few knots more than most). Flying almost level with another Lanc, who was limping. Just crossing the French Coast when up came quite a scything of flak. It got him (not by the Grace of God, us). He started diving straight down. We counted four parachutes opening, praying for more but to no avail. The Lanc struck the water burst into a terrific sheet of flame. We all fell silent until over base, everybody thinking of the three men inside.[59]

Whilst the bulk of the Heavy Bomber Force was only capable of dropping standard 1,000lb or 500lb bombs through the Mark XIV bombsight, one squadron had been specially trained to drop more sophisticated munitions with far greater precision. This was 617 Squadron, the famous 'dambusters', and their capability was founded on a number of significant new innovations and inventions, arguably the most important of which were the 'earthquake bombs'. This new generation of bomb was designed by Sir Barnes Wallis to penetrate deep underground before detonating and generating a Camouflet effect which would undermine the foundations of otherwise very difficult targets such as hardened concrete bunkers or submarine pens. These earthquake bombs were all given the generic term 'Tallboy' and by the summer of 1944 two types had been satisfactorily developed, a 4,000lb Tallboy S and a 12,000lb Tallboy M. The bomb was not just simply larger than existing bombs its casing was both slender and streamlined in order to obtain near supersonic speeds before impact and burrow itself to depths of 100 feet when it hit the ground. The bomb's steel shell was heat treated and had a specially thickened nose to avoid shattering when it struck the surface, additionally an enhanced explosive called TORPEX (40 percent TNT, 42 percent RDX) was poured under pressure into the casing for

---

58 Written on 15 August 44 by Bombardier Perry. Bdr J G Perry papers Ref 86/47/1, Imperial War Museum.
59 Campbell Muirhead, *The Diary Of a Bomb Aimer* (Tunbridge Wells, Spellmount, 1987), p.89.

XXXX	Army
XXX	Corps
XX	Division
X	Brigade
Infantry Division symbol	Infantry Division
Armoured Division symbol	Armoured Division
Paratroop Division symbol	Paratroop Division
HQ symbol	HQ
Air Landing Brigade symbol	Air Landing Brigade
+ – + –	Corps Boundary
O – O –	Army Boundary
Infantry Division symbol	Infantry Division
Panzer Grenadier Division symbol	Panzer Grenadier Division
Panzer Division symbol	Panzer Division
Fallschirmjäger Division symbol	Fallschirmjäger Division
Static Division symbol	Static Division
Kampfgruppe symbol	Kampfgruppe
High Ground symbol	High Ground
Woods/Orchards symbol	Woods/Orchards
Inundated symbol	Inundated

Key to maps. We have followed the Second World War convention of showing British and Allied Symbols in red and German and Axis symbols in blue.

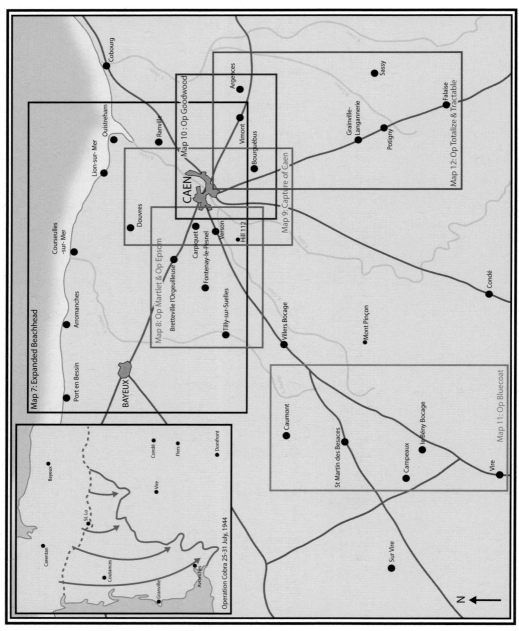

Map 1 Overview of operations in Normandy.

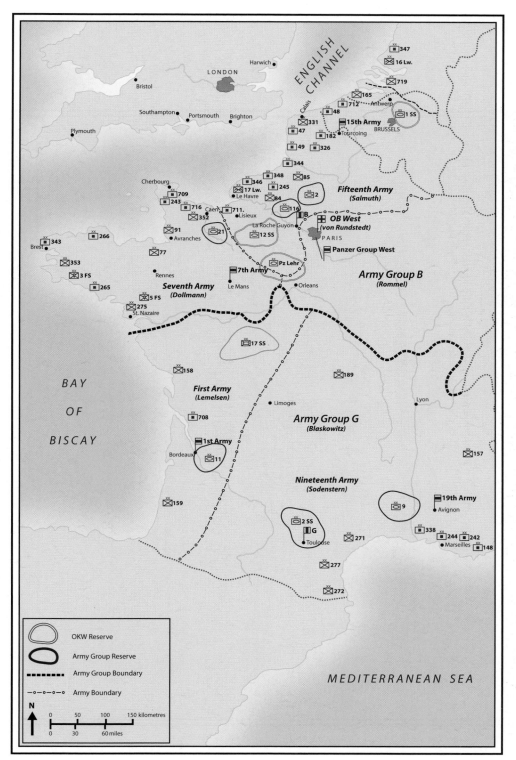

Map 2 German dispositions, early June 1944.

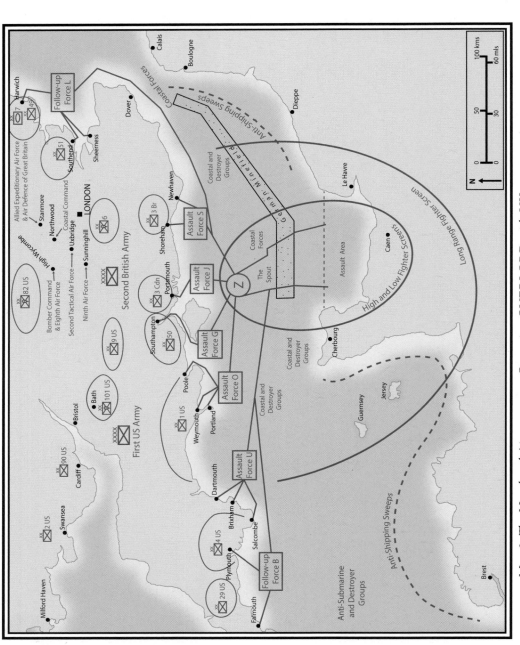

Map 3 The Naval and Air support to Operation OVERLORD with UK concentration areas.

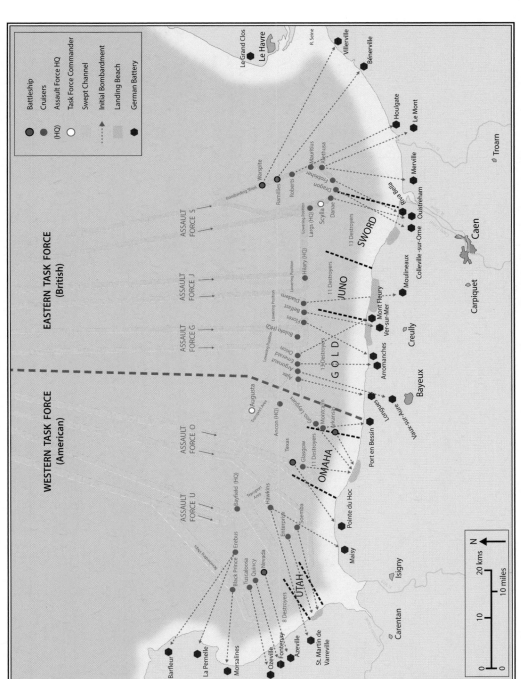

Map 4 D-Day - the assault, 6 June.

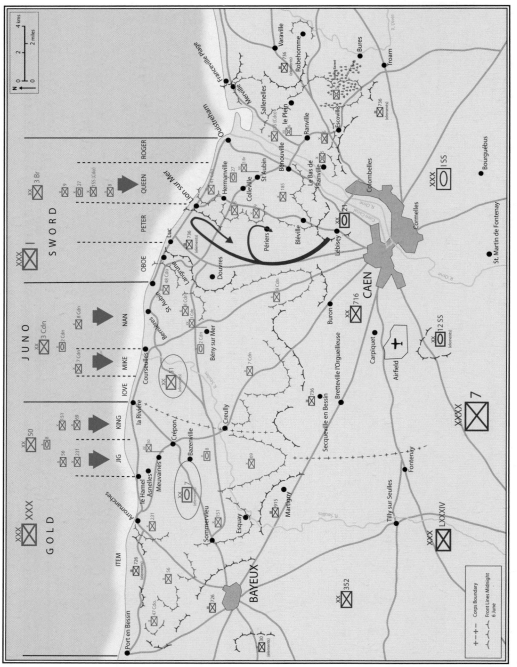

Map 5 The initial British assault up to midnight 6 June.

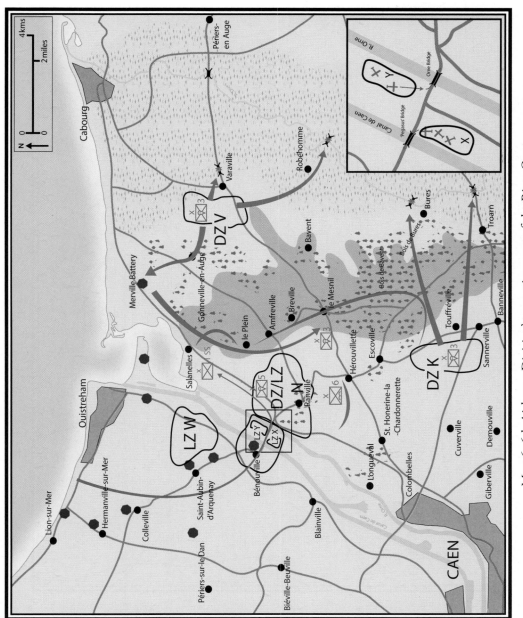

Map 6 6th Airborne Division's operations east of the River Orne.

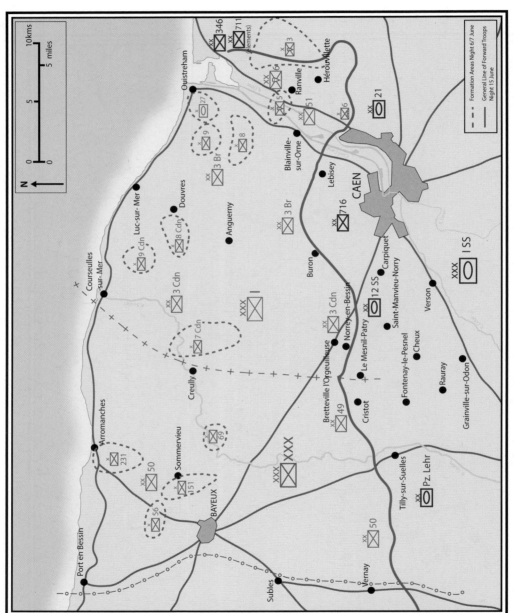

Map 7 The expansion of the British bridgehead 6-15 June.

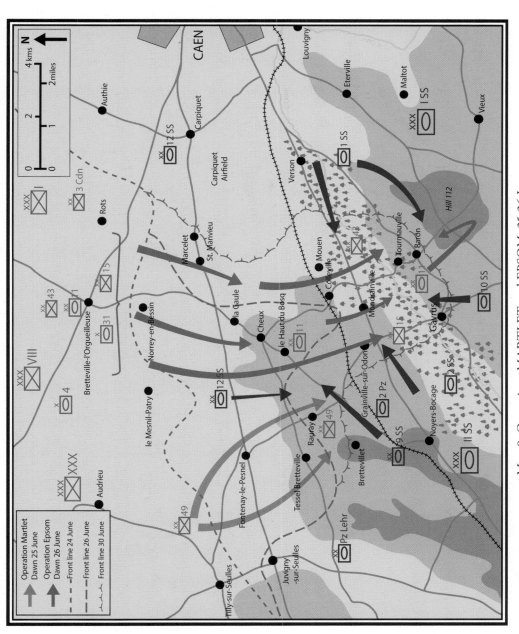

Map 8 Operations MARTLET and EPSOM, 25-26 June.

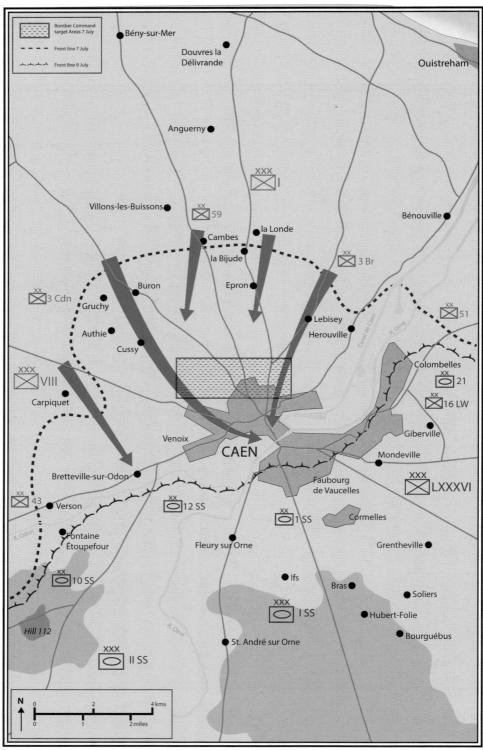

Map 9 Operation CHARNWOOD, the capture of Caen, 7-9 July.

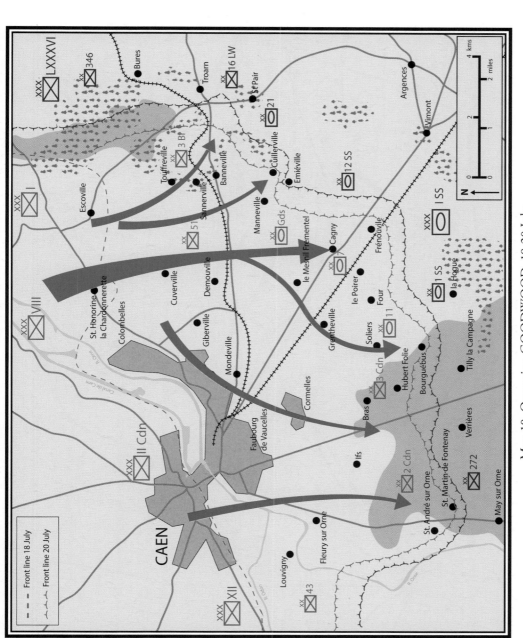

Map 10 Operation GOODWOOD, 18-20 July.

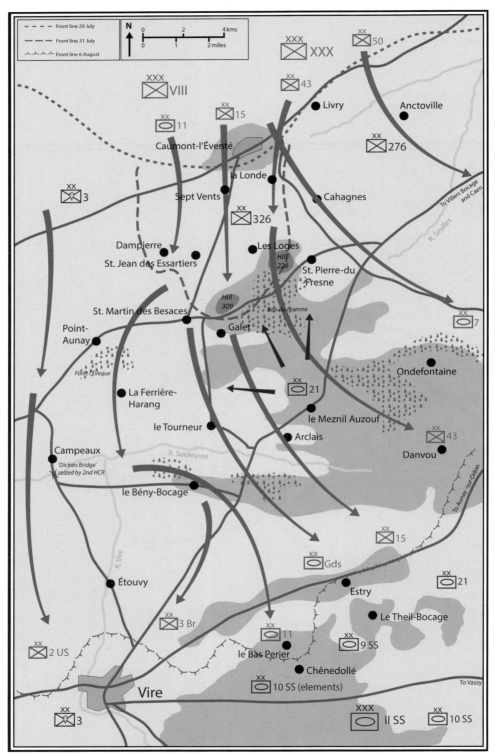

Map 11 Operation BLUECOAT, 30 July-7 August.

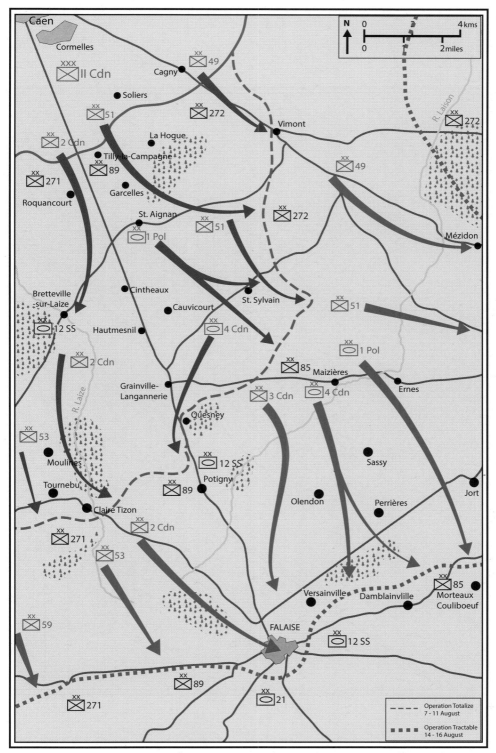

Map 12 Operations TOTALIZE and TRACTABLE, 8-21 August.

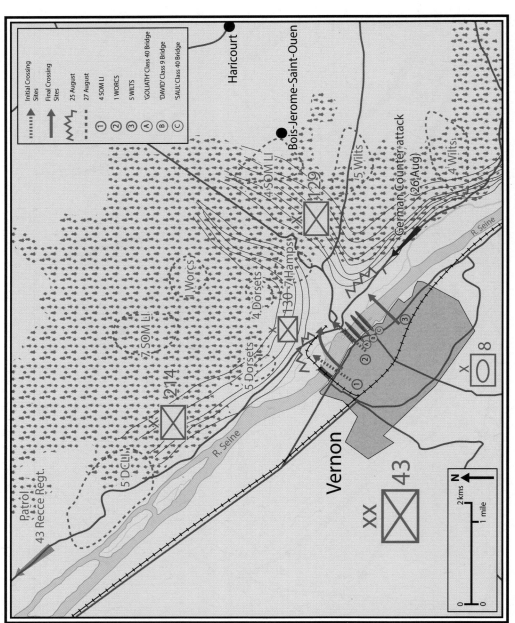

Map 13 The crossing of the River Seine at Vernon, 25-27 July.

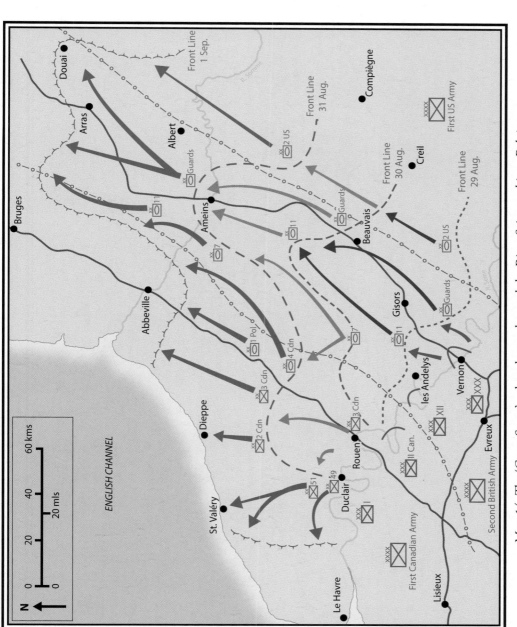

Map 14 The 'Great Swan' - the advance beyond the River Seine and into Belgium.

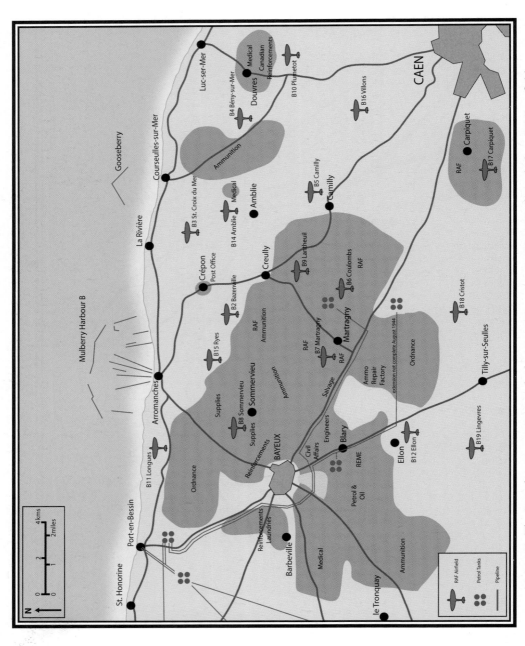

Map 15 The British maintenance and administrative set-up in Normandy including RAF airfields.

Figure 6.23 A 12,000lb medium capacity deep penetration 'Tallboy' is hoisted from a bombrack at Woodhall Spa, Lincolnshire in preparation for a raid on a V-weapon site in France, 22 June. (Crown Copyright Air Historical Branch)

a greater explosive effect. Tallboy M measured twenty-one feet in length and had a three foot diameter, the tail of the bomb was fitted with four fins that were offset five-degrees to cause the bomb to spin at 500rpm when dropped. This meant that unlike conventional munitions, which wobbled and tumbled when dropped, Tallboy bombs were ballistically stable in flight and could be dropped consistently and predictably.

The second technological innovation, which was also unique to 617 Squadron, was the advanced Stabilised Automatic Bomb Sight (SABS) which allowed bomb-aimers to exploit Tallboys predictable and consistent ballistic flight into highly accurate bombing missions. The sight consisted of a gyroscopically stabilized telescopic sight which was mounted in the nose of the Lancaster. The bomb-aimer would keep the sight over the target and feed in a number of variables including height, airspeed and external air temperature, the SABS would then automatically generate aiming corrections and release the Tallboy bomb at the right moment. Although a step forward technologically the SABS required the 617 Squadron Lancasters to fly a long steady run up to the target of five to seven minutes duration, with no deviation in either height or course. In 1944 this was not a simple matter when there was a very real danger from the highly accurate, radar predicted German 'flak'.

The final innovation was the low-level marking of the targets with incendiary flares by Mosquito aircraft, this was a technique pioneered by 617 Squadron themselves and ensured that target markers fell with an accuracy of twenty yards. A far greater degree of precision than normally

Figure 6.24 Typhoon pilots of 181 Squadron leave the briefing tent at B2/Bazenville after a midday sortie over the battlefield. (Crown Copyright Air Historical Branch)

achieved by standard RAF pathfinder squadrons which complemented both the bombing skills of 617 Squadron and the accuracy of the Tallboy bomb.

The first occasion that the Tallboy was used in support of the Normandy campaign was on the night 8-9 June against the Saumur railway tunnel. The aim was to cut this important German line of communication to the Normandy bridgehead. Twenty three Tallboys were dropped, most falling near the markers at the mouth of the tunnel causing great damage. It was however the Tallboy dropped by Flight Lieutenant Joe McCarthy which highlighted the unique 'earthquake' characteristics of Tallboy. His bomb struck the side of the mountain, penetrated some ninety feet and detonated above the roof of the tunnel. The earthquake bomb worked as intended and collapsed the tunnel, the Germans were still digging it out three months later when the Americans overran the area.

A further illustration of the effect of Tallboy and 617 Squadron was the mission against Le Havre on the night of 14 June, the reader will recall from Chapter 3 the unusually large concentration of E-boats in the harbour following the German Naval evacuation of Cherbourg on 12 June. The mission was designed not only to use Tallboy against the hardened E-boat pens where many of the craft were sheltering, but also to generate a sufficiently large 'tidal wave' that would damage many of the craft moored in the basin and outer harbour.

Three special marking Mosquitoes led by Squadron Leader Leonard Cheshire would lead the attack and mark the targets, they would be followed by 22 Lancasters from 617 Squadron each equipped with one 12,000lb Tallboy M and a further 199 normal Lancasters carrying 1,000lb and

500lb bombs. There were two aiming points for the Tallboys, the first was the roof of the E-boat pen itself, the second was the area of the tidal basin alongside the Gare Maritime where intelligence had indicated the heaviest concentrations of E-boats were.

As a result of the raid the twelve boats inside the E-boat pen were all sunk, in addition the tidal wave effect in the basin smashed many boats against each other and the harbour walls, in some cases the craft were beached. British intelligence estimated that the Germans had lost 38 vessels sunk outright with another 31 to 34 damaged. The 617 Squadron raid on Le Havre highlights not just the technical competence the RAF had achieved but also the advantage air power delivers to naval operations as well as the Army.

Few ground forces have been so well served by the air force in any war. The contribution of the air forces before and after D-Day was undoubtedly a battle winning factor and one that was appreciated at the time by the most junior of soldiers who could observe its effects on the battlefield as well as CinC 21st Army Group himself. Debates may still continue over the level of physical damage air power achieved but the moral effect must not be underestimated. Field Marshal Montgomery emphasized the importance of this aspect after the war:

> The moral effect of air action is very great and is out of proportion to the material damage inflicted. In the reverse direction the sight and sound of our own air forces operating against the enemy have an equally satisfactory effect on our own troops. A combination of the two has a profound influence on the most important single factor in war – morale.[60]

However the Royal Air Force could only strike targets such as the E-boats at Le Havre or the petrol tankers at Châtellerault if there was reliable and accurate intelligence. As will also be seen in the next chapter, the Army's plans and operations were also based on good intelligence and a thorough understanding of the enemy.

---

60 Montgomery, Field Marshal B L, 'Some Notes on the use of Air Power In support of Land Operations', HQ BAOR, October 1945, p.29. Held at Joint Doctrine and Concepts Centre, Shrivenham.

7

'Knowledge Gives Strength to Arm' – Intelligence and Reconnaissance

During the whole of the Second World War, our Intelligence was of a very high order indeed: in fact, it was unheard of for a fresh German formation to appear on my front without 24-48 hours' warning.

General Horrocks[1]

There were few areas in the campaign where the Allies outperformed the Germans as comprehensively and dramatically as in the field of intelligence and reconnaissance. This chapter combines the two disciplines because of their level of interaction. Intelligence allows the commander to direct reconnaissance to look at specific targets or areas and in return reconnaissance produces information on the enemy, contributing and feeding the intelligence machine. If it works well it is a virtuous reinforcing cycle.

Despite occasional mistakes and gaps, the Allies' intelligence system furnished commanders with high levels of accurate information about German dispositions, actions and future intentions. That this system was produced virtually from scratch speaks volumes about the talent and energy of the individuals involved in its operation and the ethos within the Allied command generally and 21st Army Group specifically. Intelligence is sometimes popularly viewed as a separate activity to normal military operations. This is an entirely false impression; if a commander wishes to have an accurate picture of the enemy and incorporate that understanding into his plans then he must invest his own time and energy in directing his intelligence staff and focusing it accordingly. This is highlighted by the critical first step of what is known as the Intelligence Cycle: 'Commanders Direction'. General Montgomery understood this well – he personally selected his intelligence staff and increased their numbers in his headquarters to furnish his needs. Moreover he was adept at guiding and directing the intelligence staff on what he wanted to know. The relationship between a commander and his intelligence officer is a subtle one, dissimilar to almost any other staff officer in a headquarters. Montgomery had an excellent relationship with his intelligence officer at 21st Army Group, Brigadier Bill Williams, one that started in the western Desert when Montgomery took over the Eighth Army. His personal confidence in his intelligence officer meant that Montgomery trusted intelligence and used it as the basis for his planning. Brigadier Williams describes his first encounter with Montgomery in the western desert, at the start of what would be one of the most important and effective relationships within HQ 21st Army Group:

---

1   Horrocks, Sir Brian, *Corps Commander* (London: Sidgwick & Jackson, 1977), p.82.

Not long after General Montgomery's electrifying arrival at HQ 8th Army, I was told he wanted to see me. I was summoned to the caravan pretty early on, 15 or 16 August, 1942, perhaps. (I couldn't keep a diary, because of the vital security of 'Ultra').

The new Army commander had uncomfortably piercing eyes which also seemed to be hooded, a disconcerting combination. He listened with his whole frame vibrantly still, never interrupting. His questions in a sharp, spinsterly voice were directly on target. He wanted to know when 'Rommel' would attack, where and what with… He devoted most of his time that first morning I spent with him (I had barely become a major and was I think, still wearing three pips) interrogating me about the enemy defence's at Alamein. The new commander of Eighth Army was one battle ahead of the rest of us. Lieutenant-General Montgomery was already devising the offensive which was to make his name.

The answers to the first three queries were reasonably clear; in fact, as clear as desert daylight. It so happened that almost never before and rarely ever again did we have evidence so hard and cold and up-to-date as to be able to give any commander a pretty precise answer. It was a fluke – a fluke, admittedly, in which a lot of hard work was involved, of which I was merely the mouthpiece that morning. Well, that was fine: but he had only just arrived and why should he believe us? Well, he did. And this established a relationship. He won his first battle, the model defensive battle of Alam Halfa, by believing in the Intelligence with which he was furnished that morning. From that tight reined success at Alam Halfa sprang the morale needed for victory at Alamein not too many weeks later.

It meant, too, that because the Intelligence had proved adequate then, he believed it thereafter – not gratefully (I doubt if gratitude was in his make up) but practically – in practice.[2]

General Montgomery assisted his intelligence staff by posing specific questions that directed their intelligence focus and collection. In addition he made certain that in preparing his army for Normandy his structure would have sufficient intelligence collection and reconnaissance elements within it. Montgomery insisted that 2nd TAF's reconnaissance element was expanded, maintaining that 'If the Recce Wing was bad it would be like having one hand tied behind your back'.[3] At a more tactical level shrewd commanders would also plan and consider how they might collect the best available intelligence on the enemy from within their own organisation. The commanding officer of 5th Duke of Cornwall's Light Infantry, Lieutenant Colonel George Taylor, describes how he restructured his battalion to ensure it was able to collect the necessary tactical information on the enemy:

I had two main intentions in rebuilding the battalion into a crack fighting unit: one was to establish an elite company that I could use as a spearhead, or reserve, the other was to have a scout platoon for reconnaissance…Two officers and 20 NCOs and men from the 4th Bn volunteered to be our scouts and the platoon was to prove its worth in seeking vital information. It was also to cut down our officer casualties, as NCOs, down to lance corporal were to carry out dangerous scouting missions with courage and efficiency.[4]'

Simply put if a commander wants to understand his enemy he must be prepared to devote the appropriate level of resources to it. In addition Lieutenant Colonel Taylor also adjusted his

---

2   Howarth, T, *Monty at Close Quarters: Recollections of The Man* (London: Leo Cooper, 1985), p.21.
3   Monty's handwritten notes for the address at Fighter Command, Friday 28 May 44, Montgomery papers. Quoted in Hamilton, Nigel, *Monty: Master of the Battlefield 1942-44* (London: Hodder & Stoughton), p.588.
4   Taylor, George, *Infantry Colonel* (Upton-on-Severn: Self Publishing Association, 1990), p.46.

battalion's tactics to take account of circumstances when enemy dispositions were unclear. Quite simply he recognized that on occasions he would have to fight for his information:

> I told them that we would attack in greater depth than was customary in most battalions, and that unless we had time to locate the enemy with a good degree of accuracy, we would attack with only one company, backed by the maximum firepower. It was realized that unless one had been in close contact with the enemy for several days we would know very little about his dispositions and that we would have to fight to make him show his hand.

Successful commanders did not see intelligence as a niche activity undertaken by separate specialists but as their own business. They understood that an intelligence failure, just like an operational failure, or a logistics failure was a command failure with lack of direction from a commander inevitably being a contributing factor.

Having established the key questions that the commander wished to know, the intelligence staff would look to the various assets available to them to answer these questions. The overarching question would also have to be broken down to subsidiary and supplementary questions that when individually answered would provide a comprehensive picture. For 21st Army Group the information could be derived from a number of different sources and agencies, including signals intelligence, air photo reconnaissance, tactical air reconnaissance, prisoner of war interrogation and analysis of captured documents. The staff could also expect information from their forward troops, either from reconnaissance patrols or by routine reporting of activities to their front. The 'fame' of Ultra tends to dominate the history books but its sensitivity meant that it was not disseminated in 'raw' form below Army level. Even at high levels where Ultra was routinely available the intelligence staff worked on the basis that all sources and agencies should be methodically exploited and fused together into a coherent assessment. Single source reporting is always regarded as potentially hazardous by good intelligence officers.

At lower tactical levels the ability to task intelligence sources such as air reconnaissance or interrogators was limited, though information from these sources did cascade down. One of the key methods of gathering tactical intelligence was through conducting reconnaissance patrols or setting up observation posts. We have already seen Corporal Ganter conducting a specialist patrol outside Le Havre to obtain engineer intelligence in Chapter 4, but patrols were also tasked for more general purposes. Patrolling was a risky business and always taken very seriously; a patrol programme was normally arranged and coordinated at brigade level with the outgoing patrol usually personally briefed by the battalion's CO. Patrols would be given a specific piece of information to find out, information which would assist the formation or unit IO in understanding the enemy opposing them. As an example on 29 June 2Lt Dugmore of 1st Hampshires was tasked with a patrol to find out the following questions:

a. Are there enemy at the hedge junction 810668?
b. Are there enemy at the gap in the wall at approx 810666?
c. Is the Château de Cordillon occupied at 808664?
    Also to bring back information concerning gaps in walls or any other information obtainable.[5]

---

5   TNA: WO 171/1305, War Diary 1st Battalion Hampshire Regiment – Patrol Report 2 Lt Dugmore 30 June 1944.

Reconnaissance patrols, or their static equivalent standing patrols, were usually small and worked to a common format. Stan Scott of 3 Commando gives a general picture of the reconnaissance patrolling he undertook in Normandy:

> The favourite number for a Recce patrol was five, all lightly armed and clad. The patrol leader's four men each had a job to do, such as navigator, and a pacer who judged distance by counting the number of his own paces, knowing how many represented a certain distance. If in some instances it was necessary to take a prisoner, two of the men could be detailed as a 'snatch party'. They all watched the patrol leader he did not watch them. He was the one who gave the signals using four fingers of one hand. No noise was made, you went out and came back without the enemy knowing you had paid them a visit.
>
> Standing patrols moved out at first darkness, took up position as near to the enemy as possible and lay there all night to look and listen. If there were fifteen men, they would spread out around three feet apart and so cover a front of about forty five yards. You had to recognize sounds like digging, lighting up fags, anything that gave away the enemy positions, even people farting! Again, get in and out without being known.[6]

When the reconnaissance patrol returned, they would be debriefed by the IO and the commander would write up a short report detailing what had been found. 2Lt Dugmore detailed his observations following the patrol to Château de Cordillon:

> The journey up to the hedge junction 810668 was ueventful. An old German Posn was found there. There were some weapon slits sited to fire all-round. There was a quantity of equipment lying around, and it seemed as though the posn was abandoned in a hurry some days ago.
>
> There was no sign of a recent occupation. In the hedge between there and the track there was a number of old posns in the ditch. The track was reached and the gap in the wall (810666) was found to be unheld. The bottom of the gap was filled up with rubble to a height of 4'9'. On the Château side there was one half-dug slit, barely more than a shell scrape. Earlier on 29.6.44 I had made a recce at 2045hrs, down to the track and had seen a German body in the hedge. When the patrol went to find it, however, it had been removed, all but the tin hat. Left near was a satchel of rations, which were all fresh. Inside the Château wall the patrol worked along towards the house. There were few slit trenches and the iron gate was open. About 250 yards from the buildings three German bodies were found. I examined them and took the shoulder tabs off two. The other one was wearing overalls. The bodies were decomposing fast and judging by the smell were at least a week old. Ground sheets had been put over their heads but no attempt had been made to bury them. All still had their rifles and were fully armed. The patrol got to within 20 feet of the main building and lay up there for 20 minutes. No sound was heard, there were no slit trenches and the whole place appeared to be quite deserted. On the way back another gap in the wall was discovered. In all there are three gaps and one gate. To the west of the Château is an orchard, there sounds of R.T. similar to those which I heard from tanks before our posn the night before. I did not investigate as there was one of our patrols in the area. The journey back was uneventful.[7]

---

6   Barber, Neil (ed), *Fighting with the Commandos the recollections of Stan Scott No.3 Commando* (Barnsley: Pen & Sword, 2008), p.80.

7   TNA: WO 171/1305, War Diary 1st Battalion Hampshire Regiment – Patrol Report 2Lt Dugmore, 30 June 1944.

Although such missions were hazardous the information brought back by these patrols was important in understanding the enemy dispositions and developing successful fighting patrols. Like other formation headquarters 51st Highland Division would capture the information gleaned from recent patrols in its regular Intelligence Summaries. Its 15 June report gives a good sense of the information recce patrols regularly produced:

> Last night our tps sent out several patrols. One patrol on the right flank had nothing to report save three enemy in the area of the old docks 0771. Further EAST slight activity and Spandau fire was reported from the edge of St Honorine at about 2230 hrs. A patrol to the area pt 35 -1269 – heard mvt and conversation at 123702 and 123698. Several half-tracked vehs were heard moving in the area 122697 and dug-in posns are suspected on the reverse slope of the pt 35 feature. A patrol who were fired on by an M.G. from the direction 122693 state that the track leading SOUTH in 1269 is 30 yds wide, definitely not mined, and well used by enemy MT.
>
> A patrol to the area of the brickworks 148687 saw a few men walking about but, apart from finding the brickworks unoccupied, had little to report. Another patrol to the village of TOUFFREVILLE confirmed that it is occupied by enemy and reported a section posn (strength approx 6 men), astride the track at 135689, and the sentry moving in the woods at 141689.[8]

Whilst simply observing the enemy could be useful, potentially greater quantities of information could be obtained if the patrol brought back a prisoner. This was sometime specified as a particular requirement by the tasking brigade or battalion, Stan Scott was tasked with exactly such a mission in the Orne Bridgehead:

> We went down the road and Spencer signalled with his hand 'One, two and three, get down.' No talking, down, watch. He took Ted Pritchard and myself and we just walked normally along the side of the road. If you started to creep or crouch and the enemy saw you, they would know something was up, whereas they would not think anything of someone walking about as if it was their own area. All of a sudden we could hear the faint sound of snoring, and we approached it. I got on one side and Pritchard the other. We bent down, got hold of this bloke and pulled him bodily out of a hole. He stood there and Spencer pushed the barrel of his Thompson into the German's guts. He said, 'Du bist gefangener.' The bloke must have thought that his mates were playing a joke! I guess he said something like, 'Don't play about!' and pushed the Thompson away. Most of us carried a knife on our thigh, in a special attachment on our trousers (some had a pocket inside as well). Spencer said, 'I'm not playing about,' and went straight in with his knife. The bloke just collapsed back into the hole. We carried on along the road and found another Jerry, but this one was sensible. He was grabbed, pulled out and didn't need any telling. He took one look and knew who had got hold of him.[9]

As well as being captured by patrols many prisoners were taken in general offensives or simply deserted of their own volition. To administer these PWs the unit would often set up a collecting point where the unit's intelligence personnel would begin the reception treatment. This initial screening and identification was very much the battalion intelligence officer's business. He would

---

8   TNA: WO 171/527, 51st Highland Division War Diary, Intelligence Summary No.188, 15 June 1944.

9   Barber Neil (ed), *Fighting with the Commandos: the recollections of Stan Scott No.3 Commando* (Barnsley: Pen & Sword, 2008), p.81.

Figure 7.1 Infantrymen of the Royal Winnipeg Rifles searching German prisoners at Aubigny, France 16-17 August. (Lieut. Donald I. Grant, Library and Archives Canada, PA-161993)

compile an initial report identifying the name of the prisoner, his time, date and place of capture, which direction was he moving in at the time of capture and finally the strength of the enemy group with which he was captured. Intelligence Officer, Lieutenant Joe Brown describes the process:

> It was the responsibility of the Intelligence Section to focus the Battalion's mind on obtaining intelligence about the enemy, particularly the identity of the infantry/grenadiers and any supporting troops. This intelligence would help to confirm or identify changes in the enemy's Order of Battle, an important factor in the planning considerations by Corps and divisional commanders formulating tactical plans. As forward troops and the first link in the chain, intelligence about the Order of Battle started at battalion level…Captured Officers and Non-Commissioned Officers would be searched first and all documents taken from them. We remove a P.o.W.'s shoulder-strap and send this with the escort; if captured and not wearing one, this would be noted. This Page from my I.O.'s Notebook details how we had to handle and treat P.o.Ws. However, the golden rule was 'Separate – Search – and Send Back Quickly'.
> …Identification of the enemy began with the colour patches which indicated the arm of service. The panel below shows the various colour distinctions. As infantry we expected to confront the greenish uniforms and white patches of the infantry (grenadiers) or green patches of the Panzer grenadiers, and/or the pink patches of armoured personnel when attacked by German 'battle groups' with infantry plus artillery or by infantry with artillery and tanks.
> When unusual colour patches were identified, they had to be reported. For example the blue of support troops, red of artillery (possible forward observation men), black of engineers, the lemon of signallers, maroon of smoke troops. If they were in the forward area that was important to know.

PW ARE THE BEST SOURCE OF FIRST-HAND INFORMATION.

IF PW ARE BROUGHT BACK QUICKLY, THIS INFORMATION CAN BE EXTRACTED QUICKLY.

THE MORE QUICKLY THIS INFORMATION IS EXTRACTED, THE MORE QUICKLY IT CAN BE USED TO HELP THE CAPTORS.

CAPTORS

DO	DON'T
DISARM completely, Prevent destruction of equipment.	DON'T make a friend of your enemy, i.e., show no sympathy.
SEPARATE officers, NCOs, OR. Forbid talking.	DON'T try to question.
SEARCH thoroughly. Prevent destruction of documents.	DON'T leave unguarded.
ESCORT :—	DON'T collect souvenirs.
(a) 10 per cent of PW (own walking wounded rather than fit men).	DON'T assume PW does not understand English ; therefore, DON'T mention place-names in their bearing.
(b) PW can be used as stretcher-bearers for own or enemy wounded for one trip only.	
REPORT on WHEN, WHERE, and HOW captured (to be brought by escort).	DON'T DELAY.

Diagram 7.1 Dos and Don'ts of PW handling.

DISTINGUISHING COLOURS WORN BY BRANCHES OF THE GERMAN ARMY.

Tk units [1] .... pink		A tk units [2] .... pink	
Hy A tk units .... pink		Mobile units [3] .... pink	
Armd recce units (+ letter A) .... pink		Armd trains (+ letter E) .... pink	
Pz Gren [1] .... grass-green		Gren & Fus. (mot) ...... white	
Recce units, part mech ... yellow		Recce (cycle) bns [4] ...... yellow	
Gren (normal) .... white			
Mtn regts .... lt green		Jäger bns .... lt green	
Engrs .... black		Arty .... red	
Sup tps .... lt blue		Sigs .... lemon	
Smoke tps .... maroon		Medical .... dark blue	

Diagram 7.2 German coloured patches worn on shoulders to earmark branch of Army.

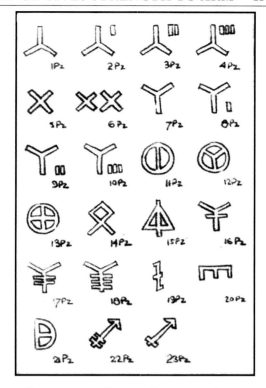

Diagram 7.3 German Formation Signs.

German divisions also had unique identifying shoulder flashes which helped the IO to identify which particular formation the PWs came from (above).

The 'pocket litter', a soldier carried, including his pay book and wallet, usually provided additional information. The German soldier often had private papers, official documents (such as his last leave pass and post office savings book) and many photographs. Most of the photographs were valueless but there were occasional breakthroughs particularly when pieces of equipment were used as a background to a group shot. As one example the first identification of the new German Mk VI Tiger Tank was discovered from a captured prisoner's photograph earlier in the war. The IO would often look out for references on any captured files or documents; the German file references 1a (Operations) and 1c (Intelligence) were always a high priority for translation and subsequent exploitation. German operation orders followed a standard pattern and the distribution list often gave useful order of battle information. A knowledge of German conventional map marking signs was another important skill intelligence officers needed to possess, as captured German maps usually had pencilled marks on them.[10] In forward areas intelligence staff and interrogators confined themselves to extracting identifications and passing the documents back to Corps headquarters for more detailed examination. A German speaking NCO or Field Security NCO would often sift and filter these documents to prevent higher headquarters from being overwhelmed. The Intelligence Officer for 56 Infantry Brigade was impressed with the capture of documents at the beginning of Operation BLUECOAT:

10 Mockler Ferryman, Intelligence Corps Museum.

A particularly valuable find was made by 2 SWB [2nd Battalion South Wales Borderers] in an Arty OP in the area of 8 Coy on the St GERMAIN ridge. This find comprised both documents and maps. Among the documents was a list of codesigns which gave away the whole of the Div Order of Battle and solved several points which had been puzzling intelligence circles for some time. There was a sketch showing the observations that the enemy had obtained for his arty that made it quite clear why he considered the ridge to be his main line of defence. Best of all was a set of maps which gave the exact posns of the defensive fire tasks and also of the guns themselves SW of VILLERS BOCAGE. These maps were reprints of the 25,000 TILLY-SUR-SEULLES and VILLERS BOCAGE sheets which the enemy had probably captured from 7 Armd Div when they first made an attack on that area. Although the enemy had superimposed his own grid system he had conveniently retained ours and it was immediately possible to phone eight figure map references of gun posns to the Counter-battery office. They were delighted.[11]

A captured prisoner would usually be sent to the Corps PW cage where trained personnel from Corps or Army interrogation pools would carry out a preliminary interrogation. This would normally be confined to obtaining information regarding identity of the enemy unit, place and time of capture; enemy units to the flanks as well as those in reserve. The interrogators would also try to establish questions on enemy intentions, resources, morale, casualties in recent fighting, boundaries between units or formations and other tactical information.

Whether the PW would talk or not depended on a number of factors. The speed with which the prisoner was brought to the PW cage was key, too slow a delay and the prisoner had a chance to 'craft' his story. The interrogator's skill was also important. Whilst there was little training on questioning technique all interrogators spoke German, indeed the view of many of these interrogators was that those who spoke the language well also had the best cultural understanding of their enemy, which reinforced their overall capability. In addition to linguistic skill former interrogators also judged that detailed knowledge of the armed forces of the enemy[12] was frequently critical. All British interrogators were officers and generally of high intelligence, perhaps by design the language and commissioning requirements also meant that the interrogators were usually in their mid-twenties or older. It was felt that greater experience of life and general maturity gave them an added confidence and edge over their interrogation subjects.

When PWs could not be speedily evacuated, units could conduct interrogation for immediate tactical benefit; though this was generally frowned upon for it often 'corrupted' the prisoner before he reached the Corps cage. The best results were obtained by an early and expert interrogation conducted before the prisoner had time to recover from the bewilderment and dejection of his capture. Even if the PW was a willing deserter, maintaining him in an obedient state was an important aspect of his handling as this extract from a HQ 6th Airborne Division memo makes clear:

The handling of deserters has a special repercussion on their interrogation. A lax bearing and a too obvious eagerness to accept their statements at unit level increases the deserter's opinion of his own importance; the time lag which has occurred in several cases before evacuation to Div Cage makes it obvious that interrogation at Bn and Bde level is far too detailed and goes

---

11 TNA: WO 171/650, War Diary of 56 Infantry Brigade, 56 Infantry Brigade Special Intelligence Summary, 3 August 1944.

12 Burrill, Col D M, *Prisoners, Intelligence & War*, A Defence Fellowship Study conducted at Kings College London University, 1988-89, p.48.

Figure 7.2   German soldiers surrender to 31st Field Company, Royal Canadian Engineers at Boulogne, 18 September. (Lieut. Donald I. Grant, Library and Archives Canada, PA-174406)

beyond strictly tactical sphere. Units are warned that in his eagerness to give information a deserter may – if he finds that he has 'sold his story' successfully – try to give infm the accuracy of which the unit may not be able to verify.[13]

A prisoner's willingness to talk was also influenced by the rank, arm and general security awareness of the PW. The interrogator's judgement in selecting his subject was important here; the officers might generally know more, but they were also less inclined to talk. Signallers and clerks, though low in rank, were often more pliable and had a wide knowledge of operations too. It was therefore important to separate and segregate officers and men soon after capture and prevent last minute security instructions being issued.

Whilst some PWs were caught against their will a significant proportion deserted freely and would be more likely to talk. A XII Corps Intelligence summary highlights the fragile morale that caused such desertions:

Between 0900hrs 4 Aug and 1600 hrs 5 Aug 27 deserters and 37 PW passed through the Corps cage. Of the former, the majority, and of the latter a high proportion were POLES, their reasons for desertion are fairly obvious. Germans, however, appear to have deserted for one or more of the following reasons:
a)   Because they see the battle is hopeless (aussichtsloss); a state of mind brought about not only by the gen situation as they see it but also because of our superiority in arty and aircraft.
b)   Because they have no sympathy with the Nazi government.

13 Note on the treatment of POWs by units of 6th Airborne Division, Airborne Forces Museum, Aldershot.

c)   Because of a grievance – often against a particular offr or NCO or sometimes because of some difficulties at home.

Some Germans are rather touchy about being called deserter and are hesitant to admit the case. One man preferred to say that he had voluntarily been captured –'Ich bin freiwillig in die Gefangenschaft gekommen' – having hidden in a ditch where he waited till found by our own troops several hours after his unit's withdrawal.[14]

XII Corps also commented on the large volume of information these deserters provided in the battle:

Deserters continued during the period to give most valuable information on enemy disposi-tions and it was estimated that the enemy front was held RIGHT to LEFT by 271, 10 SS Pz, 277 and 276 Div…During the period under review most valuable information was continu-ally received from deserters, particularly Poles, who frequently were able to pin pt on air photos such targets as HQs, tpt lines, gun posns and so on. This enabled offensive action to be taken against these targets.[15]

The reader does need to be wary of taking the source attribution in Corps and higher level intel-ligence summaries at face value. Source protection is always an intelligence officer's concern and it was common practise to protect a more vulnerable source, such as Ultra, by disguising such sensi-tive intelligence as PW derived information. Even taking this into account, a considerable body of information on the enemy was undoubtedly derived from PWs.

The final form of interrogation that could take place was 'Long Term Strategic and Tactical detailed interrogation.' This would usually take place at the Combined Services Detailed Interrogation Centre (CSDIC) based in London. At the CSDIC sophisticated techniques could be used. These included listening in to PWs conversations through hidden microphones in their cells and the use of 'stool pigeons', German PWs who had been 'turned' and were now working for the Allies. The stool pigeon was normally placed in a cell alongside the genuinely captured PWs, he would attempt to elicit further information from the PW who would unwittingly believe he was sharing a confidence with a comrade rather than betraying a secret. The sorts of information obtained by CSDIC interrogation were more strategic and operational in nature and less likely to become irrelevant through the passage of time. Information obtained could include details of the German High Command, German operating techniques, German intelligence, the opinion of senior commanders on Allied tactics as well as enemy defences further along the coast. These would all be captured in a CSDIC Special Intelligence Report.[16]

Whilst German prisoners might reveal information only with a little persuasion from interroga-tors, there were many French 'line crossers' or refugees who would pass through the frontline and were very willing pass on what they had seen to a friendly Allied intelligence officer. British Field Security sections would initially have to assess whether such individuals were saboteurs, agents or genuine refugees. Once they were established as bona fide they could be debriefed, though as civil-ians they were probably untrained in observation and reporting. Nonetheless even broad or rough

---

14   TNA: WO 171/310, XII Corps War Diary, Intelligence Summary Number 31, 6 August 44.
15   TNA: WO 171/310, XII Corps War Diary.
16   TNA: WO 208/5531, Interrogation reports on German prisoners of war: SIR 400-499; CAB 146/473, Canadian Special Interrogation Reports referring to the Normandy Campaign; WO 208/3592, CSDIC UK Interrogation of enemy POWs: Interrogation Reports; WO 208/2525 Procedure in interrogating and handling prisoners of war.

descriptions, sometimes of events far back from the front line, were all useful in pulling together the jigsaw. In early June an un-named French civilian crossed into the line on the eastern side of the bridgehead. A small extract of some of the information he passed to British intelligence officers is given below:

(b) The SEINE bridge at VERNON was still usable by pedestrians. The enemy were marching tps over and working a ferry service on either side.

(c) The aerodrome at Evreux was still usable.

(d) Lisieux is quite impassable through the town because of bombing.

(e) At 120632, between CAGNY and VIMONT on the right hand side of the rd from VIMONT an isolated house guarded by four sentries with two small armd cars parked nearby. He was definitely of the opinion that the house was the HQ of an Armd or Recce Unit.

(comment: steps have already been taken to identify and deal with this target which might well be a sort of firm base command post for 12 Pz Recce unit or a bn of 100 Tk Regt.[17]

As well as information from reconnaissance patrols, PWs and civilians there was one other good source of information that the intelligence officer and his commanding officer could control directly; snipers. Though a sniper's primary task was to kill individual enemy soldiers, his ability to move discreetly past the forward troops meant they could observe a little further into the enemy's depth and provide valuable information. It was frequent in most battalions for the intelligence officer to control the snipers.

Dismounted recce patrols and snipers were suitable in a close contact and largely static battle, but when an operation became more fluid the mobile reconnaissance elements available at both the divisional and corps level were required. The infantry division contained a reconnaissance regiment within its organization, formed from the Reconnaissance Corps, they were equipped with half-tracks and carriers as well as armoured cars. The high proportion of tracked vehicles within the unit gave them the necessarily high cross-country mobility to support an infantry division. Armoured divisions possessed an armoured reconnaissance regiment; usually equipped with Cromwell tanks. The protection, mobility and firepower of a tank should have made them ideal for reconnaissance in an armoured battle, in reality most armoured divisional commanders used them as another tank regiment, particularly when a Corps armoured car regiment was put under their command. The armoured car regiments were equipped almost exclusively with armoured cars. This meant they were suited to long distance reconnaissance tasks, mainly on roads, covering ground quickly and stealthily if required. They were originally designed as a Corps reconnaissance asset but on many occasions were tasked to work directly in support of an armoured division. General Horrocks highlighted the qualities he expected from his own Corps' armoured car regiment:

Normally, armoured cars bear a role out of all proportion to their size, as they are the eyes and ears of the Corps commander. Advancing usually on a wide front, they constantly report back by wireless to their Liaison Officer at Tactical Corps HQ and to be successful three things are required:

Firstly the man in charge of the leading scout car (usually a corporal of horse in this particular regiment)– the equivalent of a sergeant in the infantry should be very alert and intelligent.

17 TNA: WO 171/527, 51st Highland Division War Diary, Intelligence Summary No.188, 15 June 1944.

Secondly an armoured car squadron must be prepared to fight for their information; in other words, exert pressure, so that the enemy is forced to disclose his location.

Thirdly, and probably most important of all, their wireless communications must never break down.

The 2nd Household Cavalry were superb in all three respects.[18]

There were a number of different armoured cars used by the British; the American built Staghounds were large twin-engined armoured cars that were usually employed as a headquarters car at squadron and regimental level. The AEC armoured car often known as the 'Matador' was probably the least capable, simply consisting of an armoured body mounted on a Matador 4x 4 truck chassis. Though the Matador was armed with a 75mm gun and had a good cross-country performance, it was generally only used as a support section vehicle. The Support Section's role was an important element of the squadron, it contained a small number of troopers who could dismount and tackle obstacles, clear mines, manage PWs and all the other miscellaneous tasks that would otherwise distract the recce troops from their primary role. The Matador's lack of stealth was not such a handicap in this role.

The Recce troops themselves consisted of two Daimler armoured cars and two Daimler scout cars. The four-wheel drive Daimlers scout cars were small and weighed only 3 tonnes, their low profile meant they were particularly suited to the bocage of the Normandy countryside and could sneak unobserved amongst the hedgerows and sunken lanes. However they were only armed with a Bren gun and the open top meant that the crew was particularly vulnerable to shell splinters. The recce troop's Daimler armoured cars were a modern and popular vehicle amongst the crews, it too was small and fast (up to 50 mph). It had a reliable 6-cylinder Daimler engine whose five-speed gearbox could use all five ratios in reverse as well as forward. To do this a second steering position at the rear of the vehicle would be used. This, together with the ability to fire smoke, would be an important advantage for the armoured car crews in the tactical conditions of Normandy. Lieutenant Orde of 2nd Household Cavalry relates:

As beginners we learnt much from the Inns of Court Regiment, who like us, were waiting to know what was to be their next big job. Their officers came over for a drink and were subjected to a battery of questions. One fact of paramount importance stood out. It was never the enemy's light reconnaissance units which they had first encountered, but invariably either the tank or the anti-tank gun, and unless the leading scout car saw these first its chance of survival was much reduced. Once spotted the scout car had to act like lightning, put down smoke and reverse as hard as it could go. And the German 88mms were deadly up to 1,000 yards. Having heard all this, it was with interest that troop leaders inspected the first batch of electrically fired smoke generators which had just arrived. Previously smoke canisters had only been fired from two short barrels at the side of the turret of the armoured car, using a ballisite charge. The system was unreliable, the smoke frequently failing to go off. In addition, the whole turret had to be aimed, and there was a time lag of several seconds before the smoke canister hit the ground and began to screen the threatened vehicle. The new electrically fired smoke was attached to the front of both the armoured cars and scout cars and could be instantaneously fired by the driver flicking on his side-lamp switch. The vehicle under fire would then make its own screen in the manner of a destroyer, retreating behind a dense cloud of smoke. Lieutenant Kavanagh was the

---

Figure 7.3 A Staghound armoured car of the 12th Manitoban Dragoons crosses the River Seine at Elbeuf on 28 August. (Lieut. Donald I. Grant, Library and Archives Canada, PA-137296)

first to give a demonstration of this new gadget and got badly choked in the process, but it worked and was to save many lives in the future.[19]

Whilst smoke would help when in trouble, avoiding it in the first place was a far better proposition. To increase their chances of survival a cautious approach was required and the troop leader would try to ensure that as one vehicle moved, its partner behind would cover that movement with both observation and, if required, fire. Once the advancing vehicle had pushed forward a certain distance, it would go firm and allow its rearward partner to also move forward, covering its movement in turn. This tactic was known as 'snake patrol' and helped reduce the risks of a surprise encounter with the enemy. The value of good observation was also emphasized to armoured car troop commanders:

If you are expecting to meet the enemy never enter a piece of ground without first looking into it. If each of the cars in your troop follows this principle rigidly stopping at each tactical feature be it a hill, a bend in the road etc. and scanning the ground then your troop will automatically advance in the correct manner. Each car will move by bounds; each car will search the area it is about to enter and the chances are that four pairs of eyes will spot what is waiting for you. The worst thing an armoured car troop can do is to 'Bum' along and bump into the enemy unexpectedly. In practice the speed at which a contact is made is a very low

19 Orde, Roden, *Household Cavalry at War: Second Household Cavalry Regiment* (Aldershot: Gale & Polden, 1953), p.77.

one, probably if the troop leader is advancing with proper caution, no more than 10 or 15 miles an hour. Any idea that contact is made at a high speed is absurd. Only when the enemy is in rout can that happen.[20]

Moreover if the armoured car came under fire the commander's reaction to enemy contact had to be instantaneous, this could only be achieved through training and drills practiced extensively before landing in Normandy:

An armoured car contact is a quick and often passionate affair; things happen suddenly. If you are not physically and mentally prepared for a sudden crisis you will act on impulse and the chances are that the impulses will be wrong. How does one prevent that? The answer is by training your troop (and yourself) realistically and by becoming mentally accustomed to the idea of instantaneous reaction. Whenever you are going along a road ask yourself 'What would I do if, say, an enemy tank suddenly appeared at the edge of the wood?' or 'What would I do if suddenly an anti-tank gun fired from the edge of that field?' There are plenty of other skirmishes you can imagine and put to yourself. You can then sort out unhurriedly the correct answers and when in actual battle something similar to one of these situations suddenly confronts you, you will instinctively do the action you thought out and practiced on training. You will not be acting on impulse although you will be acting quickly. For example will your right hand fly first to the smoke discharger buttons or to the control box? In other words will you want to fire smoke first or give orders to your driver, or your gunner, or to the other cars in your troop? There won't be a second to lose in hesitation. And what will your left hand be doing? Grabbing a round to load as soon as the gun is empty? Holding your binoculars? Dropping the map? These all sound terribly trivial actions but if the troop leader or car commander isn't master of his every move the result may be fatal inaction or fatal muddle.[21]

The close bocage of Normandy was a very difficult operating environment for armoured cars. The fields of view were restricted and the narrow lanes had high banks and often a deep ditch on either side in which the cars could get stuck fast. Smooth and quick extractions were difficult to achieve, as Lieutenant van Zoelen's summing up of his first action indicated:

The scout car let off smoke, I let off smoke, then he got ditched, then I got ditched, but luckily the Hun failed to take advantage of our predicament.[22]

The Daimler armoured car was armed with both a 2-pounder gun and a Besa machine gun. Whilst the 2-pounder would be ineffective against heavily armoured vehicles, it was still a capable weapon against light armoured vehicles including enemy armoured cars. Though these enagements did not occur as frequently as had been thought prior to the campaign, enemy armoured cars were

---

20 Abraham, S M O'H, 'Notes on Armoured Reconnaissance'. Although Major General Abraham wrote the guide when CO of 12th Lancers in 1959 they are based heavily on his wartime experiences. He joined the 12th Lancers during the Second World War, taking part in the Desert campaign as an Armoured Car Troop Leader and as a Squadron second in command and Squadron Leader in the Italian campaign. During his service he was awarded the MC and Bar. The notes are held in the Defence Concepts and Doctrine Centre, Shrivenham, under TDRC index 4923.

21 Ibid., Index 4253.

22 Orde, Roden, *Household Cavalry at War – Second Household Cavalry Regiment* (Aldershot: Gale & Polden, 1953), p.99.

Figure 7.4
The driver of a
Humber scout car
receives orders,
Falaise, 17 August.
(Lieut. Ken Bell,
Library and Archives
Canada, PA-138494)

still occasionally encountered, particularly after the break out. Corporal of Horse Johnson relates meeting one outside Albert in September:

> Suddenly Corporal Britton says, 'Something big coming along the road.' So I ordered his scout car back to the cross-roads to wait for me. Nothing happened for a while, then we both saw each other at the same time, an eight wheeled armoured car and myself. He fired first and missed, but advanced towards me very confident. I ordered the 2-pounder to fire and Trooper Price scored a hit. Then we felt a terrible explosion and I saw flames coming through my periscope. Corporal Mellish-Smith said, 'We've had it.' 'OK,' I said; 'retire slowly,' and I was amazed when our car started to move as I thought the engine had been hit. I reloaded the 2-pounder and gave the order to fire again. Trooper Price said, 'Can't see the b____s through these flames.' So I opened up the cupola and stuck my head out and gave gun laying directions from here. Then I was spotted by the enemy gunner, who fired at my head but luckily only cut my wireless mast in half instead. I then got down, locked gun and tapped Trooper Price. He put three rounds into the German car. Had another look over the top, but was now choked with smoke so gave order to evacuate the car. We all tumbled out and ran to the scout car around the corner, jumped on the back, and said, 'Drive like hell.[23]

An armoured car regiment's key role was to obtain information to feed the higher commander's intelligence requirements. This intelligence could be about enemy positions and forces, a natural obstacle or the conditions of the roads along an axis of advance. The key advantage with manned

23 Ibid., p.224.

reconnaissance is that the troop or squadron leader can act on his own initiative to fulfil his mission. He can seek out weak points or gaps in the enemy defences or manoeuvre to maintain contact with them when they move. The regiment can also seize and exploit opportunities; on occasions this can have the effect of altering a corps or even army plan. Lieutenant Dickie Powle's actions in seizing the bridge over the River Souleuvre on the second day of Operation BLUECOAT are a good example of this. Lieutenant Powle along with other 2nd Household Cavalry elements was trying to find a gap in the enemy defence's south of St Martin des Besaces. Most of the recce troops were struggling to break free from the close battle and Lieutenant Powle's patrol had similar problems losing both an armoured car and a scout car jammed between the high banks of a lane. With his troop halved to only two vehicles; a Daimler scout car and a Daimler armoured car, Lieutenant Dickie Powle decided to press on. Corporal Bland the commander of the scout car records the journey:

> Early on we found ourselves with only two cars left. Lieutenant Powle decided to go on without them. Shortly afterwards, I spotted a German look-out guard; he ran, but luckily a grenade I threw accounted for him. The idea of the grenade was better than using our guns as it was harder for the Germans to determine what it was; this served us lucky. We quickly came upon a couple of 88mms. And a number of smaller calibre jobs, but fortunately they were without warning, and although they tried hard they missed us... We pushed on rapidly now, in order to get past this sticky spot, and got through safely. I remember Lieutenant Powle shouting a remark to me, 'We may as well try what's in front – it can't be worse than trying to neck it back through that lot!' After taking a number of enemy posts by surprise, I had occasion to look at the map and realized that we were getting close to the bridge and also a rather long radio range away from Headquarters.[24] This came as a bit of a shock. We tried to get a message through, but could not at the time make contact. It was decided I should have a crack at crossing the bridge covered by the other armoured car. It worked, and after quickly dismounting we (myself and Trooper Read) slipped up behind a German sentry and quietly finished him off. We had to dispose of any such visitors, otherwise we were sunk as there was not a hope of holding any numbers off with only two cars if the warning went off...We had decided to dismount to hold the bridge; this kept us out of sight. The cars we covered in bushes. Only Corporal Staples remained mounted to try to make contact, which he did after some brilliant operating. Anyhow the message was received that tanks would be arriving to consolidate the old bridge. They hit the same bad patch as we did on the way, but five arrived and between us we held the bridge with hardly a breath until some more arrived in the evening after nearly shooting us up.[25]

The effect of the news at the Main Headquarters of 2nd Household Cavalry Regiment was electrifying, Lieutenant Orde described how it was passed to the commanding officer who was co-located with Major General Roberts, the 11th Armoured Division commander, at his HQ.

> Then at about 1030 in the morning, just as the tanks and infantry could be seen forming up for the attack which was to result in the capture of St Martin des Besaces half an hour later, a message came through from 'C' Squadron having a vital bearing on the outcome of

---

24 Major Herbert's Squadron Headquarters near Dampierre. The wireless interference was then probably as bad as it was ever to be because there were so many British and American formations in abnormally close contact.

25 Orde, Roden, *Household Cavalry at War – Second Household Cavalry Regiment* (Aldershot: Gale & Polden, 1953), p.104.

Figure 7.5 A Canadian Humber armoured car links up with British infantry near Caen, June 1944. (Tank Museum)

the battle. Badly distorted by being sandwiched in between a routine location check and an inordinately lengthy situation report from 'One Eight Able'.[26] It was difficult to decipher, but its implications were of the utmost importance. So much so that Colonel Abel Smith grabbed the mouthpiece of his wireless set and demanded of Lieutenant Armes, the Rear Link [of C Squadron], an immediate re-check. Within a minute it came back from Major Herbert, who tended to 'take to the air' in person at moments of high drama!

The message definite and unaltered, ran thus: 'I say again, at 1035 hours, the bridge at 637436 is clear of enemy and still intact.'

This meant that Lieutenant Powle had found a way clean through the enemy lines, and was at this moment a good six miles behind them. With one armoured car and one scout car, he had slipped through west of St Martin des Besaces, somehow dodged the 88mm guns covering this sector, and, travelling through the Foret L'Eveque, had reached the River Souleuvre by the bridge carrying the main road into Le Beny Bocage and Vire beyond. This was wonderful news.[27]

It was a spectacular achievement and prompted the commander of VIII Corps to pass 11th Armoured Division over this crossing and for General Dempsey to shift his main effort from XXX

---

26 The Wireless call sign of the LO at 8 Corps.

27 Orde, Roden, *Household Cavalry at War – Second Household Cavalry Regiment* (Aldershot: Gale & Polden, 1953), p.101.

Corps, who had made more limited progress, to VIII Corps. It highlights the disproportionate influence a young reconnaissance commander can have on a battle.

When an enemy front is broken the role of the armoured car regiment in leading the pursuit and exploitation of a routed enemy becomes an especially important task, its speed and ability to travel long distances allow the commander to determine the best routes available to the formation. We shall return to this role towards the end of this book and examine their part in the 'Great Swan' alongside the other elements of the Armoured Corps. But the depth to which the reconnaissance regiments could operate in front of friendly forces was still limited by their ground based logistic support and the requirement for gaps to appear in the enemy's forward defences through which they could exploit through. However if a unit could be dropped by air beyond the front line then further information in the enemy's depth could also be obtained.

The Special Air Service Brigade had precisely this capability, though its primary mission was to conduct attacks against enemy targets themselves, rather than collect intelligence per se. The main focus of SAS operations were the German re-supply dumps some distance from Normandy. These included the forest of Orleans south west of Paris (Operation GAIN); the Morvain hills west of Dijon (Operation HOUNDSWORTH) and the Vienne between Poitiers and Limoges (Operation BULBASKET). There were five SAS battalions made up of four squadrons with three troops in each, a captain usually commanded the troop which contained four sections. 3 and 4 SAS were French units and would be used exclusively in Brittany to develop the resistance and create a 'free' area, 1, 2 and 5 SAS would be used to attack the key lines of communication. Although armed with plastic explosive and other materials for sabotage and ambush attacks on German locomotives the SAS troopers could also communicate targets and other intelligence to the SAS Brigade HQ in Moor Park near London. The Brigade maintained liaison officers with both the Allied Expeditionary Air Forces and 21st Army Group and would pass on attractive targets suitable for attack by air. One such example of an SAS target were the petrol tankers at Chateaullerault. The OC of the BULBASKET team Captain Tonkin described how the information fell into his lap:

> A small very frightened and therefore highly courageous French civilian (I think he was a railway employee) arrived at our newly established base. He told us that there were eleven petrol trains on a well camouflaged and heavily guarded series of sidings about a kilometre south-west of Chateaullerault.[28]

Capt Tonkin needed to confirm the story and pinpoint the exact location of the tankers and therefore tasked one of his officers Twm Stephens to carry out a further reconnaissance. The 60 km journey took Twm Stephens a significant period of time but by the early hours of 10 June he was able to confirm the presence of the tankers and that they were too heavily guarded for the SAS to take on. Consequently at 1717 hours that afternoon the enciphered location was radioed back to SAS Brigade Headquarters who in turn passed the information to 2 Group. They performed the low level raid (described earlier in Chapter 6) with Mosquito bombers that evening, though the crews were not told the source of the information for obvious reasons.[29] Other SAS units produced similar targeting intelligence, Operation HOUNDSWORTH identified some thirty targets warranting attack from the air including the submerged causeways that German Engineers had constructed across the River Seine.

The other major strand of reconnaissance which supported many units and formations was air reconnaissance, of which there were a number of different types. These included Tac/R where the

---

28 McCue, Paul, *SAS Operation Bulbasket* (London; Leo Cooper 1996), p.28.
29 Ibid., p.28.

Figure 7.6 Pre-invasion oblique aerial photograph showing defences at Courseulles.
(Crown Copyright Air Historical Branch)

Figure 7.7 Another oblique aerial photograph showing troops of the 3rd British Division
assaulting the QUEEN WHITE sector of SWORD Beach on 6 June.
(Crown Copyright Air Historical Branch)

Figure 7.8 Aerial photograph of a German convoy attempting to escape from the Falaise pocket in mid-August. (Crown Copyright Air Historical Branch)

pilot would report by radio what he had seen, the information being broadcast to the relevant ground headquarters through the normal ASSU network. Though Tac/R broadcasts were important, a picture always paints a thousand words, consequently the photographs produced by Photo Reconnaissance aircraft were of particular importance. The RAF produced a number of different types of air photographs. The first type were known as 'Verticals' they were produced at either 1:10,000 or 1:16,000 scale and were used to either brief, establish the topography of an area or for detailed interpretation. These photographs allowed objects as small as 3-feet to be accurately measured, allowing enemy defensive constructions to be examined in detail. A system of off-setting the cameras on the aircraft also allowed a 'Parallax' effect to be achieved, this meant that the photographs when viewed through special lenses could be seen in stereo and relief viewed and studied. An accurate appreciation of the ground is something any commander values and these 'Stereo' prints were often in demand.

Stereo photographs also allowed a trained photographic interpreter to identify equipment more easily. A good example of this practice was the identification of the E-boats at Le Havre, the reader will recall from Chapter 3 that as the US VII Corps advanced up the Cotentin peninsula the German E-boats fled the port of Cherbourg. This was picked up by signals intelligence and on the morning of 14 June Flight Lieutenant P J Kelley from 542 Squadron conducted a mission over the port in his Spitfire XI. Flying at 30,000 feet Flight Lieutenant Kelley took a series of 'Verticals' which when examined by the interpreters at RAF Medmenham showed the distinctive torpedo tube 'cut aways' that even at 30,000 feet identified the craft as the missing E-boats. The confirmation that there was now a large concentration of craft in the various basin's of Le Havre harbour triggered the successful 617 Squadron raid (covered in chapter 6) that ended the E-boat menace to the invasion fleet.

The second type of air photographs available were 'Obliques'. These could be 'close ups' of pinpoint targets, which when taken from 1,000 feet allowed examination of detail and construction. Alternatively obliques could be taken from 1,000ft to 4,000ft and give a more detailed overview of the country. Gridded obliques were also produced for the artillery so that exact positions of targets could be accurately fixed on them and subsequently related to the ground. Coastal

Figure 7.9 de Havilland Mosquito PR IX based at Wyton, Huntingdonshire.
(Crown Copyright Air Historical Branch)

silhouette obliques were also taken at sea level from 3 to 4 miles distance and were used extensively on D-Day itself.

Air photographs could be taken by a variety of aircraft. The Spitfire PR XI and XIII was excellent in the low level photo reconnaissance role and had three F24 cameras in split verticals, an oblique F24 as well as two 5-inch F8 cameras under each wing.[30] Mosquitoes, with their greater range, were also used extensively. Ronald Foster describes their equipment and operation:

> Usually our Mosquitoes carried two main cameras, 'F/36s' which took side by side photos with an adjustable overlay to obtain stereo effect. On top of each camera a film magazine was clipped each of which held 500 exposures. Another camera was also fitted an 'F/6' that produced a larger print of about nine inches square, and covered a wide and extensive ground area surrounding the actual target. One Mosquito on 544, a fighter mark, had a forward facing camera for use in very low level flights the pilot operated it from a button on the control column. We called this kite, the dicer. At times our usual aircraft were also fitted with an 'oblique' facing camera, an 'F/14' operated by the pilot who sighted along the port wing when flying close to the ground.

On D-Day itself Ronald Foster flew his eighteenth sortie against the railyards at Toulouse:

> Our last target was Toulouse, where the marshalling yards were extensive and took several runs to cover. We made some runs at 4,000ft and received some flak. We came lower and

---

30 Delve, Ken, *The Story of the Spitfire* (London: Greenhill Books, 2007), p.161.

Figure 7.10 Photographers at RAF Benson testing cameras before installing them in a Mosquito. Left to right – two F.24 14-inch vertical cameras, one F.24 14-inch lens oblique camera, two F.52 vertical cameras with 20-inch lenses. (Crown Copyright Air Historical Branch)

lower – on some of our evasion manoeuvres to avoid the thick flak we flew at less than the height of the flak towers on which some anti-aircraft guns were stationed.

On some of the runs, while Frank was operating the cameras, I dully wondered what the unusual noise was below us on the main body of the kite. Of all things, under the circumstances, the thought sprung into my mind that the sound was like being drubbed with many cricket bats. A weird line of thought to be sure, which I cannot explain. In fact it was the plane being hit, splintered and marked by shots and shrapnel that sprayed us from many directions.

The Mosquito was still flying well as we departed the area; all targets were covered.[31]

Once the aircraft had landed the photos would be quickly extracted by the ground crew and examined by an Air Photographic Interpretation Section (APIS) at the airfield itself. These would produce a 'First Phase' report mainly concerned with movement, the location of armour and any concentrations of troops. On a sortie of about 100 photos it was thought possible that the First Phase report could be disseminated within one hour of the sortie's photos being processed. A 'Second Phase' report was usually undertaken by the APIS at Army or Army Group HQ[32] but on occasions by the interpreters at Corps or Divisional HQ.[33] Major General Gale of 6th Airborne Division describes the effectiveness of his own interpreters in this regard:

The interpretation of air photographs was done by a small section of experts on my staff known as the Army Photographic Interpretation Staff. They were under the command of one

---

31 Foster, Ronald, *Focus on Europe: A Photo-Reconnaissance Mosquito Pilot at War 1943-45* (Ramsbury: Crowood Press, 2004), p.93.

32 There were 6 Officers and 34 ORs in an Army Group APIS and 12 Officers and 26 ORs AT Army level (Mockler-Ferryman, p.117).

33 Both Corps and Divisional APIS were 2 Officers and 4 ORs.

Captain McBride of the Border Regiment. When, in 1934 and 1935, I was Brigade Major of the Ferozepore Brigade in the Punjab, India I knew McBride well. He was then a very senior subaltern serving with his unit. He was an expert at his job and there were no secrets in these photos we had taken that McBride did not unearth. We found the German mortars, the holes in the hedges where he was wont to run up his self-propelled guns, and his rocket firing mortars. The tracks as well as the tell-tale footpaths and muzzle blast of the guns all showed up on the air photographs. Most nights the Germans came over and gave us a bit of bombing. One July night a bomb, which dropped just outside the office, sent a shower of splinters into the sand-bagged door-way where poor McBride was standing; and thus we lost yet another of the band.[34]

Third Phase interpretation was long-term strategic interpretation and usually only done at Army Group or at the Central Interpretation Unit at Medmenham.[35] Much important work was done at Medmenham, both in preparation for D-Day and in locating and identifying the V1 sites in northern France and the Low countries. Before D-Day Allied intelligence had predicted that most enemy movement would take place during the hours of darkness, the Army therefore stipulated a requirement for 'night photography' and the RAF developed a capability in 69 Squadron based at Northolt. Flight Lieutenant S Phillips explains:

The only night reconnaissance squadron was our own 69. We flew Mk III Wellingtons 'Wimpeys'. The guns of the nose turrets, and other gear, were removed and replaced with clear perspex nose fairings which provided me with a good visual field of view. An open shutter moving film camera and photo flash pistol were provided; plus a flare launch tube for the 54 flares (18 bundles of 3) stowed in the fuselage. The flares were dropped from 3,000 and we were to go down to 800-1000 feet for visual observation and photos. On a sortie, a particular target might be set for photos: and this would be the priority task. Flares would need to be dropped. Also an area of roads, river crossings or such to cover as visual reconnaissance. If the moonlight were good enough then no need for flares… Many of our trips were for trying to find German troops, vehicles on the move, or bivouacking by night; or under camouflage. We operated from close up for an artillery shoot under our flares or as far-ranging as 60 miles in front of our troops…

The crew was pilot: navigator 1 to get us to and from the target; navigator 2 as target area map reader, pinpoint identification, flare dropper, photo man and the rear gunner.

Flying low level at night is always a hazardous business and required great skill from the pilots of 69 Squadron. Flight Lieutenant Phillips expressed strong admiration for his own pilot Flight Lieutenant John Stuart, one of the many New Zealanders flying with the RAF:

In approaching to do photos he couldn't come in too low. There is an ideal field of view of the cameras at 800 to 1000 feet and we were expected to do that. It was always heart stopping for me when I had the photo target lined up, warned Johnny and pressed the camera tit. Now we had six flashes to come, two seconds apart all in a lovely straight line. What a target for the gunners! Yet on more than half the occasions we didn't get any flak. When we did, Johnny just held us straight on, to finish the run. Relaxing a little after climbing out and up, Johnny

---

34 Gale, Gen Sir Richard, *With the 6th Airborne Division in Normandy* (London: Marston & Co, 1948), p.113.
35 TNA: WO 205/1153, Aerial Photography: notes on provision of intelligence from air photographs and photographic interpretation in the field – HQ 21 Army Group.

would go through the routine, asking the crew 'OK Mac? Ok Phil? OK Jackie?' and with our replies came the inevitable 'Good on Yer Phil!

I was glad when the flare work was done – maybe two targets. Then I could be flare-happy within reason dropping them all over the place…we might see something really special – an armoured convoy ideally, then the hot potato was mine. I mustn't drop it through my nerveless fingers. I was supposed to say precisely '3 miles NW of Senonches, travelling towards Verneuil.' The pilot had authority to break R/T silence there and then if anything really good was seen, so up he climbs gets R/T contact and tells them 'We have 3 melons at Glos-sur-Risle two miles west of Theirville'

I had given him my pinpoint. Then it was up to 34 Wing to decide what kind of attack to send in if any.

Not all missions went totally to plan, Flight Lieutenant Phillips describes his eleventh trip to Elbeuf on 28 July:

We did some visual Recce of the roads with some bundles of flares and soon I was confident of my roads for photos, which we took. We were still very near to the built-up area of Elbeuf and its bridge. Then the searchlights coned us. The flak that came up was different – some of the lines of tracer ended in explosions. I didn't like being hit by these bursting shells and the ordinary tracer was clobbering us as well. Johnny went down, but he hadn't much sky to play with; and he jinked us violently out of it into darkness and calm. Climbing gently and setting course for Muids.

Jackie [Sgt J Dennison the tail gunner] says 'my turret won't move skipper' it didn't take Johnny long to test a few other things and find that we had no hydraulics. So off we go for home and over the sea we wind down the wheels manually and hope they'll stand the strain of a 'too fast' landing. Once again Mac and I had to take up crash stations. Jackie had no option but to stay where he was. Johnny told us about his stalling speed – he knew he wouldn't be able to come down to the usual 90-95 mph. In fact he came in at 115-120mph as our record shows.

We bounced in quite steadily then one wheel collapsed and the kite stuttered one wing along the ground, Johnny letting it go into the grass. It didn't overturn us, lucky us. Then the other wheel collapsed and we spin round in half a circle, one wing now almost cracked off and then rest, and silence. Johnny's 'off' switch had got the spluttering engines to obey and the immediate danger of fire was over. I think that Mac and I were out very smartly: even so by then the rescue boys were running from their trucks, and they did their work to get Jackie and Johnny out.[36]

The final principle collection source available to 21st Army Group was signals intelligence. The practice of intercepting wireless communications and locating the source of the enemy transmitter (known as Direction Finding (DF)) was a practice undertaken by all armies and was widely known at the time. However the technical methods of cryptography (the decoding and deciphering of intercepted code), were very closely guarded secrets. The British Signals Intelligence service went by the name 'Y' though even in 1945 the origin of where that term had come from had been lost. Sometime in 1943, probably in order to have a name understandable to both British and Americans, the term 'Signal Intelligence' was coined. However as 'Y' was known to many in the Army as responsible for both the results of field interception and the administration of the units doing the work it continued to be widely used in Normandy.

---

36 IWM 12607 03/33/1 Private Papers of S Phillips.

There were 'Y' elements available at Army Group, Army and Corps HQ consisting of cryptanalysts, translators and intelligence staff. The 'Y' service was relatively manpower intensive, as an example there were some 13 Officers and 128 ORs attached to an Army HQ. Sections whether at Army Group, Army or Corps carefully directed their own particular focus. As an illustration the 'Y' elements at Corps would focus upon intercept material which could be dealt with on the spot, and when combined with D/F, provide intelligence of direct interest to Corps. This material could include German ground and air reconnaissance reports, army co-operation traffic, and forward supply messages (in clear or simple code) between enemy lower formations.[37]

Whilst the 'Y' service were able to intercept messages sent *en clair* and decode German low and medium grade codes used at the tactical level, the high grade ciphers and codes, including Ultra, would be tackled at the Government Code and Cipher School at Bletchley Park. The technological decoding miracle of Ultra, which took place in Hut 6 of Bletchley Park, has been covered in many other books and is well known now. However such material was useless unless it got into the hands of the operational commanders. The first step in this process was for the message to be passed to 'Hut 3'. Ralph Bennet who worked in Hut 3 from 1942 to the end of the war describes the process from then on:

At whatever hour of the day or night a key was broken by Hut 6, word was immediately passed to Hut 3 and decodes soon began to reach the No.1 of the Watch. Partly for historical reasons dating back to pre-war recruitment, partly by chance, the translating watch was largely composed of civilians, although almost all the rest of the hut's personnel were in uniform…Work reached the No.1 of the watch in the form of print-outs from the de-coding machine (Hut 6 was better off than the German operators in this respect) pasted on to the back of each sheet. Intercept and decode alike were in the five-figure groups of the original transmission. Weather conditions or static might have caused some letters to be missed at the moment of intercept and others to be taken down wrongly, but in most cases an experienced No.1 had only to glance at a message to decide its urgency. The first task of the watch keeper who dealt with it was to supply the missing letters and correct the corruptions dividing the five-letter groups into words and expanding the many abbreviations used. The work of emendation could be quite straightforward with a clean text in continuous German prose, but when unfamiliar technical terms were used, or when missed or corrupt letters occurred at critical points, considerable difficulty could be encountered before the German text could be plausibly reconstructed and an acceptable translation made…

When he was satisfied that the English version fairly represented the sense of the German the No.1 handed text and translation to the Air and Military advisers, service officers who sat opposite each other at the next table in the production line. One or other, as the cases required, would use the resources of the huge card indexes maintained by his section to explore the significance of the text before him – for a correct and lucid translation could still present severe intelligence problems. Valuable information was often squeezed out of unpromising material by persistent investigation of such unlikely detail as the previous employment of a corporal (if he were known to have been engaged on radar work, for instance, his present movements might suggest those of his unit, or the opening of a new tracking station)… Having solved the problems as best he could, the Adviser annotated the translation accordingly, decided whether the item merited a signal to commands abroad, drafted the signal if he so decided, and then handed it over to the Duty Officer for teleprinter operators and coding

---

37 Mockler-Ferryman, Brigadier, 'Military Intelligence in the Second World War', 1945, Intelligence Corps Museum, pp.256-257.

clerks. Over two hundred such signals were sent out on D-Day, and an average of more than a thousand a week was maintained for the next few months.[38]

The signal would then be sent to one of the Special Liaison Units. These were attached to the highest Allied headquarters in Normandy. They allowed Army Group and Army commanders as well as some of their key staff access to Ultra intelligence, but importantly not those at Corps level. Despite the extensive use of land lines by the Germans and the German army key being the most difficult to crack, Ultra was still the most valuable source to senior commanders. It consistently gave regular and reliable information on the movement of key German divisions around the bridgehead. Most importantly Signals Intelligence, including Ultra, is usually highly predictive giving the enemy's future intentions and plans as well as his current activity. Ralph Bennet summarizes Ultra's contribution to Operation EPSOM:

> The bulk of the intercepted traffic concerned 1 SS Pz Corps. We knew the tank strength it could muster in its position on the eastern flank of the British salient across the Odon at the end of the battle on 1 July: 1 SS Pz Division had fifty four Mark IV tanks, twenty-six Mark V Panthers and thirty one assault guns, 12 SS Pz Division twenty-five IVs and twenty-six Panthers, while twenty-five of the twenty-eight Tigers with which Heavy SS Pz Abt 101 had started the day were in the repair shops by nightfall. The Corps' petrol and ammunition supplies began to run dangerously low at once, and the petrol situation was becoming 'more acute every day' on the 27th. The Corps or its component divisions frequently reported the point at which they would concentrate their main effort, and the Corps itself remained 7 Army's spearhead until the fighting died down
>
> II SS Pz Corps did not enter the battle until 29 June. At dawn 9 SS Pz Division was moving up to tackle the Allied breakthrough west of Caen, but soon postponed its effort. Next day it gave long notice of an intention to attack Cheux, a communication centre in the middle of the Allied salient, during the night 30 June to 1 July. Only a little over four hours separated the German and the British times of origin of this signal, making it among the speedier performances of Hut 6 and Hut 3, and when it was dispatched there were still several hours to go before 9 SS PZ's intended attack. It must surely have been this long notice which allowed the preparation of the tremendous artillery barrage which snuffed the attack out on the morning of 1 July and caused one of 9 SS Pz's officers to warn those approaching the locality 'Abandon hope all ye who enter here.[39]

As well as supporting operational decision making Ultra information could also be used for striking specific targets. Perhaps the most famous occasion was when the Headquarters of Panzergruppe West, the large German armoured striking force, emerged from the shadows to briefly signal their location 'Battle Headquarters Panzer Gruppe West evening ninth at La Caine'. This short message was sufficient to allow Bletchley Park to pinpoint it accurately. As a result 2nd TAF conducted a raid on the headquarters effectively putting it out of action for more than a fortnight. The origin of the source of intelligence was clearly not disclosed to the pilots, indeed to protect the source further a British reconnaissance aircraft flew over the HQ location immediately prior to the raid. This was the raid undertaken by the Mitchells of 2 Group and described in Chapter 6.

---

38 Bennet, Ralph, *Ultra in the West* (London: Hutchinson, 1979), pp.27-28.
39 Ibid., pp.85-86.

It will be apparent that there was a large variety of intelligence and information coming into headquarters at all levels. Some of this information would be single source and already processed by analysts, some would be completely unprocessed raw information. The reliability of sources would vary dramatically and sometimes be difficult to discern; as indeed would the criticality and relevance to the intelligence officer's own formation or unit. Arguably the most important step in the intelligence function is therefore processing this information. That was the role of the intelligence staff at all headquarters and though the sources, time and manpower available might vary, the critical functions of collating, evaluating, analysing and finally interpreting the information were common. This work would all need to be conducted in a focused way that answered the commander's initial intelligence direction, which in turn had focused much of the collection efforts. At lower levels the limited manpower available meant such work was inevitably rudimentary. At a brigade headquarters intelligence manning consisted of the brigade intelligence officer (normally a captain), a sergeant, a corporal and lance corporal. The brigade intelligence officer attended all conferences and accompanied the brigade commander on reconnaissance. He was responsible for a regular flow of information upwards, downwards and laterally and was also concerned with the preparation of intelligence summaries, identification of prisoners and material as well as the distribution of maps, air photographs and codes. He paid frequent visits to battalions, flank brigades, divisional headquarters and maintained close contact with the Royal Artillery and Royal Engineer staffs who fed him targeting information and engineer intelligence.[40]

A good intelligence officer would have to approach the information he possessed as objectively as possible, making sure that he or his commander were not skewing the intelligence to fit a preconceived plan or delivering to the commander what he 'wanted to hear'. Part of this objectivity rested in making sure that the intelligence officer and his commander did not become too wedded to their own previous assessments. The intelligence staff is different in this respect to other headquarters staff branches and this required a subtle handling by the commander. Brigadier Williams describes it well:

> Military Intelligence is not only spasmodic, it is always out of date: there is a built in time-lag. Better the half-truth on time than the whole truth too late. (Not a recipe for the historian but vital to the Intelligence officer). So that, although, to be useful to a commander, it must provide as clear an answer as possible (not just a set of possibilities in no order of probability, which he can pick and choose between) one more clue can readily refute it. It follows, therefore, that one complete irrelevance to Military Intelligence is vanity. Going on believing that the carefully confected from a wealth (it is more often from a paucity) of detail, is still true when it isn't raises hideous problems. Men are being killed because of your false information.[41]

It is a credit to Montgomery that he understood this subtle dynamic. Montgomery would accept that his 'I' staff were giving him the likeliest answer they could for that moment and corrections were therefore taking account the latest available information. It was also important that the intelligence officer was not overly reliant on a single source. Checking the accuracy of information with other sources, or indeed using one piece of intelligence collection to cue another were all seen as good practice. As an example 51st Highland Division checked information received from a civilian source (probably a refugee or line crosser) with air photographic intelligence. The civilian source had reported seeing two well camouflaged tanks on 28 June, imagery of the same

---

40 Mockler-Ferryman, 'Military Intelligence in the Second World War', 1945, Intelligence Corps Museum, p.111.

41 Howarth, T, *Monty at Close Quarters: Recollections Of The Man* (London: Leo Cooper, 1985), p.23.

grid references given by the civilian allowed 51st Highland Divisions photographic interpretation section to reveal:

> One set of veh[vehicle] tracks (6'-7' track) leading to a possible camouflaged object 12 x 25 ft at 07856835. Similar object and large camouflaged patch nearby.[42]

The importance of not relying on single sources at higher levels of command was also understood and the tendency Ultra had to dominate the intelligence process could be overcome with care. As Bill Williams advises:

> At an Army HQ we maintained, however, that during battle we had not done our day's work properly unless we had beaten the Ultra, unless we knew what was happening and could appreciate what would happen before it could arrive. This did not mean that we were not glad of its arrival, for at best it showed that we were wrong, usually it enabled us to tidy up loose ends, and at worst we tumbled late into bed with a smug satisfaction.[43]

The statement above underlines again that an intelligence staff is only successful if its assessments are predictive and accurate. It is no point simply reporting what is going on, a good intelligence officer must attempt to predict his adversaries future moves, for these are the assessments that are of most use to his commander in his planning. As we shall see in the next chapter these predictions help a commander seize the initiative and in Montgomery's own words force the enemy to 'dance to his tune'. Having formulated his assessments the critical final step in the intelligence process is dissemination. For information that included Ultra this presented some problems given the extreme sensitivity of the source. Brigadier Bill Williams explains how this necessary restriction was managed:

> Experienced Intelligence Officers at Corps were not likely to believe for very long that the fact that Intelligence at Army had the habit of being right was necessarily due to the intellectual capabilities of the officers on the Army staff. Anyone with a brain in his head (and we made a point of insisting on that class of person as G2 'I' at Corps) speedily recognised that the Army had got something up its sleeve. Moreover, the Corps commander had to receive the same appreciation from the Army commander as, with proper safeguards, he had received from his own 'I' staff. Nothing breaks down the confidence of a Corps commander in his 'I' staff more than if he thinks that by by-passing them he can get something better at Army. There were two alternatives: either to indoctrinate the G2 'I' of Corps, which was forbidden, or to practice the polite convention that the Intelligence Staff at Army had a habit of making the correct appreciation by virtue of some remarkable element in their glandular make up. In fact we hedged between these two alternatives by admitting, when taxed with it, that there was indeed something up our sleeve yet continuing to filter it down only in the form of an appreciation, at the same time making it clear to the G2 'I' at Corps when we knew something as distinct from when we only thought something. It was a difficult game to play; it depended upon the confidence in the G2 'I' at Corps (and they were all hand-picked) and upon a rigid

42 TNA: WO 171/527, 51st Highland Division War Diary, Intelligence Summary No.200, 29 June 1944.

43 TNA: HW 1/2918, Notes on the use of ULTRA, Brigadier Bill Williams, HQ 21st Army Group, 5 October 1945.

discipline in controlling one's wish to be helpful with the very pressing realization that to be too helpful on one occasion might mean that one would never be able to be so helpful again.[44]

Even Montgomery never saw raw Ultra but was given a verbal appreciation and advised on which aspects he could or could not use when delivering his own assessments. Fused intelligence would be passed in a number of ways. At tactical levels wireless and line communications would give timely, running commentaries and assessments to subordinate headquarters. A written intelligence summary would also be produced by formations, not so much on a daily or other formalised basis but when it was felt appropriate. An example of a typical divisional intelligence summary is included in Appendix I.

For many tactical commanders the most valuable method of dissemination were the 'over printed maps' of which many copies were made and issued. The ability to relate the enemy and his equipment to the ground is always useful and these serve as a good example of a 'fused' intelligence product. Although highly appreciated they could be a little alarming on occasions, Lieutenant John Foley a Churchill Tank commander recalls being handed one just before the attack on Le Havre:

> These Defence Overprint maps were magnificent things produced by the Ordnance chaps practically as you went into battle. They were large scale maps of the battle area, and clearly printed in blue[45] was the location of every field gun, anti-tank gun, minefield, rifle and machine-gun pit, barbed wire entanglement, and concrete obstacle. The blue printing pointed out where the anti-tank ditches ran and where the concrete dug-outs were situated. They described the state of the ground and practically gave you a weather forecast.
> They were a great help, but sometimes a bit frightening. The one for Le Havre seemed just a solid mass of blue.[46]

The Allies were fortunate in the intelligence system they possessed. It was able to predict the majority of German intentions from the tactical to the strategic level and often added focus and purpose to the targeting of Allied air and artillery. This ability to understand the enemy and predict his next move could only be properly exploited if the Allied commanders could swiftly and competently develop and execute a sound operational plan. It is therefore important to observe in the next chapter what mechanisms the British Army had in place to make use of such an advantage.

---

44 Ibid.
45 In 1944 enemy forces were marked in blue and friendly forces in red. This colour coding was reversed after the war and to this day enemy forces are now marked in red on all NATO country's maps.
46 Foley, John, *Mailed Fist* (St Albans: Mayflower Books, 1975), p.99.

8

'Penetrating the Fog' – Command and Control

I was never embarrassed by the Germans, nor do I propose to be in the future.

General Montgomery, to XIII Corps Officers, 30 June 1941[1]

Commanding, controlling and coordinating the operations of an organization as large as 21st Army Group was an obviously complex affair, it could only be managed by a combination of commanders, headquarters, staff officers and reliable communications at various levels. This chapter examines how 21st Army Group utilised this command and control system to defeat the Germans but begins with a study of the command philosophy that existed within the British Army at the time.

Command is an intensely personal affair, an individual commander's character will have a huge bearing on the precise manner in which he exercises command and any interpretation by historians runs the risk of being too subjective, revealing as much about the author's own views and personality as that of his subjects. Some commanders have laid out their own views on command, in particular General Montgomery wrote lengthy notes on 'High Command in War' whilst he was still commanding 21st Army Group. Montgomery's huge personal dominance of 21st Army Group gives us a useful understanding of the command philosophy that existed at the time. Moreover there are a number of common functions and responsibilities that all commanders in all wars have to carry out if their operations are to be successful.

The British Army was clear that the first of the commander's responsibilities is to ensure that his unit or formation is capable of performing the missions that it is likely to be assigned. The commander will naturally need to ensure his organization is equipped and trained properly but just as importantly he will need to ensure it has the right ethos and spirit. General Montgomery emphasized that this requirement to 'create the fighting machine, and to forge the weapon to his liking' was the primary responsibility of a commander. The commander's efforts would not only have focused on the fighting elements of the organization but also on his headquarters and staff officers who would need to be trained and developed to 'enable the weapon to be wielded properly and to develop its full power rapidly'.[2] General Montgomery stated in his typically forthright manner that a commander's primary method to achieve this was by creating what he termed the right 'atmosphere':

1   Horne, Alistair, *The Lonely Leader: Monty 1944-45* (London: Macmillan, 1994), p.29.
2   Montgomery, Field Marshal Bernard, 'High Command In War', Germany, 21st Army Group, 1945, p.21. Held at Defence Concepts and Doctrine Centre, Shrivenham.

In that atmosphere his staff, his subordinate commanders and his troops will live, and work, and fight. His armies must know what he wants; they must know the basic fundamentals of his policy and must be given firm guidance and a clear 'lead'. Inspiration and guidance must come from above and must permeate the force.

Once this is done there is never any difficulty, since all concerned will go ahead on the lines laid down; the whole force will thus acquire balance and cohesion, and the results on the day will be very apparent.[3]

As one example Lieutenant-General Simonds went to great lengths in detailing for his officers an operational policy explaining how he saw his infantry and armoured divisions being employed in Normandy. Similarly when Major General Roberts took over 11th Armoured Division he spoke to all of his officers in a local cinema and spelt out how the tactical handling of his division should be exercised, what the various tasks of the different arms might be as well as the cooperation required. These ideas would then of course be reinforced by the commander through various exercises and study days whilst the formation was preparing in England for the invasion. As well as ensuring proficiency in weaponry and tactics, General Montgomery was also clear that commanders must ensure that their soldiers should be full of 'binge' and 'enter the fight with the light of battle in their eyes, and definitely wanting to kill the enemy'. Ensuring his unit's morale was at its peak and able to withstand a prolonged period in battle was uppermost in a commander's mind, but a successful unit's spirit and ethos was developed in a much more nuanced manner than simply encouraging naked aggression.

The soldiers of 21st Army Group had been drawn from civilian life only a few years previously, their motivations were complex but contained a sober, practical and realistic understanding of the tasks ahead of them. Many leaders felt that part of sustaining these soldiers' morale called for a commander to make the individual soldier feel he was part of a close-knit team rather than a tiny cog in a faceless army. Those commanders that got the balance right and were successful in creating such an atmosphere left a profound impression and an enduring legacy on the men they were leading. Commanding officers of battalions and regiments in particular played a disproportion-ately large role within the Army in creating this necessary ethos. Their autonomy, seniority, power and responsibilities were so much greater than their subordinates, yet their span of command was sufficiently small for them to personally know the vast majority of individuals within their unit, certainly when it initially deployed to Normandy.

The importance commanding officers had as leaders within 21st Army meant that all of their appointments were personally scrutinized by General Montgomery. However this did not mean that they did not have their weaknesses. Lieutenant Sydney Jary recalls his commanding officer and in doing so highlights how no commanding officer is ever a one-man band and is still dependent upon a supporting team:

Out of the same drawer as our Divisional commander, he was an above average battalion commander but no leader of men. He was ambitious, brave and resourceful but insensitive to his subordinates. A good picker of officers and, most importantly he was extremely lucky. To a large extent he was saved by James Brind DSO, his 2IC, Tim Watson his Adjutant, Gordon Bennetts his IO, and Fred Hale his Quartermaster. Compassion and wisdom poured down from James Brind. A civilised and cultured man he was adored by us all: I would have followed him anywhere. Not only a sound commander but a trusted and respected leader.[4]

---

3   Ibid.
4   Jary, Sydney, article in *British Army Doctrine and Training News No.17*, pp.44-45.

The CO and his Battalion Headquarters could not realistically expect to see everything and be everywhere and it was arguably the company or squadron officers who were most critical in leadership terms. It was they who would often personally underpin the soldiers' morale, helping them to withstand the shocks and dangers of battle and leading them in accomplishing their battlefield tasks. It called for high quality officers; Corporal Proctor was a section commander in the 4th Somerset Light Infantry and highlighted the qualities that would help a young platoon commander in leading his soldiers:

> During my six years army service I knew many Officers – some good – some bad. The most obvious difference between them was not in their tactical awareness as one might expect, but in the relationships they had with their soldiers. No matter how tactically aware an Officer may be, it counts for little unless he can command the trust, loyalty and respect of his men and is able to inspire them. The good Officers, without exception, enjoyed that trust, loyalty and respect…
>
> .. Some Officers no doubt expect trust and respect to be theirs by right, and fail to realise that these two essential factors in the relationship between officers and men are not cheaply or easily given but must be worked for and earned. The Platoon should be thought of as a family, and the Officer at its head should not insulate himself against the demands – emotional or otherwise – 'his family' will make upon him. He should give them his time and his friendship, and show a genuine interest in his men as individuals with their many and varied problems. Friendship for his men does not mean an end to discipline, as trust and respect imposes its own self-discipline and he will find that the courtesies of rank will always be observed…
>
> …When things go wrong, a cool, level-headed, common sense appraisal of the situation is essential – a good Officer will never 'flap' or show indecision. In this way, trust and respect is cemented.[5]

Corporal Proctor's platoon commander, Lieutenant Sydney Jary, was also clear that soldiers needed to have both trust and confidence in their leader. He suggests that the more 'heroic' characters portrayed in films would have caused a platoon to lose faith in their leader:

> The fact is that infantry soldiers will not follow a leader who has the characteristics of some of the parts played by John Wayne and other of that ilk. They see the 'macho' officer as a threat to their very lives; who will get them killed in, at the best, an ill-conceived operation or, at the worst, in an exhibitionist display of personal valour.[6]

As command is such a personal business not every leader chose to create such a 'familial' atmosphere as illustrated in the examples above, either because they saw no need to or their dispositions were more severe. Major-General G I Thomas, the commander of 43rd Wessex Division was a notoriously fierce disciplinarian who ruthlessly commanded his staff and subordinates. His notoriety was apparent even to private soldiers, Private B Davies, 7th Royal Hampshires explains:

---

5   Jary, Sydney and Proctor, Douglas, "Reflections on the relationship between the Leader and the Led", *JR Army Medical Review* 2000 Number 146, pp.54-56.
6   Ibid.

The General earned himself the nickname 'Butcher' Thomas by his use of the units under his care and attention. The trouble is, at least to this survivor, one is left wondering just whose side he was supposed to be butchering.[7]

Nonetheless despite what many of his soldiers and officers may have thought of him, (and he did have some admirers) 43rd Wessex was widely regarded as a very credible fighting formation and remained under Thomas' command throughout the war. It illustrates that there are many different ways a commander can create the right 'atmosphere'. Fortunately for their subordinates most commanders took a different view to Major-General Thomas, this included Major-General Sir Allan Adair of the Guards Armoured Division:

I always got more results by being friendly; it is no good if officers are frightened of their commanders. I have little respect for senior officers who are continuously incapable of controlling their temper – and there were and still are, a lot of them around! Of course, a good 'rocket' has to be given occasionally.[8]

Major-General Roberts also preferred a more relaxed approach to that of Major-General Thomas and was disappointed to find that this did not exist within his own headquarters when he took over at 11th Armoured Division in December 1943:

I came to the conclusion that one officer was partly responsible. He was efficient, but could not relax and was not easily approachable. I did not think we would work happily together, so I felt we must have a change…

When I saw the officer concerned he could not understand it and was much upset and, I fear, departed feeling that he had been badly done by. Thereafter, with one or two other staff changes, the whole atmosphere changed rapidly.[9]

The sacking of an incompetent, or indeed an incompatible, subordinate was sometimes the inevitable course of action in some circumstances. However commanders also paid as much attention in selecting suitable personnel to be posted into a formation or HQ. General Montgomery famously took the selection of personnel very seriously and went to particular trouble to identify talented individuals, noting the names of those who impressed him for future use. He encouraged this practise in all his commanders:

Probably one of the most important requirements in a commander is that he must be a good judge of men. He must be able to choose as his subordinates men of ability and character who will inspire confidence in others.

It is necessary to remember that all divisions are different; some are good at one type of battle, others are good at another type of battle; the art lies in knowing what each division is best at, and having the right divisions in the right place at the right time.

It is the same with commanders in their several ranks; one is best at this, another at that; you require the right commander in the right place at the right time.[10]

---

7   Delaforce, Patrick, *The Fighting Wessex Wyverns* (Stroud: Sutton Publishing, 1994), p.8.
8   Adair, Sir Allan, *A Guards' General* (London: Hamish Hamilton, 1986), p.149.
9   Roberts, Major-General G.P.B, *From the Desert to the Baltic* (London: William Kimber, 1987), pp.153-154.
10 Montgomery, Field Marshal Bernard, 'High Command In War', Germany, 21st Army Group, 1945, p.25. Held at Defence Concepts and Doctrine Centre, Shrivenham.

Although a significant proportion of the Army's personnel had previously served in North Africa and Italy, many of them had no combat experience and commanders could sometimes only select personnel for important appointments based on observing their conduct in training and exercises. This carried the inherent risk that their battlefield performance might not match their peacetime one. Major General Roberts had to sack one of his brigade commanders and two commanding officers after 11th Armoured Division's first battle. He describes the rude awakening he received when he visited 159 Infantry Brigade during Operation EPSOM, on 28 June:

> I was shocked when I got there. The Brigadier was in a sorry state, quite over-wrought. He was standing in a slit trench with just his head and steel helmet showing above it; his brigade major was in the armoured half-track, which housed the wireless sets. There was quite a lot of noise going on, some artillery shelling, but mainly mortaring by what we then called 'moaning minnies'. These were in fact large multi-barrel mortars, which en route made a very loud moaning sound and exploded with a very loud bang. Said the Brigadier, or more correctly, shouted, 'We can't possibly stay here with this quantity of shelling – it is really – ghastly – we must withdraw.' On enquiry of the brigade major I found there had not been any casualties in Brigade HQ. So I told the Brigadier that I thought the mortar's bark was worse than its bite and went on my way across the river. There is no doubt there was a lot of mortaring, and there was also no doubt that the area of the bridge was one of the favourite targets. However I crossed safely and made my way to the units. The 4 KSLI was not doing too well, but I was glad to find Roscoe Harvey, commanding the armoured brigade, his usual imperturbable self. I went up to the top of Pt 112, but there was no way I could get to the other side it was well covered from several directions.
>
> As there was nothing more I could do, I got back to my HQ as I felt I must do something about the infantry brigade commander. I got on to the Corps HQ, explained the situation to the BGS. The Corps commander was out, but he would ring me later. He did ring, and I arranged for my brigadier to see him at 1000 hours the next morning. There was now the problem of who was to take over the brigade. The problem was easily solved; the CO of the Herefords, Jack Churcher, was undoubtedly the best CO and he had a good second-in-command who could take over his regiment; so this was arranged.[11]

Having 'forged the weapon to his liking' the commander's second responsibility would be to lead it on operations requiring the commander to both plan and execute operations. In some of the higher levels of command (division and upwards) there might be capacity within the headquarters and staff for an element of concurrency between planning and execution to occur, however at brigade level and below a lack of time and manpower normally meant the two functions could only be conducted sequentially.

Whatever the level of command concerned it is often helpful in understanding military operations to view the planning and execution function as an activity that is carried out in direct competition with the enemy. That is to say whichever side is fastest and most effective at going through its planning and execution functions will normally seize the initiative from its opponent. Obtaining the initiative is a critical advantage in battle and although often mentioned by historians, its relationship to the speedy and efficient planning and execution of operations in comparison to the enemy is sometimes overlooked. To explain this concept a little further, the side that is quicker at observing the enemy and predicting his next move, comprehensively understanding his own friendly force's dispositions, developing a feasible plan, communicating that plan

---

11 Roberts, Major-General G.P.B, *From the Desert to the Baltic* (London: William Kimber, 1987), pp.164-165.

to subordinate formations; who in turn successfully execute it; will seize the initiative from their opponent. This planning and execution process is a continuously repeating cycle which will need to be driven at a faster rate than the enemy's if the initiative is to be maintained. Gaining and maintaining the initiative is undoubtedly one of the most important concepts in war and allows a commander to surprise the enemy with a series of unexpected moves confounding his opponent's plans and forcing him to adopt a reactive approach.

Nowadays the planning-execution cycle above is referred to as the 'decision-action cycle' and the speed with which an organisation can complete this cycle is often referred to as its 'tempo' of operations. These terms may have been unfamiliar to General Montgomery but the idea of seizing and retaining the initiative through efficient planning and execution (and 'balanced forces' which could not be caught off guard) was at the very centre of his approach to warfare and lay at the heart of his campaign in Normandy:

> It is necessary to gain quickly, and to keep, the initiative. Only in this way will the enemy be made to dance to your tune and react to your thrusts.
>
> When making a plan it should be remembered that most opponents are at their best if they are allowed to dictate; they are not so good if they are forced to react to your movements and thrusts.
>
> Therefore the plan must be based on the following four principles:-
>
> (a) Surprise is essential. Strategical surprise may often be difficult, if not impossible, to obtain; but tactical surprise is always possible and must always be given a foremost place in the planning.
>
> (b) The enemy must be forced to dance to your tune all the time. This means that the commander must foresee his battle: he must decide in his own mind, and before the battle starts, how he wants the operations to be developed: he must then use the military effort at his disposal to force the battle to swing the way he wants.
>
> (c) As the battle develops the enemy will try to throw you off your balance by counter-thrusts; this must never be allowed. Throughout the battle area the whole force must be so well balanced and poised, and the general layout of dispositions must be so good, that there will never be any need to have to react to enemy thrusts.
>
> (d) The initiative, once gained, must never be lost; only in this way will the enemy be made to dance to your tune and react to your thrusts.
>
> If you lose the initiative against a good enemy you will very soon be made to react to his thrusts; once this happens you may well lose the battle. It is very easy in large scale operations to lose the initiative, and great energy and drive are required to prevent this from happening. A commander must understand very clearly that without the initiative he cannot win.[12]

It is easy to see this concept in practice in the Allies own planning and management of the Normandy campaign. The FORTITUDE deception plan for instance convinced the Germans that the D-Day landings were a diversion for a fictitious main effort in the Pas de Calais. In Normandy itself the technique was also incorporated within Montgomery's general plan which tied down the bulk of the enemy forces in front of the British (where the Germans expected the main thrust to be launched) so that the actual breakout by General Bradley's American Army could occur further to the west and against much weaker German opposition.

---

12 Montgomery, Field Marshal Bernard, 'High Command In War', Germany, 21st Army Group, 1945, p.16. Held at Defence Concepts and Doctrine Centre, Shrivenham.

This technique of seizing the initiative was not supposed to be limited to the higher operational levels, it could be equally successfully applied at lower tactical levels too. On D-Day itself a battlegroup from 21st Panzer counter-attacked into a gap between 3rd British Division and 3rd Canadian Division. However prior to the invasion in May the commander of the Staffordshire Yeomanry had predicted and planned for just such an eventuality:

> I know what the enemy will do. They will drive their command tanks onto an eminence effectively out of range of 6-pounders [about 1,000yards], make a quick plan, get back into their tanks before anv effective field artillery concentration can be brought to bear, and withdraw behind the ridge. They will form up their squadrons, give out their orders, then drive straight for their objective. What they do not know is that I have three troops of 'Fireflies' [Sherman tanks with 17-pounder guns – a well kept secret] which I will station on Hermanville ridge and leave as backstop.[13]

The British were consequently well prepared, the German Battlegroup lost thirteen tanks and this D-Day counter-attack onto the beach was effectively blunted.

The first stage in leading his formation on operations was therefore for the commander to develop a sound plan as quickly as possible. Montgomery was adamant 'that the plan of battle must be made by the commander and NOT by his staff' though some commanders admitted to adopting a more inclusive approach. Lieutenant General Horrocks for instance routinely worked out his battle plans for XXX Corps in consultation with his Chief of Staff, Logistics, Artillery and Engineer commanders and a liaison officer from 83 Group RAF.[14] To help them produce their plans commanders in the British Army would adopt a formal process known as an 'appreciation', this method ensured that they logically considered the tasks they had been set as well as all the important factors that could possibly effect the outcome of their plan. Major-General Richard Gale, commander of 6th Airborne Division, describes the process:

> He must firstly know precisely what is expected of him. What are his tasks in particular? Then he must have good and as accurate information as is possible as to the country, the enemy, and his strength in the vicinity, his reserves, particularly of armour, and the routes by which they could reach his front. He will want air photographs and maps. He will want to know all the administrative problems that any course he may adopt will involve him in, and what administrative assistance he is going to get to augment his own slender resources. He will want to know what support he can expect from the main army in the form of artillery fire, air cover, or sympathetic and diversionary action elsewhere on the battlefield.[15]

One of the first factors the commander would want to get to grips with was the effect of ground on the forthcoming battle, Major-General Gale emphasized its importance when planning future 6th Airborne operations in Normandy:

> First there is the country. Would it, and to what extent would it, assist us? Would it favour the enemy more than us? Were there weaknesses in it and could these be exploited? Ground means so much in battle. The study of ground is of the greatest importance. Just as the sailor

13 Nigel Tapp quoted in D'Este, Carlos, *Decision in Normandy* (New York: Konecky & Konecky, 1983), pp.139-140

14 Horrocks, General Sir Brian, *Corps Commander* (London: Sidgwick & Jackson, 1977), p.32.

15 Gale, Lt Gen R N, *With the 6th Airborne Division in Normandy* (London: Marston & Co, 1948), p.36.

makes the wind and tide serve him, so the commander exploits the ground. Even in modern battle with all the clutter of scientific machinery to assist it, the course of events is materially affected by ground.

Understanding the potential effect ground may have on an operation takes a practiced eye and the imagination to visualize a future encounter. Some commanders, General Dempsey for instance, had a very strong reputation at being able to visualize the shape and influence ground may have on a battle from just the contours and symbols on a map. Major-General Gale was lucky enough to plan his battle to seize and defend the Orne Bridgehead whilst back in England, he therefore had plenty of time available. He was also able to obtain a large number of air photographs and his intelligence staff had also produced an impressive clay model of the area, which showed the various features and relief of the Orne bridgehead in great detail. In the piece below Major-General Gale summarizes his appreciation of the ground on his southern and eastern flank and the conclusions he drew from it in regard to the enemy's movements, his own force dispositions as well as the risks he was prepared to take:

> The model brought out certain facts very clearly, far more so than did the map. Looking to the south the bridges form the apex of a triangle one arm of which, the river Orne, runs south-west. The other arm running south-east, is the line of villages and orchards from the bridges through Ranville to Hérouvillette.
> The river, of course, gave a considerable degree of security on that flank. The tow path and river runs much lower than the rest of the country, and as might be expected was studded with trees and orchards. A drive up this by enemy infantry would be a very restricted affair and should not be difficult to stop.
> From the south-east the line of the villages, orchards, gardens and walls leading up through Hérouvillette to the bridges would lend itself admirably to defence.
> Looking across the front or base of the triangle, from Longueval on the river to Escoville south-east of Ranville, ran a long, low and bare ridge. Within the three sides of this triangle the ground is completely open. Movement across this by armour or infantry would be most hazardous: it was in fact an ideal killing area. Thus, though there would not be much depth to Poett's [5 Parachute Brigade] position, by holding the village and the line of the river he would be in quite a secure position to deal with any immediate counter-attack of the type and strength which I had anticipated.

Elsewhere in 6th Airborne's area Major General Gale observed that the ground to the north and east of Ranville was open and flat and that from the sea a steep ridge rose that ran in a south-easterly direction from Salanelles in the north to Troarn in the south. The ridge was crossed by only three roads; one through Breville in the north, one through Le Mesnil in the centre and a final one from Troarn in the south. There were two dominating high points on the ridge at Le Plain and Le Mesnil. Major General Gale highlights the implication of such ground to his plans:

> This imposing long wooded ridge was the key to the whole position east of the Orne. He who held it could control the plain to the west, overlook Ranville and the canal and river and Poett's little bridgehead, and furthermore could see over the greater part of the British I Corps front.
> Movement, even by infantry, off the roads on the ridge was virtually impossible. By holding Le Plain, Le Mesnil and the road junction south-east of Escoville the ridge could be held, and held too, with comparatively small forces. German dispositions showed that the vital importance of this ridge had not been fully appreciated. There were some sketchy defences at

Le Plain but nothing at Le Mesnil and farther to the south. It should be possible, therefore, to seize these points, if only our plans remained secret and we had the advantage of surprise. To leave these, let the enemy man them and assault them later, would have been a costly and immense task far beyond the capacity of one division.

The approach from the east across the River Dives to this ridge was through thick woods, and the valley of the Dives itself was an obstacle to armour and vehicles. In fact the valley was a flooded and low-lying swamp. A really heavy attack supported by armour from the east could, therefore, be ruled out. By holding the ridge we could prevent movement from the east towards Caen as far south as Bures for certain, and with luck, through Troarn. By basing troops on Le Plain, Le Mesnil and the road junction east of Escoville we could have a firm base from which we could send out detachments to destroy the bridges at Varaville, Robehomme, Bures and Troarn.[16]

Analysis of the ground was usually closely followed by consideration of the effect weather might have on the battle. Mist and low lying cloud could disrupt air support but also complicate the coordination of operations, causing friendly troops to lose sight of their flanking forces or even their direction during an attack. The commander did not have to master all these facts by himself, his staff officers were there to help and provide advice where necessary or even explore options for him. As one illustration we have already seen in the last chapter how the intelligence staff would help the commander understand the enemy picture, another important factor in the commander's appreciation. Good commanders would follow Montgomery's advice to read the mind of his opponent, anticipate his next move and remain one step ahead.

Having considered the ground and enemy factors the commander would also take stock of his own friendly forces available, this did not just include his own units and dispositions but also flanking formation activity and what firepower could be brought to bear from the artillery and air forces which lay outside of his command. Criticism that the British were too reliant on large levels of artillery and air power is often misplaced. The British were excellent at exploiting the full potential of artillery and it is therefore only to be expected that, together with air support, they integrated this considerable resource and advantage into their planning.

Time is another critical factor in planning any operation, there are normally many strands to an operation and sequencing these correctly is important. Major General Gale and his team at 6th Airborne Division had to focus hard on this factor as their plan was complicated by the available hours of darkness, the timing of the fly-ins and the need to achieve surprise. As he explains all of this could only be reconciled by careful management of timings within the overall plan, he was also constrained by the requirement to protect the seaborne landings and silence the guns at Merville before first light:

The timing was thus a question of working back. How long would the troops take to assault and silence the battery? How long would the move from the dropping zone to the battery take? How long would it take to concentrate the battalion after a drop in the dark? In the first instance we could not drop the men near the battery, and the only suitable dropping zone was fully a mile and a half away and over difficult country. In a night drop a battalion in the most favourable circumstances cannot concentrate in under one hour. I did not reckon that even with everything on our side, the battalion would be ready for its difficult assault in under three hours. The assault would not take less than an hour making a total of four hours.

As a result of the experiences in the Sicily airborne landings, I was determined that first

---

16 Ibid., pp.44-46.

we must land pathfinder troops of the independent Parachute Company, to put out 'aids' for the mass of aircraft that were to follow to 'home' on. They would require at least half an hour to do this. This half-hour would have to be added to the four hours wanted by the assaulting battalion.

Now there wasn't much more than six hours of darkness to play with during the whole night at this time of the year and the fly-over from England would take an hour and a half. We had in fact no time to spare.[17]

Major General Gale also had to capture the two bridges over the Caen Canal and River Orne. As surprise was critical to the capture of these bridges they would have to be seized by gliders before anything else occurred. This operation therefore took place simultaneously with the Pathfinder's drop. Major General Gale and his team had squeezed the utmost out of the available hours of darkness and ensured that his troops not only had sufficient time but that all tasks were in their proper sequence.

This unfolding appreciation process all led inexorably towards the production of the plan itself where the commander would allocate tasks to the various subordinates under him, and produce a concept of operations on how these units or formations would operate in time and space as well as what support they could expect from artillery, engineers and airpower. One aspect that no commander worth his salt would ever overlook was the importance of administrative matters, what we would term logistics today. As General Montgomery highlights:

> In Modern warfare new factors have been introduced which make it vital that a commander should ensure that his administrative arrangements are equal to the strain imposed in carrying out his tactical plan. The chief of these factors are the speed of advance of a mechanized army, the increased vulnerability of lines of communication to attack by air or armoured columns, and the vast organization required for the maintenance of the force and for the repair of vehicles and equipment.[18]

The commander's plan ultimately had to ensure that achievable tasks were given to the correct organisations, that they had sufficient time to complete them and that they were best suited to the strengths and capabilities of the particular organisation. The commander also had to ensure that he grouped his units and formations together in the most appropriate manner to achieve their missions. This all required considerable judgement from a commander and even an experienced Corps commander could get it wrong. During the preparations for Operation GOODWOOD Major General Roberts' considered that his 11th Armoured Division, which was the lead assaulting division, had been given a number of inappropriate tasks by the Corps commander, Lieutenant General Dick O'Connor:

> We, 11th Armoured Division, were to lead, followed by Guards Armoured Division, and then 7th Armoured Division. Our final objectives were on the right of the Corps, Bras, Hubert-Folie, Fontenay. Our infantry brigade had to clear Cuverville and Démouville, two villages immediately in front of the start line, but also we were ordered to take Cagny, which was on the left flank of our advance. I thought this was all too much. Why could not the infantry (51st Highland Division), now holding the front line, get up out of their trenches and attack

17 Ibid., pp.47-48.
18 Montgomery, Field Marshal Bernard, 'High Command In War', Germany, 21st Army Group, 1945, p.21. Held at Defence Concepts and Doctrine Centre, Shrivenham.

Figure 8.1 Cromwell and Sherman tanks wait to advance south of Caen during
Operation GOODWOOD. (Crown Copyright Army Historical Branch)

Cuverville and Démouville? The advance of our armoured brigade was going to be preceded
by a rolling barrage, fired by eight field regiments; but to utilize good going it had to do
a dog-leg to the left of Cuverville and Démouville to ensure it got out quickly. In fact the
barrage was 2,000 yards wide, proceeding at 15 yards per minute, 4,300 yards south-east, and
then 2,000 yards south-west. Our objectives were on the right, but we had to take Cagny on
the left and clear the villages in the centre before we could get to our objectives on the right,
and in doing this I would have no infantry brigade to clear the way as they were tied up in
Cuverville and Démouville.

I made these points verbally to the Corps commander (Dick O'Connor) but I got no change.
Feeling rather strongly about it, I put it all on paper and sent it to the Corps commander. I got
a reply that the present plans could not be changed and if I felt they were unsound, then he
would get one of the other divisions to lead. But he would ask me only to 'mask' Cagny, not
to take it. I really had no alternative but to accept the situation and replied accordingly, but
still think it was a stupid arrangement.[19]

Once the commander had conducted his appreciation and produced his plan it was now time
to direct his subordinates as to what he wanted them to achieve. Major General Gale explains the
importance of making his intentions absolutely clear to his subordinates:

In battle a commander is not just given a role and told to get on with it. The part he has to
play is part of a bigger plan: he is, as it were, a piece of a great mosaic. The plan belongs to
the senior commander; it is his; he is the architect and nothing he can do can absolve him of
his responsibility should it miscarry. In order to ensure that the object he wants to achieve is
in fact achieved, he must lay down certain things for his subordinate commanders to do. He
must make it quite clear what these things are; why he wants them done; and in what order
of priority they stand, not only in respect of time, but also of importance. After this he will
generally allow his subordinate a free hand.[20]

19 Roberts, Major-General G.P.B, *From the Desert to the Baltic*, (London: William Kimber, 1987), pp.170-171.
20 Gale, Lt Gen R N, *With the 6th Airborne Division in Normandy* (London: Marston & Co., 1948), p.34.

The process of giving such direction was known as the 'orders process'. As in the appreciation there was a common format used throughout the Army, this not only allowed units and headquarters that did not normally work together to understand each other, but also offered a series of headings that if followed correctly would ensure no important items were inadvertently missed. This was an important consideration when commanders and soldiers were exhausted, stressed and short of sleep. The orders process normally took place in the commander's own headquarters with all of the subordinate commanders in attendance so that each had mutual knowledge of each others tasks. The orders would normally be preceded by enemy, ground and meteorological briefs which would give the subordinate commanders the most important and up to date information as well as a useful insight into what had led the commander to produce his plan. After highlighting any additional forces assigned to the organization the commander would then cover the most important aspect of all, the tasks and priorities he had set his subordinates. The orders process would usually conclude by tying up a number of coordinating or administrative details including the Fire Plan, timings, codewords, the locations of various headquarters, medical and administrative support as well as the arrangements for controlling Prisoners of War. On some occasions, particularly for large deliberate operations, written orders would be produced and an example from Operation TOTALIZE is included in Appendix J. It was however more typical for orders to simply be passed verbally with subordinate commanders scribbling the details down in notebooks.

Once the orders had been delivered the subordinate commanders would then have to extract the details relevant to their own organization, make their own appreciation and plan and deliver a set of orders that were applicable to their own forces. Time is a very precious commodity on the battlefield and in order to ensure the initiative did not pass to the enemy, this activity was conducted quickly, with a great deal of concurrent activity also taking place. This concurrent activity was usually initiated by means of a 'Warning Order' which gave subordinates a useful forewarning of possible tasks and H-Hours allowing troops to be prepared and pre-positioned in advance of receiving the actual orders themselves.

Whilst more time was available for those at higher operational commands at the lower tactical level the decision-action cycle was more rapid and there was far less time available for planning and delivery of orders. Lieutenant Colonel George Taylor observed Lieutenant Colonel Dick James, his predecessor as Commanding Officer 5th Duke of Cornwall's Light Infantry, grappling with a curtailed time period in which to make his plan, give out his orders and carry out a battalion attack on Hill 112:

> In the late afternoon, it was decided to put 5 DCLI under the command of 129 Brigade to help secure the top of the hill, Brigadier Essame told Dick James of this decision in the big house near the church at Fontaine Étoupefour. I attended this conference. Time was of the essence, as the attack was to be pushed home as the light faded, supported by tanks. Essame asked James how much time he required to work out details.
>
> Slightly flushed of face, the CO calmly worked out the time factor on a piece of paper. At least two hours, was his reply. The brigadier, adding another half hour for good measure, fixed zero hour at 20.30 hour.
>
> On these occasions, time is always the relentless enemy of the battalion commander. He has to think calmly and clearly of the essentials, while dealing with outside interference and interruptions, draw the right conclusions from his own reconnaissance and those of his subordinates, and take stock of all viewpoints.
>
> Hampered by the vagueness of local information, his decision has to be reached often when moving at speed in a carrier or scout car. He must marry in the armour with the infantry and devise the covering fire plan of the artillery, mortars and machine guns. Then he must ensure that his troops undaunted by enemy fire, are at the battle start line by the appointed hour.

Figure 8.2 Canadian infantrymen are briefed by their commander at Carpiquet airfield, 12 July. (Lieut. Ken Bell, Library and Archives Canada, PA-162525)

Heavier becomes the weight of responsibility on his shoulders as the hands of his watch seem to turn faster and faster.

We were to learn, in the grim and bloody days to come, that the time allowed, two hours and practiced for this process, should be at least doubled in times of war against a strong defensive position.[21]

The orders would cascade right down the chain of command, good commanders being careful not to eat up too much of the precious pre H-Hour time with their own arrangements and allowing time for their subordinates to plan and create their own orders. As an armoured troop commander Lieutenant Bill Bellamy was at the bottom of this chain and describes receiving his orders from his squadron commander:

Deep consoling sleep is broken, 'Wakeup. Wake up.' Creeps realisation of the cold and the blackness. Furtive movements, whispered words, dry mouths formulate assent and hear, hollow through blanketed distance. 'Troop leaders for orders, sir.' Covers thrown aside and blindly searching for boots, map board and hat, the queasy stomach of early morning turns to the hollow pitted emptiness of pent up feeling and anticipation. 'Surely my troop is in reserve. O God it must be. Make it an easy job. I wonder where we are going now?' These thoughts course feverishly through the mind while damp clothes cover a flinching body and the pulse beats abnormally quickly until there is no further excuse for lingering. Boots swish among the

---

21 Taylor, George Brigadier, *Infantry Colonel* (Upton-upon-Severn: Self-Publishing Association, 1990), pp.36-37.

tall wet grass saturated trousers flap against the legs. 'There he is. Thank God the others are there too. Am I late? No.' Sleepiness returns once more as maps are set and then the battle is drawn on them in different coloured chinagraphs. 'I would have that job! Why couldn't I do that troop's? I always lead.' Conflicting and distracting thoughts race through the brain and then suddenly – 'Any questions?' – and relief that despite the uncivil hour you had grasped it all. The long walk back, the troop conference. A sleepy somewhat outraged group of men packing the tanks and brewing the tea while the tank commanders cluster round to be put in the picture. Immediately all is well, you are awake and it is they who are sleepy. Orders are concise, positions are explained, a cup of tea, the roar of engines warming up, the crackling of wireless and then the order to advance is given. In that first move, the brain is emptied of all distractions, the whole plan clears, the map stands out as a country with elevations, breadth and depth, the stomach settles, warms, retracts and normality returns, ousting fears and uncertainties.[22]

Once battle had been joined the British Army placed a strong emphasis on quick verbal orders as the basis for speeding up their 'decsion-action' cycle. Even at Army Group level General Montgomery rather than relying on typed instructions made a point of travelling forward to subordinate headquarters to give specific orders to individuals:

A commander must train his subordinate commanders, and his staff, to work and act on verbal orders and instructions. There is far too much paper in circulation in the Army as a whole; no commander can have time to read all this paper and also do his job properly. Much of the paper in circulation is not read; much of it is not worth reading.

Operational command in the field must be direct and personal, by means of visits to subordinate HQ, where orders are given verbally. It is quite unnecessary to confirm these orders in writing; commanders who cannot be trusted to act on clear and concise verbal orders are useless.

The ability to deliver a clear set of orders was therefore an important quality a commander had to possess. Failure to do so could lead to a lack of confidence in the operation as a whole, even if the plan was a sound one. Brigadier Michael Carver, who commanded 4th Armoured Brigade, received orders from many different divisional commanders. He recalled two contrasting styles in particular:

On 3 July we were switched to the command of 53rd Welsh Division, while 11th Armoured Division was withdrawn. I was not impressed with the Welsh nor their commander, Major-General Willie Ross. He was the type of commander whose 'orders groups' tended to be like councils of war, rather than occasions when clear and definite orders reflected the grip of the commander on the situation. A few days later 43rd (Wessex) Division took over the eastern sector of the front, linking up with the Canadians on their left, and we came under them. Their commander, Major General G I Thomas was a very different character from Ross. A small, fiery, very determined and grim gunner, without a spark of humour, he would bite the head off anyone who attempted to disagree with him or question his orders, as I was soon to find out.[23]

---

22 Bellamy, Bill, *Troop Leader* (Stroud: Sutton Publishing, 2005), p.131.
23 Carver, Field Marshal Lord, *Out Of Step* (London: Hutchinson, 1989), p.193.

Once the orders were delivered the commander's focus would inevitably shift from the planning of the operation to its actual execution. This is a period where the commander though having passed the tasks onto his subordinates still retains overall responsibility for the operation's success, though he must be careful of interfering too much. Brigadier Essame who commanded 129 Infantry Brigade, part of 43rd Wessex Division, often resented Major General Thomas' meddling:

> He loved to be in close contact with the action. He always wanted to know exactly what was going on. It was his nature. He spent a great deal of time swanning around visiting his brigadiers, often interfering with their decisions as a result. A good gardener leaves his plants to grow on their own and doesn't come round every couple of days to pull them up to see how the roots are growing. Whenever he did not have enough to do he intervened in the handling not only of battalions but even companies.[24]

Whilst a commander's constant interference in a subordinates plan was rightly resented no operation ever runs entirely according to plan or as Lieutenant Colonel George Taylor more pessimistically put it 'In War, if a thing can go wrong it certainly will.'[25] The commander would therefore continue to monitor the battle as it unfolded, adjusting his plan and giving further direction as required. Lieutenant Colonel Trevor Hart-Dyke gives a good account of his actions as Commanding Officer of The Hallamshires during their attack on Fontenay on 25 June. The Hallamshire's preparation for this battle had been comprehensive. They had plenty of time to prepare for the attack, they were able to follow the Infantry school's specimen night attack orders and brief every individual soldier in the battalion on a large cloth model prepared in a barn. The commander of 49th Division had also visited the battalion to make sure all of them understood and had confidence in the plan. Their approach to securing the Forming Up Point and Start Line as well as marking the routes to them meant that last minute confusion was also avoided. Lieutenant Colonel Hart-Dyke was with his battalion in the FUP at 0245 hours, fifteen minutes before H-Hour but despite such impressive 'stage management' when the Start Line was crossed anything could happen and the commander had to be prepared to take advantage of opportunities and avert crises:

> At 'H' hour the forward companies moved off in the dark, silently and just as if it was another exercise.
>
> At battalion headquarters the roar of artillery fire added to the suspense of awaiting the success signals of the forward companies. As it became lighter, so it became foggier, until visibility was restricted to about five yards. This was a problem we could not have foreseen and could do nothing about. I could get no information out of either company, until both at last reported that they were lost in the mist and had lost touch with all their platoons. Realising that those companies could not now clear the enemy up to their objective, the stream, I sent 'A' and 'D' Companies forward to take both objectives, the second being the far hedge of the orchards beyond the Fontenay-Juvigny road. Five minutes later, realizing I now had no reserve and was, therefore, no use out of the battle, I moved forward down the slope, with the Pioneers, Carrier Platoon dismounted and the platoon of Royal Engineers to the site I had selected for my command post for the attack on the second objective, where I hoped to clarify the situation. One could see very little and the white tape eventually ran out. I had then to call on Sergeant Bennett, the Intelligence sergeant, to use his compass. Bearings had to be

---

24 Delaforce, Patrick, *The Fighting Wessex Wyverns* (Stroud: Sutton Publishing, 1994), p.8.

25 Taylor, George Brigadier, *Infantry Colonel*, (Upton-upon-Severn: Self-Publishing Association, 1990), p.15.

taken every five yards and it was a slow and eerie business. En route we ran into two carriers and at least a platoon of the R.S.F moving painfully across our front and I gave them the compass bearing to their own sector. Soon after crossing the road we came upon the track on which I had decided to set up my command post until the final objective was taken. Moving a hundred yards to the left we were thankful to find the exact spot I had selected at a track and hedge junction.

We had hardly halted when machine gun and tank fire seemed to open up on us from all directions. We dug scrapes rapidly and I thought hard. I was out of touch with all the companies, who were actually behind us. The situation was somewhat unorthodox. But what must be the situation of the 26th Panzer Grenadier Regiment, subjected to a devastating bombardment, with houses collapsing all around them and thick mist preventing them seeing what was happening or using their weapons? They must be in a desperate state. I ordered the Engineers to fix bayonets and Wizard, looking rather surprised and pained, started to lead his men off to clear the houses to the west at the road junction, while the pioneers began to move forward.'

As the Engineers and pioneers departed the follow on companies slowly began to emerge from out of the mist behind them:

I was never so relieved in my life. I divided them into two parties and sent Peter Newton with 'D' Company forward to clear as far as the river and Tony Nicholson and Mike Cooper and Peter Hewitt, one of our gunner Forward Observation Officers (F.O.O.) with the rest of the men to clear the houses at the road junction. The sappers and pioneers came back. Meanwhile, to save time and ensure they crossed the open slope behind us before the mist cleared I ordered up the Artillery Anti-Tank Troop, who were to be responsible for anti-tank defence north of the river. On arrival I fear they just unlimbered and covered arcs in all directions round my command post. The situation was now very different from what it had been a few minutes earlier.

Visibility had now cleared to about 60 yards. Peter Newton came on the air to say he had occupied 'Queen' which was the code sign for the river line, our first objective on the right sector. I ordered him to push on to 'King', which was the road on the far side of the river, and to seize the final objective on the right company sector. I did not know what was happening on the left of the sector, but it is an army axiom to exploit success, and Brigade Headquarters said that the Lincolns had reached all their objectives. I could get no news of the R.S.F., who were in 147 Brigade on my left. After this I became resigned to never getting any information about troops in other brigades, and forever after I always attached a liaison officer on my wireless link privately to any battalion with whom I was working. It transpired later that the R.S.F. had not secured their F.U.P. and Start Line and had consequently suffered heavy losses when forming up for the attack.

I now decided to push on myself and told the Engineers and Pioneers to find a route across the damaged village to bring up my anti-tank guns, as previously arranged. There was no time to be lost as the mist was clearing and an enemy counter-attack with tanks could be expected. To my relief we found a suitable route, which the Engineers quickly cleared, and, as I walked across the river bridge to my next command post at the road junction, I wirelessed Johnnie Mott to send forward the remaining fighting vehicles by groups. These consisted of the battalion 6-pounders, four company carriers, four ammunition carriers, followed by the mortars, signal and medical carriers. I found Peter Newton had disposed his company on his objective and his men were busy digging in. My carrier soon arrived and I toured down to the right and contacted the Lincolns. There were a lot of Boche dead about, the result of our artillery fire. They were very smashed up. Bill Ashby now turned up with a platoon of 'B' Company, and told me the sad news of David Lockwood's death. I ordered him to work down the north side of the road and beat Capt. Ashby to their own unit, which should be across the bridge.

Our anti-tank guns were now in action under Arthur Cowell, who was in his element. So I got onto the Brigadier and told him it was OK for the KOYLI to get cracking with their attack on Tessel Wood. I told him I had only about four mixed platoons on the objective, but felt sure I could hold it. I put my carrier in the farmyard and sat down for a rest.[26]

There are a number of points that can be drawn out from Lieutenant Colonel Hart-Dyke's account of commanding his battalion in the battle for Fontenay. The first is the commander's role in managing risk; Lieutenant Colonel Hart-Dyke takes a calculated risk in pushing his right hand company to their final objective 'King' when he does not yet know what progress has been made on his left. The reader will also recall Major General Gale's decision to apportion his resources to defend the southern flank based on which enemy approaches he thought likely. Taking risks such as these is a key responsibility for commanders at all levels; it is a necessary function for several reasons. Firstly a commander will very rarely have enough troops to carry out all the tasks he wishes and will therefore have to prioritise and judge where he will take risk, additionally he might spot a fleeting opportunity and decide to take a gamble that capitalizes on a situation before it passes. The ability to manage and take risks calls for sound judgement from a commander and is a critical quality. General Montgomery again illustrated this point in his Notes on 'High Command':

> It will be exceptional to win a battle without taking certain risks. It requires a nice judgement to decide what risks are legitimate and justifiable, and what risks are definitely not so.
>
> A commander who is not prepared to take a chance, and who tries to play for safety on all occasions will never reap the full-fruits of victory.[27]

The second aspect that is worth elaborating upon in Lieutenant Colonel Hart-Dyke's account is how he recognizes the need to keep his cool when all may seem to be going awry. Despite his companies losing their way in the mist, his own battalion headquarters' isolation and increasing enemy fire Lieutenant Colonel Hart-Dyke remains collected and recognizes that though things may appear bad for him they are probably worse for the enemy – 'But what must be the situation of the 26th Panzer Grenadier Regiment?... They must be in a desperate state' he asks himself. General Montgomery again emphasized this point:

> The battle is in effect a contest between two wills, his own and that of the enemy commander. If his heart begins to fail him when the issue hangs in the balance, then the enemy will probably win…
>
> When the issue hangs in the balance radiate confidence in the plan and in the operations, even if inwardly you feel not too certain of the outcome.[28]

Setting an example in terms of courage was also equally important, it was in fact an essential element in propping up the will to carry on fighting amongst one's own troops. A CANLOAN

---

26 Hart-Dyke, T, *Normandy to Arnhem* (Sheffield: Greenup and Thomson, 1966), pp.12-17.

27 Montgomery, Field Marshal Bernard, 'High Command In War', Germany, 21st Army Group, 1945, p.43. Held at Defence Concepts and Doctrine Centre, Shrivenham.

28 Ibid.

officer recorded the strong example set by the popular Major General Rennie, who returned to Normandy to command 51st Highland Division having been wounded earlier in the campaign. At the beginning of an attack by his new command the General was looking over the ground that was going to be attacked over, artillery fire began to fall around and it was suggested that he might like to take cover. 'What do you see behind you?' he demanded. 'The Black Watch, sir, coming up to the attack.' One of his staff officers replied. 'Then it wouldn't do for them to see me hiding, now, would it?'[29]

Finally it is worth understanding the Hallamshire's attack and Operation MARTLET's larger purpose. MARTLET was a subsidiary attack by the 49th Division on the Rauray Spur, launched on the left of the much larger major offensive by VIII Corps known as Operation EPSOM. Operation MARTLET had two aims; firstly to capture the Rauray Spur which dominated the ground 15th Scottish Division would have to advance across during EPSOM and secondly to draw the German reserves away from the area of the EPSOM offensive. To achieve these effects Operation MARTLET commenced on 25 June effectively preceding Operation EPSOM by 24 hours. Although 49th Division failed to capture the Rauray spur by the end of 25 June they did succeed in duping the German commanders to move their reserves away from the EPSOM area to reinforce the Panzer Lehr Division who were engaged with 49th Division. Kurt Meyer, the commander of 12th SS *Hitlerjugend* Panzer Division which faced the EPSOM offensive, describes the consequences for the Germans:

> That evening the Corps ordered the deployment of our last tank battalion to restore the situation in that sector the next morning. The Panzer Lehr Division was to be assisted at all costs.
>
> I vainly asked for that order to be rescinded. The chief of staff's graphic situation report that friendly reconnaissance had identified the staging of strong enemy forces –especially armor – in the sector of SS Panzer-Grenadier-Regiment 26 did not influence the Corps to change its order. My remark that an enemy tank attack was expected at any moment and the II./SS-Panzer-Regiment 12 was in a very favourable defensive positions was also dismissed. And so it was that on 26 June there was not a single tank in the divisional sector.[30]

When the EPSOM offensive started the Germans had to reverse their decision and re-deploy their tanks back to the area where the main British EPSOM attack was striking. It is worth considering these movements in terms of the decision-action cycle. Who has seized the initiative? Who is now reacting to whom? The same logic and questions are equally appropriate at the operational level during EPSOM. Although the operation's aim was to capture Hill 112 and surround Caen to the south, it also succeeded in forestalling General Rommel's own planned offensive to split the American and British beachheads by a thrust on Bayeux. Instead the formations that he had earmarked for use in this large attack (II SS Panzer Corps) now had to be employed in counter-attacks against the British EPSOM offensive. It will also be recalled from Chapter 7 that the Allies had received one of their regular Ultra messages predicting the movement of II SS Panzer Corps towards the British positions over the River Odon. Forewarned of the precise nature of the German counter-attack General Dempsey was able to 'balance' his forces by adjusting his dispositions and fireplan and the expected German attack was defeated with heavy losses to the panzer formations. Losses that Rommel could ill-afford. Again who is dancing to who's tune? EPSOM like all of the British offensives was also nested under General Montgomery's overall plan of tying down the most capable German formations in front of the British to allow the Americans to break

---

29 Smith, Wilfred, *Codeword CANLOAN* (Toronto and Oxford, Dundurn Press, 1992), p.99.
30 Meyer, Kurt, *Grenadiers* (Mechanicsburg PA: Stackpole Books, 2005), p.244.

out against weaker opposition. Operation EPSOM is judged by many historians as a failure and indeed it did not capture the territory hoped for, but it was successful in maintaining the initiative for the British and forcing the Germans into a reactive defence, tactics which had very little chance of inflicting a decisive defeat on the Allies in Normandy.

In order to maintain an effective grip on the battle a commander had to have a high degree of situational awareness on both enemy and friendly force activity. This was provided to him through his headquarters and staff who had to strike a balance between keeping the commander informed, yet freeing him from the burden of having to examine and consider every item of information and all aspects of running his organisation. General Montgomery put it very clearly arguing a commander:

> Should keep himself from being immersed in details. He must spend a great deal of time in quiet thought and reflection, in thinking out the major problems, in thinking how he will defeat his enemy.
>
> If he gets involved in details he cannot do this; he will lose sight of the essentials that really matter; he will be led off on side issues that will have little influence on the battle; and he will fail to be that solid rock on which his staff must stand.
>
> No officer whose daily life is spent in considering details, or who has not time for quiet thought and reflection, can make a sound plan of battle on a high level or conduct large-scale operations efficiently. It is for this reason that the plan must always be made by the commander and NOT by his staff…
>
> …He himself must devote his attention to the larger issues; he must NOT 'belly-ache' about details.[31]

Senior British commanders would organize their headquarters into three echelons a Tactical HQ, a Main HQ and a Rear HQ. The Tactical HQ (or 'Tac' as it was usually known) was where the commander would exercise personal command and control of the battle. It would be small, highly efficient, completely mobile and able to protect and defend itself. It would normally consist of signals, cipher and liaison personnel, defence troops and a small operations and intelligence staff for keeping in touch with the battle. At unit level Tac HQ might be little more than a Bren carrier fitted with a few radios, at brigade or divisional level tanks or half-tracks might be used to form Tac.

There are a number of advantages a commander obtains in deploying forward in a Tac HQ, perhaps the most important one is that it helped the commander get a proper perspective or 'feel' for the battle. Brigadier Carver deployed forward in his 4th Armoured Brigade Tac HQ during the fighting for Hill 112. His Brigade was due to exploit to the River Orne after Major General Thomas' infantry had captured and cleared Hill 112. Having secured ample artillery support the only other stipulation Brigadier Carver made was that the infantry should capture the square wood on the reverse slope of Hill 112:

> If it were not [captured], my tanks would be shot up from the rear as they went forward. After further heated argument and objections from the infantry, it was agreed. My plan was for The Greys to lead the advance, as they had had the easiest time in the previous operation.
>
> The infantry attack was launched during the night of 9/10 June, the Churchills of a squadron of 9th Royal Tanks supporting the final phase of the attack being almost all knocked

---

31 Montgomery, Field Marshal Bernard, 'High Command In War', Germany, 21st Army Group, 1945, p.22. Held at Defence Concepts and Doctrine Centre, Shrivenham.

Figure 8.3
A recce party of 3rd County of London Yeomanry led by Major John Aitken MC and Squadron Sergeant Major Jewell near the river Orne, 13 August. (County of London Yeomanry)

out by anti-tank fire from this wood, which the infantry had not cleared. Having confirmed this myself when I took my tactical headquarters forward, I reported it by wireless to Tiger Urquhart, the splendid sapper who was GSO1 of 43rd Division, saying that I would not order my leading regiment over the crest towards the River Orne until the wood had been cleared of enemy as had been agreed. He referred this to G. I. Thomas, who came on the set himself and said that his information from his infantry brigades was that all the objectives had been secured, and that therefore I must start my forward thrust. I said that I was on the spot, as his infantry brigadiers were not, and that, if he did not believe me, he could come and see for himself. This not surprisingly did not please him. He insisted that I should order my tanks to advance over the crest. I said that, if I did I expected that the leading regiment would suffer at least 75 per cent casualties, as a result of which they would not be able to reach their objective. He asked me which regiment I proposed to send. I told him it was The Greys. 'Couldn't you send a less well-known regiment?' he replied, at which I blew up.[32] Finally he accepted my arguments, but relations between us, poor to start with, were permanently soured.[33]

Commanders who deployed forward could also, by their own personal presence, exert an influence on those they commanded and encourage troops to do more. Lieutenant Colonel George Taylor argued:

---

32 The Royal Scots Greys were Scotland's most famous regular cavalry regiment.
33 Carver, Field Marshal Lord, *Out Of Step* (London: Hutchinson, 1989), pp.193-194.

That in a Division or Brigade headquarters a senior commander or senior staff officers should go forward at what is judged a critical time, especially after a successful attack to counter the natural inertia that sets in amongst victorious troops. After a unit has captured a strongly held position and suffered casualties a sensitive commander is apt to think we have done our stuff and I don't want to risk having more casualties.[34]

Unsurprisingly Major General Thomas applied his own unique style of 'charm' in this regard when visiting the Brigade HQ of one of his brigade commanders before a battle:

One conversation at a brigade 'O' Group with G.I.T. [Maj Gen Thomas] went like this: G.I.T to Brigadier Coad, 'Do you understand the plan?' Coad: 'Yes, sir.' G.I.T. to gunner CO: 'Do you understand the plan?' Gunner CO: 'Yes, sir.' G.I.T. to both of them 'Well then, fucking well get on with it!' turned his back on them and off he went.[35]

That commanders felt able to deploy forward in their Tactical HQs has much to do with the trust they had in the competence of their staff and headquarters at Main and Rear HQ who planned and controlled the operation in his absence. As its name implies Main HQ is the central core of the formation's HQ structure and it is here that the bulk of the planning and detailed staff work takes place; it is normally situated close to its twin 'Rear' Headquarters which focuses on the administrative aspects of the formation and with which it works hand in glove. Lieutenant-General Horrocks describes the set up he found at XXX Corps when he took over command of the Corps in early August.

A Corps HQ was normally divided into two parts: Main, concerned with the actual fighting; and Rear, concerned with administration. Although separated, they were located as close to each other as possible, depending on the nature of the country and the state of the battle. When I arrived on 4 August 1944, Main H.Q. was located at Quesnay (approximately three miles north-east of Caumont) and Rear H.Q. a few miles away in close touch with the supply depots, workshops and hospitals etc., which had been established in the beachhead. Each consisted of approximately 100 camouflaged lorries, caravans and trucks, dotted about in a wooded area 400 yards x 400 yards.

I was mostly concerned with Main H.Q., though I used to visit Rear H.Q. as often as possible. I lived in the caravan, with next door to it a lorry containing large-scale maps of the battle area; this was my main office. The Operations department consisted mainly of a camouflaged marquee, complete with field telephones, and maps of different sizes; this was manned day and night. ... The whole HQ had to be very mobile and able to move at short notice.[36]

The key to the efficient running of Main and Rear was the Chief of Staff and Chief Administrative Officer, who dealt with the day to day control and administration of the formation giving the commander freedom to think and command. General Montgomery was blessed with a patient, popular and highly competent Chief of Staff in the shape of Major General Freddie de Guingand. The duties of a Chief of Staff, similar at all levels, involved taking all detail and sufficient work off his chief's shoulders so that he could command, reflect and think. He would ensure all staff

34 Taylor, George Brigadier, *Infantry Colonel* (Upton-upon-Severn: Self-Publishing Association, 1990), p.73.
35 Delaforce, Patrick, *The Fighting Wessex Wyverns* (Stroud: Sutton Publishing, 1994), p.6.
36 Horrocks, General Sir Brian, *Corps Commander* (London: Sidgwick &Jackson, 1977), p.32.

branches worked together in a cooperative manner and that the relationships with both superior and subordinate headquarters remained cordial. Mutual confidence and communication were critical between a chief of staff and his commander, in their discussions no subject should be banned and unpleasant facts should not be hidden – although there were right and wrong times to present them. The chief of staff would have to hold frequent telephone or radio conversations with his commander when he was at Tac HQ, collecting as many subjects as possible together so as to avoiding interrupting the commander too frequently. Major General De Guingand also felt the following subjects were also important to a Chief of Staff:

(a)   Be accessible.
(b)   Let Heads of Branches, Advisers, etc., feel that you will always hear all relevant arguments before making a decision.
(c)   Don't dilly-dally over making decisions, otherwise work is held up all-round.
(d)   Encourage ideas.
(e)   Keep calm, and never be pompous.
(f)   Give credit where it is due, and when possible let the C-in-C know the originator of any particular 'bright idea'.
(g)   Watch for over-strain amongst officers and clerks.
(h)   Know when to take time off.

If members of other Services and/or Allies are attached to the Headquarters, they should be treated in exactly the same way as your own staff; subject in the case of some Allies to certain security restrictions. The point is that they should be made to feel members of the team.

When dealing with parallel RAF and Allied Headquarters, be tactful and frank. Put your own cards on the table and avoid any suggestion that you wish to play theirs for them.[37]

Headquarters at army, corps and even divisional level inevitably resembled large tented 'villages' or encampments. Moving such organizations was a tricky affair, particularly when there was still a requirement to maintain command, control and communications during the period.

At lower levels of command the unit's Main headquarters would be more spartan. An infantry battalion's Main headquarters for instance would normally consist of less than ten men and given its proximity to the frontline was usually in considerable danger, especially from indirect fire. Some units quickly learnt that the solidly built stone Norman houses made a very good company or battalion command post, particularly if they had a roomy cellar. Care however had to be taken that it was not either a former German headquarters or an obvious isolated building marked on a map as both tended to draw the full fury of the enemy's fire.[38] If no building was available then the only option was to dig in the command post and ensure it had strong overhead cover. Lieutenant Robert Woollcombe describes visiting his battalion's Main headquarters during the battle for the Odon, he illustrates the typical conditions battalion staff would work under.

The Command post itself had been speedily excavated by an armoured bulldozer from the RE. It was a large stout dug-out walled with a comforting thickness of earth; the roof shored up with strong beams – in all a pretty neat job. Three steps led down to the entrance, and selecting the moment one scuttled for it, arriving breathlessly but thankfully within.

There they all were in the murk of the faint daylight from the sandbagged entrance and

---

37   Montgomery, Field Marshal Bernard, 'High Command In War', Germany, 21st Army Group, 1945, pp.28-31. Held at Defence Concepts and Doctrine Centre, Shrivenham.
38   Taylor, George Brigadier, *Infantry Colonel* (Upton-upon-Severn: Self-Publishing Association, 1990), p.28.

the light of a couple of hurricane lamps. Giles, now the commanding officer, for Colonel Ben had been severely wounded. Giles, at the start of the command that lasted him from here to the Cease Fire. So different from Ben. A face-veil round his neck as a scarf, loud of voice and harassed. One felt the thudding of the shells outside was more in the nature of a frightful bore for Giles, but for all the hunting and shooting demeanour that never left him, Giles probably worried a lot. He was however infected with the verve of 'Bash on, Borderers,' in all circumstances. Press ever on. And since he was possessed of an obstinacy amounting to an almost daunting single-mindedness, somehow, harassed but regardless, he invariably carried all before him, ending the campaign with D.S.O. and Bar...

Giles was issuing directions – or rather shouting them – at Henry of 'D' Company, who looked, and was on his last legs. Henry looked as if he had forgotten what sleep had ever felt like. On the morning after the assault all contact had been lost with Henry's Company for 'D' Company, having unwittingly consolidated during the confusion of darkness in the middle of an enemy locality, had at dawn found themselves pinned to the ground and surrounded by Germans similarly entrenched. They were still in an extremely exposed position on point 113 itself, and Giles was wanting them to send out a fighting patrol in broad daylight. Vainly Henry tried to get a word in edge ways and explain his doubt of ever seeing the patrol again; but Giles, too preoccupied for mercy was waving all objections aside...Then there was 'Heid the ba' ['A' Company commander]. Quite quiet now. But with wakeful eye, ready for the least signal to hurl 'A' Company at anything, anywhere. Beside him young Guy, who had gained a Military Cross at St Manvieu, raised through the casualties to the command of 'C' Company. Hugh, the I.O., marking both their maps with the latest situation. And Mac the Adjutant, seated at a small table in the centre. A wireless '19' set before him. Headphones clasped to his ears. Oblivious to everyone else, his voice raised penetratingly in wireless procedure, constantly passing information back to Brigade. Mac used to be signals officer before he became Adjutant. He could have talked wireless procedure in his sleep. Here in Normandy he very nearly did so. Finally, near the entrance, the Gunner Battery Commander, who always shared the command post. His two F.O.O.s out with the companies. His face pale and tired in the feeble daylight near the doorway. His eyes unhappy, absorbed in listening. Restless. The nerves of this man, who time and again must have saved our lives with his guns and had wrought such slaughter, on edge under the shells of the enemy. And a second and gunner wireless set, crackling in the corner, one or two gunner personnel, a corporal from the intelligence section and a few signallers and runners squatting about on the floor, completed the picture.

In a few moments there was another dose of shelling outside. A series of muffled thuds sounded unpleasantly close, as though the dug-out were being thumped by a vast fist. Blast smote the walls. The ceiling trembled and a few small stones fell. And no theatrical technique could quite recapture the atmosphere in that command post. Nobody quite stopped what they were doing, but involuntarily everyone listened. Speech flickered. Even Mac paused, in the middle of his headphones. Some instinctively reached for their steel helmets. And it was then I noticed the Padre.

He had been sitting quietly on the floor at the back, looking somewhat exhausted, with nothing in particular to do. But now his eyes were tightly shut and his clenched fists were shaking convulsively above his head. The last thud went and he relaxed. Then another lot came down and again he flinched into the same attitude. After this time his eyes met mine, and he held my gaze with a kind of defiance, and I quickly looked away. For it seemed a solemn thing, the Padre silently wrestling with his fear, alone at the back of the dug-out. A man old enough to be my father, and there was no shame in it.[39]

In addition to the staff officers whose duties lay at the various headquarters most commanders also had a number of liaison officers at their disposal. These would typically be sent to neighbouring or higher headquarters where they could keep the commander abreast of the situation on their flanks or the nascent planning their superiors were undertaking. Lieutenant J G Forrest was a subaltern in the Warwickshire regiment part of the 185 Infantry Brigade in 3rd Division and selected to become a liaison officer:

> It was because I had been 'in' on the planning that my Brigadier sent me to 9 Can Inf Bde of 3 Can Inf Div, with the idea of listening in on our Bde net and keeping the Canadian Brigadier informed of what was happening on our front, since he was on 185's right.
> I paid them several visits before the landing and got on Christian name terms with the Bde staff. So that I had no difficulty in working with them, indeed I enjoyed the association very much.

Lieutenant Forrest, with a jeep and a driver, joined the 9th Canadian Infantry Brigade as it advanced towards Carpiquet. His first priority was to establish communications with 185 Brigade so that he could understand what was going on:

> After some knob twiddling I was rewarded with Peter Batt's voice, dishing out some dope to Walter Pike of the 'Warwicks', after some half hour's listening I gathered that they were getting on quite well and preparing to go ahead that day. I duly reported same, and exact positions, to the Cdn Brig and for the next two days I had little difficulty in keeping them informed.

Liaison officers could also be sent to lower formations to get a further perspective of the battle. It is widely known that General Montgomery used a team of liaison officers in precisely this manner and considered them an essential element in maintaining his situational awareness of an unfolding battle. These young officers would tour the battle area, visiting subordinate HQ down to divisions and even lower, bringing back to General Montgomery each night an accurate and vivid picture of what was going on. The importance General Montgomery attached to their reports meant that they usually had direct access to the commanders. General Horrocks for instance insisted that the liaison officers spoke with him before they departed so that as accurate a picture as possible was obtained. The advantage that a liaison officer has is that he can form judgements, often on sensitive subjects that might not be passed formally in a SITREP over a radio net or telephone line. Lieutenant Forrest recalls performing such a role during operation BLUECOAT when his brigade was dug-in around the Presles ridge:

> As was inevitable in this close country work, manpower began to be a bit of a problem. The Norfolks, who had combined to make something like a Bn strength with the Mons [Monmouthshire Regiment], were down, although their spirits were high. The Warwicks, out of our command, had driven off several counter-attacks and had sustained a lot of casualties; the KSLI although not ¾ of their strength were the best off. This was the picture I had to go and give our own General. I had the awkward job of giving him the impression (not in so

---

39 Woolcombe, Robert, *Lion Rampant* (Edinburgh: B&W Publishing, 1994), p.91.

many words) that a 'bash-on' policy at that time was 'not on' and at the same time convince
him that our tails were right up.

Liaison officers might also be used to explain or reinforce a particular order or concern of a
commander. Lieutenant Forrest had just such a task to fulfil when visiting one of the subordinate
battalions of 185 Infantry Brigade:

> The subject of my visit was a cross-tracks, about a mile to the N.E of his position, which the
> Brig was a trifle concerned about. I had to tell the CO that the Brig wished these cross-tracks
> to be in our control. I was on very good terms with the CO and he did not hide his feelings.
> 'Why' he said, 'If I send anybody out to hold those tracks I shall never see them again in this
> country' – and so on. I suppose he was only sorting the thing out in his own mind; I had to
> show understanding of his predicament and still convince him of the Brig's wishes. However,
> he decided to send a small party there to let him know if anything happened up there. I said
> I thought that ought to do very nicely (it was about the only thing he could do) and went
> back.[40]

The final essential element in helping a commander understand and control the battle is communications. This was the responsibility of both the regiments themselves who managed communications within their own units and the Royals Signals who had sizable signals detachments from
brigade upwards. The British aimed to have a communications system that was robust enough
to handle the volume of traffic, reliable enough for users to have confidence in the system and,
through the employment of a number of different methods of communications, had a degree of
built in redundancy.

The mainstay of the British communications system was wireless, the beauty of which was that it
allowed multiple stations to listen in and broadcast on the same radio net at the same time, which
therefore increased the situational awareness of all within a formation or unit. Wireless equipment
was developed extensively through the Second World War and by 1944 the commanding officer
of an armoured regiment was able to have all the tanks in his regiment listening in on the same
frequency. The wide availability of wireless throughout the chain of command was hugely important in speeding up the decision action cycle and a formation's tempo.

The British had a number of different radios to suit the different requirements of the units and
their operators. For the infantry the short range No.18 set was issued, it was light enough to be
carried on the signallers back and provided both Radio Telephony (RT – where the operator spoke
through a headset using a pressel switch) as well as using morse over Carrier Wave (CW). In theory
RT would give a range of 2.5 miles and CW up to 4 miles but the power output of the radio set was
relatively low (only 0.25 watts). In Normandy it was found that the radio's signal could be easily
interrupted by trees, buildings and undulating terrain and the ranges were often found to be much
less than those the handbooks claimed. Somewhat larger was the No.19 radio set, this had a longer
range of up to 10 miles and could also use both RT and CW.

The No.19 set was not just used in mobile vehicles but also in battalion and brigade headquarters. At brigade level the set would usually be operated by a member of the Royal Signals,
normally from a command vehicle; typically a three-ton Bedford fully equipped as a mobile wireless station. The command vehicle would normally have two No. 19 sets, one of which would be
on the Divisional Command Net and the other on the Brigade Command net, working forward
to the three battalions and other units operating with the brigade. As well as being responsible

---

40 J G Forrest papers Ref. No. 83/7/1 Imperial War Museum.

for the operation of the radio sets the small team of signallers would also have to ensure a ready supply of batteries.[41] Battery charging was a continuous operation with most operators having one battery being used and two being charged either by the engine on the vehicle or in other instances utilizing a portable (and noisy) petrol engine known as a 'chore horse'. Though the No. 19 set provided battalion and brigade headquarters with a more powerful radio and longer range than the No. 18 set the operator and commander would still need to site the headquarters carefully and work hard to achieve good communications. Lieutenant Colonel Hart-Dyke recalls communication problems as he attempted to control an attack on woods to the east of the village of Audrieu:

'A' Company's attack was due to start at 19:30 by which time Ivor Slater was to be on his start line along the northern edge of the Château woods. But at 19:30 hours we were out of wireless communication with 'A' Company and I had to tell the Brigadier that I might have to call off the attack until next day, as my plan depended upon a timed artillery programme and co-ordination between the two companies operating on a separate axis. In desperation we put Harold Sykes's [The RA Battery commander] spare set on to our frequency and then rushed out into the middle of an open field with the set and got through to 'A' Company. They were all ready on the start line, so I ordered the Field Regiment to commence its timed programme and the attack to proceed.

Half an hour of suspense followed and Ivor Slater then came on the air and to say that their first objective had been taken without serious casualties and that the artillery fire had been most effective. They had, however, been held up by enemy fire from the hedgerows, which formed their final objective, and wanted the artillery to do a repeat. This Harold Sykes laid on and 'A' Company continued their advance.

Meanwhile time was getting short for the final phase, the attack by 'D' Company on the wood. I got through to Peter Newton and asked him if he thought that he could carry out his attack without Ivor Slater's fire support from the flank. I felt 'A' Company might get held up again and might well go off the air. Peter said he thought it would be OK if I gave him a smoke screen. This I agreed to and told him I would give him the zero hour when the fire support was ready…

… All this time the Command Post was in the middle of an open field. As Peter Newton's attack went in we came under small arms fire, which, though not aimed at us was too close to be pleasant. I could not afford to move our Command Post under cover as I should lose wireless contact and then be unable to control the attack. However there were three carriers back at the farm and I shouted to the drivers to drive them between our Command Post and the direction of the enemy fire. This successfully accomplished, we all felt much happier and were able to carry on calmly directing operations.[42]

Other wireless sets were available for even greater distances, such as the No. 10 which was a mobile radio relay transmitter and carried 8 duplex telephone channels up to distances of 50 miles. These sets were more cumbersome and were reserved for the larger and more senior headquarters.

Wireless was also supplemented by the use of line or cable, whilst this method was not a practical proposition in a fast moving battle, or over very long distances, it did have the advantage of being able to carry larger volumes of traffic more securely. In forward areas line would be laid by the units themselves with Royal Signals line sections working on behalf of higher formations and incorporating existing civilian cables through exchanges into the military network. The

41   Proctor, *Quiet Little Boy Goes to War* (Bordon: Dragon Print, 1996), p.31.
42   Hart-Dyke, T, *Normandy to Arnhem* (Sheffield: Greenup & Thomson, 1966), pp.8-9.

disadvantage with line communication was that in many instances surface laid line was often cut either by shellfire or the passage of a tank or other vehicle over it. The line sections would then have the unenviable task of venturing out into the area to identify where the break was and patching it up. As the campaign progressed the line sections found that the best method of laying cable was by drooping it over the existing telegraph poles with a pronounced sag which meant that the line was more likely to absorb the shock of a blast and not break.

Stitching together this entire communications network was the responsibility of the Royal Signals. The growing sophistication and variety of communications available to the British Army meant that the Royal Signals had to be expanded as the war progressed, an infantry division's signal regiment increased from 491 personnel to 753, and an armoured division's from 629 to 753. Lieutenant Colonel M A Philp paints a vivid picture of the communications available to the commander and staff of an Infantry Brigade.

> Ops room is rather an overstatement as this really consisted of a small dugout housing at most three or at a squash four people, together with the necessary maps and papers. Into this we fed the remote controls from the Brigade Command Net and the rear link to Division. (The Q rear link to Division was fed into a separate ordinary slit trench where the staff captain functioned). There was also a telephone from the switchboard in the Signal Office. The Ops room was always manned by a duty officer and operator but if the brigade commander and brigade major wanted to discuss anything over the maps the duty officer got turfed out.
>
> As I have mentioned earlier we went to Normandy with practically all new equipment the predominant item was the 19 Set and I cannot speak too highly of its performance. From the moment they were switched on just after being brought ashore, they ran day and night for over three weeks, except when the batteries were charged, and gave not one bit of trouble…
>
> The wirelesses themselves were kept in the vehicles which were parked around and carefully camouflaged. Although I have referred to the use of remote controls the equipment for this purpose was not used as it necessitated an operator to be at the set to effect the switching and this was not only unhealthy but expensive in manpower. We overcame this problem by wiring the microphone and headsets to long jumper leads that worked directly into the set and this we found perfectly satisfactory.

Prior to landing Lieutenant Colonel Philp believed there would be many instances of mutual interference between different Allied radio nets all trying to use the same frequencies. This problem was not as grave as feared, a fact which reflects very well on the Royal Signals frequency assignment planners whose task was to deconflict the communications of the many users in the bridgehead. Instead it was the sheer volume of traffic that proved to be the biggest problem:

> After the first day or two the Brigade Command Net became very busy but was able to cope, but the traffic on the Q net rocketed to phenomenal proportions and proved quite incapable of carrying the load. The result was that the staff issued a continuous demand for Signals Dispatch Riders.
>
> In theory an SDR could only be turned out for a Flash message, but this simply didn't work, the staff just insisted on them at any hour of the day or night. Despite my protests it was not uncommon for one to be called for when an earlier one had left only ten minutes earlier. After a few days of this sort of thing, coupled with the normal SDS rounds my DRs (I only had three) were out on their feet and I had to impress drivers and anyone else I could lay my hands on to help out.
>
> As described earlier we were able fairly soon after arrival at Beauville to get lines out to the Battalions and one to Div HQ and on these we soon installed fuller phones.

Figure 8.4 The crew of a 15th Scottish Division Bren carrier south of Caumont , 30 July.
The commander is speaking on a No.19 radio set (Imperial War Museum B8198)

A Fuller phone was an an instrument developed during World War One and was intended for line telegraphy using Morse, most signal officers considered them a museum piece. Although a tricky instrument to adjust and operate it did have the advantage of being able of being superimposed on a telephone circuit to give Speech and Dial facilities.

> After a certain amount of education of the staff the effect was dramatic and the loads on the DRs dropped to manageable proportions. The advantages of our line circuits soon became apparent, staff could telephone units, messages were sent by telegraphy worked by the operators and the wireless links acted as a standby in the event of a line failure. As the operators were working the telegraph circuits the staff managed the wireless links, the operators only being called upon to adjust the set when necessary. Work quickly fell into this pattern and proved a happy example of staff and signals working as an integrated team. There was the added bonus that wireless traffic was reduced thereby increasing Security and also avoiding to some extent the use of codes and slidex[43] which always tended to slow things up.[44]

---

43 Slidex was a paper based encoding system that allowed tactical headquarters to encode and decode words or phrases in their radio communications.

44 Lt Col M A Philp papers 79/13/1 Imperial War Museum.

Good though the communications system was, some messages and staff products such as overlays could only be delivered by DRs. Driving a motorcycle near the frontline was a hazardous role, Marine Raymond Mitchell was a DR for 41 Commando RM and describes the typical work of a DR:

> Being on duty at night meant remaining fully clothed, ready to go at a moment's notice. Curled up in a blanket behind the duty signaller, ears were always attuned to the cranking of the call-up handle. A few turns meant that all was well, but when it went on and on, it was time to steel yourself for the Signaller's 'Sorry sir, I can't raise them, the line must be cut'. The inevitable consequence would be, 'Better send the DR then,' and you would squirm into your riding coat. Then shoulders hunched against the cold, a half-mile stumble through the trees, kick the engine into life and off on a lonely ride.[45]

If the night was noisy with shellfire the DR's mind would be fully occupied trying to sort out what was happening around him. If the night was quiet and particularly when he turned his engine off to consult his map, or search for a gap in a hedge on foot, then he would experience the unnerving sensation of imagining every German around was listening and waiting for his approach. Either way his arrival at a frontline unit would typically be greeted with an un-welcoming cry to *'Shut that bloody thing off!'* Raymond Mitchell describes a journey to deliver a message to 4 Special Service Brigade Headquarters:

> Brigade HQ was found without trouble. After a couple of miles along the road a good '4 SS HQ' sign in the verge directed me up a narrow track to a farm. On the return trip I had passed the glider fields and was rounding the bend towards the Orne bridges when a shell exploded in the field directly ahead, barely fifty yards away, quickly followed by another and another and another. Instinctively I 'rode to ground' – a technique learned for precisely any such self preservation situation – and landed in a shallow depression against the hedge, with my bike lying there, hugging Mother Earth, I realized that here was another 'minus' of a Despatch Rider's life – the noise of a motor-cycle engine drowns the whine of approaching shells. With the engine silenced, I could follow it all – German shells coming in towards Ranville and the bridges area, and our guns opening up in retaliation. After a while there was a lull, as if both sides were pausing for breath, so I hauled the bike upright and raced off down the hill kicking the engine into life on the move. Bike and I shot back over the bridges to the relative peace of the beachhead as if the bats of hell were close behind.[46]

Good communications as well as efficient headquarters and staff officers would all assist the commander in controlling his battle and planning for the next one. Whilst this decision-action cycle repeated itself once more the commander would also need to ensure that his formation or unit had not become blunted by prolonged exposure to combat. When Major Martin Lindsay was posted as the second-in-command of 1st Gordons on 15 July, the CO briefed him on the state of the battalion after thirty-five days fighting. The battalion had also seen extensive fighting in North Africa, Sicily and Italy:

> He gave me the low-down on the Battalion. They have lost twelve officers, including the C.O. and three company commanders, and 200 men in the thirty-five days since the start

---

45 Mitchell, Raymond, *Commando Despatch Rider* (Barnsley: Pen and Sword, 2001), pp.89-90.
46 Ibid., pp.60-61.

of the campaign, without achieving very much. Two days ago they were ordered to take the Collombelles factory area, but it was much stronger than anybody anticipated and the attack failed miserably. He is rather worried about the morale of the Battalion. The continual shelling has made a number of men 'bomb-happy'...

...The Battalion has fought for thirty-four days and is now having three or four days rest before the next show. Cumming-Bruce says that the Colombelles attack failed partly because the troops lack offensive spirit as the result of being too tired, too much use having been made of the Division.[47]

General Horrocks who arrived seven weeks into the battle of Normandy noticed a similar phenomena:

My next and most important task was to get 'the feel' of the troops in the Corps, and it soon became obvious to me that the seven weeks' hard slogging in the thick bocage country had taken their toll and the gloss had gone from the magnificently trained army which had landed in Normandy. I have always said that in a section of ten men, as a rough guide, two lead, seven follow and one would do almost anything not to be there at all. The two leaders take most of the risks and are usually the first to become casualties. When this happens on a large scale, as had occurred in the Normandy Beachhead Battle, so much better suited to defence than to attack, the cutting edge of a division becomes blunted. This was obviously what had happened to the 43rd Wessex, one of the best trained divisions which has ever left our shores.[48]

American studies in the Second World War suggest that combat fatigue would begin to effect all front-line infantrymen after as little as four weeks of sustained combat. Combat fatigue was inevitable and though the time it took to gain a grip on a man might vary, it affected all soldiers, in all armies, in every nation. Practical steps were taken by some COs to try and sustain their men and stave off combat fatigue. Lieutenant Colonel Hart-Dyke writes about the efforts made in his own battalion:

As the campaign progressed and one could count the original members of a company on the fingers of one's hands, so one had to consider the welfare and fighting fitness of these few survivors. They had seen the men of their sections and platoons go, until none were left who had fought with them. There comes a time when men, with prolonged service with the rifle companies, or as a result of some particular stress, are no longer battle worthy, though their hearts might be too big to ever admit it, during our spell at Tessel Wood I always had 8 men per rifle company and two men each from Signals, Carriers, Pioneers and Mortars living at 'B' Echelon. Each man went back for two days; one for a complete sleep round the clock; the other for a bath, and in which to make up arrears of correspondence to the folks back home. The resulting deficiency in our fighting strength was well repaid by the increase in our morale and fighting efficiency.[49]

Even at lower levels efforts were made to bring some respite from the constant danger. Sergeant Major Charles Martin describes his own attempts outside Carpiquet in early July:

---

47 Lindsay, Martin, *So Few Got Through* (London: Collins, 1946), p.13.
48 Horrocks, General Sir Brian, *Corps Commander* (London: Sidgwick & Jackson, 1977), p.34.
49 Hart-Dyker, T, *Normandy to Arnhem* (Sheffield: Greenup and Thomson, 1966), p.61.

Figure 8.5 Lance Corporal Bill Weston receives a message from dispatch rider Arnot Walter, 2 July. (Lieut. Michael M. Dean, Library and Archives Canada, PA-137516)

To provide some relief, I always had the men out periodically to move about, make a washroom call, get a break. Sometimes if the shelling was steady and the position well forward, we would need a 'get out' trench – more like a ditch – so you could belly your way to an area where it was safe to come to a crouch and then work your way to the rear. It was important for men always in action to get some time to think without fear, more or less. They needed to give the eyes and the mind a chance to rest. That meant getting back to our HQ unit – platoon or company headquarters – where some respite from machine-gun and mortar fire could be found.[50]

Higher-level commanders were also deeply aware of the importance of maintaining the morale of soldiers in a 'citizen army' during the fifth year of war. Some Historians arguably overstate the case and judge this focus by commanders on their soldier's morale to be a result of excessive concern over the 'fragility' of their spirit. Personal accounts written at the time often remark positively on the spirits of the soldiers and there are many reports of Germans judging those they faced to be determined, courageous and having high morale. The Germans too, of course, would have cases of combat fatigue but in a less open society such weaknesses would be hard to admit. Perhaps the importance that British commander's attached to maintaining morale has created a false impression that their efforts were life support for a 'seriously ill patient'. The activity and focus of these commanders might be more related to Montgomery's opinion that high morale is a battle winning asset that was always worth investing in:

Morale is probably the most important single factor in war. A high morale is based on discipline, self-respect and confidence of the soldier in his commanders and in his weapons.

---

50 Martin, Charles, Battle Diary (Oxford & Toronto: Durndurn Press 1994), p.43.

Without a high morale, no success can be achieved – however good may be the strategic or tactical plan, or anything else.

A high morale is a pearl of very great price. And the surest way to obtain it is by success in battle.[51]

The approach commanders in 21st Army Group took to warfare had much to do with the importance in achieving and maintaining high morale. Key elements of this approach were convincing soldiers that their lives would not be sacrificed wastefully, ensuring the best material and fire support was available and launching offensives where the likelihood of success was high. This approach has been criticized as over cautious, and over reliant on material however it played to the strengths of the British Army and was appropriate for maintaining the morale of British soldiers. There are of course alternative methods of maintaining morale. The Germans imbued their soldiers with ideological fervour and those who 'cracked' were either treated as having a medical disease or became one of the 13-15,000 German soldiers executed by their own side during the war. These methods were unlikely to be effective or appropriate for an Army largely composed of pre-war civilians drawn from a democratic society.

Whether preparing for battle, planning and executing an operation, or motivating a unit through successive engagements command in warfare is an intensely personal affair and each formation and unit will have adopted subtly different approaches depending on the style and character of their commander. There are some common aspects to the British approach: the shared planning and orders process, the structure of their headquarters and communications. Ultimately all of 21st Army Group worked under the common 'atmosphere' generated by General Montgomery. It is therefore appropriate that the last words in this chapter are given by him:

My final advice to any officer who may be called on to exercise high command in war is as follows:-
a)   Have a good Chief of Staff
b)   Go for simplicity in everything
c)   Cut out all paper and train your subordinates to work on verbal instructions and orders
d)   Keep a firm grip on the basic fundamentals – the things that really matter
e)   Avoid being involved in details, leave them to your staff
f)   Study the factor of morale; it is the big thing in war and without high morale you can achieve nothing
g)   Never worry
h)   Never belly-ache
i)   Keep fit and fresh, physically and mentally. You will never win battles if you become mentally tired, or get run down in health.[52]

In his own study of morale Montgomery recognised that one of the most significant props to a British soldier's spirits was his confidence that he and his comrades would receive adequate medical treatment should they become sick or wounded. We shall see what provisions the British made for the medical treatment of its casualties in the next chapter.

---

51 Montgomery, Field Marshal Bernard, 'High Command In War', Germany, 21st Army Group, 1945, p.17. Held at Defence Concepts and Doctrine Centre, Shrivenham.
52 Montgomery, Field Marshal Bernard, 'High Command In War', Germany, 21st Army Group, 1945, pp.43-44. Held at Defence Concepts and Doctrine Centre, Shrivenham.

9

'Faithful in Adversity' – Medical Services

> The soldiers all know that should they fall in battle they will have the best possible expectations of sound treatment and human consideration: this is a great factor in maintaining morale, and morale is the big thing in War.
>
> General B L Montgomery 13 January 1944[1]

The British understood the importance of good medical support to their armed Forces in underpinning the Army's combat effectiveness, the quicker casualties could be treated and recover from their wounds, the sooner they could be returned to the battle. General Montgomery also believed that effective medical services underpinned a soldier's fighting spirit, giving him the confidence that he and his comrades would be well looked after if wounded.

21st Army Group's medical services came under the command and control of the Army Medical Services (AMS). The AMS prime responsibilities were for the collection of casualties from the battlefield, the subsequent care and treatment of the sick or wounded and eventual evacuation to the UK if required. They would also advise commanders on medical unit deployments and ensure these formations were correctly supplied with the necessary medical equipment.

The Medical services were represented at the headquarters of corps, divisions and in the lines of communication areas, there was also a sizable presence at Army and Army Group level. These representatives would often double-hat as commanders of their respective formation's medical units,[2] for instance the CO of 195 Airlanding Field Ambulance (Lieutenant Colonel Anderson) would also act as the chief medical adviser to his brigade commander (Brigadier Kindersley – 6 Airlanding Brigade).

It is important to emphasise the challenge of battlefield evacuation in Normandy. Indeed the modern routine of speedy casualty evacuation by helicopter to large hospitals and surgical centres make it hard for us to appreciate the scale of manpower and resources required by 21st Army Group to make their evacuation chain work successfully. It also requires further imagination to understand the lay down and purpose of this ground evacuation chain, moving the critical casualties from the frontline to surgical support and Base Hospitals as quickly as possible. Sister Pamela Bright, a surgical nurse in a casualty clearing station in Normandy, noted the pressing need to evacuate could catch the unwary off guard:

---

1 Brooks, Stephen, 'Montgomery and the Battle of Normandy – Montgomery's notes for talk to Generals 13 Jan 44' in *Montgomery and the Eighth Army: A Selection from the Diaries, Correspondence and Other Papers of Field Marshal the Viscount Montgomery of Alamein* (Stroud: Army Records Society, 1991), p.33.
2 Nicholls, Lt Col T B, *The Army Medical Services in War* (Bailliere: Tindall and Cox, 1941), p.12.

Figure 9.1 A nursing orderly tending to a wounded British soldier at an airfield in Normandy, 12 June. (Crown Copyright Air Historical Branch)

> Evacuation of casualties took place as quickly as possible, and the efficiency of this service deserves a book of its own…An officer of the 43rd Wessex Infantry Division came into the resuscitation ward to look for the wounded of his regiment. At the sight of it all – and the smells – he felt very sick. An orderly persuaded him to lie on an empty stretcher until he felt better. The next thing he knew he was back in England![3]

Even in static conditions it might seem that despite having empty beds and sufficient staff the front line medical unit's greatest anxiety was to get rid of people rather than cure them. This was not irrational, wartime medical staff understood that a medical unit choked with sick and wounded is immobile. Being fixed in such a manner was potentially risky, as the medical unit would be unable to either follow up an advance, so that the men they are supposed to serve would be left with disorganized medical attention, or, if there was a withdrawal, it would mean that a large number of men with their attendant medical staff would have to be left behind and fall into enemy hands. Furthermore a front line medical unit that is at capacity with sick and wounded will be unable to cope with a sudden unexpected influx of casualties, caused by an unexpected enemy attack for example.

For this reason speedy evacuation was seen as a priority. Throughout the chain of medical units, from the front line to the clearing stations, the seriously wounded man was kept for the minimal amount of time for his wounds to be attended to and then quickly moved on and kept moving, until he reached either the base hospital or home.[4] This chapter will take the reader on a journey

---

3   Bright, Pamela, *Life in Our Hands* (London: Pan Books, 1957), p.18.
4   Nicholls, Lt Col T B, *The Army Medical Services in War* (Bailliere: Tindal & Cox, 1941) p.5.

through this medical evacuation chain explaining the type of treatment the soldier received at various stages as well as how the medical facilities operated.

In the first instance, at the actual point of wounding, the individual soldier would be required to conduct a little self-help. He had been taught how to use his field dressing (which was little more than an absorbent bandage) and if he could apply it, this would help reduce infection and potentially stem the flow of blood from his wound. If he was fit enough to walk, he would have understood that he must try to make his way back to his Regimental Aid Post (RAP) or perhaps one of the walking wounded collection posts set up by the front line Royal Army Medical Corps (RAMC) unit, the Field Ambulance. Lieutenant D H McWilliams was wounded during the first day of EPSOM, having gone forward to investigate a strip of wood that he felt might provide cover for attacking Germans:

> Before going across to the A Company positions, I decided to have another look at the problem and, as I was beginning to do so, I became aware of the scream of a rapidly approaching shell. For what seemed quite a long time, I debated whether to dive into a nearby (fortunately dry) ditch or whether, bearing in mind that the Jocks could probably still see me, to maintain my pose of undignified concern. The scream became ever louder and, to cut the story short, dignity lost out, in the nick of time as it happened, for the shell exploded on the very lip of the ditch into which I had just leapt, showering me with earth and debris and blasting me with a wave of heat and fumes. With studied (very studied!) unconcern, I made some flippant remark, coupled with instructions to dig faster as this probably presaged a counter-attack, when, once again, the scream began, disproving, as things turned out, the theory that you don't hear the one that gets you. This time, I did not stand on ceremony, but shouting to everyone to take cover, set a good example by hurling myself flat. Unfortunately I had moved away from the friendly ditch, and could not quite make it to any of the half-dug slit trenches, so had to be content with the ground. It was not enough, and I felt that I had sustained some damage to my right leg and jaw, as well as being (temporarily) deafened. Closer inspection revealed that the jaw had been no more than grazed, but that the leg of my battle dress was reddening rapidly high up on the thigh: sufficiently high up, in fact, to move me to open my fly buttons to check that all that ought to be there still was. Reassured on that point, I ascertained that I had both an entry and exit wound and was losing a fair amount of blood. Once my field dressing was applied, however, the flow seemed to diminish. Very soon the leg began to stiffen and it became obvious that I could no longer do my job effectively, so I handed over to my platoon sergeant, and took my leave. One of the Jocks volunteered to escort me back to the RAP (Regimental Aid Post) and, with my reversed and unloaded rifle as a crutch, we wended our way back. The leg rapidly became a solid bar, and the inconvenience of this became very apparent when we encountered what looked like a fallen power line, stretching right across the road: the only way I could get my right leg over even so small an obstacle was by canting (with support) my whole body to the left and thus getting my right foot sufficiently off the ground to clear the cable.
>
> By painful stages we made it, and I was immediately made as comfortable as possible, along with many others, pending evacuation. My helpful Jock wished me luck and departed back to the platoon.[5]

Lieutenant McWilliams was lucky in that he was wounded during a temporary lull in the battle and a fellow soldier could be spared to assist his walk to the RAP. There were some tactical

---

5   Lt D H McWilliams, 9th Cameron Highlanders papers, Ref No: 15132, Imperial War Museum.

situations, particularly during an assault, where the mission would 'trump' the casualty's own circumstances. The casualty's comrades, or even follow-on forces, would have been given strict instructions in these instances to ignore him and carry on with their allotted tasks. This would not be an easy task for the wounded man's fellow soldiers to do, but it was absolutely essential if the momentum of the attack was to be maintained or a mission successfully accomplished. During the start of Operation BLUECOAT Major J J How recalls the 3rd Monmouthshire's leading company commander was wounded and a platoon effectively wiped out, yet still the advance continued:

> Someone shouted, 'Stretcher bearers!' The cry was taken up elsewhere. Close behind me lay a softly moaning body, face down in the corn. It was Williams. He had been carrying the 'eighteen set'. It lay smashed on the ground. The back of his tunic was ripped open. I lifted a piece to reveal a huge wound...'don't worry about the bloody artillery! Get moving! Everyone's held up! Leave the wounded! Leave them! For Christ's sake get moving!' We got moving.[6]

It would be a frightening period for the casualty. If the battlefield went quiet around him he might have felt that he had been abandoned by his comrades but if the sound of fighting continued or even increased then he would not unnaturally fear either being killed, wounded once more, or captured in a German counter-attack. On some occasions soldiers would be able to assist their comrades, often at personal risk to themselves. Major Bill Apsey of the 1st Rifle Brigade was lucky his comrades came to his aid during Operation GOODWOOD:

> Two platoons moved towards Soliers and started to clear it up. All went well so I left the gunner and tank OPs who were with me to catch up with the leading platoons. I remember walking towards the crossroads and suddenly found myself sitting in the road. My leg looked a mess but no pain. Almost immediately I was on my back with my left arm useless. Damned mortars – you could never hear them coming. Somehow I crawled to the side of the road and was then conscious of a blow in the back. Third time lucky? Fourth time? Suddenly silence and my batman, Rifleman Jackson and others rushed over and put me in the back of a tank. A jab of morphia, swig of scotch and I was on my way to the Regimental Aid Post.[7]

Major Bill Apsey was badly wounded and invalided out of the Army. Though many were assisted by their comrades, for some wounded soldiers the first person who could be expected to come to his aid was a stretcher-bearer[8] sometimes after a significant period alone. The stretcher-bearers role is one that is often overlooked, though it is not an easy job by any means. A stretcher team could be composed of four, three or sometimes as little as two men. As the Mark II stretcher weighed 30 pounds, without the casualty, the physical demands of a two-man team carrying a laden stretcher are clearly significant.

The team would try to make the casualty as comfortable as possible and the technique of carrying a stretcher was important in that regard. If four bearers were employed they would step off together with the inner foot, taking short shuffling paces, and never halting with a jerk. If there were only three bearers, two of them would take the head and one the foot, if there were only two bearers the rear man must march out of step with the man in front. Were the stretcher to be carried shoulder high then the casualty will be head first, when the stretcher was carried by lowered hands

---

6   How J J, *Normandy: the British Breakout* (London: William Kimber, 1981), p.24.
7   Delaforce, Patrick, *Marching to the Sounds of Gunfire* (Stroud: Sutton Publishing 1996), pp.82-80.
8   Regimental stretcher-bearers, i.e. those drawn from within the unit as opposed to Royal Army Medical Corps orderlies who were employed further back.

Figure 9.2 Major J W Forth, chaplain of the Cameron Highlanders
of Ottawa (M.G.), helping the unit's regimental aid party to treat a
casualty near Caen, 15 July. (Lieut. H. Gordon Aikman, Library and
Archives Canada, PA-133244)

at waist height then the feet would lead first. Over hilly or uneven ground the injured part would always be carried higher than the rest of the casualty hopefully assisting in reducing the flow of blood from the wound. Therefore a man with an injured leg would be carried feet first uphill and head-first downhill.

All this was great in theory, but how conscientious the teams were in the heat of battle is debatable. What is more certain, is that the stretcher-bearers would spend a great deal of time selecting their route back to the RAP, not just avoiding obvious obstacles that might effect the casualties comfort like hedges and walls, but using tactical judgement to avoid the dangerous areas and other hazards on the battlefield.

The stretcher-bearers would have to cope with a variety of wounds, including fractures, haemorrhaging and 'shock'. They were taught the treatments of these but not in the same detail as medical students. For instance a stretcher-bearer might be able to splint a fractured limb competently but without actually knowing the name of the broken bone.[9] They would also administer morphia to reduce the patient's pain marking his forehead with a prominent 'M'. Failure to do the latter could cause the casualty to be overdosed by multiple separate injections.

An infantry unit would normally have 20 stretcher-bearers under the control of a sergeant,[10] ordinarily these individuals would be split up and handed down to provide direct support to the companies usually setting up a Company Aid Post. This may seem a small amount of manpower when one considers the casualties sustained by units in some of the major offensives. However this

9   Cotterell, Anthony, *RAMC* (London: Hutchinson, 1943), pp.38-39.
10 Nicholls, Lt Col T B, *Army Medical Services in War* (Bailliere; Tindall and Cox, 1941), p.72.

pool was often supplemented by drawing on other personnel in the regiment, recently captured PWs as they transitted to the rear, or by the RAMC orderlies from the field ambulance. These were often sent up to the battalions as reserve stretcher-bearers.

Four stretcher-bearers would typically be allocated to a company attack. As an assaulting company would normally consist of about 100 men advancing over an area 500 yards wide and possibly a mile or so deep, this was a significant amount of both ground to cover and personnel to support. Each group of infantry were normally allotted the attention of one of the stretcher-bearers who would follow them at a distance 'discreet enough to reduce personal danger as far as possible without losing contact.'[11] This individual would do what he could for each casualty; he might for instance move him into a shell hole or ditch for a little added protection, or he might carry out some very quick first aid and encourage the walking wounded to make their own way back to the RAP. The stretcher-bearers main purpose however was to note the location of those who could not move and report it to the Regimental Medical Officer (RMO) as soon as possible. This may seem a little minimalist but it is worth remembering that the stretcher-bearer was only issued with a few shell dressings, triangular bandages and morphine. It was also emphasised that the stretcher-bearer should keep up with the advancing company, rather than stay and look after the first casualties the company encountered. Failure to do so would mean there would be no medical help at all for the company once it had reached its objective.

Marking where the casualties were was a critical element in the subsequent evacuation, this was usually done by plunging a man's rifle into the ground. However in the high Normandy wheat fields even this marker could be easily overlooked. Consequently stretcher-bearers would often group together 'nests' of casualties usually on or near the 'centre-line' (the attack's axis of advance) so that they could be easily identified and picked up later.

When supporting a unit in defence the stretcher-bearers would have to ensure they sited the Company Aid Post correctly, (conveniently central to the defensive position but also sheltered from enemy observation and direct fire) besides identifying the nearest point to which it would be feasible to bring an ambulance or other vehicle for evacuation. They would be expected to know the whereabouts of every section in the company position and be able to find their way to them at night and under fire. It was a difficult and dangerous role and one that often attracted the admiration of many of their comrades. Lieutenant Colonel Hart-Dyke, of the 1st Hallamshires wrote about his medical staff's performance on the Rauray spur at the end of Operation MARTLET (1 July):

> All day our RMO Gregory-Dean worked like a Trojan under fire while so many ambulances were knocked out working between Les Haut Vents and Fontenay that evacuation of the wounded was no longer possible. During the day the regimental stretcher-bearers under Sergeant Goodliffe were heroic and two lost their lives. Lance Corporal Penn alone rescued 32 men, 11 of whom were saved under close small arms fire and one even after he himself was severely wounded. Recommended for the Victoria Cross he received the Military Medal. Later, he had to have his leg amputated.[12]

Unlike infantry units, armoured units were not allocated any stretcher-bearers at all. Given the large provision of vehicles to armoured units it was considered superfluous and casualties were often simply placed on the backs of tanks or other vehicles transiting to the rear. This may seem to be better at first hand, but the casualty would sometimes need medical care before transit to the rear as this incident during Operation CHARNWOOD bears out:

---

11   Cotterell, Anthony, *RAMC* (London: Hutchinson, 1943), p.20.
12   Hart-Dyke, T, *Normandy to Arnhem* (Sheffield: Greenup & Thomson, 1966), p.16.

One very sad case was that of a young tank officer who was brought back badly wounded slung over a tank – he was conscious but very shocked – he had compound fractures of both legs and had lost a foot. I tried to transfuse him but in his shocked state his veins had contracted to cords – John Simpson took over and dissected out a vein but even then he couldn't insert a canula – we did what we could and sent him back to the casualty clearing station (CCS) but we heard later that he died. I remember my father's advice as a Regimental Medical Officer (RMO) and Field Ambulance CO in the 1914-18 war, that it was better to leave a casualty with severe fractures where he lay until Medical help could reach him rather than move him back unsplinted.[13]

The stretcher-bearers would evacuate the casualty in the first instance to the unit's RAP, this was commanded by the Regimental Medical Officer (RMO), normally a lieutenant or captain, who had a total of 42 personnel under his command (including the 21 stretcher-bearers). The casualty's arrival at the RAP would be the first occasion that he was 'booked in' to the medical system on a Field Medical Card (AFW3118), this document would be firmly fixed to the patients clothing and accompany him back through the casualty evacuation chain. The treatment given by the Medical Officer at the RAP was pretty rudimentary and once more the primary consideration was to evacuate the serious or critical casualties quickly back through the chain, rather than try and cure them at the RAP.

The RMO was a critical man in the RAP and the view of the Army Medical Services was that was where he should remain, resisting the temptation to wander all over the battlefield giving attention to the wounded. This would reduce the risk that he might be killed or wounded thereby depriving the unit of their only doctor. Equally whilst he was succouring one man, perhaps half a mile from his RAP, there were potentially 30 or 40 casualties all requiring his attention back at the RAP. Finally all the Medical Officer would realistically be able to accomplish away from his RAP was apply first aid whilst under fire, this of course could be satisfactorily done by either the wounded soldier's comrades or the stretcher-bearers.[14] Nonetheless the temptation was often great and many RMOs clearly felt the need to leave the RAP. David Tibbs, who was the Regimental Medical Officer for 13 Para, describes the results of his foray out of the RAP in August:

After an abortive night march, soon after dawn, we were moving up the hillside at Putot en Auge. Sudden intense fire came on three sides from well-concealed positions. My medics pulled in many wounded to a sunken road and I went to a spot where three men had been individually shot down. One was dead another probably so, but the third was shouting in distress and I went out with a Red Cross flag to pull him in (he had severe injuries by bullet to his genitalia and groin). As I did so I saw the second man was still blowing bubbles of blood, so with great reluctance I returned to fetch him, only to find he had now died. Without thinking I stripped off his bandoleer of ammunition and flung it to the sunken road. As I did so there was a tremendous crack as if a gun had been fired close to my head. I felt a violent shock, like electricity, in my right arm and found myself lying on the grass. After a brief moment of confusion I realised that I had become the fourth victim of the sniper and tried to shift away before another shot followed, but found that I had no strength. Wisely no-one came out to help me but one of my own RAMC men called out 'Try Hard Sir, Try Hard!' This made me redouble my efforts and I managed to push myself on my side along to the gap

13 The Normandy Diary of a junior medical officer in 210 Field Ambulance. Army Medical Museum Archives RAMC/PE/1/382/NORM, pp.7-8.
14 Nicholls, Lt Col T B, *Army Medical Services in War* (Baillière; Tindall and Cox, 1941), p.86.

in the hedge through which I had come where hands reached out to help me. I managed to limp back to my own RAP but lost a large amount of blood and felt dreadful (the bullet had gone through the neck of my right scapula, obliquely from front to back, and had severed the subscapular artery). Pain came later but was not severe.[15]

The RAP was normally located in a building or sometimes dug into the ground itself. Some form of protection from bullets or splinters was usually advisable, though cuttings and sunken roads were avoided as notorious 'shell traps'. Nevertheless there were different approaches taken to the construction of an RAP even within the same brigade:

When we visited Andy [The RMO] in his RAP we found it consisted of a canvas screen in the middle of a field with no attempt at digging it in: Andy said it was all right as the mortar bombs always fell short or over his post and none had so far landed within fifty yards….on the way back I looked in at Benny's RAP – in contrast to Andy's flimsy above ground shelter, Benny's was dug-in deep and no-one was visible above ground. I got the impression that he ran his RAP on communal principles, discussing his policy with his staff and coming to agreed decisions, one of which was to stay below ground as much as possible, but there was no doubt that the whole unit leapt into action and that the comrades performed very well when casualties arrived.[16]

The RAP was often placed very near battalion headquarters itself so that its situational awareness of the ongoing battle could be maintained. It would need to be sufficiently close to the companies for the stretcher-bearers to move back and forth, but also sited to give evacuating vehicles a covered approach from enemy observation and direct fire. Transport near the frontline rarely moved with impunity and evacuating casualties from an RAP was always a hazardous business; as 225 Parachute Field Ambulance supporting 6th Airborne Division recorded:

At 1400 hrs on 8 June an appeal for help from 195 Airlanding Field Ambulance to evacuate casualties from the RAP at LONGUEVAL was received. The canal road was covered in its length by enemy snipers and the route was dangerous. A convoy of jeeps and trailers was, however, taken along unmolested. On arrival at the RAP of 1st Bn Royal Ulster Rifles it was found that the exit to the RAP was covered by enemy automatic weapons. Some 30 casualties were awaiting evacuation in transport outside the RAP and any attempt at evacuation was met by fire. Several stretcher-bearers of 12 Para Bn had been wounded and the RMO, Capt Kennedy. Lt Col Anderson of 195 Airlanding Field Ambulance was also hit. All casualties were evacuated by a back entrance and the RAP cleared.[17]

It was recognised that the RAP's role would be to move with the unit at all times and provide that 'first line' or integral medical support. Therefore normally a patient in Normandy would only spend the minimum amount of time at the RAP, somewhere between 10 minutes and two hours. However in some circumstances soldiers would have to spend longer and the treatment given by

---

15 Tibbs, David, 'The Doctor's Story, RMO 13 Para Bn – 225 Parachute Field Ambulance', Army Medical Museum Archives RAMC/PE/I/216/TIBB, p.13.

16 The Normandy Diary of a junior medical officer in 210 Field Ambulance. Army Medical Museum Archives RAMC/PE/1/382/NORM, p.27.

17 Narrative of 225 Parachute Field Ambulance post-operational report, 5 June-8 Sep 1944. Army Medical Museum archives Appendix E, p.2.

Figure 9.3 A casualty is brought into a 3rd British Division Regimental Aid Post by jeep, 9 July.
(Imperial War Museum B6740)

the RMO in these circumstances was likely to be greater. Captain Douglas Aitken was the RMO of the 24th Lancers. His account of trying to carry out his duties during the battle for Point 103 explains the difficulties in attempting to conduct front line medical work at night:

> Sinclair and I work away on the casualties. It's getting dark. Suddenly three very fast-travel-ling rounds come through the other end of the orchard – they must have come from an enemy tank. Only one explodes; must have been two armour piercing and one H.E. There is a call for stretcher-bearers but I have none and send off the nearest people with stretchers. Five casual-ties come in – three fairly light, and one man with the whole of his lower jaw blown away, and the other with one leg badly injured.; none of them are ours and no vehicle has been hit. I look at the man with the jaw; it is very ugly and I see no hope for him. I give him a very large dose of morphia – an assurance of a peaceful death. It is all I can do. Sinclair tends the others and I do the leg up; he has lost a lot of blood but will do. A stream of bullets passes over my head and one chips the tree above me; how fortunate I was kneeling. I say to myself that whoever fired them is unlikely to fire in exactly the same direction again and we all go on working. We have fifteen cases waiting to go, all but three are stretchers and I daren't send them. If any more come in I don't know what to do; but I can't hold any more…
>
> … Thirteen more infantry come in – a mortar landing in the middle of them and two have their legs off below the knee – there is one with both off and one with one off and the other hanging by a bit of skin and muscle. Some of the others are serious, too. We sort them out and Sinclair and I get down to the job in the dimmed light of a torch. This is so dim that is hardly worth using but it's all we dare use. We are constantly losing scissors and things when we lay them down. I remember noting never to use anything but white bandages and triangulars at night. I talk to Sinclair about blood transfusion but we agree to risk leaving it at the moment;

Diagram 9.1
Medical evacuation chain.

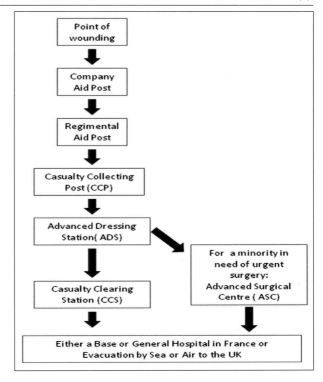

it may only open up the main arteries that we cannot find in all the mess of blood and flesh....

... We finish tying up the man with no legs; the one with one hanging on I nearly put up wrongly as I had to unwind his foot two complete turns to bring it right. I splint it and put on innumerable bandages. It is then that we hear of the section [a Field Ambulance section had set up in the adjoining field] and they go off for their much needed blood. I feel now that we should have risked the blood straight away. Perhaps they will live. Curious –the one with both legs off only wanted to evacuate his bowels – otherwise he felt nothing. All the time I was treating him he kept struggling up, 'For God's sake, Sir, I must have a shit.' I persuaded him to let me finish his dressings and then I turn him over, pack a lot of cotton wool between his legs and tell him to go ahead. He does and then says he feels O.K. and can he get up?

... One of our own fellows comes in with multiple wounds but he is the best patient yet. We talk and smoke while I do up his six wounds. I give him a huge piece of shrapnel out of his hip and he puts it away in his pocket. He seems quite oblivious to pain. It's getting dawn again and I have two minor cases on my hands. The leg cases are both living after three pints of blood each. I am very glad. I fall asleep where I am in the ditch.[18]

Whilst evacuation was a priority for the seriously wounded many individuals with superficial wounds could be simply patched up on the frontline and returned to their companies. If the casualty was to be evacuated he would be moved by RAMC stretcher-bearers, or by vehicle, back to the Casualty Collecting Post (CCP). This was another very mobile unit and normally served two different unit RAPs. It was to be accessible to four wheeled vehicles and located as close to the

---

18 Willis, Leonard, *None Had Lances: The Story Of The 24th Lancers* (Chippenham: Picton Print, 1986), pp.143-144.

RAPs as possible, on the realistic understanding that stretcher-bearers could not repeatedly carry loaded stretchers much more than half a mile. The CCP was in essence little more than a post box and designed to ensure that the RAPs were not clogged up with casualties and could remain mobile and move with its battalion when required. It was led by a medical officer and formed around a section from one of the RAMC Field Ambulance's two forward companies.

Ordinarily if a casualty was already in an ambulance or on transport he was simply sent further back the evacuation chain. Resuscitation could be done at the CCP if required, but the idea was that the CCP should not remain full of wounded and again there was a well-understood imperative to keep the casualty moving back down the evacuation chain. If the CCP was full of casualties and the battle moved on then it would be simply 'leap-frogged' by an alternate CCP who would take up the responsibility of supporting the RAPs in their new locations. Captain Helm from 210 Field Ambulance describes the support his CCP gave during Operation JUPITER:

> At the CCP all was well and as we were due to get up at 4am to be ready for the attack we all went to bed early and I slept fairly well through the noise of enemy bombs and our own guns. We were up and ready at 0430am and soon our casualties began to arrive in ambulances – I would get inside – have a quick look at everyone to see that they were fit enough to go on back to the ADS. If they all seemed well enough the ambulance went straight on. We took about one in ten into the CCP because of continued bleeding, severe pain indicating the need for morphine and fractures for splinting or re-splinting – this relatively small proportion needing immediate treatment compared to the first battle[19] was due to good work by the RMOs and their stretcher-bearers helped by our own men…At this time in spite of my efforts and agitation I was not allowed blood or plasma in the CCP – I had the feeling that our second in command thought that in my youthful enthusiasm I would transfuse too many leaving the Advanced Dressing Station (ADS) short of blood. It was clear that some of our badly wounded lads did need transfusions and that without it some would die on the bumpy four mile track back to the ADS.

The casualty's next stop would be an Advanced Dressing Station (ADS). This facility was also generated by the Field Ambulance and based around its headquarters. The Field Ambulance's two other companies would be responsible for providing the CCPs and evacuating casualties from RAPs through the CCPs to the ADS. On arrival at the ADS the ambulance would enter the car park or ambulance rank where the driver would hand in a list of the blankets, stretchers and other equipment in use in the ambulance. The next available ambulance would take exactly the same stores and equipment back to make sure the front line medical posts were not denuded of equipment or vehicles.[20] The ADS was a less mobile facility than those nearer the front and could not quickly close and move in the manner of an RAP or CCP. Part of its lack of mobility came from the fact that it would have to wait for its casualties to be evacuated which could take between one and four hours. In a similar manner to the CCPs an ADS would not close until an extra one had been opened; the ADS' would therefore leapfrog back and forth as required. To enable this process and maintain flexibility one of the three Field Ambulances within the division was kept in reserve.

As soon as the ambulance pulled up at the ADS a doctor would jump inside and begin to prioritise the patients. He would judge the condition of each patient classifying them in three groups. The first group would be those suffering from severe shock and in need of immediate resuscitation through blood transfusion (about 6%). This would be done in the ADS. The second group would

---

19   This unit's first battle was Operation Charnwood, the attempt to take CAEN from the north 7-10 July.
20   Cotterell, Anthony, *RAMC* (London: Hutchinson, 1943), pp.86-87.

consist of those who were not fit to travel without an operation (about 4%). If one had been set up this group could be operated on in an Advanced Surgical Centre (ASC) which was formed from a Field Surgical Unit and a Field Dressing Station. Finally the third group would include those wounded who were able to travel the journey back to the Casualty Clearing Station (about 90%).

The ADS would normally have the space and capacity for 50 cases at a time. Given that there were only one or two ADS per division they could quickly become congested and the importance of prioritising the casualties and directing them onwards quickly was once more paramount.[21] Captain Helm relates the pressure 210 Field Ambulance's ADS was under when it came into action for the first time in support of 59th Division's assault on the north of Caen, 7-10 July.

> Friday the barrage was even heavier than usual and we knew that one of our battalions, the 2/6th Battalion South Staffordshire Regiment was moving forward – this was to be their baptism of fire and we expected casualties. At the ADS we were working six hour shifts and Hamish, the company commander and I were supposed to be resting, but after a good night's sleep I didn't feel I could rest and was hanging around the ADS when suddenly we received the expected casualties but in unexpected numbers. About fifty arrived in ten minutes. This was quite a beginning for an untried ADS and our second in command was visibly shaken – he told me to return to my rest but Alex from HQ Company asked me to stay. The ADS staff had been well-trained, but like all of us were out of their depth at first. We tried to get a routine going for our nursing orderlies – treating those with minor injuries, all of whom were to have their wounds dressed and to be given anti-tetanus injections and sulphonamide tablets: they rapidly took this on smoothly giving the MOs time to stop haemorrhages, splint fractures and set up transfusions. I was again told to go away and rest but was rapidly recalled with another rush of wounded.

These initial casualties had been caused when, as a result of the dust kicked up by their move to their start line, the 2/6th South Staffordshires came under a mortar barrage causing significant casualties. After a brief spell off duty Captain Helm was called back after the attack had started properly on 8 July:

> Casualties began to arrive in great numbers and it looked as if we might be swamped. There were large groups waiting to be assessed in reception, some already dead, some dying, some in urgent need of transfusion, a group of terrified, disorientated lads – battle-exhausted, jittering and yelling in a corner. Somehow we got through the work transfusing a fair number but our resuscitation room was nowhere near big enough, and we needed another MO rather than a Stretcher Bearer Officer (SBO), although the excellent Chick, our SBO, and the sergeant dispenser worked hard and effectively. Alec from the HQ Company worked away steadily and efficiently and the second in command remained visibly shaken. Several SS wounded came in – a tough and dirty bunch – some had been snipers up trees for days – one young Nazi had a broken jaw and was near death but before he fainted he rolled his head over and murmured 'Heil Hitler'.
>
> Hamish and I were off duty for six hours in the evening – these six-hour shifts were unsatis-factory as by the time we had eaten, washed and shaved, there was little time left for sleep. In this thirty-six hour long battle we had about seven hundred casualties through our ADS – by no means all from our 177 Brigade and they included Germans and a few civilians. In the chaos and scale of this particular battle the majority of these casualties had by-passed their

21 Ibid., p.86.

Figure 9.4 An ambulance jeep of the Royal Canadian Army Medical Corps evacuates casualties near Vaucelles, 20 July. (Lieut. Ken Bell, Library and Archives Canada, PA-129031)

regimental aid posts and our forward company posts [the CCPs] and were brought straight back to us on stretcher jeeps and in ambulances.[22]

The next stage in the casualty's journey was to a Casualty Clearing Station, a separate unit in its own right and in theory allocated on the basis of two to a corps and one at army level. In actual practise they were all commanded and controlled at army level which gave the medical system greater flexibility. Again the CCS' would go forward and leap frog each other in turn always making sure that there was a medical 'foot on the ground' at all times. CCS' were primarily there to deliver surgical support on patients; Sister Pamela Bright describes her CCS:

Forward surgery was carried out by the two surgeons, and there were usually two Field Surgical Unit surgeons attached. This meant that there were four theatres, four complete teams, two for each eight-hour shift. Sometimes a Field Dressing Station became attached, and this increased our capacity because they were able to look after the lightly wounded and sick. There was always a blood transfusion team... Our capacity was 121 beds and 150 stretchers, and in Normandy these were always full. The staff of the CCS consisted of the commanding officer, four surgeons (two senior, two assistants), two anaesthetists, one physician, a dentist, a company officer, two or three chaplains and a variety of medical orderlies,

---

22 The Normandy Diary of a junior medical officer in 210 Field Ambulance. Army Medical Museum Archives RAMC/PE/1/382/NORM, pp.1-9.

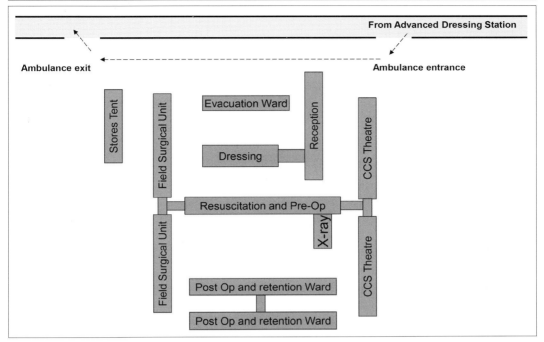

Diagram 9.2 Typical layout of a Casualty Clearing Station.

cooks, mess orderlies, X-ray orderlies. There were eight of us nursing sisters, one of whom was senior and in charge: four worked on one shift and four on the other – usually two in the wards, one in theatre and one in the resuscitation ward. The latter was a responsible job as very often it was left to the sister to decide which patient was sufficiently revived to stand an operation.[23]

Casualty Clearing Station layouts tended to vary but VIII Corps felt the ideal layout was as shown above.[24]

A good CCS had to have adequate space in reception. Without this room the functioning of the CCS would swiftly become chaotic, additionally by having the evacuation ward close to the reception, the less serious cases could be siphoned off by the attached FDS staff for minor treatment and subsequent evacuation. The resuscitation ward was usually the largest ward with four operating theatres leading directly off it so that the surgeons could monitor the waiting cases and determine with the nursing sister the priority of operation. The two post-operative or retention wards containing serious cases were deliberately not too large so that adequate supervision could still be maintained.[25] Sister Pamela Bright describes a post-operative ward:

It consisted of two long marquees divided by a small corridor where stood trestle tables scrubbed like white bread, on which were the trays, instruments, enamel ware, sterilizers,

23 Bright, Pamela, *Life In Our Hands* (London: Pan Books, 1957), pp.18-19.
24 Crew, F A E, *Army Medical Services, Campaigns, Volume IV North-West Europe* (London: HMSO, 1962), p.287.
25 Ibid., pp.287-288.

all the hugger-mugger, required in surgical work: drums full of sterile dressings, jars full of rubber drains and lengths of tubing, bottles coloured by the stuff inside them, bandages, rolls of wool, abdominal binders, all neatly stacked. There were boxes of adhesive tape, Elastoplast, potted meat jars containing safety pins, clips, spigots; and the tin of talcum powder and bottle of methylated spirits, the colour of a pale iris, stood full because we were too busy to think of rubbing bottoms.

In the far partition were the stretcher cases for whom there was reasonable hope. Some lay in odd attitudes, faces white and eyes shut, some looked about them, but they were all dirty and unshaven with battle dress torn and stained; tired beyond all telling, they slept or lay peacefully on the floor. In the nearer marquee were beds crammed together for the dangerously ill. This part of the ward looked like a place of torment with its fantastic effect of rubber tubing every-where. If a piece was not running into a man's arm or leg, it was in his nose, running down into his stomach, continually sucking out its contents to aid peristalsis of the bowel and ultimate life. Tubes were everywhere, draining large cavities and or some essential organ.

The ward was full. The men lay propped up on pillows, boards, box lids served as back rests; white sheets covered messy injuries. Under the blue striped pyjamas was the grime that you itched to remove but knew you could not because there were other far more important things to do.[26]

A patient's arrival at the CCS would see him prioritised at reception. The surgeon would then assess whether the patient needed any further treatment to stabilise him before operation and judge which of the 8-10 men waiting for surgery should be operated on first. A man wounded in the chest or belly, or in need of immediate amputation, was always a priority and the goal was to operate on him within an hour of his arrival at the CCS. During the first day of Operation EPSOM the average interval between time of wounding and arrival at a CCS was 2½-4½ hours,[27] though longer delays became inevitable when the battle of Normandy became more mobile and geographically dispersed.

When the time came for the casualty to be operated upon he would be taken into the theatre (which was simply a medium sized tent) and anaesthetized intravenously. The anaesthetist's role is significant. Too little anaesthetic and the casualty's muscles would not relax and stay taut and tense, while the patient is in no pain, it does make the surgeons work harder. Conversely if too much anaesthetic is given the patient could stop breathing. The anaesthetist also has to make sure that the casualties tongue is forward all the time; when unconscious the muscles of the tongue are liable to fall back and choke the patient.

Whilst the casualty is being administered anaesthetic the surgeon and operating room assistants would be 'scrubbing up'; washing their hands in water thoroughly, after which they would not touch anything that was not sterile. They would be wearing sterilised rubber gloves, rubber apron and a sterile gown. The surgeon then put sterile towels round the operating area, which would have already been cleaned by the operating room assistant. The size of the wound varied, if caused by a low velocity small arms round it could be quite small, whereas a bomb or shell splinter could lacerate a large area. Let us assume the casualty had a belly wound:

The surgeon cuts away the potentially infective edges of the wound, he enlarges the incision to about six or seven inches long to get into the abdominal cavity. He mops up the blood with

---

26 Bright, Pamela, *Life In Our Hands* (London, Pan Books, 1957), p.7.
27 Crew, F A E, *Army Medical Services, Campaigns, Volume IV North-West Europe* (London: HMSO, 1962), p.158.

large gauze swabs and puts his hand in the wound to feel around for any damaged organs. If he feels any he may have to enlarge the incision to reach them. If there are any bleeding blood vessels he pinches them in special forceps and ties them off with catgut, which is subsequently absorbed by the body in three weeks or so. He examines the whole length of the intestine for any signs of punctures. He pulls out a bit at a time and examines with tremendous care. If he finds a puncture he sews it up with catgut. Otherwise the contents of the intestine could leak into the abdominal cavity and lead to peritonitis. That is the whole trouble with belly wounds. It isn't the metal fragments; they just stay where they land up without doing any harm, and the surgeon doesn't spend much time searching for them. But once peritonitis gets a hold, which it can in a few hours, it rapidly poisons the whole body and kills it. The job done he sews a rubber tube eight inches long and of finger thickness into the abdominal cavity, leaving about half an inch protruding. There is bound to be some degree of peritonitis in a few days time and the tube gives the poisons a route of exit…The operation probably took thirty minutes. The patient comes round about two hours later. If he lives three days he will probably be all right.[28]

When the surgeon sewed up the patient he would probably have sprinkled a small teaspoonful of sulphonamide powder in the wound. These drugs are anti-bacterials delaying bacterial growth and allowing the white blood cells to overcome any infection. In addition penicillin would also almost certainly have been administered, normally in a course of three hourly injections. It was more likely than not that our casualty with the belly wound survived. A fact which many attributed to the availability of surgery close to the frontline as well as the use of penicillin, sulphonamides and transfusion.

Major C Denley Clark was a surgeon operating with 21 Field Surgical Unit. During the period of 14 August the surgical unit was based in St Jean des Essartiers where they were supporting the VIII Corps break out (Operation GROUSE). In a 24-hour period Major Clark and his team conducted nine operations.[29] These were mainly HE, shrapnel or gunshot wounds with the patients being evacuated from the surgical unit anywhere between 3-10 days after their operation. Some of the injuries were serious and complicated. Private Hammond of 1st Suffolks for instance suffered a penetrative wound of the lower abdomen at 1300 on 14 August. Major Clark was able to operate upon him six hours later, making an excision of the wound of entry and a lumber incision to expose the right kidney, which was shattered in its lower half. The kidney was removed and a hole through the lower margin of the pleural (lung) cavity closed. Major Clark identified considerable bleeding from a hole entering the right posterior aspect of the liver with an exit 2 inches above middle of lower margin, this was checked by mattress sutures. He also removed a piece of shrapnel from the region of the spleen. Private Hammond's convalescence in the surgical unit was uneventful and he was evacuated on 23 August.

Private Connor, of 3rd Monmouths, was brought in to the CCS suffering from a sucking chest wound, compound fracture of the right elbow and left fibula. On his arrival at the surgical unit Major Clark suspected gas gangrene had already set in. He operated on Private Connor at 1245 on 15 August. However the twenty-two year old Private Connor never recovered and died at 0700 on 16 August as a result of multiple injuries and infection in his thorax. He was the only one of the nine patients operated on by Major Clark and his team that day not to survive and is buried in Bayeux cemetery.

---

28 Cotterell, Anthony, *RAMC* (London: Hutchinson, 1943), p.30.
29 Drawn from Maj CD Clark's surgical log and case notes held within his papers in the Army Medical Museum RAMC/CF/4/525/CLAR/2.

33 FSU conducted 127 operations in the month of July, a daily average of well above 5 operations a day. Undoubtedly high quality surgery conducted close to the front line played a key role in saving many on the front line, but nurses and medical orderlies were also critical to a patient's recovery. Medical orderlies gave transfusions, administered morphine and conducted other routine tasks. Nurses were required to also conduct complicated medical procedures as well as supervise the orderlies and monitor the patient's recovery. Sister Pamela Bright records one of the difficult treatments nurses could be expected to perform:

'What do I do after I've boiled the Miller-Abbott? I've never used one before?'

'You pass it,' she said. She was filling a syringe with morphia and for a moment her eyes left the little rubber capped bottle as she turned to me, a puzzled expression on her face. 'Yes, I remember,' she went on 'it's swallowed –it's supposed to be more effective than a Ryle's tube which only aspirates the stomach: the Miller-Abbott does more it aspirates the small intestine. It has a double lumen, hasn't it?'

'Yes,' I said.

'Well, when it's down, you blow up the balloon. Let him swallow about six inches every half-hour and aspirate at frequent intervals.'

'Thanks.' I left her quickly, feeling not a bit grateful to the two Americans, Mr Miller and Mr Abbott, for their idea. I took out the tube from the sterilizer with the large forceps, put it into the receiver on my tray and went to the boy, Tom. He appeared to be very ill. His face was drawn and anxious, his eyes very bright, and they looked at me as if I was an immense distance away. His pulse was rapid and thready, his abdomen was swollen and so full of gas that I understood immediately why Major Wills was so concerned. Effortlessly he was being very sick. I tried to explain to him what I was going to do. In the ordinary way, a Ryle's tube is passed via the nose and if the patient is cooperative he suffers little inconvenience, swallowing easily, but the Miller-Abbott seemed to me to be a highly unpleasant project; for one thing, it was thicker, and, for another it had to go by the mouth. Trying to hide my fears that I might not succeed I said:

'Tom, will you drink some water?' He was greedy for it. Quickly then I put the beastly thing in his mouth and told him to swallow. He spat it out. I tried coaxing as I repeated the process. He retched, he spluttered and coughed, getting blue in the face; then he was very sick.

'Leave me alone can't you?' like a child, he pleaded. Feeling acutely sorry for him, I cursed doctors for not doing their own prescribed treatment.

Explaining gently how it would benefit him, I coaxed him to swallow more water, talking to him all the time and pushing the tube a little further with each of his gulps. And this time it passed onward, along the oesophagus into the stomach and reached the mark which indicated that it was in the small intestine. I fixed it in place with adhesive plaster on his cheek and with a Spencer-Wells forcep clipped it on his pillow. With a syringe I put a little air in through the lumen marked 'inflator' and then through the other, aspirated off pints of filthy brown fluid. I think Tom felt relieved almost at once; breathing as if he had been running, he tried to thank me. I would not have cared so much if he had not taken the personal indignity so patiently. I would rather he had sworn at me.[30]

Whilst sulphanomides and penicillin ensured that infection and sepsis were no longer the big killers they had been, blood transfusion was another medical advance that had been introduced at the beginning of the war and was in widespread use in Normandy. To understand its importance it

---

30 Bright, Pamela, *Life In Our Hands* (London: Pan Books, 1957), pp.9-10.

is probably worth explaining that when a person is wounded two things usually happen. Firstly the cut blood vessels lose whole blood until either a clot forms or the blood vessels go into spasm and stop bleeding. Secondly plasma from the blood continues to be lost through the damaged tissues as it tries to stabilise a clot over the injured area. For large injuries such as amputations or burns, large amounts of both blood and plasma can be lost, causing the injured soldier to go into shock. At this point the heart is unable to pump fast enough or hard enough to maintain blood pressure and supply oxygen to the tissues. Loss of plasma may also thicken the blood remaining in vessels, particularly at the areas of injury, this may cause further damage. A man suffering from shock is therefore pale and cold: his pulse is rapid and weak.

There are three fluids that can be injected into the casualty's veins to help him recover. Firstly 'Whole Blood' which could be taken directly from a comrade or sent up from base in a bottle. This bottle would need to be constantly refrigerated and would keep for up to 14 days. Secondly 'Plasma' which is important in both helping to replace lost fluid and also increasing the volume of circulating fluid in the blood vessels so that blood pressure is maintained and circulation in the areas of injury improved. Plasma also contains clotting factors to promote clots and scab formation at the injury site. Plasma could be stored either as a liquid or alternatively in a powdered, dehydrated form, needing only water to be added to be of use. The final fluid is 'glucose-saline', which is simply a sugar and salt solution, designed to help reduce the fluids lost through sweating. This fluid replaces whole body water, it does not stay in the blood vessels for long after transfusion and does not transport oxygen. It is not therefore useful to replace massive blood loss through injury.

Managing these fluids and ensuring that there was a ready supply in theatre was a complicated business that was carried out by Field Transfusion Units. These were co-located with the CCS and generally carried about 80 bottles of blood in their refrigerators. They would be supplied by the blood distribution sections of Blood Transfusion Units who were established in Normandy from D+5, providing two blood banks, named 'X' and 'Y', of three refrigerator vehicles each. These in turn were supplied by sea from the Army Blood Supply Depot at Portsmouth; though by D+17 the method of resupply was switched to air and this was maintained until the end of the campaign.

Ensuring a steady and available supply of blood in the early days of the campaign was a security as well as a logistical challenge. Immediately prior to D-Day it had been felt too risky to mass 'bleed' personnel or deliver the blood into the widely separated and 'sealed' invasion assembly areas without compromising operational security. As a consequence supplies of blood were limited at the very beginning of the campaign and tended towards their 'best before' age of 14 days.

As the general hospitals became established in France; the Blood Transfusion Units moved into the centre of these and the re-supply of blood steadied at about 400 pints per day. On occasions it was still necessary to locally bleed individuals and during a ten day period in early July, 1500 pints of blood were taken from individuals in Normandy as casualties resulting from the heavy fighting around Caen mounted.[31]

Once a casualty had been successfully treated in a CCS he would either be returned to duty or sent further back the evacuation chain to a General or Base Hospital. These larger hospitals were not present in the early stages of the campaign, in which case the casualty was sent straight back to the UK, but by the middle of June General Hospitals began to be built in Normandy. Initially there were three concentrations around Ryes, Reviers and La Deliverande but these became concentrated into what was known as the Bayeux Medical Area. By 20 June a definite plan for convalescence, recovery and evacuation was in effect. Two evacuation sectors, east and west, roughly corresponding to the Corps areas were defined and the existing policy of evacuating all cases not

31   Crew, F A E, *Army Medical Services, Campaigns, Volume IV North-West Europe* (London: HMSO, 1962), pp.204-205.

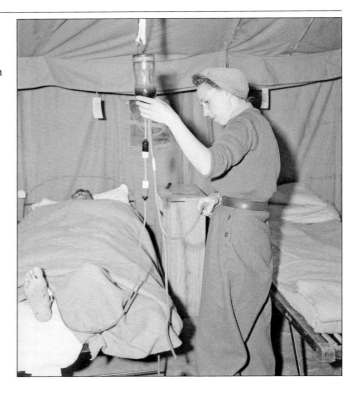

Figure 9.5
Lieutenant B Rankin (Royal Canadian Army Medical Corps) administering a blood transfusion to a wounded soldier, Montreuil, 10 September. (Lieut. Frank L. Dubervill, Library and Archives Canada, PA-128234)

likely to be fit in forty-eight hours was continued. By 26 July there were nineteen general hospitals in the bridgehead (all bar one of which were tented). These together with the Twelve CCS meant that there were sufficient beds in Normandy for all patients except those unlikely to return to duty within the week. This latter group were evacuated to the United Kingdom either by Air or Sea.

The evacuation to the United Kingdom was probably the issue that most confounded the medical planners of 21st Army Group during the D-Day planning. The specific issue was that evacuation by sea in the first few weeks of the campaign would potentially conflict with the operational priority to reinforce the bridgehead with as many combat units as possible. The medical priority to evacuate in the early stages of the campaign was particularly pressing given the very limited facilities and beds available in Normandy immediately after the landings. This quandary was first identified by the Medical Planning Section of the Administrative Planning Staff, who predicted the number and types of casualties expected during the assault phase. These included 2,000 lying cases requiring urgent surgical attention (8 per cent of the total casualties), 8,125 lying cases who would not need surgical attention (36 per cent of the total casualties) and finally 12,375 sitting cases (56 per cent of the total casualties).

The Army Medical Services, after considerable lobbying, succeeded in securing five hospital carriers and 70 converted LSTs from the Navy. The five hospital carriers, which would be available from the afternoon of D+1, were small merchant vessels which would remain well offshore and would receive casualties from water ambulances which would either come alongside or be hoisted onto the carrier's davits. The more seriously wounded and those potentially requiring surgical attention during the voyage would use the hospital carriers. It was expected that most hospital carriers would be able to take about 100 lying cases and 200 sitting cases. The majority of casualties however would be evacuated by LST of which a number would be made available from the beginning of the operation off the Anglo-Canadian Beaches. All of these would be medically manned on the basis of three medical officers, twenty sick-berth attendants or nursing orderlies and ten general duty men per ship. The load of these ships was 200 lying cases and 100 sitting cases. In addition some unconverted LSTs were also utilised and these could carry 100 sitting cases.

Normally the LST would lie offshore and be loaded by the amphibious DUKW vehicle. However if bad weather prevented this then it was accepted that the LSTs could be beached at the discretion of the naval commander and 'dry out' on the outgoing tide. Casualties could then be loaded directly from the beach.

The evacuation was to be controlled by embarkation medical officers who were allocated to each of the three beach sub-areas. Their principal task was to keep the naval officers in charge of the beaches informed of the number and type of casualties requiring transport. A DUKW would be sent out to the LSTs as they arrived and shepherd them into the relevant beach area. A company of pioneers were also provided for each beach sub-area to act as stretcher-bearers.

By July the daily requirement had been established at one medically equipped LST on each tide and one hospital carrier sailing from the Mulberry harbour at Arromanches. By the end of July these had been increased to three LST on each tide as well as the carrier, this reflected the increase in casualties taking place ashore. These medical ships would then sail to Southampton and Gosport where two Field Ambulances were located, reinforced with surgeons with special experience in the prioritisation of battle casualties. The Field Ambulances would establish dressing stations which could undertake the preliminary sorting of cases, first-aid treatment, resuscitation and urgent surgery. The condition of many of the casualties on the flat bottomed LSTs was expected to have been poor given that they would have undergone a voyage of ten to sixteen hours in a craft not attaining a high standard of medical and general amenity and notoriously unsteady at sea. It was expected that the condition of many patients would have deteriorated to a state requiring immediate life-saving treatment including resuscitation and blood transfusion.

During the voyage the small surgical team would conduct whatever operations were necessary. These teams were heavily over-worked and the difficulties encountered in conducting surgery at sea in a craft as ungainly as an LST can be readily imagined. On many occasions the casualties arrived in a shocking state. Surgeon Lieutenant G R Airth RNVR served on LST 302 and recalls a particularly large number of casualties arriving on 12 June:

> The first 'duck' with casualties had just gone aboard, and I was able to join in pronto. There were some ghastly injuries; and some of the men had taken 48 hours to reach us; morphia had been plentiful but treatment non-existent. We got the theatre going immediately, and removed many pieces of shrapnel. We knew that some men would die whatever we did, so we just tackled the cases that could be saved, and gave the others morphia. The senior man Gilchrist did the operating, I gave all the anaesthetics, transfusions etc. All intravenous anaesthetics – nothing like them for speed. Got 60 casualties in the first rush, and expected another 400; we remained on the beach till high tide – about 2330 when we were to push off, but no more arrived. All this time Jerry was strafing us spasmodically, our wide-open tank door faced hostile guns, and my fear was that someone would lob a lucky shot straight into the ship.
>
> But it didn't happen. The only damage we did sustain was by one of our own ships. It came blinding along in the dark, at 8 knots to beach, hit a cable, swung to starboard, and hit us a fearful crack, skated up our side and beached in contact with our bow doors. The words that were said between the two captains were choice. Not till the morning did I see the whacking great hole in our side, three feet above the water line while we unloaded. Well, we were so busy in the op. theatre that we never heard the ramp come up and the bow doors close. But we did hear the scream of the engines as we went hard astern; heaven be praised she backed off first go. We lay three miles offshore till 0300 yesterday, then joined a convoy for home. We went on operating till 0400, had three hours in bed, fully clothed, then up for a snack, and back to it.

The most massive effort was for an amputation through the thigh for gas gangrene. But the poor fellow was too far gone; despite several pints of blood, he did not rally. Another was quite the opposite – blood was life-saving – he sat up after the first pint – came on board the colour of paper. This went on all yesterday, the only thing that really worried us was the noise of the engines – unusually loud; found out why when I went up on deck for the first time last night, we were towing another LST.[32]

On 3 August the LST 302 beached at 1200 and by 1400 was loaded up with casualties. The deteriorating weather conditions did not make Surgeon Lieutenant Airth's job any easier particularly during operations where the steadiest of hands was required:

Am about to remove piece of shrapnel from man's lower eyelid. Am frankly windy of this, as the ship has a 20 to 30 degree roll, has been worse and may become worse again, when I'm in the middle of it and can't stop. We have had this roll ever since we set off from the mustering place at 0630 this morning, and it was worst when we stopped for 90 minutes at 0800 to let minesweepers get ahead of us. Very necessary – Jerry dropped a lot of mines, right in our path during the night. 'No 1' even saw one coming down, in the moonpath. Apart from the heavy swell, it's a marvellous afternoon – if we had time to enjoy it; but with a large and severely wounded family in one's care, there's been no time to stroll on deck.

1650 Glad to say have been 100% successful over the matter of the shrapnel, and have retained it. Remarkably lucky for him – it struck his lower eyelid, about ¼ inch below the lashes and travelled obliquely inwards towards the eyeball, and towards the angle of the eye. It just did not perforate the deep surface of the lid, and so enter the eye. Planned this small op with some care; first fixed his head on and between the pillows, so that the angle of left eye and bridge of nose were level with each other: then filled L. eye socket with sterile warm liquid paraffin – this was to keep out blood, which pours from any face wound, surgical or due to 'enemy action'. Then raised large wheal of local anaesthetic in the skin of eyelid. Used local instead of general anaesthetic in order that, should I injure the eyeball, he would let me know before the damage was irreparable.

Made incision ¼ inch long as exactly as possible in crease of eyelid, to render scar invisible. Terrific haemorrhage as expected, pressure with tiny swabs, on forceps followed by many charges of adenalin, [Used to staunch flow of blood] all repeated each time went a little deeper, eventually gave a dry field, with black irregular lump in bottom – the shrapnel. When had removed this, the inner lining of eyelid lay bare – ie it was lying within 1/16 inch of the eyeball itself. A close shave indeed. Sewed up the wound with superfine silk, and sewed only the deep parts of the skin together, so that there were no 'stitches' to leave marks, then brought the ends together over a minute paraffin dressing. No after pain and there should be no scar.[33]

In case LSTs carrying casualties put in at other ports, medical teams were also established at various other harbours along the south coast, often using staff from medical units providing cover to embarking troops. From the south coast ports the casualties were sent to one of three geographical and functional groups of hospitals. The first or 'port' group of hospitals were for those casualties who on disembarkation clearly required urgent hospital treatment or were not fit for travel. The Second or 'transit' group of hospitals existed south of a line drawn from the Thames estuary to

---

Figure 9.6 Surgeon Lieutenant Graham Airth's operating theatre on LST 302. (Robert Williams)

Figure 9.7 A view of the internal tank hold of LST 302, showing casualties waiting to be evacuated back to the UK. (Robert Williams)

Bath; all casualties would be sent here as it was believed that about half the number of casualties would require further operative surgery. The remainder would be evacuated as soon as possible to the third group 'home base' hospitals situated north of the Bath-Thames estuary line. Transport between the disembarkation ports and port hospitals would be by ambulance car, transit between the port and transit or home base hospitals would be by one of the 28 ambulance trains.[34] Captain David Tibbs, RMO of 13 Para, whose wounding in August was covered earlier in the chapter, continues the story of his entire evacuation.

> I was taken, at first by jeep, and then by ambulance back to Bayeux, to the blessed haven of a well organised, tented hospital with QA [Queen Alexandria's Imperial Military Nursing Service] nurses. It was wonderful and my fullest admiration goes out to the RAMC and QA hospital organisation. My wound was seen to by an operation and the next day the surgeon told me that I would never move my shoulder joint again (fortunately not true). I found myself amongst the earliest to receive penicillin, at that time a brick red fluid dispensed by multiple injections from an enormous syringe to everyone, and causing an intolerable ache for some hours afterwards. A few days later I was taken back to England in a huge tank landing craft filled with British and German wounded all mixed up; squabbles were inevitable! I was initially placed on a lower bunk with a German above who delighted in swinging his booted foot over the edge near my face, a situation soon remedied by reminding a medical orderly that I was a RAMC medical officer and wished to be in the upper bunk. At night before we sailed, a German plane dropped bombs round us making one feel very helpless lying with hundreds of others in this cavernous hold of the ship thinking of the carnage a hit would cause. We landed at Portsmouth where our kindly WI (Women's Institute) ladies, dispensing goodies, were shocked by some young SS German soldiers who spat at them. From there we went by train to Basingstoke for a few nights and here I heard my first buzz bomb which came overhead and then cut off. I felt real fear for an eternity until a heavy explosion nearby let me know it had fallen on someone else…From here I was transported by ambulance-train to Newcastle-on-Tyne where I spent three weeks before convalescence leave on the Isle of Wight.[35]

Casualty evacuation by air began on 13 June, a week earlier than had been anticipated in planning. It was initially a little ad hoc but by 18 June it had been placed under the command of HQ 11 Line of Communication Area and became much better organised. A Medical Air Liaison Officer was appointed to 83 Group RAF and 81 Base General Hospital was made the collecting centre and focal point for those to be evacuated by air. A single airfield was also identified (B14 near Amblie) as the sole point of air evacuation. An RAF casualty evacuation unit was established at the airfield, but its capacity was limited and on several occasions a Field Dressing Station or even a Casualty Clearing Station was established nearby to help hold and treat casualties prior to their journey. During the month of June a total of 3,176 casualties (2113 lying) were evacuated by air.[36]

The arrival and reception of casualties by air into the UK was organised and controlled by an Air Evacuation Headquarters, formed from HQ Salisbury Plain District, and based at Stratton

34 Crew, F A E, *Army Medical Services, Campaigns, Volume IV North-West Europe* (London: HMSO, 1962), pp.65-66.
35 Tibbs, David, 'The Doctor's Story, RMO 13 Para Bn – 225 Parachute Field Ambulance', Army Medical Museum Archives RAMC/PE/I/216/TIBB.
36 Crew, F A E, *Army Medical Services, Campaigns, Volume IV North-West Europe* (London: HMSO, 1962), pp.190-191.

St Margaret. It had representatives from all three services, the civilian Emergency Medical Services (EMS) and the Canadian Army. All transport aircraft were to fly into airfields situated in the Swindon area (Blakehill Farm, Down Ampney and Broadwell). Occasionally the airfield at Watchfield was also used to preserve the security of airborne operations mounted from the previous three airfields. The RAF established a casualty evacuation centre of 200 beds at each airfield with facilities for urgent surgery and resuscitation. In a similar manner to casualties evacuated by sea the nearby EMS hospitals of Stratton St Margaret and Oxford were available for urgent cases. For the remainder an ambulance train would take patients from a newly constructed railway siding near Shrivenham to the various home base hospitals.[37]

Ken Tout, a tank commander in the Northants Yeomanry, was wounded later on in the campaign, in NW Europe. His account gives a good description of the air evacuation chain and the random manner in which casualties were placed in home base hospitals.

We are lifted into the long cavernous box of an aeroplane with double tier beds slung from the wall all the way along the fuselage. As a 'walking-wounded' I am asked to watch the plasma bottle mounted above a badly mutilated Durham Light Infantryman…In spite of his weakness, the Durham man manages a smile. 'Squat on the edge of my bunk, Geordie,' he suggests.

Engines boom like a full troop of tanks. Thin fuselage walls shudder and stretch as we begin to move. A wide-open door in one wall offers an opportunity for any aerophobes to jump out at the last moment. Or for anyone of more suicidal tendencies to take a high dive in mid-ocean. The plane lifts off with all the resilience of an old bucket with a hole in the middle.

Now in the sky an unbroken hierarchy of suffering takes effect. Those of us with plebeian ailments, like stomach ulcers or appendicitis or my splintered leg, gather round and minister to the real hierarchy of pain – the engineer with two legs missing, the Highlander with shot lungs and double pneumonia, the artilleryman with half a face blown away and half a brain showing, my own light infantryman with blood still staining his bandages…Now there is the altitude. And the cold. And the swaying. And the diabolical noise. And the smell of other men's decay and degeneration. And the vast distances before we again come to earth… The cold grey sea is behind us. And the green fields of England smile up at us. And soon the golden towers of Oxford send their ancient radiant greetings up towards us as the plane dips, and the booming engines hiss into quietness and the clumsy flying box becomes a graceful, gliding bird, lifting swiftly over the Oxford hills and down among the tree-tops and flattening along a lush, green, unending meadow as though the soft spinning tires hesitate to bruise those butter-rich wild flowers strewn across our triumphal path.

Down. Thump. Rattle. Squeal. And all our aristocracy of pain are alive and lifting themselves painfully to look with misting eyes at the soil, the bracken, the green woods of Blighty.[38]

Ken Tout had landed at one of the airbases near Swindon, along with his fellow casualties he was transferred to the railhead subsequently ending up, by complete coincidence, near his home town of Hereford.

Casualties suffering from battle exhaustion were treated somewhat differently to those with physical injuries, their wounds may have been slightly harder to diagnose but it was understood that the closer the casualty was treated to the frontline the greater his chance of recovery and being returned to duty. Prior to D-Day there had been a great deal of preparatory work conducted by

37 Ibid., pp.67-70.
38 Tout, Ken, *Tanks Advance! Normandy to the Netherlands 1944* (London: Robert Hale, 1987), pp.210-214.

Figure 9.8 A patient is lifted on to a waiting Dakota for evacuation back to the UK, June 1944.
(Crown Copyright Air Historical Branch)

the psychiatrists attached to each Corps of the Army, educating RMOs on the care of acute battle exhaustion, handling the resulting discipline and morale problems that could ensue and weeding out men deemed unsuitable for combat.

The first corps exhaustion centre was deployed in Normandy on D+8 and there was then a steady build up of these centres, usually formed from an RAMC Field Dressing Station. By the end of June each corps had its exhaustion centre and these were backed up by three Army level exhaustion centres and a large rehabilitation centre. In the second half of June the percentage of battle exhaustion casualties steadied at about 13 per cent of all casualties. Battle exhaustion tended to affect seasoned campaigners perhaps more than the new, but leadership and the character of one or two individuals could have both a positive and negative effect. The Second Army Psychiatrist recorded in a report at the end of June:

> One anti-tank unit was known to be in an unhealthy state from a psychiatric point of view. The explanation was provided a few days ago when the commanding officer was evacuated showing a severe state of anxiety. A whole platoon of a certain battalion was evacuated to the Corps exhaustion centre owing to the irresponsible behaviour of its subaltern commander and the presence in its midst of a severe chronic neurotic (with the exception of whom all made good recoveries and returned to duty).[39]

---

39 Crew, F A E, *Army Medical Services, Campaigns, Volume IV North-West Europe* (London: HMSO, 1962), p.207.

Figure 9.9 A soldier is evacuated by Dakota from France, 16 June.
(Lieut. Ken Bell, Library and Archives Canada, PA-131430)

However most individuals were not weak in one way or another but had simply been exposed to too much fighting.

Though corps and army exhaustion centres had been set up there was still a shortage of both accommodation and skilled medical personnel to treat the battle exhaustion casualty. This necessitated that some casualties had to be evacuated to the UK which meant that their return to duty was less likely. It was recognised that establishing divisional exhaustion centres was key. These would sift the casualties going to the corps exhaustion centre, but also had the advantage that the division was the stable entity within which the unit belonged. Regimental Medical Officers could still maintain contact with the casualties and the treatment of battlefield exhaustion casualties in forward medical units within the sound of gunfire was far more likely to have a positive effect for the patient. The divisional exhaustion centres were formed once more from the RAMC Field Dressing Stations and run by specially selected medical officers under the guidance of the Corps psychiatrist. This evolution was probably just in time as the incidence of battle exhaustion casualties rose steadily during July till it reached 21.7 per cent of total casualties for the week ending 22 July (a total of 2,370 casualties).

Nonetheless results in July were both impressive and immediate, principally because it now became possible to retain battle exhaustion casualties for up to seven days treatment. Fifty per cent of the casualties were returned to full combatant duties and 10-20% returned to Lines of Communication or base duties in Normandy. During July a specific concern became the stability of the reinforcements arriving in depleted or worn down units. The Second Army psychiatrist wrote in his report at the end of July:

Apart from the general quality of reinforcements, three points stand out. The first is that a unit that has suffered a very large number of casualties consists almost entirely of reinforcements can hardly be considered a coherent body of men…When such a unit goes into action a very high breakdown rate must be expected, since the emotional ties among the men, and between the men and their officers (which is the most single potent factor in preventing breakdown) barely exist…The second is that reinforcements should be integrated into their units in sizeable bodies…The third point is that untrained reinforcements frequently become psychiatric casualties. Stories of clerks, cooks, storemen and the like being sent forward as riflemen reinforcements are all too frequent. Such men apart from breaking down themselves can be a real menace to their units.[40]

The general sense of 21st Army Group's Medical services is one of efficient planning and execution. There were notable successes in reducing casualty and sick rates compared to previous wars and Montgomery outlined the more successful innovations at the end of the War:

Air transport has been of great importance in the evacuation of casualties. By this means over a hundred thousand wounded men were evacuated to base hospitals from front-line units. In the sphere of transfusion, great quantities of blood and blood plasma were used. A co-ordinated service of air transport and refrigerator trucks ensured that fresh blood was always at hand for surgeons working directly behind the lines – even during the rapid advance into Belgium.

Another interesting fact is that, in the last war, two out of every three men wounded in the belly, died. Field surgical units, operating close behind the lines, greatly reduced this danger. In the Normandy campaign two out of every three men wounded in the belly recovered.

The healing of war wounds has been revolutionised by the use of penicillin. Many men who in the last war would have been permanent invalids, were fit and ready to go back into the line within a month of being wounded.

To sum up, the doctors were prepared to lay 15 to 1 that once a man got into their hands, whatever his injury, they would save his life and restore him to health. It is a fine thing that these odds were achieved with a handsome margin.[41]

There were 58,594 soldiers recorded as wounded within 21st Army Group during the period from 6 June up till the end of August. There is sometimes a danger in quoting statistics such as these to lose sight of the human dimension. That it was an important contribution to morale has been stated before but perhaps much more importantly the medical staff of all three services regularly prevented lives and families from being destroyed on a daily basis. This simple fact is clearest to those that passed through their care and their gratitude was often profound. Earlier mention was made of Private Hammond who was brought in to 33 FSU on 14 August with wounds to his lower abdomen. Following evacuation to the UK and considerable treatment in the UK he was able to write to his surgeon, Major Clark, about his experiences of the medical chain. His words eloquently capture the medical services contribution to the campaign and seem the most appropriate way to conclude this chapter:

---

40 Crew, F A E, *Army Medical Services, Campaigns, Volume IV North-West Europe* (London: HMSO, 1962), p.209.

41 Montgomery, Field Marshal B L, Despatch, *The London Gazette*, 3 September 1946.

Figure 9.10 A Dakota is unloaded of casualties at RAF Down Ampney, 18 August.
(Lieut. Jack H. Smith, Library and Archives Canada, PA-128183)

R Hammond (1 Suffolks)
1 Richmond Rd
Kirkley
Lowestoft
Suffolk

Dear Sir,

I think the best thing to do before I get down to writing this letter is to try to refresh your memory concerning myself. It may be a difficult thing to do because by now many wounded men have been through your hands and the likelihood of you only remembering one seems remote.

Here goes! Whilst serving with the above named Battalion in the Falaise Gap area I had the misfortune of becoming wounded… I was given the usual treatment as given to other cases by the very competent RAMC forward post orderlies and sent back to 33 FSU. The most I knew then concerning my injuries was that a piece of shrapnel had penetrated my right lung and that I couldn't breathe. On arrival I was almost at once operated upon. I couldn't say for sure when I awoke but when I did I didn't feel quite so bad. The following day I had the great pleasure of meeting you Sir, and on finding out the state of my injuries knew that you had undoubtedly saved my life. The shrapnel had penetrated my liver, also my kidney making it necessary for you to remove some. My pleural cavity came into light also. The incision was terrific and I was cut from navel to spine.

After eleven days you decided that I could be moved to a hospital in England. I was treated grandly by the nurses and orderlies of 33 FSU and long to thank them personally, but I'm afraid I don't remember their names, also that I'm unable to get to see them under the present circumstances. If they are still with you sir, will you thank them for me please.

Figure 9.11 German and British wounded await attention at a Regimental Aid Post south of Caumont, 31 July. (Imperial War Museum B8299)

I remained in the General Hospital at Bayeux for one day. I was then flown to England. My destination was the Mid-Glamorgan Hospital at Bridgend and after a spell of a few months I was moved to Chase Farm Hospital Middlesex remaining there one month. Then came the great day, I was moved to my hometown hospital the Lowestoft and North Suffolk. While I was in these three hospitals I was the centre of great wonders and many doctors including a Major-General admired your work and complimented you on the grand job you had done on me. I too join them in their appraisal.

Now I am discharged from Hospital and living with my parents. I have been granted a 100% pension also. My general condition up to date is grand, though I still have some pain, I also use a stick but hope to dispense with this eventually. I've explained my case sir, as near as I can compile it and hope you remember me. Forgive me for not writing before, but I'd like to thank you for all the fine work you done to save my life.[42]

The soldiers of 21st Army Group had high levels of confidence that their medical services would look after them if wounded. This confidence had a very positive effect on sustaining their morale and as General Montgomery continuously reminds 'morale is probably the most single important factor in war.'

---

42 Letter Hammond to Clark drawn from the papers of Major CD Cark in the Army Medical Museum RAMC/ CF/4/525/CLAR/2.

10

'Grim Summer' – Life in Normandy 1944

We must never forget those grim days of desperate struggle and achievement.

Field Marshal Montgomery of Alamein, 1947[1]

The Normandy campaign would mark all who served there and many aspects were common to all. For some however, this was the first trip they had ever taken to a foreign country, other servicemen were well-travelled, perhaps having served overseas previously or taken a foreign holiday in more peaceful times. Whatever the case the Normandy countryside, food and people together with the campaigning requirements of living, eating, and simply surviving were experiences that all servicemen collectively faced.

The dangers however were not equally shared, some soldier's duties meant they seldom ventured near the frontline. Even amongst frontline soldiers the infantryman was always in greater danger and suffered proportionally higher casualties as a result. Despite these differences the threat of death affected everyone who crossed the channel that summer to a greater or lesser degree.

With the exception of the Airborne Division and those who landed in the first wave of D-Day most soldiers began their deployment to Normandy in a similar manner, the movement of men and vehicles increasingly following a prescribed and routine pattern as the operation matured. The preparation's soldiers made for this momentous journey were also similar. Once the series of pre-invasion exercises had been concluded in late spring most soldiers spent long periods preparing their equipment and vehicles for operations in Normandy. The waterproofing of vehicles for wading ashore was a particularly time consuming affair recalled by many. John Foley describes the preparation required to ensure his Churchill tanks were ready to land:

> This was a tedious and back-breaking job, and took us best part of six weeks. Every rivet in the belly of the tank had to be rasped clean and painted with waterproof paint. Inspection plates had to be sealed with a rubbery solution; extension funnels had to be fitted to the tank exhaust pipes and the air inlet louvre. Yards of balloon fabric were pasted in position around the turret ring, the driver's visor, and gun mounting.[2]

In the final moments the invading troops would journey from their barracks to a series of marshalling areas and transit camps set up along the south coast, large divisional columns taking to the route at the same time. Lieutenant Colonel M Crawford, commanding officer of 8th

---

1   Scarfe, Norman, *Assault Division* (London: Collins, 1947), p.13.
2   Foley, John, *Mailed Fist* (St Albans: Mayflower, 1975), p.30.

Figure 10.1
3rd County of London Yeomanry Sherman
tanks await embarkation at Worthing.
Waterproofing of vehicles had been
completed and the regiment stood by at
6 hours Notice To Move (NTM).
(County of London Yeomanry)

Middlesex, recalls his battalion's journey from Sussex to a transit camp near the port of Tilbury
on 15 June:

Moved off at 0130 hrs. Very annoyed to find that Corke (driver of Humber 4x4) had failed
to fix back axle light although he has had nothing to do for the past week. Column started
off at very fast pace to go via Battle to Div Start Point at Goudhurst then route Pembury,
Riverhead, Farnborough, London Bridge, East Ham, to marshalling area somewhere near
Tilbury. This was unexpected as we imagined that we would go from some port in the south
such as Shoreham or even Hastings itself. Car was running very badly, just this side of Battle,
stopped altogether. Owing to the engine being waterproofed very difficult to locate trouble.
Managed to stop my jeep and Tech Adj. Hughes and the L.A.D breakdown. Hughes got it
running again, trouble seemed to be in Carburettor. Tried to catch up the column, got about
6 miles beyond Battle when car stopped again. This time unable to locate fault so left Humber
with Hughes and all my kit, and with Spear (Adjt) got in front seat of Jeep; driven by Lenney
we caught up with column at Pembury. Div. Column continued drive without halts, very bad
march discipline one moment crawling, the next minute 30-40 mph.

As we approached London, after Farnborough Kent, the Metropolitan Police took us over,
and got us through London in most marvellous way. It was now 0600hrs. No one about
except some Yank soldiers and their girls, looking rather bedraggled, waiting for the trams to
start after an obvious night out. All traffic other than the convoy brushed aside by the police.
As we got over London bridge and into the city more people about and when we got to the
East End, such places as East Ham, East Sheen etc there was the most wonderful demonstration by the people of London, all the poor people rushing out giving us tea, buns, potato
chips, cigarettes and soap. Not only to us as Middlesex but to the whole divisional column.

As we had no breakfast the tea and buns were very welcome. It was very touching and made me feel that the spirit of the Country is very good at heart and that one should not believe what the Daily Mirror writes. Arrived at the R.C.R.P at Woodford (Route Control Road Post) where Monty King who had gone in advance met us and conducted us with Movement Control Staff to our Marshalling Area T6, this turned out to be nothing else than Purfleet ranges. This time the column was very bad again, as soon as the Metropolitan Police had given us up, it went to pieces. Half our column got lost near Egypt. The Camp itself which is supposed to be run on the Hotel system, the camp staff doing everything, appears to be very badly run. The whole place being very dusty and dirty.[3]

On arrival at the transit camps maps were distributed, orders passed and the vehicles and equipment checked once more. After that there was little for the soldiers to do except wait. Films and canteens were laid on but most soldiers could not take their mind off the invasion and a nervous atmosphere descended on the various transit camps, relief finally coming with the journey to the embarkation port.

If a soldier travelled on an American ship he could expect good food, coffee as well as hot showers. Such was the American affluence and generosity that many would load their vehicles with tins of peaches and other such luxuries. The only advantage the British ships seemed to have over their American counterparts was that they were not 'dry'. Lieutenant Colonel Crawford seems to have been particularly unlucky and found one of the few American ships where the hospitality was poor:

Drove to East India Docks, where we expected to embark on ship on which our vehicles had been already loaded. However when we got there, all vehicles still on shore. Found Evill, [Major T Evill was the officer responsible for all British Army soldiers on the ship] our ship an American Liberty ship the 'George Wythe' had only just come in. Could do nothing about it. It was Sunday and dock hands being paid double overtime were getting 10/– a day so proceeded to load very slowly. We were impatient. Hung about sheds at the back of the dock all day. Dirty and unpleasant. However as vehicles went into 5 holds, things went quicker than was expected. George Wythe is an M.T ship, which being raised from docks by dereks on ship. Trouble over LAD trailer which was eventually overcome by much argument. Embarked at 1800 hrs. Scare that 3 of HQ Coy missing. Wheadon 3 ton driver and 2 pioneers Rivers and Johnson. However they reappeared within ½ hour. All B Coy present, 3 of their D.R's Von Bergen, Cunningham and Zappoloni, having been absent all day but reappearing at 1745 hrs. Having got everybody on board, Captain (American) informed us we would not sail until 1030 hrs next day. However kept everyone on board. Evill read our orders etc. No cooking arrangements available for us but living on compo packs. I have been given tiny little cabin in stern, normal place for ships hospital – communal wash house with American naval AA gun crew. Very dirty, which I shared with John Spear, Peter Allen having refused offer in order to be with his company. No arrangements made for officers sleeping, latrines or washing. There are 600 bunks piled on top of each other in holds 4 & 5. Total of us on board 25 officers, 624 other ranks, 143 vehicles. Gross tonnage of George Wythe 7800. John Spear had incident with drunk US naval rating in wash house called 'Red'.

After the inevitable briefings and lifeboat practise the ships were ready to depart. 8th Middlesex on the *George Wythe* were ready to set sail on 19 June.

---

3   Lieutenant Colonel M Crawford papers, reference no. 5471, Imperial War Museum.

Pilot came aboard and we set sail at 1100 hrs. Had to go into a lock where the troops threw any remaining English money over the side to small children on either side of lock. It is reputed by a policeman watching that they are making £2 to £3 a day. Into the river, had to drop anchor quick, could not make out why. Picked up another pilot and sailed down river until we reached Southend at 1600 hrs where we found a huge convoy collecting. Our captain was taken away to see the captain which means we will sail tonight. Convoy formed up at 1830 hrs and sailed at 1900 hrs, very interesting to watch coast of county of Kent which we knew well also forts which we had seen often out to sea. Went to bed at 2300hrs as it was dark and could see very little, although Spear wanted to watch us go through the Straits of Dover. Apparently we missed a good spectacle as Jerry guns opened fire on convoy. We were awakened by destroyer coming alongside asking from a loudspeaker if we had any casualties, fortunately the answer was no. So went asleep again. One of the M.T. ships in the convoy was hit and set on fire and it had to leave and put into Dover.

June 20th

Everyone slightly relieved, as we continue sailing along hugging the south coast of Britain. The captain and crew of the George Wythe being yanks did not cooperate or mix at all with us, terrific struggle to get permission for officers to use boat deck. Definitely no one allowed to use ship's officers' shower baths. Convoy turned south at 1400 hrs and we expected to see coast of Normandy at 1700 hrs, however strong NE. wind got up making the sea quite choppy, and this delayed us until 2200 hrs when we arrived in the middle of of the Navy, battleships, cruisers, monitors, destroyers. All engaged on shelling the Huns, drawn up like a Spithead Review. A most impressive spectacle. There is no doubt that we must have complete supremacy in the air. Sailed right through the fleet, saw the Rodney and dropped anchor about a mile from the coast. Too heavy a sea running for us to disembark.[4]

Lieutenant Colonel Crawford's temper probably did not improve as his unit was to spend a further 72 hours on the *George Wythe* until the rough seas began to die down. Most soldiers were able to disembark almost immediately on arrival off Normandy. But even for the follow on waves there were still many hazards on the beaches that had not yet been cleared, the large underwater craters in particular meant disembarkation should not be taken lightly. Ken Tout, who was commanding a small Stuart tank belonging to his regiment's reconnaissance troop, recalls his landing at Le Hamel on 15 June:

We are the first tank to roll off the ship, but in front of us the single truck must disembark. An American sailor in black, glistening thigh-boots ambles down the ship's ramp. Walks cautiously into the sea. Anti-climax! The surge of tiny breakers hardly reaches his knees. He walks out a yard or two. Splashes around the sea, still some hundred yards or so from dry sand. He waves the lorry to descend.

The three-tonner quickly gathers speed down the steep ramp and hits the water with an explosion of spray which douses the American guide. The lorry runs on a few yards into the sea. And disappears!

We sit at the top of the ramp, Johnny's hands about to release our own brakes, my mouth ready to give the order. We gape at the swirling waters where the three-tonner was. Just a yard or two away the American seaman stands, only up to his shins in water which has swallowed a large truck. Two frightened faces appear in the water at his side and start swimming for life.

---

4   Ibid.

The American hauls them out and they too stand shin deep in the still rippling water.

The American slides his boots tentatively forward. Moves in a circle, a huge circle round the watery grave of the truck. Comes back up the ramp. 'There's a deep crater. Must be a mine crater, ' he yells to me. 'Will go see if the captain can move off and come in again further along the beach.' But in a moment or two he's back again. 'Captain says tide is turning soon. No time to back out and come in again. Have to try it. Come down slowly, carefully. It's your skin!'

Our engine is still running, throwing up blue fumes in the faces of the tanks and seamen around and behind us. I explain over the I/C to Johnny. 'Bloody Hell!' he exclaims 'We didn't waterproof for fifty feet of water. Can I get out and walk, mate?'

The American in his thigh-high, thigh–dry boots, is again standing in the shallow water, indicating ominously with his right hand. Johnny, the fastest and most reckless of drivers, eases the gear sticks with the tenderness of a surgeon assisting a complicated birth. We begin to roll. Faster. Still faster. Too fast. Far too fast. 'Hold it, Johnny! Hold it! Right hand down! NOW! Hard!'

We hit the water crab-wise. Tilt and skid. Swinging right. Not quickly enough. Tilting and swinging. Tilting more and swinging harder. The American seaman backs away frantically. Then we are heading right, heading across the bows of the ship, away from the deep hole, driving for the beach. And the high booted American guide already turns away from us and fixes his attention on the mighty Sherman sliding down the ramp behind us. In front of us a chain of impatient marshals ('Beach marshals, not field marshals,' I think frivolously) waves and waves and waves us on. Don't stop! Hurry! Keep moving! Get off the beach!' Their mouthed words are unheard but the intention is clear.[5]

Whilst the majority of soldiers would deploy as part of a unit with the comforting presence of comrades and familiar organisation around them, others would deploy as individual reinforcements. In these circumstances the Army can seem an unfriendly place and the soldier is starkly reminded that he is a tiny cog in a very big machine. Major Martin Lindsay was summoned from England to deploy as a replacement for the one of the casualties in the 51st Highland Division. After sailing from Southampton he arrived at Gold Beach on 14 July:

We left the Prince Albert in a tank landing craft which steered for a large white pole not unlike a polo goalpost. At the foot of it a notice informed us that this desolate piece of featureless sand was King Beach. Stranded on the shore were several burnt-out craft which had blown up on land mines and a few tanks which bogged themselves in the heavy, clay-like sand. The only beach official appeared to be an elderly captain crouching like a cave-dweller in a lean-to made from ration boxes and tarpaulin sheets…

… I jumped a lift in a passing truck and came to a much knocked-about village, and there I found Ian Mackenzie, who had crossed with me, in a group of officers. We asked about the fighting which had lately taken place. Then one of them said, 'Fifteenth Scottish Division is attacking tonight. They cross the start line at 1 a.m.' This was a nasty shock for Ian, as his posting is to a Highland Light Infantry battalion in that division. He hurried off to the town major's office to try to borrow a jeep, and I felt sorry for him being pitched into a night attack within an hour or two of joining.[6]

---

5   Tout, Ken, *Tanks, Advance!* (London: Robert Hale, 1987), pp.31-32.
6   Lindsay, Martin, *So Few Got Through* (London: Collins, 1946), pp.9-11.

As the soldiers advanced further inland they would have become acutely aware of the various dangers that existed in the Normandy beachhead. Shelling was in many ways the most destructive danger that faced individuals. It could come with little warning and could be highly lethal. Artillery and mortar fire was often fired speculatively by the Germans and large buildings, gullies, major roads were all routinely fired upon by their artillery. Battery Sergeant Major A H Lacey of 7th Field Regiment Royal Artillery recalls the particular danger of loitering around crossroads, a favourite German target.

> I returned to the cross roads at LION SUR MER and noticed that the Rook flag I had planted at the cross roads had been blown up. Remembering a warning 'Keep off cross roads' I retired to the doorway of a wooden chapel about one hundred yards from the cross roads. A couple of minutes later I saw about six Commandos standing on the cross roads pushing the bolts of their rifles backwards and forwards and then 'Crash'. The British Army had lost 6 good men, as I saw them being pulled to the side of the road.[7]

Soldiers became very adept at listening for the sound of approaching shells and mortar fire, taking cover as soon as they heard them. Soldiers would feel distinctly unsafe out of their slit trench. Even between bombardments, they would make sure they kept a keen eye on the nearest available trench when moving around and were ready take a running or standing jump into it should they hear incoming rounds. Captain Hal Foster recalls an O Group given by the CO of 1st Dorsets, Lieutenant Colonel 'Speedy' Bredin:

> Rather than have us come to Battalion HQ he had set up a chair with a small umbrella to protect against the sun…As we gathered round most, I think, noted one single three-foot deep' slit trench nearby…The O group had just nicely started when the first Jerry 'range' shot came in, followed by a pretty fair stonk of the area. In my own case I was second from the top as we hit the one trench. When the stonk lifted we sheepishly crawled out of our cover to find 'Speedy' sitting under his umbrella (a little paler) and saying, 'Well, gentlemen, now that is over shall we resume?'[8]

Captain Jocelyn Pereira of 5th Coldstream Guards recalls his first experience of shelling when his unit took over a position at St Mauxvieux. His account illustrates how prolonged and wearing German artillery and mortar bombardments could be:

> We sat there amid an air of uneasy expectancy; then suddenly I heard a distant umph, umph, umph, umph. Everyone in the open scuttled into trenches and something came singing through the air with a high pitched 'eeeeee' that ended in a sort of angry 'ssst' and a CRRUMP, CRRUMP, CRRUMP, CRRUMP, as four shells landed in the field just behind us. More came over, landing all-round us. And even though the fragments went sizzling over our heads the deafening detonation of each shell seemed to have a force that nothing could stop and concussions hit you almost as though the shell had been right on top of one. It was the most frightening thing that ever happened to me. I didn't want to die just then, just like that, and to sit there seemed to be like a sentence of death. The air was full of smoke and fumes. Someone shouted out for stretcher-bearers, and a more lightly wounded man went limping away towards the R.A.P. with another helping him along. His ashen-white face streamed with

7   Major General N P H Tapp papers, reference no. 11423, Imperial War Museum.
8   Smith, Wilfred, *Codeword CANLOAN* (Toronto & Oxford: Dundurn Press, 1992), p.93.

Figure 10.2 Lance Corporal Peter Chimilar of the Canadian Provost Corps placing a warning sign by the side of the road, Haut-Mesnil, 14 August. (Lieut. Donald I. Grant, Library and Archives Canada, PA-131267)

sweat and he looked as though the shock had left him half-unconscious groping for he knew not what. Grimly we went on discussing the position. I was surprised to find that I could mark up the map with a steady hand; it was not at all a reflection of how I felt.

It was the most unpleasant day that I ever lived through. In retrospect the shelling was not as bad as many places we were in, but at the time every step down the sun-drenched lanes seemed to be haunted by the waiting tension between each stonk. At first we hardly knew the difference between the sound of our own guns firing and the Germans.

I thought: This is barely endurable for a day; how can I go on for months and months? After a few days we learnt to recognize the sound of the German shells and could judge more or less where they were arriving. You can get used to something which is going to miss you, but a direct stonk is different: you can hardly become accustomed to a noise that may at any moment herald your death. If anything, as one gained in experience one's nerves seemed gradually to become less resilient under the strain, but the first day was the worst.[9]

Whilst bad luck played a large part in any casualties sustained by unobserved, speculative harassing shellfire, the closer a soldier got to the front line, the more likely he was to come under the far more lethal enemy observed indirect fire. The riskiest moment in these circumstances would frequently occur when soldiers were moving and were therefore without the benefit of cover immediately to hand. Major Martin Lindsay was frequently responsible for moving his troops

---

9   Pereira, Jocelyn, *A Distant Drum*, (Aldershot: Gale & Polden, 1948), pp.10-11.

from one position to another. Throughout his diary he rightly stresses his concern over whether the enemy are in a position to be able to observe such movements. On 15 August his battalion was ordered to occupy the village of Glatigny and he set off with a small reconnaissance party to select areas for his companies to occupy:

> Glatigny seemed to be under enemy observation because first the tanks on the far side of the village and then the village itself, just after we had entered it, got heavily and accurately shelled, though I was hanged if I could see where the observation was from, unless it was a village, one of the many Le Mesnils, on the left. I took some of my party down a lane running along a ridge leading out of the village. Suddenly there was the usual whistle in crescendo which signalled a covey of shells on the way. With one accord we all lay flat and heard them landing all-round us. Then there was a particularly loud crack as a shell burst twelve feet away – I paced out the distance later. I thought it was in the road beside me, for the dust was such that we were in pitch darkness for what seemed a minute, and our nostrils were choked with gunpowder – or whatever the bursting charge may be – so that it was some hours before I could rid myself of the acrid smell. I could hear somebody whimpering in the darkness behind me and Donald Howorth shouting, 'Lie still, you bloody fool.' When I could see I found that the Signal Sergeant, Rae, was dead, and the R.S.M. Thomson, slightly wounded in the head but bleeding profusely, and Howorth was tying him up. He himself had a few punctures in his thigh. Only Petrie, second-in-command of C Company, and myself were untouched.
>
> I went back along the track to where there were, most conveniently, some empty slits dug by 2nd Seaforths, who had just moved out. I told the company commanders to put their men into them, and that we would not occupy Glatigny until dark as I thought it was under enemy observation.[10]

The protection a slit trench gave meant that many soldiers regarded their shovel or entrenching tool as important an item of equipment as their weapon. Digging in would not only provide protection from German shelling but also from the nightly Luftwaffe air raids. Although these air raids were not sufficient to seriously threaten the overall invasion, they could have a serious local effect. Major Martin Lindsay recalls the chaos caused by one particular night raid on 19 July, as well as his disgust at a unit that had failed to dig in properly:

> At 11 pm just as I was going to meet them, we had an air-raid. They came over low and lit up the whole countryside with dazzling clusters of parachute flares. Our A.A. was pretty ineffective and we had no nightfighters up. They dropped five bombs very close to this farmhouse and two officers in my small advance party were hit. I am afraid that Gilchrist's wound is a spinal one, but the other fellow is all right. We lay on the floor of the dining room for the first one or two, then ran outside to a dug-out.
>
> When all was quiet again I went to look for the Battalion, but missed them as they had been sent another way owing to the road being blocked by burning transport. Some artillery ammunition trucks had been hit and set on fire and the shells kept exploding. I had a nightmare ride on the back of a motor-bike, and was upset and annoyed to find that neither I nor the driver had a field dressing when some gunners at the roadside stopped us and asked for some. Eventually, tired, cross and sweating, I found the Battalion, and the guides led the companies and transport off into the areas we had chosen. Then a young and rather shaken officer of the Fife and Forfar Yeomanry arrived to ask for assistance. Their A echelon had

---

10 Lindsay, Martin, *So Few Got Through* (London: Collins, 1946), pp.50-51.

Figure 10.3 German artillerymen load a Nebelwerfer 15cm multi-barrelled rocket launcher, June 1944. (Bundesarchiv, Bild 101I-299-1821-27A, photo: Scheck).

caught it badly in the bombing and three officers had been killed, wounded or missing. None of them had dug slit-trenches. Incredible – and in the fifth year of the war! One would say it served them right were it not such a tragedy.[11]

Whilst shelling and bombing could affect all within the beachhead, the closer one got to the frontline the more apparent other threats became. Snipers were a constant menace in forward areas and 'sniper scares' a frequent occurrence. Many commanders pointed out to their soldiers that the individual was not a trained sniper per se but far more likely to be a simple rifleman, who having been left behind by his withdrawing unit, hoped to 'bag' an important target rather than immediately surrender. Whatever the case commanders were an attractive target, as Keith Jones recalled whilst travelling through Cheux in his small Humber scout car during Operation EPSOM:

A brigade LO drove back along the line of vehicles, warning each crew that the place harboured snipers. Thinking that among the buildings it was also easy to lob grenades I slid the front hatch of the Humber closed over Nobby's head, unlatched and slammed home all pistol ports, while Nobby eased down his visor to the bullet-proof glass block. I had stowed my map board, grabbed my steel helmet from the radio top and regained my seat, which I was about to lower, when I noticed that our wheels were awash in water as we bumped into the 'street' past the first grey stone building. I watched to see if the water was going to get any deeper, pondering what might have caused the flood (a damaged water tower or pump? water used to fight the fires?), when a sudden swipe past my ear that stung the whole cheek reinforced the crack of a single shot. A neat round hole had appeared in the Bren-gun butt clamped in front of my head.

---

11 Ibid., pp.21-22.

My thinking slowed to a snail's pace, questioning whether the hole had been there earlier. Unbelievingly I turned to see if some chump behind had accidentally loosed off a round. That act woke me up, because every vehicle in view was closed down tight. My own seat went down with a bump. I pulled the hatch to above my dreamy head, replacing the infantry–style steel helmet on the radio top as the car lurched on through the village.[12]

German sniping activity would usually illicit an anti-sniping patrol or some other response from the British soldiers. Lieutenant Colonel Leach, recalls snipers around 5th Royal Horse Artillery's gun batteries during operations near Villers Bocage:

During the afternoon [14 June] the enemy harassed two guns with shelling, mortaring and snipers. This caused a steady drain of casualties to men and vehicles. The snipers were a perpetual nuisance as they could dominate the whole area, but they caused surprisingly few casualties.

Many hunts took place. The C.O. was determined to capture one sniper whom he had spotted and after a careful stalk was somewhat surprised to capture his own signal officer who was hunting a sniper. The American L.O. and a gunner from G Battery had a competition to see who could hit a sniper first at 400 yards. Little did they know that the truck on which they were lying was carrying 300 gallons of petrol. The gunner won with his second shot.[13]

Mines would also prove to be a problem in the forward areas. The Germans had sown a variety of mines and though many would be quickly cleared as the Allies advanced others would take longer to uncover and disarm, making travel near the frontline a hazardous affair. Major Martin Lindsay was aware of the danger mines posed, yet it was not sufficient to prevent him from becoming a casualty in Belgium.

Yesterday I was sent to recce a concentration area in some woods, but before choosing one I had to be sure that there was a good track forward for vehicles. I noticed that there were sandbags on the floor of the jeep on my side, but none on the driver's. I asked Macdonald why this was so, and he replied that he had taken them out to clean the car. 'You drivers always have a good excuse for having no sandbags, but one day you may well be sorry,' I growled at him splenetically.

The Derbyshire Yeomanry had been through all these woods. We started to drive down a ride and I told Macdonald to stick to the tracks of the armoured cars. A few minutes later there was a blinding yellow flash with a deafening bang, and I found myself sitting on my bottom in the middle of the sandy track, a jeep's length behind. I was still clutching my map. I glanced quickly at my feet and was glad to see that they were both still there. I shouted: 'Are you all right?' and was relieved when Macdonald answered: 'Yes,' after a whimper or two. I got slowly on to my legs and hobbled over to the jeep, to satisfy myself that no limb was missing, though he had obviously broken something as he was in pain and could not move. The whole of the front of the jeep was wrecked. In half an hour it would be dark, and I was now terrified of being benighted in the woods. In my dazed condition it seemed as if life itself depended upon getting 500 yards to a main cross-track. I felt sick and there was a horrid acrid smell of the powder exploding charge in my nostrils, ears and hair. But worst of all was the stiffness in my legs; my trousers were torn and bloodstained and I felt as if somebody had slashed me across the shins with a crowbar.

---

12 Jones, Keith, *Sixty-Four Days of A Normandy Summer* (London: Robert Hale, 1990), pp.35-36.
13 Lieutenant Col L R Leach papers, 17201, Imperial War Museum.

When I came in sight of the corner I saw a jeep and shouted. Roddy Sinclair, the Brigadier, was in it, and never have I been more pleased to see anybody. At that moment some Derbyshire Yeomanry arrived, and we sent them down the track to rescue Macdonald. By the time we reached the Klooster my legs had stiffened up considerably and I had to be carried down the steps to the R.A.P. in the cellar. I was annoyed to find that I have a few small punctures in the front of each shin, a few inches below the knee.[14]

Those travelling in heavy armour such as tanks would normally survive an encounter unscathed though the vehicle might shed a track or wheel. Smaller armoured vehicles such as Bren carriers however could be easily overmatched by German mines. In August, Reginald Fendick was travelling in one of his platoon's carriers near the Alliere River. His carrier was the leading vehicle of the MMG company who were being sent forward to help consolidate a recently captured objective:

From the bridge, we went up narrow, tree-lined lanes and came to a drive through the grounds of a small château. The RAP of the East Yorks was just setting up in a cellar of the Château, and I paused and had a word with the MO, to ask him if there had been any mine clearing along the way yet. He thought a party of Sappers had gone along the drive a short time before, so I motored on. The drive ended at a 'T' with a secondary road, and I directed Sailor Seaman, my driver to turn left, to get to the nearby main road which went up the ridge to our objective. Sailor swung a little wide on the turn, so the right track went partly onto the verge. I was standing, leaning forward over the front, actually looking for signs of mines in the road as we turned. I remember very clearly feeling a gentle puff of wind on the right side of my face, and my lights went out. What follows is known to me only from what I was told later.

A double-set Teller mine (that is, two mines set one on top of the other, so they went off simultaneously) went off under the right front bogie of the carrier. It ripped the floor of the carrier wide open, peeling the steel like a banana skin back over my seat, which was just behind me as I stood. It cut Sailor off at the waist and he was killed instantly. I was thrown high into the air, and landed flat on my back, several yards up the road, in which there were more mines buried…but I didn't hit any of them. By O'Dowd and Bert Barrett, who were in the back of the carrier, were badly shocked, but not wounded, and they crawled out. Someone, I think Bob Boyle, came up and checked me, and I am told that I spoke to him and asked him to help me up. But I have no recollection of that. They took all the kit off the wreck, got me on a stretcher, and took me with O'Dowd and Bert back to the East York's RAP, which we'd just passed. Sailor was buried nearby, and then John Milne took 1 Platoon under his wing and they went on with their job.[15]

The dangers posed by mines, shells, mortars and small arms could easily unnerve individuals particularly those exposed to them for the first time. Battery Sergeant Major A H Lacey of 7th Regiment Royal Artillery recalls one such individual on Sword Beach.

The ramp was down and the self-propelled guns were moving off on to the beach before we realized it, but our S.P refused to start and we were left alone on the craft for a period of about four minutes. During this period, a Hun bearing malice towards the Reconnaissance Party, started to stop us with machine gun fire. The slogan was 'Heads Down'. Serjeant Wheatley

14 Lindsay, Martin, *So Few Got Through* (London: Collins, 1946), pp.118-119.
15 Fendick, R F, *A CANLOAN Officer* (Buxton: MLRS Books, 2008), pp.94-95.

said 'I can see him'. I replied 'Shall I lift my head?' but he replied 'No, just lift your eyebrows 'cos those tracers are about two feet from your head.' Regardless of his warning I looked up and saw on our right flank the machine gun firing from the upper storey of a house beyond the range of our Sten guns, and to my amazement and disgust a Bombardier of the 33rd Field Regiment was crouching in the turret of the S.P. instead of manning the Browning, which was his duty as No 2 on the gun. I ordered him to man the Browning and silence the machine gunner and the lame reply was 'I am sorry sir, I am only supposed to fire at aircraft with the Browning'. However much I shouted at him and called him a windy bastard, I could not induce him to tackle the job. The situation was made healthier, however, by one of the sailors on our craft, who gave the Hun a real good straffing with his Oerlikon gun, and we heard no more from that quarter.[16]

In these circumstances it was up to leaders to grip the individual concerned. Lieutenant D H McWilliams recalls just such an occasion with one of the soldiers in his unit, 9th Cameron Highlanders, at the beginning of operation EPSOM:

It appeared that one of the two or three reinforcements who had recently arrived, presumably to replace the LOBs, was unwilling to accompany us on our date with destiny, and had refused to don his equipment or 'pick up his musket'. This was serious, because the maintenance of morale at that point was vital and 'one bad apple etc. etc.' I found the individual (by our standards, pretty mature and certainly over thirty) standing among an interested gathering of Jocks, who were no doubt wondering what 'Big Bill' (the nickname which the Jocks had awarded me, hopefully as a mark of 'acceptance') would do. I began with the sweet voice of reason and persuasion, but found that to have no effect. Although the recalcitrant was both apologetic and polite, he professed himself quite unable to face what was to come. Whereupon, I dropped the mask and, remembering that an officer must 'get hold of his men', that is literally what I did, seizing him bodily, cramming him into his equipment and forcing his rifle into his hand. Having read subsequently what General Patton said during the famous 'slapping incident' in Italy, I recall my own choice of words as being remarkably similar. Meanwhile the Jocks made supportive noises. In retrospect, I am not particularly proud of the incident, but still cannot see any practical alternative at that stage in our preparations.[17]

Convincing frightened soldiers to accept the constant danger was a tall order, but to their credit many soldiers did respond to such leadership and stuck it out. Geoffrey Picot of 1st Royal Hampshires describes one such individual:

One evening one of my sergeants told me that a private – let us call him George – wanted to see me. I had noticed him in a slit trench many a time, meek, dumb and expressionless. He told me he could stand it no longer, and said he wanted to get back into a building and rest for a few nights. I had every sympathy with him, but had I sent him back and put him on a supply vehicle every other chap whose nerve was beginning to fail would say he too could stand it no longer and could he be sent back behind the line? And soon I would have no platoon left. Boredom, loss of nerve, bomb happiness had to be fought and overcome. I spoke quietly to George and said he must stick it out. He said he couldn't. I said he had to, and that had to be that.

16 Major General N P H Tapp papers, Reference No. 11423, Imperial War Museum.
17 ID H McWilliams (9th Cameron Highlanders) papers, Reference No. 15132, Imperial War Museum.

He went back to his position, and stayed there. He stuck it out. Months afterwards, when conditions were much happier, I was amazed at the change in him. The dumb, listless face now wore a small contented one, more happy and confident.[18]

For many soldiers continuous exposure to danger began to blunt their combat effectiveness even if they had been able to stand up well initially. Stanley Whitehouse noted how his own spirits steadily reduced as the campaign in North-West Europe progressed:

About this time I began to experience more acute symptoms of 'bomb happiness', or 'shell shock' as it was called in the earlier Great War. I had been in the line now almost continuously, for more than six months and as week succeeded week I was having to dig deeper and deeper into those innermost resources of resolution, endurance and zeal to combat the gnawing, nagging fearfulness that filled my waking, and often sleeping, hours. As the campaign progressed I came to realize that for all the enemy's skill and doggedness he was more easily overcome than my troubled, tortured mind. I had long since forsaken that spirit of adventure, that devil-may-care attitude that had sustained me in the early days, when mates all around me were being killed and horribly maimed, and the whiplash of the murderous Spandau and the crunch of the mortars had men quivering in the bottom of their 'slitters'.[19]

Major Lindsay also began to notice a similar effect not just on himself, but others who had also been able to perform well at earlier periods of the campaign or indeed war:

In the last hour I have been reading a Sunday Times review of Moran's 'Anatomy of Courage.' It quotes his theory that courage must be husbanded. 'Courage is willpower, whereof no man has unlimited stock, and when in war it is used up, he is finished. A man's courage is his capital and he is always spending.' How right he is! I can think of an officer with a M.C. and Bar and several N.C.O.s with M.Ms who bear this out. They were all decorated for fine leadership in North Africa and Sicily and must presumably have been the pick of the Battalion. The officer was finished before he was killed and the N.C.O.s – the few that remain – are virtually useless to-day. They have all had to carry on far too long. I can quote my own case too. Until a month or two ago, though I hated being shelled, I used positively to look forward to the thrill of battle. Now, though I have not yet got to the stage of dreading an action, I get no pleasure out of it and look forward to end of the war.[20]

Surviving enemy fire was difficult enough for the frontline soldier, but on top of this he also had to perform his operational duties and endure the austere environment. As ever those nearest the frontline, especially the infantry, bore the greatest discomforts and hardships. Lieutenant Sydney Jary recalls the challenges of living in squalid conditions:

One felt and was dirty and in the small hours of the morning, with boot laces cutting into swollen feet, a foul-tasting mouth and an aching stomach, life had little to commend it. The dirt and discomfort worried me more than the danger. Danger, for some reason that I have never understood, exhilarates. But despite every effort to keep clean, it did not always prove

18 Picot, Geoffrey, *Accidental Warrior* (Lewes: Book Guild, 1993), p.89.
19 Whitehouse, Stanley & Bennett, George, *Fear is the Foe: A Footslogger from Normandy to the Rhine* (London, Robert Hale, 1988), p.125.
20 Lindsay, Martin, *So Few Got Through* (London: Collins, 1946), p.13.

possible, and that was unbearable. Never once since have I not been grateful to sink into a hot bath or slide into a bed with clean sheets. We went to extraordinary lengths to keep dirt at bay... Once, in Normandy, I washed and shaved in the rainwater in the deep ruts made by carts. Afterwards I discovered that, four hundred yards away, the opposition had been over-looking my ablutions: a decent lot, who obviously approved of personal hygiene.

The Platoon seldom went unshaven and never once did I have to reprimand a man for uncleanliness. Their personal standards avoided the lice which plagued the Germans. In some exposed positions, which were either close to the enemy or under clear observation, our natural functions were severely inhibited. Newspaper or food cans were our resort, but they brought their own disadvantages. Throwing a newspaper containing excreta from a slit trench could produce dire consequences not only from the enemy but also, in Normandy, from the summer's heat. In these circumstances we tried to become nocturnal animals but not always with success.[21]

Those who occupied positions even a short distance back from the front line found it easier to sleep, keep clean and carry out their various ablutions. Some, such as Major Robert Kiln, even seem to have relished certain aspects of outdoor living:

On the gun positions, or where we were in settled position, proper latrines were always dug. These consisted of a deep narrow trench, over which one either squatted or usually sat on a pole – flat and as smooth as possible! Hygiene was rigorous, the rules were clear: never dig a latrine within thirty feet of a stream, well or river: never uphill of a water supply: always fill in afterwards and always mark the site so that the next occupiers know what to avoid.

When we were mobile, we carried entrenching tools, and each person dug his own hole and squatted. I always preferred a backrest, and would find a convenient tree, dig my hole, and then squat with a nice backrest, light my pipe and enjoy the summer morning air.[22]

Fatigue was one of the biggest trials that faced frontline soldiers, long summer days and constant operational demands resulted in chronic tiredness. Those who imagine bright eyed and fresh faced soldiers brimming with aggressive energy would be surprised by the actual reality of combatants punch drunk with lack of sleep and drained of energy. Private Stan Whitehouse describes the effect constant and deep fatigue could generate:

We patrolled, cleaned weapons, grabbed a bite and stood to when the enemy was believed to be pushing forward. At odd hours of the day and night we tried to snatch an hour's catnap before being rudely awoken for some urgent detail. Our bodies – and minds – desperately cried out for sleep, deep luxurious sleep, away from the ear-splitting, nerve shattering noise all around us. So great was our need for rest that we dozed off whenever we stopped moving. The problem was alleviated to some extent when one platoon from each company was sent back over the canal during the day to rest up in some empty houses. It was heavenly stretching out on dry, bare floorboards instead of enduring cramp, pins and needles and other tortures huddled in a tiny, cold, damp 'slitter'.[23]

---

21 Jary, Sydney, *18 Platoon* (Winchester: The Rifles, 2009) pp.70-71.

22 Kiln, Major Robert, *D-Day to Arnhem with Hertfordshire's Gunners* (Welwyn: Garden City, Castlemead Publications, 1993), p.127.

23 Whitehouse, Stanley and Bennett, George, *Fear is the Foe* (London: Robert Hale, 1997), p.32.

Figure 10.4 Captain W Noble of the Highland Light Infantry of Canada snatches some sleep, 20 June. (Lieut. Ken Bell, Library and Archives Canada, PA-133103)

Part of the problem in combating fatigue was the lack of routine and the uncertainty of campaigning. Even in supposedly quiet periods units could be given a new task with little warning or forced to move just as they had finished establishing a position. All units suffered from the constant uncertainty of active service to one degree or another. This was an experience that 5th/7th Gordons were very familiar with; as the humorous author of their war diary related at the time:

> The Battalion were told that there would be no move that day, this was taken as a portent by the battalion (now well trained in such matters) that we would move very shortly. Training won the day and we were ordered within half an hour to attack Grandchamp MR 418919.[24]

Despite the fatigue many soldiers were initially struck by the beauty of the Normandy countryside in high summer, though this rural idyll swiftly took on a nightmarish quality as the battle raged and destruction mounted. The smell of the countryside in particular began to take on a distinctly unpleasant form:

> We still had to move across country, avoiding roads, and we breathed in quantities of dust which strips of khaki parachute tied round our mouths and nostrils could barely keep out, and tank interiors required much housekeeping to keep clean. One thing impossible to keep out was the stench of dead cows. I am sure all Normandy veterans have firm memories of smells and odours, if not from cordite, then from putrefying animals and men. In particular, there was a special scent clinging to all things enemy – a cloyingly sickly sweet odour. Perhaps

---

24 TNA: WO 171/1301, War Diary of 5th/7th Gordons, 18 August 1944.

it was the German Army issue soap. Whatever its origin, it insinuated itself into our nostrils like the smell of cordite.[25]

Normandy's location as prime farming land, coupled with the large quantities of horse transportation that still existed in the German Army, meant that large numbers of dead, bloated and rotting cows and horses were a particular feature of the campaign. The sight of unmilked, wounded or dead animals was a familiar and depressing experience for the soldiers. Sapper Keane of 260 Field Company, Royal Engineers remembers this well:

> There had been plenty of cows about before the fighting started. Quite a number of them got killed or, had to be put down because of their injuries, so it was a common sight to see fields scattered with dead cows. Unfortunately they quickly went rotten, fermented inside and, eventually the carcasses inflated and burst. It was very important not to be around when this happened, the stench had to be experienced to be believed.
>
> I was around at one time when some farmers were putting down some injured cows, they were doing this by the old fashioned method of holding a steel spike to the animal's head and hitting it with a club hammer. One of our lads didn't hold with this primitive method and offered to shoot the next one with a revolver. This proved even worse, because, he held the gun in the wrong place and at the wrong angle and, as a result, it took several shots to kill the unfortunate animal.[26]

In addition to the dreadful smell in the air, the long hot summer and constant traffic soon turned the battlefield into a very dusty environment. For those driving vehicles or marching by the side of the road the thick billowing dust was yet another environmental hardship that had to be endured:

> During the Beachhead period, the weather was very changeable: alternating between very hot and dry, which meant heavy dust on all the tracks, and wet, which meant heavy mud in slit trenches and on roads and tracks. The soil in the beachhead area was, for the most part, quite fine and powdery, which was good for fast digging of slits, but bad for dust or mud.
>
> When it was dry, we had to wear eye-shields whenever we moved on the roads. These were plastic shields with a plastic headband, and a strip of elastic, originally issued as anti-gas protection. The eye shields folded around the side of the face and were held along the side part by two snap fasteners. They were very close fitting which was probably good to keep the dust out, but the plastic edges cut into the cheeks, and I always found them uncomfortable. By this time all anti-gas precautions had been abandoned as the threat was thought to be negligible but a few items like the lightweight oil capes and the eye-shields, were retained for personal weather protection.
>
> Nothing could keep one from breathing the dust. We always felt guilty if we had to move on a dry dusty track where the rifle regiments were marching along, as our dust caused them acute discomfort and we couldn't help it.[27]

The dust was not simply a discomfort. German observers were well practised at spotting the dust clouds thrown up by a travelling vehicle and then swiftly bringing down artillery or mortar

---

25 Hammerton, Ian, *Achtung! Minen!* (Lewes: Book Guild, 1991), p.118.
26 Sapper Keane papers, 20114, Imperial War Museum.
27 Fendick, RF, *A CANLOAN Officer* (Buxton: MLRS Books, 2008), pp.62-63.

Figure 10.5 Infantrymen of the 8th Canadian Infantry Brigade take a brief rest during their advance into Caen as a Sherman tank kicks up more dust, 18 July.
(Lieut. H. Gordon Aikman / Dept. of National Defence / Library and Archives Canada / PA-129128)

fire. Consequently there were many areas of the beachhead where large screens of hessian sacking on poles had been erected along the enemy side of roads, to mask vehicle movement from enemy view. These screens often bore signs saying 'dust brings shells' as a reminder to the fast driver. Such dangers made the problems of re-supply much harder.

Whether in defence or attack the requirement to ensure that the unit was supplied with ammunition, food and water was critical, a failure to do so could quite easily lose a battle. The tactical system of supply in the British Army rested on a series of echelons all of which would carry a certain amount of supplies. F Echelon consisted of the fighting elements of the unit, the unit's individuals and fighting vehicles (such as the Bren carriers) and they could carry a limited amount to keep going. A1 echelon was under the commanding officer's control and would be kept anywhere from 2 miles to 200 yards behind his frontline depending on the ground and the threat. A1 echelon was normally a small party of lorries and carriers, it included the medical officer's vehicle, the fitters' vehicle as well as fuel, ammunition and ration lorries. The rifle companies would normally send one or two of their vehicles, usually under the CSM, to A echelon to pick up supplies and then distribute them amongst the men. The balance of the unit's vehicles and administrative parties, which were not needed for the daily supply of the unit, were grouped under the senior administrative or 'Q' officer of the brigade and known as B echelon. This echelon consisted of vehicles such as stores lorries, office lorries and so forth. In order to keep the battalion resupplied the A or B echelon vehicles would travel between the various Royal Army Service Corps supply points for ammunition, rations and fuel known as Delivery Points, here they would draw the unit's daily requirements.

The unit's Quartermaster and his staff were key to the running of this system and a good QM was worth his weight in gold. It would be his efforts and those of the company quartermaster

Figure 10.6 Canadian infantrymen cook supper near Authie, 9 July.
(Lieut. H. Gordon Aikman, Library and Archives Canada, PA-162681)

sergeants (CQMS) that would ensure that the company or squadron had all the supplies including ammunition, water and rations. For soldiers these issued rations were not simply a source of energy and sustenance, but a welcome, if temporary, distraction from the daily trials of life in Normandy. Major Robert Kiln describes the rations that were supplied to his gunners:

> Our rations consisted of the '14 man pack'; this was a box about two feet by nine inches, which contained a complete diet for fourteen men for a day or seven men for two days and there were six different menus. They were really superb; mostly tinned or dried food; but of excellent variety. Army biscuits about 2½ inches square and ½ inch thick, though some were smaller, tinned stews, steak and kidney puddings, corned beef, spam, tinned bacon, Ambrosia rice pudding, cheese, marmalade and strawberry jam remain in my memory, as well as boiled sweets, chocolate bars and of course tins of cigarettes and latrine paper.
>
> My favourites were corned beef with strawberry jam on an army biscuit, bacon and mara-malade on a biscuit, or creamed Ambrosia rice with dollops of jam. Garton Ash remembers the steak and kidney puddings and currant duff.[28]

Major Robert Kiln's enthusiasm for the quality of Army rations was not universally shared. Canadian artilleryman Major George Blackburn takes a different view and highlights some of the disadvantages of the issued rations, together with the difficulties in cooking them:

---

28 Kiln, Major Robert, *D-Day to Arnhem with Herfordshire's Gunners* (Welwyn: Garden City, Castlemead Publications, 1993) pp.126-27.

For a while at least there'll be a certain excitement in receiving a Compo box. Finding you've been given the one with the can of peaches is like winning a lottery....

...A great deal of time is spent reading directions and experimenting with methods of heating the contents of cans of 'M & V' (meat and vegetable stew), 'Steak and Kidney Pudding' (a can lined with thick dough and filled with a solidified concoction posing as chopped beef and kidney), 'Sultana Pudding' (resembling a dried out fruit cake that can be sliced and eaten cold with slices of canned cheddar), and 'Treacle Pudding' (a caramel-coated creation that is especially pleasant when warmed up). One thing you quickly learn is that if the contents of a can requires heating to be really palatable, then it must be heated through and through – something not easily accomplished in the case of the 'Steak and Kidney Pudding', due, you suspect, to the efficient insulation provided by the thick mass of dough lining the tin and surrounding the glutinous mess within.

It won't be long before repetition destroys all enjoyment of these rations, but so far Compo meals have been in some ways superior to many past meals developed by the cooks from fresh rations. A notable exception was breakfast the first morning: pre-cooked bacon. Cold it plopped out of the can in a sickly white, cylindrical blob. Heated, it turned into liquid grease, which when poured off left a pitiful residue of red strings representing the lean meat that had streaked the fused rashers.

In each box there are two tins of 'boiled sweets' (hard candies that contain no sugar), small slabs of very hard and remarkably tasteless chocolate (one per man per day) and two tins of cigarettes, one flat and one round, allowing seven cigarettes per man per day.[29]

Soldiers on the frontline would usually have to cook the rations themselves. The close proximity to the enemy meant that standard field cooking equipment was often too noisy or cumbersome to use on the frontline or simply not available at all. Most soldiers used the Benghazi Cooker or Burner. This was simply an empty metal container filled with sand and doused with petrol. When the sand was lit the cooker would produce plenty of heat but it did deposit greasy black soot on everything within range and the burning time was always unpredictable. Despatch Rider Raymond Mitchell describes the disadvantages and hazards of these home-made cookers:

It was frustrating for a cook to see the flames of his cooker starting to plop out just as the water for making tea was coming to the boil and this sometimes goaded him into acting rashly. The prudent thing was to wait patiently until the sand had cooled down or at least drag the hot stove outside before refuelling, but some cooks poured petrol on the hot sand. The inevitable result was a grey mist of petrol vapour flowing over the galley floor (we were surprised to learn that it was heavier than air) and with other stoves burning nearby, there would be a panic evacuation until a massive WHOOOOMP signalled that the freshly-fuelled stove had been rekindled by a neighbour. Few cooks in the forward areas had any eyebrows.[30]

For many soldiers some form of centralised cooking was occasionally available, the Army Catering Corps' role in boosting morale should not underestimated and the Army took great pains to deploy cooks as far forward as possible. The cooks would free the soldiers from the burden of cooking their own meals and ensure that wherever and whenever possible frontline soldiers enjoyed a centrally cooked meal such as a stew or breakfast. These were often brought forward by the CQMS in thermos containers if the operational circumstances dictated. Such sound

29 Blackburn, George, *The Guns of Normandy* (London: Constable 1998), p.48-49.
30 Mitchell, Raymond, *Commando Despatch Rider* (Barnsley: Pen & Sword, 2001), p.73.

administration paid dividends, particularly in the later winter months where the energy a hot meal delivered was literally life saving. Although frequently deployed on the frontline Lieutenant Reginald Fendick's MMG Platoon was lucky enough to have a dedicated platoon cook, something for which his men were clearly very grateful.

> In an MG platoon we had our own platoon cook, in our case Pte C Bennett of the Army Catering Corps, so we always did as well or better than any other infantry. Because we were a small body, 30-odd men at full strength, often less, we usually had an abundance of rations, not to mention what we were to pick up locally from abandoned farms. And Bennett was a real expert at making even the plainest food attractive.
>
> He was always up close with the platoon, never further back than the carriers. Subject to the battle situation, there was hot tea at stand-to in the morning, a good hot breakfast, regular meals through the day, usually topped off with some kind of snack, and tea during the evening and for sentries being relieved during the night. Even during hot periods of action, Bennett usually managed to whip up something, and the drivers would bring it up to the guns. On more than one occasion he set up his cooker close behind the gun line, and the chaps would pick up their grub during breaks in firing.[31]

Unsurprisingly tea was one of the major props of the British soldier's morale. CANLOAN officer Reginald Fendick describes tea as 'a necessity for my British lads'. Sadly he comments that the pressed blocks his platoon was issued made 'poor weak tea', Major George Blackburn's criticism of compo tea is even harsher:

> Unquestionably, the feature of Compo rations destined to be remembered beyond all others is Compo tea: tea made from tea leaves already mixed with powdered milk and powdered sugar. Directions say to 'sprinkle powder on heated water and bring to boil stirring well, three heaped teaspoons to one pint of water'
>
> Every possible variation in the preparation of this tea is being tried, but so far it always ends up the same way. While still too hot to drink, it is a good-looking cup of strong tea. Even when it becomes just cool enough to be sipped gingerly, it is still a good tasting cup of tea, if you like your tea strong and sweet. But let it cool enough to be quaffed and enjoyed, and your lips will be coated with a sticky scum that forms across the surface, which if left undisturbed will become a leathery membrane that can be wound around your finger and flipped away.[32]

Efforts would frequently be made to improve the Compo rations. Sometimes this was simply through experimentation and imagination. Reginald Fendick recalls with evident satisfaction meeting a number of officers 'who'd been with 1/7th Middlesex in North Africa. They taught me to make a very good steamed pudding out of crushed Compo biscuits in lieu of flour, with marmalade, raisins, chocolate, etc. It was steamed in a bit of cloth hung over boiling water in a Compo biscuit tin.'[33] On other occasions the rations were best improved through acquisition of local produce, a practise that would not only test the British soldier's linguistic skills, but allowed them to supplement their rations with eggs, milk and even cheese. Some of the French cheeses, particularly the local produced Camembert, proved a little too much for the 1944 soldier's palate. John Foley describes how his tank troop resolved the issue of Camembert:

---

31 Fendick, RF, *A CANLOAN Officer* (Buxton: MLRS Books, 2008), p.60.
32 Blackburn, George, *The Guns of Normandy* (London: Constable 1998), p.50.
33 Fendick, RF, *A CANLOAN Officer* (Buxton: MLRS Books, 2008), p.100.

One of the things which surprised me most was the speed with which Five Troop acquired a degree of fluency in Norman French. Westham and Hunter (between whom a surprisingly cordial friendship had sprung up) would go off with a couple of tins of date pudding. At the first farmhouse Hunter would address Madame in passable Grammar School French, only to receive a curt shake of the head. But Henry Westham would proffer one of the tins with a broad smile and something that sounded like 'Aaves voo dayz erf, silver plate?' and at once be inundated with fresh eggs and delicious Camembert cheeses. Funny thing, none of the troop liked the peculiar tang of the fluid Camembert cheese, but they never returned from one of their foraging expeditions without bringing one for me. Usually it was handed over with some touching little speech like: 'You 'ave this. Then there'll be more eggs for us.[34]

Whilst much of the food would be legitimately purchased or bartered, many soldiers would freely help themselves to unguarded items or animals. The slaughtered animals that scattered the countryside were routinely butchered and provided occasional fresh (and not so fresh) meat. At other times the looting of abandoned French homes took place, this was a serious military offence though many in positions of authority, such as Major Martin Lindsay, overlooked such transgressions:

We had a good dinner to-night: rabbit and some excellent white wine. Somebody had obtained a four-gallon container of this from a drunken Canadian in exchange for a Gordon cap-badge which the Quartermaster will replace. 'Scrappy' Hay, who commands 5-7th Gordons in this Brigade, came in afterwards. He said that his view of foraging is that he just doesn't enquire what happens to rabbits and hens in unoccupied farms. There is a story of a dialogue between a staff officer and a Gordon who was plucking a fowl, as follows:
S.O., 'You know you will be shot if anybody sees you with that hen?'
Gordon, 'Well, Sir, we mae git shot ony time so it maks nae difference.'
S.O. (disgusted), 'I suppose you are one of those desert fellows.'[35]

Soldiers might have been restrained from looting French homes but the capture of significant German garrisons provided considerable, unhindered opportunities for looting. The fall of the German Fort at Le Havre is one such example, as the 5th/7th Gordons war diarist records:

The capture of the Fort seemed to be a very stiff proposition and it was not until late morning that a decision, as to how this was to be accomplished was taken. This decision was taken owing to an ammunition dump blowing up and making a breach in the very solid wall of the Fort. What caused the explosion is not known, but it was thought that it was unlikely that the enemy did it himself. The possibility of one of our mortar bombs having a lucky hit was more probable.
'D' Coy (Major L.I.G McLean) was ordered to take the Fort and in support they had the Div artillery, 'C' Squadron 144 RAC, Flails, AVRE's and Crocodiles. The whole attack was laid on for 1600 hours. Everything was ready, and just as the assault was to be launched, rather dramatically, the enemy put up the 'white flag'.
The affair now took on a very different complexion and 'D' Coy who were preparing for a somewhat gory battle, modestly withdrew into the background, while senior officers who had been sitting in the comparative safety of the O.P. made a 'mad' rush to be in at the kill first.

34 Foley, John, *Mailed Fist* (St Albans: Granada, 1975), p.49.
35 Lindsay, Martin, *So Few Got Through* (London: Collins, 1946), p.25.

The hope of getting a certain amount of loot being the main incentive.

On arrival inside the Fort it was found that the garrison consisted of 7 officers and 242 O.R's.

What can only be described as rather an orgy then started. It was found that the enemy had blown up most things of value, but there were considerable stores of wines and spirits, which the F.F.I (who had appeared from nowhere), and the 'Jocks' were quick to realise. The difficulty of keeping out the F.F.I, and by this time all units in the district, was considerable. Meanwhile the garrison were all patiently waiting in the main square to surrender to someone. Order was restored and the prisoners eventually marched away.

In this connection there were two incidents worth relating.

One Officer, who went away empty handed from the fort, after repeated efforts to get past the guard, was heard to say that it was far harder to get into the Fort, when it was held by the 5/7 Gordons, than by the Germans.

Some officers were however luckier. The brigade major managed to steal five cases of champagne from a 5 cwt truck, as well as some bottles which he was able to lay his hands on in the limited time at his disposal. He went proudly back to Bde HQ with his gains, where he stated that he had procured some champagne and liqueurs for the mess. When asked what the liqueurs were, he said in all innocence 'I don't quite know what it is, but I think it is very good, and it is called ENCRE'.[36]

Though alcohol was available through official NAAFI supplies, it was only available in small quantities. Local sourcing brought easier rewards, good wine was often readily available as was the local cider, but what seems to have made the most impact, both physically and mentally, was the locally brewed apple brandy – Calvados. This drink however was not for the unwary – Lieutenant Ian Hammerton's troop had assisted a local farmer in extinguishing a fire in his farmhouse and were looking forward to a well-deserved reward:

The farmer was naturally delighted that his home had been saved and asked us to wait a moment while he dived into the cellar. 'Ah!' we thought, 'he's gone to get something for us.' He emerged with a small tray on which there was a tiny earthenware jug and a number of thimble sized glasses.

'The old meany,' someone muttered, with visions of tankards of cider. The thimbles were filled and handed round with many 'Mercis'. POW! What had hit us? I took only a sip but my beret nearly parted company with my head. This was my first introduction to Calvados, that notorious apple spirit.[37]

Though the power of homemade Calvados was often too much for all but the most hardened of drinkers, it was still actively sought after and consumed by a practised minority. Troop Leader Bill Bellamy recalls the dangers of its use even for strictly 'medicinal' purposes such as stemming the pain of a fellow subaltern's toothache:

The driver of the squadron ARV (armoured recovery vehicle) was a man of great resource, a skilled 'discoverer' of local produce, and Tony was one of his favourite officers. Hearing of his discomfort, he came along and offered him a mug of Calvados.

'Wash it round your mouth, sir,' he proposed, 'you'll find it better than all those medicines.'

36 TNA: WO 171/1301, War Diary of 5th/7th Gordons.
37 Hammerton, Ian, *Achtung! Minen!* (Lewes: Book Guild, 1999), p.110.

Tony did as he suggested, at first, with care taking small lady like sips and emptying the first mug slowly. A second mug was provided, as the treatment was proving beneficial, and he emptied this second mugful with remarkable speed. However, all that this achieved was an intensification of his thirst and despite my protestations a third mug was provided. He didn't manage to drink much of this as, although by now he had lost his toothache, he was as drunk as a lord. His troop sergeant and I had the greatest difficulty in restraining him from dancing off around the leaguer, singing and shouting. Eventually, the drink and the sun put him to sleep so that, to our relief, peace reigned.

Poor Tony, he woke up a few hours later, not only with raging toothache but also with a terrible head. I borrowed the squadron jeep and took him back towards the beachhead to find the dentist. They discovered an abscess under one of his teeth and I sat at the mouth of the tent while the dental officer took the offending tooth out and drained the cavity. Most impressive, I thought, to sit in the sunshine and have a tooth extracted. Tony didn't see it in quite the same light.[38]

Whilst soldiers would have to take what creature comforts they could grab whilst serving on the frontline, there were occasions when a unit might be brought out of the line for a more organised rest. On these occasions the ability to properly rest and carry out essential elements of administration was much greater. Lieutenant Stuart Hills describes the excitement that these periods out of battle would generate:

Whenever we came out of action, as we did for a while after Berjou, there was a feeling of exuberance in spite of the casualties. We did not bubble like effervescent schoolboys but we knew that for a short spell the numbness would disappear from our minds and bodies and that, for a change, we could be human beings rather than automatons of destruction. We would spend a night in delicious sleep after a hard-fought battle and rise next morning when the sun was high in the sky. We would then indulge ourselves royally with a breakfast cooked from long-preserved rations which we had not had time to touch whilst in action. We would smoke our cigarettes, talk aimlessly among ourselves, replenish our tanks and do whatever maintenance jobs were necessary. We stripped naked in the warm sunshine and washed luxuriously in pails and dixies until we shone like marble. Then we would stretch out in the sun, read, sleep or attack our correspondence. Cooking, though remained the main business of the day and given the ready availability of the local produce, I do not think I have eaten better in my life.

Sometimes when rest periods were more official, we of course had ENSA shows and organised baths. But, given good weather, what I liked most was to be left on my own. In those summer days the sun used to set very late and it was then that a good number of men used to get together for a sing-song. In my troop there was a splendid player of the accordion, Trooper Bennett. As the sun fell in the sky so we would sit around a fire, drinking our NAAFI beer ration laced with Calvados, and sing our hearts away. Occasionally I would be asked to perform and no one seemed to care how many mistakes I made or if I did not know all the words. Music is a fine thing for morale and these gatherings helped ours, as a sense of pride and well-being swelled in our chests. Many of the familiar faces had gone, but we were the men who had 'been and seen' and we were secretly proud of both the Regiment and ourselves.

It was only on late evenings such as these, when one was happy and contented, that the Army and the 'cause' meant anything to the ordinary soldier, for in battle or moments of

---

38 Bellamy, Bill, *Troop Leader* (Stroud: Sutton, 2005), pp.65-66.

Figure 10.7 Pilots of 414 Squadron RCAF relax with a game of cards. They are, left to right, Flight Lieutenant J Seaman, Flying Officer J A Roussell, Flying Officer L May (who survived baling out on 16 June 1944) and Flying Officer J Younge (who failed to return from a sortie on 6 September 1944). (Crown Copyright Air Historical Branch)

> stress, everything except concern for one's own safety was pushed into the background. And then, as darkness fell, we would slip away to our separate tanks, which stood there like huge black stones, and kip down by them, smoke our last cigarettes and sleep.[39]

If the unit was fortunate enough to be taken out of the line for more than a few days then more thorough preparations could be made. These periods should not simply be thought of as a 'holiday' as many commanders would also use them as a period to integrate battle casualty replacements, undertake some training and overhaul their equipment and vehicles more thoroughly. Lieutenant Colonel George Taylor, the CO of 5th Duke of Cornwall's Light Infantry, for example expected his companies to begin training on the second day they were pulled out of the line. The battery commanders of the Hertfordshire Yeomanry also had to balance the desire to re-charge their men's spirits with the requirement to ensure the guns were properly cleaned and serviced. This tension resulted in a fractious start to what was otherwise recalled as an idyllic period of rest at the little hamlet of St Andre, a few miles south of Bayeux. This period, which began on 19 July, was the first occasion the guns had been out of action since D-Day.

> The regiment's rest area was in a typical Norman high-hedged field next door to a small hamlet and just across the road from the 'Château'. Actually, the Château was a modest country house with a French family in residence, who had two charming daughters.
> Regimental Headquarters was naturally housed in the Château, but Claude had done well,

---

39 Hills, Stuart, *By Tank Into Normandy* (London: Collins, 2002), pp.141-142.

Figure 10.8 Infantrymen of the North Nova Scotian Highlanders celebrate their entry into Vaucelles with French wine, 20 July. (Lieut. Ken Bell, Library and Archives Canada, PA-136397)

he had taken over two small cottages; one for an Officer's Mess, one for a Sergeant's Mess and best of all, a large barn as a general Battery Mess Room and shelter. He had even got to work and collected tables and benches.

We discussed our plans, and decided that we would have a real slap-up lunch on our first day. Claude then went off to organize supplies. Various vans and lorries disappeared, to come back with good Norman beef, eggs, butter, cheese and barrels of cider. Our first lunch was to be a real treat after six weeks of tinned food, and accompanied by cider for every man.

We all settled into our area on a fine evening and slept well. I was up at 0630, with our first parade of all troops scheduled at 0800, to start maintenance and cleaning of all our guns and equipment. There were grim grey skies that morning, and a persistent wetting downpour. At 0730 I called a conference with my troop commanders and the battery sergeant-major (BSM), and decided that we would postpone the 0800 parade until the rain lifted. I could see little point in unwrapping guns and weapons only to get them wet. So all members of my battery stayed in their tents or bivouacs and I retired too to have a second cup of coffee.

At 0830 my BSM rushed in and informed me that the Colonel was approaching. Out I went, saluted smartly, and got a right old dressing down. Why weren't you on parade? He would have no slackness in his regiment. Maintenance was our first job, and if I wanted to keep my job, I had better smarten things up pronto. George Fanshawe then stormed off to the next battery to deal out the same treatment to them…

… I wondered whether I was wise to go ahead with our plans for lunch. I stuck to my plans, and at 1230 everyone stopped maintenance and cleaned themselves up for lunch. The barn was beautifully laid out with tables and seats, food all ready and rows of barrels of cider. As the troops filed in, they collected their cider and food, and the officers and sergeants moved around helping and serving. Just as it was getting under way, up came Sawyer and whispered 'The runner has just reported that the Colonel is on his way.' Hell! I thought, that is the end of my reign as Battery Commander. I met George at the entrance with a smart salute, and in he strode. Dead silence while he strolled around, looking at the cider and the roast beef. He strode over to me and said, 'Bloody good show Bob, best thing I have seen today.' I had the courage to offer him a mug of cider, which he drank, and then went off with a beaming grin to talk to my officers and men. The sun broke through actually and metaphorically.[40]

These periods of rest were a good moment for soldiers to catch up with correspondence. Letters were usually a good source of morale for soldiers and something like 20,000 letters a day were being dealt with by one corps postal depot alone.[41] Lieutenant Stuart Hills described them as the 'most beneficial tonic a fighting soldier could receive'. Though he also recalled seeing men in tears of sorrow as well as joy as they opened their precious letters from home, illustrating that letters could sometimes contain bad news as well as good.[42] Company Sergeant Major Charles Martin of the Queen's Own Rifles recalled one of his soldiers receiving a particularly distressing letter. His account further illustrates the leader's role in looking after his men, including their domestic problems, as well as the efficient telegram and welfare service that was sometimes available:

I was checking our positions and making my rounds when I met Jack, sitting on the edge of his slit trench. I could tell he was upset. We sat together and talked for a while. Then it came out he had had a letter from his wife. The girl had sent it before D-Day to England, and now it had followed us here. Apparently it was one of those unfortunate things that sometimes get set to paper – she'd heard he was running around, having a high time etc. etc., while she was waiting it out in Canada. Well, she warned him, two could play at that game. And if just by chance she turned up pregnant, nobody could blame her and it would be all Jack's fault.

In cases like this, we always urged a talk with the padre, but Jack seemed to think the only thing was for me to write to his wife.

Why he thought I should be the one was beyond me, but that was it and nothing else would do. This was a tough one. To start with, I told Jack to write a letter while I waited. Pretend you never received this last, I said, and just tell her how much you care. This is what he did. I took his letter and the one from his wife over to the padre, Captain Andrew Mowatt. Seemed he thought a letter from me would be a good idea as well, so I put together some words about the rough emotional shape I'd found Jack in that day and how important it was for him to have the support at home.

While I was waiting for Captain Mowatt to censor both letters, the Knights of Columbus canteen pulled up. They had a notice announcing that telegrams could be sent home. And even better, a soldier could send flowers by special arrangement. I was about the first in line and got off a bouquet to Vi [Sergeant Major Martin's wife] in England. And I got word to more or less everyone at home by sending a wire to Canon Banks, the rector of two Dixie-area churches – St. Peter's Church at Erindale and my own St. John's Church farther east. I knew he'd read my message the following Sunday to both congregations.

40 Kiln, Major Robert, *D-Day to Arnhem with Hertfordshire's Gunners* (Welwyn: Garden City, Castlemead Publications, 1993), p.119-120.
41 Ellis, L F, *Victory in the West* Volume 1 (London: HMSO, 1962), p.484.
42 Hills, Stuart, *By Tank Into Normandy* (London: Collins, 2002), p.143.

Initially, I'd only thought of me and mine for flowers and telegrams. Then a brainwave struck. What about the Jack problem? So I sent flowers to Jack's wife too. And I did my best at composing a very sentimental note and put Jack's name to it. I never did find out the exact outcome; all I know is that they later had a good-sized family.[43]

As Sergeant-Major Martin indicates above, all outgoing letters would have to be censored by the platoon or troop commanders. Whilst serious security breaches were rare, a soldier's interpretation of the truth could be stretched to a degree that would surprise many young officers. As Lieutenant Geoffrey Picot illustrates censoring letters was often not a popular chore:

I spent the first half hour with my platoon sitting on the grass censoring their letters. This was not a difficult task. Soldiers could write what they liked as long as there was nothing which, if the letter fell into the hands of the enemy, could help the enemy. Broadly speaking, that meant that no mention must be made of particular battalions or divisions or other formations, that there must be no reference to places such as Bayeux or Arromanches, and that there should be no discussion of weapons.

Not wishing to linger on personal remarks and knowing that my soldiers knew perfectly well what to write about, I was racing through these letters quickly when another officer approached me and, evidently thinking (surprisingly) that I might know more than he did, asked me: 'Do you think I ought to pass this letter? This chap is telling his girlfriend that he performed enormous heroics on the beach and with the aid of only a handful of pals stormed through the enemy defences, killing and capturing them in great numbers.'

'So what?' I asked.

'Well he didn't do anything of the sort. In fact he was always lagging behind.'

'So what?' I repeated. 'He's not giving any military information away. What he tells his girlfriend is not our business – nor how many girlfriends he tells it to.'

Horace Wright, an experienced campaigner, agreed, and gave me this advice: 'Never use the scissors. If there is something you cannot pass, take it back to the soldier, explain why, and ask him to write the letter again.'[44]

During longer periods of rest excursions might also be possible. Journeys to the beaches to bathe were common for those who were brought out of the line to relax, trips to a field cinema might also be arranged, though Major Martin Lindsay did not enjoy this as much as expected:

This evening we went to see 'The Lodger,' but it was not much fun. The marquee was not dark enough for a successful film show and the seats consisted of compo boxes. Even the unaccustomed smell of powder and scent that wafted back from a row of Canadian sisters in front did not adequately compensate for my numb bum.[45]

Alternatively Bayeux, the only large and undamaged town to have been captured by the British in the first few months, was a popular destination to unwind. Sidney Beck of the Hertfordshire Yeomanry describes its attractions:

43 Martin, Charles, *Battle Diary* (Toronto & Oxford: Dundurn Press, 1994), pp.24-26.
44 Picot, Geoffrey, *Accidental Warrior* (Lewes: Book Guild, 1993), p.64.
45 Lindsay, Martin, *So Few Got Through* (London: Collins, 19460, p.35.

Figure 10.9
An unidentified
Canadian infantryman
of 9th Canadian
Infantry Brigade writes
a letter home, circa
8-9 June. (Lieut. Frank
L. Dubervill, Library
and Archives Canada,
PA-132800)

Our chief recreation lay in trips to Bayeux for ENSA shows and to sample the Normandy wares (and women?). If memory serves me right, the films showing were 'Wintertime' with Sonja Henje and 'Going my Way' with Bing Crosby. Although we had seen both films in those far off days in Romsey, we did not much mind seeing them once again. There was the usual ENSA Concert Party at the Bayeux Theatre, with plenty of jokes about the sea-sick soldiers and how the comedian found his way to Normandy by following the train of vomit bags in the Channel!! For most of us it was our first visit to a Continental Theatre and we were interested in the little private boxes on ground level and the crude latrine arrangements.

There was the cathedral to see, the replica of the tapestry, and that quaint carved wooden pulpit. On the Sunday afternoon there was a football match between a British Services team and the Bayeux Sporting Club. It was a lovely sunny afternoon and many of the local inhabitants turned out in their Sunday best to watch the game. Just over two months previously, German soldiers had played here, but they never played any French teams and the people did not come to watch.

We were surprised by the excellent football the French played, their goalkeeper giving a very fine display. I cannot remember the result, but I fancy the French won by the odd goal. But I do remember that once a rabbit dashed across the field and the players and spectators, as one man, forgot the game. In his headlong dash, the rabbit left the pitch littered with the bodies of players who had made vain dives to catch him. The crowd jumped to their feet and cheered like mad before the frightened creature made a headlong dive into the crowd near the goal posts. An Irish Guardsman caught him and in a trice the rabbit was dead and being tucked away in a Battle Dress blouse. It took some time to get the game re-started.[46]

---

46 Kiln, Major Robert, *D-Day to Arnhem with Hertfordshire's Gunners* (Welwyn: Garden City, Castlemead Publications, 1993), pp.121-122.

After the breakout there would be opportunities to explore larger liberated towns and cities in France, Brussels too would become a popular destination for those fortunate enough to have a 24 or 48 hour leave pass. Major Martin Lindsay together with his battalion's intelligence officer, David Martin, were fortunate enough to enjoy a trip to Paris in September, particularly 'lucky' given that an order placing it out of bounds had been received by the battalion only the night before. They set off early in the morning being driven by the officers' mess corporal, Robb and his jeep driver, Akers:

> We went on through St Denis and the suburbs and down to the Rue des Capucines. Looking for a place to park the car, we saw a lot of jeeps and trucks outside the American Red Cross. We went inside and I asked the charming and sophisticated woman who was running it if we could make use of it, and leave the jeep in their car park. Then a Mme. De Montague came up with her daughter and asked for news of some of the Black Watch. David and I promptly asked them both to lunch. They said: 'No, you must come and have lunch with us at the flat, but have you any tins?' We thought this a bore, so insisted that they should lunch with us. It was a bad lunch at the Ritz – the stew was German Army rations and not as good as our compo – but the martinis were excellent and it was all extremely cheap.
>
> After lunch we went round the shops, almost the first we have seen as most of the others had been blitzed. To us it seemed a wonderful and quite pre-war display. But I couldn't get any Tangee lipstick for Joyce. It was a lovely afternoon and we had a lovely time. Paris as usual seemed very gay, and we wondered if it had not been equally gay during the occupation. The restaurants were all going just as well as in London. We each had a luxury haircut, but spent most of the time just sauntering down the boulevards. Our kilts were a tremendous success, the first seen in Paris since 1940.
>
> At five we assembled at the Red Cross and I was horrified to find that the jeep had disappeared. The American lovelies all thought it very funny. I went to the British H.Q. feeling that it was all rather tricky, with Paris out of bounds. However, the Lieut-Colonel to whom I had to report is in the Blues with my brother-in-law. He said he felt rather uncomfortable about Paris being placed out of bounds, and I was able to assure him that nothing causes more ill-feeling than the present system whereby the fighting troops capture a town, then some rear H.Q. arrive, settle themselves in comfortably, and then place it out of bounds. Or so it seems to us, for Rouen, Le Havre and Paris are all in the same category. He fixed us up with passes to stay in the hotels that have been requisitioned, David and I in the Bedford in Rue de l'Acade, and Robb and Akers in the Metropolitan in Rue Cambon; he also told us of a truck going to the Division next day, and that it might first be worthwhile visiting the barracks where picked up American vehicles are taken. The Americans lose ten jeeps a day in Paris, he said.
>
> I had a somewhat gloomy evening in the Bedford, feeling very guilty about losing the jeep and over-staying the one day's leave which Harry had given me. The barracks was packed with American vehicles of all descriptions but alas not our jeep.
>
> The HD truck had come to fetch two Argyll absentees, so we travelled back in suitable company.[47]

As Martin Lindsay's trip to Paris illustrates, short breaks such as these would invariably bring the British soldiers into contact with the French population. These enjoyable periods were sometimes in stark contrast to the experience British soldiers had with the French population near the frontline. Many British had expected to be treated as liberators, but in the early days of the

47 Lindsay, Martin, *So Few Got Through* (London: Collins, 1946), p.87.

campaign, when the frontline was largely static the cost of being liberated was often tragically high for the local French to bear cheerfully. Peter Ross a staff officer with Headquarters XXX Corps recalled one Norman farmer's wife unenthusiastic reaction to liberation:

> On D+1 Pete sent me to a farm near Le Hamel to tell the owners to bury the carcasses. As I walked up the straight narrow little path the farmer's wife appeared at the door. She was a thin-faced, dark woman, and I felt uncomfortable as she eyed me with distrust. I explained why I had come. She made no answer. Thinking she might not have understood my French, I said it again.
>
> Looking at me with contempt she said, 'Who do you think will do that? I am alone. My husband was killed by the Germans, and my son was killed by one of your bombs. He was fifteen. The hands have all gone. And now the horses are dead, so I cannot even work the farm.'
>
> She stopped talking, but continued to stare at me. Tears came into her eyes. She pressed her lips together and held herself erect as though determined not to give into her despair in front of me. I realized the atrocious insensitivity of what I had ordered her to do.
>
> 'Madame,' I said heavily, 'I am deeply sorry. We'll send some soldiers to bury the horses.'[48]

In such circumstances it is easy to comprehend why the British were not universally popular with the Normans. It makes the stoicism of those who were prepared to assist their liberators even more admirable, Brigadier Derek Mills-Roberts was struck by one such Frenchman's fortitude early on in the campaign.

> We pressed on until we came out of the gate of a long meadow on to a road which ran through Le Plain. There a soldierly figure, dressed in corduroy trousers and a tweed jacket, greeted us courteously: he quickly explained that he was the owner of the solidly built farm which lay in front of us and that it would make an excellent observation post.
>
> I said, 'You know what that means?' His farm would be likely to be badly damaged by German guns if it was used for this purpose.
>
> He answered quite simply, 'I am an ex-warrant officer of the Cuirassiers of the Guard.' He was completely unperturbed.
>
> His farm dominated the right-hand half of the village and was a most important feature. The farmer gave us useful information about the enemy.[49]

In spite of the destruction inflicted upon them many of the French would welcome the Allied soldiers into their homes or offer whatever comforts they had available. As the breakout occurred and gathered pace the degree to which towns had been damaged decreased and the liberations became much more festive. Geoffrey Picot recalls the experience during the 'Great Swan' when, for a brief moment, it seemed as if the war was coming to an end:

> I shall never forget those tumultuous days at the end of August when France warmed to its liberation. Apples and pears were thrown at us as we passed through the villages, bottles of local 'fire-water' were placed in our hands, little delicacies of food that we knew people could ill spare were showered upon us whenever we stopped for a moment, and it was all given with moving eagerness.

---

48 Ross, Peter, *Valiant Dust* (Dublin: Lilliput Press, 1992), p.144.
49 Mills-Roberts, Derek, *Clash by Night* (London: Kimber, 1956), p.101.

Figure 10.10 Trooper Brooker of 3rd County of London Yeomanry enjoys female attention at Grand Villiers, 2 September 1944. (County of London Yeomanry)

The young and middle-aged waved flags, shook our hands, danced in the streets, kissed and behaved with enthusiasm and excitement.

A woman walking on her own along a country road clapped her hands continuously and said 'Merci, merci' all the time our column of 130 vehicles rumbled past her.

Old men wept for joy; old men who had fought their war and won it a quarter of a century previously and had lived through the shame and horror that had come to them when the next generation did not win over again what was really the same war...

... In some villages the population brought chairs out of doors and sat on these all day long as different troops drove through. It was indeed for them the occasion of a lifetime. On all faces were such expressions of thankfulness and joy as I had not seen anywhere before. I was confident that they would remember Britain with gratitude for the rest of their lives.

For us also it was unforgettable. All the troops were deeply moved.[50]

Even these bright clouds of liberation sometimes had a dark and sinister lining. The prospect of further fighting for the British still lurked at the back of many soldier's minds and for the French? Four long years of occupation had generated many scores that needed settling. Ken Tout and his Sherman tank crew sombrely recalled the liberation of one French town:

For us this is a mere halt along an unending road towards an uncertain objective beset with unimagined dangers. For them this is the Day of Peace and Liberation and consummation of

---

50 Picot, Geoffrey, *Accidental Warrior* (Lewes: Book Guild, 1993), p.166.

Figure 10.11 An elderly man attacking a collaborator in Bernay, 4 September.
(Lieut. Donald I. Grant, Library and Archives Canada, PA-190010)

the hopes of years. So they laugh and dance and tilt the wine bottle while we sit watchful in our tank, chewing an apple but storing the wine against future celebrations.

The jollity does not last long. Someone brings a kitchen chair out onto a green apron of land in front of a farm building dragging a thickset farm girl with pale face and red eyes. They sit her roughly on the chair. The sparse population of the miniscule village gathers round. One of the men grabs the girl's hair and the other wields a pair of sheep-shears, chopping through the long locks and ripping the strands from the scalp. The tiny crowd jeers and laughs and shouts 'Collaborator![51]

It is easy to feel sympathy for the French girls who were shaved and humiliated that summer, many having committed nothing more serious than having a German boyfriend. The majority of Allied soldiers who witnessed such scenes catalogued them as a strictly French affair, distasteful and shameful to watch, but not something they felt they should necessarily interfere with. The most common practice seems to have been to let the French get on with it whilst they focussed on the Germans. Major Robert Kiln recalls one officer who did decide to intervene in a small town near Amiens on 31 August:

> Just before midnight, the whole column was bypassing the centre of the town, which lay two hundred yards to our right. A lot of noise was coming from the town square, so I set off on foot to investigate with one of my troop commanders, Roy Marshall. Roy had joined 342nd Battery in Normandy to replace Geoffrey Street. He was an exceptionally able officer, having won both the Military Medal and the Military Cross, a rare distinction, and was older and more experienced than I was, although I was his major.

---

51 Tout, Ken, *Tanks Advance!* (London: Robert Hale, 1987), p.134.

Figure 10.12
The CO of 3rd County of London Yeomanry
enjoys champagne with Cpl Quye at
Auxy Le Château, 3 September.
(County of London Yeomanry)

Roy and I soon reached the town square, which was full of lights and people. In the centre were four or five girls, all weeping and being held by a group of French men, having their hair cut off and heads shaven amid acclaim from an ugly-looking crowd. It was a pathetic sight in the pouring rain, and I was wondering what to do, when Roy went into action. Drawing his revolver, he advanced and in passable French ordered them to stop and release the girls. This they refused to do and an ugly scene looked likely. At that moment one of our bombardiers, carrying a Sten gun, arrived to tell us that the column was about to move again. His arrival, armed, tipped the balance. Reluctantly the girls were released, and they made off. We then shook hands with some of the French, and I persuaded Roy that our main priority was to advance on Amiens! Similar scenes must have been going on all over France. This performance at midnight in the pouring rain was a macabre and nasty affair, and in great contrast to the scenes of rejoicing we were now witnessing every day.[52]

The frenetic pace of the breakout in late August and early September meant that the periods to properly enjoy French, or Belgian, hospitality were inevitably transitory, but there were occasional moments when the joy of liberation was able to briefly permeate a soldier's existence. Major Robert Kiln again provides an illustration:

We retreated down the road to a little village with a crossroads just to the west of Brussels. Here our troops were due to make a left turn to the north, bypassing Brussels, and up to Antwerp, about thirty miles away. We arrived to find one of our SPs parked by the roadside,

---

52   Kiln, Major Robert, *D-Day to Arnhem with Hertfordshire's Gunners* (Welwyn: Garden City, Castlemead Publications, 1993), p.153.

apparently broken down. We stopped to investigate and found the No.1, a sergeant, in the local café on the crossroads. The breakdown appeared to be a 'tactical' one, and as his commanding officer I was just about to start laying down a bit of discipline. However, as I crossed the threshold of the café, Madame, a magnificent red-haired woman about twice my size, seized me in her arms, kissed me warmly and called me 'mon brave colonel' (a calculated flattery of promotion). I then had to dance and drink with her. My sergeant, looking not at all abashed, was sitting with a glass of wine and a girl on his knee, grinning at me. What the hell! It had been a long day and a little liberating would do us no harm. So I made a rota of duty on the crossroads to direct all our vehicles away from Brussels and up to Antwerp, and settled back to enjoy Madame's hospitality.

It was now seven or eight o'clock, when in came our sergeant to say that the Colonel was approaching. He had the good sense to appraise Madame, who took in the situation in a flash and was at the door with her most attractive barmaid to welcome George Fanshawe while I hid in the darkest corner. George got the full treatment. 'Ah mon brave General', a voluptuous embrace and a glass of champagne from the barmaid, and George too is captured.[53]

For other British soldiers left behind by the rate of advance of the armoured columns there was more of an opportunity to, as the Army expression went, 'get one's feet under table'. A chance to meet the local French and understand them a little better, such encounters would also become increasingly common with Belgian and Dutch families when the winter weather and largely static frontline meant that many British soldiers would be billeted in local towns and houses. However if encounters with the French could be unfamiliar and confusing, those with the Germans gave even more cause for alarm and suspicion. It is hard to comprehend what it must have been like for the British to have met their enemy on the battlefield for the first time, particularly for soldiers who had spent the previous four years training to kill them. The propaganda and perception in many soldier's minds rarely matched their first encounters with the enemy. Lieutenant Robert Woolcombe describes capturing his company's first German prisoner near St Manvieu during Operation EPSOM. St Manvieu was held by members of the 12th SS *Hitlerjugend* Division who had already achieved a fearsome reputation for ruthlessness in the previous weeks' fighting with the Canadians:

Suddenly we froze at a burst of fire from Black's Bren gun, firing from his hip, and instantly an apparition rose screaming from the corn and rushed towards us, throwing itself at my feet. It was an SS.

He must have sensed I was the patrol leader. He may have been watching us. Quickly a heavy Luger pistol was taken off him, made in Belgium and fully loaded. But he was in no state for offensive action. By a neat bit of shooting Black had hit him, and his left shoulder was streaming with blood. He knelt at my feet clutching my knees, frantic with pain and terror.

'Don't shoot – don't shoot! Have pity! Don't shoot!'

He knew that much English.

We understood. To key up their resistance they had been told the British shot all prisoners. He now expected death in cold blood.

For a few speechless seconds we gazed at him. Black alone stood apart, a little upside down, surveying the results of his handiwork. For myself it was a strange experience to stare down at this Nazi clutching my legs and pleading for his life. One did not blame him for his terror. Nevertheless, he was of the 'Herrenvolk.' One felt no compassion.

---

53 Ibid., pp.121-122.

We hoisted him to his feet. His helmet, covered by a canvas camouflage casing, had tumbled off, exposing a shock of blond hair. His eyes blue, his face under a several-day growth of fair down. By his paybook he was twenty. He would not walk unaided, so one of the patrol and I carried him, his arms over our shoulders.

'Don't shoot – oh, have pity' he still sobbed, beside himself from shock and his wound.

'No, we don't shoot,' said a Jock.

We carried him into the Company positions, the centre of all eyes, and set him down like a trophy at Company Headquarters. He was quieter now. He looked at me. He would have killed me in that field. Impossible to tell what he thought now. A stretcher-bearer attended to his wound; two bullet holes had torn the flesh. I had never seen Gavin so taken aback – he had sent us out on text book routine, thinking nor more of it.

'Well done, my boy,' he said incredulously. It was the acme of praise.

The prisoner was taken away.[54]

On other occasions the prisoners were captured in less dramatic circumstances. The large proportion of Russian and Polish conscripts in the German Army meant that there were often significant numbers of German soldiers who were looking for the first opportunity to surrender. Corporal Graham Roe, of the Hallamshires, recalls one such encounter whilst repairing the signal cables that had been cut by shellfire:

It was my custom to lie down on my back to repair the cable across my chest. I did not present a target for an enemy sniper and I had a better view of anyone approaching me. It was a sunny day but the sun was in my eyes. Suddenly I found myself looking into the muzzle of a rifle. I could make out the silhouette of two burly soldiers in field grey. My heart sank. This was either the end or I would be taken prisoner. I sat up with a jerk. The words of Psalm 46 came into my thoughts, where God is my refuge and strength and a very present help in trouble. I waited. One of them with an apology for a smile, handed me a leaflet promising a safe passage, if they brought the leaflet in, and surrendered. One of them banged his chest and said, 'Me Ruskie.' Plucking up my courage I said in German 'Bleiben sie da' and finished joining the cables.[55]

Many British soldiers first encountered German PWs was as they moved up to the frontline. Columns of PWs would become a familiar sight on the Normandy roads particularly as the battle of the Falaise Gap reached its conclusion when some 20,000-27,500 prisoners would be taken by the British on a daily basis.[56] Witnessing some of the fiercer elements of the German Army was often a sobering experience for those about to engage in battle for the first time. Private Rex Wingfield recalled seeing his first Germans:

From in front came the muffled shush-shush. Round the corner came a column of German prisoners – hundreds of them. This was the first time we had seen them in the flesh and they seemed horribly tough. Automatically I checked on the coloured braid of their epaulettes and identified Artillery, Signals, Infantry, Armoured troops – all looking about eight feet tall and twice as bloodthirsty. These were some of the first prisoners from the Falaise Gap. I saw the last ones later. I shall never forget them. These troops moving past now were well-preserved

54 Woollcombe, Robert, *Lion Rampant* (Edinburgh: B&W Publishing, 1994), p.60.
55 Delaforce, Patrick, *Marching to the Sounds of Gunfire* (Stroud: Sutton, 1996), p.106.
56 Ellis, L F, *Victory in the West* Volume 1 (London: HMSO, 1962), p.446.

Figure 10.13 German prisoners captured by the 3rd County of London Yeomanry, north of the Falaise pocket, 13 August. (County of London Yeomanry)

specimens. They promised us that we should soon be killed by their own units. We might, of course, be lucky and be taken prisoner. We asked them why they were so cocky, as they were prisoners. They didn't like that one little bit. Some spat at us, but the rest shuffled past in sullen silence.[57]

The majority of German prisoner's were treated well by the British, who usually felt no particular ill will towards them. The apparent exception to this good behaviour was that of looting which as we have already seen was a frequent practise. Lieutenant Bill Bellamy recalls his troop's behaviour when they captured their first eight prisoners sheltering in a nearby barn:

They all lined up on the road looking pathetic, young, anxious, hollow-eyed and very apprehensive. None of us could speak much German, so any exchanges had to be by sign language. I was surprised at my feelings of friendliness towards them. I couldn't even dislike them and found myself wanting to offer them a meal while they waited to be collected.

My sentiments were not shared by all, and when I told one of the troop to collect their pay-books, he took the opportunity to go through their pockets, indicating that they should hand over their watches etc. When I saw this I was livid and made him return everything and leave them alone. It seemed totally wrong to me that because they were prisoners, we should rob them of personal items. Bill Pritchard disagreed with me, on the basis that as soon as they were back in the area of the prisoners' cages then others would take everything of value from them, the 'others' being people who had had no hand in their capture. While I could understand his argument I couldn't agree with it, and they left us with their personal possessions

57 Wingfield, R M, *The Only Way Out* (London: Hutchinson, 1955), p.24.

intact, we retaining their weapons. Perhaps I was wrong in adopting the attitude that I did, but then my father had been captured by Rommel in the desert, he had been well treated by the Germans which meant a lot to him, and I suppose that to some extent I reflected this.[58]

Other units adopted a less principled stand on the looting of prisoners. Major Martin Lindsay clearly saw it as a routine and acceptable part of warfare. He recorded an influx of prisoners on 11 September:

> A lot of prisoners were coming back, and it was most encouraging to see that they were being led by their officer. They lined up in front of me. 'There you are,' I said to the men who were near me, 'The Master Race. Help yourselves.' They soon had a fine collection of watches, fountain pens, pocket knives, and not a few French Francs. Then I put the prisoners on improvising the track. Some of them had our pink leaflets on them. They seem very good propaganda to me. On one side was printed, 'Why die in the last week of the war? You are between two Allied armies and the sea, and your holding out will help no one.[59]

The dead Germans that littered the battlefield were also a constant reminder of the destruction being meted out in the Normandy battle. For many who had never seen a dead body before, it was a deeply shocking sight. Ken Tout recalls the youthful curiosity that prompted him to explore the interior of a burned out tank near Creully in early July:

> We did not expect to intrude on the privacy of the crew still seated inside, charred to the size of wizened monkeys and to the consistency of burned sausages. The roasting of human flesh and the combustion of ammunition and the defecation of a million voracious flies created an aura of such sense-assaulting horror that we recoiled. We retreated even before our minds could aspire to the pity and loathing which would have sent us hurrying from the presence of those incinerated mummies.
>
> Then there was our encounter with a dead German near that same place. We had smelled the presence of death. And we had found him sleeping undisturbed from some previous battle. Bobby McColl had ordered us to bury him where he lay. We were used to digging slit trenches for our own shelter and, in the soft Norman earth, it was no great toil to dig an enduring shelter for this alien in a strange uniform. We dug deep, not out of respect for the dead but because we must continue to eat and sleep nearby. With some reluctance, but hurried on by our own revulsion, we grabbed his limbs to swing him into the trench. The arm which I seized disintegrated under my fingers, and the clumsy body slumped to the grass again. We vomited into the handkerchiefs which we had tied over our noses. Then, taking our spades, we unceremoniously shovelled the decomposing pieces of human residuum into the deep pit.[60]

But of course a comrade was just as likely to be struck down as a German. Lieutenant Jocelyn Pereira captures the impact numerous deaths could have on a unit. At the time his battalion, 5th Coldstream Guards, was in a defensive position, on a ridge in front of La Marvindiere:

---

58 Bellamy, Bill, *Troop Leader* (Stroud: Sutton Publishing, 2005), pp.106-107.
59 Lindsay, Martin, *So Few Got Through*, (London: Collins, 1946), p.85.
60 Tout, Ken, *Tanks, Advance* (London: Robert Hale, 1987), p.55.

It was a bad time for the Battalion, and if I had been writing this then I would never have said 'three hundred casualties,' for that is a figure only and makes nonsense of all that we felt. You cannot say: 'Mark Howard, Bunty Stuart Brown – write down two killed'; and yet there seems to be no way in which one can express the meaning of our losses in the human terms in which they occurred. For three years we had worked and trained and lived together until there was something more than a battalion – there was a community of spirit and feeling that made the Battalion as much a part of oneself as one was a tiny fraction of the whole. And now, when the evening light began to turn the tall hedges into long, black shadows across the bocage meadows, one felt suddenly as though the darkness that was beginning to separate trench from trench and each man from his neighbour was like the loneliness that was coming upon the Battalion as the friends one had had diminished one by one, killed or wounded.[61]

It was the death of close friends that often struck the soldiers hardest. Lieutenant Bill Bellamy recalls the death of a much loved and vastly experienced Squadron Leader, Piff Threlfall, on 24 July. At the time the squadron was near the village of Ifs and although a short distance from the frontline was on a reverse slope and therefore out of the enemy's view. Just prior to the shelling two Bren gun carriers of the Northumberland Fusiliers had arrived and fired their Medium Machine Guns in the indirect fire role at suspected German troop movement. Such actions inevitably prompted a violent response by the Germans:

My tank was sited directly behind Piff's and Jack was next to me, on my right. Everyone was in their tanks, except for the three of us, as there was still a bit of shelling going on, although it was not very close. Piff was smoking his inevitable pipe, I can't picture him without one, sitting on the ground with his back against his tank. Map-board on knee and his very discoloured and worn old 8th Hussar green and gold side hat perched on the top of his head. Suddenly the shellfire came much closer and both Jack and I, feeling a little foolish, made for the shelter of our tank turrets. Piff, unperturbed, sat there quietly smoking. The next salvo fell directly to the front of his tank and as I watched him from the top of my turret, he fell quietly over on to his side. Evidently the shell splinters had passed under the tank and hit him in the back. Both Jack and I jumped down from our tanks and rushed to pick him up, both hoping that he was stunned or lightly wounded; but he had been killed outright and we were left, two grown men, unashamedly weeping in front of any of the squadron who cared to look. He was the most wonderful man to have as a squadron leader, unflappable, experienced, a good counsellor and a friend to all of us. We all loved him and although we had other good squadron leaders, those who had been privileged to serve under him never forgot him.[62]

Whether the dead were British or German the logistical arrangements for disposing of bodies were conducted by the soldiers themselves. Initially bodies were buried where they fell at a point in the battle when such administration was practical. Lieutenant Robert Woollcombe recalls being placed in charge of a burial party tasked with burying some of the EPSOM dead near St Manvieu:

They were scattered along the hedges, round the field. The complete course of a platoon attack could be traced in detail. The platoon commander, a lieutenant, looking faintly surprised, a slight twist to his neck and not a mark but for some congealed stains where his battle-dress covered the kidneys. In a breast pocket a slab of chocolate as I had in mine, and a snapshot

---

61 Pereira, Jocelyn, *A Distant Drum* (Aldershot: Gale & Polden, 1948), p.49.
62 Bellamy, Bill, *Troop Leader* (Stroud: Sutton Publishing, 2005), pp.76-77.

Figure 10.14 A road near Chambois, south-east of Trun, filled with wrecked German vehicles and dead following an attack by Typhoons of 83 Group. (Crown Copyright Air Historical Branch)

of his wedding a month earlier. Here a corporal huddled over his Sten gun, taken completely unawares. His face pudding-like, and the boiled sweets still in his pocket.

A corporal from 'C' Company was among the burial party. 'I know him! He was in my ward in hospital last Christmas – that bloke!' he exclaimed stupidly, his face a picture of ludicrous astonishment. With a big nose and a startled, lugubrious voice, a living corporal, blankly, gaping at the dead one.

So we collected them and laid them side by side, and took the personal effects off them; most of which work, owing to the loathing of the Jocks to touch their own dead, fell upon the corporal and myself. A long shallow trench was dug. Others as they were found were brought to us, in ones and twos from the fields around, slung in groundsheets, by stray parties detailed for the purpose. They were deadweights, and the faces bored into you. One of them, very fair skinned with blond hair, had a strange name ending in '-ski'. He was unblemished except for a neat red hole in the centre of the forehead. His blue eyes stared before him in sightless amazement. A trouser-button was open and his genitals showed like wax. Another was a carrier driver whose vehicle had been hit by an anti-tank shell or gone up on a mine. His arms and a leg were in rough splints and his mouth was open, dried like leather and twisted as if in a last shout. Then came the surprised platoon commander, and we covered them over with earth.[63]

The unit Padres played a key role at these moments and usually received great respect and admiration for this aspect of their work. Leslie Skinner was a particularly popular Padre and took the

63 Woollcombe, Robert, *Lion Rampant* (Edinburgh, B&W Publishing, 1994), p.69.

Figure 10.15 Captain Callum Thompson, a Canadian chaplain, conducts a funeral service in the Normandy beachhead, 16 July. (Lieut. Donald I. Grant, Library and Archives Canada, PA-190111)

duties of looking after the dead terribly seriously, particularly the tanks crews of his own unit the Sherwood Rangers.

> Once a tank has been hit and the wounded, if any, got away, other tanks of the troop know that one or more of their comrades remained in that knocked-out tank. They draw comfort from me – or anyone else – just going to look – even if the actual removal for burial had to wait until later. The morale and 'spiritualness' of the men actually doing the fighting seems to me to be paramount and trying to do the things I did and do, is the best I can do.

The importance of the tasks still did not make them any easier to perform. Padre Skinner recalled having to deal with the aftermath of a battle on 17 August:

> Buried the three dead and tried to reach remaining dead in tanks still too hot and burning. Place absolute shambles. Infantry dead and some Germans lying around. Horrible mess. Fearful job picking up bits and pieces and re-assembling for identification and putting in blankets for burial. Squadron Leader offered to lend me some men to help. Refused. Less men who live and fight in tanks have to do with this side of things the better. They know it happens but to force it on their attention is not good. My job. This was more than normally sick-making. Really ill vomiting.[64]

---

64 Reverend Skinner papers 10908, Imperial War Museum.

Padre Mark Green who served the 24th Lancers also recognised the importance of sensitively handling the dead but still found it an emotionally draining experience:

> Late in the morning I was at the 4th/7th Royal Dragoon Guards R.A.P. on the other side of the hill from ours talking to Hedleigh Davies, their Padre, when a tank drove up and stopped. The Doctor, Hood, went to see what was the matter. The crew tumbled out of the tank, looking extremely shaken. They explained that they had been shot up and the tank commander, a young subaltern, was dead inside the turret. Would the M.O please get him out? The M.O. climbed up, looked in, and came down quickly, looking as white as a sheet... and he was one of the bravest and staunchest men I ever met. Hedleigh Davies and I decided to get the crew to drive the tank to some more secluded spot, which they did. Somehow we got the young subaltern out, though never before had we seen such a ghastly sight; and several times we nearly gave up completely. Later in the afternoon I buried him. It was a hasty funeral, and I remember feeling so utterly worn out physically and emotionally that as I said the words of the Burial service I was in tears.[65]

For those who were lucky enough to survive an engagement the only prospect to look forward too was further fighting. Even at the end of the Normandy campaign there was still eight months before the Germans finally capitulated, the grim summer would turn inexorably into a grim winter. Moreover as the campaign progressed and the casualties mounted the statistical inevitability of becoming killed or wounded became almost intolerably obvious to frontline soldiers. Major Martin Lindsay recalled the wounding of Major Bruce Rae, the last of the twenty or so rifle company officers who had landed with 1st Gordons at Normandy:

> That is what is so superlatively gallant about these chaps. They go into battle time after time, knowing perfectly well that they are dicing against the mathematical odds, which indeed they sometimes jocularly observe. For an officer to go into a dozen actions without being killed or badly wounded is like a coin coming down heads six times running. He knows that his luck cannot possibly last, yet he would die of shame were some one else to take his place.[66]

65 Willis, Leonard, *None Had Lances – The Story Of The 24th Lancers* (Chippenham: Picton Print, 1986), p.124.
66 Lindsay, Martin, *So Few Got Through* (London: Collins, 1946), p.57.

11

'From Mud, Through Blood To The Green Fields Beyond' – Armour

There was something different about these tanks and armoured cars. The Allies were advancing, we knew, but they were many miles away; but then a young tank commander looked up at me and waved. The impossible had happened – they were British!

Citizen of Brussels 3 September 1944[1]

On 4 September 3rd Royal Tank Regiment crossed over the Escaut canal at Warcoing and advanced to Ronse and Renaix, where the population went wild with joy.[2] They continued their advance the next day, liberating the great port of Antwerp. It would have been understandable if some of the tank crews had reflected on events since they crossed the River Seine at Vernon on 28 August. In just six days the regiment, along with many other Allied units, had covered 230 miles, exceeding the rate of advance achieved by the Germans in May 1940. Some tank crews might have cast their minds further back to the Normandy battles where British armour had supported the infantry in breaking out of Normandy, defeating the cream of Germany's armoured forces in the process. Yet despite these significant achievements for some historians it has become the trend to view the performance of British armour in 1944 as poor, or even peripheral to Allied victory. This chapter aims to give the reader an understanding of how armour supports operations and the experiences a tank crew would encounter in Normandy. It will also demonstrate that the contribution of the Allied armoured crews was significant, competently executed and often very courageous.

A tank is essentially a front line armoured fighting vehicle with three important characteristics; 'Firepower', 'Protection' and 'Mobility', the combination of all three will also determine the tank's overall survivability. These three characteristics are the essential features of the tank's design and are achieved in a number of ways. Firstly its tactical 'mobility' is a function of its tracks, engine, gearbox, suspension and running gear. Its 'firepower' usually consisted of a large calibre gun in a revolving turret, known as its main armament, as well as secondary machine guns. These gave the tank both offensive and defensive capabilities. Finally the tank's 'protection' was provided by armour plate which allowed the crew to operate the tank safe from many battlefield hazards. Protection could also be viewed in a wider context, factors such as low noise or a small silhouette making it difficult for the enemy to locate the tank. Tank designers understood that the tank's characteristics of firepower, protection and mobility not only interacted with each other, but that

---

1 Horrocks, Sir Brian, *Corps Commander* (London: Sidgwick and Jackson, 1977), p.77.
2 Delaforce, Patrick, *The Black Bull: From Normandy to the Baltic with 11th Armoured Division* (Stroud: Sutton Publishing), p.150.

Figure 11.1 A camouflaged 3rd County of London Yeomanry Sherman tank at Bois Halbut, 14 August. (County of London Yeomanry)

engineering and cost limitations often resulted in a series of compromises between these characteristics. For example a tank with a larger gun and thicker armour would normally have less speed and agility, alternatively a fast and more maneuverable tank would normally need to be light and would therefore possess both thinner armour and a smaller gun. All tanks therefore have their own strengths and weaknesses as a result of these compromises, the German and British tanks in Normandy were no different.

British tank design in the Second World War had a poor record. Although responsible for the invention of the tank, the British had allowed the design and supply of tanks to dwindle between the wars and when the conflict did break out British tanks were undergunned and mechanically unreliable. It is telling that both Alam Halfa and El Alamein, the desert battles that turned the war in Britain's favour, were to be won by an Army whose most powerful armoured capability rested in its fleet of American built Sherman and Grant tanks. As the war progressed there were improvements to this poor start and the British built Cromwell and Churchill tanks were superior machines, both of them playing a significant part in the Normandy campaign. Nevertheless it would be the American built Sherman tank that would equip most British armoured divisions and brigades.

The three main tanks used by the British; the Cromwell, Churchill and Sherman,[3] were divided into two different categories of armour – infantry support tanks and cruiser tanks. This reflected the British ideas on the 'proper' roles of armour at the time and the two types of tank would be organized into two distinctly different armoured formations. The 'infantry support' tanks were

---

3   The British also had the M3 Stuart Light tank, though this was used solely for reconnaissance purposes.

found in the independent tank brigades within 21st Army Group whose mission was to provide the infantry divisions with the armoured support they needed to accomplish their assigned tasks. In Normandy this role typically involved supporting an infantry offensive operation against enemy positions, for some Churchill regiments this meant continuous chopping and changing between infantry formations. The infantry support task meant their tanks needed heavy protective armour, machine-guns and a large calibre gun capable of firing HE shells to destroy the trenches, bunkers and enemy infantry that would hamper an infantry advance. As infantry support tanks would work directly alongside the infantry a good cross-country performance was seen as more important than a particularly fast turn of speed. The Churchill tank had been developed and built by the British during the Second World War for exactly this role. It had seen active service in North Africa and Italy and the latest improvements, particularly thicker armour, had been incorporated into the Churchill MK VI and VII which equipped most tank brigades. The Churchill was armed with a 75mm gun and two Besa machine guns, it was relatively slow (12-15 mph) though its cross-country performance was very good indeed.

Whilst heavily armoured, slow-moving infantry support tanks like the Churchill would be suitable for providing close support to the infantry, the British recognized the need for a second type of tank. This needed to be a faster tank, able to exploit success once the enemy's defences had been breached by the infantry, a tank that could manoeuvre into the enemy's rear. These were the 'Cruiser' tanks and would equip the armoured divisions and armoured brigades. In 1944 there were two Cruiser tanks available to 21st Army Group; the American built Sherman tank and the British built Cromwell tank. They both carried the same 75-millimetre gun as the Churchill tank, but were less well armoured and consequently much lighter and faster, the Cromwell was able to travel at speeds up to 40 mph and the Sherman supposedly at 24 mph (though many commanders have stated that the tank could exceed this). Both of these Cruiser tanks were optimized for the break out battle and the subsequent pursuit and exploitation that the armoured divisions in Normandy would hopefully conduct. However the British found that breaking out of the Normandy bridgehead was not as easy as they had supposed and a large part of these tank's fighting would be spent acting more as infantry support tanks than cruiser tanks in the bloody battles of attrition throughout the summer. The crews of the Shermans and Cromwells would also discover that the compromises that had been made in both protection and firepower to enhance their vehicle's mobility had left their tanks dangerously exposed to the more heavily armed and armoured German Tiger and Panther tanks. Some commanders, including Montgomery himself, thought these distinctions between 'infantry support' and 'cruiser' tanks were unhelpful. Montgomery would have preferred a 'Capital' tank that could serve both functions, German tanks were arguably designed in exactly this manner.

The Churchill, Sherman and Cromwell all carried a crew of five, including a driver, a co-driver/bow machine-gunner, a loader/wireless operator, a gunner and the tank commander himself. The tank itself was usually part of a troop of four tanks, with four troops to a squadron and four squadrons to a regiment. A troop was normally commanded by a young lieutenant and a squadron by a major, a lieutenant colonel would command the regiment. All of these leaders had their own tanks which provided them with the protection and mobility to command their part of an armoured battle. In terms of firepower the majority of British tanks were equipped with a 75mm medium velocity general purpose gun as its main armament.[4] This was located in the revolving turret and was fired either by the gunner on his own initiative, or at the command of the tank commander who had the best all-round visibility and could direct the gunner to slew the turret around to

---

4   There were some Churchill tanks that retained the 6-pounder but most had been converted to 75mm. There were also some Crowmwells armed with a 95mm support gun.

engage a target he had not seen. Ken Tout describes occupying his Sherman gunner's position prior to Operation TOTALIZE. He gives a good description not only of the controls he operated to fire the gun but where the other members of the crew were also positioned in the tank:

I reach for my headset, two earphones joined by a thin, curved piece of metal which fits down over my black beret. From now on we shall be able to talk to each other only through the microphones and earphones. Behind my head the huge engine kicks into life and drowns the reverberating barrage of the guns for the moment. My right hand instinctively finds the metal grip which controls the turret. I twist left, and the turret swings back, smooth, swift and silent, powered by its efficient Westinghouse system.

I sit upright on my narrow seat. The rough, hard turret wall is close to my right shoulder. My left shoulder is pressed into the equally unyielding guard of the big gun. There is some room for my feet, and I feel around with my left foot to find the firing buttons set there on the turret floor. In front of me the turret wall sweeps up closer and confining. At eye level are a periscope, giving me a general view of a segment of the outside world, and a telescope fixed to the gun, giving me a very much enlarged firing view and aiming sight...

...On the other side of the great 75mm breech sits Stan, with rather more room than I have. I do not need to move. He does. At any moment he may need to swing away from his wireless set, pick up a 75mm shell – an armful indeed – and slam it into the breech of the gun. The Browning machine-gun is also on Stan's side of the 75mm, mounted co-axially – and so called the 'co-ax' – so that when I traverse the turret and elevate or depress the gun mounting the 75 and the Browning move together, respond to the same gun sight through which I take a single aim, and if fired by the separate floor buttons, will hit the same target without further adjustment.

Figure 11.2
Ken Tout served in Normandy with the
Northamptonshire Yeomanry as both a Sherman
tank gunner and commander. (Ken Tout)

Keith McAlpine is positioned behind and above me. There is a collapsible seat at about level with my shoulders, on which he can sit, although generally the commander stands with his head out of the turret. There is also a higher seat which he can use when travelling outside the battle area.

Down in front of us the driver's compartment is low but fairly spacious as to width. Harvey needs fair space to move the two brake levers, large sticks rather like old-fashioned levers used in railway signal boxes. There is also a large gear lever. Bookie has no driving controls but in front of him he has another Browning machine-gun which protrudes through its own small mantle in the front of the tank below the turret ring. He both loads and fires that gun. This means that we can fire in two directions at once. The co-driver can fire over most of the front area even though the turret has been swung to one side, or even to the rear, and is firing at another target.[5]

The Sherman would carry about one hundred 75mm shells (45 of which were in the turret, the remainder were carried in bins within the tank's hull) and twenty-five boxes of belted ammunition for the Browning machine guns. These shells came fixed in one piece and could be either Smoke, Armour Piercing 'Shot' or High Explosive (HE). The HE shells were frequently used to destroy non-armoured targets such as buildings, infantry positions and anti-tank guns. Keith Jones was a tank commander with 1st Northamptonshire Yeomanry, he recalls using the 75mm main gun on his Cromwell Tank to destroy a suspected OP that was directing artillery fire onto his unit during Operation GOODWOOD:

The village revealed no obvious targets in gun emplacements, pillboxes or trenches, no doubt too well camouflaged. The farm buildings looked like farm buildings, solidly built and probably reinforced. One had a long, red tiled roof. I remembered a remark someone made about tiled roofs at the Oxford tactical course.

'Put one on delay, Bill and load. Seventy-five traverse left, 400, on!' The traverse stopped. 'Stanley, can you see that lovely red-tiled roof?' He assented. 'Just in case the OP controlling these stonks we've had is operating from there I want you to get a bull's eye. Take your time, fire when on.'

I had just seen Bill reach across and tap Stanley's arm as the breech slid closed. I fancied I heard Stanley murmur as he pressed his eye socket to the rubber:

'Oh, aye!'

The tank rocked as the gun recoiled. The immediate noise entered my right ear with real pain. The ejected shell case hit the back of the canvas chute, then fell to the turret floor with a sound that was to become familiar:

'Phong!'

We watched, open-mouthed like kids before a firework spread its glitter, Albert through his open driving aperture, Harry and Stanley through their telescopes, Bill and I out of our hatches. The shell entered the centre of the tiled roof, exploding not on impact but immediately inside the building, lifting many tiles into the air on our side and the other, baring an enormous area of roof.[6]

There is real skill in hitting a target like a house some distance away, but smaller targets like enemy tanks were even harder. Judging distance was a particularly important aspect of this

---

5   Tout, Ken, *Tank!* (London: Robert Hale, 1985), pp.43-44.
6   Jones, Keith, *64 Days of a Normandy Summer* (London: Robert Hale, 1990), pp.106-107.

Figure 11.3 A Cromwell Mk V tank of 1st RTR, 7th Armoured Division, advancing through Cantaloup near Caumont during Operation BLUECOAT, 31 July-1 August. Lloyd carriers of 3rd Independent Machine Gun Company can be seen in the background. (Tank Museum)

gunnery skill, the commander would have to estimate the range, the gunner then choosing an aiming graticule in his sight based on that range. Incorrect range estimation would normally mean a first round miss and that was likely to give away the tank's position to the enemy with sometimes fatal consequences.

Allied tank commanders believed the primary threat to their tank was another enemy tank; it was therefore common practice for the tank to travel with an AP shot already loaded and ready to fire instantaneously should an enemy tank appear. Even if the first target actually encountered by the British tank was one for which the AP round was not necessarily suitable for, the 'shot' would still be fired and the gun quickly loaded with HE. Ken Tout recalls having to engage an infantry dug-out position with the AP shot loaded in his Sherman tank.

Streaks of light shoot out of the ground on our left. The Sherman in front starts to traverse left. I twist the pistol-grip, spin the turret, eye to telescope, crosswires swinging and dipping at the source of the firing. Keith orders, 'Gunner, fire! Reload HE. Driver, swing left. Co-driver, fire when on.'

I stamp on the firing button of the 75mm, then on the co-ax button. The huge breech of the 75mm leaps back into the turret, jams against its springs, slides forward again into place. It thunderclaps in my left ear. The automatically-opened breech coughs stifling cordite fumes in my telescope, the mighty muzzle flash of the 75mm obscures and blinds momentarily as a tracer spark leaps across the brief space and slams into the ground by the German machine-gun. Stony Stratford [the name of the tank] rocks back on its haunches under the power of the 75 recoil. Streaks of smaller tracer from our Browning follow the same trajectory as the larger shot, sparking around a hardly visible dug-out. The tank in front also bangs off a 75mm shot.

All this within a second, without breathing, without thought. Our 75 had been loaded with AP (armour-piercing shot), not necessarily effective against men in a hole in the ground but a very discouraging package to receive, travelling at two thousand feet per second with force sufficient to split open any tank but a Tiger. Now Stan is ramming a high-explosive shell into the breech. He slaps my leg, signing 'loaded' – even while I think, 'Those must be SS fanatics in that slit trench.' A touch on the traversing grip, stamp on the button, flame, thunder, shock, leaping tracer hitting target. Then fire, massive, sudden, vivid, brief. A flame of sunset condensed a thousand times, mixed with a thousand lightnings with their accompanying thunders, compressed into an area in, and above, and around the dug-out. Expired in a split second. But in that brief flame a whirling mass of sandbags, a shattered machine-gun, metal objects, equipment, boxes, helmets, pieces of human bodies, all clear, distinct, in Technicolor, quickly dying.[7]

It would be wrong to ignore the effectiveness of the tank's machine guns, most British tanks in Normandy were armed with two machine-guns, one in the bow and a second in the turret. On the Sherman these machine-guns were .30 Brownings, very reliable and capable of firing 600 rounds per minute out to a range of 1,500 yards. Churchill and Cromwell tanks were equipped with the Czech-designed Besa machine-gun which was able to fire a 7.92mm round up to 850 rounds per minute out to the same distance. The suppressive fire these guns could bring to bear on identified enemy positions was extremely valuable and they were also used in a prophylactic manner to fire into areas of cover such as hedgerows or tree lines where snipers, Spandau or Panzerfaust teams might lurk. Ken Tout describes the use of the machine guns in his Sherman:

'Gunner, take the edge of the village straight ahead and douse it with co-ax. Co-driver, same target. Fire in your own time.'

I make a small adjustment of height and direction, a touch on the traverse grip to the right, a push on the elevating wheel forward and downward. Stamp briefly on the co-ax button. The familiar dotted line of fire leaps across the space as the Browning thuds for a moment or two. The tip of the tracer hits what might be the roof of a house in the huddle of shapes. I depress the guns fractionally. Through the telescope I can see our artillery shells bursting along the target. I can hear their explosions coming with the rhythm and frequency of a dog barking excitedly. I touch the floor button again with my foot, feeling the metal disc clearly through my illegal thin-soled shoe. Hobnailed War Office issue boots do not make for efficient firing in a Sherman. (Perhaps that's why we have a better firing record than 'regular' regiments.) Tracer streaks again, right on target. I put my foot down and keep it down, at the same time twisting the traverse grip in my right hand. Tracer hoses the distant village edge as the Browning thuds solidly away.

Down in the front compartment Bookie is also firing his Browning, which he controls directly by hand (which I cannot do because my Browning is invisible and inaccessible to me on Stan's side of the big gun). My tracer overlaps and merges with the tracer from other tanks. Alien tracer, probably enemy, crosses our front from the right. The multiple lines of fire crisscross and interconnect like the warp and wool of a brightly-coloured oriental carpet.

I keep the Browning firing until the entire belt of 250 bullets is exhausted. A dull click. Stan whips the old box away, pushes in a new box, threads the metal end of the new belt under

7   Tout, Ken, *Tank!* (London: Robert Hale, 1985), pp.64-65.

Figure 11.4 A Panzer Mk IV of 21st Panzer Division travelling at speed in Normandy, June 1944. (Bundesarchiv, Bild 101I-493-3356-05, photo: Siedel)

Figure 11.5 A German Panzer Mk V 'Panther' in northern France. (Bundesarchiv, Bild 101I-301-1955-32, photo: Bernhard Kurth)

the flat cover of the Browning and out through the other side. Cocks the gun manually. Slaps my thigh. Loaded! Again I tread the button. Traverse back and forward along the front of the village.[8]

The HE shells of the tank's 75mm main armament and machine guns were suitable for engaging 'soft targets' but only AP rounds would be effective against armoured targets. The AP round had a muzzle velocity of 2,050 feet per second and was effective against a number of armoured vehicles, relying upon a combination of its density, hardness and velocity to deliver enough kinetic energy to penetrate the armour. Stuart Hills a tank troop commander with the Sherwood Rangers recalls his first engagement near Rauray on 25 June:

> A wooded area jutted out to our left, and suddenly Arthur spotted a Panzer Mark IV. 'Enemy hornet,' I heard through the intercom. Remembering my training at Lulworth, I ordered: 'Eleven o'clock. Two thousand five hundred yards. Gunner, traverse left, steady, on. Enemy tank. Armour piercing (AP). Fire when ready.' The first shot bounced once before hitting the Panzer. There was a plume of blue smoke from its exhaust as it lurched into reverse and stalled. It started to move again and a second shot hit it as it disappeared into the wood. The shots would not have penetrated but they might have damaged a track. This was my first tank-to-tank engagement and it had not been as conclusive as I might have wished.[9]

This engagement was hardly likely to be conclusive, given that even at 2,000 yards the 75mm AP round could only be expected to penetrate 47mm of armour plate and a Mk IV's Panzer's frontal armour plate was 80mm thick. In reality a tank commander would often have to manoeuvre and close the range, or attempt a shot at the weaker side armour of the German tanks (The same German Mk IV Panzer had only 30mm side armour). Stuart Hills' account gives us an early indication of what was to be one of the greatest difficulties of the Normandy campaign, namely that the majority of Allied tank guns could not hope to penetrate German tanks except under favorable conditions. Fortunately the Mk IV Panzer Lieutenant Stuart Hills encountered above was broadly comparable to the British tanks and was also the most common German tank in Normandy, accounting for about 50% of German tanks. There were however other, more potent, threats in the German inventory, the MK V Panther and the Mk VI Tiger were particularly notorious. A German Mk VI E Tiger tank had frontal armour 100mm thick and side armour 80mm thick, even if the British tank closed to 100 yards its 75mm gun could only penetrate 74mm of armour and would therefore not defeat the Tiger's armour. The British tank commander faced little choice other than manoeuvring to both close the range and turn a flank so that he could shoot at the thinner rear or side armour. This was much easier said than done.

That some of the German tanks had such thick armour did not come as a complete surprise to the British. In 1943 they had tested the existing 75mm and 6-pounder anti-tank guns against a captured Tiger tank's frontal armour and disturbingly discovered that the rounds could not penetrate at any range. They quickly understood the requirement to provide their tanks with a heavier gun and developed the Ordnance Quick Firing 17-pounder. This gun could fire a larger AP round but also a Discarding Sabot (DS) round, the latter increasing the velocity of the round to 3,950 feet per second. The DS round was able to penetrate 161mm at 2,000 yards and 221mm at 100 yards making it the most successful solution the Allies had to overcoming the German Panthers and Tiger tanks. In 1943 Macleod Ross, a British tank expert, travelled to the United States and

---

lobbied the Americans to fit the 17-pounder gun to all Sherman tanks that were then coming off the production lines. The Americans were suspicious (after all British wartime tank design had not exactly covered itself in glory so far) and they rejected the idea. Thankfully Macleod Ross was able to persuade Whitehall to convert Sherman guns to 17-pounders in British factories. Given the poor condition of British industry at the time this was not an easy process, but by 6 June one in four British Shermans had been equipped with 17-pounders, the new design was christened the Sherman Firefly. The new Firefly tanks were able to take on the Tiger and Panther tank's frontal armour at ranges up to 1,900 yards. Unsurprisingly cramming in a gun as large as a 17-pounder into a Sherman tank required that the tank and turret in particular had to undergo substantial modifications, including losing the co-driver and the bow machine gun.[10] Ken Tout describes a Firefly tank:

> The Firefly tank is an ordinary Sherman but, in order to store its massive shells, the co-driver has been eliminated and his little den has been used as a storage space. The electrical traversing gear makes it easy to swing the gun around but heaven help me if I ever have to traverse the 17-pounder by hand, as with the 75 at Noyers. The flash is so brilliant that both gunner and commander need to blink at the moment of firing. Otherwise they will be blinded for so long that they will not see the shot hit the target. The muzzle flash spurts out so much flame that after a shot or two, the hedge or undergrowth in front of the tank is likely to start burning. When moving, the gun's overlap in front or, if traversed, to the side is so long that driver, gunner and commander have to be constantly alert to avoid wrapping the barrel around some apparently distant tree, defenceless lamp-post or inoffensive house.[11]

Despite these disadvantages the Sherman 'Firefly' was effective, even against the fearsome Tiger tank, this was amply demonstrated during TOTALIZE when tanks of the 1st Northamptonshire Yeomanry were attacked by a German armoured column on 8 August:

> No. 3 Troop (Lieut. A. James) of 'A' Squadron, the forward troop covering the right flank, were the first to make contact. Sjt Gordon commanding a 17-pounder Tank reported three Tigers advancing slowly north, in line ahead, along the Falaise-Caen road. These were seen at a range of 1200 yards. On hearing Sjt Gordon's report, Captain Boardman, the squadron second in command, ordered him to hold his fire and moved over to the troop position where he could control the shooting. When the range had closed to 800 yards Captain Boardman gave the order to fire. Sjt Gordon engaged the rear tank of the three. Two shots from Tpr Ekins, the gunner set it on fire. Time 1240 hours. The second tank traversed right and fired three shots at Sjt Gordon, but anticipating this he had already reversed into cover. Unluckily as he did so, either his turret flap hit a branch of an apple tree or it received a glancing blow from the enemy's shot; whatever the cause it came crashing down on the Serjeant's head almost knocking him out. Sjt Gordon, completely dazed, climbed out of his tank and as he did so was wounded by shrapnel, for it must be remembered that the Squadron's position was continually under mortar and shellfire. Lieut. James dashed over to Sjt Gordon's tank, took command, quickly moved into a new fire position and Tpr. Ekins fired one shot at the second tank. It exploded in a flash of flame. Time 1247. By this time the third Tiger was in a panic, milling about wondering how he could escape. To add to his confusion, Captain Boardman

10 Jarymowycz, Roman, *Tank Tactics: From Normandy to Lorraine*, (Mechanicsburg PA: Stackpole Books, 2001), p.262.

11 Tout, Ken, *Tanks, Advance!* (London: Robert Hale, 1987), p.106.

Figure 11.6 Sherman Firefly tanks of 3rd County of London Yeomanry de-waterproof near Banville, 7 June. (County of London Yeomanry)

peppered away with 75mm AP, which stopped him but did not put him on fire. Two shots from Tpr. Ekins settled the matter and this Tiger also started to burn. Time 1252. Three Tigers in twelve minutes is not bad business. Captain Boardman later described it rather like Practice No.5 on the ranges at Linney Head.[12]

The second Tiger to be destroyed by Trooper Ekins in the account above is that of Michael Wittmann, the German 'Panzer Ace'. Michael Wittmann was famous for destroying a number of 7th Armoured Division tanks at Villers bocage and effectively blunting a British advance in the process, yet in this instance he appears to squander the Tiger tank's considerable technological advantage. Not only did the Tigers (believed to number 5) fail to knock out a single British tank, but it also appears that they failed to hit a single target with any of the shots they fired. This largely unknown tank engagement highlights a double standard in some histories and the folklore of Normandy more generally. The historian Brian A Reid makes the point that 'If an Allied tank commander had done something this tactically unsound, it would have been told and retold over the years as typical example of American, British or Canadian tactical incompetence. Wittmann's action, however, has survived in popular lore as an example of courage and audacity; he may have been a dead hero, but the key word is dead, not hero. And that applied not only to him, but also to most of his men.'[13]

---

12 Neville R F, *The First Northamptonshire Yeomanry in North-West Europe* (Brunswick: J.F. Meyer, 1946), pp.29-30.

13 Reid, Bryan, *No Holding Back: Operation TOTALIZE Normandy August 1944* (Toronto: Robin Brass Studio,

Compared to their German counterparts, British tanks were also disadvantaged in terms of protection. In the cruiser tanks the bid to make the vehicle faster and therefore lighter had meant that armoured protection was sacrificed. The 30-32 ton Sherman tank had 76mm thick frontal armour and 51mm thick side armour, the Cromwell tank, weighing 27 tons, had 75mm frontal armour and 63mm side armour. This was not much use when the main armament of the modest German MK IV panzer (the 75mm KwK 40) could penetrate 84mm of armour at 1000 yards and the ubiquitous 88mm gun which was mounted in the Mark VI, B Tiger tank as well as many anti-tank guns could also penetrate 168mm of armour at the same distance. It should be pointed out that the different thicknesses on all tanks between their frontal and side armour reflect the view that the front of the tank is the area most likely to be facing the enemy and therefore warrants the greatest protection. Tank crews were trained to ensure that their frontal armour is pointed at the area of greatest threat whenever possible to increase their vehicles survivability, reversing out of a firing position for instance was a common tactic.

The disadvantage the Allied crews operated under was stark, not only did Allied tanks struggle to overmatch some German armour but conversely German tanks could generally penetrate the Allied tanks' front or side armour at almost any range. What was additionally mortifying for the Sherman crews was the tendency for their tanks to catch fire when struck by German shells. So common was this phenomena that Allied crews called their tanks 'Ronsons', based on the manufacturers advertising boast that their cigarette lighters lit 'first time, every time'. The ever-observant German soldiers christened the Shermans simply 'Tommy Cookers'. Contrary to popular belief the flammable nature of the Shermans was not as a result of the petrol engines in the tanks but rather that any penetration in the frontal arc of the Sherman would bring the enemy AP shot or Panzerfaust projectile into contact with the Sherman's ammunition stock. If the ammunition casing was ruptured it was almost inevitable that the propellant would ignite. 21st Army Group's Number 2 operational research group study of destroyed British Shermans in Normandy noted that 82% of Shermans had caught fire when hit. It takes little imagination to understand that the effect of such fires was often horrific. Captain John Stirling of 4th/7th Royal Dragoon Guards recalls his Sherman coming under fire near the little hamlet of Brettevillete:

> We had to do a five hundred yards attack with infantry which looked fairly simple. Near the little hamlet of Brettevillete I saw an SP moving about in a farm and fired six rounds of HE at it. Sergeant Harris reported over the air that he was being fired on from the farm and I made a long-since 'Famous Last Words' remark. 'It's alright. It's only a mortar.' I saw a flash from the wood above the village. The next moment a shell hit the turret with a terrific bang. After that everything was vague and ponderous like it is in a dream. I heard Murphy shout, 'Bail out, bail out.' It seemed cowardly to leave the tank when we could still fight it. Then I saw the gun mantlet spinning slowly down the gun with a great hole in it. I realised the tank was useless and we must bail out. I struggled up and was half-way out when I saw the flash again and again that terrible crash as we were hit.
>
> Something hit me in the back and I was flung to the ground. I got up and hobbled about a bit. I was alone. The tank was on fire now and from inside the turret came the screams of a trapped animal. I got up on the front. Both the driver's hatches were open and empty. With an effort I scrambled up on the turret. Murphy's hands were grasping upwards. I caught them in mine and gave him a hand. 'Come on, Murphy,' I almost whispered. His eyes were closed and sightless. Where his legs used to be were two little black charred stumps. The hands were

Figure 11.7 A German Panzer Mk VI 'Tiger' of 101 SS Heavy Panzer Battalion, I SS Panzer Corps, July 1944. (Bundesarchiv, Bild 101I-299-1805-21; photo: Scheck)

limp and clammy in the last nervous convulsions of death that was spreading a yellow stain across his face. The operator was peacefully dead on the floor.[14]

Captain Stirling was moved down the medical evacuation chain and transported by air to the hospital at RAF Wroughton. He returned to duty in Normandy seven weeks later. Whilst Cromwell tanks were just as thinly armoured as Shermans, the Churchill Mk VII tank's armour was much thicker; 150mm at the front and 95mm at the side. This undoubtedly gave it better protection but it was by no means invulnerable and it too had to operate cautiously on the battle-field. It was not just Sherman tanks that could potentially 'brew up', as Patrick Gordon a Churchill wireless operator/loader with 9th Royal Tank Regiment recalls:

The worst day for A Squadron was at Maltot on 10 July. We were moving across a field of yellow rape and through my periscope I could see tank after tank stop and catch fire although there were no signs of German tanks firing. One began to feel uneasy and the constant sound of small arms fire against the turret made us realize that things were going to be tough. Ted Spight from one of the brewed up tanks appeared just in front of us looking very dazed so we opened up a pannier door and laid him on the tool box behind the driver. Soon afterwards we were hit and *Iceni* rocked to a standstill. The interior of the turret suddenly became intensely hot, a dry scalding heat. I kept my eyes shut, shielding my face with my hands. The left hand was not wearing the leather gauntlet glove with which we were issued, the right hand had

---

14 Major J D P Strirling papers, Ref No. 3303, Imperial War Museum.

a glove on. After seemingly minutes, but it can only have been a very short period, I stood up and pushed open my turret hatches. We were yelling and I tried to release the clip which held the bag for holding the empty shell cartridges, but it jammed and could not be budged. I tried to do this in order that both Jock and Dickie could move over to my side of the turret in order to get out because Jock could not open his cupola flaps as shortly before we were hit something had struck the top turret and jammed it shut. I pulled myself out of the turret and fell over the side hitting the tracks and toppled on to the ground. As I laid there I could see a large hole slightly forward of the turret (I believe it was an '88 shot) and flames started coming out of the turret together with the sound of exploding ammunition. The dreadful cries of my crew trapped in *Iceni*, even now nearly fifty years later, occasionally return to remind me of the horror of 10 July 1944. To my everlasting sorrow I was unable to help even one of those young men with whom I had lived in intimate contact that was part of a tankman's life when in action.

My face became swollen and very tight making it difficult to see and the skin of my left hand hung down in black strips from an arm which was bloodless and white. Lt Shep Douglas, my troop leader, crawled along the field. 'Who are you' he said, not recognizing one of his own troop to who he had given orders earlier that morning. I followed him across the field of rape, crouched low because we could hear gunfire, to a gap in the hedgerow where infantry were in position. The look of horror on their faces which changed to looks of pity when they saw me will remain for ever in my mind. It is a look which I would never want to inflict on another human being.[15]

A tank's protection is not simply a measure of the thickness of its armour, but is also about utilising whatever cover, camouflage and concealment was available as means of protection. Captain Whitelaw,[16] of the 3rd Tank Battalion the Scots Guards, also equipped with Churchill tanks, highlights this. Having captured Point 226 south of Caumont during the early stages of Operation BLUECOAT he deployed his squadron's four troops facing south through to east

The mortaring and shelling on the hill suddenly intensified. Then I saw the Left hand tank of my Left forward troop go up in flames closely followed by the other two. Immediately I started to return to the hill. As I was driving up the field I saw all three tanks of my left flank troop go up in flames, and as I approached the top of the hill, I saw a tank moving from right to left in front of me. Suddenly it appeared to me (wearing a headset) as if the turret of this tank had been quietly lifted off and put down on the ground some yards away. It was only when I saw the flames that I realized that this tank had in fact exploded following a hit on the ammunition bin. This tank subsequently turned out to belong to the Second-in-Command of the battalion who had come over to see what was happening. He and his crew were blown up.

At this time I realized that the fire was coming from our Left rear because of the angle of hit on the tanks. However, needless to say I still had no idea of the exact position of the enemy tanks or guns. It subsequently turned out to come from the farm buildings in the wooded area on the Right, at the bottom of this hill.

I should like to emphasise now that all six tanks in my two Left hand troops together with the Battalion Second-in Command's tank and my second squadron HQ tank had all been knocked out in the time that it took me to drive up one fairly small field – in fact a matter of a

---

15 Beale, Peter, *Tank Tracks – 9th Bn RTR at War 1940-45* (Stroud: Sutton Publishing, 1995), p.ix.

16 This is 1st Viscount Whitelaw, who went on to have a very successful political career, holding a series of Cabinet posts as well as becoming deputy prime minister under Margaret Thatcher.

little over a minute. I mention this because it shows how very accurate and quick the German shooting was.

Captain Whitelaw's tanks had been engaged by two Jagdpanthers. These were fearsome self-propelled (SP) guns, heavily armoured and equipped with 88mm guns and superb optics. The attack by the Jagdpanthers in this instance was an unusual tactic by the Germans who tended to use SP guns in a static defensive role. The attack caused Captain Whitelaw to reflect on the dispositions of the Scots Guards' tanks:

> It was obviously a carefully co-ordinated attack planned by the Germans in the CAHAGNES area who had seen us move onto the hill some three hours previously. It was very well carried out and the shooting was of a very high order. Further battle experience would certainly have made my reserve troop and the reserve squadron shoot much quicker. This would have prevented the destruction of my Right hand forward troop but not the initial tank losses. From my point of view the main lessons learnt were that my tanks should have been more carefully concealed than they were and that I should have been even more suspicious of the unknown Left flank. The vital necessity of carefully concealed tank positions impressed me most forcibly. I think that more attention to this would have been the best hope of cutting down our heavy losses.[17]

Both British and German tanks moved very cautiously around the battlefield using dead ground and the reverse of slopes to get into a position which exposed the minimal amount of the vehicle to any potential threat. The commander's sight deliberately is one of the highest points on the turret and it allows him to observe whilst the remainder of the tank is hidden, if he were to use his binoculars from his cupola then even less of the tank need be exposed. It was a hard act to get these 'hull down' or 'turret down' positions to work all the time; but when it could be applied it meant that the enemy tank gunner faced great challenges in hitting what was often a very small target indeed. Ken Tout recalls a German Mk IV panzer moving clumsily into a turret down position:

> 'Gunner, traverse right. On! Mark IV hull down on strip of bare skyline.'
>
> My eye is attracted by a tracer from one of our tanks shooting towards the point indicated by Keith. What idiot Jerry commander is poking his head over a bare skyline? Hands adjust controls. Pity the poor crew in that Mark IV. Target so small that the fine crosswires almost blot it out. Pity the poor Jerry gunner. Stamp on button! The smoke. The Noise. Germans must be getting short of commanders too. My own tracer emerging from its cloudy birth and striking at the skyline just low of target. Near enough to splash earth and steel splinters in the idiot commander's eyes. Perhaps near enough to ricochet into the Mark IV's turret. In the eternal split-second of supercharged thought I wonder how Keith can have identified that tiny square bulge as a Mark IV. It is no more than a squared-off dirty fingernail paring showing over the crest, a thousand yards away. It does not look large enough to receive one of our 75mm shells. Its own gun is not showing. Possibly the commander did not realize that a scrap of his turret is protruding above the skyline as he surveys us through his periscope.
>
> Stan [The Loader] slaps my leg. Even as I stamp the floor button, in the eye glance before our own smoke and flame obscure my vision, I see the tracer from a neighbouring Sherman heading out in the same direction. My tracer almost collides with the other shot, right on

---

17 Operation BLUECOAT Battlefield tour: Directing Staff edition, HQ BAOR, Germany, 1947, p.40.

Figure 11.8 Churchill tanks carrying infantry in Normandy August 1944. (Tank Museum)

the same spot of the target. A modest puff of smoke arises from the point of impact. The tiny line of turret disappears. But immediately a larger puff, plume, gusher of smoke broadens and blackens the skyline at the same spot.[18]

A tank's protection will also depend on how difficult he is to detect once he has fired. Some German tanks like the Panther used propellant with a lower 'flash' which made it harder to spot once an engagement had begun. In contrast the flash and smoke from a Sherman Firefly's 17-pounder was so large that it highlighted its position to even the most casual of observers. Similarly dust produced by a travelling tank often gave away its movement and position, a good tank commander would usually slow down on the approach to a firing position to prevent throwing up too much dust and avoid hard turns as well. The noise and smoke from the tank engines could further assist the enemy in locating a British tank. Conscientious tank commanders went to great lengths with squadron or regimental fitters to ensure that their tanks were running on a mixture that didn't create the large blue clouds of smoke that were particular characteristics of some tanks, including the Cromwell, when starting up.[19] Other commanders would be reluctant to turn their tanks engines off when attending O Groups, or in concealed overwatch of an enemy position, they would only have to start them again, often with a burst of new blue grey smoke potentially compromising their position. Keeping the batteries charged, so that the radios worked and the

---

18   Tout, Ken, *Tank!* (London: Robert Hale, 1985), pp.125-126.
19   Bellamy, Bill, *Troop Leader* (Stroud: Sutton Publishing, 2005), pp.26-33.

Figure 11.9 Sherman tank of 3rd County of London Yeomanry, June.
(County of London Yeomanry)

turret traverse could be operated was often another sensible reason to keep the engine running. On the frontline any movement attracts an observer's eye and this could also allow the tanks to be spotted, as the Allies were generally in the offensive, and therefore often moving, it was much harder for an Allied tank to remain concealed than a German vehicle. One German commander emphasized how easy it was to remain hidden when static:

> Your most effective weapon is the ability to keep still…Allow the enemy tank to approach as close as possible before engaging…[the] British opened fire on tanks too early…A tank in motion cannot shoot effectively with its cannon; the gunner can only aim accurately when the vehicle is stationary. Therefore there is no need to get 'nerves' because an approaching tank swivels its turret this way and that…If the tank fires its MG only you can be pretty sure you have not been spotted.[20]

The Germans went to extraordinary efforts to conceal their tanks from both ground and air observation, covering tracks, regularly replacing the local foliage strapped to the vehicle when it started to wither, or failed to match the immediate surroundings. Although the British did not concern themselves quite so much with concealment from the air, British tanks would also make considerable effort to protect themselves through camouflage; draping hessian or local foliage over

---

20 RG 24 10553 CMF Info letter No.10 *'How to deal with Panzers – A German view'* quoted in Jarymowycz, Roman, *Tank Tactics* (Mechanicsburg PA: Stackpole Books, 2001), pp.274-275.

their tanks. Troop pennants attached to radio antennas were quickly dispensed with once they were found to give the Germans both warning and a sighting mark as British tanks appeared over the brow of a hill.[21]

The ease with which a tank can manoeuvre and take advantage of the ground is a function of the third key characteristic of the tank; its 'mobility'. This can be divided into 'strategic', 'operational' and 'tactical' mobility. A tank's tactical mobility performance is the result of a number of factors. The weight of the tank for instance is very important, the heavier the tank the more power is required from the engine to move it, or the designer accepts a slower performance. The Germans put large engines in their tanks so that although the 32 ton Sherman tank may have been lighter than some its German counterparts (e.g. the 45 ton Mk V Panther and the 54 ton Mk VI Tiger E) this did not translate into a speedier performance. The Sherman was still only able to travel at 24 mph compared to the much heavier armoured and armed 34 mph Panther. Even the Tiger tank could travel at up to 25 mph.

Top speed however is often not as important as the ability to accelerate quickly from a standing start. This is a vital characteristic in battle and a function of the transmission and gearbox as well as the power to weight ratio of the tank. In this area the Sherman was better than the Tiger or Panther.

The design of a tank's tracks are also important in delivering tactical mobility. Small narrow tracks deliver a greater ground pressure than large broad tracks and are therefore more likely to sink into the ground. This was less of a problem in the mainly dry conditions of Normandy but would certainly become more apparent in the autumn period. It was a surprise to many Allied tankmen to discover that because of its wider tracks the much heavier Panther was able to cross softer and boggier ground than the narrow tracked but lighter Sherman. Finally, tactical mobility was a function of the suspension system on the tank. A powerful engine may allow the tank to go fast across country but it was up to the suspension system to absorb the bumps from the undulating terrain and allow the crew to operate the tank's equipment. A poor suspension system would naturally limit a tank's speed even if the engine was powerful. Regardless of whatever technology was incorporated into the tank a good driver was also essential in getting the best of the tank's mobility. Though British tanks rarely fired their main armament on the move the importance of a good driver to the fighting efficiency of the tank is often overlooked. Private Norman Smith, a Cromwell tank driver, explains that a good tank driver was firstly responsible for maintaining the vehicle in a reliable condition. The crew's lives would depend on the tank engine starting instantaneously if fired upon:

> A very good tank driver also knows how to give his crew a reasonably balanced 'ride', so that they can get on with their jobs of gunnery and wireless and, in the case of the commander, observation. This demands a little more from the tank driver than the skills traditionally required of a chauffeur: looking ahead, not accelerating and braking suddenly. Going across country through hedges, over ditches, into ruined buildings the tank driver needs considerable judgement in order to avoid throwing his crew about like dice in a shaker. It is quite easy to get hurt inside a tank without anyone shooting at you; safety belts were not provided and if they had been would not have been worn as you need quick movement, especially the loader/wireless operator. If the tank brewed, the split second releasing a safety belt would have had you fried. A good driver knows what demands he can make of the tank's suspension, mixing his braking and accelerating in rapid alternation sometimes.[22]

---

21 Newton, Cecil, *A Trooper's Tale* (Grashills: Aldbourne, 2004), p.35.
22 Delaforce, Patrick, *Marching to the Sound of Gunfire* (Stroud: Sutton Publishing, 1996), p.103.

The driver would normally have two tiller bars or steering columns in a tank; each braking a different track, by pulling these tiller bars back and forth the driver could use the tracks to steer the tank. A gearbox would also control the speed of the tracks and some tanks possessed highly sophisticated ones that allowed the relative speed of the tracks to be altered and used to steer the tank (the Churchill tank for instance possessed the Merrit-Brown gearbox). This effect was more pronounced at lower gears and allowed the tank to spin 360 degrees on its own axis; this was called a neutral turn. Despite these advancements Second World War tanks were generally neither easy nor forgiving vehicles to drive, this was particularly the case over rough and uneven terrain and practice was an undoubted benefit.

The tank driver inevitably had limited visibility, particularly when closed down, and it would therefore be up to the tank commander to give him the necessary instructions. This was important, not just because the tank commander had the better view, but also because he would be the individual with the best tactical awareness of what was going on and could judge how to manoeuvre and position the tank in relation to both the enemy and friendly forces. Keith Jones was sent in his Cromwell tank to reconnoitre squadron positions for engaging an approaching group of German tanks during Operation BLUECOAT:

> As we approached the junction, I told the crew what we were going to do. It would be an acute-angle turn to the right, probably needing first gear. The driver went down his gear box to get the tightest turning circle, four to three. Three to two.
>
> I recall feeling satisfaction at what we had achieved in such a short time. On 'A' set we could hear the squadron moving out to take up the positions reported. We slowed towards the threshold of the junction, and I could feel my adrenalin working with anticipation of completing the trickiest part of the assignment. I had no inkling that I was about to make a serious blunder.
>
> The tank was almost at the corner when I heard a number of guns firing and felt two projectiles zip past the turret. If I had had any doubt about my perception, the operator disappeared precipitately below hatches. Staying head out, I spoke sharply into the microphone on intercom.
>
> 'Driver, speed it up! We're being shot at!'
>
> I could hear the enemy's quick-firing machine-guns as well now. The counter-attack must have reached a point just over the brow of the road from us.
>
> Faithfully the driver put his foot down on the accelerator instead of changing down one more gear to first. He lugged simultaneously on the right tiller bar, for the acute turn was upon us. The tank eased round as she would in second, not tight enough. Up she went onto the crown of the main road, skidded across and down the other side. There was at most a three-foot grass shoulder and then, deceptively deep, a ditch. A tank's length and we were in it, all twenty-eight tons of us, the port beam coming to rest along its far side, the tank at an angle near to 45 degrees, the driving sprockets threshing under 600 brake horsepower to no avail at all, stuck.[23]

The tactical mobility of a tank has an obvious impact to the course of an engagement or battle, but the effect of a tank's operational and strategic mobility is also important, this was one area where British tanks compared favorably to their German counterparts. The lightness of the British tanks meant that they were somewhat easier to transport across the channel in either shipping or landing craft. It was also a practical proposition to pass Shermans and Cromwells across rapidly

23 Jones, Keith, *64 Days of a Normandy Summer* (London: Robert Hale, 1990), pp.147-148.

Figure 11.10 Wounded German soldiers being ferried to an aid post on the hull of a Cromwell tank of 2nd Welsh Guards, 3 September 1944. They were captured after the Guards shot up a German convoy that blundered into their path, 20km from Brussels. (Tank Museum)

constructed engineer bridging; such as the Class 40 bridging over the River Seine seen in Chapter 4; at almost twice the weight of a Sherman a Tiger tank would have required substantially stronger bridging which would have taken much longer to construct. Finally the reliability of the Allied tanks is not to be underestimated. German tanks may have matched Allied tanks for speed despite their heavy weight, but they could only do so by consuming a large amount of petrol and through large, complex and temperamental engines. The stresses and strains on components like suspension and running gear meant that heavy tanks like the Panther and Tiger suffered from continual reliability issues and always required considerable maintenance. This was more significant than many imagine. A study by 2nd New Zealand division in Italy during 1944 discovered that many Tiger tanks simply broke down and had to be abandoned. The German support system could not cope with the thirsty and temperamental nature of these complex pieces of machinery and any extended manoeuvre or movement by the German armoured divisions would severely impact on the reliability and availability of these tanks and test the German support system to its limits. When the break out from the Normandy bridgehead occurred the Allied advantage in having a reliable and easy to maintain tank would become more apparent. The operational research section of 21st Army Group examined 223 German tanks between 8-31 August, of these three quarters had either been abandoned or 'scuttled', most of these tanks had either broken down or run out of fuel. In stark contrast the British armoured brigade's Cromwells and Sherman tanks travelled an average of 317 miles during the ten-day pursuit from the River Seine to Brussels and yet on average only six tanks per day were lost to mechanical breakdowns.

The task of repairing, maintaining and recovering broken down or damaged tanks fell to the armoured regiment's Royal Electrical Mechanical Engineers (REME) personnel. Captain Pat MacIver was the Electrical and Mechanical Engineer officer (known as an E.M.E) of the 24th Lancers and describes the role of a unit's REME personnel:

> The L.A.D. was the Light Aid Detachment of the Royal Electrical and Mechanical Engineer, a small mobile workshop in support of the squadron fitters. Every vehicle, especially each fighting vehicle, became personal to its crew who loved it for better or worse and sometimes, regrettably, 'until death do us part'. In the 24th Lancers, where pride and fellowship were strong, the system worked particularly well. The squadron fitters would maintain and repair anything they could with hands tools. Under training conditions this was like the mechanically-minded owner of a good car doing his best not to let it out of his hands into a garage.
>
> 'The garage' in this case was rather special, a mobile workshop which was proud to be part of the Regiment and to go wherever they went. This L.A.D. cared for instruments such as watches, compasses and gun-sighting equipment (including the gyro-stabiliser which came with the Sherman tanks). It cared for the tank guns and machine guns, and for the rifles and pistols. And, of course, it cared for the Armoured Fighting Vehicles and 'B Vehicles' which were those essential load-carrying trucks that brought ammunition and fuel, rations and mail and reinforcements forward, returning with 'the empties' of which some were human cargo. The L.A.D. had a mobile machine-shop which included an instrument workshop, and a 15-cwt truck equipped for electric and gas welding. There was a binned stores lorry which carried spare parts, and a heavy recovery vehicle to pull vehicles out of ditches and to tow them back for repair. The couple of dozen R.E.M.E tradesmen were almost as possessive of the regiment as were the squadron fitters, for if the L.A.D. had to pass a vehicle or gun back to the Brigade Workshop R.E.M.E that equipment was lost to the Regiment, at least temporarily.[24]

On operations in Normandy the LAD of an armoured regiment would always be busy. The 24th Lancers were pitched into battle very quickly after their arrival:

> Most of the tanks were runners which had been knocked out by gunfire, and this called for a new pattern of work for the L.A.D. Battle casualties had never been simulated in training, and the technical problems were very interesting. Shells penetrated tanks in an infinite variety of ways and places and no two problems were the same, but it was always a matter of patching holes and making good the damaged equipment, often replacing it by cannibalization. Sometimes an armour piercing shell passed into the hull and damaged the turret cage, W/T set, driver's controls or the like: these, or an engine change were easy problems. Damage to the turret ring could be 'beyond local repair', as was the brew-up when an enemy shell exploded ammunition in our tank. A difficult case occurred when the enemy shell ignited phosphorous grenades stowed in our tank: apart from the fire damage, the phosphorous stains were corrosive to the skin.
>
> While battle casualties could be full of technical interest, they brought personal misery with the pieces of flesh, the severed foot in a boot, the bloody clothing, all becoming maggot-ridden – and the personal belongings, reminders that these were our friends. The R.E.M.E. undertook the unpleasant task of clearing the tank prior to starting work, until someone took

---

24 Willis, Leonard, *None Had Lances – The Story Of The 24th Lancers* (Chippenham: Picton Print, 1986), pp.51-52.

pity and arranged for an R.A.M.C hygiene corporal to be attached to the L.A.D. for this work.[25]

The REME was not only responsible for the repair and maintenance of tanks and other Army vehicles and equipment, it also had to quickly and efficiently recover disabled armoured vehicles from the battlefield so that they did not fall into enemy hands and could be subsequently repaired. For this task the REME were equipped with Armoured Recovery Vehicles (ARVs) effectively tanks whose turret and main armament had been removed and could tow tanks off the battlefield.

To take advantage of his vehicle's firepower, protection and mobility the tank commander needed to both communicate to his crew and other tanks in the troop, squadron or regiment. Tanks very rarely operated alone, instead they derive protection from mutual support and created greater shock and surprise amongst the enemy when their firepower was concentrated and they were employed in numbers. This required a slick command and control system which was facilitated by a communication system of radios and internal communications (intercom) that were fitted into each tank. All British tanks generally had a similar system, based around the No.19 radio set. John Foley describes how they worked in his Churchill tank:

> There were three different systems in the tank: there was the 'A' set, used for longish range speech and morse back to squadron headquarters or further if necessary. There was the 'B' set, a very short-range radio used by the Troop Leader for talking to his other two tanks, and the intercom which simply allowed the tank commander to talk to the crew of his own tank.
>
> Of course with three microphones hanging around his neck the unfortunate Troop Leader would be in a bigger tangle than he usually is, so the back room boys thought up the bright idea of having just one microphone and a simple control box on the turret wall near the commander's pedestal.
>
> The control box consists of a small three-way pointer which can be moved until it points, appropriately enough, to either 'A', 'B' or 'IC'. And according to which way the pointer is pointing, so the microphone is in that particular circuit.
>
> Sounds simple, doesn't it? But many a well-meaning Troop Leader has dictated a model Situation Report to his squadron leader, only to receive a courteous acknowledgement, from his driver together with the suggestion that he tries again, this time on the 'A' set.
>
> The opposite, of course, can sometimes have drastic results.
>
> Like the time we were taking part in a Squadron mock attack across country. Things were going too well and I was just beginning to wonder where the snag was when I heard Corporal Robinson's voice coming over the 'A' set.
>
> 'Driver, slow down.'
>
> 'Driver slow down, I said. Take it easy going through this hedge.'
>
> Desperately I tried to call him on the 'B' set to tell him to alter his control switch but of course he couldn't hear me.
>
> 'Smith! Slow down!' Corporal Robinson, his dark brown voice rising to bright blue. 'Are you mad? There's a damn chalk pit just the other side of this hedge. Driver halt!'
>
> I closed my eyes and removed my headset in order to hear the crash, but just as the phones touched the turret roof I heard:
>
> 'Oh Christ!'
>
> It was followed by an aggressive 'click' and I knew that Corporal Robinson had spotted his mistake in what they call the nick of time.

---

25 Ibid., pp.149-150.

Trouble was, the Squadron Leader had also heard that broadcast and I received a shrill rebuke and a lecture about N.C.O.s who couldn't work a simple three-way switch.

So it was with some gratification that on a gunnery exercise the next day I heard the familiar voice of the Squadron Leader coming over the air saying:

'6-pounder traverse left. Traverse left, I said! Come on Jones. What the hell's the matter with you? Get that gun moving! Traverse...oh!'[26]

The radio was an important form of communication in allowing any commander to move his tanks across the battlefield as efficiently as possible and direct their fire power onto the most appropriate target. It was therefore vital that the crew should be able to work the radios and that they were kept operational. Major Jock McGinlay emphasized this aspect but also noted that the radios could be used for other gentler aspects when away from the frontline:

RHQ had the idea that, once the radios were netted in on the battalion frequency, no one should interfere with the set. In theory this may been right and the Royal Signals personnel attached to each battalion made sure that every set was in perfect tune. We had to have alternative frequencies in case of accidents and we were all supposed to know how to change. Each dawn, the CO's tank sent out a signal and we all had to make sure we were spot on to that signal. The result was that most tank crews were scared stiff to go near the set – quite the wrong idea, in my opinion; each tank crewman should be able to do every job in the tank.

To this end I got my troop together and said they could listen, as I intended, to the BBC each night, just as long as they kept quiet about it and as long as they took turns each morning at getting back onto the battalion net. Woe betide anyone failing to be spot on net. The result was a very happy troop and a confident one as far as the wireless was concerned. In my own tank we even went as far as to have four pairs of headphones terminating in a tobacco tin inside the bivouac under which we slept alongside the tank, with a master lead to the set, connected up to Hi Gang! and all the other programmes the BBC were pumping out.[27]

In this book we have covered many different pieces of equipment and machinery that soldiers had to operate, but the tank is perhaps unique. For the five-man tank crew it was not just a piece of military hardware but their permanent home and refuge. Its armoured protection meant that when on the frontline the crew would fight, live, sleep, talk, eat and carry out every other aspect of human existence from within it. Many of course would die within its narrow confines. At the back of each crewman's mind would be the knowledge that his small refuge might become a blazing inferno in a matter of seconds requiring him to exit at the fastest possible speed. The limited space in a tank and the awkwardness in getting in and out at the best of times, meant that being a tank crewman was not a job for those who suffered from claustrophobia:

As the stench in the tank diminished – or we all became accustomed to it, I spent more time in the turret. Being inside a tank has something in common with the kind of prison cell in which you are lowered down through a hole in the roof, which is also the only way out. A tank is not so deep as a cell. When you stand in army boots on the revolvable floor your forehead is just below the cupola ring, if your height is almost six foot. To step up onto the Cromwell pedestal raised you about a foot, enough to collect an airburst or snipers bullet. There was a small leather-covered stool projecting from the turret ring, onto which you could

26 Foley, John, *Mailed Fist* (St Albans: Mayflower Books, 1975), pp.18-19.
27 Forty, George, *Tank Warfare in the Second World War* (London: Constable, 1998), p.119.

Figure 11.11
County of London Yeomanry move through St Martin des Besaces in early August, the turretless vehicle passing the Sherman on the right is a Royal Electrical and Mechanical Engineers Armoured Recovery Vehicle.
(County of London Yeomanry)

hook yourself for a change of posture and a further elevation. Finally, when not at immediate risk as a target, a commander could park his bottom on the rim of the cupola, with the hatch lids open one each side protecting his thighs from small arms fire or a sudden squall. If you preferred to have your hatches open fore and aft, like those on the operator's side, there was a simple bolt to pull back on the cupola, which would then traverse to the desired position and bolt into a hole drilled at ninety degrees from the previous one.

Driver and co-driver each had their separate hatches in the two forward corners of the hull. It was possible to pass something forward or back from their compartment to the turret, and in a real emergency to crawl through. The turret gunner was in front of the commander, so nearest to the co-driver when the turret traversed front. The gunner normally got in and out by the commander's cupola. For all concerned, entrance and exit were something they were used to, so long as they stayed alive and athletic. For a wounded crew member getting out was another matter. If in the rear link we thought about it, we also avoided discussing it. Yet we could expect to find, like all other crews, that when a tank is hit, the motivation to bail out is a reflex action, like the corks in five bottles simultaneously drawn – provided that is, all five are unimpaired.[28]

The long summer days and short nights of the Normandy campaign meant that the tank crew were in operation for very long periods of time with little time for either rest or administration. In addition they would be in the closest proximity to each other for hours on end. The tank crew had to operate as a team with any individual idiosyncrasies or pettiness subdued. Differences in rank, background and character would need to be quickly overcome. Troop commander Stuart Hills describes how this tricky balance between familiarity and military discipline was achieved:

---

28 Jones, Keith, *64 Days of a Normandy Summer* (London: Robert Hale, 1990), pp.63-64.

Living so close to each other we tended to drop all formality and the crew called me by my Christian name, yet in action very strict discipline prevailed over the intercom and they answered every order immediately. Trust was a key commodity, because our very lives depended on our ability to work well together: tank crews which fell out with each other were much more likely to end up dead.[29]

There were many chores to be undertaken on the tank. Looking after the tank's main armament and machine guns was arguably one of the most important tasks and the consequences of a misfire or gun jamming in action were too terrible to contemplate. Ken Tout describes the process of cleaning the guns on a Sherman tank:

The 75 gun is a good friend but a hard master. It needs endless cleaning, servicing, checking, pampering. To clean the barrel there is a stiff brush with an extremely long handle, like those used by old-time chimney sweeps to clean narrow chimneys. Two of us together can summon up enough strength to force the tight fitting brush up the seemingly endless barrel. Rifle grooves inside the barrel cause the brush to spin, making it doubly difficult to control. Once the barrel has been thoroughly scoured and polished from without, the breech can be tackled from within. The big gun's recoil mechanism and breech fill the centre of the tank turret. We crouch around the gun in confined space and wrestle with the breech block, a heavy, uncooperative lump of polished steel which, if carelessly handled, has been known to crunch fingers beyond repair. The loader, alias the wireless operator, is provided with a thick glove, to guard against burns from the hot brass of expended shell cases and also to protect fingers against the clashing menace of the breech block.

The next chore is the cleaning and checking of the smaller guns, the browning .300 machine-guns – neat, squared, black, mass-produced but highly efficient American weapons. Whilst I extract and dismantle the turret Browning and then the other Browning from the co-drivers compartment, Stan gets busy on his wireless set, checking out all his spare valves to see that everything is in working order. Stan, Keith and I can all strip a Browning blindfolded, disconnecting it bit by bit down to its dozens of component parts, large and small. The Browning has a very strong spring to counteract its recoil when fired. It is a special art to be able to twist the highly compressed spring, take the massive pressure of it, twist it out of its socket and remove it from the gun. It only need's a finger's slip to turn the Browning into a vicious crossbow discharging the spring at a range of inches to smash through skin, muscle and bone. Tanks are hazardous places in which to live, even when the German 88s are not firing.[30]

In addition to ensuring the guns were cleaned and fit for operation the crew would also have to 'zero' the main armament checking the accuracy of the gun and ensuring it was collimated with the gun sights. In peacetime this could be done going to a nearby ranges and actually test firing the weapon. In wartime such an option was often not practical and a simple work around was used instead:

My last task is to check the gun sights. Crawling under the gun and into the loader's perch, I exert all my eleven stone ten pound force on the breech lever and swing open the breech block. I can now peer up the brilliant, silver-blue steel barrel to the bright, cobalt-blue sky beyond.

29 Hills, Stuart, *By Tank into Normandy* (London: Cassell, 2002), p.99.
30 Tout, Ken, *Tank!* (London: Robert Hale 1985), p.26.

Oh yes, August Holiday Monday at home today! I crawl back under the open gun, stretch up, hook fingers over the turret hatch and haul myself onto the flat dome of the turret, down the lesser angle of the front of the driving compartment, onto the ground.

I pull two hairs from the abundant growth on my head. The muzzle end of the big gun has tiny slits in cross shape and, with a little grease, I fix the hairs to form a cross at the end of the orifice. Back up the steep tank front, in through the turret hatch, down and under the gun. Wedged in the loader's seat, I look up the barrel again and see the cross hairs outlined against the sky. Under the gun again and squirm into the even tighter gunner's seat. Jam my eye against the telescope fixed to the gun. Fine lines on the telescopes indicate exactly where the gun is, or should be, pointing. My left hand reaches out for the wheel which raises and lowers the gun. I depress the gun until the distant cornfield comes into sight, then a lorry nearer at hand. My right hand turns the wheel which traverses the entire turret by manual power.

The turret turns so that the gun sight comes to bear precisely on the top of the white identification star painted on the door of the lorry. Now all I have to do is check that the hair cross seen through the gun barrel is also dead on the same spot. If not, I adjust the telescope sight to correspond to the actual aim of the gun as indicated by my two surrendered hairs, freely given up for King and Country.[31]

Other duties which would occupy the crew's time would include the maintenance of the two tracks, so called 'track bashing'. Each track consists of a series of independent links held together by large steel retaining pins. During peacetime and regular road travel rubber pads would be fitted to each track but for combat the simple cross-country steel tread would be used. These tracks would need to be inspected regularly for wear, damage or any obstructions that might jam the sprockets, idlers or running gear. If damaged or worn links needed replacing, the track would be slackened and the retaining rivets knocked out. Each link was heavy in its own right and therefore manipulating and maintaining an entire track was a tiring business usually involving the whole crew rather than one man. It was not uncommon for a tank to shed a track through either a tight aggressive turn or by picking up a troublesome object in its sprocket, fixing the track back on always entailed splitting the track and driving the tank back on to it, again another time consuming affair.

Second World War British tanks had no night vision systems and consequently were virtually blind at night, if they stayed on or near the frontline they would certainly be vulnerable to attack by German infantry. Consequently British tanks would retire to the rear at dusk to replenish, rearm and rest their crews. On occasions the crew would dig trenches about a foot deep and pile the soil at the side. The tank would then be driven over the trench and this would give excellent protection for the crew from artillery or mortar fire whilst they slept.[32] Though this was a safe practice in dry conditions, stories of tanks sinking in to soft wet ground and crushing individuals meant that it was a less popular method as the weather deteriorated. Alternatively the crew could use a tarpaulin fixed to the rail alongside the skirt of the tank above the tracks. This could be pulled out sideways and supported by poles at the corners to make a bivouac under which the crew could sleep. There was just room for five to lie side by side, the crews normally sleeping fully dressed except for their boots and the tank commander at one end of the row so that he would

31 Ibid., p.28.
32 Boardman, C J, *Tracks in Europe: The 5th Royal Inniskilling Dragoon Guards 1939-46* (Salford: City Press, 1990), p.121.

immediately be available if called for.[33] The final sleeping alternative that was adopted if the threat from artillery, mortar, or even direct fire, was sufficiently high was to sleep in the tank itself. Though obviously cramped and uncomfortable it was a relatively frequent practice. During the night before Operation GOODWOOD Keith Jones grappled with the dilemma of whether to sleep in or outside his tank:

> The driver and co-driver had tolerably comfortable leather-padded seats and back rests. For the turret crew the opportunities to relax were notoriously more limited. I took the shovel from its place to which Stanley had returned it, and began attacking the ground behind the tank. It must have been the hardest subsoil in the beachhead. When I had got down a bare three inches, Harry volunteered to take it on. If the Paras and the Scotties could dig it, a Norfolk farming lad could dig it, he reckoned – until he had been at it for ten minutes. After that he declared that, wherever the Airborne or the Jocks had dug-in before, it could not have been just here. He handed me back the shovel and disappeared into the forward hull.
>
> Stan proposed to curl himself round the junction box on the turret floor. Then part of Bill could use the ammunition bins on his side of the gun, while I was invited to 'drape' myself across the gunner's seat, the pedestal and an ammo bin on my side.
>
> Stan explained: 'Better than having to sleep upright.'
>
> I said I should stretch out behind the tank and come inside only if we were shelled, in which case I should try not to wake anyone. Then I had one more go with the shovel, arranging my bedding in the shallow grave, and got in fully dressed, noting that half of me protruded above ground-level.[34]

Given the long periods of time that tank crews would spend in their armoured vehicles it is not surprising that great efforts were undertaken by many to improve their vehicles. This would often result in a number of unofficial modifications being undertaken, all designed to improve both the 'efficiency' of the tank as well as provide an additional level of comfort. Liberties would also be taken by the crew in what to wear. The advantage in being a member of a tank crew is that hidden in the bowels of a tank you are rarely able to be seen by senior officers or NCOs, who would normally be expected to pass harsh judgements on your appearance. In addition the 'relaxed' nature of the Royal Armoured Corps regiments, particularly the Territorial Army Yeomanry regiments, encouraged the tank crew to adopt a standard of dress that owed more to comfort and practicality than military uniformity:

> We strike camp. Roll our bedding bundles inside ground sheets, tie them tightly, lash them to the flat rear deck, keeping the bundles long and flat so as not to impede the traversing 75mm gun. Spare kit in storage bins. It looks like a hot night, so four of us opt to travel in our one-piece denim overalls with only a pair of pants or shorts underneath. I wear a singlet as a kind of sweatshirt. Stan wears a khaki shirt under his denims. Bookie and Harvey go bare chested. In theory we wear battledress, thick, suffocating, under the denims.
>
> The British Army has never been able to come to terms with the fact that regulation hobnail boots can be dangerous on an iron tank. Early on in my training a tank started unexpectedly as I was climbing up the front. The iron nails in my boots skated on the armour plate and I found myself diving under the tank, fortunately just clear of the churning tracks. So of the

---

33 Hills, Stuart, *By Tank Into Normandy* (London: Cassell, 2002), p.98.
34 Jones, Keith, *64 Days of a Normandy Summer* (London: Robert Hale, 1990), p.78.

five only Bookie, who has always worn boots, is regulation shod. Even he has removed the hobnails. Harvey and Stan wear PT pumps, giving good purchase on the armour plate but quite illegal. I wear a strong pair of brown shoes from Stead & Simpson.

In contrast Keith, who feels the cold, dons full battledress, shirt, blouse, thick trousers, denim overalls on top. He has a pair of jaunty black civilian leather boots. All of us wear the black beret of the tanks, with the silver horse badge eternally galloping over an oval patch of bright blue cloth. Bookie sometimes wears the special tanker's steel hat, a plain basin-shaped helmet without the infantry rim. But the tin hat is unpopular and unwieldy inside the tank. Driver and commander will wear goggles as protection against the thick dust clouds cast up by columns of tanks when on the move.[35]

Having completed their administrative duties the tanks would normally return to the front line just before dawn. In static phases, or pauses in the battle, they would usually observe the battle-field from a 'hull down' position, keeping the bulk of the vehicle in dead ground behind a slope. The crew would be constantly on the lookout for tanks or any other potential target. Under such circumstances it would be impossible for the tank crewmen to exit the tank for even the most pressing of reasons. Conducting routine bodily functions was not sufficient justification and alter-native arrangements were adapted.

Stanley asked if he could risk getting out for a leak. From the higher ground further south, enemy guns answered him by plastering us once more. I suggested Bill might extract an empty shell-case from the bottom of our gun's canvas chute and pass it to Stanley for the emergency. This took a minute or so. Stan said he would try. In the event he could not manage anything whilst seated on the gunner's stool. I flattened myself against the back of my turret so that he could stand almost upright and try again. The enemy stonk ceased, and with it Stanley announced his personal relief.

It proved catching. Harry asked if Stan could pass him the shell-case for use in the forward compartment. Stanley traversed the turret until Harry could reach through and take the case from him. Harry banged his face on the hull Besa stock as he levered himself up to the edge of his seat to use the improvised container.

Albert might as well use the thing while it was there. He knocked the case and spilled a drop in getting it past the gear lever located between his knees. By the time he had finished, Bill was ready to reach forward and take it. As another stonk began, he added his own contribution. Then he looked enquiringly across the gun breech at me. I took deliv-ery cautiously just behind and below the gun. The long brass cylinder was heavier than expected, and really warm.

I was just performing when on the radio all squadron commanders were summoned to order group at a rendezvous given in letter code. Thoughtful always, Bill wrote it down for me. I finished what I had begun before grabbing the microphone to acknowledge the order. Fastening my thin metal fly buttons, I pitched the no-longer-empty shell case out of the cupola as clear of the tank as I was capable. I knew we were all hot, tired and apprehensive. The dispatch of the liquid-filled case triggered in me a brief euphoria. Switching to intercom, I announced that a valuable contribution had just been made to the local French agriculture. The engulfing stonk stopped as if on cue.[36]

---

35 Tout, Ken, *Tank!* (London: Robert Hale, 1985), pp.40-41.
36 Jones, Keith, *64 Days of a Normandy Summer* (London: Robert Hale, 1990), pp.110-111.

Figure 11.12 A German infantryman takes aim with a Panzerfaust, June 1944.
(Bundesarchiv, Bild 101I-721-0375-28A, photo: Koll)

Nothing quite magnifies the extremes of the external ambient temperature like a tank. When it is hot outside, and there were many hot days in the Norman summer of 1944, then the crew would cook. In winter time the crew would freeze in a vehicle that took on the properties of a fridge. The dust, hot temperatures and bright sunlight could all begin to degrade the crew's performance over time. Bill Bellamy recalls the other difficult environmental conditions:

Dust thrown up by the tracks presented us with an additional problem as our front mudguards had been ripped away by the dense hedgerows and the dust and grit always seemed to blow into our eyes. This was especially bad for the driver and co-driver, as they were actually sitting between the tracks, peering out through small round apertures which funnelled the dust stream into the tank. By the end of the day we were all filthy, mouths full of grit and eyes raw. Conjunctivitis was prevalent, more especially among those who 'lived downstairs'. Despite that, the problem was mild at this time [June] compared to the dust which we experienced later in the July battles. I was unable to wear goggles, as that prevented me from using my field glasses, yet it was vital to keep a close eye on every quarter. I can't remember any operation during which I had my head inside the turret, it was always out and I kept my two turret lids open, using one on either side to give me some protection.

When the sun shone, it seemed to glare down on us from dawn to dusk and, although this had its pleasant side, it was a great disadvantage when one had to keep alert. On a number of occasions, I developed a kind of binocular blindness and found it impossible to see with any clarity. Luckily my crew members were keen and competent, and helped by taking over the watch duties when I felt my vision deteriorating.[37]

The operational experience, performance and tactics of the tank and its crew were not just dictated by the capabilities of the tank but also by the type of ground. In this regard there were two very different areas the crews encountered in the first two months of the Normandy campaign. Firstly the close 'bocage' country to the west of Caen, secondly the more rolling, large open fields to the east of the city. In August as the British broke out into northern France during the 'Great Swan' the countryside changed once more becoming even more open and flat. For many of the tank crews whose military experience was either fighting in the desert, or training in the wide open armoured training areas, like Thetford or Salisbury Plain, the close nature of the bocage came as something of a shock. Captain John Stirling of 4th/7th Royal Dragoon Guards recalls:

> If ever a piece of country was ideal for defence by tanks and a nightmare for them to attack in, it was Normandy in summer. The countryside is so like England. Luxuriant green grass and foliage. Tall, thick hedges bounding small pasture fields, little sunken lanes with grassy banks, clumps of grey stone buildings forming a farm or a village. A delightful spot for a picnic, but a death trap for an invading army. In this cover a tank or a gun could hide completely and bide its time. You only became aware of its existence when your leading tank went up in flames, and often several more went up before you had any exact idea of the position. It was difficult to see to shoot more than a few hundred yards. Instead of tanks picking a position to a flank and sitting there shooting while the infantry went forward, now they had to go forward side by side with the infantry and were duly picked off.[38]

The challenge to the mobility of the British tanks was immense. Not only did the thick hedges limit visibility and provide cover for the enemy but they were also very difficult to traverse. In this tangled countryside the slower but more agile Churchill tanks performed better than the Shermans. Indeed so good was the Churchill's ability to cross difficult countryside that during Operation BLUECOAT Churchills from 6 Guards Tank Brigade succeeded in penetrating deep into the enemy's rear, simply because the Germans did not expect any tank to be able to operate in that area and had neglected their anti-tank defences. Ken Tout describes the hazardous process of traversing bocage from his gunner's position in a Sherman tank:

> 'Driver, advance!' The Sherman climbs up the bank. I get a view of the tree tops above the hedge. We level off and stay perched on the bank. This is the evil moment when the Sherman shows its thinly plated bottom to any gunner or bazooka man sitting out in the field beyond. It is a naked, unprotected feeling. Hickey revs the engine a little, we begin to topple, a giant hand seems to rip the hedge aside, we crash down to earth and are through!
> We come looking for guns, for flame, for smoke, for the frantic sudden movement of mechanical monsters behind hedges. Or the solitary field-grey hero nursing a bazooka and challenging us to move our big gun more swiftly than his modest iron tube. But this is an empty field. A tiny field. Not big enough to kick a football in. Certainly not the space for a game of cricket. A tiny grazing area defended by high ramparts of hedgerow. And nothing to see. Another tiny private world of our own. Conquered by us. And nobody the wiser.
> We roll up to the opposite hedge, merely a couple of rotations of our tracks and we are again

---

37 Bellamy, Bill, *Troop Leader: A Tank Commander's Story* (Stroud: Sutton Publishing, 2005), pp.62-63.
38 Major J D P Stirling papers, Ref No. 3303, Imperial War Museum.

Figure 11.13 A German paratrooper equipped with a Panzerschreck anti-tank rocket launcher. Most German paratroopers were engaged against American forces during the Normandy battle, though the British and Canadian forces would encounter them during the autumn and winter battles of 1944. ((Bundesarchiv, Bild 101I-587-2263-29, photo: Hegert))

pressing into the greenery. The commander must be able to see something from up above. I return to my botany studies. I should end this campaign an expert on privet, hawthorn, bramble and such. Troop corporal reports to troop leader. I sit and wonder whether the end of our barrel is projecting through the hedge to the amusement of a crew of German anti-tank gunners the other side. My continued existence suggests that this is a fallacy.

We get the word to move again. Presumably 3 Able and 3 Charlie are also forsaking their little conquered fields to brave another hedge. We crawl towards the sky, tip, balance, wait for the crash of anti-tank shots through our exposed bottom plates, then crash down frontwards into a new green world – as tiny as the previous one. Behind us the infantry will be moving up and peeping through the horrendous hole we have just made in a farmer's hedge.[39]

Such countryside required the closest cooperation with the infantry who would be required to search out the hidden German anti-tank guns and Panzerfaust teams. The Panzerfaust 30 (translated as 'armour fist') was one of the most effective weapons used in the Normandy campaign. It was a light (5.2kg) disposable rocket launcher that was fired by one individual, it had a range of only 30 metres but at that range its shaped charge warhead could penetrate 200mm of armour. The weapon was fired by holding it under the crook of an arm and lining up the tip of the warhead with a crude sight on the tube itself. The tube contained the propellant to launch the rocket itself and there was therefore a small backblast behind the firer. The Panzerschreck (translated as 'tank terror') was also used by the Germans in Normandy, but was available in more

---

39 Tout, Ken, *Tanks, Advance* (London: Robert Hale, 1987), p.76.

limited numbers than the Panzerfaust. It was a heavier (11kg) reusable rocket launcher whose rockets could also penetrate 200mm of armour but benefitted from a longer effective range of 150 metres. The disadvantage for the firer was the large amount of smoke and blast the weapon produced when fired, which meant that the operator was easier to locate. The Panzerschreck certainly did not compare well with the Panzerfaust's short burst launch and more subdued signature. Although British tanks were at their most vulnerable to Panzerfausts when on the move through the bocage, they could also be stalked by a German 'tank-hunting party' when static. Camouflage, regularly switching firing positions and the proximity of nearby infantry were the tank's best defence against such parties. Bill Bellamy and his troop were in a static position near Villers bocage:

Once again it was a wonderfully warm sunny day, everything was silent, the woodland was full of birdsong, and butterflies flitted about on the bracken. Smith was on lookout with me when he quietly nudged my arm, indicating that I should look to my near right. I could hardly believe my eyes. There on the other side of the wall but within 50 yards of my tank, was a three-man Panzerfaust crew with a Feldwebel in charge of them. The two soldiers were older men but the Feldwebel was young, deeply tanned and very much in charge, clearly directing their movements through the undergrowth. The colour of their greenish-grey uniforms and the red edging around their epaulettes seemed to be etched against the back-cloth of the greens of the scrubs around them. In fact the whole episode still stands out in my mind in real 'technicolor' detail. They were searching for us, bending low so as not to be seen over the top of the wall, but for some extraordinary reason although they appeared to be looking straight at us, the camouflage, plus the fact that the sun was behind us, must have prevented them from spotting us. They stopped at a track junction and, because of the waist-high bracken fern, were themselves completely invisible to our infantry. They had not been spotted by either of my other two tanks, probably for the same reason. What was even more frustrating was the fact that my gunner was unable to get a sight on them as they were just too close to the wall, which totally blocked his view. As they stood there, peering in our direction, I made a mental note never to take up a supporting position again without the gunner having a field of fire.

I called down quietly to the platoon commander, who at that moment was standing just by the front of my tank, asking him to lend me a Bren gun or his Sten gun so that I could fire at them. He flatly refused saying that such weapons as he had, he needed, and walked away from the tank towards the left but behind the wall. Meanwhile, Alan Howard, who was in the right-hand tank, and on a slight rise in the ground, had spotted some movement but couldn't determine if it was the Queen's or some enemy. He came up on the 'B' set and asked if it was enemy and whether he should fire his turret machine gun. I think that the sound of this call, crackling out over my headphones, disclosed our whereabouts, to the Germans, as the man with the Panzerfaust lifted it on to the shoulder of the second man and pointed it in our direction. I shouted over the wireless for Corporal Howard to fire, and at the same time fired at them with my pistol, although they were really out of range unless one was very lucky or a very skilled. I think that I had fired about twenty rounds in my life and all those on a range under clinical conditions, so I certainly wasn't the latter. At the same moment the Panzerfaust was fired, and I actually saw it in flight. It went about 5 yards to the left of my tank, hitting the parapet of the stone wall at exactly the spot where the young officer from the Queen's was walking. It decapitated him as if by surgery, and his body seemed to continue on its way for a few paces before falling. It was revolting and totally unexpected. It distracted me for a few vital seconds and, although I heard the sound of Alan Howard' tank firing, when I looked

Figure 11.14 A heavily-camouflaged Sturmgeschütz III turns in a built-up area of Normandy. (Bundesarchiv, Bild 101I-721-0387-11, photo: Theobald)

> back to the woodland I could not see any sign of the three Germans. It was all over in a couple of minutes but it remains as one of my most vivid memories of the war.[40]

In addition to hand-held infantry weapons, the bocage allowed the Germans to very effectively employ their many medium calibre anti-tank guns; such as the 7.5cm Pak 40. Being both easy to conceal and move into firing positions they were deployed in a very similar manner to the way the British employed their 6-pounder anti-tank guns. The weapon had a maximum range of 1,700 yards and at a more typical engagement range of 1,000 yards could penetrate 84mm of armour (or to put it another way the frontal armour of a Sherman or Cromwell tank).

The other German weapon system that was suited to the bocage and whose role has sometimes been underestimated are the German assault guns or self-propelled guns. These tracked armoured vehicles looked a little like tanks, but had no turret and instead mounted the main armament in a fixed casement in the vehicle's hull. The obvious disadvantage of this was that the whole vehicle had to turn in order to traverse the gun. On the other hand assault guns were cheap and easy to build and the lack of a turret meant they had a low profile. A Sturmgeschütz III (StuG III), the most common assault gun used by the Germans in Normandy, was only 7 feet high compared to the Sherman's 9 feet, making it ideal for defence amongst the hedgerows of Normandy. Assault guns or self-propelled guns could be armed with a variety of main armaments up to and including 88mm in calibre. The StuG III for instance was armed with the same high velocity 75mm gun as the Pak 40, making it a very potent opponent. Ken Tout recalls their effectiveness:

---

40 Bellamy, Bill, *Troop Leader* (Stroud: Sutton Publishing, 2005), pp.60-61.

Figure 11.15 Sherman tanks of the Fort Garry Horse near le Rabet take part in Operation TRACTABLE, the tank in the foreground is a Flail tank from 79th Armoured Division. (Lieut. Donald I. Grant, Library and Archives Canada, PA-113659)

I screw my eye up close to the gun sight and slowly traverse along the 2 Troop area, taking advantage of the considerable magnification to explore the intimacies of that little wilderness of trees and shadows in front of an even darker hedge. Nothing moves there…

…The SLAM-CRASH of an aimed shot – direct, violent, massive – smashes across the humdrum background of barrage. Where? What? '2 Baker. I'm bloody hit! Bail out! Hornet at…Gawd…' (…?...) (God, that's Astley gone!)

Hornet – enemy tank or SP. Where? Where? where, where, where…I squeeze the grip right …left…traversing quickly staring into the camel-shaped tree. Hornet at …where, where, where, the hedge solid topped, fairly level has a gap, a gap. A gap? Why? What 'Charlie, left of roof, hornet in hedge over…' I adjust left, down, crosswires on! Stamp! Flame at muzzle. Frustrating smoke. Smoke. Smoke. Clearing to show spark of tracer leaping high into gap but another tracer from near gully flies into gap ahead of my tracer as Stan slaps my leg, loaded, down a bit, fire! Stan slaps. Stamp. Fire. Traverse. Sight. Slap. Stamp. Fire…

…A feather of smoke, more permanent than the transient clouds exhaled by shell bursts, wavers up to the left of the roof. I put my foot on the other pedal as solidly as on the accelerator of a car. The co-axial Browning rattles away, every fifth bullet trailing tiny tracer sparks. The first sparks dig into the roots of the hedge. I move the gun control gently up and down in a hosing motion with my left hand whilst traversing the turret slowly with my right hand. The Browning sends out fiery arrows at the hedge, perhaps half a mile away. Other tanks are brassing up the hedge in a similar fashion. I keep my foot down, mentally ticking off the tens of bullets fired. A sharp click announces the end of the belt of bullets. My tiny hose of fire quenches. Beyond the hedge the single column of smoke still rises, much thicker now. Around the Robertmesnil roof a wider cloud of smoke indicates a building on fire. Whether farmhouse or barn we have no means of telling.

Keith: 'Gunner, cease fire. Operator, load AP again.'

Stan: 'Co-ax reloaded…75 loaded AP'

Me: 'I feel better for that little bit of anger.'
Bookie: 'I hope Corporal Astley feels better too.'
Me: 'What do you mean?'
Bookie: 'I mean look over to the right of the track. More smoke.'[41]

The variety of threats likely to be encountered in the bocage; the Panzerfaust teams, medium calibre anti-tank guns, assault guns as well as tanks themselves meant that British armour had to operate carefully. The situational awareness of the crew of a tank is very limited in such close country, the gunner and loader will be looking through narrow periscopes and even the commander, who can at least stick his head out of the cupola will be somewhat deafened by the engine noise of his tank. Under such circumstances assistance from the infantry and other arms was essential in dealing with the enemy. Stuart Hills, describes, from a tank commander's perspective, how this flexible cooperation between arms would work:

> In this sort of country, the infantry proceeded along the sides of the roads in advance of the tanks, as this lessened the chance of tanks being hit by Panzerfausts. If Spandau fire opened up on the infantry, they immediately went to ground in adjoining ditches and it was then that the tanks had to move forward to take retaliatory action with their own machine-guns or 75-millimetre HE shells. This might involve moving through gaps into the fields beyond the lanes, but we were wary of getting too far ahead of our infantry and they liked us around to give them shelter and protection.
>
> When the country was more open, the infantry would move ahead and, if fired upon, the tanks would respond with smoke shells to provide initial protection. The tanks would then advance, but the biggest danger was the possible presence of enemy tanks. We could also call up our own supporting artillery from the Essex Yeomanry who would put down additional covering fire. The infantry were obviously unable to advance if enemy tanks were in the vicinity and they could give us no protection from those tanks or self-propelled guns –which were usually the dreaded 88-millimetres – so we would use smoke to give ourselves cover. If we had an RAF Forward observer with us, he could call up aircraft, but if we were on our own, we had to get on to Brigade over wireless to secure help from a spotter plane and then call down the ubiquitous Typhoons.
>
> When we entered a town or village, tanks did the softening-up first by destroying all possible positions where enemy infantry might be lurking. We simply hosed down the buildings with shells and machine-guns, and then called through our infantry for systematic house-to-house clearance. There was always the danger of Panzerfausts in such an environment, just one infantryman who might be lurking behind a wall or doorway waiting to attack us from virtually any possible direction.[42]

Infantrymen were well aware of this symbiotic relationship between tanks and infantry and understood the vulnerabilities and risks the tanks operated under when in the bocage. Infantry platoon commander Sydney Jary took a sympathetic view of their predicament:

> I was left with a profound pity for them. Hopelessly out-gunned by the German Mk IV, Mk V (Panther) and Mk VI (Tiger) tanks, they suffered grievous casualties. The German 75mm and 88mm anti-tank guns also wreaked a terrible havoc. To add to these perils the German

---

41 Tout, Ken, *Tank!* (London: Robert Hale, 1985), pp.104-105.
42 Hills, Stuart, *By Tank Into Normandy* (London: Cassell, 2002), pp.119-120.

Figure 11.16 The dreaded German dual-purpose 88mm gun. Used in the anti-tank role it was deadly. (Bundesarchiv, Bild 101I-496-3469-24, photo: Zwirner)

infantry had by far the most effective short-range and anti-tank weapons. Their bazooka was larger and had a longer range than that used by the American infantry and was in all respects superior to our PIAT. Their small Panzerfaust was probably the best conceived weapon of its type in any army. Lurking in woods and hedgerows, German infantry, armed with either of these weapons exacted a heavy toll of any of our tanks that strayed from the immediate protection of our rifle sections.

Denied scope for manoeuvre, our tanks were reduced to the role of blind, slow and highly vulnerable infantry support guns. Their primary task was to knock out enemy machine-gun positions with 75mm high-explosive shells and these they could seldom see. Consequently, and it was very difficult, we had to devise a means of identifying these cunningly concealed targets for the tank commander. We soon learned not to climb onto the tank and shout. Due to engine noise he could seldom hear and, for us, it proved a lethal pastime. We tried firing Very lights towards the target and also Bren bursts of all-tracer rounds, but neither was satisfactory. The most successful arrangement was for the tank commander to throw out a head and breast microphone set, but even then engine noise made it difficult.[43]

Cooperation with the infantry was vital and usually entailed the tank commander sticking his head out of the turret. Tank telephones, a handset in a box on the exterior of the tank that linked to the tanks intercom system, were to be developed later on in the war, but many tank and infantry

43 Delaforce, Patrick, *Marching To The Sound Of Gunfire* (Stroud: Sutton, 1996), p.109.

commanders would be killed in Normandy by snipers or German rifleman whilst trying to coordinate with each other.

If the bocage west of Caen was difficult to operate in, then the more open country to the east of the city might have been expected to offer better opportunities for armour. On the face of it the ground was good 'tank country' but sadly the Germans had time to set up a mutually supported defence in considerable depth, incorporating their most powerful weapons; the 88mm anti-tank guns as well as Tiger and Panther tanks to great effect. The wide open fields played to the strength of these weapons; namely their long range fire that could penetrate and destroy the British Cromwell and Sherman tanks before the latter could advance close enough to retaliate. Firing from well concealed, hull down, or dug-in positions they ensured that their own protection was high.

The 88mm anti-tank gun was the most feared of the German anti-tank weapons in the Second World War. At 1,000 yards it could penetrate up to 187mm, at 2,000 yards it could penetrate up to 137mm of armour; still almost twice the thickness of a Sherman's frontal protection. The effect of an 88mm strike was devastating. Lieutenant Derek Philo, a troop commander in 5th Royal Inniskilling Dragoon Guards, describes being struck by an 88mm gun at the incredibly short range of 100 yards:

> I ordered the gunner to traverse left, in the general direction of the suspected opposition, and warned the crew that we were going to move forward as quickly as possible and go straight across the road. From there we could get into a good position to observe and fire. Trooper Eddie Booth, the driver, knew his job and was ready to move. I gave the order 'Driver, advance to cover' and we set off with a surge of power which rocked me back against the turret ring. We were right in the middle of the road when we halted with a jolt. The driver being closer to the ground and concentrating on the way ahead, had spotted mines right in the centre, where normally there would be a white line. We halted about two feet short of them.
>
> I ordered 'Driver reverse'. We then learned that the enemy gun was a very well positioned 88mm and firing at a devastating range of about a hundred yards. The shot entered the co-driver's hatch and went out through the driver's side, killing both men instantly. The turret was jammed. We couldn't move, nor could we use the gun. We had no alternative to bailing out. I had gained the distinction of being the first tank in the Regiment to be knocked out by an 88mm.
>
> The two crew members, Eddie Booth and Billy Hodgson, had been killed before we had a chance to fire a shot. To further complicate our escape the turret hatch had come down very heavily on my head when we were hit and almost knocked me unconscious. I grabbed a smoke grenade and threw it out of the turret to cover our exit, but it fell on the engine deck and almost choked us, I was still unaware that the two forward crew members were dead and hoped to be able to get them out. Fortunately, the German gun crew must have thought we were on fire and did not fire again. The three turret crew almost fell out of the turret, half blind and choking with the thick smoke. The other tanks in the troop, now aware of the gun position, quickly deployed and dealt with it. The Germans who manned it were mere boys. I was able to report what had happened, but I knew that the first class account of the damage done by an 88mm would do nothing to reassure the others. The medical officer's half-tracked ambulance came forward and we were taken back. 'Doc' Forrester gave me a drink of something and I went out like a light. I was to remain away from the Regiment until the following December.[44]

44 Boardman, C J, *Tracks in Europe; The 5th Royal Inniskilling Dragoon Guards 1939-46* (Salford: City Press,

A single 88mm gun was dangerous enough but where the Germans felt a major Allied attack was likely they would deploy an antitank screen of many guns sited to give mutual support to each other and arranged in depth. These dug-in guns could usually be neutralised by a combination of air support and/or artillery, however during Operation GOODWOOD the British quickly out ran the bulk of their artillery support, stuck as it was on the other side of the River Orne, the preliminary air bombardment had also not touched the tank and anti-tank positions sighted on the Bourguébus ridge. The British had underestimated the depth of the German defences and were now to experience the effect of concentrated mutually supporting tank and anti-tank fire. The 2nd Fife and Forfar Yeomanry were tasked to take the Bourguébus ridge and suffered heavy casualties as their attack withered in the face of this combined fire. Lance Corporal Ron Cox was a young loader/operator in the regiment and describes his part in the attack:

> I did not see Major Nicholls' tank hit; it was out of sight of my periscope. But I did see what happened to the 2ic's tank. It brewed as soon as it was hit and the three turret crew bailed out, the gunner and radio operator both with their clothes smouldering. Then Lieutenant Sammy Millar, our troop leader, whose tank was halted just in front of us, was the next to be hit. Our crew commander, Sergeant Wally Herd, could see the carnage going on around him as he stood huddled down with his head just above the turret…
>
> … The whole crew remained perfectly calm and almost totally silent, apart from the occasional 'Bloody hell!' as another tank went up. After what seemed hours but was probably only a few minutes Wally Herd, whose coolness, I'm sure, saved our lives that day, ordered 'Driver reverse.' The tension was electrifying. I remember thinking 'Good old Wally, he's getting us out.' There was absolutely no cover, except the uncertain billows of smoke that might obscure us one moment and reveal us the next. Suddenly there was a tremendous crash and the tank shuddered and rocked.[45]

Lance Corporal Cox's tank had been struck by a shell which broke a track, immobilizing the vehicle. The crew successfully bailed out, fortunately in the nick of time because the tank was struck a second time. In such circumstances artillery was often the best method of dealing with the 88mm gun. But that would suppose that the target could be accurately located. If that was not the case then the tank commander could consider using his smoke shells to mask the general areas of the gun and prevent him engaging the unit.

> Suddenly regimental net reported losing tanks to 88mm gunfire on the right. I traversed our turret in the general direction, scanned the area up to a thousand yards distant through binoculars, along the rising ridge as well as down the slope of a re-entrant: nothing firing and nothing moving anywhere. Were the enemy shots coming from tanks located higher up the ridge in the heat haze? There were several patches of sunken or dead ground between our position and the haze obscured distance.
>
> I ordered a few rounds from our own gun, on percussion spread about in the nearer sectors: perhaps a blast would flap a camouflage net, draw some retaliation…Nothing. Another tank was reported hit, B or C Squadron's? I had seen nothing fire the shot. I fired two more rounds still with no effect.
>
> 'We have a few smoke, Skipper.'

1990), p.124.
45 Dunphie, Christopher, *The Pendulum of Battle – Op GOODWOOD 1944* (Barnsley: Leo Cooper), 2004, p.75.

Bill might have come to the end of one bin of HE, seen some smoke projectiles there and thought we could use them before we traversed to get at another bin. Equally well he might have thought they could resolve our present problem. I thought of the tactical course dictum that smoke is a two-edged weapon. I hesitated. Then 'A' set reported another tank casualty.

'We'll try a couple, Bill. Keep your fingers crossed.'

I picked an area 900 yards further along the ridge on its eastern edge, judging it to intervene between the regiment and whatever gunsights might be trained on us from beyond. We put down the two smoke and a third which Bill produced. None of us had seen 75mm smoke used before.

In what felt like still air under a sizzling sun, the initial effect looked negligible. As the little distant puffs developed, spreading and thickening, we could see that there was some kind of a local white screen. Then slowly, where we could have sworn there had been no wind, the screen began moving back towards us. Light airs from the south! Another tank was reported hit. I winced. The tactical course had been right: it would have been better if I had never used the stuff.

Next moment C Squadron announced spotting an 88mm gun emplacement they had previously knocked out which had now sprung to life again. They silenced it once more, and our tank losses from armour piercing shot ceased for the time being.[46]

The open ground to the east of Caen was perfect for the 88mm anti-tank gun, but troublesome though these were, they were at least usually static. The same gun on the Tiger tank made it one of the most feared German tanks of the war. Though mechanically unreliable and only deployed to the Normandy front in three rather understrength battalions the Tiger captured the dark imagination of most Allied tank crews. This was scarcely surprising given its combination of lethal firepower and heavy armoured protection that made both its front and sides impenetrable to most British tanks. Captain Tony Heywood of the 1st Grenadier Guards armoured battalion recalls encountering a Tiger in his Sherman tank during Operation GOODWOOD:

By this time Tiger tanks had engaged us from Emieville. We lost a number of tanks and had the unpleasant experience of seeing our own 75mm rounds bouncing off the German tanks. I could see one of our 17-pounders engaging two enemy tanks, but his shots were going wide, so I moved my tank alongside to give corrections. As we got into position my operator said 'I think 4 Charlie has had it'. Sure enough smoke started to erupt from the turret and the crew quickly bailed out. Now the Tiger turned his attention to me. We managed to get three quick shots off at him, and watched in horror as they bounced off. The Tiger fired, and somehow missed us. We quickly fired smoke, and as we reversed I could see that the Tiger was also withdrawing.[47]

Captain Heywood was lucky, usually the only chance a Sherman had to defeat a Tiger, if in a standard Sherman, Cromwell or Churchill, was to attempt to manoeuvre to the rear. John Foley encountered a Tiger in his Churchill and attempted to do precisely that, ordering the remaining tanks in his troop to stay firm whilst he manoeuvred his tank across open ground to get a shot at the Tiger's vulnerable rear armour.

46 Jones, Keith, *64 Days of A Normandy Summer* (London: Robert Hale, 1990) pp.108-109.
47 Dunphie, Christopher, *The Pendulum Of Battle: Operation Goodwood 1944* (Barnsley, Leo Cooper, 2004), p.123.

We were in position, about forty yards from the road. The Tiger had not yet gone by, but a little way up the road to the right I could see the cottages vibrating from the passage of the super-heavy tank.

'It'll all depend on you, Pickford,' I told the perspiring operator across the turret from me. 'The quicker you can load, the more shots we'll get off.'

He nodded to show he understood, and McGinty cuddled closer into his telescope.

I saw the front of the Tiger's track starting to cross the gap – and then I was staring straight down the barrel of an indecently long 88 millimetre gun. He hadn't been going for the bridge at all; he had been coming after us. The tank commander of the Tiger must have thought we were still in our defensive position some way back, because in the brickdust and smoke he didn't see us at first. My entrails turned to ice as I stared at the heavily armoured front of the Tiger. And then I yelled 'Fire!'

McGinty fired, and even before the gun had run back into its mounting, Pickford had slammed home another shell and the breech had clanged shut.

'Fire!' I yelled again.

The crew of Avenger were able to get off three shots all of which bounced off the Tiger's thick frontal armour:

McGinty had just got off the third round when the Tiger gunner recovered from his surprise. I was peering forward through the gloom when suddenly, and without any noise that I can remember, a sharp spike of yellow flame stabbed out of the muzzle of the 88mm gun in front of us.

Sparks flew from the front of Avenger, and she reared back on her hind sprockets, the nose lifting slightly off the ground.

A sudden heat singed the back of my neck and a rapid glance over my shoulder showed flames and smoke pouring from the engine hatches.

'Bail out – round the back of the tank!' I hollered, and snatching off my headset I dived from the turret straight to the ground.

Crosby, Pickford and McGinty joined me as a second shell crashed through the length of the tank and into the engine compartment.

Feverishly I looked around for some sort of cover, and a shallow saucer-like depression in the ground some distance away was the only thing I could see.

'Into that hole over there. Move!' I said, and keeping bent double we ran across and into the hollow.

Then I realised one of us was missing.[48]

John Foley's driver Hunter had been killed when the Tiger shell's struck. When facing armoured goliaths such as Tigers British tank commanders were forced to develop imaginative ways to deal with such a menace. Lieutenant Stuart Hills used a judicious blend of smoke and supporting arms to deal with a Tiger tank that was destroying the Shermans in his column. The reader will note that the Tiger's commander was taking advantage of his gun's impressive range and successfully engaging the British tanks from 2,000 yards. The account also demonstrates the sophistication of the British in rapidly employing combined arms against a difficult target:

---

48 Foley, John, *Mailed Fist* (St Albans: Mayflower Books, 1975), pp.80-82.

On August 2 the squadrons went their own way and our own role became more intense and dangerous. We started at dawn, with my tank about fourth from the front. The infantry of the 7th Hampshires were with us, walking alongside the tank and covering our flank. Then we arrived at a T-junction, which was mined, along with the fields around it. The column halted to allow the sappers to come up and clear the mines, when suddenly a Tiger tank emerged from cover and moved to the high ground overlooking the road. It opened fire at about 2,000 yards and hit the tank further back in the column. With both ends of the road now blocked, we were bottled up and the Tiger was out of our range.

I shouted: 'Gunner, traverse right. Steady on Tiger, Smoke. 1,750 yards fire when ready.' Our shot landed just in front of the Tiger and the smoke soon obscured it from view. We fired again, this time just to the left of the tank, aiming to keep plenty of smoke between us and it. Other tank commanders did the same, while the air officer accompanying us called up four Typhoon fighter-bombers off the cab-rank to fire their rockets at the Tiger. We fired some red smoke to identify the target, and then the planes came in, very low and with a tremendous roar. The second plane scored a direct hit and, when the smoke cleared, we could see the Tiger lying on its side minus the turret and with no sign of any survivors. It was an awesome display of firepower and demonstrated only too clearly how important control of the skies was to our ultimate success.[49]

Whether in the bocage or the more open ground east of Caen, the British armour was essentially carrying out two tasks: assisting infantry in the break in battle and armoured exploitation of a broken enemy. Infantry support tanks were not only useful during the break in battles in Normandy, they also played a key role in overcoming the highly developed fortifications such as those of Le Havre. John Foley describes how his crew cooperated with the infantry in overcoming these difficult defences:

The previous night's bombing had left huge craters everywhere but it had also destroyed a lot of the defence works. Anti-tank guns there were, but the bombing had written off their protective machine-gun posts. And in some cases the bigger guns had been bombed, leaving the Spandau pits unharmed.

We very soon reached a working agreement with the infantry; we would take care of the machine-guns for them, if they would sort out the anti-tank guns for us.

And it worked like a charm.

We would roll slowly forward until a burst of unpleasantness met us, and then we would turn our combined guns on to whatever was causing the trouble. Sometimes we had to put down a hasty smoke bomb, and retire a little way down the hill; and sometimes the infantry would dive into the bomb craters while we fired shells at the pillbox until the little white flags began to appear.

On my right Tony Cunningham had the bad luck to come on an anti-tank gun and Spandau post together and in action. But by cunningly using his smoke thrower and guns alternately he managed to persuade these particular Germans that the war held no future for them.

At last we reached the top of the hill and were able to spread out and allow a couple more troops to pass through and continue the good work.[50]

---

49 Hills, Stuart, *By Tank Into Normandy* (London: Cassell, 2002), p.121.
50 Foley, John, *Mailed Fist* (St Albans: Mayflower Books, 1975), p.102.

On some occasions the German defences had been beaten down by an earlier artillery or air bombardment. This aided the British armour and meant that they were more likely to achieve the shock and surprise a mass of tanks can generate on the enemy. The effect of this was often to undermine the will of the enemy in a way that a more conventional infantry attack could not do. Major Bill Close, a squadron commander in the 3rd Royal Tank Regiment, gives a sense of this phenomena during the early stages of Operation GOODWOOD.

> We set off after the barrage which advanced ahead of us. Control was fairly easy initially, but with the tremendous dust and the explosions only 100 yards ahead it became increasingly difficult. Tanks were about thirty yards apart. I was in between and just behind my leading troops, with my third and fourth troops behind me. On my left was B Squadron. I suppose our regimental frontage was about 600 yards. Soon we met the first dazed and shaken German infantry who tried to give themselves up. We rather gaily waved them back where the motor platoons of G Company had their hands full rounding up parties of bewildered Germans and pointing them to the rear. I clearly remember seeing David Stileman behind me, like a florid cockerel marshalling his chicks. As we got level with Cuverville on our right there was a small amount of anti-tank fire, so I told my two right-hand troops to brass up the hedgerows with their machine guns, just to keep the enemy's heads down, while we pressed on towards the first railway line.[51]

Although the British did succeed in advancing 6 miles into the German defences it was not sufficient for them to effect a break out during Operation GOODWOOD, the depth and strength of the German defences were just too strong. However Operation GOODWOOD successfully supported Montgomery's plan to tie down the bulk of the German forces, particularly their armoured forces, in the British Sector. This ultimately allowed the Americans under Bradley to break out in the West. Although the first weeks of August would continue to see tough fighting in Normandy the broken German front gradually began to give way, initially progress remained bloody and painfully slow; the consequent pressure on the exhausted armoured crews was high:

> I called together my tank commanders in the troop for a last-minute conference, which was all the more important as we were to be the leading troop in the squadron. We took it in turns between the three of us to be the lead tank, and this time it was to be my turn. To be the leading tank, of the leading troop of the leading squadron of the leading regiment, with the axis of advance along a narrow lane into a village known to be held by enemy armour and infantry, was to put it mildly, bloody dangerous. It was just as unpleasant for the infantry, but at least they could dive into the nearest ditch, whereas a Sherman tank could barely rotate its turret, let alone hide.
>
> We were by now all too familiar with that fearful sense of anticipation whenever we turned a corner or crested a hill. We almost expected the crash of an anti-tank gun or a Tiger's 88-millimetre, that virtually simultaneous explosion of a shell hitting the tank, followed by a moment's pause to recover from the shock, and then the order to bail out. If we were lucky, we would scramble from the tank, trying to avoid the inevitable Spandau bullets or the arrival of a second shell, before we dashed to the nearest ditch and covered our heads. I had seen this happened to others and I was under no illusions about my own invulnerability. And now I had to lead again. My attitude at such times was one of anger and resentment, which was

---

51 Dunphie, Christopher, *The Pendulum of Battle: Operation GOODWOOD 1944* (Barnsley: Leo Cooper, 2004), p.60.

self-defeating if allowed to go too far. It was difficult to hide such vexation from the crew, who perhaps felt I should do more to protect them, but I never felt any bitterness towards me. On the other hand, the generals came under heavy fire from me, with some extremely rude things said about their parentage and other matters.[52]

As the German front collapsed the long awaited opportunity for the Allied armoured divisions to pursue and exploit a broken army presented itself. Once the River Seine had been crossed by 43rd Wessex Division at Vernon the commander of XXX Corps, General Horrocks, decided to use his armour's operational mobility and advance deep into the rear of the enemy. He describes this pursuit by the two armoured divisions within XXX Corps:

> The race for the Rhine was now on, and the next few days were the most exhilarating of my military career. The German Fifteenth Army, holding the coastal area, and still awaiting our major invasion in the Pas de Calais, suddenly found their lines of communication threatened by a powerful armoured thrust. With the Guards Armoured Division on the right and the 11th on the left, we swept through the inadequate ad hoc defences which were all the Germans could manage in the time, like a combine harvester scything through a field of corn. The armoured car screens formed by the 2nd Household Cavalry Regiment on the right and Inns of Court on the left, would report enemy defensive positions, hidden Panthers and so on; if the opposition was likely to be serious, our leading tanks which had been advancing down the road would deploy across country to attack the enemy from the flank or rear, supported by their artillery which could drop into action at a moments notice. If the opposition proved tougher, the Motor Battalion and/or lorried infantry brigades would de bus and attack from the front – this, however, was rarely necessary. All this sounds easy, but success depended on high-class training and above all perfect wireless communication.[53]

General Horrocks highlights that to maintain the momentum of the advance in the 'Great Swan' he decided to use that other element of the Royal Armoured Corps, the armoured car regiments. These armoured car regiments not only scouted ahead of the armoured columns but could also dash forward and seize key bridges before they were blown. 'Faith', 'Hope' and 'Charity' were three such bridges over the River Somme at Sailly-Laurette, Corbie and Vecquement and on 31 August the 2nd Household Cavalry Regiment were tasked with capturing all three. So began a tough night for the 2nd Household Cavalry Regiment as Lieutenant Orde relates:

> A night march through enemy territory is at the best of times a tense affair. The drivers peer out of their visors, intent on avoiding falling asleep or landing in the ditch. The car commanders also stare ahead, trying to penetrate the gloom for signs of the enemy and check-up on the right route. The operators live in a strange world of their own at the bottom of the turret, tormented by crackles and demonic wireless noises while map boards and chinagraph pencils drop on to their heads. Gunners grip the trigger mechanisms as much for support as anything else, for they are almost blind at night. Over everyone the desire for sleep descends in recurrent and overpowering waves …
> … Villages began to slip by. Most of the inhabitants realized that the British had crossed the Seine and were on their way forward, but none had imagined that they could be arriving so soon and in the middle of the night. They believed that the Germans were still passing

---

52 Hills, Stuart, *By Tank Into Normandy* (London: Cassell, 2002), pp.125-126.
53 Horrocks, Lt Gen Sir Brian, *Corps Commander* (London: Sidgwick and Jackson, 1977), p.70.

Figure 11.17 3rd County of London Yeomanry Sherman tanks advance towards the Somme river during the break out, 2 September. (County of London Yeomanry)

through and not many had stirred from their beds. But occasionally a keen-eared Frenchman would detect the difference between the sound of the fleeing enemy transport and the more sustained roar of the pursuing British cars, and then he knew it must be 'Les Anglais'. We saw them stir, silhouetted figures pulled back the curtains, flung open their bedroom windows and shouted their heartfelt greetings as they cheered the cars on their way …

General Horrocks had set 2nd Household Cavalry Regiment a demanding timeframe and would have known that the risk to the Recce troops would have correspondingly increased. In such a pursuit the commander inevitably has to sacrifice security and caution for speed. Lieutenant Orde continues:

There could be no question of tactics – The squadrons simply went forward at the pace of the leading scout car and, apart from the advance guard troops, very nearly nose to tail. Nor was it only the troop in the lead which did the shooting, because so little aware of the true situation was the enemy that he would frequently blunder into the middle of the column from a side turning. At other times he would come bowling down the road, visiting farms in search of provender, straight into the sights of the advancing Besas… Meanwhile every crew and vehicle appeared to be imbued with but one common purpose – to speed flat out for the Somme. For the first time since landing in Normandy, the armoured cars felt that they had been given a job really suited to their cavalry role, and nobody in the British Army was going to catch them. The scout cars were in their element, the armoured cars were beginning to wonder whether their ammunition would last out, and even the Staghounds forgot the world of wireless and galloped on, neck and neck with the clanking Matadors. ...[54]

All three bridges were to fall to the British that morning. Lieutenant Hanbury had been given the task of capturing 'Hope' at Corbie. As his troop approached the bridge they came across Germans trying to set up a hasty protective screen. Corporal of Horse Thompson describes the action at the bridge:

> It was easier than shooting pigeons, with Mr Hanbury's and Corporal Brook's cars dealing with the front and that great shot Trooper Elmore picking them off on the flanks. After we passed these people there was nothing until we reached the village, the entrance to which was a right hand turn. After the first scout car and armoured car had got round this corner, something opened up at the rear of Mr Hanbury's car. I noticed this from my position about fifty yards behind him so when I turned the corner myself I had my guns ready to engage them. There was a machine-gun post and goodness knows what else, but I have never seen people move so quickly as when Elmore got cracking with the Besa. The whole Troop arrived at the bridge, leaving the German dead en route. I was placed at the approaches to the bridge while Mr Hanbury's car and the scout cars dashed over to the far side. All the bombs (there were four), 250lbs., and electrically detonated were laid out in readiness, but we had just beaten the enemy to it and none were connected up.[55]

Lieutenant Jonkheer Groenix van Zoelen's Troop captured 'Charity' which was also mined and quickly came under counter-attack from the Germans which they were able to beat off. Finally 'Faith' fell to Lieutenant Peak and Lieutenant Franklin's troops. With the crossings secured by the armoured cars the pursuit began to pick up momentum once more with the Allied daily advance often covering fifty miles a day. Lieutenant Stuart Hills remembered the same exhilarating period from the Sherwood Rangers perspective, which was part of 8 Armoured Brigade, he was particularly grateful that the countryside had changed to good 'tank country':

> How different we found it from the closeness of the bocage, which had hindered us as much as it had helped the German defenders. Now all the advantage lay with the speedy Shermans, which could by-pass potential sources of trouble and rely on their mechanical efficiency to make ground very quickly. The Germans had of course covered the same stretch of country at comparable speeds in 1940 during their dash to the French coast. It was good tank country and now the success of their blitzkrieg tactics was easier to understand.
>
> The Sherwood Rangers were able to adopt the old desert formation – one squadron in open formation in the lead, RHQ just behind, and the other two squadrons on either flank. We worked as an armoured regimental group, supported by a battery of guns from the Essex Yeomanry and a company of motorized infantry from the 12th/60th King's Royal Rifle Corps, under Derek Colls. The commanders of both these groups travelled with our RHQ group, which allowed the best possible coordination of arms. To travel at top speed across hard, open country on a lovely morning, knowing that the Germans were on the run, was exhilarating to say the least, and everyone was in the best possible spirits. It was almost like taking part in a cross-country steeplechase or going on a pre-war motoring tour. In every village we passed

---

54 Orde, Roden, *Household Cavalry at War: Second Household Cavalry Regiment* (Aldershot: Gale & Polden, 1953), p.204.
55 Ibid., p.210.

we received terrific welcomes. Occasionally we would stop to receive the fruits of our success in the form of something to eat or drink, but usually we passed through in a cloud of dust, hardly able to see or hear the cheering groups of liberated French.[56]

Nothing underlined the catastrophic defeat the Germans had suffered quite like the 'Great Swan' of late August and early September. The advance went on for several weeks only petering out on the border with Holland in the second week of September as the armour out ran its logistic tail. The clash in Normandy was over and the decisive battle in the West decided in the Allies favour. But for many tank crewmen the excitement of the pursuit could never erase the horrific battles of attrition in Normandy and the cost paid by the armoured crews. For those lucky enough to survive, the encounters in Normandy would scar them for life; there are many grim ways to die on a battlefield but the fate of armoured crews was particularly horrific. Knowing that was the risk they undertook day after day against the best of the German armoured formations and tanks makes their courage even more admirable. The Royal Tank Regiment has three striped colours which adorn their belts, ties and penants. These colours are brown, red and green. The colours originated in the First World War and symbolised the armoured soldier's dream of progressing 'From mud, through blood to the green fields beyond'. That description seems appropriate to the Normandy campaign too as the British armour assisted the infantry in breaking through the strong defences of the bridgehead before being able to exploit and pursue the German army in the 'Great Swan'. What is admirable is that the British armour persevered in difficult terrain, often in less capable tanks against a stubborn and highly capable foe. It was perhaps this courageous persistence which prompted Montgomery to think of his armoured troops when he wrote about the importance of the human factor in the Autumn of 1944:

In war it is the man that counts, and not only the machine. A good tank is useless unless the team inside it is well trained, and the men in that team have stout hearts and enthusiasm for the fight; so it is in all other cases. With good men anything is possible.[57]

---

56 Hills, Stuart, *By Tank Into Normandy* (London: Cassell, 2002), p.149.
57 Montgomery, Field Marshal Bernard, 'Some Notes on the Conduct of War', Belgium, November 1944, HQ 21st Army Group. Held at the Defence Concepts and Doctrine Centre, Shrivenham.

12

'Our Greatest Generation'

We must never forget those grim days of desperate struggle and achievement. We are still going through difficult times; we are not yet out of the wood. Let us face up to the problems of the future by drawing strength from the memory of our splendid achievements in the past.

Field Marshal Montgomery of Alamein[1]

This book's main aim was to illustrate how an Army works and operates, highlighting the complexity of land operations as well as the organisational efficiency required to make an Army operate effectively. There are hundreds of detailed lessons that can be drawn from 21st Army Group's operations in Normandy but a smaller number of major points that will help us, as Montgomery suggests, 'face up to the problems of the future'.

Firstly we must recognise the organisational skill required in preparing an Army for war at the scale and sophistication of 21st Army Group. It is deeply impressive that in just a little over four years, following a humiliating withdrawal at Dunkirk, Britain was able to develop an Army that went on to conduct an opposed amphibious landing. An Army that, with its American Allies, undertook a gruelling 90 day offensive, decisively defeating one of the best equipped and most experienced armies the world has ever seen.

The performance of this Army on the battlefield is all the more impressive given that only a small element of the Army had seen service in North Africa or Italy. The majority of the divisions and soldiers were new to battle and their success derived from their ability to adapt what they had been taught in training to the character of the Normandy battle. There were many shocks for the British in Normandy, yet 21st Army Group quickly adapted their plans and tactics on landing in Normandy. They effectively developed the manner in which their arms cooperated with each other, introduced new equipment and exploited their strengths shrewdly. Their effective use of artillery and air power in particular were hallmarks of their campaign. This is in contrast to the German Army, whose response to the Normandy landings was to commit their soldiers to a largely positional defence south of the Seine, supported by costly and predictable counter-attacks which held no prospect of operational success and only delayed the inevitable.

That 21st Army Group was able to organise and adapt has much to do with the pre-war Regular and Territorial Army soldiers who formed the backbone of leadership within the Army at both officer and soldier level. Although very small in number it was these individuals who would become the brigade commanders, commanding officers and the platoon sergeants or sergeant majors. It is worth noting that most western nations today have tiny military forces, a fraction of the size of even the small 1930s pre-war armies; little thought and less resource seems to be given to how these might have to expand exponentially should the threat change. This should cause us concern, to use Montgomery's words we are still 'not yet out of the woods' and live in an uncertain world. The current human capital within our existing peacetime armies needs to be viewed by the nation

---

1   Scarfe, Norman, *Assault Division* (London: Collins, 1947), p.13.

less as an inefficient drain on public spending but more as the critical investment a nation should make for its security, one that may prove decisive should the threat change.

Secondly we must recognise that there is a minimum level of operations which tests an Army's organisational efficiency and ability to conduct combined arms manoeuvre at a scale and complexity that is truly demanding. This level of warfare is the division, it is at this size that all the major arms and services of an Army are commanded and controlled, it is also at this level that the tactical begins to meet the operational level of war. Currently Britain is the only nation in Europe still able to deploy a division, with three subordinate brigades on operations; many nations have lost this important aspect of their Army's institutional resilience which will cause them significant problems should they require to expand or re-generate. The preservation of this divisional capability should be seen by Britain as a critical pillar of its national security, other western nations would also do well to follow this example.

Finally Normandy underlines the critical importance of inter-service cooperation. Where the services worked well together the impact on the enemy was often decisive. Where single service vested interests pre-dominated then mediocrity and wasted effort swiftly followed. The campaign in Normandy was a predominantly land operation and required recognition from the other services that Germany could only be beaten by a decisive land operation. The cost of this land campaign in Allied lives was stark, 21st Army Group were to lose 16,138 killed, 9,093 missing and 58,594 wounded between D-Day and the end of August.[2]

So much for the future but how should we 'draw strength from the memory of our splendid achievements'? What should we particularly remember? The ability of an Army to organise itself, innovate and conduct combined arms manoeuvre are important factors in the victory in Normandy, but they did not offer a magic solution in itself. The second aim of this book was to highlight the human aspects of warfare and emphasise that victory would still have to be won by soldiers, sailors and airmen. It would be they who had to possess the courage, sufferance and motivation to overcome the fierce German defences and defeat their adversary. Reading their many accounts, papers and diaries, many of which were never destined to be published, one cannot but admire the self-deprecating and understated modesty of that generation. An era where a ferocious German counter-attack would be simply described as 'difficult', a bout of shelling 'tiresome' and a withering blast of Spandau fire as 'a nuisance'. This was not a naïve generation, they were informed by their father's experiences in the Great War and went to Normandy well aware of the nature of battle and its inevitable butcher's bill. Unlike the Germans they were not hoodwinked by malicious political philosophies or deluded by false ideas of their own super-human martial qualities.

There was instead a practical and pragmatic element to their morale and motivation. Reluctant soldiers in many cases, they brought in to the Army the cynicism of the factory floor but also a strong workmanlike sense that the Germans had to be defeated at their own game of war; and that this was the quickest way to return to their families. Most of the veterans admitted to be being frightened at one time or another. A small minority of the Army were so frightened they were unable to complete their jobs. At a greater scale a very small number of units were not fit for purpose too, either because they were badly led, had experienced a catastrophic run of bad luck, or suffered heavy casualties that had severely damaged the unit's cohesion. It is unrealistic to argue that weak individuals and bad units did not exist in 21st Army Group, of course they did, warfare is mankind's most testing human endeavour and not every person or unit is able to meet that challenge continuously. But for every incapable man there were sufficient individuals who could shoulder the burden and for every weak unit there were others that were reliable and strong.

---

2   Ellis, L F, *Victory in the West* Volume 1 (London: HMSO, 1962), p.493.

That the effectiveness of the British Army was able to be sustained throughout the grim summer of 1944 says as much about the replacement officers as it does for those who initially landed with their units. As Lieutenant Geoffrey Picot noted of 1st Royal Hampshires:

> If a Bn suffers light casualties, it is easy to absorb their replacements. Morale, cohesion and team spirit can be maintained. But when there are heavy casualties particularly among the senior officers, it is much more difficult to maintain these qualities. The private soldiers naturally do not respond so well to command by strangers. By now, of ten key men in our fighting outfit, battalion and rifle company commanders and their second in command, I think only one was still with us. It is surprising that the Bn continued to fight so well, although I doubt whether it ever again performed so superbly as it had on D-Day.

The Army leadership understood its citizen soldier's motivation and character and wisely they adapted their own techniques and plans to account for it and to get the most from their men. They took Montgomery's advice and studied the factor of morale within their own organisation and recognised that 'high morale is a pearl of very great price'. In return the Army's soldiers were confident that the Germans would be beaten and remained committed to their task.

This was not just about good senior leadership but about the motivation of the soldiers themselves. It would be the comradeship within the platoons and troops that carried the men through the grim summer and bitter winter to final victory in 1945. Lieutenant Reginald Fendick captured his regard for his own platoon and though the proportion of 'old regular soldiers' is perhaps higher in his unit than in others, his comments and emotions are very similar to those made by other veterans about their own units, of whatever regiment or corps:

> All the platoon were first class, typical Cockneys, most of them, could always crack some sort of joke to relieve the pressure, and the worse things got, the tougher they got. When I went around the slits during that horrible night, I always got a cheery greeting and a joking remark: 'Sir, can't you do something about all this noise; we can't sleep'. They loved to 'argue the toss' and could argue any subject by the hour, but they were sharp-witted, and very quick on the uptake. A lot of them were professional soldiers, and all had been trained by the professionals, and they would really jump to it when the chips were down. No waffle then, just a quick 'Right' and away. Physically, most were on the small side but wiry.
>
> They would never quit; that would 'let the side down', and they had a very strong sense of team play, of 'mucking in' together. They were a very mixed lot, some well educated, some with little, and from many levels of British society. But there was no class friction or any sign of resentment among them, ever.
>
> Many were very frightened when under fire, but carried on. To me, that is a measure of true bravery, when a badly frightened man continues to do his duty. And it is fostered by the comradeship and Regimental spirit found in a good unit.[3]

The quiet modesty of these men has however meant that their achievements have been overlooked in the post war years. Perhaps having patently won they felt no need to explain or justify their performance, most just wanted to get on or restart their civilian lives. In contrast the Germans felt their defeat keenly and did sense a requirement to voice their own undoubted prowess. This has inevitably been to the detriment of the British veterans' reputation whose self deprecating nature has meant his voice has not been fully heard or his achievements properly understood. Historians

---

3   Fendick, R F, *A CANLOAN Officer* (Buxton: MLRS Books, 2000), pp.83-84.

need to tread carefully when viewing German claims of their own excellence; the German Army and SS was not an institution where mistakes, criticism and weakness could be treated in an open minded manner. Any institution which deludes itself into thinking it is part of a master race is going to struggle both publicly and privately to recognise excellence or superiority in others.

History has so far been unkind to the British soldier in Normandy, yet I believe it is their quiet courage and competence which underpin the 'splendid achievements' of the past. This book highlights their heroic goodness as well as the spirit that animated them and I hope goes a small way to redressing the balance. Perhaps they were our greatest generation? They would of course be embarrassed by such a title, instead I suspect they would prefer to summarise their achievements in the understated manner of veteran Norman Scarfe when describing his own infantry unit:

'We thought we could be relied on.'

Figure 12.1 Private R Pankaski waiting to advance towards the village of Ifs during Operation SPRING, 25 July. (Lieut. Ken Bell, Library and Archives Canada, PA-163403)

Appendix A

Order of Battle for 21st Army Group

The lists below cover the main formations and units employed within 21st Army Group. The organisation is produced in list form but of course the Army Group was structured on armies that contained two or more corps and corps that would contain several divisions. These structures were very flexible and regularly altered as circumstances demanded. Armies, corps and divisions would be routinely reinforced by GHQ and army-level troops depending upon the operation. The divisions were only very rarely broken up and are listed here as complete entities.

TWENTY-FIRST ARMY GROUP[1]
Commander-in-Chief   General Sir Bernard L Montgomery
Chief of Staff   Major-General Sir Francis W de Guingand

GHQ AND ARMY TROOPS
79th Armoured Division
Major-General Sir Percy C S Hobart

Brigade	Unit	Role
30th Armoured Brigade	22nd Dragoons	Sherman Crab Flail tanks
	1st Lothian and Border Horse	
	2nd County of London Yeomanry (Westminster) Dragoons	
	141st Regiment RAC	
1st Tank Brigade	11th Battalion Royal Tank Regiment	Churchill Crocodile Flamethrowers
	42nd Battalion Royal Tank Regiment	
	49th Battalion Royal Tank Regiment	
1st Assault Brigade Royal Engineers	5th Assault Regiment RE	AVREs
	6th Assault Regiment RE	
	42nd Assault Regiment RE	
Divisional Troops	79th Armoured Divisional Signals	
	1st Canadian Armoured Personnel Carrier Regiment	Armoured Personnel Carriers

---

1   Information extracted from Ellis, L. F., *History Of The Second World War – Victory In The West*, Volumes I and II', London, Her Majesty's Stationary Office, 1968, pp.501-563.

Army Independent Brigades

Brigade	Unit
4th Armoured Brigade	The Royal Scots Greys
	3rd County of London Yeomanry (Sharpshooters) (to 28 July 1944)
	3rd/4th County of London Yeomanry (Sharpshooters) (from 29 July 1944)
	44th Battalion Royal Tank Regiment
	2nd Battalion The King's Royal Rifle Corps (Motor)
6th Guards Tank Brigade	4th Tank Battalion Grenadier Guards
	4th Tank Battalion Coldstream Guards
	3rd Tank Battalion Scots Guards
8th Armoured Brigade	4th/7th Royal Dragoon Guards
	24th Lancers (to 29 July 1944)
	The Nottinghamshire Yeomanry
	13th/18th Royal Hussars (from 29 July 1944)
	12th Battalion The King's Royal Rifle Corps (Motor)
27th Armoured Brigade (to 29 July 1944)	13th/18th Royal Hussars
	1st East Riding Yeomanry
	The Staffordshire Yeomanry
31st Tank Brigade	7th Battalion Royal Tank Regiment (to 17 August 1944)
	9th Battalion Royal Tank Regiment (to 31 August 1944)
	144th Regiment Royal Armoured Corps (23-31 August 1944)
33rd Armoured Brigade	1st Northamptonshire Yeomanry
	144th Regiment Royal Armoured Corps (to 22 August 1944)
	148th Regiment Royal Armoured Corps (to 16 August 1944)
	1st East Riding Yeomanry (from 16 August 1944)
34th Tank Brigade (to 24 August 1944)	107th Regiment Royal Armoured Corps
	147th Regiment Royal Armoured Corps
	153rd Regiment Royal Armoured Corps
2nd Canadian Armoured Brigade	6th Armoured Regiment (1st Hussars)
	10th Armoured Regiment (The Fort Garry Horse)
	27th Armoured Regiment (The Sherbrooke Fusiliers Regiment)
56th Infantry Brigade (Became integral part of 49th Division from 20 August 1944)	2nd Battalion The South Wales Borderers
	2nd Battalion The Gloucestershire Regiment
	2nd Battalion The Essex Regiment
1st Special Service Brigade	3 Commando
	4 Commando
	6 Commando
	45 (Royal Marine) Commando
4th Special Service Brigade	41 Commando
	46 Commando
	47 Commando
	48 (Royal Marine) Commando

21st Army Group Anti-Aircraft Troops

HQ Anti-Aircraft Brigades	74th, 76th, 80th, 100th, 101st, 105th, 106th and 107th
Heavy Anti-Aircraft Regiments	60th, 86th, 90th, 99th, 103rd, 105th, 107th, 108th, 109th, 112th, 113th, 115th, 116th, 121st, 146th, 165th and 174th; 2nd Canadian
Light Anti-Aircraft Regiments	20th, 27th, 32nd, 54th, 71st, 73rd, 93rd, 109th, 112th, 113th, 114th, 120th, 121st, 123rd, 124th, 125th, 126th, 127th, 133rd, 139th, and 149th,
Searchlight Regiments	41st

Other 21st Army Group Formations and Units

Armoured	
	GHQ Liaison Regiment RAC (Phantom)
	2nd Armoured Replacement Group
	2nd Armoured Delivery Regiment
	25th Canadian Armoured Delivery Regiment (The Elgin Regiment)
Royal Artillery	
HQ Army Groups Royal Artillery	3rd, 4th, 5th, 8th and 9th; 2nd Canadian
Heavy Regiments	1st, 51st, 52nd, 53rd, and 59th
Medium Regiments	7th, 9th, 10th, 11th, 13th, 15th, 53rd, 59th, 61st, 63rd, 64th, 65th, 67th, 68th, 72nd, 77th, 79th, 84th, 107th, 121st and 146th; 3rd, 4th and 7th Canadian
Field Regiments	4th RHA, 6th, 25th, 86th, 147th, 150th, and 191st, 19th Canadian
Royal Engineers	
HQ Army Groups Royal Engineers	10th, 11th, 12th, 13th and 14th; 1st Canadian
GHQ Troops Engineers	4th, 7th, 8th, 13th, 15th, 48th and 59th
Airfield Construction Groups	13th, 16th, 23rd, 24th, and 25th
Army Troops Engineers	2nd, 6th and 7th; 1st and 2nd Canadian
Royal Signals	
	21st Army Group Headquarters Signals
	Second Army Headquarters Signals
	First Canadian Army Headquarters Signals
Air Formation Signals	11, 12, 13, 16, 17 and 18 Signal Regiments
	1st Special Wireless Group
Infantry	
	4th Battalion The Royal Northumberland Fusiliers (Machine Gun)
	First Canadian Army Headquarters Defence Battalion (Royal Montreal Regiment)
Royal Marine	
Armoured Support Group	1st and 2nd Royal Marine Armoured Support Regiments
Army Air Corps	
Glider Pilot Regiment	1st and 2nd Glider Pilot Wings
Special Air Service	
	1st and 2nd Special Air Service
	3rd and 4th French Parachute Battalions
European Allies	
	1st Belgian Infantry Brigade
	Royal Netherlands Brigade (Princess Irene's)

ARMIES, CORPS AND DIVISIONS

Second Army

General Officer Commanding-in-Chief   Lieutenant-General Sir Miles C Dempsey
Chief of Staff   Brigadier M S Chilton

First Canadian Army

General Officer Commanding-in-Chief   Lieutenant-General H D G Crerar
Chief of Staff   Brigadier C C Mann

I Corps

Lieutenant-General J T Crocker

I Corps Troops	
Royal Armoured Corps	The Inns of Court Regiment RAC (Armoured Car)
Royal Artillery	62nd Anti-tank, 102nd Light Anti-Aircraft, 9th Survey Regiment
Royal Engineers	I Corps Troops Engineers
Royal Signals	I Corps Signals

VIII Corps

Lieutenant-General Sir Richard N O'Connor

VIII Corps Troops	
Royal Armoured Corps	2nd Household Cavalry Regiment (Armoured Car)
Royal Artillery	91st Anti-tank, 121st Light Anti-Aircraft, 10th Survey Regiment
Royal Engineers	VIII Corps Troops Engineers
Royal Signals	VIII Corps Signals

XII Corps

Lieutenant-General N M Ritchie

XII Corps Troops	
Royal Armoured Corps	1st The Royal Dragoons (Armoured Car)
Royal Artillery	86th Anti-tank, 112th Light Anti-Aircraft, 7th Survey Regiment
Royal Engineers	XII Corps Troops Engineers
Royal Signals	XII Corps Signals

XXX Corps

Lieutenant-General G C Bucknall (to 3 August 1944)
Lieutenant-General B G Horrocks (from 4 August 1944)

XXX Corps Troops	
Royal Armoured Corps	11th Hussars (Armoured Car)
Royal Artillery	73rd Anti-tank, 27th Light Anti-Aircraft, 4th Survey Regiment
Royal Engineers	XXX Corps Troops Engineers
Royal Signals	XXX Corps Signals

II Canadian Corps
Lieutenant-General G G Simonds

II Canadian Corps Troops	
Armoured	18th Armoured Car Regiment (12th Manitoba Dragoons)
Royal Canadian Artillery	6th Anti-tank, 6th Light Anti-Aircraft, 2nd Survey Regiment
Royal Canadian Engineers	II Canadian Corps Troops Engineers
Royal Canadian Signals	II Canadian Corps Signals

Guards Armoured Division
Major-General A H S Adair

Divisional Troops	2nd Armoured Reconnaissance Battalion Welsh Guards
	Guards Armoured Divisional Engineers
	55th and 153rd Field, 21st Anti-Tank and 94th Light Anti-Aircraft Regiments RA
	Guards Armoured Divisional Signals
5th Guards Armoured Brigade	2nd (Armoured) Battalion Grenadier Guards
	1st (Armoured) Battalion Coldstream Guards
	2nd (Armoured) Battalion Irish Guards
	1st (Motor) Battalion Grenadier Guards
32nd Guards Brigade	5th Battalion Coldstream Guards
	3rd Battalion Irish Guards
	1st Battalion Welsh Guards

7th Armoured Division
Major-General G W E J Erskine (to 3 August 1944)
Major-General G L Verney (from 4 August 1944)

Divisional Troops	8th King's Royal Irish Hussars
	7th Armoured Divisional Engineers
	3rd and 5th Regiments RHA; 65th Anti-Tank and 15th Light Anti-Aircraft Regiments RA
	7th Armoured Divisional Signals
22nd Armoured Brigade	4th County of London Yeomanry (Sharpshooters) (to 29 July 1944)
	1st Battalion Royal Tank Regiment
	5th Battalion Royal Tank Regiment
	5th Royal Inniskilling Dragoon Guards (from 29 July 1944)
	1st Battalion The Rifle Brigade (Motor)
131st Infantry Brigade	1st/5th Battalion The Queen' Royal Regiment
	1st/6th Battalion The Queen' Royal Regiment
	1st/7th Battalion The Queen' Royal Regiment

11th Armoured Division
Major-General G P B Roberts

Divisional Troops	2nd Northamptonshire Yeomanry (to 17 August 1944)
	15th/19th The King's Royal Hussars (from 17 August 1944)
	11th Armoured Divisional Engineers
	13th Regiment RHA; 151st Field, 75th Anti-Tank and 58th Light Anti-Aircraft Regiments RA
	11th Armoured Divisional Signals
29th Armoured Brigade	23rd Hussars
	2nd Fife and Forfar Yeomanry
	3rd Battalion Royal Tank Regiment
	8th Battalion The Rifle Brigade (Motor)
131st Infantry Brigade	3rd Battalion The Monmouthshire Regiment
	4th Battalion The King's Shropshire Light Infantry
	1st Battalion The Herefordshire Regiment

3rd Division
Major-General T G Rennie (to 13 June 1944)
Brigadier E E E Cass (acting)
Major-General L G Whistler (from 23 June 1944)

Divisional Troops	3rd Reconnaissance Regiment RAC
	3rd Divisional Engineers
	7th, 33rd and 76th Field, 20th Anti-Tank and 92nd Light Anti-Aircraft Regiments RA
	3rd Divisional Signals
	2nd Battalion The Middlesex Regiment (Machine Gun)
8th Brigade	1st Battalion The Suffolk Regiment
	2nd Battalion The East Yorkshire Regiment
	1st Battalion The South Lancashire Regiment
9th Brigade	2nd Battalion The Lincolnshire Regiment
	1st Battalion The King's Own Scottish Borderers
	2nd Battalion Royal Ulster Rifles
185th Brigade	2nd Battalion The Royal Warwickshire Regiment
	1st Battalion the Royal Norfolk Regiment
	2nd Battalion The King's Shropshire Light Infantry

6th Airborne Division
Major-General R N Gale

Divisional Troops	6th Airborne Armoured Reconnaissance Regiment RAC
	6th Airborne Divisional Engineers
	53rd Airlanding Light Regiment RA
	6th Airborne Divisional Signals
3rd Parachute Brigade	8th Battalion The Parachute Regiment
	9th Battalion The Parachute Regiment
	1st Canadian Parachute Battalion
5th Parachute Brigade	7th Battalion The Parachute Regiment
	12th Battalion The Parachute Regiment
	13th Battalion The Parachute Regiment
6th Airlanding Brigade	12th Battalion The Devonshire Regiment
	2nd Battalion The Oxfordshire and Buckinghamshire Light Infantry
	1st Battalion The Royal Ulster Rifles

15th Scottish Division
Major-General G H A MacMillan (to 2 August 1944)
Major-General C M Barber (from 3 August 1944)

Divisional Troops	15th Reconnaissance Regiment RAC
	15th Divisional Engineers
	131st, 181st and 190th Field, 97th Anti-Tank and 119th Light Anti-Aircraft Regiments RA
	15th Divisional Signals
	1st Battalion The Middlesex Regiment (Machine Gun)
44th (Lowland) Brigade	8th Battalion The Royal Scots
	6th Battalion The Royal Scots Fusiliers
	7th Battalion The King's Own Scottish Borderers
46th (Highland) Brigade	9th Battalion The Cameronians
	2nd Battalion The Glasgow Highlanders
	7th Battalion The Seaforth Highlanders
227th (Highland) Brigade	10th Battalion The Highland Light Infantry
	2nd Battalion The Gordon Highlanders
	2nd Battalion The Argyll and Sutherland Highlanders

43rd (Wessex) Division
Major-General G I Thomas

Divisional Troops	43rd Reconnaissance Regiment RAC
	43rd Divisional Engineers
	94th, 112th and 179th Field, 59th Anti-Tank and 110th Light Anti-Aircraft Regiments RA
	43rd Divisional Signals
	8th Battalion The Middlesex Regiment (Machine Gun)
129th Brigade	4th Battalion The Somerset Light Infantry
	4th Battalion The Wiltshire Regiment
	5th Battalion The Wiltshire Regiment
130th Brigade	7th Battalion The Hampshire Regiment
	4th Battalion The Dorsetshire Regiment
	5th Battalion The Dorsetshire Regiment
214th Brigade	7th Battalion The Somerset Light Infantry
	1st Battalion The Worcestershire Regiment
	5th Battalion The Duke of Cornwall's Light Infantry

49th (West Riding) Division
Major-General E H Barker

Divisional Troops	49th Reconnaissance Regiment RAC
	49th Divisional Engineers
	69th, 143rd and 185th Field, 55th Anti-Tank and 89th Light Anti-Aircraft Regiments RA
	49th Divisional Signals
	2nd Princess Louise's Kensington Regiment (Machine Gun)
70th Brigade	10th Battalion The Durham Light Infantry Regiment
	11th Battalion The Durham Light Infantry Regiment
	1st Battalion The Tyneside Scottish
146th Brigade	4th Battalion The Lincolnshire Regiment
	1/4th Battalion The King's Own Yorkshire Light Infantry
	Hallamshire Battalion The York and Lancaster Regiment
147th Brigade	11th Battalion The Royal Scots Fusiliers
	6th Battalion The Duke of Wellington's Regiment (to 6 July 1944)
	7th Battalion The Duke of Wellington's Regiment
	1st Battalion The Leicestershire Regiment (from 6 July 1944)
56th Brigade (from 20 August 1944)	See under GHQ Troops

50th (Northumbrian) Division
Major-General D A H Graham

Divisional Troops	61st Reconnaissance Regiment RAC
	50th Divisional Engineers
	74th, 90th and 124th Field, 102nd Anti-Tank and 25th Light Anti-Aircraft Regiments RA
	50th Divisional Signals
	2nd Battalion The Cheshire Regiment (Machine Gun)
69th Brigade	5th Battalion The East Yorkshire Regiment
	6th Battalion The Green Howards
	7th Battalion The Green Howards
151st Brigade	6th Battalion The Durham Light Infantry
	8th Battalion The Durham Light Infantry
	9th Battalion The Durham Light Infantry
231st Brigade	2nd Battalion The Devonshire Regiment
	1st Battalion The Hampshire Regiment
	1st Battalion The Dorsetshire Regiment

51st (Highland) Division
Major-General D C Bullen-Smith (to 26 July 1944)
Major-General T G Rennie (from 27 July 1944)

Divisional Troops	2nd Derbyshire Yeomanry RAC
	51st Divisional Engineers
	126th, 127th and 128th Field, 61st Anti-Tank and 40th Light Anti-Aircraft Regiments RA
	51st Divisional Signals
	1/7th Battalion The Middlesex Regiment (Machine Gun)
152nd Brigade	2nd Battalion The Seaforth Highlanders
	5th Battalion The Seaforth Highlanders
	5th Battalion The Queen's Own Cameron Highlanders
153rd Brigade	5th Battalion The Black Watch
	1st Battalion The Gordon Highlanders
	5th/7th Battalion The Gordon Highlanders
154th Brigade	1st Battalion The Black Watch
	7th Battalion The Black Watch
	7th Battalion The Argyll and Sutherland Highlanders

53rd (Welsh) Division
Major-General R K Ross

Divisional Troops	53rd Reconnaissance Regiment RAC
	53rd Divisional Engineers
	81st, 83rd and 133rd Field, 71st Anti-Tank and 116th Light Anti-Aircraft Regiments RA
	53rd Divisional Signals
	1st Battalion The Manchester Regiment (Machine Gun)
71st Brigade	1st Battalion The East Lancashire Regiment (to 3 August 1944)
	1st Battalion The Oxford and Buckinghamshire Light Infantry
	1st Battalion The Highland Light Infantry
	4th Battalion The Royal Welch Fusiliers (from 5 August 1944)
158th Brigade	4th Battalion The Royal Welch Fusiliers (to 3 August 1944)
	7th Battalion The Royal Welch Fusiliers
	1st Battalion The East Lancashire Regiment (from 4 August 1944)
	1/5th Battalion The Welch Regiment (from 4 August 1944)
160th Brigade	2nd Battalion The Monmouthshire Regiment
	4th Battalion The Welch Regiment
	1/5th Battalion The Welch Regiment (to 3 August 1944)
	6th Battalion The Royal Welch Fusiliers (from 4 August 1944)

59th (Staffordshire) Division
Major-General L O Lyne

Divisional Troops	59th Reconnaissance Regiment RAC
	59th Divisional Engineers
	61st, 110th and 1116th Field (to 31 August 1944), 68th Anti-Tank (to 26 August 1944) and 68th Light Anti-Aircraft Regiments (to 22 August 1944) RA
	59th Divisional Signals
	7th Battalion The Royal Northumberland Fusiliers (Machine Gun) (to 24 August 1944)
176th Brigade (to 26 August 1944)	7th Battalion The Royal Norfolk Regiment
	7th Battalion The South Staffordshire Regiment
	6th Battalion The South Staffordshire Regiment
177th Brigade (to 26 August 1944)	5th Battalion The South Staffordshire Regiment
	1/6th Battalion The South Staffordshire Regiment
	2/6th Battalion The South Staffordshire Regiment
197th Brigade (to 26 August 1944)	1/7th Battalion The Royal Warwickshire Regiment
	2/5th Battalion The Lancashire Fusiliers
	5th Battalion The East Lancashire Regiment

4th Canadian Armoured Division
Major-General G Kitching (to 21 August 1944)
Major-General H W Foster (from 22 August 1944)

Divisional Troops	29th Reconnaissance Regiment (The South Alberta Regiment)
	4th Canadian Armoured Divisional Engineers
	15th and 23rd Field, 5th Anti-Tank and 8th Light Anti-Aircraft Regiments RCA
	4th Canadian Armoured Divisional Signals
4th Armoured Brigade	21st Armoured Regiment (The Governor General's Foot Guards)
	22nd Armoured Regiment (The Canadian Grenadier Guards)
	28th Armoured Regiment (The British Columbia Regiment)
	The Lake Superior Regiment (Motor)
10th Infantry Brigade	The Lincoln and Welland Regiment
	The Algonquin Regiment
	The Argyll and Sutherland Highlanders of Canada (Princess Louise's)

2nd Canadian Division
Major-General C Foulkes

Divisional Troops	8th Reconnaissance Regiment (14th Canadian Hussars)
	2nd Canadian Divisional Engineers
	4th, 5th and 6th Field, 2nd Anti-Tank and 3rd Light Anti-Aircraft Regiments RCA
	2nd Canadian Divisional Signals
	The Toronto Scottish Regiment (Machine Gun)
4th Brigade	The Royal Regiment of Canada
	The Royal Hamilton Light Infantry
	The Essex Scottish Regiment
5th Brigade	The Black Watch (Royal Highland Regiment) of Canada
	Le Regiment de Maisonneuve
	The Calgary Highlanders
6th Brigade	Les Fusiliers Mont-Royal
	The Queen's Own Cameron Highlanders of Canada
	The South Saskatchewan Regiment

3rd Canadian Division
Major-General R F L Keller (to 8 August 1944)
Major General D C Spry (from 18 August 1944)

Divisional Troops	7th Reconnaissance Regiment (17th Duke Of York's Royal Canadian Hussars)
	3rd Canadian Divisional Engineers
	12th, 13th and 14th Field, 3rd Anti-Tank and 4th Light Anti-Aircraft Regiments RCA
	3rd Canadian Divisional Signals
	The Cameron Highlanders of Ottawa (Machine Gun)
7th Brigade	The Royal Winnipeg Rifles
	The Regina Rifle Regiment
	1st Battalion The Canadian Scottish Regiment
8th Brigade	The Queen's Own Rifles of Canada
	Le Regiment de la Chaudiere
	The North Shore (New Brunswick) Regiment
9th Brigade	The Highland Light Infantry of Canadal
	The Stormont, Dundas and Glengarry Highlanders
	The North Nova Scotia Highlanders

1st Polish Armoured Division
Major-General S Maczek

Divisional Troops	10th Polish Mounted Rifle Regiment
	1st Polish Armoured Divisional Engineers
	1st and 2nd Polish Field, 1st Polish Anti-Tank and 1st Polish Light Anti-Aircraft Regiments
	1st Polish Armoured Divisional Signals
10th Polish Armoured Brigade	1st Polish Armoured Regiment
	2nd Polish Armoured Regiment
	24th Polish Armoured Regiment (Lancer)
	10th Polish Motor Battalion
3rd Polish Infantry Brigade	1st Polish (Highland) Battalion
	8th Polish Battalion
	9th Polish Battalion

Lines of Communication and Rear Maintenance Area
Major-General R F B Naylor

Headquarters Lines Of Communication	Nos. 11 and 12 Lines of Communication Areas
	Nos. 4, 5 and 6 Lines of Communication Sub-Areas
	Nos 7 and 8 Base Sub-Areas
	Nos. 101, 102 and 104 Beach Sub-Areas
	Nos. 10 and 11 Garrisons
Engineers	Nos. 2, 3, 5 and 6 Railway Construction and Maintenance Groups
	No. 3 Railway Operating Group
	No. 1 Canadian Railway Operating Group
	No. 1 Railway Workshop
	Nos. 2, 6, 8, 9, 10 and 11 Port Operating Groups
	Nos. 1, 2, 4 and 5 Port Construction and Repair Groups
	Nos. 3 and 4 Inland Water Transport Groups
	No. 2 Mechanical Equipment (Transportation) Unit
Signals	Nos. 2 and 12 Lines of Communication Headquarters Signals
	No. 1 Canadian Lines of Communication Headquarters Signals
Infantry	5th Battalion The King's Regiment
	8th Battalion The King's Regiment
	2nd Battalion The Hertfordshire Regiment
	6th Battalion The Border Regiment
	1st Buckinghamshire Battalion The Oxfordshire and Buckinghamshire Light Infantry
	5th Battalion The Royal Berkshire Regiment
	18th Battalion The Durham Light Infantry

Appendix B

Allied Naval Forces in Operation Neptune

Allied Naval Commander-in-Chief   Admiral Sir Bertram H Ramsay, RN
Chief of Staff   Rear-Admiral G E Creasy, RN
Eastern Naval Task Force
Rear-Admiral Sir Phillip Vian, RN
HMS *Scylla* (Cruiser)

Force G – Gold Beach HMS *Bulolo* (HQ Ship)			
Assault Groups	**Bombarding Force K**		
50 Inf Div (XXX Corps)	Gunboats/Monitors	Cruisers	Destroyers
G1 231 Inf Bde Gp	HNMS *Flores* (Dutch Gunboat)	HMS *Orion* HMS *Ajax* HMS *Argonaut* HMS *Emerald*	HMS *Grenville* HMS *Jervis* HMS *Ulster* HMS *Ulysses* HMS *Undaunted* HMS *Undine* HMS *Urania* HMS *Urchin* HMS *Ursa* HMS *Cattistock* HMS *Cottesmore* HMS *Pytchley* ORP *Krakowiak* (Polish)
G2 69 Inf Bde Grp			
G3 56 Inf Bde Gp, 151 Inf Bde Gp			

Force J – Juno Beach HMS *Hilary* (HQ Ship)			
Assault Groups	**Bombarding Force E**		
3 Cdn Inf Div (I Corps)	**Cruisers**	**Destroyers**	
J1 7 Cdn Inf Bde Gp	HMS *Belfast* HMS *Diadem*	HMS *Faulknor* HMS *Fury* HMS *Kempenfeldt* HMS *Venus* HMS *Vigilant* HMS *Algonquin* HMS *Sioux* HMS *Bleasdale* HMS *Stevenstone* HNMS *Glaisdale* (Norwegian) FFS *La Combattante* (French)	
J2 8 Cdn Inf Bde Gp			
J3 9 Cdn Inf Bde Gp			
J4 1 and 4 SS Bdes			

Force S – Sword Beach HMS *Largs* (HQ Ship)			
Assault Groups	**Bombarding Force D**		
3 Brit Inf Div (I Corps)	**Battleships**	**Cruisers**	**Destroyers**
S1 9 Inf Bde Gp	HMS *Warspite* HMS *Ramillies* HMS *Roberts* (Monitor)	HMS *Mauritius* HMS *Arethusa* HMS *Frobisher* HMS *Danae* ORP *Dragon* (Polish)	HMS *Kelvin* HMS *Saumarez* HMS *Scorpion* HMS *Scourge* HMS *Serapis* HMS *Swift* HMS *Verulam* HMS *Virago* ORP *Slazak* (Polish) HNMS *Stord* (Norwegian) HNMS *Svenner* (Norwegian) HMS *Middleton* HMS *Eglinton*
S2 185 Inf Bde Gp			
S3 8 Inf Bde Gp			

Appendix C

Allied Air Forces

Allied Expeditionary Air Force
Air Commander-in-Chief   Air Chief Marshal Sir Trafford Leigh-Mallory
Deputy Air Commander-in-Chief   Major-General Hoyt S Vandenberg USAAF
(to 6 August 44). Major-General Ralph Royce (from 7 August 44)
Royal Air Force. Second Tactical Air Force
Air Marshal Commanding   Air Marshal Sir Arthur Coningham

Wing	Squadrons	Aircraft
34 Reconnaissance Wing	16, 69, 140 Squadrons	Spitfire, Wellington, Mosquito
3 Naval Fighter Wing	808 Fleet Air Arm (FAA), 885 (FAA), 886 (FAA), 887 (FAA) Squadrons	Seafire
Air Spotting Pool	26, 63 Squadrons 1320 Special Duty Flight	Spitfire Typhoon

No. 2 Group – Air Vice Marshal B E Embry

Wing	Squadron	Aircraft
137 Wing	88, 226, 342 (Fr) Squadrons	Boston, Mitchell
138 Wing	107, 305 (Pol), 613 Squadrons	Mosquito
139 Wing	98, 180, 320 (Dutch) Squadrons	Mitchell
140 Wing	21, 464 (RAAF), 487 (RNZAF) Squadrons	Mosquito

No. 83 Group – Air Vice Marshal H Broadhurst

Wing	Squadron	Aircraft
39 (RCAF) Reconnaissance Wing	168, 400 (RCAF), 414 (RCAF) Squadrons	Mustang
	430 (RCAF) Squadron	Spitfire
121 Wing	174, 175, 245 Squadrons	Typhoon
122 Wing	19, 65, 122 Squadrons	Mustang
124 Wing	181, 182, 247 Squadrons	Typhoon
125 Wing	132, 453 (RAAF), 602 Squadrons	Spitfire
126 (RCAF) Wing	401 (RCAF), 411 (RCAF), 412 (RCAF) Squadrons	Spitfire
127 (RCAF) Wing	403 (RCAF), 416 (RCAF), 421 (RCAF) Squadrons	Spitfire
129 (RCAF) Wing	184 Squadron	Typhoon
143 (RCAF) Wing	438 (RCAF), 439 (RCAF), 440 (RCAF) Squadrons	Typhoon
144 (RCAF) Wing	441 (RCAF), 442 (RCAF), 443 (RCAF) Squadrons	Spitfire
Air Observation Posts	652, 653, 658, 659, 662 Squadrons	Auster

No. 84 Group – Air Vice Marshal L O Brown

Wing	Squadron	Aircraft
35 Reconnaissance Wing	2, 4, 268 Squadrons	Mustang, Spitfire
123 Wing	198, 609 Squadrons	Typhoon
131 (Pol) Wing	302 (Pol), 308 (Pol), 317 (Pol) Squadrons	Spitfire
132 (Nor) Wing	66, 331 (Nor), 332 (Nor) Squadrons	Spitfire
133 (Pol) Wing	128, 306 (Pol), 315 (Pol), 602 Squadrons	Mustang
134 (Cz) Wing	310 (Cz), 312 (Cz), 313 (Cz) Squadrons	Spitfire
135 Wing	222, 349 (Belgian), 485 (RNZAF) Squadrons	Spitfire
136 Wing	164, 183 Squadron	Typhoon
145 (Fr) Wing	329 (Fr), 340 (Fr), 341 (Fr) Squadrons	Spitfire
146 Wing	193, 197, 257, 266 Squadrons	Typhoon
Air Observation Posts	660, 661 Squadrons	Auster

No. 85 (Base) Group – Air Vice Marshal J B Cole-Hamilton (to 9 July 1944)
Air Vice Marshal C R Steele (From 10 July 1944)

Wing	Squadron	Aircraft
141 Wing	91, 124, 322 (Dutch) Squadrons	Spitfire
142 Wing	264, 604 Squadrons	Mosquito (N/F)
147 Wing	29 Squadron	Mosquito (N/F)
148 Wing	409 (RCAF) Squadron	Mosquito (N/F)
149 Wing	410 (RCAF), 488 (RNZAF) Squadrons	Mosquito (N/F)
150 Wing	561 Squadron, 3, 486 (RNZAF) Squadrons	Spitfire Tempest
Airfield Construction Wing	5022, 5023, 5357 Squadrons	
Beach Squadrons	1, 2, 4 Squadrons	
Balloon Squadrons	974, 976, 980, 991 Squadrons	
Port Balloon Flight	104 Squadron	

Royal Air Force Regiment Group – Colonel R L Preston

Mobile Wings	1300, 1301, 1302, 1303, 1304, 1305, 1306, 1307, 1308, 1309, 1310, 1311, 1312, 1314, 1315, 1316, 1317, 1318.
Armoured Squadrons	2742, 2757, 2777, 2781, 2806, 2817
Light Anti-Aircraft Squadrons	2701, 2703, 2734, 2736, 2773, 2794, 2800, 2809, 2819, 2834, 2843, 2872, 2873, 2874, 2875, 2876, 2880, 2881
Rifle Squadrons	2713, 2717, 2726, 2729, 2798, 2816, 2827
Special Duty Squadron	2739

Royal Air Force, Air Defence of Great Britain
Air Marshal Commanding   Air Marshal Sir Roderic Hill

Group	Squadron	Aircraft
No. 10 Group	1, 41, 126, 131, 165, 610, 616 Squadrons	Spitfire
	263 Squadron	Typhoon
	151 Squadron	Mosquito (N/F)
	68, 406 (RCAF) Squadrons	Beaufighter (N/F)
	276 (Air/Sea Rescue (A/SR)) Squadron	Spitfire, Warwick, Walrus
	1449 Flight	Hurricane
No. 11 Group	33, 64, 74, 80, 127, 130, 229, 234, 274, 303 (Pol), 345 (Fr), 350 (Belgian), 402 (RCAF), 501, 611 Squadrons	Spitfire
	137 Squadron	Typhoon
	96, 125 (Newfoundland), 219, 456 (RAAF) Squadrons	Mosquito (N/F)
	418 (RCAF), 605 Squadrons	Mosquito Intruder
	275 (A/SR), 277 (A/SR), 278 (A/SR) Squadrons	Spitfire, Warwick, Walrus
No.12 Group	316 (Pol) Squadron	Mustang
	504 Squadron	Spitfire
	25, 307 (Pol) Squadrons	Mosquito (N/F)
	Fighter Interception Unit	Beaufighter, Mosquito, Mustang, Tempest
No.13 Group	118 Squadron	Spitfire
	309 (Pol) Squadron	Hurricane

Royal Air Force, Airborne and Transport Forces
Commander   Air Vice-Marshal L N Hollinghurst

Group	Squadron	Aircraft
No. 38 Group (Airborne Forces)	295, 296, 297, 570 Squadrons	Albermale
	190, 196, 299, 620 Squadrons	Stirling
	298, 644 Squadrons	Halifax
No. 46 Group (Transport Command)	48, 233, 271, 512, 575 Squadrons	Dakota

Royal Air Force, Coastal Command

Air Officer Commanding-in-Chief   Air Chief Marshal Sir W Sholto Douglas

Group	Squadron	Aircraft
No. 15 Group	59 Squadron	Liberator (Very Long Range (VLR))
	120 Squadron	Liberator (VLR Leigh Light (L/L))
	422 (RCAF), 423 (RCAF) Squadrons	Sunderland
	811 (FAA) Squadron	Avenger, Wildcat
No. 16 Group	119 Squadron	Albacore
	143, 236, 254, 455 (RAAF), 489 (RNZAF) Squadrons	Beaufighter
	415 (RCAF) Squadron	Wellington, Albacore
	819 (FAA), 848 (FAA), 854 (FAA), 855 (FAA) Squadrons	Avenger, Swordfish
No.18 Group	86 Squadron	Liberator (VLR)
	210 Squadron	Catalina
	330 (Nor), 333 (Nor) Squadrons	Catalina, Mosquito, Sunderland
	1693 Flight	Anson
No 19 Group	144, 235, 404 (RCAF) Squadrons	Beaufighter
	58, 502 Squadrons	Halifax
	53, 224 Squadrons	Liberator (L/L)
	206, 311 (Cz), 547 Squadrons	Liberator
	248 Squadron	Mosquito
	10 (RAAF), 201, 228, 461 (RAAF) Squadrons	Sunderland
	172, 179, 304 (Pol), 407 (RCAF), 612 Squadrons	Wellington (L/L)
	524 Squadron	Wellington
	816 (FAA), 838 (FAA), 849 (FAA), 850 (FAA) Squadrons	Avenger, Swordfish
	Attached – 103 (USN), 105 (USN), 110 (USN), and 114 (USN) Squadrons	Liberator

Appendix D

Divisional Organisation

	Armoured Division		Infantry Division		Airborne Division	
Brigades and their Main Units	Armoured Brigade	1	Infantry Brigades	3	Parachute Brigades	2
	Armoured Regiments	3	Infantry Battalions	9	Parachute Battalions	6
	Motor Battalion	1			Airlanding Brigade	1
	Infantry Brigade	1			Airlanding Battalions	3
	Infantry Battalions	3				
Reconnaissance	Armoured Reconnaissance Regiment	1	Reconnaissance Regiment	1	Airborne Armoured Reconnaissance Regiment	1
Artillery	Field Regiments	2	Field Regiments	3	Airlanding Light Regiment	1
	Anti-Tank Regiment	1	Anti-Tank Regiment	1	Airlanding Anti-Tank Batteries	2
	Light Anti-Aircraft Regiment	1	Light Anti-Aircraft Regiment	1	Airlanding Light Anti-Aircraft Battery	1
Engineers	Field Squadrons	2	Field Companies	3	Parachute Squadrons	2
	Field Park Squadron	1	Field Park Company	1	Airborne Field Company	1
	Bridging Troop	1	Bridging Platoon	1	Airborne Field Park Company	1
Signals	Armoured Divisional Signals	1	Infantry Divisional Signals	1	Airborne Divisional Signals	1
Machine Guns	Independent Machine Gun Company	1	Machine Gun Battalion	1		
Special Units					Independent Parachute Company (pathfinders)	1
Supply and Transport	Brigade Companies	2	Brigade Companies	3	Composite Companies	2
	Divisional Troops Company	1	Divisional Troops Company	1	Light Composite Company	1
	Divisional Transport Company	1				
Medical Services	Field Ambulance	1	Field Ambulances	3	Parachute Field Ambulances	2
	Light Field Ambulance	1	Field Dressing Stations	2	Airlanding Field Ambulance	1
	Field Dressing Station	1	Field Hygiene Section	1		
	Field Hygiene Section	1				

	Armoured Division		**Infantry Division**		**Airborne Division**	
Ordnance	Ordnance Field Park	1	Ordnance Field Park	1	Ordnance Field Park	1
Workshops	Brigade Workshops	2	Brigade Workshops	3	Divisional Workshop	1
	Light Anti-Aircraft Regiment Workshop	1	Light Anti-Aircraft Regiment Workshop	1	Airlanding Light Aid Detachments (with units)	7
	Light Aid Detachments (with units)	12	Light Aid Detachments (with units)	11		
Provost	Divisional Provost Company	1	Divisional Provost Company	1	Divisional Provost Company	1
Strength	Officers 724, Other Ranks 14, 240 Total Strength 14, 964 All Ranks		Officers 870, Other Ranks 17,477 Total Strength 18,347 All Ranks		Officers 702, Other Ranks 11,446 Total Strength 12,148 All Ranks	
Vehicles	3,414 vehicles including: Cruiser Tanks: 246 Light Tanks: 44 Tracked carriers, armoured: 261 Scout cars, armoured: 100 Trucks and lorries: 2,098		3,347 vehicles including: Tracked carriers, armoured: 595 Armoured cars: 63 Trucks and lorries: 1,937		1,708 vehicles including: Cars 5-cwt ('Jeeps'): 904 Trucks and lorries: 567	
Weapons	Rifles and pistols: 9,013 Machine carbines: 6,204 Light Machine Guns: 1,376 Medium Machine Guns: 22 Mortar, 2-, 3- and 4.2-in: 160 PIATs: 302 Field guns, 25-pdr: 48 Anti-tank guns, 6 and 17-pdr: 78 Anti-aircraft guns, 20 and 40mm: 141		Rifles and pistols: 12,265 Machine carbines: 6,525 Light Machine Guns: 1,262 Medium Machine Guns: 40 Mortar, 2-, 3- and 4.2-in: 359 PIATs: 436 Field guns, 25-pdr: 72 Anti-tank guns, 6 and 17 pdr: 110 Anti-aircraft guns, 20 and 40mm: 125		Rifles and pistols: 10,113 Machine carbines: 6,504 Light Machine Guns: 966 Medium Machine Guns: 46 Mortar, 2-, 3- and 4.2-in: 535 PIATs: 392 Pack howitzers, 75mm: 24 Anti-tank guns, 6 and 17 pdr: 68 Anti-aircraft guns, 20mm: 23	

Appendix E

Tanks – Armour, Speed and Weight

Type	Maximum Armour		Main Gun	Maximum Speed	Weight	Remarks
	Front	Side				
British and American						
Stuart	44mm	25mm	37mm	40 mph	12.5-15 tons	Reconnaissance. Several versions
Sherman	76mm	51mm	75mm	24 mph	30-32 tons	Some British Shermans converted to 'Fireflies' by fitting 17-pdr gun
Churchill, Marks I to VI	90mm	76mm	75mm	15 mph	37 tons	Some with 6-pdr gun
Churchill, Mark VII	150mm	95mm	75mm	12 mph	41 tons	In one (flame-thrower) regiment of 79th Armoured Division; a few in 34th Tank Brigade
Cromwell	75mm	63mm	75mm	40 mph	27 tons	
German						
Mark IV	80mm	30mm	75mm KwK 40	25 mph	25 tons	Half the tanks in the armoured division were of this type in most cases
Mark V (Panther)	100mm	45mm	75mm KwK 42	34 mph	45 tons	Half the tanks in the armoured division were of this type in most cases
Mark VI, E (Tiger)	100mm	80mm	88mm KwK 36	23 mph	54 tons	
Mark VI, B (Tiger)	180mm	80mm	88mm KwK 43	25 mph	68 tons	

Appendix F

Tank and Anti-Tank Guns – Performance against Armour

Gun	Projectile	Penetration against homogenous armour plate at 30 degrees angle of attack				Remarks
		At 100 yards	At 500 yards	At 1,000 yards	At 2,000 yards	
British and American						
75mm, Mark V	APCBC[1]	74mm	68mm	60mm	47mm	In Sherman, Churchill and Cromwell tanks.
6-pdr, Mark V	APCBC	93mm	87mm	80mm	67mm	Towed British anti-tank gun and in some Churchill tanks. DS 'Sabot' introduced in Normandy for the first time
	DS[2] ('Sabot')	143mm	131mm	117mm	90mm	
17-pdr, Mark II	APCBC	149mm	140mm	130mm	111mm	Towed British anti-tank gun and in some Sherman tanks. DS 'Sabot' introduced in August.
	DS ('Sabot')	221mm	208mm	192mm	161mm	
German						
75mm KwK 40	APCBC	99mm	92mm	84mm	66mm	In Mark IV tanks
75mm Pak 40	APCBC	99mm	92mm	84mm	66mm	Anti-tank gun, towed and self-propelled
88mm KwK 36	APCBC	120mm	112mm	102mm	88mm	In Mark VI, E (Tiger) tanks
75mm PaK 42	APCBC	138mm	128mm	118mm	100mm	In Mark V (Panther) tanks
88mm Kwk 43	APCBC	202mm	187mm	168mm	137mm	In Mark VI, B (Tiger) tanks, Jagdpanthers and towed anti-tank guns

---

1 APCBC: Armoured Piercing Capped Ballistic Capped.
2 DS: Discarding Sabot.

Appendix G

Mortar and Artillery Capabilities

Mortars	Weight of Shell	Maximum Range	Normal rate of fire	Remarks
2-inch mortar	2.5 lbs	100-500 yards		Held in infantry platoon HQ
3-inch mortar	10 lbs	500-1,500 yards (Charge I) 950-2,800 yards (Charge II)		Six per infantry battalion. Four in airborne and airlanding battalions
4.2-inch mortar	20 lbs	1,050-2,800 yards (Charge I) 1,500-4,100 (Charge II)		16 held in heavy mortar company of machine gun battalion
Field				
75mm pack howitzer	14 lbs	9,500 yards	3 rounds per minute	Airborne divisions only
25-pdr gun/ howitzer	25 lbs	13,400 yards	3 rounds per minute	Standard field gun
25-pdr SP ('Sexton')	25 lbs	13,400 yards	3 rounds per minute	One regiment per armoured division
105mm SP ('Priest')	33 lbs	12,150 yards	3 rounds per minute	In two assault divisions for initial landing
Medium				
5.5-inch gun	80 lbs	18,100 yards	1 round per minute	Standard medium gun
Heavy				
155mm gun (US)	95 lbs	25,400 yards	1 round in two minutes	155mm and 7.2 inch guns were in equal numbers in Heavy regiments
7.2-inch howitzer	200 lbs	MK I 16,500 yards	1 round in two minutes	
		MK II, 19,600 yards	1 round in two minutes	
Anti-Aircraft				
20mm (Hispano)	8.5 oz	Effective ceiling 3,000ft Horizontal range 1,000 yards	650 rounds per minute	
40mm Bofors	2 lbs	Maximum ceiling, 23,000 ft Horizontal range, 10,800 yards	60 rounds per minute, single shot. 120, automatic	Standard light gun
3.7-Inch	28 lbs	Maximum ceiling, 48,000 ft Horizontal range 15,800-18,000 yards	10-25 rounds per minute (with mechanical fuse setter)	Standard heavy gun

Appendix H

VIII Corps Fire Plan for Operation BLUECOAT

Fire Support

One additional field regiment was placed under command of 11 Armoured Division, so that both attacking divisions had three field regiments, and these resources were supplemented by VIII AGRA, which consisted of four medium regiments and one heavy regiment.

Time concentrations for phase 1 were issued by RA VIII Corps but thereafter each division was responsible for laying on its own barrages, concentrations and DF tasks.

Counter-battery tasks were to be coordinated by the CCRA VIII Corps in the area between the Corps boundary on the right and a line running north and south 500 yards east of Caumont.

The three divisions and 8 AGRA were each to be supported by one air OP flight

Air Support

A large air support programme was laid on but the operation was to take place whether this could be carried out or not.

This programme included:

a) Heavy and medium bomber attacks in two waves on selected area targets shown on the map.
b) Fighter-bomber attacks on close targets on 11 Armoured and 15 (S) Div fronts.
c) Fighter-bomber attacks on opportunity targets.
d) Armed recce on all approaches to the battle area
e) Tactical and photographic reconnaissance

The following table gives detail of the attacks in (a) above:

Time	Area	Type of bomb	Aircraft
0730 –0830 (XXX Corps)	D	Fragmentation; cratering not acceptable	200 heavy bombers
	E	HE	200 heavy bombers
	F	Fragmentation; cratering not acceptable	200 heavy bombers
	G	HE	100 heavy bombers
0855-0955 (VIII Corps)	A	Fragmentation preferred; if not possible, cratering acceptable	300 medium bombers
	B	Mixture of fragmentation and HE; cratering acceptable	350 medium bombers
1555-1655 (VIII Corps)	C	Mixture of fragmentation and HE; cratering acceptable	216 medium bombers

No HE bomb was to be larger than 500 pounds. The targets in the XXX Corps sector are included to indicate the scale of the air effort in support of Operation 'BLUECOAT'.

The programme for fighter-bomber attacks on close targets ahead of VIII Corps was:

Mortar positions	(X and Y)	0615 hours
Machine gun positions	(Y and Z)	0630 hours
Lutain Wood	(W)	0645 hours

The Air Support Signals Unit (ASSU) was deployed with two nets serving VIII Corps. Tentacles were attached to most brigades and divisional HQs with a Visual Control Post allotted to 29 Armoured Bde (11 Armoured Div).

Lt Col R J Streatfield, who commanded 190 Field Regiment RA supporting 15 Scottish Division, made the following comments on the Fire Support Plan for Operation BLUECOAT:

There were four principal factors affecting the artillery plan; I will give you a few details of each factor as I come to it:

The first factor was short notice. On 27 July, the Corps commander learnt that this action might be on, and he and CCRA therefore took two Air OPs and flew over the ground. Then on 28 July the CCRA came with his forward HQ and parked it alongside HQ RA 15 (S) Div at Balleroy and at 7pm that evening he held his first preliminary conference. Then on 29 July, the day before D-Day, at 1200 hours, he held his first main Fire Plan conference. At 1800 hours that evening he held his second one and by midnight the whole of the Fire Plan for the three phases, including the traces and the concentration tasks, had been issued. That could not have been done except by very good staff work between RA VIII Corps and RA 15 (S) Div, and that was made easy by the two HQ being in one place. It follows therefore that the plan had to be extremely simple to get it out on time.

The second factor was ammunition. Provision of ammunition was very difficult, not because the ammunition was not there, but because there was very little time and very little road space to get it up. On the night of 28 July, 300 rounds per gun for the field artillery was dumped in the FDLs, that was all we had – just adequate, but not enough for a pre-bombardment and preliminary counter battery programme, and to support the fighting troops as well; and so we had to decide which it was to be.

The third factor was information. The information as General Verney has already said, was extremely sketchy, chiefly because surprise was the Corps commander's main requirement for this attack, and no patrolling was being done. The OPs had been able to get a little ground information, when 15 (S) Div artillery was supporting the attack by 3 US Div on this sector on 24 July, but as will be obvious when we see the ground, this did not amount to very much. As a result we had very few targets on which to do a pre-bombardment; and it tended to indicate the use of barrages rather than concentrations.

The fourth and last factor was the question of positioning the artillery. That was difficult, because there was only the one road down which we could get the guns and it was impossible to take them across country; therefore, we had to cover all three phases and support the troops when they got to the objective from our original positions; both field and medium guns had to be sited as far forward as possible; they were moved up the night before D-Day.

Now I will say a word about the artillery available. It was not a very big gunner concentration, such as we came to know later on in the campaign. We had the usual two regiments of 11 Armoured Div plus 25 Fd Regt, and 77 Med Regt, one of the medium regiments of 8 AGRA, in direct support. There were the three field regiments of 15 (S) Div and 63 Med Regt

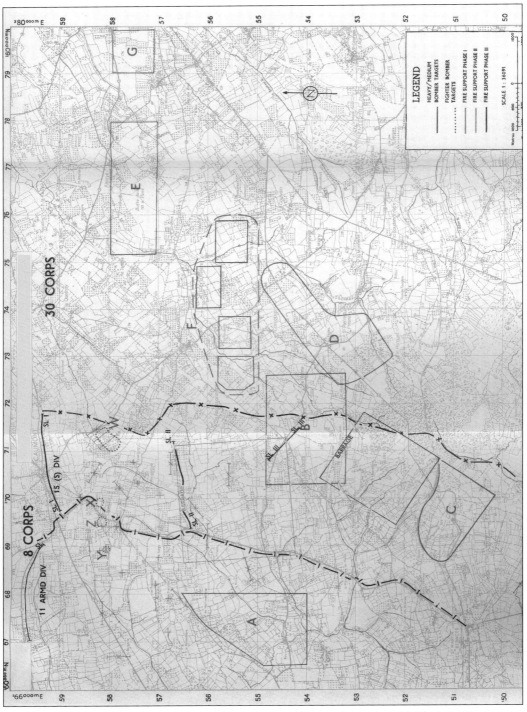

Diagram H.1 Fire Support and Air Support during Operation BLUECOAT.

in direct support; and there was the rest of 8 AGRA, which consisted of two more medium regiments and one heavy regiment.

The affiliations were perfectly normal; 131 Fd Regt with 227 (H) Inf Bde, 181 Fd Regt with 44 (L) Inf Bde and 190 Fd Regt with 46 (H) Inf Bde. Their OP teams married up in the normal way, with the usual OP teams from my regiment with 9 Cameronians. In addition, we had some OPs in the tanks of 6 Gds Tk Bde. They had practised manning OP tanks in Yorkshire, and when we sent them over to marry up the evening before they had no difficulty; we had one OP in a tank with each battalion. We also had the usual tie up of medium OPs, one OP team from the direct support regiment with each attacking brigade. The only difficulty with the tank OPs, which will come out tomorrow, was that, in Phase III, 4 Tk Coldstream Guards and 3 Tk Scots Guards, having been already used in phase II were not able to change over their OPs, because there were not enough tanks to go round.

Generally the gunner plan was to have no preliminary bombardment or counter battery; the whole weight of the artillery support was to be used to support the attacking troops and I will briefly explain the plan for each phase of the attack. These plans were very simple.

In Phase I, from H minus 2 to H plus 20 minutes, we fired concentrations on nine targets which we thought were strongpoints in the area of the attack. After that everything was at call. During that Phase the CO of the field regiment who was acting for the CRA said on the air at 0900 hours that Phase II would start at 0955 hours, and that gave us time to get ready for the barrage. The barrage was the support for Phase II, and there are one or two points to be stressed about the barrage. Firstly it was a very broad one – about 2300 yards wide – and therefore all three regiments of the divisional artillery were used, and all the batteries were spread over the front line of the barrage. The barrage lasted 110 minutes and there was no main pause in it. The rate of fire was 'slow' and the speed of advance was 100 yards in four minutes.

Secondly 75% of the ammunition used was airburst, with the 222 fuse [Time initiated] and not the with the VT fuse [Barometric pressure initiated] which we got later, and which was much better. I think there were two main reasons for this; first, the tanks were going to lead and they accepted the danger; and secondly, we had found when fighting in the 'bocage' country, that the ground-burst 25 pounder did extraordinarily little damage to the Boches who were always well dug-in. If we got a good airburst, it always compelled him to go to ground.

Those were the two reasons for the decision; because of the little ammunition available, and because it was rather a broad barrage with not very many shells coming down, and we hoped that in that way we would spread more alarm and despondency than would have been possible with the ground-burst.

In Phase III again, there was a smaller barrage with much the same idea, 75% airburst and again no main pause. In this barrage we had only two field regiments in the front line of the barrage, with the other regiment, 190 Fd Regt, superimposed, so that, as the direct support regiment of 46 (H) Inf Bde, it could be taken off for opportunity shooting if necessary. I should say that in both these barrages we had medium regiments superimposed 300 yards ahead, two medium regiments in the first barrage, and one in the second. DF tasks for all phases were made out, put on traces and issued down to company level, so that they were well known.

Appendix I

51st Highland Division Intelligence Summary No 200

Based on Information up to 1900 hrs 29 June 44

PART I.

1.   OPERATIONS.

Another quiet day with very little to report. Last night air bursts were reported over ESCOVILLE at 2015 and at about 2300 hrs our arty shelled enemy activity in the triangle area. This caused some retaliation with arty, mortar and M.G. fire in this sector which continued off and on until dawn. There was some intermittent arty activity on other sectors during the night, but generally speaking it was quieter than usual. The enemy, however, was, like ourselves, actively engaged in patrolling, and one or two clashes were reported.

At 0130 hrs an enemy patrol came into contact with one of our parties protecting some mine-laying at 103706. At about 0430 hrs a similar scuffle took place and unfortunately one of our own returning patrols took evasive action and suffered several casualties through getting into our own A.pers mine-field. Another enemy patrol penetrated into the wood on the southern edge of ESCOVILLE, but action was carefully avoided as it was thought that the enemy was mainly out to locate our posns in that village.

Today there has been very little indeed to report, and the only item of interest was some vehicles observed infiltrating into the wood at 097675 during the afternoon.

Patrols.

On the left a patrol to 133699 were fired on in that area and heard enemy near them. Mortars, M.G. fire and flares confirmed that the enemy remained active both in the area of the triangle and the BUTTE de la HOGUE. The patrol moved, however, down the western edge of the woods in 1270 and established fairly firmly that the enemy are not occupying the forward western edges. Another patrol penetrated the woods at about 133703 where grenades were thrown at them and the patrol split into two parties. One officer and one O.R. are still believed to be missing. It seems clear that there is at least a section posn at this point; at the same time the enemy do not appear to be up to the forward edge of the EAST – WEST track on the 706 Northing in 1370.

In the centre a patrol moved down the track towards pt 35, and lay up for some time at 123702; the activity in this area was considerable with M.G fire and flares, and in addition one S.P. gun was thought to be firing from just over the ridge at 126697.

Further WEST another patrol moved down the central track between the 10 and 11 Eastings. They found a wire fence on the EAST side of the track from 109711 to 108709; this consisted of three strands of ordinary wire on steel posts. Similar fences ran EAST from the NORTH and

438

SOUTH ends. On reaching the area 105700 they were fired on by M.G.s thought to be at 111698 and 100700, and were unable to advance further. The leader was fairly confident that tk movement was heard in the area of CUVERVILLE. An enemy patrol was encountered moving rapidly WEST at 107715.

On the right the enemy continued to be active and noisy both in the Château and the factory areas. A line of pits was found from 088703 to 091702 and fresh pits at 087701. The houses at 084701 and 087699 were still found to be occupied. NORTH of the rd sentries were found at 097699 and enemy movement in both directions (CUVERVILLE-COLOMBELLES) was heard; digging close to the rd was also heard at 076705.

Other Fronts

WEST of the river our neighbours after very heavy fighting yesterday, in which considerable casualties were caused to both sides, have consolidated their hold on the CHÂTEAU de la LONDE.

Further to the WEST our tps have crossed the ODON in some strength and have captured ESQUAY 9561 and the high ground to the NE of it.

Air.

(a) Tac/R has shown a considerable amount of movement and concentration of MT and armd vehs in the area NW of FALAISE, which is clearly the main reinforcement area at present for counter-attack against our thrust over the ODON.

(b) Enemy losses 28 Jun:-
27 MT destroyed, 28 damaged.
24 enemy aircraft destroyed with 3 probables and 10 damaged.

PART II.

ENEMY DEFENCES.

Infm from a civilian source on 29 Jun with comments by APIS, 51 (H) Div:-

(a) In the trees NORTH of the rd 085676 there is a troop of ? 10.5cm gun hows.
Comment: Nothing seen in cover 25 Jun, but there are tracks along the line of trees and the site is possible.

(b) NEBELWERFER have been seen firing from the trees in 07436762 and more have been reported in the area of 06906846.
Comment: Nothing identifiable seen.

(c) At MONDEVILLE there is an O.P. manned by 5 men in the tower of the SALLE de FETES at 07066847. The tower looks like a church tower and the building is about 100 metres away from the stadium.
No comment possible.

(d) Two well camouflaged tks seen 28 Jun at 07866830 and at 07746823,
Comment: One set of veh tracks (6'-7' track) leading to possible camouflaged object approx 12 × 25 ft at 07856835. Similar object and large possibly camouflaged patch nearby.

(e)   There are two pillboxes in MONDEVILLE – one at 06586818 near a café and the other at 06626826 near a grocers shop.
Comment: Nothing seen at the precise location but possibly in the basements of the buildings. Possible works at 06606834 and 06546826.

(f)   At GIBERVILLE the Bakery at 08546879 is being used as an MG repair shop. There are supposed to be about 25 Germans there. Few Germans are seen in the village itself but the Château is occupied and guarded by a sentry. The road from 080695 to GIBERVILLE to 092670 to GRENTHEVILLE is much used by the Germans. Some vehs were seen on Sunday near the culvert at 08306780.
Comment: Impossible to check. The use of the road seems likely.

(g)   Some 50 tks were reported to have been in the area 085679 to 089679 till Thursday 20 Jun.
Comment: No cover of the date. Number of tks seems excessive.

(h)   The source was warned by members of a Resistance group to avoid the wood 090696 as it was reported to be full of Germans. He was shot up by M.G. fire from the area of the GENDARMERIE near the cement works 08457008.
Comment: Wood known to be occupied by tps and has been well shelled by our arty.

(i)   Heavy A.A. installations near the station at SOLIERS 074636.
Comment: No heavy A.A. seen at point indicated by souce in fair cover 25 Jun. Source saw 4 heavy A.A. guns early on 26 Jun but only very faint sign of possible activity can be seen on the cover. There is an established tendency for Heavy A.A. in this area to be rapidly re-arranged, so the source's report may be perfectly valid.

2.   <u>BEHIND THE LINES.</u>

The French civilian who gave the info above was accompanied by two officers, one R.A.F. and one R.C.A.F. They had been living mainly in GIBERVILLE since D-Day when their aircraft carrying supplies had to make a forced landing. Their impression is that GIBERVILLE has never been a very important enemy centre, though there has been quite a lot of traffic through the village by night. During their stay behind the lines they had moved around quite a lot particularly to the SOUTH where they had visited BOURGUÉBUS and TILLY la CAMPAGNE but had seen no tks or Armd Cars. Much of our air and arty effort against the village was actually in vain since on one or two occasions the only target, apart from half a dozen Germans, was provided by the villagers.

It should be noted that these officers were extremely well treated and helped in every way by many of the villagers at the greatest personal risks to themselves. These people have now been forcefully evacuated by the Germans and obliged to leave many of their possessions some of which they have buried.

When the time comes for Allied tps to enter the village the least that can be done is to restore them everything as intact as circumstances allow.

Appendix J

5th Camerons Operation Order No 3 for Operation TOTALIZE

OPERATION TOTALIZE

<u>5 CAMERONS OPERATION ORDER NO. 3</u>
Phase I A[1]

<u>6 Aug 44</u>

Maps: 1/25000 CAEN 40/16 SW
1/25000 BRETTEVILLE 40/14 W

INFORMATION

1. <u>Enemy.</u>
    In view of the Allied thrusts and successes in the WEST some changes in dispositions have been and are being made by the enemy.
    It is believed that he is not in as great strength as previously in front of this operation and that the 1st SS Panzer Div is stretched along the Corps front.
    Full details of enemy dispositions and up to date information will be given out by the IO just prior to the actual operation.
2. <u>Own Tps.</u>
    On completion of Phase I the Bn will be ready to commence Phase Ia. At the same time as this is started the 5 SEAFORTH will attack and take SECQUEVILLE-LA-CAMPAGNE 0959.

INTENTION

3. 5 Camerons will clear and hold the area WOOD 1058-1057.

METHOD

4. This operation will be divided into four phases: –
    <u>Phase I.</u>   Move from present area to FUP.
    <u>Phase II.</u>   Assault from FUP to edge of objective.
    <u>PhaseIII.</u>   Clearing the objective.
    <u>Phase IV.</u>   Reorganisation.

---

1   In order to better illustrate the style and content of operation orders that were prevalent at the time I have taken the liberty of amending this order slightly. This has been limited to solely including details where the order refers to previous orders and does not contradict either the content of the order or the direction given.

5.   Phase I.
     (a)   Coys will move to the FUP in the following orders:-
           B Coy
           Bn HQ
           C Coy
           D Coy
           A Coy
     (b)   Routes.
           B Coy will move direct to ROAD and TRACK Junc 075584 – east along road to ROAD
           and TRACK Junc 078585 – south-east along track to area TRACK Junc 081579.
           Bn HQ as for B Coy.
           C Coy will move direct to road by the L of LONGUICHON – north-east along road as
           for B Coy to area 082583.
           D Coy will move direct to TRACK Junc 076580 – across country to ROAD and TRACK
           Junc 075584 – then as for B Coy to area TRACK Junc in WOOD 062585.
           A Coy will move behind C Coy to area 077583.
     (c)   Control Posts.
           The IO will establish control posts at the following places:-
           1)   ROAD and TRACK Junc 075583.
           2)   ROAD and TRACK Junc 078585.
           3)   TRACK Junc 081585.
     (d)   Guides.
           Coys will each provide four guides to report to the IO in the Bn HQ prior to the move.
           One guide per coy will lead the coy from their present posns to the FUP.
           The other three guides per coy will be used by the IO to mark the FUP as required.

6.   Phase II.
     (a)   The Bn will attack with three coys up:-
           Right   B Coy
           Centre   C Coy
           Left   D Coy
           Reserve   A Coy
           (a)   S.L. Track running north and south from north TRACK Junc 086586 to south
                      TRACK Junc 086578.
           (b)   Rate of advance. 100 yds in one minute.

7.   Phase III.
     (a)   First Objective.
           Right – B Coy.   Will clear WOOD up to line of TRACK north 103582 to south 106579.
           Centre – C Coy. Will clear WOOD up to line of TRACK north TRACK Junc 103583
           to south B Coy's boundary.
           Left – D Coy.   Will clear triangular copse up to line of TRACK north 100585 to south
           C Coy's left boundary.
           A Coy will remain in the area of the TRACK at 095584 until these objectives have been
           secured. Bn HQ will also remain in this area.
     (b)   Second objectives.
           On the capture of the first objective the fwd coys will check on the line of TRACK
           running north-west – south-west.
           A Coy will then be prepared to pass through B Coy.

Second objectives will be attacked as follows:

Right   A Coy
Centre C Coy
Left   D Coy

Limit of second objectives north-east end of WOOD.
Rate of advance – 100 yds in six minutes.

8. Phase IV.

On completion of Phase III coys will then reorganise in the following areas:-

B Coy   area 103576
A Coy   area 108580
C Coy   area 109583
D 2 reserve area 099582

Bn HQ will be established in clearing 101584

On completion of this attack 153 Bde will pass through 5 CAMERONS and clear remainder of WOOD Eastwards.

9. Supporting Arms.

(a) Arty.

Concentrations will be fired on to the WOOD lifting 200 yds every twelve minutes.
Smoke and HE will be used to blind the right flank incl CONTEVILLE and POUSSY.
Additional fire support and DF tasks will be issued on a separate arty trace.

(b) 4.2" Mortars.

These will fire as per Bde Fire Plan.

(c) Tks.

One Sqn of tks will be in support of the Bn in carrying out this attack, and will move with forward with the infantry in the mixed assault echelon.
Further details will be issued later.

(d) MMGs.

Pl under comd will move forward with 'F' Ech and will be used to protect the right flank.
MMGs of 154 Bde will also support this operation.

(e) 3" Mortars.

These will move forward with 'F' echelon to area TRACK Junc 099586 where further posns and tasks will be allotted to them as the CO directs.
MFCs with B and A Coys.

(f) Carriers.

Will move forward with 'F' ech to the area of Bn HQ.

(g) A.Tk.

Will move forward with 'F' Ech and will be allotted to coys as follows :-

B Coy   Pl less one section
A Coy   One sec.

Tp 6-pdr RA – task to be responsible for the north face of the objective.
Two will move fwd with D Coy's F Ech and two will move fwd with C Coy's .

(h) Pioneers.

Will remain behind with 2 i/c and give any assistance required in moving firward of 'F' Ech.

ADMIN

10. Tpt.
    (a) 'F' Ech will move forward on call from Bn HQ.
    Composition of 'F' Ech is shown at Appdx A.
    'F' Ech will be assembled in coy groups by the OC, SP Coy, who will be responsible for the marshalling of the entire echelon.
    Route forward – ROAD and TRACK Junc 081586 – along road north-east to ROAD and TRACK Junc 086589 – to TRACK Junc 094589.
    A TCP will be established at the D.P. under Capt I. MACDONALD.
    Responsible guides will again report there to lead veh groups into coy posns.

11. Med.
    Two med jeeps will move with the MO along with Bn HQ.
    Eight amb cars will be located in area BRAS 053633
    A ADS will be established north of CORMELLES

12. POW.
    A Div cage will be established in WOOD at 054647

13. Stragglers' Post.
    A stragglers' post will be established at the TRACK at 052648

14. Rations.
    A hot meal will be issued in the Assembly area before moving. Each man will carry breakfast and tiffin rations for the following day. The remainder of the day's rations will be carried in coys' carriers. Water bottles will be full.
    Fresh rations will be issued up to evening of 7 Aug. On morning 7 Aug QM will draw three days compo rations from SRP., THIS FOR 8 AND 9 Aug and one day's reserve.
    14a.   Wire. All carriers and vehs will carry a roll of Dannert wire.

15. POL.
    On D normal 250 miles running will be held by the Bn.
    A reserve dump will be established as required in 'A' ech locality by MTO.

16. Rec.
    Two recovery posts will be established in the area of the TRACK running north-south at 052650.

17. Amn.
    Each coy will be allotted one extra carrier for the purpose of carrying ammunition. These carriers will be assembled in coy groups at 'F' Ech.

INTERCOMN
18. Bn HQ will move at the head of A Coy up to and including the capture of the first objectives. After this it will be established in clearing 101584.

19. 18 Sets.
    One with each rifle coy.
    One with Bn HQ.
    One with the Carrier Pl.
    One with the Mortar Pl.
    One with the 2 i/c.

20. 38 Sets. As per present allocation.

21. Bde success signal will be codeword LAGGAN.
    Coy success signal will be by the codeword STIRLING followed by coy call sign.

22. 452 Bty RA, Tp 6-pdr RA and Pl 1/7 Mx will be on the Bn 18 Set net.

23. H Hour not before 1200 D+1

24. HQ, 152 Bde located in area LORGUICHON.

ACK
Captain
Adjutant, 5 CAMERONS

Bibliography

UNPUBLISHED SOURCES/OFFICIAL DOCUMENTS

Interviews/Correspondence With Veterans

Field Marshal the Lord Bramall KG GCB OBE MC JP DL, King s Royal Rifle Corps
Major Joe Brown CBE, Royal Scots
Gunner Joseph Dutch, 126th Highland Field Regiment
Major General Robert Ford GCB CBE, 4th/7th Dragoon Guards
Sapper Brian Guy, 246 Field Company RE
Ian Hammerton MBE, 22nd Dragoon Guards
Major Sydney Jary MC, 4th Somerset Light Infantry
Major John Majendie MC, 4th Somerset Light Infantry
Warrant Officer Les Pring MM, 128th Highland Field Regiment
Captain Jack Swaab MC, 127th Highland Field Regiment
Ken Tout OBE 1st Northamptonshire Yeomanry

Interviews/Correspondence with Modern Experts

Brigadier Jeremy Bennet OBE, late Royal Artillery
Major Bart Cookson, Royal Tank Regiment
Colonel James Coote DSO OBE, Princess of Wales's Royal Regiment
Mr Norman Franks, author and expert on RAF second world war operations
Dr Rob Johnson, Director of the Changing Character of Warfare Programme, Oxford University
Dr Justin Pepperell, Consultant Physician Taunton and Somerset NHS Trust
Lieutenant Colonel Harry Scott, Household Cavalry Regiment
Lieutenant Colonel Simon Stockley, Royal Engineers

Army Medical Museum

225 Parachute Field Ambulance post operational report 5 Jun –8 Sep 1944, Army Medical Museum archives.
Clark, Major C D, surgical log and case notes held within his papers in the Army Medical Museum RAMC/CF/4/525/CLAR/2.
Helm, W H, 'The Normandy Diary of a junior medical officer in 210 Field Ambulance'. Army Medical Museum Archives RAMC/PE/1/382/NORM.
Tibbs, David, 'The Doctor's Story, RMO 13 Para Bn – 225 Parachute Field Ambulance'. Army Medical Museum Archives RAMC/PE/I/216/TIBB.

Imperial War Museum

Private Papers Collections:

Ref	Title
17	Lane A J – Royal Engineers, 263 Field Company
191	*Wyvern News* Weekly Supplement No.4, France, 30 July 1944
339	Major D Vernon – Royal Engineers, 24th Field Company
569	Baker A E – 4th/7th Royal Dragoon Guards
1471	Brigadier E E E Cass CBE DSO MC – 8th Infantry Brigade
1548	Accounts describing the Mulberry Harbours
1882	Byford P F – Signaller 53rd Welsh Division
2778	Perry J G – Royal Artillery, 15th Medium Regiment
2833	Lieutenant Colonel E Jones MBE – 1st Battalion South Lancashire Regiment
3269	R T Greenwood – 9th Battlion Royal Tank Regiment
2505	Wilkes A A – Royal Engineers – 931 Port Construction and Repair Company
3856	Holdsworth D – 2nd Battalion Devonshire Regiment
3985	P T Cash MC – Royal Artillery
4141	Forrest G J – 2nd Battalion Warwickshire Regiment
5471	Colonel M Crawford DSO – 8th Battalion Middlesex Regiment
5838	Sheldrake R D – Royal Artillery, 55th Anti-Tank Regiment
6350	Personal Recollections of the Westminster Dragoons who Landed in Normandy on D-Day
7188	Lieutenant Colonel M A Philp – Royal Signals (185 Infantry Brigade)
7913	E A Smith – Troop Sergeant, Reconnaissance Troop, 2nd Battalion Grenadier Guards
8031	Major R E Ward –Royal Engineers, 42nd Assault Engineer Regiment
8066	Captain W H Helm – 210 Field Ambulance (Also in Army Medical Museum Archives)
8509	Corbett J – Royal Signals, Y Service
10908	Reverend L F Skinner TD – Sherwood Rangers Yeomanry
11055	Captain E M B Hoare DSC RN – 18th Minesweeping Flotilla
11423	Major General Nigel Tapp KBE CB DSO – Royal Artillery, 7th Field Regiment
12085	Captain D G Aitken – RAMC, 24th Lancers
12607	Phillips S – RAF, 69 Squadron
13717	Major J A R Mitchell – Royal Tank Regiment (Firefly)
13574	Diary of Surgeon Lieutenant G R Aith RNVR LST 302
15132	Captain D McWilliam – 9th Battalion The Cameronians
17201	Lieutenant Colonel L R H G Leach MC – 5th Royal Horse Artillery
19506	Dixon J B – 4th Battalion Wiltshire Regiment
19507	Mee K V – Royal Engineers, 1st Assault Brigade, 79th Armoured Division
19538	Lieutenant E A Brown – 73rd Anti-Tank Regiment
20020	Clark G C – 2nd/6th South Staffordshire Regiment
20114	Keane D W G – Royal Engineers, 260 Field Company
20347	Ellis, H C – Royal Engineers, 1st Assault Brigade, 79th Armoured Division

Military Intelligence Museum

Mockler-Ferryman, Brigadier, *Military Intelligence in the Second World War,* 1945, Intelligence Corps Museum

The National Archives

CAB 101/308 *Victory In The West* Volume 1 Draft circulation and comments
CAB 106/1060 Reports on the Normandy Campaign 1944 6 June – 10 July by Brigadier James Hargest
CAB 146/473 Canadian Special Interrogation Reports referring to the Normandy Campaign
CAN 106/963 "Immediate" Reports of actions in Normandy 1944
HW 1/2918 'Notes on the use of ULTRA' Brigadier Bill Williams, HQ 21st Army Group, 5 Oct 1945
WO 171/12 War Diary Second Army G Branch
WO 171/223 War Diary Second British Army GS (I)
WO 171/310 War Diary 12 Corps
WO 171/456 War Diary 11th Armoured Division
WO 171/466 War Diary 15th Scottish Division
WO 171/479 War Diary 43rd Wessex Division
WO 171/513 War Diary 50th Infantry Division
WO 171/527 War Diary 51st Highland Division
WO 171/613 War Diary 8th Armoured Brigade
WO 171/627 War Diary 29th Armoured Brigade
WO 171/633 War Diaries 31 Tank Brigade
WO 171/640 War Diary 33rd Armoured Brigade
WO 171/646 War Diary 44 Infantry Brigade
WO 171/650 War Diary of 56 Infantry Brigade
WO 171/856 War Diaries 4th County of London Yeomanry
WO 171/859 War Diary 1st Northamptonshire Yeomanry
WO 171/859 War Diary 7th Royal Tank Regiment
WO 171/865 War Diary 1st Royal Tank Regiment
WO 171/1085 War Diary 80th AA Brigade
WO 171/1250 War Diary 1st Armoured Battalion Coldstream Guards
WO 171/1253 War Diary 1st Battalion Grenadier Guards (Motorised Battalion)
WO 171/1266 War Diary 5th Battalion Black Watch
WO 171/1267 War Diary 7th Black Watch
WO 171/1270 War Diary 5th Battalion Queen's Own Cameron Highlanders
WO 171/1299 War Diary 1st Battalion Gordon Highlanders
WO 171/1301 War Diary 5th/7th Gordon Highlanders
WO 171/1305 War Diary 1st Battalion Hampshire Regiment
WO 171/1307 War Diary 1st Battalion Herefordshire Regiment
WO 171/1314 War Diary 2nd Battalion Princess Louise's Kensingtons
WO 171/1364 War Diary 6th Royal Scots Fusiliers
WO 171/1372 War Diary 4th Battalion Somerset Light Infantry
WO 171/1394 War Diary 4th Battalion Wiltshire Regiment
WO 171/3575 War Diary 211 Civil Affairs Detachment
WO 205/99 Operation Overlord: intelligence and security planning

WO 205/404 Reports from operations other than immediate reports for action: correspondence and maps. Vol 1

WO 205/1085 Miscellaneous documents forwarded as duplicate copies to SHAEF Rear

WO 205/1153 Aerial Photograohy: notes on provision of intelligence from air photographs and photographic interpretation in the field

WO 208/2525 Procedure in interrogating and handling prisoners of war

WO 208/3193 Military Intelligence Special Tactical Studies

WO 208/3249 Notes on Combined Services Detailed Interrogation Centre

WO 208/3465 Interrogation of POWs in the field: report by Major Shergold

WO 208/3592 CSDIC UK Interrogation of enemy POWs: Interrogation Reports

WO 208/5531 Interrogation reports on German prisoners of war: SIR 400-499

WO 285/9 'First 100 Days' Commander Second British Army's personal war diary

Official pamphlets accessed through Defence Concepts and Doctrine Centre Tactical Doctrine Retrieval Cell/Military Library Research Service

21st Army Group *Notes On War Field Marshal B L Montgomery*

British Army Of The Rhine September 1945 *Infantry Notes No.14*

British Army Of The Rhine April 1946 *Morale In Battle: Analysis*

British Army Of The Rhine, August 1946 *Royal Engineers Battlefield Tour Normandy to the Seine*

S M O' H Abraham, *Notes on Armoured Reconnaissance* (The notes are held in the Defence Concepts and Doctrine Centre, Shrivenham under TDRC index 4923.

Staff College 1947 Battlefield Tours of OP NEPTUNE, GOODWOOD, TOTALIZE, BLUECOAT

War Office 1939 Carriers, *Machine Gun Instruction Book*

War Office 1942 *Bren Light Machine Gun*

War Office 1942 *Small Arms Training*

War Office 1943 *Infantry Training Part V: The Carrier Platoon*

War Office 1943 *Infantry Training Part VI: The Anti-Tank Platoon*

War Office 1943 *The tactical handling of the Armoured Division and its components*

War Office June 1943 *The Tactical Handling of the Armoured Division and its components*

War Office July 1943 *Anti Tank Tactics*

War Office 1944 *Handbook For the Ordnance QF 25 Pounder/Gun Howitzer*

War Office 1944 *Infantry Training Part VIII Fieldcraft, Battle Drill, Section and Platoon Tactics*

War Office 1944 *Small Arms Training Volume I, Pamphlet No.9 The 3-inch Mortar*

War Office 1944 *The British 6-Pounder Anti-tank Gun*

War Office February 1944, *Field Engineering*

War Office 25 March 1946 *Small Arms Training Vol. I Pamphlet No.28 Sniping*

War Office 1950 *The Development of Artillery Tactics and Equipment* (Brigadier A L Pemberton)

War Office 1952 *Military Engineering*

War Office *Military Training Pamphlet No.23 Operations*

War Office *Military Training Pamphlet No.63 The Co-operation of Tanks with Infantry Divisions*

Royal Artillery Institution

Letter from RMH Cree, 'The Crossing of the River Orne', Royal Artillery Institution Archives MD 1843.

'Memoirs of Maj Gen G D Fanshawe 1943-45' (Part IV), Royal Artillery Institution Archives MD 1661.

Neilson, Captain Ian, 'Normandy 1944 – The Role Of the Air Observation Post', Paper held in the Royal Artillery Institution archive MD 2878

'Searching for Gunner Whitaker', Royal Artillery Institution archives RAI A/C 2005.08.04

PRINTED SOURCES

Adair, Allan, Edited by Oliver Lindsay, *A Guards' General,* London, Hamish Hamilton, 1986.

Admiralty, Battle Summary No.39 *Landings in Normandy – Operation Neptune, June 1944,* London, Admiralty, Archives Of the Royal Navy, 1947.

Anderson, Richard C, *Cracking Hitler's Atlantic Wall – The 1st Assault Brigade Royal Engineers on D-Day,* Mechanicsburg, PA, Stackpole Books, 2010.

Anon, *By Air To Battle* Cambridge, Patrick Stephens, 1978.

Anon, *Taurus Pursuant, A History Of 11th Armoured Division* British Army Of The Rhine Stationery Office, 1945.

Astley, Ivor D. *Tank Alert,* Ilfracombe, Arthur H Stockwell, 1999.

Balkoski, Joseph, *Beyond The Beachead – The 29th Infantry Division in the Normandy Beachead,* Mechanicsburg, PA, Stackpole Books, 1989.

Ballantyne, Iain, *Warspite,* Barnsley, Pen and Sword, 2001.

Barber, Neil, *The Day the Devils Dropped In – The 9th Parachute Battalion In Normandy – D-Day to D+6,* Barnsley, Pen and Sword, 2002.

Barber, Neil, *Fighting with the Commandos, The recollections of Stan Scott, No.3 Commando,* Barnsley, Pen & Sword, 2008.

Barris, Ted, *JUNO – Canadians at D-Day June 6, 1944,* Toronto, Thomas Allen Publishers, 2004.

Baverstock, Kevin, *Breaking The Panzers – The Bloody Battle for Rauray Normandy, 1 July 1944,* Stroud, Sutton Publishing, 2002.

Beale, Peter, *Tank Tracks, 9th Battalion Royal Tank Regiment at War 1940-45,* Stroud, Sutton Publishing, 1995.

Belchem, David, *All In The Day's March,* London, Collins, 1978.

Bell, Noel, *From The Beaches To The Baltic – G Company, 8th Battalion The Rifle Brigade*, Aldershot, Gale & Polden, 1947.

Bellamy, Bill *Troop Leader – A Tank Commander's Story,* Stroud, Sutton Publishing, 2005.

Benamou, Jean-Pierre, *Normandy 1944, An illustrated Field-Guide 7 June to 22 August 1944,* Bayeux, 1982.

Bennett, Ralph, *Ultra in the West – The Normandy Campaign of 1944-45,* London, Hutchinson and Co, 1979.

Bennett, Tom, *617 Squadron – The Dambusters at War,* Wellingborough, Patrick Stephens, 1986.

Bidwell, Shelford and Graham, Dominick *Fire-power, The British Army Weapons & Theories Of War 1904-1945,* Barnsley, Pen and Sword, 2004.

Black, Jeremy, *Rethinking military history,* London, Routledge, 2004.

Blackburn, George, *The Guns of Normandy,* London, Constable, 1998.

Boardman, C J, *Tracks in Europe, The 5th Royal Inniskilling Dragoons Guards 1939-1946.* Salford, City Press Services, 1990.

Bolland, A.D. *Team Spirit – The Administration Of an Infantry Division during "Operation Overlord",* Aldershot, Gale & Polden, 1948.

Borthwick, Alastair *Battalion – A British Infantry Unit's actions from El Alamein to the Elbe 1942-1945,* London, Baton Wicks, 1994

Boscawen, Robert, *Armoured Guardsmen – A War Diary, June 1944 – April 1945,* Barnsley, Pen and Sword, 2001.

Bouchery, Jean, *From D-Day to VE Day, The British Soldier*, Paris, Histoire & Collections, 1999.

Bowyer, Michael J F, *2 Group RAF, A complete History 1936-1945,* Manchester, Crecy Books, 1992.

Bradley, Omar N, *A Soldier's Story,* New York, Henry Holt and Company, 1951.

Brickhill, Paul, *The Dambusters,* London, Evans Brothers, 1951.

Bright, Pamela, *Life In Our Hands – Nursing Sister's War Experiences,* London, Pan Books, 1957.

Brisset, Jean, *Charge of the Bull – A History of the 11th Armoured Division in Normandy 1944,* Norwich, Bates Books, 1989.

Brooks, Stephen, *Montgomery and the Battle of Normandy,* Stroud, History Press for the Army Records Society 2008.

Bruce, Colin John, *Invaders – British and American Experience of Seaborne Landings 1939-1945,* London, Chatham Publishing, 1999.

Buckley, John, *British Armour In The Normandy Campaign 1944,* London and New York, Frank Cass, 2004.

Buckley, John, *The Normandy Campaign 1944 Sixty Years On* London and New York, Routledge, 2006.

Bull, Stephen, *World War Two Infantry Tactics – Company and Battalion,* Oxford, Osprey, 2005.

Bull, Stephen, *World War Two Infantry Tactics – Squad and Platoon,* Oxford, Osprey, 2004.

Bull, Stephen and Rottman, Gordon L, *Infantry Tactics of the Second World War,* Oxford, Osprey, 2008.

Carrington, Charles, *Soldier at Bomber Command,* London, Leo Cooper, 1987.

Carver, Michael, *Out Of Step – The Memoirs Of Field Marshal Lord Carver,* London, Hutchinson, 1989.

Chalfont, Alun, *Montgomery of Alamein* London, Magnum Books, 1976.

Churchill, Winston, *The Second World War,* London, Cassell, 1948.

Clark, David, *Angels Eight – Normandy Air War Diary,* Bloomington IN, 1st Books, 2003.

Clark, Lloyd, *Operation Epsom – Battle Zone Normandy,* Stroud, Sutton Publishing, 2004.

Clark, Lloyd, *Orne Bridgehead – Battle Zone Normandy,* Stroud, Sutton Publishing, 2004.

Claytoon, Aileen, *The Enemy Is Listening,* New York, Ballantine Books, 1980.

Close, Bill, *A View From The Turret,* Tewkesbury, Dell & Bredon, 1998.

Cooper, Belton Y, *Death Traps – The survival of an American Armoured Division in World War II,* New York, Ballantine Books, 1998.

Cooper, Bryan, *The E-boat Threat,* London, Macdonald and Jane's Publishers, 1976.

Copp, Terry, *Fields of Fire – The Canadians in Normandy,* Toronto, University of Toronto Press, 2003.

Copp, Terry, *The Brigade, The Fifth Canadian Infantry Brigade in WWII,* Mechanicsburg, PA, Stackpole Books, 2007.

Cotterell, Anthony, *RAMC,* London, Hutchinson & Co, 1944.

Crew, F A E, *Army Medical Services, Campaigns, Volume IV North-West Europe,* London, HMSO, 1962.

D'Este, Carlo, *Decision in Normandy* New York, Konnecky and Konnecky, 1994.

Daglish, Ian, *Operation BLUECOAT,* Barnsley, Pen and Sword, 2003.

Daglish, Ian, *Operation Goodwood,* Barnsley, Pen and Sword, 2004.

Daglish, Ian, *Over the Battlefield – Operation Bluecoat – Breakout From Normandy,* Barnsley, Pen & Sword, 2009.

De Guingand, Freddie, *Operation Victory,* London, Hodder & Stoughton, 1947.

Delaforce, Patrick, *Marching To The Sound Of Gunfire, North-West Europe 1944-45* Stroud, Chancellor Press, 1996.

Delaforce, Patrick, *Monty's Ironsides – From The Normandy Beaches To Bremen With The 3rd (British Division),* Stroud, Sutton Publishing, 2002.

Delaforce, Patrick, *The Black Bull – From Normandy to the Baltic with the 11th Armoured Division,* Stroud, Sutton Publishing, 1993.

Delaforce, Patrick, *The Fighting Wessex Wyverns – From Normandy to Bremerhaven with the 43rd (Wessex) Division,* Stroud, Sutton Publishing, 2002.

Delve, Ken, *The story of the Spitfire, an Operational and Combat History,* London, Greenhill Books, 2007.

Demoulin, Charles, *Firebirds! Flying the Typhoon in Action!,* Shrewsbury, Airlife Publishing, 1987.

Doherty, Richard, *Only the Enemy In Front (Every other beggar behind...) The Recce Corps at War 1940-1946,* Bath, Bath Press, 1994.

Doherty, Richard, *The British Reconnaissance Corps in World War II,* Oxford, Osprey, 2007.

Doherty, Richard, *Ubique – The Royal Artillery in the Second World War,* Stroud, The History Press, 2008.

Dunphie, Christopher & Johnson, Garry, *Gold Beach – Inland From King,* Barnsley, Pen and Sword, 2002.

Dunphie, Christopher, *The Pendulum Of Battle, Operation GOODWOOD, July 1944,* Barnsley, Pen and Sword, 2004.

Dyson, Stephen, *Tank Twins – East End Brothers In Arms 1943-45,* London, Leo Cooper, 1994.

Ellis, Chris and Chamberlain, Peter, *Handbook Of The British Army 1943,* London, Purnell Book Services, 1975.

Ellis, John, *The Sharp End Of War,* Newton Abbott, David and Charles, 1980.

Ellis, L. F., *History Of The Second World War – Victory In The West, Volumes I and II,* London, Her Majesty's Stationery Office, 1968.

Falvey, Denis, *A Well-Known Excellence – British Artillery and an Artilleryman in World War Two,* London, Brassey's, 2002.

Farrell, Charles, *Reflections 1939-45: A Scots Guards Officer in Training and War,* Bishop Auckland, Edinburgh, The Pentland Press, 2000.

Fellows, Rex, *Fragments of Battle,* Matlock, Newton Mann Publishers, 1995.

Fendick, Reginald F, *A CANLOAN officer – The memoir of a Canadian Junior Infantry Officer On Loan to the British Army for the Liberation of Europe, 1944-45,* Buxton, MLRS Books, 2000.

Fleming, Tom, *My Daily War Diary 1940-1946,* Gateshead, Atheneum Press, 2003.

Fletcher, David, *Chuchill Crocodile Flamethrower,* Oxford, Osprey, 2007.

Flower, Desmond, *History Of The Argyll & Sutherland Highlanders 5th Battalion, 91st Anti-Tank Regiment,* London, Thomas Nelson and Sons, 1950.

Foley, John, *Mailed Fist,* St Albans, Mayflower, 1975.

Ford, Ken, *Assault Crossing, The River Seine 1944,* Newton Abbott, David and Charles, 1988.

Ford, Ken, *Caen 1944, Montgomery's break out attempt,* Oxford, Osprey, 2004.

Ford, Roger, *Fire From The Forest,* London, Cassell, 2003.

Fortin, Ludovic, *British Tanks in Normandy,* Paris, Histoire and Collections, 2005.

Forty, George, *Leakey's Luck – A Tank Commander With Nine Lives,* Stroud, Sutton Publishing, 2002.

Forty, George, *Road to Berlin –The Allied Drive From Normandy,* London, Cassell, 1999.

Forty, George, *Tank Warfare In The Second World War,* London, Constable, 1984.

Foster, Ronald H, *Focus On Europe – A Photo Reconnaissance Mosquito Pilot At War, 1943-45,* Ramsbury, Marlborough, Crowood Press, 2004.

Franks, Norman, *Typhoon Attack,* London, William Kimber, 1984.

French, David, *Raising Churchill's Army – The British Army and The War against Germany 1919-1945* Oxford, Oxford University Press, 2001.

Gale, R. N., *With the 6th Airborne Division in Normandy,* London, Marston & Co., 1948.

Gale, Richard, *Call To Arms,* London, Hutchinson, 1968.

Gethyn-Jones, Eric, *A Territorial Army Chaplain In Peace and War*, West Sussex, Gooday Publishers, 1988.

Gilbert, John, *Only Death Could Land – The Canadian attack on Carpiquet*, St Catharines, Ontario, Gargunnock Books, 2006

Glass, Fiona and Marsden-Smedley, Phillip, *Articles of War – The Spectator Book of World War II*, London, Grafton Books, 1989.

Golley, John, *The Day Of The Typhoon – Flying with the RAF Tankbusters in Normandy*, Bury St Edmunds, Wrens Park Publishing, 1986.

Gooderson, Ian, *Air Power at the Battlefront, Allied Close Air Support 1943-45*, London, Frank Cass, 1998.

Graveley, T B, *Signal Communications*, The War Office, 1950.

Greenwood, Trevor *D-Day to Victory – The Diaries of a British Tank Commander*, London, Simon & Schuster. 2012.

Hamilton, Nigel, *Monty*, New York, McGraw Hill, 1981.

Hammerton, Ian, *Achtung! Minen! The Making of a Flail Tank Troop Commander*, Sussex, Book Guild, 1991.

Harrison Place, Timothy, *Military Training in The British Army 1940-1944*, London, Frank Cass, 2000.

Hart, Stephen A, *Sherman Firefly vs Tiger, Normandy 1944*, Oxford, Osprey, 2007.

Hart, Stephen Ashley, *Colossal Cracks Montgomery's 21st Army Group in Northwest Europe. 1944-45* Mechanicsburg PA, Stackpole Books, 2007.

Hartcup, Guy, *Codename MULBERRY – The planning, building & operation of the Normandy Harbours*, Barnsley, Pen & Sword, 2006.

Hart-Dyke, Trevor, *Normandy to Arnhem – A story of the Infantry*, Sheffield, Greenup and Thompson, 1966.

Hastings, Max, *All Hell Let Loose*, London, Harper Press, 2011.

Hastings, Max, *Ovelord, D-Day and the Battle For Normandy 1944*, London, Book Club Associates, 1984.

Hastings, Robin, *An Undergraduate's War*, London, Bellhouse Publishing, 1997.

Hawkins, Ian, *Destroyer, An Anthology Of First Hand Accounts Of The Wat At Sea 1939-1945*, London, Conway Maritime Press, 2003.

Hay, Ian, *One Hundred Years of Army Nursing*, London, Cassell, 1953.

Henderson, Johnny & Douglas-Home, Jamie *Watching Monty*, Stroud, Sutton Publishing, 2005.

Henry, Chris, *British Anti-tank Artillery 1939-45*, Oxford, Osprey, 2004.

Henry, Chris, *The 25-pounder Field Gun 1939-72*, Oxford, Osprey, 2002.

Hill, Stuart, *By Tank Into Normandy*, London, Cassell, 2002.

Hinsley, F H, *British Intelligence in the Second World War*, London, Her Majesty's Stationary Office, 1988.

Hogg, Ian, *Tank Killing – Anti-Tank Warfare By Men And Machines*, Basingstoke, Sidgwick & Jackson, 1996.

Holborn, Andrew, *The 56th Infantry Brigade and D-Day – An Independent Infantry Brigade and the Campaign in North-West Europe 1944-1945*, London, Continuum, 2010.

Horne, Alistair with Montgomery, David, *The Lonely Leader –Monty 1944-1945*, London, Macmillan, 1994.

Horrocks, Brian with Belfield, Eversley & Essame, H, *Corps Commander*, London, Sidgwick and Jackson, 1977.

Horrocks, Brian, *A Full Life*, London, Collins, 1960.

How, J.J. *Hill 112, Cornerstone of the Normandy Campaign*, London, William Kimber, 1984.

Howarth, David, *Dawn of D-Day*, London, Collins, 1959.

Hue, Andre, *The Next Moon* London, Viking – Penguin Books, 2004.

Hunt, Eric, *Mont Pincon,* Barnsley, Pen and Sword, 2003.

Jary, Sydney, *18 Platoon* London, Hardy Publishing, 2009.

Jarymowcz, Roman, *Tank Tactics – From Normandy to Lorraine,* Mechanicsburg PA, Stackpole Books, 2009.

Jones, Keith, *Sixty-Four Days Of A Normandy Summer – With A Tank Unit After D-Day* London, Robert Hale, 1990.

Keegan, John, *Six Armies in Normandy,* London, Penguin, 1993.

Kershaw, Robert, *Tank Men – The Human Story Of Tanks At War,* London, Hodder and Stoughton, 2008.

Kiln, Robert, *D-Day to Arnhem With Hertfordshire's Gunners* Welwyn Garden City, Castlemead Publications, 1993.

Kilvert-Jones, Tim, *Sword Beach – British 3rd Infantry Division/27th Armoured Brigade,* Barnsley, Pen and Sword, 2001.

Kirby, Norman, *1100 Miles With Monty –Security and Intelligence at Tac HQ,* Stroud, Sutton Publishing, 2003.

Lane, A .J., *What More Could A Soldier Ask Of A War?* Sussex, Book Guild, 1990.

Laurier Military History Series *1st Canadian Radar Battery 1944-45,* Waterloo Ontario, LCMSDS Press, 2010.

Lavery, Brian, *Assault Landing Craft – Design, Construction & Operations,* Barnsley, Seaforth, 2009.

Lee-Richardson, *21st Army Group Ordnance, The story of the campaign in North-West Europe,* BAOR, Germany 1946.

Lewin, Ronald, *Montgomery as Military Commander,* London, Batsford, 1971.

Lewin, Ronald, *Ultra Goes To War,* London, Grafton Books,1988.

Lewis, Adrian R *Omaha Beach – A flawed victory,* University of North Carolina Press, 2001.

Lewis, Jon E. *Eyewitness D-Day,* London, Magpie Books, 2004.

Lincoln, John, *Thank God And The Infantry,* Stroud, Sutton Publishing, 1994.

Lindsay, Martin, *So Few Got Through,* London, Collins, 1946.

Lovegrove, Peter, *Not least in the crusade – a short history of the Royal Army Medical Corps,* Aldershot, Gale and Polden, 1951.

Lucas, James & Barker, James, *The Killing Ground – The Battle Of The Falaise Gap August 1944,* London, Book Club Associates, 1978.

Lucas, James, *Battlegroup!* London, Cassell, 1993.

Lucas, James, *Death in Normandy – the last battles of Michael Wittman,* Halifax, Shelf Books, 1999.

Lund, Paul & Ludlam, Harry, *I Was In The War Of The Landing Craft,* London, W. Foulsham & Co, 1976.

Mace, Paul, *Forrard – The Story of the East Riding Yeomanry,* London, Leo Cooper, 2001.

Maher, Brendan A. *A Passage To Sword Beach – Minesweeping in the Royal Navy,* Annapolis, Maryland, Naval Institute Press, 1996.

Mangilli-Climpson, *Larkhill's Wartime Locators - Royal Artillery Survey in the Second World War,* Barnsley, Pen and Sword 2007.

Martel, Giffard Le Q. *Our Armoured Forces,* London, Faber and Faber, 1945.

Martin, Charles Cromwell, *Battle Diary – From D-Day and Normandy to The Zuider Zee and VE day,* Toronto and Oxford, Dundurn Press, 1996.

Martin, H.G, *The History Of The Fifteenth Scottish Division 1939-1945,* Edinburgh and London, William Blackwood and Sons, 1948.

McBryde, Brenda, *A Nurse's War* London, Hogarth Press, 1986.

McCue, Paul, *Operation Bulbasket,* London, Leo Cooper, 1996.

McGregor, John *The Spirit of Angus* Chichester, Phillimore and Co, 1988.

McKee, Alexander, *CAEN: Anvil Of Victory,* London, Souvenir Press, 1964.

Melville, A, *First Tide*, London, Skeffington & Son, 1945.

Meyer, Hubert, *The 12th SS – History of the Hitler Youth Panzer Division,* Mechanicsburg PA, Stackpole Books, 2005.

Meyer, Kurt, *Grenadiers – The Story Of Waffen SS General Kurt "Panzer" Meyer,* Mechanicsburg, PA, Stackpole Books, 2005.

Millar, George, *Maquis,* London, William Heinemann, 1945.

Millin, Bill, *Invasion,* Sussex, Book Guild, 1991.

Mills-Roberts, Derek, *Clash By Night – A Commando Chronicle,* London, William Kimber, 1956.

Milner, Marc, *D-Day to Carpiquet – The North Shore Regiment And The Liberation Of Europe,* New Brunswick, Goose Lane Editions, 2007.

Mitchell, Raymond, *Commando Despatch Rider,* Barnsley, Pen and Sword, 2001.

Moberly, R B, *2nd Battalion Middlesex Regiment (D C O) Campaign in N W Europe,* Cairo, Schindlers Press, 1946.

Montgomery of Alamein, *Normandy To The Baltic,* London, Hutchinson & Co., 1947.

Montgomery of Alamein, *The Memoirs Of Field-Marshal The Viscount Montgomery Of Alamein, K.G.,* London, Collins, 1948.

Mucklow, Gordon, *60 Days With The 5th Battalion Duke Of Cornwall's Light Infantry,* Privately Published, 1993.

Muirhead, Campbell, *The Diary of a Bomb Aimer,* Tunbridge Wells, Spellmount, 1987.

Neal, Don, *Guns And Bugles – The Story Of The 6th Bn KSLI –181st Field Regiment RA,* Studley, Brewin Books, 2001.

Neillands, Robin and De Norman, Roderick, *D-Day 1944 – Voices From Normandy,* London, Weidenfeld & Nicholson, 1993.

Newton, Cecil, *A Trooper's Tale,* Marlborough, Wiltshire, privately published, 2000.

Nicholls, T B, *Organization, Strategy And Tactics Of The Army Medical Services In War,* London, Bailliere, London, 1941.

North, John, *N W Europe 1944-5 The achievement of 21st Army Group,* London, HMSO 1953.

Orde, Roden, *The Household Cavalry At War: Second Household Cavalry Regiment,* Aldershot, Gale & Polden, 1953.

Overy, Richard, *Why The Allies Won,* London, Pimlico, 2006.

Owen, James and Walter, Guy, *The Voice of War – The Second World War Told By Those Who Fought It,* London, Viking, 2004.

Pakenham- Walsh, R.P. *Military Engineering (Field),* The War Office, 1952.

Pakenham-Walsh, R.P. *The History Of The Royal Engineers, Volume IX,* Chatham, Mackay & Co, 1958.

Parham, Maj Gen H J and Belfield E M G, *Unarmed into Battle, the story of the Air Observation Post,* Winchester, Warren & Son, The Wykeham Press, 1956.

Pereira, J, *A Distant Drum –War Memories of the Intelligence Officer of the 5th Bn. Coldstream Guards 1944-45,* Aldershot, Gale and Polden, 1948.

Perret, Bryan, *Through Mud and Blood – Infantry/Tank Operations in World War Two,* London, Robert Hale, 1975.

Picot, Geoffrey, *Accidental Warrior –In The Frontline From Normandy Till Victory,* London, Penguin, 1993.

Powdrell, Ernest, *In the Face Of the Enemy, A Battery Sergeant Major in action in the Second World War* Barnsley, Pen and Sword, 2008.

Pridham, C H B, *Superiority of Fire,* London, Hutchinson, 1945.

Pritchard, Jack, *Seven Years A Grenadier,* Rushden, Northamptonshire, Forces & Corporate Publishing, 1999.

Proctor, D. *Section Commander,* Bristol, Sydney Jary, 1990.

Reid, Brian A. *No Holding Back,* Toronto, Robin Brass Studio, 2005.

Renouf, Tom, *Black Watch,* London, Abacus, 2011.

Reynolds, Michael, *Sons Of The Reich, II SS Panzer Corps,* Havertown PA, Casemate, 2002.

Richardson, Charles, *Send For Freddie – The Story Of Montgomery's Chief Of Staff, Major General Sir Francis de Guingand, KBE, CB, DSO,* London, William Kimber, 1987.

Ritgen, Helmut, *The Western Front 1944: Memoirs of a Panzer Lehr Officer,* Winnipeg, Manitoba, JJ Fedorowicz Publishing Inc., 1995.

Roberts, G.P.B. *From the Desert To The Baltic,* London, William Kimber, 1987.

Ross, Peter *All Valiant Dust – An Irishman Abroad,* Dublin, Lilliput Press, 1992.

Rosse, The Earl of & Hill, E.R., *The Story Of The Guards Armoured Division,* London, Geoffrey Bles, 1956.

Rottman, Gordon, *World War II Combat Reconnaissance Tactics,* Oxford, Osprey, 2007.

Rottman, Gordon, *World War II Infantry Anti-Tank tactics,* Oxford, Osprey, 2005.

Rottman, Gordon, *World War II Infantry Assault Tactics,* Oxford, Osprey, 2008.

Routledge, Brigadier N W, *History of the Royal Regiment of Artillery: Anti Aircraft Artillery,* London, Brassey's, 1995.

Ryder, Peter *Guns Have Eyes* London, Robert Hale, 1984.

Sainsbury, J. D, *The Hertfordshire Yeomanry Regiments, Royal Artillery,* Welwyn, Hart Books, 1999.

Saunders, Tim *Hill 112 – Battles Of The Odon 1944,* Barnsley, Leo Cooper, 2002.

Saunders, Tim *Operation EPSOM,* Barnsley, Leo Cooper, 2003.

Scarfe, Norman, *Assault Division – A History Of The 3rd Division From The Invasion Of Normandy To The Surrender Of Germany,* London, Collins, 1947.

Schofield, B. B. *Operation Neptune,* London, Ian Allan, 1974.

Scotland, A.P. *The London Cage,* London, Evans Brothers, 1957.

Scott, Desmond *Typhoon Pilot,* London, Arrow Books, 1982.

Scott, Peter *The Battle Of The Narrow Seas,* London, Country Life Publishing, 1945.

Shannon, Kevin and Wright, Stephen, *One Night In June,* Wrens Park Publishing, 2000.

Shilletto, Carl, *The Fighting Fifty-Second Recce – The 52nd (Lowland) Divisional Reconnaissance Regiment RAC,* York, Eskdale, 2000.

Shores, Christopher & Thomas, Chris, *2nd Tactical Air Force* vols 1-3. Hersham, Ian Allan, 2004.

Smith, Wilfred I, *Code Word CANLOAN,* Toronto & Oxford, Dundurn Press, 1992.

Speidel, Hans, *We Defended Normandy,* London, Herbert Jenkins, 1951.

Steers, Bob, *Field Security Section,* Bexhill on Sea, Olivers Printers, 1996.

Strong, Kenneth, *Men of Intelligence,* London, Cassell, 1970.

Swaab, Jack, *Diary of a Gunner Officer,* Stroud, Sutton Publishing, 2005.

Swaab, Jack, *Slouching In The Undergrowth – The Long Life Of A Gunner Officer,* Stroud, Fonthill, 2012.

Taylor, George, *Infantry Colonel,* Worcester, Self Publishing Association, 1990.

Tent, James Foster, *E-Boat Alert – Defending The Normandy Invasion Fleet,* Shrewsbury, Airlife Publishing, 1996.

Terraine, John, *The Right Of The Line – The Royal Air Force in the European War 1939-1945,* London, Hodder and Stoughton, 1985.

Thomas, Chris, *Typhoon Wings of 2nd TAF 1943-45,* Oxford, Osprey, 2010.

Thornburn, Ned, *The 4th K.S.L.I In Normandy,* Shrewsbury, 4th Bn K.S.L.I Museum Trust, 1990.

Tillotson, Michael, *The Fifth Pillar – The Life and Philosophy Of The Lord Bramall KG,* Stroud, Sutton, 2005.

Tout, Ken, *A Fine Night For Tanks – The Road To Falaise,* Stroud, Sutton Publishing, 2002.

Tout, Ken, *Tank! – 40 hours of battle, August 1944,* London, Robert Hale, 1985.

Tout, Ken, *Tanks, Advance! Normandy to the Netherlands, 1944,* London, Robert Hale, 1987.

Tout, Ken, *To Hell With Tanks,* London, Robert Hale, 1992.

Townshend Bickers, Richard, *Air War Normandy,* London, Leo Cooper, 2004.

Tucker-Jones, Anthony, *Falaise The Flawed Victory, The Destruction of PanzerGruppe West, August 1944,* Barnsley, Pen and Sword, 2008.

Verney, GL, *The Deset Rats – the epic story of the indomitable 7th Armoured Division,* London, Hutchinson, 1957.

Warner, Phillip, *Horrocks – The General Who Led From The Front,* Reading, Sphere Books, 1985.

Watkinson, G L. *Royal Engineers Battlefield Tour – Normandy To The Seine,* British Army Of The Rhine, 1946.

Watts, J C *Surgeon at War* London, George Allen & Unwin, 1955.

Wavell, *Generals and Generalship,* Aylesbury, Penguin, 1941.

Weeks, John, *Men Against Tanks – A History Of Anti-Tank Warfare,* Newton Abbott, David & Charles, 1975.

Westphal, Siegfried, *The German Army In The West,* London, Cassell, 1951.

Whitaker, Denis and Whitaker Shelagh, with Copp, Terry, *Normandy the real story – How ordinary Allied Soldiers Defeated Hitler,* New York, Ballantine Books, 2004.

Whitehouse, Stanley and Bennett, George B, *Fear is The Foe – A Footslogger from Normandy to the Rhine,* London, Robert Hale, 1997.

Williams, Dennis, *Stirlings in Action with Airborne Forces,* Barnsley, Pen & Sword, 2008,

Willis, Leonard, *None Had Lances – The Story Of The 24th Lancers,* Chippenham, Picton Press, 1986.

Wilmot, Chester *The Struggle For Europe,* London, Collins, 1952.

Wilson, Andrew *Flamethrower,* London, Kimber, 1956.

Wilson, Edward *Press on Regardless – The Story Of The Fifth Royal Tank Regiment in World War Two* Staplehurst, Spellmount, 2003.

Wingfield, R.M. *The Only Way Out,* London, Hutchinson, 1955.

Winterbotham, F.W. *The Ultra Secret,* London, Wiedenfield and Nicholson, 1974.

Womack, J. A., *Summon Up The Blood,* London, Leo Cooper, 1997.

Woollcombe, Robert, *Lion Rampant,* London, Leo Cooper, 1955.

Zaloga, S J, *M10 and M36 Tank destroyers 1942-53,* Oxford, Osprey, 2002.

Zaloga, S J, *Sherman Medium Tank, London, Osprey, 1993.*

Index

INDEX OF MILITARY UNITS

INDEX OF PEOPLE

INDEX OF PLACES

INDEX OF MISCELLANEOUS TERMS

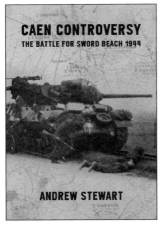

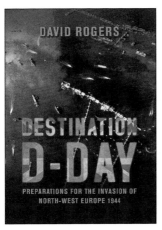

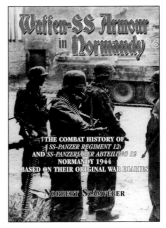